MW00982455

Global Marketing Management

Global Marketing Management: A Strategic Perspective

BRIAN TOYNE
University of South Carolina

PETER G. P. WALTERS
University of South Carolina

ALLYN AND BACON
Boston • London • Sydney • Toronto

Series Editor:	Henry Reece
Cover Administrator:	Linda K. Dickinson
Cover Designer:	Susan Hamant
Manufacturing Buyer:	Bill Alberti
Editorial Production Service:	York Production Services

Copyright © 1989, Allyn and Bacon
A Division of Simon & Schuster
160 Gould Street
Needham, Massachusetts 02194-2310

All rights reserved. No part of the material protected by this copyright notice may be reproduced or utilized in any form or by any means, electronic or mechanical, including photocopying, recording, or by any information storage and retrieval system, without the written permission of the copyright owner.

Library of Congress Cataloging-in-Publication Data

Toyne, Brian.
   Global marketing management: a strategic perspective / Brian Toyne, Peter G.P. Walters.

    p.   cm.
   Includes bibliographies and indexes.
   ISBN 0-205-11829-1
   1. Export marketing—Management. 2. International business enterprises—Management. I. Walters, Peter George Pakenham, 1946– . II. Title.
   HF1416.T66 1989
   658.8′4—dc19
                                       88-7677
                                        CIP

Printed in the United States of America

10 9 8 7 6 5 4 3   93 92

Contents_____

v

PART III   CORPORATE DIMENSIONS OF THE GLOBAL MARKETING EFFORT _____ **265**

Preface

In the last decade, international marketing has changed significantly. New demands have been placed on marketing managers to coordinate and configure their domestic and foreign marketing programs to achieve synergistic results. These demands have resulted in the development of new concepts and new materials to help companies meet the competitive need to globalize the marketing effort.

Domestic and foreign markets have become increasingly integrated and competitive. To successfully meet today's challenges, a company's marketing efforts must be simultaneously responsive to national market conditions and supportive of overall corporate and business-unit strategies. We have accordingly chosen to take a strategic approach in our discussion of the major dimensions of global marketing.

International marketing textbooks have traditionally taken either an environmental or a managerial approach. As a result, much of the material presented therein concentrates on building sensitivity to economic, political, and cultural differences and on how these differences influence local marketing-mix decisions. These differences are discussed in detail in our book. However, we also have given special attention to the need to treat selected domestic and international marketing opportunities as an interdependent array of opportunities to be differentially developed to meet strategic objectives.

Although this book has benefited from its authors' non-academic business experiences, it is primarily the result of experiences teaching international business and international marketing courses in graduate business schools and executive programs. The text has been written mainly for graduate and advanced undergraduate students. Its main objective is to examine those marketing management skills essential for handling the problems of a global company. While the book is designed primarily for students, it should also be useful for marketing managers interested in studying present and projected patterns of global competition.

The text has two features that we believe will significantly enhance learning: a five-part "minibook" organization and extensive use of case studies. In Part I, the student is introduced to the major approaches to international marketing; special attention is given to global marketing. Key dimensions of the national and international environment are also reviewed. Part II analyzes global market opportunities. This section presents an in-depth discussion of international market research and highlights the issues and problems associated with demographic and cultural analyses of foreign marketing opportunities. Part III provides an in-depth discussion of the various corporate dimensions of global strategic market planning. This analysis provides a solid foundation for Part IV, in which strategic and tactical issues, problems, models, and methodologies in global product policy, pricing, distribution, and promotion are reviewed. Special attention is given to issues relating to export strategy. In Part V, we discuss the organization and control of the global marketing effort.

The sixteen cases are global in scope; they represent a variety of industries and countries. Our goal in including them is to confront the student with the key issues and problems facing today's international marketer. The cases therefore exemplify current issues and problems. They challenge the reader to apply principles of analysis and insights presented in the five parts. We trust they will make navigation outside the classroom smoother.

ACKNOWLEDGEMENTS

Writing a textbook, especially a new one, is a major undertaking that cannot be accomplished without the active support and help of a large number of people.

We are indebted to our institution, the College of Business Administration, the University of South Carolina, for its support and encouragement. We are especially grateful to William R. Folks, the former Director of the International Business Program, and Jeffrey S. Arpan, the current Director, for their encouragement.

Throughout the development of this book, a number of reviewers have made important contributions. They provided many thoughtful comments and valuable suggestions for improvement. We have been fortunate in receiving counsel from the following, whom we would like to acknowledge and thank:

Lyn S. Amine, University of Wisconsin, Whitewater
Andreas Falkenberg, University of Oregon
Ram Kesavan, University of Detroit
Michael Landeck, St. Mary's University
Irene Lange, California State University at Fullerton
Marilyn Liebrenz-Himes, George Washington University
Stephen W. Miller, St. Louis University
John Ryans, Jr., Kent State University
Robert Thornton, Miami University
James Weekly, University of Toledo
James R. Wills, University of Hawaii at Manoa
Attila Yaprak, Wayne State University

Of those involved in the preparation of the manuscript of this book, Christa G. Hatting deserves special mention. She typed many of the chapters in this book and her efficient and uncomplaining help—despite numerous revisions—is greatly appreciated. We are also grateful for the typing support we received from Dee Williams and Luz Rodriguez.

We would also like to acknowledge and thank the publishers and authors who permitted the reproduction of cases and other materials used in this book. Their names are noted in the text. A special thanks is extended to Kendell Roth, University of South Carolina, who made significant contributions to Chapter 9, and to Frank L. DuBois and Thomas Rogers, two Ph.D. students who contributed original cases for this book.

Finally, we should like to thank our families for their understanding and support during the several years we have been working on this book. Special thanks go to Zaida, and Aasny, Annika, and Erik.

Brian Toyne
Peter G.P. Walters
December 1988

ABOUT THE AUTHORS

Brian Toyne (Ph.D., M.B.A., Georgia State University) is Professor of International Business at the University of South Carolina. In addition to his teaching responsibilities at the University of South Carolina, he has taught at Georgia State University and the Helsinki School of Economics and has been involved in corporate-sponsored executive training programs for many years. He has written numerous books and articles on international business, U.S. competitiveness, and industrial policy. His publications include articles in *Academy of Management Review, Columbia Journal of World Business, Industrial Marketing Management, International Journal of Physical Distribution and Material Management, International Marketing: Strategy and Planning, Journal of Business Research,* and *Journal of International Business Studies.* He has been a member of the State of South Carolina Export Advisory Committee and a consultant to the United Nations Industrial Development Organization on various projects dealing with the industrialization of Third-World countries. For the 20 years prior to his academic career, Dr. Toyne worked in several aerospace companies in England, Canada, and the United States in engineering and management.

Peter G.P. Walters (Ph.D., M.B.A.) is Assistant Professor of International Business at the University of South Carolina. He studied at the London School of Economics for his B.Sc. (Econ.) degree and received his Ph.D. from the Institute of International Business, Georgia State University. He has also taught at Georgia State University, The Norwegian School of Management in Oslo, and the American Graduate School of International Management. He has worked as a consultant to the U.S. Commerce Department. Dr. Walters' publications have focused on exporting and international marketing and his research mainly on exporting and international product policy. His publications include articles in *Journal of International Business Studies, European Journal of Marketing, International Marketing Review,* and *Management International Review.* Prior to beginning his academic career, Dr. Walters worked for four years in a large international firm.

Part I
Global Marketing:
Its Management
and Environment

In Part I, we introduce you to the scope and nature of global marketing operations, and then we focus on the environmental context. Initially, we give particular attention to the various approaches to marketing overseas, patterns of international business operations, and theories of international business behavior. Our focus then shifts to the international operational context, that is, the economic, trading, political, and legal dimensions of the national and international environments. We also give special attention to international systems, organizations, and institutions that the international marketer must understand.

Chapter 1: briefly describes the various philosophic approaches adopted by companies when marketing in foreign countries. It also explains the major dimensions of the global marketing management process. This discussion provides the overall framework for understanding how the topics discussed in later parts of the book relate to the global marketing process.

Chapter 2: describes patterns in the recent development of international business activities and presents key elements of the theory of the dominant forms of international involvement. This enables managers to develop a framework for better understanding the basic forces driving international business and marketing operations.

Chapter 3: focuses on the *home* and *host* country dimensions of the international operating environment. Together, these comprise the *national* context for international marketing. An understanding of these environmental forces is central to effective global marketing decisions.

Chapter 4: discusses the specifically *international* dimension of the operating environment, which is made up of international institutions, agreements, and systems that affect international marketing activities. Although these contextual factors can often be ignored by domestic firms, they are central to international firms.

Case Studies: Widget Wars
Nitrofix Ghana

Chapter 1
Overview of Global Marketing Management

Global marketing is a relatively recent phenomenon. It is the result of a company combining its domestic and foreign marketing activities in such a way that they jointly and synergistically contribute to its corporate objectives.[1] In recent years, more and more companies have realized that selecting and exploiting foreign market opportunities requires direction and purpose. They also have recognized that competition for these foreign opportunities has become more intense and global. For example, General Foods and Nestlé are global competitors, and their marketing activities around the world must consider this when selecting market opportunities, developing marketing programs, and allocating marketing resources. Ford, Toyota, and Volkswagen must do the same in the auto industry, as must Xerox and Canon in the copier industry.

Globally oriented companies are increasingly using their overarching corporate strategy as the reference point for integrating and coordinating their domestic and foreign marketing activities.[2] Thus the selection of foreign market opportunities, mode of market entry, type of market presence, allocation of resources, and selection of target markets and marketing strategies all need to be consistent with and supportive of the company's strategic mission and long-term objectives and goals. As a consequence, foreign marketing activities are no longer fragmented by national borders and separate from domestic marketing activities. When Boeing develops a new commercial aircraft, or IBM a new generation of computers, they are as cognizant of foreign demand as they are of domestic demand when making their production and marketing plans and determining their financial needs.

> **Global marketing** is the process of focusing an organization's resources on the selection and exploitation of global market opportunities consistent with and supportive of its short- and long-term strategic objectives and goals.

More simply, global marketing is the realization that a firm's foreign marketing activities, in whatever form they take, need to be supportive of some "higher objective" than just the immediate exploitation of a particular foreign opportunity. This higher objective is the long-term welfare of the firm as defined by its strategic goals. This is as true for a company taking its first tentative steps overseas as an exporter as it is for a Philips or a Hewlett-Packard planning the worldwide introduction of a new generation of products.

This book is about global marketing and the management of this process. As such, its focus is on the global environment; the identification and selection of global market opportunities; and the marketing techniques, approaches, conceptual frameworks and methods used to exploit these opportunities. This does not mean the more traditional modes of doing business across national boundaries are ignored. Exporting and licensing are just as relevant in a global marketing strategy as the widespread production and other direct investment activities of giant multinational corporations.

GLOBAL MARKETING AND ITS ANTECEDENTS _____

Foreign and domestic marketing are the same in that the purpose is to create and manage profitable exchange relationships between an organization and its markets (individuals, organizations, and institutions).[3] This is done by satisfying the needs or wants of a particular market more effectively and efficiently than competitors. Essentially the same marketing principles, concepts, and techniques are used internationally as at home. That is, domestic and foreign marketers are seeking similar goals—a properly managed response from their markets—and use similar marketing tools.

However, foreign and domestic marketing are dissimilar in three important ways. First, differences in the environmental characteristics of domestic and foreign markets often require different applications of marketing principles, concepts, and techniques. Second, foreign marketing involves crossing national borders and is thus concerned with a unique set of issues and problems. Third, special techniques and methods are sometimes needed.

The way companies respond to these special challenges and problems is strongly influenced by their foreign marketing philosophy. Three basic philosophies may be identified and these are:[4]

☐   Market extension philosophy

☐   Multidomestic market philosophy

☐   Global market philosophy

Firms that evolve into global companies generally adopt these philosophies sequentially. But it is not inevitable that all companies seeking to establish profitable exchange relationships in foreign markets will become global corporations. Some companies do not advance beyond a market extension or multidomestic market orientation. Others use all three orientations, selecting the one most suitable for a particular set of circumstances. There are many reasons for this. The company may be quite satisfied with the profits it is earning from its market extension or multidomestic market orientation. Or because of ignorance, lack of competitors, or other reasons, the company's management may not see any reason for shifting from their current approach.

The Market Extension Philosophy

The market extension philosophy is one of the oldest concepts guiding a company's overseas marketing activities. Today, this philosophy is generally associated with small and medium-size exporters and companies in the first stages of internationalizing their operations.

A company operating under a *market extension orientation* assumes its foreign markets either are of secondary importance to its home market or can be satisfied with the same product. Foreign markets are viewed primarily as outlets for surplus production or as opportunities to smooth domestic production, increase volume to gain scale, or raise profit margins.

A company guided by a market extension philosophy views its foreign marketing activities as primarily separate from its domestic marketing philosophy and activities. A sales or production orientation is generally adopted, which implies the firm is interested only in either extending the life of its product or increasing its sales volume with minimum marketing effort. Thus a company adopting this orientation tries to exploit foreign market opportunities using the products and marketing mix policies developed for its domestic or home market. Only mandatory changes in the international marketing mix are made and costs are minimized. However, consumers do not buy physical objects or services for their own sake; they buy them to satisfy a need, and this need may vary from country to country. Thus the firm's foreign marketing effort can be suboptimal to the extent that the foreign market's potential is not fully developed.

The assumption underpinning this orientation is that foreign customers are mainly interested in product availability. This philosophy may be used in at least two situations. The first is where a company seeks to satisfy unsolicited orders from overseas but is not interested in developing and managing this demand. The second situation is where costs have to be minimized and overseas consumers and the foreign operating context are not very different from the situation at home.

The Multidomestic Market Philosophy

The multidomestic market concept is a more recent phenomenon and builds on the beliefs that (1) individual foreign market opportunities can make significant contributions to the company's long-run welfare, and (2) efficiencies can be realized if the foreign market activities of the firm are integrated and coordinated in a way that accentuates the company's competitive advantages in production and marketing *across foreign markets.* The focus is mostly on maximizing the company's effectiveness and efficiency in exploiting economies of scale, experience, and scope in production and marketing.

> A company adopting a *multidomestic market orientation* assumes foreign marketing opportunities are as important as home market opportunities. Basically, the multidomestic market orientation is the result of an *internal* awareness that better market performance can be obtained by integrating and coordinating foreign marketing activities and experience with the purpose of fully exploiting overseas opportunities.

Unlike a company with a market extension orientation, a company adopting a multidomestic market orientation is interested in fully exploiting each foreign market's potential. Thus marketing strategy (target market and marketing mix) is differentiated to fit each foreign market's needs and conditions. A high priority is also given to creating an effective mechanism to transfer marketing skills and experience from one market to another.

The Global Market Philosophy

A major distinction between a multidomestic market orientation and a global market orientation is that the latter focuses on pursuing market opportunities to synergistically achieve corporate objectives and goals. It is, in effect, a systems approach to domestic and foreign marketing. Domestic and foreign market opportunities are not selected solely for their *individual potentials*; rather, they are chosen for their *relative potential contributions* to overarching corporate objectives.

A company adopting a *global market orientation* makes no distinction between domestic and foreign market opportunities. Opportunities are selected by means of portfolio assessment and exploited in a way that is supportive and consistent with the company's strategic objectives. Thus the basis for selecting market opportunities and allocating resources to the marketing effort is the long-run welfare of the company within the competitive environment of its industry and a global assessment of competitive reaction.

In this book, we classify companies that have adopted a global market orientation as *global companies*; these we subdivide into companies pursuing *global-market segmentation* strategies and companies pursuing *national-market segmentation strategies*.[5] Some *global companies* compete in industries characterized by universal needs or market segments not restricted by national boundaries and adopt *global market segmentation strategies*. Firms that manufacture cameras, watches, and household electronic products like televisions, radios, video players, and soft drinks have successfully used this approach. Other *global companies* compete in industries that are essentially national, such as foodstuffs, clothing, and household packaged goods, or service special national market segments. This may result in the need to develop *national marketing strategies*. The underlying similarity of these two types of global companies is the exploitation of domestic and foreign market opportunities to achieve globally oriented corporate objectives. The major difference between these companies is the relative emphasis placed on internal and external distinctive advantages. Internal advantages include such company factors as foreign marketing experience, tested foreign market management and marketing systems, and low production costs. External advantages include such market factors as company image, brand awareness and loyalty, and access to international–national distribution networks.

Colgate, Unilever, and Pillsbury are examples of global companies pursuing *national-market segmentation* strategies. Each has many local-branded products tailored to the individual characteristics of foreign markets and marketed using sophisticated techniques and policies (packaging, advertising, merchandising, and so on) developed as a result of their overseas and domestic experience and marketing skills. In contrast, Canon, Caterpillar, General Electric, IBM, and Xerox are examples of global companies pursuing *global-market segmentation* strategies. Each has several global-branded products tailored to meet the needs of a particular group of customers regardless of their nationality. They capitalize on their worldwide reputations, technology, production efficiencies, and delivery capabilities to serve the same market segments in many countries.

GLOBAL MARKETING MANAGEMENT

One of the differences between domestic and global marketing management is that the latter must handle many issues and problems unique to doing business between and within foreign countries. These issues and problems often require changes in the *application* of the marketing concepts, principles, and tools used in the home market before they can be used in foreign markets. They also require marketing managers to undertake coordination tasks not encountered domestically and to adopt novel approaches.

These unique issues and problems result in a set of marketing activities, which we here subdivide into three groups: *international marketing management, foreign marketing management,* and *global marketing management.* Although the distinction we make among these three groups of marketing activities is not generally found in practice, and the terms are often used differently by others, it helps develop a better understanding of the scope and complexity of global marketing.

First, the development and maintenance of profitable exchange relationships in foreign markets requires that a company directly (or through an intermediary) cross national borders. Management of the marketing activities associated with crossing national borders is *international marketing management.* Second, the company marketing in one or more foreign countries is faced with markets that may differ substantially in their market conditions and characteristics from the company's home country. Management of the marketing activities associated with marketing in other countries is *foreign marketing management.* Third, the foreign and international marketing efforts of a global company must be "harmonized" so that they are consistent with, supportive of, and contribute to the company's overarching objectives and goals. Management of the marketing activities associated with seeking to harmonize a company's international and foreign marketing activities is *global marketing management.* Table 1-1 summarizes some of the distinguishing features of these three dimensions of marketing management.

International Marketing Management

International marketing is specifically concerned with those differences that affect the marketing effort *because a company, involved in exporting or foreign marketing, must cross national borders and deal with a different set of environmental conditions.* International marketing consists of all the *facilitating* and *reconciling* activities and decisions that enable the company to market within and between foreign countries. The management of these facilitating and reconciling activities is *international marketing management.*

> **International marketing management** is responsible for the creation, implementation, maintenance, and control of all activities needed for a company to (1) cross national borders, (2) support foreign marketing activities, and (3) evaluate foreign marketing performance.

As this definition suggests, three types of international marketing capabilities are needed:

1. The ability to handle the impediments and barriers erected by governments that hinder the free flow of goods and services across their borders.
2. The ability to handle the differences that always exist when exporting to, or operating in, two or more countries.
3. The ability to support and evaluate the exporting or foreign marketing effort.

TABLE 1-1
Some Distinguishing Features of Foreign, International, and Global Marketing

International Marketing	Foreign Marketing	Global Marketing
Definitions		
Marketing activities that cross national borders	Marketing activities undertaken by a company in a country other than its home country	Coordination, integration, and control of marketing activities to ensure the company's objectives and goals are simultaneously achieved within and across foreign markets
Activities and responsibilities		
Provide the facilitating and reconciling activities required to cross national borders, deal with different environments (such as language, time zone, and currency differences), and support and evaluate foreign marketing efforts	Establish the marketing presence, and manage the activities required to fulfill the company's marketing effort in the foreign market Create, implement, and control the marketing strategies designed to simultaneously achieve the company's objectives and meet the needs or wants of the targeted markets or market segments	Synergistically integrate the international and foreign marketing efforts of the company Ensure that the strategic objectives of the company are achieved and maintained within and across foreign markets Develop and maintain the company's distinctive competitive advantages in each of its foreign markets

How much these *facilitating* and *reconciling* capabilities are needed, and how they are developed and structured, depends on the company's involvement in exporting or foreign marketing and the strategic importance of this involvement by region or country. Some of these capabilities can be purchased; others must be developed internally. Moreover, some of them may be located at corporate headquarters, some at a regional or area level, and some at the foreign affiliate level.

Capability to Cross National Borders

Although many capabilities are required to effectively and efficiently cross national borders, we discuss them under (1) the handling of government regulations and (2) the handling of special market restrictions.

The Handling of Government Regulations. Crossing national borders requires complying with a myriad of government-mandated regulations and requirements that restrict or, at best, hinder the free flow of goods and services, people, and factors of production. These impediments include tariffs and quotas and require complying with nontariff barriers (NTBs) such as safety and health standards, product standards, advance deposits, and exchange controls. Often, special documents may be needed, such as export and import licenses, consular invoices, visas, and work permits.

Since there is considerable variance in the regulations and requirements imposed by countries, special assistance is frequently needed. Thus many companies create marketing units to assist their foreign affiliates. These units have the task of advising and guiding foreign affiliates on the regulations and requirements to be met; providing for the proper documentation; timely delivery of goods and other inputs; and arranging for the payment of tariffs and compliance with NTBs. They may also be responsible for ensuring that the products meet local standards. Other companies may hire the services of outside specialists like forward freighters, customs brokers, banks, and export management companies.

The Handling of Special Market Restrictions. On occasion, countries impose prohibitions on capital flows and imports to reduce, for example, a trade deficit, a drain on scarce foreign currency reserves, or with Brazil, Mexico, and other debtor nations, in response to International Monetary Fund (IMF) borrowing requirements. For instance, in 1984, the Colombian government imposed a total prohibition on imports. This prohibition adversely affected the local marketing efforts of several U.S. companies, including Colgate, Quaker Oats, and Unisys (then Burroughs). Colgate-Palmolive, able to switch to local suppliers for many of its needed inputs, continued operating though at a reduced level. Quaker Oats, unable to purchase oats locally, had to close down its rolled oats operations several times while it sought relief from the prohibition. At the same time, it began to investigate the potential for other types of products that could be made from locally purchased foodstuffs. Unisys also imported all its products for the Colombian market, so it was severely affected by the prohibition. It sought to overcome the problem by arranging countertrade agreements with affiliates in other South American countries. That is, Unisys set up an arrangement between two foreign marketing units to satisfy simultaneously the purpose underlying the governmental restriction, a zero-net outflow of foreign currencies, and the main-tenance of its local market.

Each affected company had to find solutions to a sudden change in its local environment. Changes are not unusual, especially in countries experiencing economic and politial problems. Since the changes unfavorably influenced the company's marketing effort and mode of operation, flexibility and creativity are often needed in product innovation, sourcing, pricing, and delivery.

Capability to Handle National Differences

Foreign marketing often requires working in a foreign language, in a different time zone, and in a different currency whose rate of exchange may be constantly changing relative to that of the home country's currency. We review the problems associated with national differences under (1) the handling of communication problems and (2) the handling of foreign currencies.

The Handling of Communication Problems. The problems of language and time zone differences affect the ability of the company and its foreign affiliate (or distributor) to communicate with each other. Interpreters and people familiar with local conditions are generally required to avoid difficulties. For example, advertising copy, sales promotion materials, maintenance and repair manuals, and many other marketing-related documents may need to be translated into the local language. Company policies and procedures, such as planning aids for strategic marketing administration, marketing research, and relations with government agencies and suppliers, may also need to be translated into or from the local language. Moreover, direct communication between countries is not always easy. Mail, even if sent by air, may take days, often weeks, and telephone connections may take hours to make and be of poor quality.

To reduce these problems, some companies arrange for special delivery of important letters, reports, and other documents and create centralized communication and information centers at the corporate or regional levels to expedite the translation of documents and the flow of communications. They may also use telex machines and other communication devices. Still, the problems and costs of working across time zones cannot be entirely avoided and may require additional personnel to staff communication centers.

The Handling of Foreign Currencies. The problems of currency differences and exchange rate fluctuations are generally handled by the financial function. But it remains the responsibility of marketing personnel to understand the implications that these differences and fluctuations may have on the foreign marketing effort. As we discuss later, currency differences can affect such things as the foreign marketing budget, pricing, and performance evaluation.

Support and Evaluation of the Foreign Marketing Effort

Besides handling cross-border impediments and national differences in language, currency, and time, international marketing requires supporting the foreign marketing effort and evaluating its performance. These activities fall into three categories: (1) transportation and in-transit warehousing, (2) foreign marketing support, and (3) budget and performance evaluation.

Transportation and In-Transit Warehousing. All activities needed to facilitate and expedite the flow of physical goods are international marketing management's responsibility. This is often done by hired agents, like forward freighters, especially if the company is small or inexperienced or the volume of shipments is small. Larger companies often create in-house international transportation units responsible for scheduling, shipping, and storing in-transit goods destined for foreign markets.

Foreign Marketing Support. Foreign marketing effort is strongly dependent on the marketing resources, capabilities, and experience of the parent company and foreign affiliates. These include the company's worldwide product research and development, marketing research, and advertising resources and capabilities. The experience the company has gained from marketing its products in the home market and other foreign markets, may also be of value and transferrable. It is the responsibility of the international marketing management to ensure that these resources, capabilities, and experience are made available to the foreign marketing management. This generally requires creating, maintaining, and controlling special marketing units at the corporate, regional, or local levels and issuing policies and procedures designed to stimulate the flow of products, resources, and information *in both directions.*

Budget and Performance Evaluation. Generally, foreign marketing is undertaken with specific objectives and goals in mind, such as to increase overall sales and profits, to gain additional economies of scale, to offset demand irregularities in the home market that adversely affect production capacity utilization, and to counter a competitive move by a major competitor. To achieve one or more of these objectives, the company must gain a predetermined market position, or market share, in one or more foreign markets. This, of course, takes money, management time, and other resources. It is the responsibility of the international marketing management to participate in budget preparation and allocation and evaluate the individual efforts of the foreign marketing management.

Foreign Marketing Management

Foreign marketing is marketing in a country other than the company's home country, such as when a U.S. company is marketing in Spain or France or a German company is marketing in the United States or Brazil. Domestic marketing is marketing in the company's home country, as when a U.S. company is marketing in the United States or a French company is marketing in France. The management of the marketing effort in a foreign country is *foreign marketing management.*

> **Foreign marketing management** is responsible for the creation, implementation, and control of *marketing strategies* and the management of the *marketing process* in a country other than the company's home country in order to achieve the company's corporate and business objectives in that country.

Foreign marketing management is more complicated than domestic marketing management for two reasons. First, the competitive environment of the foreign country and the characteristics of its market may differ from those of the home market. Thus, the company may not be as familiar with its foreign markets and their marketing context. Second, the operational aspects of marketing activity, such as the company's market presence, width and depth of its product offering, and availability of marketing research and advertising agencies, may also differ from those in the home country.

Country Environment and Market Characteristics

Substantial differences among countries can exist in the economic, competitive, technological, political and cultural dimensions of their environments. These differences affect the demand situation in the marketplace and the way the targeted market responds to the various elements of the marketing mix. Differences in the environmental dimensions of a country also affect the scope and content of the marketing management process. The selection of markets, or market segments, and the allocation of budgets are partly a function of the markets' environments. How the marketing tasks are performed is also affected by the environment. For example, the ability to conduct marketing research, undertake particular types of promotion, store and deliver goods, and provide after-sale service are partly a function of the country's marketing infrastructure, stage of economic development, and business practices.

Company Characteristics

The foreign marketing management task is also affected by company decisions such as the strategic importance of the foreign market, the market position to be obtained and sustained, and the form of its market presence. If the foreign market is important, it will probably receive more management attention, be allocated more resources, and be a fully integrated part of the company's core activities. Thus the width and depth of the product offerings will probably be greater in significant markets. Moreover, the scope of marketing activities undertaken locally, such as marketing research, product development, and after-sales activities, will tend to be broader in these markets. Smaller, less critical foreign markets may be served by independent distributors and agents. Marketing back up such as after-sales services may be supplied by one of the larger subsidiaries or a regional office; for example, IBM is represented in Yugoslavia by a state-operated distributor, supported by IBM's Austrian subsidiary.

Global Marketing Management

In today's world, global marketing management has become increasingly important within the modern, global company. No firm competing regionally or worldwide can afford to pursue marketing strategies that are based soley on national characteristics or potentials. To succeed in these situations, the marketing effort must consider the global aspects of the company's marketing effort and its competitors. Companies must develop characteristics that, compared with national, regional, and global competitors, generate advantages in the marketplace. Marketing resources must also be effectively allocated in line with short- and long-term strategic objectives.

Critical to the development of these competitive advantages is the creation of a *global marketing management process* capable of coordinating, integrating, and controlling the company's marketing efforts to ensure that they contribute to corporate strategic objectives and goals. Global companies are finding it increasingly important to centralize parts of the marketing management process and to decentralize others. For example, in many companies, product development and design is centralized at corporate headquarters, whereas pricing, advertising and promotion, and distribution decisions may be left to the local marketing manager. The decision to centralize or decentralize these marketing mix activities depends on the competitive structure of the company's industry, the categories of products it manufactures, and the structure and characteristics of the marketplace.[6]

Besides its marketing strategy responsibilities, the global marketing management is responsible for developing and maintaining the company's overall competitive advantages across and within all its markets (domestic and foreign), such as trademarks, company name, economies of scale, marketing procedures, and cross-market experience. Further, because of a growing tendency for global companies to develop global marketing management processes (centralized marketing information banks, corporate guidelines on branding, product development, and so on), local marketing programs are increasingly adaptations of a standardized core that accentuate the company's advantages. There is also a tendency to use standardized marketing practices.

Global marketing management is responsible for (1) seeking integration and synergism among the company's domestic, foreign, and international marketing activities, (2) maintaining the strategic objectives of the company's overall marketing effort, and (3) developing and maintaining the competitive advantages that power the company's global marketing effort.

As we noted, we distinguish in this book between global companies marketing to *global-market segments* and global companies marketing to *national-market segments*. But often the distinction becomes blurred. Multibusiness companies can be marketing to both global- and national-market segments. The distinction beween global- and national-market segments also becomes blurred when marketing mix strategies are developed that are predicated on government mandate. That is, governments (domestic and foreign) may intervene in the marketing activities of companies by imposing rules, regulations, and constraints that directly or indirectly hinder a company's marketing strategy (tariffs, nontariff barriers, product standards and specifications). We discuss these considerations extensively later in the book.

THE APPROACH OF THE BOOK

A central theme of this book is that global marketing encompasses all traditional modes (exporting, licensing, foreign production, and so on) used for developing and maintaining profitable exchange relationships between an organization and its foreign markets. The three orientations (market extension, multidomestic market, and global market) adopted when marketing overseas are all also relevant depending on circumstances.

The reasons global marketing and its antecedents are different from domestic marketing are to be found in the differences that exist between and among the marketing environments, and the need to cross national borders. The difference between a global market orientation, a multidomestic market orientation, and a market extension orientation is internal to the company and is the result of how an organization views its foreign market opportunities.

This book is divided into five parts, which we now briefly describe.

Part I: Global Marketing: Its Management and Environment (Chapters 1–4). In Chapter 1, we present a definition of global marketing and its elements, and we briefly discuss the global company and its evolutionary stages. In Chapter 2, we present an overview of patterns in the development of international business and the body of theory that has been developed to explain the behavior described. In Chapters 3 and 4, we identify and analyze the major dimensions of the national and international environments within which international firms must operate. Initially, we focus on the economic, political, and legal environment in overseas markets and, where relevant, at home. We highlight the relevance of these elements of the operational environment and approaches to measuring and analyzing their impact. The global marketing manager must also be sensitive to fundamental institutions and systems that transcend national boundaries and have an impact on international business activities. Thus in Chapter 4, we discuss key features of the international trading environment; commodity arrangements; economic integration; and international monetary, financial, and legal arrangements. In this review, we give special attention to describing the role of relevant international institutions such as GATT, the IMF, World Bank, UNCTAD, and the OECD.

Part II: Analyzing Global Market Opportunities (Chapters 5–8). In this section of the book, we examine the similarities, differences, and unique features of the global buyer. In Chapter 5, we examine the variations encountered in worldwide buyer demographics and discuss interpretation problems when comparing country demographics. In Chapter 6, we introduce the factors identified as determinants of buyer behavior around the world. We introduce a global buyer behavior model and examine its elements. In Chapter 7, we cover data and methodolgial issues and problems encountered when conducting marketing research overseas. In Chapter 8, we discuss the various issues and problems of conducting global market opportunity assessments. We also examine some of the more generally used assessment techniques and identify their strengths and weaknesses. We also explore the development of global marketing information systems.

Part III: Corporate Dimensions of the Global Marketing Effort (Chapters 9–11). In Chapter 9, we examine the basic components and concepts necessary for an understanding of corporate strategy and the corporate strategic planning process. We stress the need to identify environmental success requirements, corporate competences, and corporate differential advantage vis-à-vis competitors. In Chapter 10, we introduce the issues and problems confronting global companies when developing global corporate objectives and strategies. We also examine four generic strategies developed by global companies and the factors that must be considered when selecting a particular strategy. In Chapter 11, we discuss the dimensions and types of global marketing strategies and how these relate to the company's overall global strategy and the characteristics of the national markets it serves.

Part IV: Dimensions of Global Marketing Strategy (Chapters 12–17). In Chapters 12 and 13, we explore the issues and problems of developing international product strategies. Initially, we focus on managing the product diffusion and adoption process in foreign markets. We then give attention to the product presentation in these markets and emphasize the possibilities for and advantages and disadvantages of standardization strategies. Chapter 14 deals with developing and managing pricing strategies for international markets. In Chapter 15, we identify and discuss the three types of distribution strategies the global marketing manager needs to develop and implement, and we explore the issues and problems of integrating global and national distribution systems. In Chapter 16, we examine the market-related and company-related issues and problems of developing global and national promotion strategies and selecting an advertising agency. In Chapter 17, we examine special issues and problems in the management of export operations.

Part V: Organization and Control of Global Marketing Activities (Chapters 18–19). In Chapter 18, we examine the various organizational structures used by international companies, the factors influencing the choice of structure, and the advantages and weaknesses of the various alternatives. In Chapter 19, we examine how national and global marketing activities are controlled. We also discuss the issues and problems that need to be examined when attempting to integrate global and national marketing activities.

SUMMARY

Global marketing is the process of focusing an organization's resources on the selection and management of global market opportunities consistent with and supportive of its short- and long-term strategic objectives and goals. Thus foreign markets are selected for many reasons, including their ability to contribute to the company's short- or long-term earnings, their competitive importance, and the cost-reducing effect they will have on production. A conscious effort is made to manage the level, timing, and composition of demand in each foreign market to achieve the company's short- and long-term objectives and goals.

Three orientations or philosophies can guide organizations involved in exporting or foreign marketing. A market extension orientation holds that foreign markets should be viewed simply as extensions of the company's home market. This orientation assumes foreign customers are either more interested in the availability of products than in their particular features or have needs similar to customers in the home market. Thus a company adopting this concept will make minimum modifications to its products and to other elements of the marketing mix when servicing foreign markets. The multidomestic market orientation is based on the assumption that foreign markets are significantly different from the company home market. Thus the company will make extensive modifications to its products or other elements of the marketing mix to fully exploit foreign market opportunities. The global market orientation, while recognizing that the home and foreign markets are different, holds that these markets should be viewed as a portfolio of opportunities to be differentially exploited according to strategic need and emphasizes the need for coordination and integration of policy at the strategic level.

Three distinct yet mutually supportive groups of activities are involved in managing overseas marketing efforts: international marketing, foreign marketing, and global marketing. International marketing management encompasses all facilitating and reconciling activities required to cross national borders and act with foreign markets. Foreign marketing management includes all marketing activities traditionally undertaken when developing and managing the level, timing, and composition of demand but in a country other than the company's home country. Global marketing management encompasses all activities needed to coordinate and integrate a company's international and foreign marketing efforts to achieve its corporate objectives and goals and maintain its competitive advantages.

DISCUSSION QUESTIONS

1. What are the differences between a market extension philosophy, a multidomestic market philosophy, and a global market philosophy?
2. Why is it that all companies do not need to adopt a global market philosophy when marketing in two or more foreign markets? Could you cite companies that do not particularly need this orientation? Which companies need it the most?
3. What is the difference between international marketing management and foreign market management? Explain how each supports the other.
4. Give examples of global companies that are pursuing (a) global-market segmentation strategies and (b) national-market segmentation strategies, and explain the differences.
5. Discuss some of the problems that may be encountered by a French company when marketing its products in (a) the United States and (b) West Germany.
6. Would there ever be a case for a company to use more than one of the three philosophies described in this chapter when marketing in foreign markets? Explain.

ADDITIONAL READING

Boddewyn, Jean J., "Comparative Marketing: The First 25 Years," *Journal of International Business Studies,* Vol. 12, Spring–Summer 1981.

Hayes, R. H. and W. J. Abernathy, "Managing Our Way to Economic Decline," *Harvard Business Review,* July–August 1980.

Hill, Charles W. L., Michael A. Hitt, and Robert E. Hoskisson, "Declining U.S. Competitiveness: Reflections on a Crisis," *Executive,* Vol. 2, February 1988.

Hout, Thomas, Michael E. Porter, and Eileen Ruden, "How Global Companies Win Out," *Harvard Business Review,* September–October 1982.

Mitroff, Ian I. and Susan A. Mohrman, "The Slack Is Gone: How the United States Lost Its Competitive Edge in the World Economy," *Executive,* Vol. 1, February 1987.

Terpstra, Vern, "The Evolution of International Marketing," *International Marketing Review,* Vol. 4, Summer 1987.

ENDNOTES

1. See William H. Davidson, *Global Strategic Management* (New York: John Wiley & Sons, 1982), for an extensive discussion of the implications stemming from the adoption of a global strategic perspective.
2. Ibid., p. 2.
3. Roger A. Kerin, *Strategic Marketing Problems,* 4th ed. (Boston: Allyn and Bacon, 1987), p. 1.
4. See Sandra M. Huszagh, Richard J. Fox, and Ellen Day, "Global Marketing: An Empirical Investigation," *Columbia Journal of World Business,* Vol. 20, no. 4 (1986), pp. 31–43, for a similar classification of foreign marketing philosophies. Since many individuals and firms attach different meanings to the words used in this book, please note that the distinctions and definitions may not be used, or have the same meaning, when encountered elsewhere.
5. See C. K. Prahalad and Y. L. Doz, *The Multinational Mission* (New York: The Free Press, 1987), for a similar approach to classifying globally competitive companies.
6. Christopher Lorenz, *The Design Dimension: Product Strategy and the Challenge of Global Marketing* (New York: Basil Blackwell, 1986).

Chapter 2———————
International Business
Operations: Patterns and
Theory———————

INTRODUCTION

We now broaden our focus and describe international business and patterns characterizing its recent development. We also review key elements of the theory of the dominant forms of international involvement, international trade, and foreign direct investment. This discussion provides a solid theoretical platform for the analysis of global marketing operations in later chapters.

INTERNATIONAL BUSINESS

International business is concerned with transactions that involve the transfer of goods, services, and factor inputs (such as labor, capital and technology) across national boundaries. Three major factors differentiate international and domestic business and are the source of many problems unique to international marketing. These factors are (1) environmental heterogeneity, (2) "distance" problems, and (3) nationalism.

The international manager faces an environment that is commonly both complex and heterogeneous. Foreign markets tend to differ from one another on many dimensions, some of which have important policy implications. An awareness of these differences and of appropriate policy responses is imperative. This requires access to relevant information and an ability to understand its significance.

International marketers must also deal with elements not common to or very significant in domestic marketing. Key elements of the international environment include governmental controls over international flows of trade, investment, and labor; the international monetary system; global financial markets; and diverse international political, legal, and economic environments.

Problems arising from distance between the firm and its overseas markets also characterize international business. These problems stem from cultural, geographic, and economic differences. Misunderstandings and control and coordination problems are some of the more common results of increased distance.

Since foreign-controlled enterprises have sometimes been used as vehicles for economic exploitation and cultural imperialism, it is not surprising that international firms are particularly vulnerable to nationalism. Negative consumer perceptions and interference and control by host country governments are two of the most likely manifestations of the suspicion with which foreign firms are regarded in many countries.

Because of the richness and complexity of the operating environment and differing corporate objectives, the policies of international firms are characterized by diverse entry modes and marketing policies. Basic entry modes include direct and indirect *export;* nonequity *contractual arrangements* such as licensing, turnkey, and management contracts involving the sale of knowledge, expertise, and proprietary rights rather than physical products; and *foreign direct investment,* in which overseas assets are acquired for the purpose of controlling foreign business activities. Joint R&D, marketing, and production are becoming increasingly common because of the substantial resource demands on knowledge, and expertise inherent in overseas operations.

The activities of *multinational corporations* (MNCs) merit particular attention. Various definitions of these enterprises have currency. Some highlight corporate behavior and goals as key criteria. Others focus on structural variables such as organization, staffing, and the nature and distribution of overseas operations. However, there is a consensus that MNCs are characterized by foreign direct investment.

Finally, it should be noted that Americans working for foreign MNCs in the United States are also involved in international business even if their primary focus, as is most likely, is on managing operations within the United States.

Measurement Problems

Identifying data that present a detailed picture of the changing pattern of international business is a problem for three reasons. As already mentioned, a wide variety of modes of operation is feasible. No international agency systematically collects data on the full range of international business activities; and national statistical agencies often fail to collect relevant data. Even when relevant data are collected, international comparisons are difficult because of methodological and definitional differences.

Most countries do however collect good data on flows of merchandise trade. Patterns of exporting and importing are thus fairly well documented. Data on investment flows are often less comprehensive and of lower quality. For other forms of transnational business activity, such as licensing, other nonequity contractual modes and service trade, incomplete data is the norm. However, it is possible to develop a fairly clear picture of developments in the world economy on two fronts, (1) patterns of international trade and (2) foreign direct investment.

Patterns of International Trade

World Trade Flows

International trade consists of flows of both goods and services across national boundaries. Although flows of merchandise trade are tracked fairly accurately in most countries, such is often not the case for the international sale of services, where the diverse range of activities involved has limited the completeness and reliability of available data. Thus, the analysis focuses on the export and import of tangible goods, that is, merchandise trade flows. However service transactions account for over 20 percent of the trade of many countries, and appears to be growing more rapidly than merchandise trade.

Since World War II, the value of world trade has expanded rapidly and, apart from a decline in 1981–1983, continuously. In 1950, world exports were worth some $58 billion. By 1960, their value had increased to $118 billion. A decade later this figure would reach $286 billion, and by 1980, some $1,883 billion.[1] This growth is misleading because of changes in the unit price of exports. For example, the average annual increase in the *volume* of world trade from 1950 to 1980 was 6.7 percent, nearly half the 12.3 percent, average growth in the *value* of trade. More recently, the value of world trade increased twelvefold from 1963 to 1983 but when high inflation is taken into account, this translates into only a tripling in the volume of trade.

This impressive growth, key features of which are shown in Table 2-1, is unusual historically and is due to a number of special features of the post-war international economic environment.

There has been rapid economic growth internationally over the last four decades. This and the consequent growth in income have been a major stimulus to trade. However, world trade has increased significantly more rapidly than production and income since the 1950s. A useful measure of this disparity is the income elasticity of world trade, that is, the percentage change in world trade divided by the percentage change in world income. Trade elasticity has been estimated as close to 2 in the period from 1950 to 1970 but as evident in Table 2-2, it has declined more recently. On average, world output expanded by just over 4 percent per annum in the 1971–1980 period, compared to a 5 percent annual growth in the volume of world trade. Trade elasticity was thus 1.25 in this period. During the early 1980s, as international trade stagnated, average trade elasticity declined to an average of 1.1.

Other factors identified as important stimulants to the growth of trade include reduced barriers to trade resulting from multilateral negotiations under the auspices of the GATT (General Agreement on Tariffs and Trade); the increased economic integration in Europe; sharp falls in transport costs due to technical improvements such as containerization; greater ease and rapidity of global communication and travel; and the rise of MNCs, many of which undertake very substantial intracorporate importing and exporting.

In the 1950s and 1960s, the Bretton Woods international monetary system (to be discussed in Chapter 4) resulted in relatively stable exchange rate relationships that facilitated international trade. This stability ended in the early 1970s, when floating foreign exchange rates became common. International trade has become accordingly more complex. Although hedging strategies can help to reduce foreign exchange risk, it is now more essential than ever to understand the impact of foreign exchange movements on international marketing operations. (Chapters 4 and 14 discuss this topic in greater detail.)

Table 2-3 shows that the industrial and oil exporting nations' share of world exports increased during the period from 1950 to 1980, while the share of the

TABLE 2-1
Growth of World Trade*

	1950–60	1960–70	1970–80	1950–80
World:				
Value	7.1	9.4	20.7	12.3
Volume	6.4	7.9	5.5	6.7
Industrial countries†	8.7	10.1	18.9	12.5
Oil exporters†	5.5	9.1	33.0	15.2
Nonoil LDCs†	3.4	6.5	21.0	10.1

* Merchandise trade at annual compound percentage change
† In terms of value of exports
Source: *A Survey of International Trade Developments Since 1950* (IMF, 1982), p. vii.

TABLE 2-2
Growth of World Output and Trade

	1971–75	1976–80	1981–85	1983	1984	1985	1986†	1987‡
Output*:								
World	4.2	3.9	2.7	2.9	4.7	3.0	2.8	2.7
Developed market economies	3.1	3.5	2.3	2.6	4.8	2.8	2.4	2.3
Developing countries	6.1	4.9	1.4	0.8	2.0	2.2	3.2	2.9
Centrally planned economies	6.2	4.5	4.5	5.2	6.2	3.2	4.3	4.1
Trade§	5.0	5.1	2.8	2.5	9.0	2.3	4.0	3.0
Implicit income elasticity of world trade¶	1.2	1.3	1.1	0.7	1.8	1.3	1.4	1.1

* GDP
† Estimate
‡ Projected
§ Average of growth rates of world volume of exports and imports
¶ Ratio of world trade to world output growth rates
Sources: *World Economic Survey 1986* (United Nations), p. 12; and *Trade and Development Report 1987* (United Nations).

TABLE 2-3
Source of World Exports*

	1950	1960	1970	1980
Industrial countries	62.9	72.6	77.4	66.3
Oil exporters	7.3	6.2	6.0	16.9
Nonoil developing countries	29.8	21.2	16.3	16.8

* Percentage distribution calculated from U.S. dollar values
Source: *A Survey of International Trade Developments Since 1950* (IMF, 1982), p. vii.

nonoil less developed countries (LDCs) fell sharply. During the 1950s and 1960s, the industrial countries gained most. In the 1970s, as a result of sharp oil price increases, the oil exporters greatly increased their share of world trade, but this situation was reversed in the 1980s.

The product breakdown of world trade flows shown in Table 2-4 indicates a sharp fall in the relative significance of agricultural exports. This precipitous decline, from 29 percent of the value of world exports in 1963 to only 12.5 percent in 1985, suggests a greater self-sufficiency in food and raw materials (frequently as a result of increased protectionism in many countries). The income elasticity of demand for many agricultural products was low, and substitution of fabricated goods for natural raw materials was also important. In the 1970s, rising oil prices had a major impact on mineral trade. During the 1980s, as the price and volume

TABLE 2-4
World Trade by Product Group*

	1963	1973	1980	1985
Agricultural products	29	22	15	12.5
Minerals	17	17	29	21.5
Manufactures	54	61	56	66.0

* Percentage distribution based upon current U.S. dollar value.
Source: *International Trade*, 1984–1985, GATT Table A1.

of international oil shipments have fallen, this trend is being reversed. At the same time, manufactured exports have shown a sharp rise in relative importance.

Most international trade involves a mutual exchange of manufactures between rich industrial countries. The data on interregional flows of trade shown in Table 2-5 underline the dominance of the developed countries both as sources and recipients of trade flows. LDC exports account for only some 22 percent of world trade, with around 60 percent of these exports destined for developed markets. However, the trading activity of the centrally planned economies is even less important, accounting for only around 10 percent of world trade.

As world trade has grown more rapidly than world output, it has become relatively more important in most national economies. Figure 2-1 charts this key trend. Note especially that although the United States and Japan are major world traders, the relative importance of their international transactions is much less than in most other industrial countries.

During the early 1980s, growth in world trade faltered. The underlying reasons for the sluggish and irregular growth pattern evident then were slow economic growth and a widespread lower income elasticity of world trade. Among the causes of the lower elasticity were increased protectionism in some countries, a sharp fall in demand for OPEC oil, the growing significance of the service sector that is not trade-intensive, and unstable currency and financial markets.

TABLE 2-5
Interregional Flows of Trade*

Exports ⟶ To From	Developed	OPEC	Other Developing	Centrally Planned	Total
Developed	52.2	3.2	9.4	2.7	67.5
OPEC	4.0	0.1	2.7	0.2	7.0
Other developing	8.7	0.9	4.1	1.8	15.5
Centrally planned	2.5	0.2	1.8	5.5	10.0
World	67.4	4.4	18.0	10.2	100.0

* Figures show percentage of world exports during the first six months of 1986.
Source: *UN Monthly Bulletin of Statistics*, December 1986.

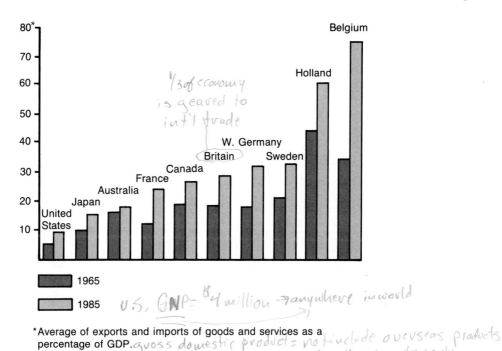

FIGURE 2-1   **The Relative Significance of International Trade** (*Source: The Economist*, November 1, 1985, p. 105.)

Exports of manufactures have fared well in recent years, with average volume growth of 5 percent per annum during 1980–1985. Agricultural exports grew by only 2 percent per annum in this same period, and exports of minerals declined at a rate of 3.5 percent per annum. These volume shifts have been complemented by price changes in which the relative price of agricultural and mineral products compared to manufactures has fallen. As a result, in 1986, manufactured goods replaced primary commodities as the leading source of export revenue for developing countries.

Sluggish United States exports resulted in 1986 in the replacement of the United States by West Germany as the world's leading exporter. At the same time, the world's leading trading countries achieved record trade imbalances as the United States had a massive trade deficit and West Germany and Japan earned record trade surpluses.

Despite the unbalanced trade pattern brought about by a very large United States deficit, increased economic growth has stimulated international trade flows in the mid-1980s. The volume of world trade increased by 3.0 percent in 1985, and 3.5 percent in 1986 and the first half of 1987. As oil exports increased, trade in mining products was up sharply in 1987. Agricultural trade, however, continued to stagnate, falling 1 percent in early 1987.

U.S. International Trade

That the United States has been the world's major trading nation for most of this century is due to its huge domestic economy. As is evident from Figure 2-1, foreign trade occupies a much less important position in the United States economy than it does in other industrial nations.

During the last three decades, United States dominance of world export markets has declined as other trading nations have been rapidly increasing their exports. In 1960, the United States accounted for 18 percent of world merchandise exports. By 1970, the United States share had fallen to 15 percent and, in 1985, stood at 11.4 percent. Table 2-6 indicates that other major trading countries have also lost market share to Japan and newly industrialized countries (NICs).

The relative significance of foreign trade for the United States economy increased steadily up to 1980, as shown in Figure 2-2. The ratio of trade to GNP increased to around 24 percent in 1980, and subsequently declined to some 20 percent in 1985. The primary reason for this decline is that United States merchandise exports stagnated in the early 1980s and, by 1985, were still some 7 percent below the 1981 record of $234 billion. By 1986, United States merchandise exports accounted for only 5.1 percent of GNP as compared to 8.1 percent in 1980. This amount is well below that of other major trading competitors; comparable 1985 percentages for West Germany, Canada, the United Kingdom, and Japan were 29.1 percent, 26 percent, 22.3 percent and 13.2 percent, respectively. Except for continued growth in United States imports—which were worth $387 billion in 1986, over 50 percent more than in 1980—the relative importance of foreign trade in the United States would have fallen back even more sharply.

The high value of the dollar was the primary constraint to United States export growth in the early 1980s. However, the fall in the dollar since 1985 is stimulating export growth and the foreign trade ratio is increasing as import levels remain high. During 1987, the volume of United States exports increased by 15 percent to $253 billion. Imports were valued at $424 billion in 1987, an increase of 9.6 percent as compared to 16.4 percent growth in export value. The effects of the weakening dollar thus seem finally to be embedded thoroughly in the economy with further rapid export growth likely in the late 1980s.

Despite stagnating during the early 1980s, United States exports are very important; they accounted for around 20 percent of domestic manufactured and agricultural goods and nearly 5.5 million jobs in the United States in 1985. Of United States merchandise exports in 1986, 78 percent were manufactured goods, 12 percent agricultural commodities, and 10 percent mainly minerals and other materials. The leading export industry groups were in order of relative importance,

TABLE 2-6
Relative Share of World Merchandise Exports

	1970	1975	1980	1985	1986
United States	15.4	13.6	12.1	12.3	11.4
France	6.4	6.7	6.3	5.9	6.4
West Germany	12.1	11.4	10.5	10.6	12.2
United Kingdom	7.0	5.6	6.0	5.8	5.5
Japan	6.9	7.1	7.1	10.2	10.8

Source: *Business America*, June 23, 1986, and November 23, 1987.

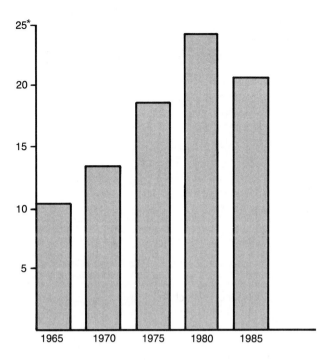

*Imports and exports of goods and services as a percentage of GNP.

FIGURE 2-2   U.S. Economic Involvement in Foreign Trade (*Source:* U.S. Commerce Department.)

capital goods; industrial supplies and materials; foods, feeds, beverages; and automotive products. Service exports are also important. Commerce Department estimates indicated that about 2,000 United States firms generated over 70 percent of United States manufactured exports,[2] and many firms never export.

The United States has been maintaining its share of *manufactured exports* from industrial countries in recent years. An estimated 17.5 percent share in 1985 compares with shares of 16.8 percent and 18.4 percent in 1980 and 1970, respectively. Despite this solid performance, the rise of imports, particularly high-tech goods (traditionally a field of world-leadership for the United States), has proved worrisome. In 1980, for example, the balance of United States high-tech exports to imports was a surplus of $26.7 billion. This figure has declined rapidly, falling to $18.8 billion in 1983, $3.6 billion in 1985, and in 1986, moved into the red with an estimated deficit of $2.6 billion.[3]

Table 2-7 shows that the major trading partners of the United States are primarily other large industrial countries augmented by NICs such as Taiwan, South Korea, and Mexico. A regional trend of growing significance is United States trade with Pacific countries, which has recently surpassed transatlantic trade between the United States and Europe. This development is primarily due to the very sharp rise in the 1980s of trade with Japan, Taiwan, South Korea, and Hong Kong, much of which is import business.

TABLE 2-7
Leading U.S. Trading Partners in 1986

U.S. Export Markets*	$ Billions	U.S. Suppliers†	$ Billions
World Total	217.3	World Total	387.1
1. Canada	45.3	1. Japan	85.5
2. Japan	26.9	2. Canada	68.7
3. Mexico	12.4	3. West Germany	26.1
4. United Kingdom	11.4	4. Taiwan	21.3
5. West Germany	10.6	5. Mexico	17.6
6. Netherlands	7.8	6. United Kingdom	16.0
7. France	7.2	7. South Korea	13.5
8. South Korea	6.4	8. Italy	11.3
9. Australia	5.6	9. France	10.6
10. Taiwan	5.5	10. Hong Kong	9.5
11. Belgium & Luxembourg	5.4	11. Brazil	7.3
12. Italy	4.8	12. Venezuela	5.4
13. Brazil	3.9	13. Switzerland	5.4
14. Saudi Arabia	3.4	14. China	5.2
15. Singapore	3.4	15. Singapore	4.9
16. Venezuela	3.1	16. Sweden	4.6
17. China	3.1	17. Netherlands	4.4
18. Hong Kong	3.0	18. Belgium & Luxembourg	4.2
19. Switzerland	3.0	19. Saudi Arabia	4.1
20. Spain	2.6	20. Indonesia	3.7
21. Israel	2.2	21. Spain	3.0
22. Egypt	2.0	22. Australia	2.9
23. Sweden	1.9	23. Nigeria	2.7
24. Malaysia	1.7	24. Malaysia	2.5
25. India	1.5	25. Israel	2.5

* Merchandise exports, 1986 f.a.s. value
† Merchandise imports, 1986 c.i.f. value
Source: *Business America*, March 30, 1987, p. 6.

Foreign Direct Investment

Global Patterns

Foreign direct investment (FDI) has been defined as "the establishment or purchase by residents of one country of a substantial ownership and management share—which is deemed to constitute an 'effective voice in management'—of a business enterprise or real property in another country."[4] This form of international engagement has historic antecedents in direct European investment in America, Asia, and Africa from as early as the seventeenth century.

Since the end of World War II, FDI has increased rapidly, providing the foundation for the current operations of many powerful MNCs. The scope of direct investment has also widened considerably, with investment in service industries (banking, insurance, tourism, retailing, and so on) as well as in more traditional activities such as manufacturing, mining, and distribution. By 1960, the value of the world stock of FDI was estimated at $66 billion. Subsequent growth has averaged over 10 percent per annum. By 1981 the value of the stock of FDI had increased by 730 percent to $546 billion. The net result of this investment was that by the late 1980s, some 10,000 companies had FDI interests giving them control over at least 90,000 foreign affiliates. The big MNCs, however, still have a dominating position, with the 500 largest investors controlling some 80 percent of these afffiliates.[5]

Up to around 1960, FDI from the United States and United Kingdom was dominant. Since then, FDI from other West European countries and Japan has become more important because of investment in manufacturing and marketing operations in Western Europe and North America.

Table 2-8 shows that the major foreign investors are the rich industrial countries in Western Europe, North America, and Japan. In 1981, 95 percent of the stock of FDI was held by firms based in these countries. The high volume of FDI (relative to the size of the domestic economy) undertaken by Swiss, Dutch, and Swedish MNCs is particularly noteworthy.

Some 65 percent of the stock of FDI was held by Anglo-American firms in 1960. This figure had fallen to 48 percent by 1985. In the intervening years, the relative importance of West German, Japanese, Swiss, and Swedish FDI increased dramatically.

As is apparent from Table 2-9, the primary investing countries are also the major recipients of FDI. In 1981, for example, 75 percent of world FDI was located in North America, Western Europe, and Japan, with 36 percent accounted for by

TABLE 2-8
World FDI Classified by Country of Origin

	1960		1981		1985	
Country of Origin	Value* $Billions	% of Total	Value $Billions	% of Total	Value $Billions	% of Total
United States	31.9	48.5	226.4	41.5	232.7	34.0
United Kingdom	10.8	16.4	65.5	12.0	97.2	14.1
West Germany	0.8	1.2	45.5	8.3	56.9	8.3
Japan	0.5	0.8	37.0	6.8	57.5	8.4
Switzerland	2.0	3.0	36.4	6.7	41.7	6.1
Netherlands	7.0	10.6	32.4	5.9	47.2	6.9
Canada	2.5	3.8	25.6	4.7	39.5	5.8
France	4.1	6.2	24.5	4.5	33.4	4.9
Sweden	0.4	0.6	7.9	1.5	12.1	1.8
Belgium-Luxembourg	1.3	2.0	6.4	1.2	7.3	1.1
Italy	1.1	1.7	5.9	1.1	12.9	1.9
Australia	0.2	0.3	2.5	0.5	7.5	1.1
Other developed countries	2.5	3.8	12.0	2.2	39 }	5.7 }
Developing countries	0.7	1.1	17.6	3.2		
World total	65.8	100.0	545.6	100.0	684.9	100.0

* The value of the overall stock of FDI

Sources: *International Direct Investment: Global Trends and the U.S. Role* (Department of Commerce, 1984). *International Financial Statistics Yearbook* (IMF, 1986).

TABLE 2-9
World FDI Classified by Host Country

	1960 *% of* *Total*[1]	*1980* *% of* *Total*[1]
Host country		
United States	13.9	15.5
Canada	23.7	10.3
United Kingdom	9.2	10.2
Australia/S. Africa	6.6	6.2
Japan	0.2	1.5
Host region		
Western Europe	22.9	37.7
Latin America	15.6	14.9
Africa	5.5	2.8
Asia	7.5	6.9
Southern Europe	0.9	0.9
Middle East	2.8	1.9
Other unallocated	—	2.2

[1] Percentage of world stock of FDI
Source: J. M. Stopford and J. H. Dunning,
Multinationals: Company Performance and Global
Trends (Macmillan, 1983), Table 1.7.

the United States, Canada, and the United Kingdom. The drop in the relative significance of Canada as a host country and the big increase in FDI in Europe were significant trends from 1960 through 1980. This change was due mainly to increased FDI from the United States in Western Europe.

Disinvestment in petroleum and mining projects, plus the political and economic instability of some LDCs, has resulted in relatively less FDI in developing countries, particularly Africa. In 1960, investment in these countries represented some 32 percent of the FDI stock. By 1980, this figure had fallen to around 27 percent.

During the 1980s, FDI continued to increase rapidly, the United States being a favored target for FDI. The significance of FDI from the United States has continued to fall as flows from Japan and Western Europe have grown rapidly.

Some 50 percent of the stock of world FDI has been made in manufacturing ventures. Around 20 percent is accounted for by materials-based activities, with the remaining 30 percent focused on diverse service activities. However, national patterns vary. For example, some 75 percent of West German investment is concentrated in manufacturing activities. Service activities accounted for some 46 percent of the stock of Japanese FDI in 1983.[6]

An important issue concerns whether FDI occurs at the expense of exporting. This is a difficult topic to research, but there is evidence showing that firms with a high proportion of FDI assets have a higher propensity to export than do firms from the same industry with lower relative FDI.[7] Although it is evident that local production will replace some exports, continued intracorporate exports and above-average exports to markets where local manufacture does not occur are common in many MNCs. Although exports may have been even higher in some firms in the absence of FDI, it seems that FDI and exporting are often complementary activities. This complementarity is due to better market contact, information and consumer service resulting from FDI, especially investment in marketing subsidiaries; substantial intrafirm shipments of components, services, and finished goods in many MNCs; and the inevitable loss of some export markets (due to protectionism, for example) without FDI.

The United States Position

Prior to World War II, British FDI was of greatest significance. During the postwar period, the United States has become the major source and recipient of FDI.

In 1950, FDI holdings of United States firms were valued at $11.8 billion compared with $3.4 billion of foreign-owned direct investment in the United States. Subsequently, flows of FDI into and out of the United States have expanded very rapidly. It is apparent, from Table 2-10, that the value of United States FDI holdings still exceed the value of comparable foreign-owned assets in the United States. However, it is also evident that the gap is closing. During the 1980s, United States FDI has stagnated. At the same time, incoming FDI has increased very rapidly.

An overview of the United States FDI position in 1985 is presented in Tables 2-11 and 2-12. Data therein indicate that investment in the manufacturing and petroleum sectors accounted for 41 and 25 percent respectively of the stock of United States FDI. Investment in overseas marketing subsidiaries and financial services, such as banking and insurance, accounted for 10 and 16 percent of the investment stock.

Nearly 75 percent of United States investment is located within other developed countries. In the developing world, South and Central America and Asia accounted

TABLE 2-10
U.S. FDI and Overseas FDI Position in the
United States

	U.S. Stock of FDI*	Stock of FDI in U.S.*
1980	215.4	83.7
1981	228.3	108.7
1982	207.8†	124.7
1983	207.2	137.1
1984	213.0	164.6
1985	232.7	183.0
1986	259.9	209.3

* Book value in billion dollars

† The data from 1982 onward is not directly comparable with the earlier data because of changes in the data base resulting from the 1982 benchmark survey of U.S. FDI.

Source: *Survey of Current Business*, August 1987.

TABLE 2-11
U.S. FDI Position by Major Industry

	Billion $ (1985)	
Petroleum	58.3	
Manufacturing	95.6	
Food		9.3
Chemicals		19.8
Metals		5.5
Machinery		18.7
Electrical		8.8
Transport		11.8
Other		21.7
Wholesale trade	23.8	
Banking	14.7	
Insurance, real estate, etc.	21.9	
Services	5.3	
Other	13.1	
Total	232.7	

Source: *Survey of Current Business*, August 1986.

respectively, for 12.5 and 6.4 percent of FDI from the United States. Major target countries included Canada, the United Kingdom, West Germany, Switzerland, Brazil, and Japan.

In 1985, foreign direct investment holdings in the United States were valued at $183 billion, still some $50 billion behind the level of FDI holdings by United States firms. The service sector accounted for some 43 percent of this FDI—with much of this investment channeled into marketing subsidiaries—followed by 33 percent in manufacturing activities and 15 percent in the petroleum industry. Table 2-13 shows the FDI position by major industry.

Some 85 percent of FDI into the United States has originated in other industrial countries, mainly Western European. (Western Europe was the source of 75 percent of the investment stock.) Major investing countries include Japan, the United Kingdom, the Netherlands, West Germany, and Switzerland. Table 2-14 charts the overseas FDI position in the United States by major source countries.

During 1980–1985, FDI into the United States increased rapidly despite the strength of the dollar over much of this time. Apart from the sheer size of the United States market, other factors motivating this investment included the dynamism of the United States economy, increased protectionism in some industries, and favorable foreign investor perceptions of American political stability and commitment to free enterprise. The attraction of purchasing cheaper dollar assets resulting from the fall in the value of the dollar since 1985 is likely to result in a continued short-term, rapid increase in incoming FDI.

Foreign direct investment by the United States has been less dynamic in recent years, a trend that seems likely to continue over the next several years.

TABLE 2-12
U.S. FDI Position by Host Country

	Billion $ (1985)	
Developed	172.8	
Canada		46.4
Europe:		106.7
EEC:		82.1
France		7.8
West Germany		16.7
Netherlands		7.1
United Kingdom		34.0
Switzerland		16.2
Japan		9.1
Other:		10.5
Australia		8.6
Developing countries	54.5	
South America		18.6
Brazil		9.5
Central America		10.4
Mexico		5.1
Africa		5.0
Middle East		5.1
Asia		14.9
Other		0.5
Other	5.4	
	232.7	

Source: *Survey of Current Business*, August 1986.

This trend has several causes: a depreciated dollar increases the cost of overseas acquisitions; many major target countries for American FDI in Europe and the developing world have experienced slow economic growth during the 1980s, and; United States investors have been troubled by signs of political instability and government intervention in some markets. However, the size and scope of the activities of United States firms and continued investment opportunities overseas should ensure that FDI by the United States will continue to increase.

Other Forms of International Operations

We now turn to evaluating available information on nonequity contractual forms of international activity and of trade in services. A lack of appropriate data constrain our analysis, which must therefore be much less detailed than that presented for trade and FDI.

Nonequity Contractual Modes

Nonequity contractual modes of international operations are not easily classified or differentiated. Very often they entail complex arrangements. Typically, they involve technology transfer in one form or another and embrace elements of at

TABLE 2-13
Overseas FDI Position in the
United States by Major Industry

	Billion $ (1985)	
Mining	4.1	
Petroleum	28.1	
Manufacturing:	60.8	
Food		11.1
Chemicals		19.5
Metals		7.5
Machinery		9.5
Other		13.2
Wholesaling	27.5	
Retailing	6.7	
Banking	11.5	
Other finance	4.7	
Insurance	11.1	
Real estate	18.6	
Other	9.9	
Total	183.0	

Source: *Survey of Current Business,* August 1986.

least one of the following: the right to do, the means to do, and the ability to do. Nonequity contractual arrangements therefore generally involve the sale or exchange of corporate knowledge, expertise, and proprietary rights with a foreign business enterprise in return for fees, royalty payments, or other services. Two major categories of arrangements are licensing agreements, and management contracts.

In a *licensing agreement* exactly what is sold varies from agreement to agreement. Commonly, such contracts deal with the sale of new or improved technology relating to plant/equipment/production-processing techniques and the sale of proprietary rights to new or improved products, services, trademarks, and brand or company names. Typically, these corporate assets will be either well-guarded secrets or heavily protected by patents or copyrights.

In *the management contract,* the firm sells management expertise. *Turnkey* and *franchising* arrangements are common variants. Turnkey deals are complex, for they often involve licensing of production and process technologies, management contracts, and exports. Current examples include deals by Western oil firms to build petrochemical plants for Arab customers in the Middle East.

Information on the relative significance of royalties and fees—the major revenue from contractual modes—is difficult to obtain. However, balance-of-payments data may be used to estimate earnings from royalties and fees as a proportion of total returns from both FDI and overseas contractual operations. In the mid-1970s, in countries such as the United States, the United Kingdom and the Netherlands, these ratios were under 20 percent, a figure that suggests the greater relative importance of FDI. In France and Sweden, the comparable ratios were over 50

TABLE 2-14
Overseas FDI Position in the United States
by Source Country

	Billion $ (1985)	
Canada	16.7	
Europe	120.9	
EEC;		106.0
France		6.3
West Germany		14.4
Netherlands		36.1
United Kingdom		43.8
Other:		14.9
Switzerland		11.0
Japan	19.1	
Latin America	17.1	
Middle East	5.0	
Other	4.2	
Total	183.0	

Source: *Survey of Current Business*, August 1986.

percent, showing a greater significance of nonequity overseas contractual business. These data imply that the relative importance of foreign contractual operations varies significantly between countries.

International Trade in Services

Measuring trade in international services is difficult because of definitional problems and a lack of data. Many definitions emphasize that service products are intangible and short-lived when compared with physical goods. However, such is not always the case. Many services, tourism for example, do involve tangible products as major components. (The definition issue is discussed in more detail in Chapter 13.) At this point, we need focus only on those products intended primarily to provide a service. We will further assume that, in contrast to most other "goods," these services are consumed more or less as they are produced and tend to be labor intensive. Such services therefore include insurance, banking, transport, tourism, consulting, and other similar professional activities.

Statistics on international trade in services are hard to come by for a variety of reasons. It is, however, possible to use balance-of-payments data to obtain an overview of international service flows. In the early 1980s, for example, service exports we estimated at between 15 and 20 percent of total global exports. Typically, the richer countries export more services than do most developing countries.

Barriers to trade in international services are widespread, typically taking the form of government mandated discrimination against foreign suppliers. Pressure to remove such barriers is likely to increase in GATT negotiations. However, many countries, particularly those in the developing world, oppose greater liberalization.

Despite these problems, many international service firms are growing rapidly and FDI in service activities is growing faster than is investment in other areas.

In the case of the United States, exports of business services are estimated at around 20 percent of merchandise exports, accounting for over 1 percent of the United States' GNP. The United States is the world's largest exporter of services, with a particularly strong position in high-tech information, financial and specialized businesses, and professional services. The major United States markets for service exports are Canada, Mexico, Western Europe, and Japan. Providing protectionist barriers are reduced, many NICs also offer attractive opportunities for United States service firms.

World Production

The relative stagnation of world output and income in the early 1980s must be viewed against earlier decades of growth. World output and income expanded rapidly during the three decades following World War II. Growth rates in the 1960s and 1970s were good, as Table 2-15 attests.

TABLE 2-15
Growth of Volume of World Production

	1963	1973	1979	1983
Total, all commodities (1963 = 100)	100	180	220	230
Agriculture	100	128	147	154
Mining	100	171	199	184
Manufacturing	100	197	249	259

Source: GATT, *International Trade*, 1983–1984, Table A1.

Increases in manufacturing output have provided the backbone for growth. Growth in agricultural and mining production has been less impressive, as is apparent from Table 2-15. Data on services are not available, but that sector has seen a dynamic expansion in many countries.

TABLE 2-16
Performance of Industrial and Developing Countries*

Country Group	1965–73	1973–80	1980–85
Industrial countries			
GDP growth	4.7	2.8	2.2
GDP per capita	3.7	2.1	1.7
Developing countries			
GDP growth	6.6	5.4	3.3
GDP per capita	4.0	3.2	1.3

* Average annual percentage change
Source: *World Development Report 1986*, The World Bank, 1986, pp. 44, 45.

Despite the relatively slow growth of many natural-resource industries, it is evident from Table 2-16 that during the 1960s and 1970s both GDP and GDP per capita grew most rapidly in the developing countries. However, this growth was skewed in favor of the NICs and oil exporters; many developing countries, notably those in Africa, had painfully slow growth. In recent years, many centrally planned economies have enjoyed relatively good economic growth, although the average standard of living in these countries continues to lag well behind standards enjoyed in well-developed market economies.

World output slumped from 1980 to 1982 when average growth declined to less than 1.5 percent per annum. Since then, output and incomes have increased more rapidly as the sharp rebound in the United States economy, which accounts for over 25 percent of the world economy, stimulated a recovery from the recession. During the 1980s, many developing countries have been hit particularly hard as their terms of trade deteriorated and their debt problems became more serious as real interest rates increased and export earnings stagnated. The economies of developed and centrally planned countries have been more robust in the 1980s.

THE BALANCE OF PAYMENTS

The balance of payments provides an accounting record of economic transactions between the residents of the reporting country and the residents of the rest of the world over a specified period. These accounts are based on double-entry bookkeeping principles; the overall payments statement therefore must balance. This is not so for the different accounts that together make up the overall balance of payments. We will focus on three major sections of the balance-of-payments statement: the current account, the capital account and the official reserves account. These accounts are shown in Table 2-17, which breaks down the United States balance of payments in 1986.

The Current Account

The *current account* section of the balance of payments is generally of the greatest interest to the international marketer, for it tracks imports and exports of goods and services (including interest, dividend, and royalty payments) and unilateral transfers. This last group of transactions shows the value of gifts, private and public, given and received, and includes such items as military and foreign aid grants, immigrant remittances, and private gifts.

Flows of tangible physical products and commodities are tracked in the *merchandise trade* balance. These transactions—and service-related flows resulting from transport, tourism, banking, insurance, and dividend and interest payments—constitute the major components of the current account. Tracking these flows is important because of their direct link to the domestic economy and their size; normally they make up the largest component of the overall balance of payments statement. Exports of goods and services, for example, are major sources of revenue, profit, and employment, and they generate funds to pay for imports.

Capital and Official Reserve Accounts

The *capital account* records capital flows into and out of the reporting country. Only the *net* changes in foreign claims and liabilities are shown, not gross flows

TABLE 2-17
1986* U.S. Balance of Payments *in dollar units*

Debit entries or outpayments (−)		Credit entries or inpayments (+)	
Current account			
Imports of goods	369	Exports of goods	222
Imports of services	127	Exports of services	149
Net unilateral transfers to foreigners *gifts*	15	*tourism, banking, insurance*	
Capital account			
(Capital outflow)		(Capital inflow)	
Net increase in U.S. assets abroad other than official reserves	100	Net increase in foreign assets in the United States other than official reserves	180
Official reserve account			
		Net increase in foreign official assets in the United States	33
		Credits	584
Net increase in U.S. official reserve assets	0	Errors and omissions	27
Total debits	611	Total credits	611
Balances			
Balance on merchandise trade:	−147		
Balance on current account:	−140		

* Provisional figures, billions of U.S. dollars
Source: *Survey of Current Business*, March 1987.

(handwritten: $147 billion trade deficit)

(for many short-term assets such as bonds are bought and sold many times in a year). The capital account also includes long-term direct investment and portfolio investment flows as well as short-term capital flows generated by bank deposits, bonds, and other commercial and financial paper transactions.

The *official reserve account* measures transactions between official monetary authorities (primarily central banks), and reflects transfers of gold and foreign exchange, and lending and borrowing between government-controlled institutions. Transactions with international financial institutions, mainly those with the International Monetary Fund (IMF), will also show up in this account.

Most official reserve transactions finance imbalances in the remainder of the balance of payments. They also result from central bank intervention in foreign exchange markets. Hence their name as compensatory measures. Not all international transactions show up on the balance sheet, however.

Currency flight and other underground transactions often go unrecorded and undetected. Some international economic transactions are carried out illegally, as is the case of currency smugglers, who exchange smuggled money for hard currency and invest overseas. It is thus necessary to add an additional entry, errors and omissions, to balance the overall account. (See Table 2-17.)

Patterns in the Balance of Payments

It is evident from Table 2-18 that dramatic changes in the balance of payments of many countries took place during the mid-1980s. Until 1982, the United States was the world's primary creditor nation. Subsequent massive payments deficits on the current account have resulted in a complete reversal of this situation; and by 1986 the United States was the world's largest net debtor. Other developed countries, notably West Germany and Japan, have earned very large current account surpluses in recent years.

Many developing countries also experienced severe balance-of-payments difficulties. Their problems had multiple causes: depressed commodity sales and low prices, serious debt servicing problems caused by high interest rates, lower levels of inward investment flows from developed countries, and an inability to borrow in private international capital markets.

In this century, the United States has typically earned surpluses on the merchandise and current accounts of its balance of payments. Since 1971, apart from

TABLE 2-18
World Balance of Payments on Current Account by Country Group, 1981–1987*

Country Groups	1981	1982	1983	1984	1985	1986†	1987†
			(Billions of dollars)				
Developed market economies	−7.2	−6.1	−5.8	−44.7	−27.7	11.4	−15.0
Excluding United States	−20.1	−5.7	31.8	54.1	96.1	152.0	145.7
Major industrial countries:	20.8	15.5	1.6	−44.5	−34.1	−18.1	−40.5
Canada	−5.5	1.7	1.2	2.0	−1.8	−6.7	−7.0
France	−2.8	−9.4	−3.1	1.0	2.0	3.0	−4.5
West Germany	1.7	10.5	10.6	13.4	28.4	37.0	44.6
Italy	−7.9	−5.1	0.8	−2.6	−3.9	4.3	5.0
Japan	6.2	8.1	22.2	36.4	55.6	86.3	86.7
United Kingdom	16.3	10.0	7.6	4.3	9.4	−1.4	−4.6
United States	12.9	−0.3	−37.6	−98.8	−123.8	−140.6	−160.7
Developing countries	−40.6	−95.8	−66.8	−45.8	−22.4	−43.7	−36.1
China	2.0	5.9	4.4	2.4	−11.4	−7.8	−7.5
Socialist countries of Eastern Europe	3.6	13.7	17.1	18.0	2.4	−2.2	−0.9

* Excluding government transfers
† Preliminary estimates
Sources: *World Economic Survey 1986* (New York: United Nations); *Handbook of International Trade and Development Statistics*, (New York: United Nations, 1986); and *The Economist*.

1975, the merchandise trade account has been in deficit. However, strong service earnings more than counterbalanced these small deficits, and during the 1970s the United States earned a surplus on its current account balance in most years.

During the 1980s, stagnant export earnings and a rapid increase in imports plunged the merchandise trade balance heavily into the red. A continued surplus on the services account was maintained, but it was swamped by the size of the merchandise trade deficit. A willingness by foreigners, notably the Japanese and Western Europeans, to increase long- and short-term United States investment holdings, and lower United States overseas investment have financed the current account deficit. Unfortunately, as interest and dividend remittances from the United States outstrip U.S. earnings overseas, the service surplus will be reduced. It is thus imperative that a significant improvement in the United States merchandise trade account occur.

The depreciation of the dollar since 1985 has brought some improvement in the trade imbalance. In real (volume) terms, the United States merchandise trade deficit has improved steadily since mid-1986, mainly because of strong growth in exports. Between 1986 and 1988, imports remained at a high level, partly because around 25 percent of United States imports—mainly food and oil— are priced in dollars; their price is thus unaffected by dollar depreciation. Although the merchandise trade deficit is anticipated to drop somewhat from 1987's $171 billion, huge foreign capital inflows will still be needed in the 1990s to finance the current account deficit (in 1987, around $160 billion). Unfortunately this implies greater interest payments to foreigners (which increased by some $11 billion in 1987 and are projected to increase a further $12 billion in 1988). Just to stabilize the current account deficit at its 1987 level, a $12 billion improvement in the merchandise trade account was thus needed in 1988. This indicates a need for a large and continuing improvement in the merchandise trade balance in the nineties.

INTERNATIONAL TRADE THEORY

This section discusses two issues central to international trade theory.

1. What are the gains from international trade?
2. Which goods should a country export and which products should it import?

An understanding of the concepts of absolute and comparative advantage is crucial when addressing both questions. Our analysis will therefore explain these concepts and their relevance for international specialization and trade. We will then survey recent theories of trade.

Absolute Advantage

Adam Smith, an advocate of free trade, argued in his *Wealth of Nations* that countries should specialize in the production of those goods in which they have an absolute advantage. Surplus output should be exported in return for goods in which a country has an absolute disadvantage. A nation enjoys absolute advantage for those goods it is able to produce more efficiently, and thus more cheaply, than can other countries.

A simple example illustrates the concept of absolute advantage and the advantages of international trade and specialization. Assume a two-product, two-country world with perfect competition, and no transport costs. Further assume that one production unit—a given mix of land, labor, and capital—can produce six bushels of wheat or one yard of cloth in the United States. The same production unit can produce three yards of cloth or one bushel of wheat in the United Kingdom.

Assume autarky (self-sufficiency) in both the United States and the United Kingdom, with two production units available in each country, one unit devoted to wheat output and one unit to cloth production. This results in the following production matrix:

	Output	
	U.S.	**U.K.**
Wheat (bushels)	6	1
Cloth (yards)	1	3

Since the United States can produce six times as much wheat as the United Kingdom using the same input of resources, it is apparent that the United States has absolute advantage in the output of wheat. The United Kingdom is three times more efficient at making cloth, and thus has absolute advantage for this product.

If complete specialization occurs in each country in line with absolute advantage, the following production matrix, with the same resource commitment, results:

	Output	
	U.S.	**U.K.**
Wheat (bushels)	12	0
Cloth (yards)	0	6

Is it now possible for each country to trade and enjoy a higher standard of living, without having worked any harder, than that attained under autarky? The answer is clearly yes since world output of wheat has increased by five bushels and world output of cloth by two yards. The only requirement is that both countries arrive at mutually beneficial barter terms of trade, terms that allow a sharing of the incremental output of wheat and cloth generated by specialization. In the case of the United States, international trade is beneficial as long as six bushels of wheat are worth more than one yard of cloth. Failing this, it is more beneficial to switch production at home if more cloth is needed. Similarly, the United Kingdom is interested in trade only when three yards of cloth are worth more than one bushel of wheat.

An example of mutually acceptable terms of trade is therefore two wheat for one cloth. At this exchange rate, the following outcome would be one of a number of possible outcomes clearly superior to the consumption levels feasible under autarky:

	Consumption		
	U.S.	**U.K.**	
Wheat (bushel)	8	— 4 shipped to U.K. →	4
Cloth (yards)	2	← 2 shipped to U.S. —	4

Comparative Advantage

Nearly fifty years after the publication of Smith's *Wealth of Nations,* the English economist David Ricardo argued that international trade was still desirable even when one country is more efficient than another in every line of production. According to Ricardo, countries should base specialization on *comparative advantage* rather than absolute advantage.

Comparative advantage exists whenever the *relative* ability of countries to produce goods differs. Countries should specialize in producing goods where they enjoy the greatest *relative* advantage (or *relatively* least disadvantage) as measured by relative prices under autarky.

The following example illustrates the nature and significance of the comparative advantage model. Assume a situation of autarky that is the same as that described in the absolute advantage example with one exception: the productivity relationships are changed so that one production unit can make either six wheat or four cloth in the United States and either one wheat or two cloth in the United Kingdom. As in the previous examples, assume that two production units are available in each country, with one used for wheat production and one for the output of cloth. The following output matrix will then characterize autarky:

	Output		Opportunity Cost	
	U.S.	**U.K.**	**U.S.**	**U.K.**
Wheat (bushels)	6	1	4/6 Cloth	2 Cloth
Cloth (yards)	4	2	6/4 Wheat	1/2 Wheat

The United States now enjoys absolute advantage in the output of both wheat and cloth and, according to Adam Smith, there is no basis for mutually beneficial international trade. However, the United States is *relatively* most efficient in producing wheat since resources used in wheat production in the United States are now six times more productive than in the United Kingdom. In the case of cloth, the United States is only twice as efficient as the United Kingdom. The United Kingdom is therefore relatively least inefficient in the output of cloth and thus enjoys a comparative advantage in cloth production.

This analysis can be confirmed by measuring the opportunity cost of wheat and cloth in both the United States and the United Kingdom. The opportunity cost of one bushel of wheat—in terms of yards of cloth—is 0.66 in the United States and 2 in the United Kingdom. Thus, every bushel of wheat produced in the United States represents giving up the chance of making only 0.66 yards of cloth as compared to 2 yards produced in the United Kingdom. Wheat is therefore relatively cheaper, in terms of the amount of cloth foregone, in the United States.

It follows that the United States has comparative advantage in output of wheat. Similar logic indicates that, in terms of the amount of wheat given up, cloth is relatively cheapest in the United Kingdom, and the United Kingdom thus enjoys comparative advantage in its production.

Two other important determinants of both comparative and absolute advantage in the real world (besides the productivity relationships considered so far) are foreign exchange relationships and the cost of factor inputs. Let us now incorporate both these elements into the example to demonstrate that the comparative advantage model is robust and can handle these vital components of an actual economy.

Assuming that one production unit costs $10 in the United States, and £10 in the United Kingdom, then the following cost of production data obtain:

	Cost per Unit	
	U.S.	**U.K.**
Wheat per bushel	$\frac{\$10}{6} = \$1.67$	$\frac{£10}{1} = £10$
Cloth per yard	$\frac{\$10}{4} = \$2.5$	$\frac{£10}{2} = £5$

Assume further that the exchange rate between the pound and the dollar is set according to barter terms of trade in which one wheat (cost $1.67) equals one cloth (cost £5). The exchange rate will therefore be $1.67 = £5, or $1 = £3.

Given these relationships, international trade is clearly beneficial. For each bushel of wheat exported at a cost of $1.67, the United States receives a yard of cloth that would have cost $2.5 to make domestically. The United Kingdom also benefits since for each bushel of wheat received that would have cost £10 to make at home, it is necessary to ship a yard of cloth that costs only £5 to produce.

We may conclude that a *country's comparative advantage situation* will be vitally affected by (1) the *productivity* of available factor inputs—principally land, labor, and capital; (2) *the cost* of these inputs in terms of the local currency; and (3) the value of this currency in terms of other currencies—*the foreign exchange rate.* Changes in any of these variables will have important implications for national comparative advantage.

It should also be evident that countries benefit from concentrating on the output of those products where they enjoy comparative advantage and that surplus production of these products should be exported in return for needed imports. In an environment of international specialization and free trade, global output will be maximized and consumers will enjoy higher standards of living than under autarky.

The Hecksher-Ohlin Model

According to Ricardo, differences in labor productivity are the underlying reason for variance in comparative advantage. Ricardo's position has been criticized for assuming that labor is the only factor of production and for not giving an explicit explanation for the cause of differences in labor productivity.

It was left to two Swedish economists, Eli Hecksher and Bertil Ohlin, to offer a direct explanation of the reasons for differences in national comparative advantage in their famous *factor endowments theory,* developed some sixty years ago. According to the model, the underlying reason for international trade is differences in the factor endowments of different countries. Relative factor abundance will lead to low factor costs. The theory posits that countries will export products that intensively use their most abundant resources. Wheat, for example, requires large inputs of fertile land. Since this production factor is in relatively abundant supply in the United States, cost of land is relatively low. Consequently, relative costs of United States wheat output are low, and the United States enjoys a comparative advantage in the output of this product.

Some have criticized the Hecksher-Ohlin framework because it is based on assumptions that have become increasingly unrealistic in today's economy. Particular exception has been taken to the assumption that technology is the same in all countries and the seeming disregard of nonprice competition. Leontief's famous 1953 study of patterns of international trade has also given the model less credence. Contrary to the expected outcome for the most capital-intensive country in the world, Leontief found that the United States exported labor-intensive products and imported capital-intensive goods.

Other Theories

Because of the aforementioned problems with the classical and neoclassical body of trade theory and the difficulty of developing a theoretical framework that can completely account for such a complex phenomenon as international trade, economists have developed a number of other trade theories. From an international marketing perspective, the two most interesting are the product life cycle model and Linder's theory. Both focus on patterns of trade in manufactured goods. Thus, they do not have the general application of the Hecksher-Ohlin model.

Linder's Theory

Staffan Linder distinguishes between trade in primary products, which he believes is a function of factor endowments as outlined in the Hecksher-Ohlin model, and trade in manufactures.[8] In the case of the latter, he argues that patterns of international trade are determined principally by demand factors, not factor intensities.

In the Linder model, products are produced initially for domestic consumption because of a limited knowledge and understanding of the needs of foreign consumers and of the cost of developing export products. The domestic product range therefore delimits the potential export range, and international trade is fundamentally an expansion of domestic trade.

It follows that the potential for trade in manufactures is greatest between countries with similar consumer needs and preferences. Linder argues that the principal determinant of the demand structure is the level of per capita income, and that most trade in manufactured goods takes place among countries that are very similar on this dimension and other factors that influence the structure of demand, such as consumer taste.

The International Product Life Cycle Theory

The international product life cycle (IPLC) theory, originally presented by Raymond Vernon in 1966,[9] attempts to explain patterns of international trade and foreign direct investment. Innovation, variance in national technological capability, and the IPLC play central roles in this theory. In essence, Vernon argues that, as a product moves through its life cycle, factor input requirements will change and the location of production centers with comparative advantage will thus alter. Consequently, as a product moves from initially requiring large R&D factor inputs to requiring increasing unskilled labor and capital inputs, it becomes more attractive to manufacture overseas. Reversals in initial trade flows result, and foreign direct investment is stimulated. This process can best be described in terms of the fundamental determinant in the model, the IPLC. Figure 2-3 shows three stages of development—new product, maturity, and standardization.

New Product Stage. Most new products are developed and initially produced in the more advanced economies, particularly in the United States. Primary reasons for this situation are the large numbers of high-income consumers with a taste for new products and the plentiful supply of skilled technical workers, who provide a comparative advantage in R&D capability.

In this phase, the good is produced in the innovating country (assumed to be the United States in this example though such is frequently not the case) and local consumption constitutes the main demand segment. Overall demand is limited and is characteristically price inelastic. Since the design and production of the good are still in the experimental stage, the manufacturing and R&D centers must be in constant close contact. The advantages of domestic production thus outweigh any production cost penalties. Limited overseas demand is serviced by exports from the innovating country.

Maturity Stage. Overall output and demand increase rapidly during this phase, particularly in other advanced overseas markets. The product becomes more uniform, production methods more routinized and price competition more important. For these reasons, overseas manufacture becomes attractive, particularly in industrial economies where production costs are competitive and transport costs or protectionist measures limit imports.

Exports from the United States remain high in the early part of the maturity phase. However, as unit costs fall overseas, foreign production, either by the innovator or competing firms, becomes more attractive and increasingly displaces United States export sales. Imports of the product begin to penetrate United States markets as initial trade flows start reversing.

Standardized Product Phase. The product and technology are now standardized and readily available. Intense price competition is typical and cost minimization crucially important. Foreign output increases rapidly as production falls precipitously in the United States, and also declines rapidly in other industrial countries. Manufacture of the good is increasingly centered in newly industrializing countries and other developing countries where plentiful supplies of low-cost labor are available for routine, often capital-intensive, mass output of uniform products.

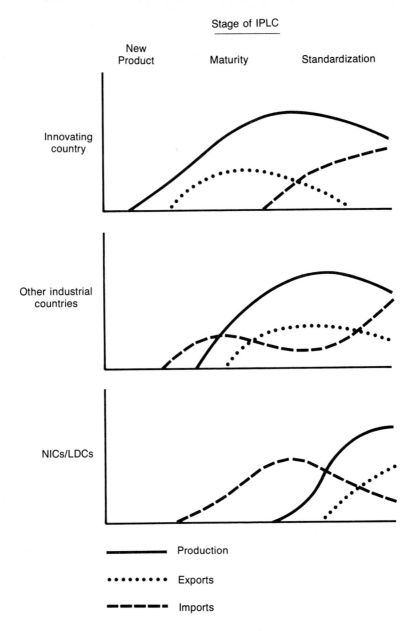

FIGURE 2-3   The International Product Life Cycle Model

Exports from these countries expand rapidly to source demand in the developed markets. As imports boom in the rich countries, their export sales drop sharply to very low levels.

A number of studies indicate that the IPLC model is useful in helping to understand patterns of United States trade and FDI. Thus United States exports tend to be R&D intensive, are expensive, are characterized by high income elasticity, and go largely to consumers in other industrial countries. The United States has also traditionally bought a high proportion of standard imports that sell mainly on the basis of price.

The IPLC model does not, however, satisfactorily account for a good deal of United States trade and investment, and it is even less useful in explaining flows of trade and investment in other countries. Note, therefore, that although the model is relevant when describing the initial international expansion of many United States firms, its explanatory value is not universal.[10]

Concluding Comments

The preceding discussion shows that international specialization in line with national comparative advantage and international trade is mutually beneficial to trading nations. In the Hecksher-Ohlin model, differences in factor endowments provide the reason for variance in comparative advantage and, therefore, the basis for trade. Newer models, which are best viewed as complementary to rather than conflicting with the Hecksher-Ohlin model, demonstrate the importance of other factors in influencing flows of trade in many manufactured goods. The Linder model, for example, demonstrates the central role of the structure of demand on trading patterns. The IPLC model is more dynamic; showing how comparative advantage among nations for the production of a good may shift as the product moves through its life cycle.

FOREIGN DIRECT INVESTMENT THEORY

The distinguishing feature of multinational enterprises is that they achieve managerial *control* over assets in overseas markets through foreign direct investment (FDI). Although capital flows due to FDI are smaller than portfolio investment flows, the theory of FDI has attracted a great deal of attention because it is central to understanding the activities of multinational enterprises.

Motives for FDI

FDI can take many different forms apart from the more obvious possibilities such as investment in overseas marketing and manufacturing subsidiaries. Historically, FDI in resource-based activities, such as agricultural plantations and mining, has been very important. More recently, much investment has been channeled into service-based activities such as banking, insurance, and tourism.

Research indicates that motivations for FDI are diverse. In the case of *natural resource seekers,* such as petroleum and mining MNCs, the major attraction is the benefits arising from owning and controlling natural resources that are unavailable or in short supply at home. *Cost and efficiency* investors are primarily attracted by the possibility of producing goods and services overseas more efficiently, and thus less expensively, than at home. Sometimes FDI becomes an undesirable necessity for *market protectors,* firms that wish to protect foreign market share originally developed through exports. Natural barriers to exporting, posed by transport costs and an inability to deliver a satisfactory level of service to end users, are often reinforced by artificial barriers created by protectionist measures. Finally, *information seekers* are motivated by a desire to establish "listening posts" in foreign markets and obtain valuable knowledge and experience by virtue of controlling operations in advanced, competitive, overseas markets.

The Eclectic Model

Given the diversity indicated above, both in terms of the form of FDI and motivations for such investment, it is not an easy task to develop a comprehensive theory of FDI.

Most recent theories of FDI are based on a *market imperfections paradigm.*[11] In this framework, multinational enterprises are seen as oligopolists deriving specific *ownership advantages* from control over assets not readily available to competing firms. These assets are most usually of an intangible nature (trademarks, copyrights, and knowledge) and allow for product differentiation that competitors are unable to replicate because of the proprietary and protected nature of these assets.

The existence of oligopolists with ownership-specific advantages does not of itself account for FDI. In the *eclectic model,* two additional elements—*internalization* and *location specific advantages*—are incorporated into a comprehensive explanation of FDI.[12] Internalization theory is of particular importance and is the focus of recent work on the theory of FDI.

In the eclectic model, firms possessing ownership-specific advantages are attracted to FDI because of the benefits of locating operations within foreign markets. The key forces at work are usually cost related. Foreign location may be advantageous because of the availability of inexpensive local factor inputs or the high cost of shipping exports. Even when the cost equation does not favor overseas location, revenue-related factors may have a powerful impact. For example, artificial barriers to exports or the ability to better serve customers from a foreign facility may be important.

The final element in the model concerns the advantages of internalizing economic transactions within the firm rather than utilizing external markets. The central proposition here is that multinational enterprises find internalizing economic transactions within the firm by means of foreign direct investment is advantageous because of market imperfections which cause high transaction costs for firms using external markets. Internalization theory is an interesting international application of Oliver Williamson's seminal work on markets and hierarchies.[13]

The internalization framework helps explain why firms will favor FDI rather than nonequity contractual alternatives when exporting is not viable. In the case of licensing, for example, associated transaction problems include the costs of identifying, negotiating with, and controlling potential licensees. Other problems arise because knowledge is a public good; this greatly complicates pricing. When these problems make external market transactions undesirable, firms will internalize across national boundaries through FDI. Successful internalization is possible because of the ownership-specific advantages possessed by the firm that are projected by means of FDI. Thus, despite the inherent problems (at least initially) of operating overseas, MNCs are still able to enjoy competitive advantage over local enterprises, which enjoy substantial benefits purely from being local.

Other Theories of FDI

Most of the cutting edge work on the theory of the multinational enterprise (MNE) has focused on the development of internalization models. However, other theories of FDI are still current and deserve a brief review.

The international product life cycle (IPLC) model is both a theory of international trade and FDI. Firms wishing to take advantage of shifts in national comparative advantage for production of a good as it moves through the maturity and standardization phases of the PLC must be prepared to undertake FDI. However, there are particular problems using the model to account for a good deal of FDI, for example in raw materials and low technology industries. The theory also does not account for a preference for investment rather than other alternatives, such as licensing, when exporting from home is not viable.

Oligopolistic rivalry has been seen to have important explanatory power. Knickerbocker argues that in loose-knit oligopoly, firms are likely to replicate the major strategic initiatives, such as FDI, adopted by competitors.[14] Consequently, if one firm invests overseas, it triggers a bunching effect as rivals imitate its behavior. Although various empirical studies give some credibility to this model, it is only a partial account of FDI; it does not account for the initial foreign investment that is the catalyst for subsequent investment flows.

Foreign direct investment has also been interpreted as a strategy to reduce risk by means of *international diversification*. The risk exposure of firms can be reduced by investing in a number of countries whose national economic cycles are not correlated. Market risk exposure, therefore, falls as the firm escapes dependence on a single national economy, the state of which poses risks for all businesses located in the particular market. Imperfections in financial markets, due to such factors as government controls, greatly limit the ability of many individual investors to developed diversified, global investment portfolios. Since MNCs are much less inhibited by such controls, they provide an indirect means of international diversification. Their stock will thus be more valuable to investors because of the diversification achieved due to their FDI activities. Once again, there is debate on the validity of this perspective. Much of the debate centers on the extent and impact of imperfections in international financial markets, an area in which there is conflicting empirical evidence and opinions.

SUMMARY

Patterns of international business and relevant theoretical frameworks for understanding these activities are the main focus in this chapter. International business transactions involve the transfer of goods, services, and factor inputs across national boundaries. In the international context special problems result from environmental heterogeneity, distance, and nationalism. International trade has expanded very rapidly during the postwar period. Major factors in this expansion were the rapid growth in world output, reduced protectionism, more efficient international communication and transport methods, and greater regional economic integration. As a result, international trade has significantly increased in relative importance in most economies.

Sharp changes in patterns of trade have occurred in the postwar era. Most trade involves a mutual exchange of manufactured goods between rich industrial countries. Agricultural trade has become relatively less important and there have been big changes in market share between trading nations. During the early 1980s, international trade stagnated as economic growth slowed and the income elasticity of world trade fell. In the mid-1980s, international trade started growing again, despite instability caused by major swings in the international value of the dollar. Although the United States is the major world trader because of heavy United States import demand, West Germany replaced the United States as the world's leading exporter in 1986.

Foreign direct investment has increased rapidly in the postwar era in volume and scope. The relative importance of Anglo American FDI has declined since 1960 as investment from other Western European nations and Japan has increased. The major sources and hosts for FDI are the rich industrial countries. The United States is both the major world recipient and source of FDI, and during the 1980s inward FDI has been increasing more rapidly than outgoing FDI from the United States.

The development of international trade in services and nonequity contractual modes (such as licensing, management contract, and turnkey projects) is not easy to measure. However, available data indicates that both activities are significantly less important than merchandise trade and FDI. World output grew rapidly from 1950 to 1970, but growth then slowed, particularly in developing countries.

Balance-of-payments statements provide an accounting record of economic transactions between residents of one country and the rest of the world. The major components of the balance of payments are the current, capital and official reserve accounts. During the 1980s, the United States current account performance deteriorated sharply. Many developing countries also experienced balance-of-payments problems. Some other countries, notably West Germany and Japan, have generated heavy current account surpluses in recent years.

An understanding of the concepts of absolute and comparative advantage is important when considering benefits from international trade and appropriate patterns of international production specialization. Adam Smith argued that countries should specialize in line with national absolute advantage. David Ricardo showed that international trade is still advantageous when a nation enjoys absolute advantage in the output of all goods. He argued that nations should specialize in producing those goods where they enjoy comparative advantage.

Hecksher and Ohlin argued that the underlying reason for international trade is differences in national factor endowments. They predicted that countries will export products that use intensively a nation's most abundant resources. The validity of some of the assumptions underlying the classical and Hecksher-Ohlin theories has been challenged, and a number of alternative trade theories have been developed. These models demonstrate the influence of other factors in the real world on patterns of trade, particularly in manufactured goods. Linder argues that demand factors are especially important and predicted that much international trade will occur between countries that exhibit a similar demand structure. The IPLC model emphasizes the significance of innovation, variance in technological capability and the product life cycle for patterns of international trade. It sees comparative advantage as changing with the stages of the product's life cycle.

The theory of FDI is central to an understanding of the diverse activities of multinational enterprises. Most recent theory is based on a market imperfections paradigm. Three linked ideas are delineated in the eclectic model of FDI: oligopolists possessing ownership-specific advantage, location-specific advantage, and internalization. Internalization theory is particularly important, for it focuses on the advantages of internalizing economic transactions within the firm rather than utilizing external markets.

Various other theories of FDI have been developed. These include the IPLC model, the oligopolistic rivalry theory (in which initial FDI by one firm is seen to trigger a wave of imitative FDI by rivals), and a model in which FDI is a strategy for international diversification.

DISCUSSION QUESTIONS

1. What is the difference between a turnkey project and licensing?

2. Comment on the following statement: "Linder's theory of international trade provides a strong rationale for standardization strategies in global markets."

3. Why is the "internalization" argument a crucial element in the eclectic theory of FDI?

4. Explain how the international product life cycle model is a theory of both international trade and FDI.

5. "Since a country's balance-of-payments statement must balance, this data is of little interest." Assess this statement.

6. What is tracked in the official reserve account of the balance of payments and why are these flows important?

7. Explain the major differences between the absolute and comparative advantage theories of international trade.

8. Over the last forty years, why has world trade increased more rapidly than global production?

ADDITIONAL READING

Caves, R. E., *Multinational Enterprise and Economic Analysis* (New York: Cambridge University Press, 1982).

Chacholiades, M., *Principles of International Economics* (New York: McGraw-Hill, 1981).

Dunning, J., "The Eclectic Paradigm of International Production: A Restatement and Some Possible Extensions," *Journal of International Business Studies,* Spring 1988.

Korth, C. M., *International Business: Environment and Management* (Englewood Cliffs, N.J.: Prentice-Hall 1985).

Rugman, A. M., D. J. Lecraw and L. D. Booth, *International Business-Firm and Environment* (New York: McGraw-Hill 1985).

Robock, S. H. and K. Simmonds, *International Business and Multinational Enterprise* (Homewood, Ill.: Richard D. Irwin 1980).

ENDNOTES

1. *International Financial Statistics Yearbook,* IMF, 1986.
2. *Business America,* May 11, 1987.
3. Joint Economic Committee of Congress Report, referenced in *The State,* January 4, 1987, p. 5.
4. *International Direct Investment: Global Trends and the U.S. Role,* U.S. Department of Commerce, 1984, p. 1.
5. Dunning, J. H. and J. M. Stopford, *Multinationals: Company Performance and Global Trends* (New York:Macmillan, 1983, p. 3).
6. *Environmental Aspects of the Activities of Transnational Corporations: A Survey* (UN, 1985) p. 108.
7. See J. H. Dunning and R. D. Pearce, *The Worlds Largest Industrial Enterprises:* Gower, 1981 and Swedenborg, B., *The Multinational Operations of Swedish Firms,* Almaquist and Wiksell, 1979. Stockholm.
8. S. B. Linder, *An Essay on Trade and Transformation* (New York: John Wiley & Sons, 1961).
9. R. Vernon, "International Investment and International Trade in the Product Cycle," *Quarterly Journal of Economics,* May 1966.
10. I. H. Giddy, "The Demise of the Product Cycle Model in International Business Theory," *Columbia Journal of World Business* (Spring 1978), pp. 90–97.
11. See, for example, S. H. Hymer, *The International Operations of National Firms: A Study of Direct Foreign Investment* (Boston: MIT Press, 1976); A. M. Rugman (ed.), *New Theories of the Multinational Enterprise* (London: Croom Helm, 1982); P. J. Buckley, and M. Casson, *The Economic Theory of the Multinational Enterprise* (New York: Macmillan, 1985).
12. J. H. Dunning, *International Production and the Multinational Enterprise* (London: George Allen & Unwin, 1981).
13. O. E. Williamson, *Markets and Hierarchies: Analysis and Antitrust Implications* (New York: Free Press, 1975).
14. F. T. Knickerbocker, *Oligopolistic Reaction and the Multinational Enterprise* (Boston: Harvard University Press, 1973).

Chapter 3
The National Environment: Major Economic, Political, and Legal Dimensions

International firms operate in a complex environment that can be described in terms of three major components. These are the home country, the host country, and international environments. This chapter focuses on the home and host country dimensions, which together compose the *national* operating environment. Particular attention is given to the economic, trading, political, and legal elements of the national context. The roles demography, culture, and consumer behavior play in the *national* environment are discussed in Chapters 5 and 6.

The acquisition and analysis of data relating to these different elements of the operating context is of fundamental importance in developing strategies for international markets. It is therefore very important that managers are aware of the type of information needed, data sources, and problems faced when evaluating the various components of the operating environment.

The environment in the country where a company is based provides a launching pad for the firm's overseas operation. Therefore, the situation at home will affect both the nature and location of a firm's international activities. For example, economic variables such as domestic factor endowments, costs, and the international value of the local currency will have important implications for the sourcing modes used to penetrate foreign markets. Domestic, legal, trading, and political factors will also affect many decisions on issues such as target markets and the products to be marketed overseas.

Whereas the home country environment is limited to one country, the host country environment is likely to comprise multiple, distinct national markets that are complex and heterogeneous. Apart from their diversity, host country markets will be less familiar and more difficult to understand than the home environment, at least in the initial stages of market entry.

THE ECONOMIC ENVIRONMENT ————————————————————

Economic Fundamentals

The implications of detailed economic information are best understood in the context of the particular economic system in place in the market of interest. Information of particular relevance, in this regard, relates to the nature of the economic system, economic structure, and level of economic development in the particular market being considered.

The Economic System

A fundamental distinction can be made between *market* and *central command* economies. As will be seen, all economies share some features of both systems and no perfect examples of either system exist. In practice, all national economies are *mixed* economies; they fall at some point on a continuum between the poles of the perfect market economy and the perfect central command system. The particular point on this continuum at which an economy falls is important, for it suggests essential information on that economy's underlying dynamics.

In a market economy, the driving mechanism is the interaction of market forces that, through the price system, govern resource use and the production and distribution of goods and services. Fueling this mechanism are such ideas as perfect competition, freedom of enterprise, and consumer sovereignty. Governments play no significant economic role in such a system.

In a central command economy, the impact of market forces is limited. How resources are used and products distributed is dictated by central government bureaucrats. For this system to function, complex planning methods and public ownership of the means of production are essential. Plans are very detailed; they specify such variables as production levels, prices, and patterns of distribution.

Although no perfect example of either system currently exists, some economies exemplify one or the other extreme. In Hong Kong, for example, the existence of many small competing firms and a government policy of minimal economic intervention result in a system with many of the characteristics of the pure market economy. The United States is not as good an example. Both federal and state governments intervene in economic matters as producers of both goods and services and through extensive economic regulation. Such features as subsidies, taxes, and nonmarket organizations (such as oligopolies and trade unions) also compromise the pure market economy model.

Many of the Marxist economies in Eastern Europe lie fairly close to the central command economy model. Still, to a muted degree, market forces do affect economic decisions, and despite extensive public ownership and planning in these countries, some economic activities are not regulated by the state. In the Soviet Union, for example, many fresh farm products are produced by peasant farmers on private plots of land and sold in unregulated markets. In the 1980s, a notable trend towards an opening up of more of the economy to free market forces and private enterprise is discernible in much of Eastern Europe and China.

Economic Structure

A common classification scheme distinguishes among three sectors in an economy.[1] These three sectors are (1) the *agricultural* sector, comprising agriculture, forestry, hunting, and fishing; (2) the *industrial* sector, comprising mining, manufacturing, construction, electricity, water, and gas, and; (3) *services*, comprising all other forms of economic activity. An alternative taxonomy distinguishes among four sectors: the *primary* sector (all activities based on natural resources), the *manufacturing* sector, *utilities* (power and water), and *services*.

Examination of Table 3-1 reveals important differences in the economic structure of countries. Typically, the LDCs are much more dependent upon agriculture than are the rich countries, where manufacturing and service activities are of much greater relative significance. Even within a given economic sector, the nature of economic operations in one country differs sharply from that in another. Capital-intensive factory farming, for example, is as different from subsistence farming as are apples and oranges. In LDCs, manufacturing activities such as textiles and food processing are based on labor-intensive operations using readily available raw materials. In the West, high-tech manufacturing, dependent on large inputs of capital and skilled labor, tends to dominate.

TABLE 3-1
Economic Structure

| | Distribution of Gross Domestic Product* | | | | | |
| | Agriculture | | Industry | | Services | |
	1960	1984	1960	1984	1960	1984
Low-Income countries	50	36	17(11)†	35(15)	33	29
Middle-Income Countries	22	14	31(22)	37(22)	47	49
Industrialized Countries	6	3	40(30)	35(25)	54	62

* The figures shown are average percentages for each group of countries.
† The figures in parentheses show the proportion of GDP accounted for by manufacturing activity.
Source: The World Bank, *World Development Report*, 1980, 1984, Table 3.

Economic Development

Rapid economic growth—measured by overall GNP and per capita income—is a primary objective in most countries. The reasons are obvious. Growth in income levels is generally accompanied by improvements in health, education, nutrition, and by a wider availability of consumer products. Concurrently, rapid economic growth brings about changes in economic and social structure, changes that are not always desirable. This is particularly true of fast-growing LDCs in which traditional social structures may be replaced by less desirable patterns (such as massive urbanization) that lead to major social problems.

The process of economic growth and resulting structural changes are commonly termed *economic development.*[2] The most usual yardstick for measuring economic development is per capita GNP. Using this data permits countries to be classified in a variety of ways. The World Bank distinguishes between five groups of countries on the basis of GNP per capita, as shown in Table 3-2. Although per capita GNP data is widely used as an indicator of economic development and relative market

TABLE 3-2
Level of Economic Development

Income Group	Number of Countries	Total GNP*	Average GNP Per Head	Population†
$400 and less	32	616	280	2,239
$401 to $1,635	44	502	800	628
$1,636 to $5,500	36	1,221	2,460	496
$5,500	39	8,150	11,380	716
No data	33	n.a.	n.a.	576

* Billions of U.S. $ in 1983
† Mid-1983 millions
Source: The World Bank, *1986 World Bank Atlas*, p. 20.

potential, it is a criterion with serious flaws. One of the most obvious is that this data does not take into account population level. For example, although its standard of living is among the highest in the world, Kuwait has a population of only 1.2 million. This low figure makes Kuwait a much less attractive market than many much poorer (in terms of GNP per head) but more populous developing countries. Therefore, when measuring market potential, it is necessary to consider both population data and average income data. Table 3-3 provides such data for a representative selection of countries.

Feedback on national economic development strategies, particularly in the case of LDCs, is often useful. Economic performance is affected by variables such as the relative emphases given to agriculture and manufacturing, balanced growth or concentration on one economic sector, and export-led growth or import substitution.

Key Economic Variables

Having sketched the nature and structure of economic systems, we now fill in our outline with more detailed economic information. The amount of data needed will vary with the perceived importance of markets and the cost of acquiring information. Typical areas of interest include (1) natural resource endowments, (2) demographic data, (3) measures of economic performance, (4) the infrastructure, and (5) economic policy.

Natural Resources

Natural resource endowments vary sharply. Clearly, nature has not been equally kind in dispensing its bounty. The importance of these resources to economic activity is most obvious in the case of some commodity exporters. In Libya and Saudi Arabia, for example, oil-based sales account for nearly 100 percent of export earnings. Less obvious examples of the significance of natural resources abound. In Norway, water resources are a fundamental shaper of traditional economic activity. Easy access to the sea, gained by virtue of a very long coast line has resulted in significant shipping and fishing industries. Even more important, abundant rainfall combined with an alpine topography makes possible the cheap hydroelectric power essential to power-intensive activities such as the aluminum industry.

Resource endowments are important not only in accounting for the pattern of economic activity in a country but also for what they imply. Climate, for example, affects the conditions of use for many products, and physical location and topographic features affect ease of market access and internal distribution.

Demographic Information

The size, structure, and nature of a population are of fundamental concern to marketers. Demographic indicators such as population size, age structure, birth and death rates, and percentage of working population are clearly important. (We discuss these in more detail in Chapter 5.)

At this point, it is worth noting that demographic information is important because it has implications for the level and pattern of demand in a given market and for the nature of the local labor force.

TABLE 3-3
Consumption Potential of Selected Countries

	Population (millions) Mid-1985	GNP Per Capita 1985 U.S. $	GNP (1985) (bil. of U.S. $)
Industrial Market Economies			
United Kingdom	56.5	8,460	478.0
Netherlands	14.5	9,290	134.7
France	55.2	9,540	526.6
Japan	120.8	11,300	1,365.0
Germany, Fed. Rep.	61.0	10,940	667.3
Australia	15.8	10,830	171.1
Canada	25.4	13,680	347.5
Norway	4.2	14,370	60.4
U.S.	239.3	16,690	3,993.9
Italy	57.1	6,520	372.3
Central Command Economies			
Hungary	10.6	1,950	20.7
Poland	37.2	2,050	76.3
Upper Middle-Income Economies			
Brazil	135.6	1,640	222.4
Portugal	10.2	1,970	20.1
Malaysia	15.6	2,000	31.2
Mexico	78.8	2,080	163.9
Korea, Rep. of	41.1	2,150	88.4
Argentina	30.5	2,130	65.0
Algeria	21.9	2,550	55.8
Venezuela	17.3	3,080	53.3
Hong Kong	5.4	6,230	33.6
Lower Middle-Income Economies			
Zambia	6.7	390	2.6
Bolivia	6.4	470	3.0
Indonesia	162.2	530	86.0
Philippines	54.7	580	31.7
Egypt, Arab Rep. of	48.5	610	29.6
Nigeria	99.7	800	79.8
Thailand	51.7	800	41.4
Peru	18.6	1,010	18.8
Turkey	50.2	1,080	54.2
Low-Income Economies			
Bangladesh	100.6	150	15.1
Tanzania	22.2	290	6.4
India	765.1	270	106.5
China	1,040.3	310	322.5
Kenya	20.4	290	5.9
Haiti	5.9	310	1.8
Pakistan	96.2	380	36.6

Source: The World Bank, *World Development Report, 1987*, Basic Indicators, Table 1.

Economic Performance

The significance of overall GNP and per capita national income data has already been mentioned. The most interesting data deals with the recent rate of growth of GNP and the reasons for the performance achieved. Over time, differences in growth rates have a significant cumulative impact on relative standards of living. In 1986, for example, the average income of the Japanese—calculated at average exchange rates—was only some 5 percent less than that for the United States. However, in 1965, Japan's average was a quarter of America's.

Other performance-related data include past and current statistics on unemployment, consumer prices, productivity, foreign trade, the balance of payments, the exchange rate for local currency, and foreign reserves. Information on such variables as investment, savings, taxes, money supply, and interest rates is also germane to any evaluation of economic performance.

When focusing on particular issues of interest, it is useful to categorize data. For instance, the notion of a country's level of external dependence may be examined by considering the following categories of data: the level and pattern of flows of trade and investment into and out of a market, the balance of payments, foreign reserves, overseas investments, and foreign indebtedness. All are readily charted. See Figures 3-1 and 3-2 and Table 3-4 for information on the dependence of the United States on foreign trade, its international investment position, and comparative trade balances.

The Infrastructure

Infrastructure refers to that network of facilities and services necessary for the functioning of an economy. Of critical importance are energy supplies, transport and communications facilities, and commercial and financial services.

Without effective transport and communication systems, the specialization of activities that characterizes modern economies becomes very difficult. Measurement of the coverage and effectiveness of road, rail, sea, and air transport systems and of associated freight handling facilities is essential. So, too, is the gathering of telephone-, telegraph-, and media-related information and any data on the relative efficiency and availability of utilities.

The availability and quality of support services in such areas as marketing, distribution, banking and insurance are important variables between markets. For example, the extent and quality of services available from advertising agencies and market research bureaus affects the development and implementation of marketing programs overseas.

Economic Policy

Government policies on fiscal, monetary, and other economic matters directly affect current and future economic performance. Governments are also directly responsible for the management and provision of many vital goods and services, particularly infrastructure-related services. The efficiency of governments in managing such resources thus concerns us here. Government incentives and controls, particularly as they impinge on foreign firms merit review. As for incentives, the major possibilities are low taxes, subsidies, and financial support for domestically based exporters and for incoming direct investment. Critical control areas include

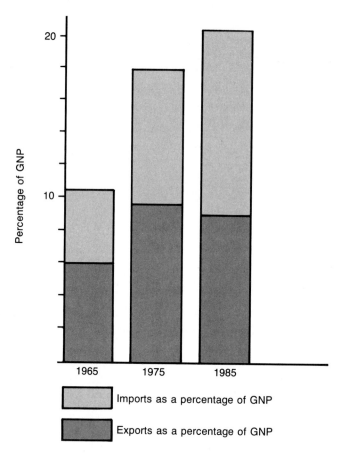

FIGURE 3-1   The Significance of International Trade for the U.S. Economy (*Source:* U.S. Commerce Department.)

prices, imports, foreign exchange, and the regulation of the payment and remittance of royalties and dividends both internally and across national boundaries.

Evaluating Economic Information

Basic Principles

Economic data provide vital information for international marketers faced with decisions on such issues as target markets overseas, market entry modes, market potential, and the nature of the international marketing mix. There is an according need for ongoing monitoring of the economic environment in current and prospective markets overseas. When monitoring, there is sometimes a tendency to focus exclusively on current and historical data and to not pay adequate attention to the implications of gathered information. Usually the future pattern of economic

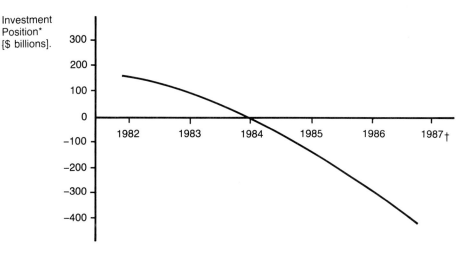

*Defined as U.S. assets abroad less foreign assets in the U.S. at year end book value.

†The figure for 1987 is an estimate.

FIGURE 3-2   **The U.S. International Investment Position*** (*Source:* Morgan Stanley, "Tracking the U.S. Trade Deficit," February 17, 1988, p. 7.)

development is of the most interest. There is thus a critical need to develop forecasts.

Most economic data, particularly macroeconomic statistics, would be extremely expensive if they had to be acquired through primary research. Fortunately, this is rarely necessary; most governments have a strong interest in tracking key economic variables. The central statistical agencies in most countries collect and

TABLE 3-4
Merchandise Trade Balance for Selected Industrial Countries

| Country | Trade Balances* | | | | |
	1983	1984	1985	1986	1987
United States	−57.8	−108.1	−132.9	−149.6	−171.2
Canada	14.4	15.9	12.8	7.5	7.8
Japan	31.5	44.0	55.9	92.5	96.1
West Germany	16.6	18.8	25.3	52.6	65.8
United Kingdom	−1.3	−5.7	−2.6	−12.4	−16.3
France	−5.9	−2.8	−2.6	0.1	−5.1
Italy	−7.9	−10.9	−11.9	−2.1	−5.7†

* Billions of U.S. dollars, f.o.b. basis

† Twelve months to August, 1987

Sources: *International Economic Review*, November 1986, March 1988; *The Economist*, February 20, 1988, p. 110.

publish large amounts of economic data. These and other secondary sources of published statistics serve as a major source of economic data.

Collection and Analysis Problems

A wide variety of problems characterizes the collection and interpretation of economic data. Most of these complications come under three headings: missing data, unreliable data, and misleading data. To illustrate these difficulties, let us focus on what ought to be a relatively simple problem, the collection of GNP-per-head data in overseas markets. It is clearly desirable to collect and evaluate data that are up to date, reliable, and directly comparable from market to market. As will be seen, obtaining such data is often difficult.

In some countries, mainly poor LDCs, there may be no agency specifically charged with collecting statistics. Even when such an agency exists, it may be understaffed and inadequately financed. Consequently, that agency may not be capable of generating up-to-date information. In addition, both rich and poor countries must combat the problem of classified data. Strategically significant data are not always readily available. Missing data, then, are a major source of headaches to the collector.

Assuming data are available, how reliable is the information? Poor or inconsistent census and collection techniques reduce the reliability of data. In the case of GNP, which can be defined in at least three ways, different approaches to measurement can cause comparability problems. GNP figures dramatize the seriousness of reliability. In many countries, both developed and underdeveloped, important areas of economic activity have not been measured. In Colombia, for example, the cultivation and export of cocaine is a major industry and foreign exchange earner. However, official GNP data are unlikely to pick up such illegal activities. Similarly, much underground economic activity goes unreported in countries where marginal tax rates are high. In Italy, it is estimated that underground economic activity produces goods and services valued at over 15 percent of official GNP.

Population statistics may also be questionable. In some countries, political pressures may cause racial, tribal, or other groups to overstate the size of their particular population segment and this will distort GNP per capita data.

Even when reliable, up-to-date information is available, data may be highly misleading. In the case of GNP figures, an obvious problem relates to the extent of the division of labor. Do-it-yourself activities are not considered a component of GNP. Consequently, the GNP in countries where people are highly self-sufficient, as in many LDCs, will be biased downward when compared to that of countries with a higher level of specialization.

A second major problem is the lack of a common currency. GNP data has to be translated into a single common denominator currency for it to be useful. This requires the use of foreign exchange rates. Insofar as the rates used reflect purchasing power parity, then such "translation" is not a major problem. However, there is evidence that exchange rates deviate from purchasing power parity values for significant periods. This deviation, plus the volatility of many exchange rates, can cause major comparability problems. For example, from 1985 to 1986, the fall in the value of the U.S. dollar resulted in an increase of over 30 percent in the dollar value of Japanese GNP per head, which had nothing to do with increased Japanese productivity. The effect of such a variance between market and purchasing power parity exchange rates is shown in Table 3-5. The data therein indicate that in 1986 the standard of living in Japan and West Germany, relative to that in the United States was overstated.

A recent dispute between Italy and Great Britain regarding the size of their respective economies further illustrates the problems with GNP data.[3] The Italians claimed that their GNP exceeded that of Britain. As evidence of a higher standard of living, Italians pointed to higher auto ownership, 359 per thousand compared to 312 in Britain.

The British replied that the trend reflected short-term lira strength, a questionable underground economy adjustment, and an economic boom built on shaky foundations. They also pointed out that indices such as TV ownership (336 per thousand in Britain to 243 in Italy) and number of telephones (521 per thousand in Britain to 405 in Italy) indicated Britain's greater strength.

Averages can also mislead. In the case of GNP-per-head, we need to consider the distribution of income. If income distribution is highly skewed, for example, by a small minority of the population earning very high incomes and the majority earning low incomes, who is left as "average"? A low average in countries with a large population may disguise the existence of upper and middle class consumer segments that are of great significance, as in India, which has large groups of middle-class consumers with levels of disposable income much higher than the national average.

Because of the problems noted above, great care must be taken when collecting and evaluating economic data. Although many of the examples discussed relate to GNP data, most of the problems exemplified are fairly general and occur frequently in analysis of economic data.

Given the great importance of published economic data, it is necessary to be familiar with relevant secondary source material. Exhibit 3-1 lists some of the more useful publications essential to the international analyst.

TABLE 3-5
Comparisons of Average GNP Per Person, 1986

	Purchasing Power Parity Level		At Average Exchange Rates
	$	Index*	Index*
United States	17,200	100.0	100.0
Japan	12,200	70.9	94.0
West Germany	12,900	75.0	85.5
Britain	11,400	66.3	55.6
France	11,800	68.6	74.4
Italy	11,300	65.7	58.7

* United States = 100
Source: OECD. Organization for Economic Cooperation and Development.

EXHIBIT 3-1 ———
International Economic Environment: Some Selected Publications ————————————

United Nations
Statistical Yearbook
Demographic Yearbook
Yearbook of National Accounts and Statistics
World Energy Supplies
UNESCO Statistical Yearbook

International Monetary Fund
Direction of Trade Statistics
Balance of Payments Statistics
International Financial Statistics
Government Financial Statistics Yearbook
Annual Report on Exchange Arrangements

World Bank
World Bank Atlas
World Development Report
Commodity Trade and Price Trends
World Product and Income

Miscellaneous
Business International—Business Asia, Business Eastern Europe,
Business Latin America, Worldwide Economic Indicators
OECD—Main Economic Indicators, Annual Economic Surveys, Economic Outlook
GATT—International Trade
EFTA Annual Report
EEC—Basic Statistics of the Community
International Labor Organization—Yearbook of Labor Statistics
Nordic Council—Yearbook of Nordic Statistics
World Handbook of Political and Social Indicators

THE TRADING ENVIRONMENT —————————————————————————————————

All governments seek to regulate international flows of trade. At the least, their goal is to ensure that certain types of exports (such as armaments) do not reach the wrong hands and that domestic industries are not destroyed by low price imports dumped in the home market. (Dumping is considered in more detail in Chapter 14, in the context of pricing policy.) We now turn to the nature of trade barriers and the rationale behind regulation of international trade.

Trade Barriers

Barriers to trade take one of three major forms: (1) tariffs, (2) quotas, and (3) nontariff barriers.

Tariffs are taxes placed by governments on exports or, more commonly, imports. Tariffs are therefore both a source of revenue and, more importantly in the case of imports, a protective measure. There are several types of tariffs. *Ad valorem* tariffs are levied as a fixed percentage of the value of the commodity being taxed. Thus a 20 percent import tariff will result in a tax of $20 on an imported good valued at $100. The *specific* duty is a fixed tax levied on each physical unit imported or exported. For example, if watches were subject to a $20 specific import duty, then both the importer of a Rolex and a Timex watch would have to pay the same tax of $20 regardless of the value of the watch. The specific tariff is thus regressive. *Compound duties* combine the ad valorem and specific tariffs by establishing a fixed unit tax and adding a variable amount to this base rate that is related to the value of the good.

Tariffs directly impact on the price of a good. As tariffs force prices up, demand is indirectly affected and usually falls. However, in contrast to the quota, consumers can still obtain the good providing they can pay the increased price because there is no physical limit to the number of items traded.

Direct limitations on the physical volume or, less commonly, value of imports or exports are known as *quotas*. Quotas do not generate revenue for the government imposing them; they are used almost exclusively to protect domestic industries from international competition.

The direct effect of a quota is on the quantity supplied of the good. Indirectly, prices are also affected; they nearly always go up as availability declines. This rise often benefits the supplier of the good, increasing profit margins. It has been estimated that the "voluntary" export restrictions placed on exports of Japanese automobiles to the United States in 1981 have resulted in consumers paying some $2,000 more for a car than would have been the case in a free market. This has two main causes: Japanese suppliers raised prices and exported only their most expensive "loaded" models; and this allowed American and European manufacturers to also raise their prices.

Restricting Japanese auto exports to the United States has helped U.S. manufacturers. OECD estimates indicate that 1985 sales of U.S. cars were accordingly some 500,000 higher and that domestic auto makers' benefited by around $1 billion in profits. Up to 35,000 U.S. jobs were also saved, and Japanese manufacturers increased their investment in U.S. capacity.

However, the cost has been high. Higher auto prices and less consumer choice were the most obvious effects. (It is estimated that the cost to the U.S. economy of each job saved is around $250,000). In addition, the competitive strength of Japanese auto firms has benefited from moving up market and from wider U.S. profit margins.

Nontariff barriers [NTB] include all other means of artificially limiting trade. Among the most important forms of NTB are subsidies to local manufacturers; "voluntary" export restraints; government procurement policies; foreign exchange controls; and technical, administrative, and other government regulations, controlling such matters as customs clearance, product standards, and documentation, which are designed to impede trade flows. Government controls, such as the export control laws in the United States, designed to interfere with the flow of trade for strategic or political reasons may also be important.

NTBs have increased in importance with the reduction of such high-profile trade restraints as tariffs and quotas. This is a serious problem, for it reduces the impact and effectiveness of measures, such as those negotiated under the auspices of GATT, to reduce barriers to trade.

In order to better understand the impact of import and export restrictions, we now discuss the cases of the U.S. steel and log industries. These cases highlight both the rationale for and arguments against control. Furthermore, most of the points raised have general validity outside the specific contexts of the steel and log industries.

Import Controls—The Case of the U.S. Steel Industry

In recent years important sectors of the U.S. steel industry have lost their competitive edge as production costs have increased rapidly and imports have captured a growing share of the market. As its ability to compete has declined, the industry has increased pressure for protection against imports, with some success. In 1978 a trigger price mechanism was put into place. It established a minimum price for some steel imports to protect the U.S. steel industry from foreign dumping. By the late 1980s, voluntary quota restrictions for some steel imports had been negotiated with foreign suppliers in 29 countries. The arguments used to justify import controls on steel and the reply to the industry view have generality outside the industry, and are now briefly reviewed to illustrate the pros and cons of protectionism.

Those arguing for steel import controls claim that imports result from unfair competition, that steel is a strategic industry, and that protection is needed to save jobs. Foreign steelmakers are accused of dumping steel in the United States at unfairly low prices because of foreign government subsidies and lax environmental standards, and are willing to suffer losses to build up U.S. market share. Unless this development is checked, say protectionists, U.S. consumers will become dependent upon foreign suppliers for strategically important products and thousands of jobs will be lost. Since many steelworkers are unwilling to relocate, high welfare and social costs will result.

Other arguments made for protecting the industry are that increased imports worsen the U.S. balance of payments and do not allow U.S. firms to earn the profits needed for modernization. Insofar as import barriers encourage foreign steelmakers to invest in the United States, capital inflows will generate jobs for Americans. Import controls will also give the government a bargaining chip in negotiations with foreign governments that have themselves imposed trade barriers.

The major arguments against protecting the steel industry are that protectionist measures result in an inefficient allocation of resources in the United States and harm the steel consumer. Critics of the steel industry claim that the inability of many U.S. firms to compete is the result of low investment, poor management, and excessive wages for steel workers. They accept a smaller industry and see it as releasing resources for more effective use in other sectors of the economy. Those firms that do not produce the right product and have poor cost control, they argue, ought to die. Their demise will stimulate surviving firms to become more efficient and will allow them to benefit from lower cost inflation as the cost of local inputs (such as labor) stabilizes or falls. Freer trade will also benefit consumers since their freedom of choice will not be constrained and prices will be held down. Protection for the industry might also stimulate countervailing protectionist measures by affected countries.

If there is indeed a serious risk that free trade will lead to the demise of most of the U.S. steel industry, then strategic arguments for protection should be heeded. However, probably the most important reason for recent import controls is political, not economic. Firms suffering large losses and workers losing their jobs have complained bitterly to Washington. Their combined political impact has been great. Consumers and others who bear the main brunt of protectionism by paying higher prices and enjoying fewer choices have often been neither cognizant of the penalties they are paying nor sufficiently motivated to act. These basic dynamics of the political process account for a large proportion of the trade barriers erected in the United States and other countries.

Steel quotas expire in 1989, and steel lobbyists started pushing hard in 1987 for protection into the 1990s. However, the industry has benefited from recent strong demand and is not as united as previously. Finished steel imports were the main target of the 1984 quotas. Since then, semi-finished steel imports of slab steel have increased rapidly as U.S. steel companies have shut down raw steel-making capacity, concentrating instead on adding value to imported slab. But quotas have also constrained these slab imports. Insufficient domestic supply of slab of the quality and tonnage needed has resulted in a rise in steel prices, by up to 25 percent in 1987, and inavailability problems. Still, the political power of the industry remains strong and continued protection is likely.

Two more significant additional arguments for protection remain to be discussed, the infant industry and terms of trade arguments.

The *infant industry argument* is commonly used in LDCs and NICs to justify protectionism, not infrequently for a local steel industry. The essence of this argument is that local producers in key industries can thrive if they are afforded a temporary period of protection during which they can grow, progress along the learning curve, and achieve the economies of scale necessary to compete both at home and internationally. Once the requisite experience and size have been obtained, then a viable local industry that can compete internationally without protection should be in place. Unfortunately, history indicates that all too frequently the baby never grows up. Large and inefficient industries are developed which become a continuing drag on the local economy. Because of the size and political clout of the local manufacturer, they cannot be jettisoned.

The *terms of trade argument* is a substantial rationale for import restrictions. It can be demonstrated that the imposition of a tariff by a *large country*—one big enough to influence the world price of a good—may result in a fall in the pre-tariff price of the imported good. In such a situation, the international terms of trade of the country imposing the tariff will improve. However, the resulting fall in volume of trade (the good will still cost more once the tariff is paid), and less efficient resource allocation in the importing country will result in counterbalancing welfare losses in that country. Any improvement in the net welfare of the country imposing the tariff occurs at the expense of the exporter of the good. The exporter is thus likely to retaliate, thereby removing any advantage derived by the importer. Despite this problem, it may be possible to arrive at an *optimum tariff* that maximizes the importer's benefits from the terms of trade effect relative to the cost of lessened trade and less efficient resource allocation.

Export Controls—The Log Export Case

Over at least the last twenty years, there has been an ongoing debate, centered in the Pacific Northwest, on the desirability of uncontrolled exports of U.S. logs to Japan. Woodworking unions and sawmill owners have generally opposed the growing trade with Japan and have called for log-export controls. Their opposition has met with some success. During the 1970s, measures to ban log exports from federal land were imposed.

Arguments in favor of export control are that the Japanese will buy lumber and processed lumber from the United States if they cannot buy logs, that Japanese log demand increases the price of softwood timber in the United States, and that exporting unprocessed logs in effect exports jobs to Japan. Proponents of export control say that logs should be processed in the United States, thus adding value and jobs in the Northwest, boosting export revenues, and deflating domestic log prices.

A contrary point of view, one supported by many forest products companies, is that U.S. sawmills are not able to meet the needs of Japanese consumers as efficiently as do Japanese sawmills. The Japanese claim that they are able to achieve higher yields from each log and to better provide the sizes needed in Japan. The Japanese also point out that they take less than 10 percent of the U.S. consumption of softwood and argue that it is U.S. demand that has the major impact on prices. More importantly, alternative suppliers of logs, notably the Russians, are eager to attract Japanese business with no strings attached.

The log export case highlights a number of generally important points. (1) The call for export controls is generally strongest in the case of raw materials, particularly those in finite supply produced by few countries. (2) The main reasons for seeking control are to increase domestic added value, to provide jobs, and to influence prices at home and on export markets. (3) Key factors influencing the degree of success of such policies include the availability of substitute products from alternative sources and the effectiveness of domestic suppliers in adding value to the basic raw material.

Political and strategic objectives often underlie export controls, although in the log export case these factors argue against control. (It is not in the U.S. interest to promote trade between Russia and Japan.) Political and strategic factors account for control of exports such as armaments and other sensitive products and for a ban on trade with certain countries (such as United States trade with Cuba).

When a country supplies a large proportion of the global production of a good, restrictions on export sales may raise overseas prices and a nation may thereby improve its terms of trade. However, the costs from a lower volume of exports have to be weighed against the benefits of better trade terms. Export trade restrictions may also bring about retaliation from affected countries.

THE POLITICAL ENVIRONMENT

Political processes and events typically involve patterns of interrelationships that develop between the various interest groups operating in a country. These groups are motivated primarily by a desire to gain, maintain, and increase their own power and influence. The major actor in this political arena is, in most countries, the national government. Along with the bureaucracy, it enjoys great power by virtue of its ability to regulate, tax, and participate directly in economic, social, and political activities. Other groups also enjoy varying degrees of power. In some countries, certain interest groups may even enjoy a degree of influence rivaling that of the government.

The national political environment is strongly affected by indigenous variables that form the context of all political activity. Among these key variables are ideology, the prevailing economic system, and nationalism. These strongly influence the political environment and are likely to be of special interest to international firms. In order to assess their exposure in this area, international operators have, during the eighties, given increasing attention to evaluating political risk in overseas markets.

Political Risk

There is no consensus on the meaning of the term political risk. One definition equates the term with government interference in business operations. A second interprets political risk more broadly, focusing on events and characteristics of the environment. Critical variables of interest include direct constraints imposed upon firms, such as discriminatory taxes, and latent factors such as the nature of political opposition.

An evaluation of the various definitions has lead Kobrin[5] to a number of important conclusions about the impact of politics upon a firm. He concludes that one should *distinguish* between *political events* and their *impact* upon the firm. Whether and how political events affect a firm depends on general environmental conditions and on factors *specific* to the firm and the industry within which it operates. Political instability is *not* the same as political risk.

Risk implies that the probability of outcomes can be derived. In the case of political risk, the probable variation in corporate performance resulting from such outcomes is the focus of interest. Positive as well as negative variations from political occurrences are possible. For example, a revolution leading to the toppling of a Marxist regime may very well improve prospects for foreign MNCs.

Key Dimensions of the Political Environment

We now consider ideological climate, political processes, and nationalism in more detail. However, the implications for individual firms of political events and situations will be strongly affected by other factors, such as the industry in which the firm is operating, and its historic and current policies and performance. Furthermore, although the primary focus is on the environment in overseas markets, it is also important not to overlook the significance of the political climate in the home country.

The Ideological Climate and Political Processes

Political scientists frequently distinguish between *democratic* and *authoritarian* regimes. These contrasting approaches to governance and management of political processes rest on different ideological foundations.

Democracies subscribe to the right of citizens to not only choose their ruler but also to exercise continuing influence and control over the decisions made by their elected representatives. Freedom before the law, equity, political equality, and a government answerable to the people further characterize democracies. Political opposition is seen as both desirable and legitimate. Institutions for the orderly and peaceful transfer of power are in place.

Governments in authoritarian regimes are, in contrast, generally not elected and the people's influence tends to be limited. In such systems, a small group of leaders pursues policies without systematically taking into account the popular consensus. Typically, the policies pursued have a rigid ideological foundation, and opposition is neither cultivated nor generally tolerated. However, exceptions and variations exist. Some authoritarian rulers do enjoy significant public support and may pursue enlightened policies. Controlled elections and limited opposition may also be allowed. Frequently, support for the ruling group is institutionalized in a single-party system.

There is usually a close link between the nature of the political system and economic activity. Eastern European communist governments are characterized by central command economic systems. In the West, democratic governments tend to support market economies. However, some authoritarian regimes in Latin America and Southeast Asia support free enterprise, market-based economic systems; and in many Western countries, government control of and direct participation in economic activities is of considerable significance.

Nationalism

Nationalism, a basic and pervasive political force, is present to some degree in all countries. It has been defined as "devotion to one's nation ... the doctrine that national interest and security are more important than international considerations."[6] For many international firms, nationalistic pressure is a significant source of problems. Foreign organizations are, at best, regarded with suspicion by nationalists and are often targeted for rigorous scrutiny and control. At worst, such firms may be regarded as dangerous abberations that should be removed from the local business scene.

In general, the higher the incidence and level of nationalist sentiment the greater the problems posed for foreign firms. In Sandinista Nicaragua, for example, nationalism is a powerful force and anti-American sentiment is strong. Despite such feelings, many MNCs—including U.S. firms such as I.B.M. and Exxon—continue operations there and are responsible for some 15 percent of the national output of goods and services.[7] One Nicaraguan government official has stated that the foreign investment law guarantees profit repatriation for firms that export or replace imports and is designed to attract foreign business.

However, many foreign firms have been nationalized and many others have exited from Nicaragua. Before the Sandanista takeover some 160 U.S.-owned businesses operated in the country. Over 30 U.S. companies were expropriated by the government between 1979 and 1985; by 1988, only about 25 U.S. firms were still operating there. No new major U.S. firms have begun operations since the revolution.[8]

The Nicaraguan government now regulates wages, prices and the availability of foreign exchange and has imposed strict occupational safety and environmental standards. The marketing of exports has been centralized, and the operations of the financial sector are closely controlled. Foreign banks are barred from taking local deposits and offering checking accounts. Still, for those firms remaining in Nicaragua, economic pressures caused by the depressed economy, the U.S. trade embargo, and foreign exchange shortages are more important problems than direct political pressure.

Nationalism is not limited to LDCs. It exists in all countries and can pose significant problems in the rich industrial countries. For example, nationalist pressures in Western Europe have hampered attempts by General Motors and Ford to acquire locally owned automobile companies in the United Kingdom and Italy. In both cases there was strong opposition to economically attractive proposals, and there is no doubt that an undercurrent of nationalistic and anti-American sentiment was a major factor in the public debate. In the United States itself, foreign companies confront many regulatory hurdles if they try to buy defense-related businesses.

Often nationalist pressure builds up in opposition to perceptions that a foreign government is interventionist. In Japan, for example, U.S. pressure to open up the highly protected rice market to farmers in the United States has been counterproductive. The rice issue impacts upon deeply rooted Japanese notions of self-sufficiency, self-respect, and the welfare of Japanese farmers. Rice politics are explosive, and Washington has deemed it foolish to press the issue. A similar example is found in the Taiwanese cigarette market. There, pressure to open the market to foreign products has caused a nationalist backlash. A vigorous antismoking campaign, with strong anti-U.S. overtones, developed following Taiwanese agreement to open the market to U.S. imports.

Government Intervention

The regulative ability of governments means that they enjoy a high level of potential power vis-à-vis international firms. Although most attention is given to the relationship between firms and host country governments, the power of home country governments to control the overseas activities of domestic firms must not be overlooked.

Local acquisition of a firm's assets is the most extreme form of intervention. Several other levels of governmental intervention can be delineated. Robinson differentiates among the following actions:

> *Expropriation* refers to a formal taking of property with or without the payment of compensation; *confiscation*, to an expropriation without compensation. *Nationalization*, refers to limiting certain economic activity to local citizens, which may lead to forced sale, expropriation, or even confiscation if aliens are already present. *Socialization* refers to placing an economic activity in the public sector.[9]

Host country governments commonly limit the local activities of foreign firms in many other ways. Such government control can have profound implications for corporate performance in the marketplace. Common examples of government intervention include:

☐   Price controls

☐   Import regulation

☐   Foreign exchange controls

☐   Dividend and royalty remittance controls

☐   Tax regulations

☐   Regulation of licensing agreements and foreign direct investment.

In the case of *home government* intervention, controls relate mainly to exporting and FDI. (Export controls are discussed in Chapter 14.) The most common FDI concern is the impact of such investment on the domestic economy.

In Norway, for example, direct investors must acquire a license from the Central Bank before projects overseas can be undertaken. The reasons advanced for control are that it is necessary to ensure that foreign investment does not harm domestic employment and regional policy, and that the outflow of capital is not detrimental to the domestic economy, particularly with regard to the balance of payments and foreign exchange situation. Obtaining an investment license is usually not difficult, but the Central Bank seeks to maintain continuing control. Typically, Norwegian foreign investors are required to submit annual financial data on their operations. The accumulation of undistributed profits overseas requires approval, as does any transfer in ownership or change in the nature of the foreign subsidiary's operations.

Alongside their regulatory powers, governments are also able to participate directly in economic activity through the activities of government-owned firms. In much of Western Europe, for example, government-controlled firms play a major role in the national economy.

The extent to which governments take over certain economic activities and industries limits opportunities for foreign firms. Although there is a trend towards privatization in countries such as Britain and France, political factors also complicate denationalization. In France, for example, the government has been heavily involved in complex negotiations to sell CGCT, a state-owned manufacturer of telecommunications equipment. Foreign firms involved in these discussions have included AT&T from the United States, Philips from the Netherlands, Sweden's L.M. Ericsson, and Britain's Plessey. All these firms are interested in obtaining the stake in France's highly regulated and protectionist digital switching equipment market currently controlled by CGCT. Both West Germany and the United States were directly involved in intense and sensitive lobbying amid complaints that the French had decided to limit foreign ownership opportunities.

Political Stability

A major concern of managers is the level of political stability in countries of interest. In markets where a firm is well entrenched and satisfied with the business environment, there is generally a corporate desire for continuity. In markets where the current regime is perceived to be opposed to the interests of the firm, instability, which might force a change in the government, may be preferable.

Important stability criteria include measures of social cohesion, the distribution of wealth and income, regional cohesion, and indices of political and other forms of protest such as demonstrations, riots, and terrorist activity. Economic variables will also have a powerful impact on the political situation. Attention should therefore be given to the performance of the economy on such critical dimensions as the standard of living, economic growth, income distribution, inflation, and unemployment. A country's level of dependence upon other countries as measured by such factors as the balance of payments, international debt, and the international investment situation will also be important.

Finally, it is evident that international political relationships among nations will affect perceptions regarding political risk in individual markets. The major factors to be considered in this regard are discussed in the next chapter.

Measuring and Reacting to Political Risk

It should now be apparent that two separate steps need to be undertaken for the effective evaluation of a firm's political risk both at home and overseas. The first stage involves forecasting political developments in countries of interest. The more important next step is identifying both opportunities and dangers likely to result from projected developments. Special attention should be given to the likelihood that foreign governments will adopt measures that threaten existing patterns of international operations.

The Measurement of Risk

Most political risk screening methodologies develop a general measure of national risk not related to a firm's particular situation. One method is based upon subjective evaluations, often generated by expert consultants in a Delphi process. The other common approach is to develop a variety of quantifiable measures of the political environment.

Two examples of subjective assessment are the Political Risk Country Reports produced by the firm of Frost and Sullivan[10] and the Business Environmental Risk Index developed by Haner.[11] Frost and Sullivan develop, on the basis of the judgment of a world-wide panel of experts, 18-month forecasts of regime stability, political turmoil, restrictions on international business, trade, and economic policy for some 85 countries. They also review major political factors in these countries and prepare an additional five-year political and economic forecast. The BERI forecasts, for around 45 countries, are based upon expert opinion regarding 15 key criteria relating to political stability, government efficiency, nationalism, financial factors, and operational variables such as currency convertibility.

A good example of the quantitative approach is provided by the Political System Stability Index developed by Haendel, West, and Meadow.[12] Their index is made up of 15 measures of the political environment grouped into three categories. These categories are the *socioeconomic characteristics* index, which measures population homogeneity and economic growth prospects; the *societal conflicts* index, measuring the potential for violent change; and the *governmental processes* index, which evaluates chances of peaceful political transition. Scores are developed for each of the criteria and combined into an overall score for a country.

Although many of the variables used in quantitative models can be measured fairly precisely, it is much more difficult to determine their political implications because much depends upon the overall context. In countries where riots are commonplace, continuing civil disturbance implies dissatisfaction but may not result in significant change. In other nations, serious disturbances may be rare, but a single riot may be sufficient to topple a government.

An essential problem with both the approaches outlined above is that they ignore industry- and firm-specific factors. Political instability is not the same as political risk, and firms are unequally affected by political change. Consequently, the implications of forecasts should be very carefully reviewed in the context of each firm's particular situation.

Managing Political Risk

Measurement of the political environment and analysis of the implications for the firm of anticipated political development should of course precede decision making. The initiatives that will then be appropriate will be strongly affected by the nature of current and planned operations in the markets of interest.

In the case of activities still in the planning stage, a variety of options are feasible. The most obvious is that of avoiding markets where risk seems high. A more sophisticated approach is to evaluate the likely impact of political events on corporate performance. In financial terms, political risk may be accounted for by either adjusting project cash flows or the rate used to discount future cash flows. Other options include taking out insurance against political risk if this is possible; negotiating with foreign governments prior to market entry; and structuring projects to take account of risk exposure.[13] It may, for example, be appropriate to maximize local financing, seek local partners, and ensure that the local operation is not viable without the assistance of the parent firm.

With regard to ongoing operations, Schapiro[14] suggests five policy responses to increased exposure to political risk. These are planned divestment, short-term profit maximization, changing the cost-benefit ratio of expropriation, developing local stakeholders, and taking advantage of political events by opportunistic policy changes. Some of these policies are designed to resist the implementation of discriminatory initiatives. Others seek to ensure that the firm is best positioned to continue achieving corporate objectives despite undesirable changes.

An interesting example of corporate divestment is provided by South Africa. During 1986, the rate of divestment by MNCs increased rapidly as such notable firms as Exxon, I.B.M., General Motors, Honeywell, and Barclays Bank sold their South African subsidiaries to local owners. The weak economic situation in South Africa, arising from political disturbances, and the consensus prognosis for continuing political unrest in the future were major factors in these divestment decisions. It is also clear that involvement in South Africa represents a political liability when doing business at home and in other parts of the world. In the United States, for example, a growing number of pension funds, university endowments, and state governments are dropping securities of firms with South African operations. In Britain, the South African connection has harmed Barclay's image and is believed to be an important reason for the bank's declining share of the important student market.

Some firms have attempted to manage this problem by demonstrating their opposition to apartheid. Kodak, for example, refused to sell its products to the South African police and the army, and supported an ongoing anti-apartheid advertising campaign. Despite efforts such as these, the divestment trend continues. Kodak has now withdrawn from South Africa, along with over 140 other U.S. firms. This leaves only around 100 U.S. companies still operating in South Africa.

THE LEGAL ENVIRONMENT

An international firm operates in a legal environment that may be described on three distinct dimensions. These are home country law, the laws in foreign markets of interest, and international law. Attention is now focused on the national legal context. (The significance of international law is discussed in Chapter 4.)

The Domestic Legal Environment

In most countries there are many regulations that will impact on a firm's overseas operations. These laws reflect domestic political forces and economic interests. Frequently, the relevant laws are formulated specifically for the purpose of regulating firms' overseas activities. Certain domestic laws not designed specifically to control overseas business operations, may also be interpreted as having an extraterritorial impact. Areas in which laws passed by the home country government commonly have implications for the overseas operation of domestic firms are now reviewed.

Antitrust Laws

A good example of the extraterritorial principle is provided by the U.S. antitrust laws. They are perceived by the U.S. courts to have jurisdiction over corporate acts overseas so long as these acts have consequences within the United States. This means that business practices of U.S. and foreign companies could be vulnerable to antitrust oversight in the United States, irrespective of where they occur.

Robinson[15] has identified a number of examples of actions that could be reviewed in U.S. courts. These include:

☐ Foreign acquisitions by U.S. companies that reduce actual or potential competition in the U.S.

☐ Participation by a U.S. firm in a foreign cartel

☐ The acquisition by a foreign firm of a competing U.S. firm or the merger of two foreign firms that formerly competed in the United States

☐ Various restrictive clauses in licensing agreements such as cross licensing and market exclusion clauses

☐   Overseas joint ventures by U.S. competitors

☐   Agreements between a U.S. firm and a foreign firm to divide foreign markets and fix overseas prices.

Regulating Outgoing Trade and Investment

National regulation of export activities typically focuses on the types of product that may be traded, the destination of exports, and export procedures such as documentation and customs requirements. (Relevant U.S. laws are considered in more detail in Chapter 14.)

Outgoing flows of investment, particularly foreign direct investment, are subject to strict control in many countries. The example of Norway, discussed earlier, illustrates the type of regulations that many governments put in place. Control over outgoing foreign investment is not currently enforced in the United States, but it has been resorted to in the past, as in 1968 when regulations limited the freedom of U.S. MNCs to undertake foreign direct investment.

In many countries, particularly those in the developing world, capital flight is a serious problem and governments have rigorous foreign exchange and capital outflow controls. These are designed to limit private and corporate short- and long-term overseas investment. Despite stringent regulation, large illegal capital movements still occur. (These are discussed in Chapter 4.)

Regulating Corporate Conduct Overseas

Some governments have established standards of corporate conduct for do-mestically based companies in foreign markets. In most countries, any regulations tend to be rather broad and do not severely inhibit the flexibility of corporate executives with regard to such sensitive issues as bribery.

Such is not the case in the United States, where the *Foreign Corrupt Practices Act (FCPA)*, which was passed in the aftermath of the Watergate scandal investigations in 1977, severely constrains the opportunities for U.S. firms to make questionable payments overseas. The FCPA makes illegal the bribing by U.S. firms of foreign politicians or high-level government officials in order to obtain preferential treatment and special favors. In the case of low-level government officials, however, it is permissible to make payments to encourage expeditious performance of a task that is a legitimate part of their governmental responsibilities. Thus, a payment to an overseas customs official to expedite the clearance of imports that can be legally brought into a country is not illegal under the FCPA. However, all such "grease" payments have to be recorded and accounted for, and they are thus open to public scrutiny.

The law also makes dangerous any adoption of the common strategy of using third parties (such as overseas firms of attorneys and consultants) to make ques-tionable payments on behalf of the firm. Under the Act, management has a "duty to know" what activities third parties are engaging in on behalf of the firm. The law forbids payment to corporate agents while knowing or "having reason to know" that funds will be passed on to foreign officials as bribes.

Critics of the FCPA contend that it is an ambiguous and overly harsh law. It is claimed that U.S. businessmen have to be so cautious that significant amounts of overseas business are being lost to foreign companies not shackled by comparable laws. Other criticisms are that the law is difficult to enforce, fails to distinguish between lesser and greater bribes, harms U.S. foreign-policy interests, and fails to deal with those who solicit bribes.

Business has taken particular exception to that part of the Act which controls payment to corporate agents. It is claimed that the having-reason-to-know clause imposes unfair burdens on companies since they are being held responsible for actions that are really beyond their control. Furthermore, it exacerbates relations with agents, and makes difficult effective recruitment of foreign lobbyists and contacts. The vagueness of the having-reason-to-know clause is also a problem; the clause is open to widely different interpretation.

A second controversial section of the FCPA involves the requirement to keep accounting records "in reasonable detail" with respect to any questionable payments. The law is criticized, once again, as being too vague; it can be construed to include small and inconsequential payments such as tips.

A definitive evaluation of the effect of the FCPA is impossible. What is evident is that few prosecutions have been undertaken and that in the case of proven violations, the penalties levied have been light. U.S. exports and overseas investments have also continued to increase rapidly since 1977 despite the FCPA.

Up to 1987, only three foreign bribery cases had been brought under the FCPA. The 1986 case was the first against a major firm. It concerned payments by Ashland Oil to an advisor to the sultan of Oman who helped Ashland gain a lucrative oil supply contract with Oman. The terms of the contract are estimated to have saved Ashland over $20 million per year. Payment was made indirectly by buying a 75 percent share in mining claims, that proved to be worthless, which the advisor had bought for $0.87 million. This investment cost Ashland $28.7 million. Ashland settled the charges by consenting to an injunction against future violations without admitting or denying any violation.

Despite few prosecutions, the law appears to have had a significant impact on behavior. A survey of 185 major U.S. MNCs carried out by the General Accounting Office has shown that 84 percent of the survey companies have toughened policies regarding questionable payments, and 80 percent have strengthened their auditing. Only 5 percent of the companies thought the Act was ineffective and 76 percent believed the law has been effective in reducing questionable payments.

A number of efforts have been launched to amend the FCPA. Most initiatives involve eliminating the duty-to-know clause. In its place would be substituted a provision making it illegal to direct or authorize payment of a bribe by an agent. It has also been suggested that the reasonable-detail provision should be dropped in favor of a requirement that records be kept according to what is "material;" that is, only those payments having a significant impact on profits, revenue, or the balance sheet.

Another example of an area where the U.S. government seeks to regulate corporate behavior in a firmer manner than in many other countries regards the pressure by some Arab nations to restrict trade with Israel. In reaction to this policy, parts of the Export Administration Act of 1979 and sections of the Internal Revenue Code forbid U.S. firms from taking actions that advance restrictive trade practices or boycotts imposed by foreign governments against countries friendly to the United States. Compliance with these anti-boycott regulations are undoubtedly a handicap for some U.S. firms when attempting to develop Middle East markets. Over 40 firms have been penalized for violations of the rules.

The Legal Environment in Foreign Markets

Knowledge of and compliance with relevant laws in overseas markets is mandatory for international companies. In the case of firms with extensive overseas operations, a wide array of different legal frameworks need to be taken into account. Diversity in national legal systems and relevant laws is very great and poses substantial problems for international firms.

An understanding of the basic nature of the legal system in markets of interest is fundamental. An important distinction should be made between *code* and *common* law systems. In the former, law is based upon a well-defined legal code laying out the law for all probable issues. This approach is followed in much of continental Europe. In the United States, Britain, and many former British colonies, common law systems—where the law is seen to be the institutionalization of custom and practice, and where the courts are the final arbiters of what is the law—have developed. Customs and practices are seen as part of statutory law. As a result, precedent and court interpretation are much more important than in code law countries.

It is crucially important to remember that surface similarities in the basic legal system often mask critical differences. These differences have a major impact on business activities. The actual detail of host country law is therefore of primary interest. Some of the more important areas of legal concern for international marketers are briefly reviewed below.

Laws that impact the primary modes of entering the market of interest—imports, licensing, foreign direct investment, and joint ventures in particular—are of major importance. In many countries, numerous strictly enforced regulations must be taken into account by foreign firms. These are often laws that intentionally restrict entry by foreign firms.

For instance, basic rules concerning documentation, packaging, and customs procedures must be adhered to by exporters. The nature of licensing and joint-venture arrangements are strictly controlled in many countries. In Mexico, for example, special provisions in licensing agreements designed to limit the freedom of action of the Mexican licensee will often be precluded by the law. In India, regulations not only ensure that a joint venture is the norm for inward foreign investment, but they also mandate a majority Indian interest in the case of most projects.

Inward foreign direct investment is strictly controlled in many countries. Major considerations include appropriate utilization of national resources, financing arrangements, ownership, and control. Such issues may be the subject of specific laws or are subject to control in the negotiation process prior to the formal government approval frequently required for incoming foreign-investment projects.

Regulations relating to product standards, packaging, advertising content, promotion, distribution, trademark and brandmark protection, and prices is also of immediate concern. As will be seen in later chapters, these laws have a major impact on marketing policy.

Differences in the national legal context reflect varying national situations, needs, and priorities. Sometimes they also are the result of a conscious differentiation strategy. One obvious approach to limiting foreign competition is to make the legal environment facing foreign firms either very restrictive or very different from that abroad. Unfamiliar and unusual regulatory frameworks, for example with regard to product standards, increase uncertainty and raise the cost of market entry.

Finally, it is critical that interpreting the host country legal environment is not left to amateurs. Expert opinion and advice is essential; the best source of which is attorneys familiar with the workings of the local legal system and the implications of relevant local laws.

SUMMARY

This chapter examines economic, trading, political, and legal dimensions of the environment faced by international firms in home and host countries.

Fundamental features of the economic environment include the economic system, economic structure, and the level of development of overseas markets. All economies share some features of market and central command economic systems and thus lie at some point on a continuum between these two poles. Various classifications are available for distinguishing between the various sectors in an economy. The process of economic growth, combined with concurrent changes in the economic and social structure, is termed economic development. A widely used, though imperfect, measure of economic development is given by GNP-per-head data.

Information on the basic nature and structure of the economic system in overseas markets needs to be supplemented with more detailed economic data. Typical areas of interest include natural-resource endowments, the demographic situation, measures of economic performance, the infrastructure, and economic policy.

When gathering and analyzing economic data, a number of basic principles must be kept in mind. Among these principles are the need to forecast and the significance of secondary source economic data. Major problems in the process of economic evaluation often arise because of missing, unreliable, or misleading data.

Trade barriers can be classified into one of three groups—tariffs, quotas, and nontariff barriers. These measures are most commonly used to restrict imports, but may also be employed to regulate exports. Key arguments used to justify import controls include the need to protect domestic jobs and strategic or infant industries, to counteract dumping, to improve the balance of payments, to obtain bargaining leverage, and to improve a nation's terms of trade. However, protectionist action invites retaliation, often hurts the consumer, and encourages the inefficient utilization of resources.

Major reasons for export controls include a desire to influence world and domestic prices for the good, a wish to maximize domestic added value and jobs, and political and strategic factors. However, export restrictions are sometimes ineffective when substitutes are available from other nations, may be politically damaging, invite retaliation, and often reduce the volume of export sales.

Normally, the key actors in the political environment are national governments, which enjoy great power due to their ability to tax, regulate, and participate directly in economic activities. Interest groups also influence the political process. They, along with the ideological environment, nationalism, and the economic system, are major determinants of the political environment facing the international firm.

It is very important that a clear distinction is made between political events and their impact upon the firm. The impact of political events on a firm is heavily influenced by factors specific to the firm and the industry in which it operates. It follows that the environment and firm must be separated and that political instability is not the same as political risk.

Effective evaluation of a firm's exposure to political risk requires forecasting political developments in markets of interest. It is then necessary to identify opportunities and threats to the firm's operations that are likely to arise from the projected developments. Two general approaches to measuring political risk have been developed. The first is based primarily upon subjective evaluations. An alternative approach involves developing a range of quantifiable measures of the political environment. Typical factors of interest include measures of population homogeneity, the potential for violent change, the political process, civil disturbance, and economic performance.

A variety of strategies for managing political risk may be identified prior to market entry. These include avoidance of high-risk markets, taking out insurance against identified risks, and negotiating with foreign governments. Projects may also be structured to take account of risk exposure. Regarding ongoing operations, policy responses to risk include divestment, short-term profit maximization, and taking on local partners.

The national legal environment is made up of domestic law and host country laws. In the case of home country law, account must be taken of those laws specifically designed to regulate the firm's overseas activities and those that are deemed by the home government to have extraterritorial impact. Principal areas of interest include laws regulating outgoing flows of trade and investment, antitrust activities, and corporate conduct overseas.

Compliance with the legal framework in overseas markets is essential; the relevant host country laws must be carefully evaluated. Areas of special interest include laws regulating market entry modes and the marketing mix.

DISCUSSION QUESTIONS

1. Why might comparative data on GNP per head in the United States, Japan, Italy, and India present a misleading picture of relative standards of living in these countries?

2. Comment on this statement: "U.S. protectionism saves jobs for American workers and is therefore desirable."

3. What are the primary advantages and disadvantages of *quantitative* country risk assessment models and *subjective* models?

4. Significant changes have been taking place in the economies of many communist countries in Eastern Europe. What has been happening, and what implications do these developments have for Western firms interested in doing business in Eastern Europe?

5. "Political instability is not the same as political risk." Comment on this statement.

6. "The Foreign Corrupt Practices Act is a severe handicap for U.S. MNCs." Do you agree? What changes, if any, are needed in the Act?

7. "Tariff barriers are preferable to quota restrictions on international trade." What is your view?

8. The U.S. government interprets some U.S. laws as having extraterritorial impact. Should U.S. firms be limited by U.S. laws when doing business in foreign markets?

ADDITIONAL READING

Brewer, T. L., *Political Risk in International Business* (New York: Praeger, 1985).

Doz, Y., "Government Policies and Global Industries," in *Competition in Global Industries*, M. Porter, ed. (Boston: Harvard Business School Press, 1986).

Fadiman, J. A., "A Traveler's Guide to Gifts and Bribes," *Harvard Business Review,* July–August 1986.

Gardner, H. S., *Comparative Economic Systems* (New York: Dryden Press, 1988).

Gillespie, K., "The Middle East Response to the U.S. Foreign Corrupt Practices Act," *California Management Review,* Summer 1987.

Greenaway, D., *Trade Policy and the New Protectionism.* (New York: St. Martins Press, 1983).

Kindra, G. S., *Marketing in Developing Countries* (New York: St. Martins Press, 1984).

Nath, R., *Comparative Management: A Regional View* (Cambridge, Mass.: Ballinger, 1987).

Raddock, D. M., *Assessing Corporate Political Risk* (Totowa, New Jersey: Rowman and Littlefield, 1986).

World Bank, *World Development Report 1987* (New York: Oxford University Press, 1987).

ENDNOTES

1. See *World Development Reports* (The World Bank, various issues).
2. Hodgson, J. S. and M. G. Herander, *International Economic Relations* (Englewood Cliffs, N.J.: Prentice-Hall, 1983).
3. See *The Wall Street Journal*, February 27, 1987.
4. See *The Economist*, February 6, 1988.
5. S. J. Kobrin, "Political Risk: A Review and Reconsideration," *Journal of International Business Studies*, Spring–Summer 1979.
6. See *Webster's New World Dictionary* (Cleveland, Ohio: William Collins, 1976).
7. See *The Wall Street Journal*, November 14, 1986.
8. See *The State*, October 11, 1987.
9. R. D. Robinson, *International Business Management* (Hinsdale, Illinois: Dryden Press, 1978).
10. See *Political Risk Yearbook* (New York: Frost and Sullivan).
11. F. T. Haner, *Best's Review*, July 1975.
12. D. H. Haendel, G. T. West, and R. G. Meadow, *Overseas Investment and Political Risk* (Philadelphia: Foreign Policy Research Institute, 1975).
13. A. C. Shapiro, *Multinational Financial Management* (Boston: Allyn & Bacon, 1982).
14. Ibid.
15. Robinson, op. cit.

Chapter 4
The International Environment: Major Dimensions and Institutions

INTRODUCTION

The relevance of the national environment in home and host countries to international firms (reviewed in Chapter 3) is rather obvious. Firms operating overseas also encounter international environmental factors that cannot be ignored. This international environment is made up of international institutions, agreements, systems, and arrangements that impact on international flows of trade, investment, and know-how, and that also affect market conditions in individual countries. We now discuss the economic, financial, political, and legal dimensions of this environment.

INTERNATIONAL ECONOMIC ENVIRONMENT

The Trading Environment

Despite the arguments for free trade (discussed in Chapter 3), the trade policies of many countries have historically been dominated by a desire to protect domestic industry from foreign competition. Such policies were very evident during the 1930s, when the onset of the global Depression and the high tariff levels imposed in the United States following the Smoot-Hawley Tariff Act of 1930 triggered a vicious circle of retaliatory protectionist measures around the world. These measures, along with the fall in general income levels, sharply reduced the volume of international trade.

Barriers to trade were significantly reduced in the late 1930s, primarily as a result of bilateral trade negotiations. Following the end of World War II, the United States and other major trading nations were anxious to encourage international economic cooperation, particularly in the managing of international trading and financial relationships. The limited impact of bilateral tariff reductions demonstrated a need for a more comprehensive and effective approach to reducing barriers to international trade. Recognition of this problem resulted in the establishment in 1947 of the General Agreement on Tariffs and Trade (GATT).

The General Agreement on Tariffs and Trade

The GATT agreement established general guidelines for the conduct of international trade. GATT also provides the primary forum for the negotiation of multilateral reductions in tariffs and other barriers to international trade. The original 23 parties to the agreement have now expanded to include all the important Western trading countries. The current members account for around 80 percent of world trade. As a result of this growth, GATT is the major organization dealing with international trade issues. There are few members from centrally planned economies, and recent attempts by the Soviet Union to join have been rebuffed on the grounds that the Soviet commitment to planning and state control of trade is incompatible with GATT's free market principles.

GATT's basic objective is the removal of barriers to international trade through a gradual, incremental approach based on multilateral negotiations. A central tenet in this process is the principle of nondiscrimination. Thus the notion of "most favored nation" treatment was established, which requires that each member country apply the same tariff rate to all other GATT members. If, for example, the United States reduces tariffs on imports of shoes from one member, then the new rate must be applied on shoe imports from all other GATT members.

Two other basic GATT principles are the prohibition of quantitative trade restrictions, except in certain specified circumstances, and the notion of consultation and negotiation to solve trade disputes. Although GATT has limited power to ensure compliance, members who contravene these principles lay themselves open to retaliation from other countries.

The intent of the GATT rules is threefold: to encourage the reduction of trade restrictions, to generalize the liberalization that occurs, and to put in place a framework for the negotiated settlement of trade disputes.

Since 1947, seven rounds of trade negotiations have taken place. Each round involves painstaking, complex negotiations on a multilateral basis. The most recent Tokyo Round finished in 1979 after four years of bargaining. The results of the successive GATT rounds have been impressive in terms of reducing tariffs on manufactured goods. The reductions agreed to during the Tokyo Round covered some 90 percent of industrial trade between the major trading nations. For the European community and United States, the average fall in tariff rates agreed to was about 30 percent. Over the total lifetime of the treaty, it has been estimated that the average tariff on manufactured imports in major countries has fallen from 40 to 5 percent.[1] Much less impressive is GATT's track record on reducing tariffs on agricultural products. Relatively little has been accomplished to reduce pro-liferating nontariff barriers [NTB] although a start was made during the Tokyo Round. Recent estimates indicate that up to 50 percent of world trade is affected, in one way or another, by nontariff barriers.[2] The current Uruguay Round is aimed at addressing the problems of NTBs and other obstacles to world trade.

The essential problem facing GATT today is that in recent years there has been a shift in the basic protectionist techniques adopted by many countries. The methods being used have resulted in selective protectionism in direct contradiction of the principle of nondiscrimination. Unfortunately, the GATT organization, a secretariat of some 300 based in Geneva, is not equipped to deal with many of the nontariff measures that have been adopted.

Many of the restrictions imposed are negotiated on a voluntary, bilateral basis and thus fall outside GATT's control. These popular market-sharing arrangements are in direct contravention of GATT's nondiscrimination tenet. Trade patterns become distorted as countries decide who can enter their market and on what terms. Other barriers are commonly justified as being necessary to counter unfair trade. Article 19 of the agreement allows temporary emergency protection of domestic industries damaged by a flood of cheap imports. Severe balance-of-payments problems may also be used to justify temporary restrictions under these safeguard provisions.

Unfortunately, many countries have resorted to protectionism, using the safeguard arguments outlined above, even though their situation does not justify such action. Although GATT members can ask for a dispute panel to be appointed to review an alleged breach of the rules by another member, any panel recommendations are nonbinding. This is unfortunate, for it is estimated that world exports would be some 40 percent higher if the GATT treaty was observed to the letter.

Some bilateral trade arrangements, which infringe GATT's basic principle of nondiscrimination, are permitted under the GATT rules and do have beneficial effects. Discrimination is permitted when groups of countries negotiate an economic integration relationship such as a free-trade area or common market. When such arrangements occur on a specialized, bilateral basis (such as the New Zealand– Australia and the United States–Israel agreements) compatibility with the spirit of GATT is more questionable.

The Generalized System of Preferences (GSP) begun in 1971 also contravenes the nondiscrimination tenet. This arrangement allows rich countries to grant preferential tariffs for selected products imported from developing countries. It is generally considered desirable and compatible with GATT, and it affects some 20 percent of LDC exports to developed countries.

The limited success of GATT in regard to liberalizing trade in agricultural products has disappointed many LDCs who perceive the treaty as having primarily benefited the rich industrial countries. The LDCs are also frustrated by barriers to their manufactured exports, particularly textiles. In 1986, some 30 percent of LDC exports were seriously affected by nontariff barriers, compared with under 20 percent of exports from industrial countries.

Many industrial countries believe that trade in services, such as banking, insurance, and consulting, should be brought under the aegis of GATT, and they criticize the resistance of developing countries to this proposal. GATT does permit LDCs to protect some infant industries from more efficient overseas competitors. The industrial countries are pressing for the end of this protectionism in a number of the richer NICs in Asia and Latin America.

The preceding analysis makes apparent that there is much to discuss during the current GATT negotiations, the Uruguay Round, started in 1987. The Uruguayan agenda calls for comprehensive negotiations to extend GATT rules to trade in agricultural products and services. On the agenda also are discussions on the protection of intellectual property patents, trademarks, and copyright; restrictions on foreign investment that limit trade; the phasing out of current violations of GATT rules; and the strengthening of GATT's dispute settlement and enforcement procedures.

The negotiations on service trade are likely to be particularly difficult because most services are not shipped across national boundaries and have to be delivered on the spot. Market access is therefore often possible only if foreign direct investment and the employment of expatriate managers is also allowed.

There is more hope for real progress in rule enforcement. Many countries agree on a need for more effective dispute resolution. Key goals are the streamlining of dispute procedures and making it harder to ignore the decisions of the dispute panels.

The New Protectionism

Despite significant reductions in the incidence and level of barriers to international trade over the last forty years, protectionism is still alive and well in many markets. As countries have been obliged to lower tariffs under GATT, they have often resorted to less obvious, but equally pernicious, protectionist measures, such as voluntary restraints, market-sharing agreements, subsidies, and other nontariff barriers. In some industries—notably steel, textiles, automobiles, agriculture, and services—protectionist barriers to unfettered trade are endemic. Thus, at the same time that the agreements resulting from the Tokyo Round are being implemented (in eight annual stages from 1980), there is strong evidence that a decreasing share of world trade is conducted on the basis of free and fair competition. GATT's rules are being increasingly circumvented and ignored in many countries.

Contrary to the free-market philosophy expounded by the Reagan administration, protectionism is on the rise in the United States. Political expediency and the United States deficit on the current account of the balance of payments have resulted in many protectionist measures in the last decade. In 1978, a trigger price mechanism set a minimum price for steel imports. In 1981, a voluntary export restraint program was implemented for imports of Japanese autos. The list continues with the steel quota program of 1984 and 1985, quota controls for textile imports, and extensive agricultural subsidies. Estimates made by the World Bank indicate that in 1983 43 percent of United States imports were affected by nontariff barriers, second only to France where the comparable figure was over 50 percent.[3]

The most common justification for protectionism is that it is retaliation against unfair trading practices in other countries. Thus a primary rationale for United States grain subsidies is to counter Common Market subsidies and the protectionist character of its Common Agricultural Policy. Japan also is a prime target for retaliation. But although Japan directly protects its agricultural, coal- and oil-refining industries and indirectly limits foreign access in other sectors, it is probably as much in compliance with GATT requirements as are most other industrial countries, including the United States. Many of the problems encountered when exporting to Japan, such as the complex nature of the distribution system and the attitudes of Japanese consumers, are issues that fall outside the GATT framework.

The developing countries have been highly critical of many features of the current trading environment. Although they have grounds for dissatisfaction, many LDCs practice overt protectionism. Brazil and India, for example, are determined to protect their nascent computer industry by shutting out most computer imports. Many other examples of protectionism exist in the LDCs and NICs.

Among the more recent and damaging protectionist arrangements that ignore GATT principles of nondiscrimination and universality are voluntary restrictive agreements and orderly marketing agreements. Through such schemes one nation coerces another into "voluntarily" restricting exports of given products. In this manner protection is achieved without violating GATT rules. Consider the example below.

The Multi-Fibre Arrangement (MFA) was designed to provide temporary protection from cheap imports for the textile industry in the rich Western countries. The agreement had its genesis in a scheme for controlling trade in cotton textiles in 1961 and has flourished since then. Discussions were concluded in 1986 for a fourth extension of the MFA for another five years. Over fifty countries were involved in these discussions. The MFA provides an orderly framework for world trade in textiles, allowing textile-importing nations in the West to negotiate bilateral, quantitative restrictions on textile imports. The United States has such agreements with over twenty textile exporters. Although the MFA does allow for a gradual increase in exports, a major portion of the $100 billion world textile trade does not take place in the context of GATT's fair trade rules.

Many other examples of voluntary agreements designed to restrict imports exist. In addition, many nations resort to other restrictions that are either justified by reference to GATT's safeguard provisions or involve NTBs, such as the manipulation of product standards or inspection regulations (which are difficult to control).

In spite of these problems, the overall international trading environment has been significantly liberalized in the post-war years. Although the outlook for the future is uncertain, the Uruguay Round of GATT negotiations offers hope for further progress. The Reagan administration, despite wobbling on individual issues, frequently attempted to hold the line against strong protectionist sentiment in Congress. In Europe, the expansion of the European Community (EC) and the 1977 implementation of a trading agreement between EC and EFTA nations created the world's largest free-trade area. The Japanese have also recently taken measures to open up their markets to foreign imports.

Important pressures, which could lead to more protectionism around the world, are still strong. In the developing world, resentment against the trading policies of the rich countries is strong. This resentment, chronic balance-of-payments and debt problems in some countries, and a desire to foster local industries has encouraged highly visible protectionism in many LDCs and NICs.

In the industrial countries, major problems are posed by protectionism in agriculture, the United States balance-of-payments deficit, and the success of the Japanese in manufactured exports. Barriers to trade in services, limits on foreign direct investment, and the lack of protection for intellectual property rights are matters of concern for the United States and other Western countries; these concerns could be used to justify the imposition of protectionist measures.

Another contentious trade issue concerns antidumping measures, introduced by the EC in June 1987, designed to counter screwdriver operations (the assembly within the EC of imported components into products that were previously imported). The rationale for such measures, which are directed primarily against Japanese firms, is that they are needed to counter strategies where overseas firms set up low value-added assembly operations for cheap imported components in the EC in order to avoid dumping controls. Since the legislation was passed, the EC Commission has launched antidumping investigations of the European assembly operations of Japanese manufacturers of typewriters and photocopiers.

In the United States, the large trade imbalance, heavy lobbying by industries threatened by import competition, and widespread perceptions of unfair trade practices in many overseas markets have given momentum to protectionism. More protection for some exposed industries has resulted and the Trade Bill, passed in 1988, tightens the process of trade regulation in the United States by mandating vigorous official investigation of unfair trade practices. However, the legislation erects no new major trade barriers and does not contain the controversial "Gephardt" amendment that would have forced countries with large trade surpluses with the United States to reduce these imbalances by 10 percent per annum or face retaliation.

The late 1980s saw the United States adopt a more aggressive policy of retaliation against countries perceived to have engaged in unfair trading practices. Examples of actions taken in 1987 and 1988 include:

☐ Threatened retaliation against the EC forced withdrawal of restrictions on United States grain sales to Spain. Ongoing discussions on contentious issues such as subsidies to agriculture and the European Air-bus have occurred.

☐ Restrictions placed on exports to the United States of some Japanese firms alleged to have dumped semiconductors in the United States. Continued pressure has also been put on the Japanese government to remove quotas on agricultural imports and to reduce protectionism in the construction and service sectors.

☐ Punitive tariff increases imposed on $105 of Brazilian exports to the United States in retaliation for barriers against imports of United States computers.

☐ Criticism of South Korea, Taiwan, Hong Kong, and Singapore for maintaining unfair trade and investment barriers and holding down the value of their currencies against the United States dollar. These countries will also lose GSP tariff-free treatment in 1989 for some $10 billion of their exports.

Commodity Arrangements

Much of world trade in primary products occurs on terms set in commodity markets where prices fluctuate with demand and supply. These markets are centered in New York, Chicago, and London, active centers of trade in such products as metals, foodstuffs, fibers, beverages (tea, coffee, and cocoa), and lumber. The prevailing price in these markets tends to exert a major influence on commodity deals wherever they occur.

A characteristic of the markets for many primary commodities is that both demand and supply tend to be price inelastic in the short term. Many primary goods are regarded as basic necessities that cannot be easily substituted. On the supply side, new mines and agricultural plantations cannot be opened overnight. Because of these factors, shifts in demand and supply for many primary goods cause sharp price movements and thus strong fluctuations in the costs of primary product processors and in the earnings of commodity exporters.

Commodity Agreements

Since there is a common interest in reducing price volatility, a number of commodity agreements to bring together primary producers and consumers have been attempted. Typically, the parties to an agreement commit to stabilizing the commodity's price within a predetermined range. The two primary intiatives designed to enforce the price policy are the establishment of a buffer stock and controls over supply.

These initiatives require multilateral agreement and the system is supposed to function as follows. When the price of the good approaches the upper limit, inventory from the buffer stock is sold and producers are permitted to increase output and exports. Conversely, if the price falls too far, the buffer stock manager purchases the good and places it in inventory. Suppliers are then instructed to reduce production and exports. Many practical problems need to be worked out. The buffer stock arrangement does not work for perishable goods; it requires substantial up-front financing since the costs of holding inventory are high; a sustained effort to hold up prices in the face of slow demand is very expensive.

Obviously, the cooperation of rich consumer countries is vital to the success of commodity agreements. But they have shown little interest in commodity agreements to improve the condition of LDCs.

Successful arrangements also require the producing nations to adhere to production controls and export quotas. However, disagreements on the allocation of quotas and pressures to maximize short-term income encourage cheating. Even if the parties to an agreement cooperate, activities of producers outside the arrangement can compromise its effectiveness. High prices may also encourage the development of substitute products.

The experience of the International Cocoa Organization (ICO) illustrates many of these problems. The major consuming nations have refused to accept Third World demands for higher prices. In 1985, the United States pulled out of the ICO, as did its biggest producer, the Ivory Coast. Since 1985, prices have stagnated and the buffer stock was not used for several years because of a lack of funds. A new agreement was therefore implemented in 1987, calling for the stabilization of cocoa prices within a given price range. The arrangement did not stop a price slide, and by early 1988 prices had fallen to a five-year low. The slide occurred because production exceeded demand by 100,000 tons and, although the buffer stock manager purchased 75,000 tons of cocoa in early 1988, insufficient funds were available for further big purchases. Under the agreement, producers should then have started withholding supply from the market by agreeing to export quotas. However, Brazil and the Ivory Coast, two leading producers, could not afford to stockpile and needed to generate export revenue. Other producers did not have suitable warehouse facilities to hold extra cocoa without its deteriorating. Furthermore the marketing activities of private firms is beyond ICO control. For all these reasons, the ICO's market stabilizing activities were not very effective in 1987 and 1988.

Probably the most successful commodity arrangement, until recently, has been the International Tin Agreement of 1956, which involved seven producing nations, 85 percent of world production, and 22 customer nations that consume some 95 percent of world output. The agreement succeeded in stabilizing prices for many years. However, relatively high prices resulted in increased output from nontraditional suppliers like Brazil and encouraged demand for substitutes.

In 1985 the Tin Agreement collapsed in the face of strong downward price pressure. Heavy purchases for the buffer stock, and an unwillingness by participating governments to increase financing, meant that the buffer stock managers were eventually unable to meet their commitments. As a result, the price of tin fell by more than 50 percent in late 1985 and has not recovered since. Other failed arrangements include the wheat and sugar pacts. Although an agreement on rubber still exists, intervention prices are so low that the arrangement has limited impact.

Producer Agreements

An alternative approach to cooperation between producers and consumers is for commodity exporters to form cartels in an effort to control price setting unilaterally. Such collective action can raise prices and maximize the profits of the cartel. In order for it to work, producers must be at least willing to cooperate in regulating output and price levels. Long-term success also presupposes relatively price inelastic demand and an absence of suitable substitutes.

A number of commodity producers, mostly LDCs, have attempted to develop export cartels to increase prices. The most common rationale behind such action is that the international terms of trade are weighted against commodity exporters who face volatile prices that, in the long term, have risen much more slowly than the average for manufactured products. In the view of many LDCs, the rich consuming nations are not genuinely interested in making commodity agreements work and cooperation with other exporters is therefore necessary.

Perhaps the best example of a successful producer cartel is the Organization of Petroleum Exporting Countries (OPEC). However, as will be seen, OPEC's success has been due in part to exceptional circumstances. The effectiveness of the cartel has also declined significantly in recent years.

Up to the early 1970s, international trade in oil was dominated by intracompany sales. The major oil companies were vertically integrated concerns that undertook the exploration, production, transportation, refining, and marketing of oil. Consequently, these firms were able to set the prices charged for oil exports. In order to bolster their power vis-à-vis the oil firms, the major exporting countries—which were almost exclusively LDCs—banded together in 1961 to form OPEC. Although the real price of oil fell in the 1960s, OPEC did succeed in halting the erosion in the value of their oil exports and the oil companies did agree to increase royalty payments.

Low prices stimulated demand during the 1960s. This increase, and the greater control over output achieved by the nationalization of local oil operations in many OPEC countries, set the scene for the dramatic increase in oil prices that began in 1973. Most of the oil importing countries argue that the sharp increase in the real price of oil during the 1970s is primarily attributable to OPEC's success as a cartel and that the competitive price would have been significantly lower than that sustained. Oil exporters counterclaim that the pe-1973 price was artificially low and induced too rapid a depletion of resources. They justify their action as a reaction to their exploitation by a cartel of oil MNCs and artificially lower prices.

Regardless of one's position on the nature of the post-1973 oil market, there is no doubt that OPEC did have a major impact. More recently, the real price of oil has drifted downwards. By late 1985, prices had collapsed from $28 a barrel, reaching as low as $8 a barrel in the summer of 1986.

This fall in oil prices reflects a number of factors demonstrating the weaknesses of producer cartels. Successive price increases in the 1970s stimulated the rapid exploitation of non-OPEC oil sources and of alternative sources of energy. As demand for OPEC oil declined sharply in the 1980s, producers were faced with the problem of coordinating a cutback in OPEC output and exports. In this environment of retrenchment, differences in national interest and political rivalries resulted in some members ignoring agreed production and export quotas. A fierce battle for market share in 1985 and 1986 was triggered inside OPEC. This intracartel competition precipitated the collapse in oil prices; only in August 1986 did OPEC oil ministers cobble together an agreement on voluntary output quotas. This agreement pushed up prices to the $14-per-barrel level. Subsequently, prices increased to around $18 per barrel and then stabilized with increased demand.

In the United States, for example, 40 percent of the oil supply was imported in 1987 as compared with only 27 percent in 1985. However, significant differences still divide OPEC's members. Unless oil demand continues to increase significantly, the unity of the cartel is likely to be tested still further.

It is apparent that even when oil prices were rapidly increasing, there was still disagreement on the extent to which OPEC could set "artificially" high prices during the 1970s. Recent events also indicate that it is difficult for producer cartels to hold prices above the competitive level in the medium term. The corollary of cartelized pricing, in most situations, is a long-term fall in demand, generating pressures that make the maintenance of cartel solidarity difficult.

For all the above reasons, most commodity exporters have given up attempts to develop producer cartels and have turned to involving both consumers and producers in multilateral commodity agreements. Most efforts in this direction, however, have had limited impact on international markets.

The diamond business provides another example of the impact of a producer cartel on world price levels. De Beer's Central Selling Organization (CSO) controls 80 percent of the world's uncut diamond market. The CSO has purchased contracts with De Beer's own mines in South Africa and Namibia and other mines in Botswana, Zaire, Sierra Leone, and Australia. De Beers also has a sales arrangement with the Soviet Union, another major producer.

As the dominant middleman, the CSO sells diamonds to dealers based in major cutting centers such as Antwerp, Bombay, Tel Aviv, and New York. De Beers markets diamonds ten times a year at "sights"—selected dealers are offered a box of diamonds at a fixed price. Despite fluctuating retail price levels, the CSO has never cut its prices. It seeks to maintain price stability by continuing to buy from its suppliers even when demand is depressed. It holds excess supply in inventory, releasing it to world markets when demand and retail prices increase.

Despite a collapse in retail diamond prices in the early 1980s, and growing sales by mining companies that do not sell to the CSO, De Beers has managed to reverse the slump in diamond prices and continues to exercise great power through a hard-nosed and efficient sales organization. Major reasons for CSO effectiveness is that it controls the pipeline between the diamond mine and the dealers and vigorously promotes diamond sales. For example, in 1987 alone, De Beers spent $110 million on diamond advertising and promotion. This expenditure supported global market research and public relations and advertising designed to "perpetuate the mystique of diamonds as the ultimate expression of love."[4] The effectiveness of this two-pronged strategy in enabling De Beers to influence world diamond markets perhaps has lessons for other producer cartels.

The OECD

The Organization for Economic Cooperation and Development (OECD) was formed in 1960 to facilitate economic cooperation between its 24 rich industrial member countries. Intergovernmental discussion on economic and social policy issues is advanced via specialized committees supported by expert groups and a large secretariat of some 1,700 Paris-based professional economists and other experts.

Issues dealt with include agriculture, development assistance, trade, and general policy. In addition, the OECD has formed a number of semi-autonomous bodies to focus on particular problems. The International Energy Agency, for example, formed in 1974, coordinates the response of the OECD members to the activities of OPEC and the rise in the price of oil.

Apart from supporting the activities of the OECD committees and agencies, the OECD secretariat also collects, analyzes, and publishes large amounts of economic, social and financial data on member countries. This vast data bank provides the basis for regular economic reports and forecasts for OECD members.

Examples of OECD initiatives include the OECD code of conduct, introduced in 1976, designed to establish minimum standards of behavior for multinational enterprises and to foster nondiscrimination of foreign firms by host governments. More recently, the Tax Committee of the OECD has developed guidelines to improve information flows on a wide range of tax issues between government agencies in member countries. These proposals, published in 1986, are likely to form the basis for a convention aimed at curtailing tax evasion. The OECD is thus a forum for discussion, consultation, and analysis; an important data bank; and a source of useful publications on national and international economic and social issues.

ECONOMIC INTEGRATION

The development of economic blocs, notably in Western Europe, has been an important feature of the international environment since World War II. Because economic integration has important implications for firms operating in markets affected by this movement, we now give special attention to this topic.

Economic integration takes a variety of forms but essentially involves economic cooperation, designed to bring about greater mutual economic interdependence among nations. The most common schemes are designed to reduce barriers to trade between participating members. More ambitious forms of integration aim to facilitate international movement of factor inputs and the coordination of economic, financial, and exchange-rate policies.

Reducing restrictions to international flows of trade and investment creates both opportunities and threats for firms. The creation of a free-trade area, for example, reduces the protection enjoyed by firms in their home market and opens up opportunities in the markets of other members of the trading bloc. For firms based in countries outside the bloc, exclusion is a source of potential problems because of discriminatory barriers that may be erected against nonmembers. At the same time, enhanced opportunities arising from economic union encourages outside firms to invest in manufacturing capacity within the bloc.

Apart from trade and investment liberalization, economic integration facilitates other forms of cooperation. The formation of the European Community (EC) has led to greater harmonization of some laws within member countries, thereby reducing barriers to entering EC markets. However, these developments have also been criticized as merely adding an additional level of bureaucratic regulation and control.

Economic Effects of Integration

Two major economic effects impact on the welfare of participants in an economic bloc. The first of these, *trade creation,* has a positive impact. This is due to the greater availability of cheap imports. Trade creation occurs when economic union induces a shift from high-cost producers, typically located in the importing country, to lower-cost producers of the good located inside the union. For example, it is likely that consumers of locally produced goods in Spain (an EC member since 1986) will now be benefiting from the removal of barriers to the import of cheaper- or higher-quality goods produced by more efficient EC firms. The Spanish consumer thus benefits from greater choice, more competition, and lower prices.

The *trade diversion* effect of economic integration will lower consumer welfare within the union. Trade diversion occurs when member countries buy from each other products that were formerly acquired from more efficient external producers. For example, Spanish membership in the EC has resulted in higher tariffs on imports of United States corn and sorghum and the elimination of barriers to EC exports to Spain. Efficient United States farmers will therefore lose business to less-effective European farmers, and consumers in Spain will now have to pay more for these products.

In addition to these effects, the formation of an economic bloc may bring about important changes in the economic structure of member countries. Greater competition, economies-of-scale benefits from access to larger markets, and more investment and innovation are among the more important changes likely to occur. These dynamic effects of economic union should lead to more effective resource utilization and faster economic growth in participating countries.

Types of Economic Integration

A convenient classification scheme distinguishing among six different stages of economic integration has been provided by Hodgson and Herander.[5] The simplest scheme is the *preferential trading* agreement, in which participants reduce restrictions on trade among themselves, but retain barriers to imports from countries not party to the agreement. An example of such an arrangement is the trade pact signed in July of 1986 between Argentina and Brazil. Their pact calls for the gradual elimination of tariffs, quotas, and administrative or technical obstacles to mutual trade. Its goal is to triple trade in five years. Although the Argentina–Brazil arrangement is contrary to the principle of nondiscrimination, Article 24 of the GATT does allow for preferential trading agreements in specified circumstances such as a movement toward the formation of a free-trade area or customs union and as part of the GSP system. There is an important condition, however: such agreements must not cause trade barriers to third parties.

A *free-trade area* is formed when member countries agree to eliminate barriers to trade with other participants simultaneously, maintaining their own individual trade restrictions on imports from nonmembers. Such agreements do not necessarily remove barriers to intramember trade in all products. A good example of a free-trade agreement is the United States–Canada trade pact signed in January 1988. The key provision of the agreement is the elimination of all tariffs and many other trade barriers over a ten-year period starting in 1989.

The next stage of integration is a *customs union,* which has all the features of a free-trade area as well as the harmonization of members' trade restrictions on imports from nonmembers. When the customs-union arrangement is extended to include the removal of barriers to the movement of labor and capital between participants, then a *common market* is formed. Lowering barriers to factor mobility is of considerable significance, but does not require a high level of economic policy coordination.

When monetary or economic unions are formed, a higher level of economic coordination is necessary. In the *monetary union,* essential steps include the establishment of a currency bloc, where the foreign-exchange rates of members are pegged—set at a fixed rate to each other—and the harmonization of monetary and fiscal policy.

An *economic union* has all the features of a monetary union. In addition, participants give up to a central policy-making institution the power to set economic policy. Monetary and fiscal policy is thus developed and coordinated at the supranational level and a unified monetary and banking system is established.

The European Community

The European Community (EC) is undoubtedly the most important example of successful post-war economic integration. It originated in the formation of the European Coal and Steel Community in 1952 by the six core members of the EC: Belgium, the Netherlands, Luxembourg, France, West Germany, and Italy. The 1952 agreement established free trade in coal and steel among member countries.

The success of this arrangement resulted in further negotiations among the original six and in the 1957 signing of the Treaty of Rome, which established the European Economic Community. The immediate objectives of the treaty were the establishment of a customs union with the dismantling of tariff, quota, and nontariff barriers to trade; and the establishment of a common external tariff. The treaty also contains provisions for the free movement of labor, capital, and services among EC members; calls for common policies on economic matters, such as external trade, agriculture, transport, and competition; and provides for harmonization of laws and social policy.

Customs-union status was achieved by 1968, and substantial progress on most of the other issues has occurred since. In the area of labor, formal restrictions on intra-EC mobility have been eliminated. Capital mobility has also been encouraged; however the Rome Treaty allows controls if capital movements are disruptive. These safeguards have inhibited the free flow of capital in many of the EC countries, notably Italy, France, and Belgium. Substantial progress has been made in coordinating economic, social, and even foreign policy, and in standardizing some areas of law. Most of the EC countries, the most notable exception being Britain, also participate in the European Monetary System (EMS), a step toward monetary union.

The European Commission continues to press for reduction of remaining barriers, mainly of a nontariff nature, to intra-EC movement of goods, services, and factor inputs. Examples of recent action include the push to end transport and airline cartels within the EC, the development of common product standards for the EC, and plans to abolish all remaining exchange controls in 1989.

The most important recent development in the evolution of the EC is the Single European Act, initially outlined in 1985. The implementation of this agreement will require the enactment of some 300 new regulations designed to dismantle virtually all remaining intra-EC trade barriers by 1992. Its goal is to develop a European market free of nontariff barriers to trade and other restraints on internal competition. Key steps planned to realize this objective are:

☐   Lifting border controls limiting intra-EC movement of goods and labor

☐   Developing common EC industrial standards

☐   Harmonizing rates of value-added tax in the EC

☐   Opening local and central government contracts to competition from within the EC

☐   Allowing banks, insurance companies, and other financial services firms to trade freely within the EC.

Although it is likely that not all these measures will be achieved on schedule, there is little doubt that the EC will be a significantly more competitive market by 1992. Most major European firms are planning for a future home market of 320 million consumers. Already there is evidence of pan-European mergers and takeovers as some European firms seek to achieve the critical mass necessary for success in a more competitive environment.

For United States firms, these EC developments present both opportunities and threats. For efficient United States MNCs such as I.B.M. and Ford, which have extensive manufacturing networks within the EC and long experience in integrating their European operations, a freer market could be beneficial. For firms that export mainly to Europe there are obvious dangers. For example, the EC could adopt industrial standards that discriminate against United States-based suppliers. However, the threat of retaliation by the United States and other countries and the European commitment to world economic growth should constrain EC protectionism.

The EC was established in the expectation of heightened economic advantages and a desire to offset the competitive threat posed by the United States during the 1950s. Political benefits were also anticipated. It was believed that a united Europe would act as a counterbalance to the two superpowers.

The EC has indeed achieved significant success in stimulating European efficiency and trade in *manufactured* goods. The Common Agricultural Policy, which guarantees minimum prices for many *agricultural* products, has also stimulated output. However, the protectionist nature of the arrangement has had serious economic costs. Efficient farmers outside Europe have been prevented from selling food within the EC. This policy has resulted in a wasteful excess supply of certain food products in Europe and in higher prices.

The EC faces many problems, including an inefficient and expensive agricultural policy, financing problems due to insufficient revenue and high farm spending, and divisions among member countries. It is thus unlikely that the vision of a "United States" of Europe (which implies political integration), or even the more limited goal of an economic union, with a single currency and economic policy, is achievable in the foreseeable future.

The EC is now an area of major economic significance both as a market and as a producer and trader. Despite the problems noted, testimony to the success of the EC is provided by a doubling in the original membership to twelve. In 1973, Denmark, Ireland, and the United Kingdom joined. They were followed by Greece in 1981 and Spain and Portugal in 1986. The population of the Community exceeds 320 million, GDP is greater than that of the United States, and the EC accounts for some 20 percent of world trade.[6]

Evolution toward a monetary union is a distinct possibility. In 1988 two former prominent European leaders, Helmut Schmidt and Valéry Giscard d'Estaing, pushed for further development of the EMS, calling for establishment of a European Central Bank and the free use of a common currency (the European Currency Unit) in all EC countries. Their plan is unlikely to be implemented soon, given objections from the German Bundesbank and lukewarm support in some countries, notably Britain (not even a member of the current EMS).

European Free Trade Association (EFTA)

In 1960, Austria, Denmark, Norway, Portugal, Sweden, Switzerland, and the United Kingdom joined together to form a free-trade area for manufactured products. The agreement has been successful and current members include Finland and Iceland. However, EFTA's importance has been reduced by the withdrawal of the United Kingdom, Denmark, and Portugal. EFTA does not provide for agricultural free trade, and the scope and goals of the agreement are much more limited than that of the EC.

Despite these limitations, EFTA has filled a useful role. Most EFTA members were loath to join the EC, for political or economic reasons, and the organization has limited the economic damage of non EC membership and provided for a unified front in negotiations with the EC. In this regard, it is significant that the two blocs negotiated a 1977 agreement for free trade in industrial goods between EFTA and the EC. This agreement limits the economic impact of non-EC membership and has resulted in the formation of the world's largest free-trade area.

Because over 50 percent of EFTA's exports go to the EC, there is concern about the EC's blueprint for 1992. As outsiders, EFTA members could be hurt. Clearly, the EC's plans are designed mainly to benefit EC firms, and EFTA does not have the bargaining power of the United States. EFTA is thus lobbying hard within the EC. There have been suggestions that they might seek to align with the new EC rules to reduce nontariff barriers in order to obtain favorable treatment.

The Council for Mutual Economic Cooperation

The Council for Mutual Economic Cooperation (COMECON) was formed in 1949 and its membership consists of Bulgaria, Cuba, Czechoslovakia, East Germany, Hungary, Mongolia, Poland, Romania, the USSR, and Vietnam. All these countries are communist allies of the USSR, and the basic aim is to provide a framework for the joint planning and coordination of production and trade. The aim is not to promote free, but rather *balanced,* trade on a bilateral basis. This is perfectly possible in economic relations between centrally planned economies, but is economically highly inefficient. It is perhaps for this reason that some COMECON countries appear to be more interested in earning foreign exchange in the West than in trading with their COMECON partners.

Other Arrangements

Outside Europe, the economic integration movement has enjoyed less success. Although many schemes for economic cooperation have been implemented, the majority have had limited economic impact. Basic problems that have proved intractable are a lack of political consensus and trust between participants and a fear of unequal division of benefits. In the developing world, there is the additional problem that many countries export similar basic commodities.

Latin America

The principle attempt by the countries of Latin America to cooperate on a multilateral basis is the *Latin American Free Trade Association* (LAFTA), established in 1960 by Argentina, Bolivia, Brazil, Chile, Colombia, Ecuador, Mexico, Paraguay, Peru, and Uruguay. The agreement called for free trade to be phased in among participants. The liberalization process enjoyed some initial success. However, progress was soon halted by resistance from domestic firms threatened by import competition.

In 1980, the *Latin American Integration Association* (LAIA) was formed to replace LAFTA. It consists of the ten original LAFTA members plus Venezuela. Emphasis is still on promoting free trade, but multilateral tariff reductions on a wide scale are unlikely to occur. The most likely scenario is that of bilateral trade agreements, following the pattern of the 1986 trade treaty between Argentina and Brazil.

The *Andean Group,* consisting of Bolivia, Colombia, Chile, Ecuador, Peru, and subsequently Venezuela, was formed in 1960 as a subgroup of LAFTA. Its basic aim was to promote cooperation between smaller LAFTA countries so that they could compete more equally with larger members. The arrangement has succeeded in promoting some import substituting industrialization, where member countries are given regional production monopolies in certain industrial sectors, such as petrochemicals and vehicles, in order to facilitate efficiency and economies of scale. Agreement on common rules for incoming foreign direct investment has also increased the bloc's negotiating power with foreign MNCs. As with LAFTA, the pact was most successful in its early stages. It has been weakened by the withdrawal of Chile.

Other Regions

In much of Africa, the Middle East, and Asia there has been limited economic integration and the development that has occurred has often had limited impact. This is not to say that economic cooperation is absent. Formal and informal economic arrangements have been entered into, and some have had a significant effect.

Some agreements have been based on former colonial relationships. Thus francophone West African states are associated in the *West African Economic Community,* and a number of ex-British colonies in the Caribbean have formed a common market, *CARICOM.* There is a good deal of *informal* economic integration in the Arab world, where there is a high degree of factor mobility between countries. Thus flows of labor move from large, populous countries such as Egypt to the rich Middle East oil producers, and capital flows in the reverse direction.

In Asia, the *Association of South East Asian Nations* (ASEAN)—set up in 1967 by Indonesia, the Philippines, Thailand, Malaysia, and Singapore and subsequently joined by Brunei—has real potential as a vehicle for economic integration. During the 1970s, political and social cooperation were emphasized. In the 1980s, increased industrialization in the region and a harsher trading environment have increased the attractions of intra-Asian trade. Thus there are prospects for real movement toward trade liberalization and industrial cooperation within ASEAN.

THE INTERNATIONAL FINANCIAL ENVIRONMENT ⸻

International monetary and financial arrangements are important to the international operating environment; they have a major impact on a firm's overseas operations. The workings of foreign exchange markets are of immediate concern to most companies. Understanding how global financial markets and international financial institutions operate is therefore necessary.

The chaotic nature of international monetary relations during the 1930s was something that the United States and Britain were determined to avoid in their plans for a new, postwar international economic order. The intention was to develop a system, based upon multilateral agreement, which would encourage international trade, investment, and economic cooperation.

Key elements in an international financial system were agreed to at a conference held in 1944 at Bretton Woods in New Hampshire. Essential features of the postwar "Bretton Woods" system were the formation of the International Monetary Fund and the World Bank, and agreement on a fixed exchange-rate regime, and rules for controlling exchange-rate movements.

The International Monetary Fund

The International Monetary Fund (IMF) was established to fill a variety of roles. Its principle task is to supervise the working of the international monetary system. In addition, the Fund controls a pool of foreign currency and gold and is responsible for issuing a new reserve asset, Special Drawing Rights (SDRs), first allocated in 1970. Control over these funds, which in terms of usable resources were estimated at around $35 billion in 1988, enables the IMF to operate as a short-term lender to countries with severe balance-of-payments problems. The IMF also provides an important forum for discussion and negotiation on international financial issues.

The Fund has 151 members and includes nearly all the industrial market economies, most of the LDCs, and some countries in Eastern Europe (but not the Soviet Union). It has a permanent staff of nearly 2,000, much of which is based in Fund headquarters in Washington, D.C.

Following the collapse of the Bretton Woods system in 1971, the IMF's supervisory role has been less important. (There has been no agreement on a new exchange-rate system and associated rules to replace the defunct fixed-rate regime.) However, the IMF still fills an important role as a lender, provides a vital forum for discussing international financial issues, and has played a leading role in dealing with the international debt crisis in the 1980s.

A good deal of controversy surrounds the IMF's lending activities. Significant loans are usually contingent upon the recipient country imposing a deflationary package of economic measures. Typical IMF demands are a cut in government expenditure, the establishment of realistic exchange rates, reductions in the growth of the money supply and government subsidies, and measures to promote exports. Its double aim is to improve the balance of payments and then position an economy for future growth. The scope and stringent nature of the IMF's loan conditions are resented by many debtor nations, who argue that the IMF's policies are a prescription for high unemployment and social unrest. Since many of the countries seeking loans are poor LDCs, debate has often been heated. The IMF is regarded by some of these countries merely as a tool of the rich Western nations.

Recently, the IMF has taken a number of actions to address some of the harsh criticism leveled against itself. In 1987, an $8.4 billion special fund was created to help the poorest LDCs. Loans from this fund are on concessionary terms for periods up to 10 years. This is a significant change, for the Fund has traditionally focused almost exclusively on short-term loans with maturities of no longer than 18 months. The Fund has also been very active in promoting mediation between the Western commercial banks and the debtor countries. There is also discussion of easing some loan terms and developing programs to cushion LDC borrowers against deteriorating global economic conditions.

The World Bank

The World Bank, which has 151 members and is commonly regarded as a sister institution to the IMF, has traditionally operated as a development bank channeling finance and technical assistance to developing countries through its major institution, the International Bank for Reconstruction and Development. The primary focus is on project financing, mostly for investments designed to improve the economic and social infrastructure. Funds are not available to help countries finance balance-of-payments and debt problems. Typical, recent World Bank projects include loans to India to build fertilizer factories, to Nigeria for the improvement of the national rail system and port authority, and to Mauritius for agricultural diversification projects.

Some of the Bank's funding is provided by rich donor countries, but most of its monies are raised on the international capital markets. The Bank is the largest borrower in these markets, raising some $10 billion to $12 billion annually in as many as 18 currencies. This means that the majority of the Bank's loans are made at near commercial interest rates. Some highly concessional assistance is provided by the World Bank's International Development Association (IDA) to the poorest LDCs. Another subsidiary, the International Finance Corporation, channels some funds to private-sector investment projects.

Although the Bank is less controversial than the IMF, there is pressure for it to move away from just project financing. The United States, in particular, wants the Bank to use more of its loans to push recipients to more market-oriented economic policies. In this role the Bank would prod debtor countries to overhaul trade, investment, and regulations that often stand in the way of the economic changes recommended by the IMF.

During the 1980s, the Bank has responded to these pressures and placed greater emphasis behind promoting the deregulation of economic activity, fiscal prudence, competitive exchange rates, and privatization in debtor countries. Greater cooperation with the IMF is also being advocated. A start has already been made in this direction with the creation, in 1986, of a $3 billion Structural Adjustment Facility to help poor, debtor countries to revamp their economies. This program will require the Bank and the IMF to work together to develop broad three-year "policy frameworks" for the restructuring of debtor economies.

One implication of making World Bank loans conditional on economic restructuring is that the Bank's generally positive image in most LDCs may become tarnished. If this occurs, the Bank's influence in the developing world may be diminished. Supporters of a more interventionist role argue that lowered esteem is unlikely since many LDCs wish to move toward more market-based economic policies and should be receptive to the Bank's advice.

In 1988, the Bank recommended that its capital be increased by some $75 billion to enable it to increase lending from $14.1 billion in 1987 to around $20 billion annually. Most of the capital will come from the rich industrial countries.

Exchange Rate Systems

Bretton Woods

Under the Bretton Woods system, foreign exchange rates were fixed, with there only being the possibility of ±1 percent fluctuation around the par values established. In practice, countries pegged the value of their currency to the dollar, which was in turn pegged to gold. The dollar was the key currency in this gold exchange standard system, where the United States government was committed to exchange dollars for gold at a fixed rate of $35 per ounce of gold.

In cases of "fundamental disequilibrium"—a situation of severe and intractable balance-of-payments problems—a country could, subject to IMF approval, adjust the par value set for its currency. Prior to this action—almost always a devaluation—IMF members were obligated to attempt to defend the par value and concurrently adjust internal monetary and fiscal policies in order to return to external balance. During the period of internal readjustment, countries were able to finance balance-of-payments deficits by borrowing from the IMF.

In the late 1950s and early 1960s, the Bretton Woods system enjoyed considerable success in promoting international economic efficiency. Transaction costs fell, foreign exchange risk was low, and trade and the international capital markets expanded rapidly. To sustain this structure, the system had to cope with the fundamental problems of international liquidity, confidence, and adjustment. For sufficient international liquidity to be generated, countries had to depend increasingly upon holding dollars as part of their international reserves. Consequently, it became imperative that confidence was maintained in the international value of the dollar. If confidence eroded, then the United States commitment to exchange dollars for gold at the $35-per-ounce gold price would be severely tested.

So long as balance-of-payments imbalances were not particularly large and countries were willing to finance a United States deficit by holding rather than converting dollars, the inefficiencies of the international adjustment system were not particularly serious. In the late 1960s, however, a series of crises highlighted the flaws in the system and confidence in the United States commitment to defend gold began to erode. In August 1971, following a serious run against the dollar, events reached a head. The United States suspended its gold conversion commitment.

This precipitated negotiations on building a new monetary system and efforts were made in 1972 to implement an adjustable peg system. But this approach proved to be unworkable, and in 1973 most major trading countries moved to a system of generalized floating.

Current Arrangements

Although often described as a floating-rate system, current international monetary arrangements do not really deserve this name. Since the demise of the Bretton Woods framework, no agreement has been reached on rules that would impose order on the international monetary situation. The revised IMF articles, finally approved in 1976, allow countries to float or to peg, do not regulate national policy on international reserves, and do not impose rules for exchange-rate adjustment.

Although many of the major trading nations, including the United States, Japan, and the United Kingdom, allow their currencies to float, central bank intervention on an individual or coordinated basis does occur from time to time. More importantly, because they are pegged to another currency, many currencies do not really float. The most common currency to which others are pegged is the United States dollar, but some currencies are pegged to the currency of a former colonial power or to a basket of currencies. Most of the EC members have pegged their currencies to each other, forming the European Monetary System bloc of currencies that float as a group against other currencies.

Although the United States dollar is not as important today as it was under Bretton Woods, it still plays a central role in international monetary affairs and continues to be a crucial reserve currency. Because of this role, the importance of international trade and investment into and out of the United States, the dominance of the dollar in the Euro-currency markets, and the fact that a number of important commodities, such as oil, are priced in dollars, the value of the dollar is of major concern in the international market place.

There are many points of view regarding the effectiveness of current international monetary arrangements. Some commentators believe that more flexible exchange rates have facilitated international adjustment in an era of high inflation and economic shocks that would have overwhelmed more rigid systems. Others disagree, pointing to the very large current account deficits of the United States in recent years, massive Japanese and West German trading surpluses, and the chronic debt problems of some LDCs and NICs. These problems are cited as evidence that international adjustment is not functioning effectively.

There is little doubt that foreign exchange risk has become a much more serious problem over the last fifteen years. Exchange rates have proved to be highly volatile, with significant variation from purchasing power parity rates being common in at least the short term. Transaction costs have also increased as buy-and-sell spreads in the foreign exchange markets have widened.

The volume of foreign exchange traded in the world's leading markets has increased sharply and central bank estimates indicate that global turnover was over $200 billion per day in 1986.[7] The London market accounted for around $90 billion of this amount, up from some $25 billion daily in 1979. London was followed by New York and Tokyo in 1986, with daily volumes of $50 billion and $48 billion, respectively. (See Figure 4-1.) An indication of the major currencies traded in New York is shown in Figure 4-2.

FIGURE 4-1   Foreign Exchange Volume

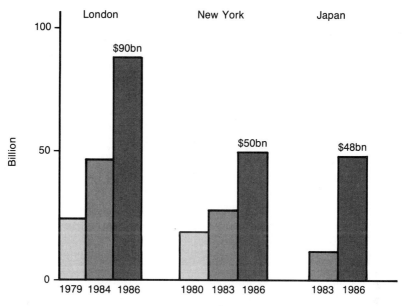

(Source: *The Economist; The Wall Street Journal.*)

FIGURE 4-2   The Composition of Foreign Currencies Traded in New York*

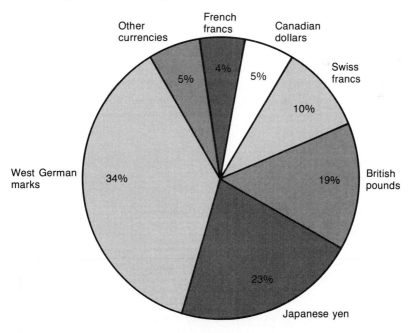

*Average daily figures, March 1986.

(Source: *Federal Reserve Bank of New York.*)

Some of the more important reasons for the rapid growth and volatility of the foreign exchange markets include the large sums that have been accumulated and invested abroad by countries, unable or unwilling to invest domestically, such as oil exporters and more recently Japan; interest rate volatility that has stimulated investors to move funds globally; reductions to barriers to the international movement of capital; and increased corporate hedging activity. In addition, facilitating factors such as widespread computerization and the development of new currency instruments, especially options and futures, have been important.

The impact of the greater uncertainty and cost of doing business in foreign currencies is hard to measure. However, the effect has probably been greatest at the margin, since international flows of trade and investment have increased very sharply since the early 1970s. It should also be noted that a wide range of options is available to firms wishing to reduce the impact of currency swings on their operations.

Although more structured systems for managing international monetary relationships may be desirable, there is little prospect for real movement in this direction. There is no consensus on appropriate reforms; and the consequences of the lack of a real "system" have not been serious enough to concentrate attention on the need for change.

International Capital Markets

International firms are able to participate in overseas financial markets, as a lender, borrower, and speculator, in a variety of ways. Traditionally, the major options have included doing business with local banks or multinational bank subsidiaries in other countries, issuing bonds in foreign markets, and, less commonly, issuing equity overseas. Over the last 30 years, the emergence of the Euromarkets has created important new borrowing and lending opportunities overseas. At the same time, there has been dramatic growth in offshore banking, and international capital mobility has been encouraged by freer international markets. During the late 1970s and 1980s, many governments eased currency controls and opened up their domestic financial markets. The United States dismantled capital controls in 1974 and has ended withholding taxes on interest earned by foreign investors. Britain ended exchange controls in 1979, Germany and Switzerland eased restrictions on incoming foreign direct investment in 1978 and 1980 respectively, and Japan has started to allow foreign financial companies to operate within its borders and permits foreign companies to borrow yen.

The development of the Euromarkets and deregulation have greatly facilitated the international flow of capital, and international financial markets are now much more integrated than formerly. Firms and financiers can now more readily raise funds in most currencies. However, increased financial interdependence, the existence of huge sums of highly mobile capital, high-speed communication systems, and complex new financial instruments create problems as well as opportunities. In particular, capital mobility and reduced regulation make the system more vulnerable to unexpected shocks, especially in situations that prompt investors to dump dollar assets.

The Euromarkets

The Euromarkets may be defined as "a series of markets—ranging from bonds to swaps and deposits—where financial instruments are bought and sold with Eurocurrencies."[8] A Eurocurrency is a currency deposit made in a bank located outside the political jurisdiction of the currency's country of origin. A dollar deposited in a bank in London, Frankfurt, Singapore, or Tokyo would create Eurodollars, the most widely used Eurocurrency. The size of the market is very large, with the Eurocurrency deposit market estimated at some $3.94 trillion in June of 1987.[9] London is the leading center for the Euromarkets.

The essential reason for the existence of the Euromarkets is that, in contrast to domestic financial markets, they are largely free from government regulation. Thus Eurodollar deposits in London was not subject to minimum reserve or other controls that the British government may impose for local currency deposits, and they are not affected by United States banking regulations. Consequently, dollars placed in Eurocurrency deposits can be traded relatively freely, and for this reason, and the economies of scale resulting from the large size of average transactions, the banks operating in the market are able to offer attractive interest rates to both depositors and borrowers. In the case of international firms, Euromarkets are attractive both as a location for short- and medium-term foreign currency deposits and as a source of funds. However, borrowing opportunities are largely limited to big, blue-chip firms that are well known in the markets.

Eurobonds

Eurobonds are bonds sold outside the country of the currency in which the bond is denominated. They are issued outside the restrictions that apply to domestic bond issues, are originally issued in several finance centers, and syndicated and traded primarily in London. Eurodollar bonds are dominant, with a 71 percent share of the market in 1985. Other significant currencies of bond denomination include German marks, Japanese yen, British pounds, French francs, and Dutch guilders.

The new issue market has increased sharply in recent years to $188 billion in 1986, but the market declined in 1987.[10] International bank syndicates play a major role in the marketing of Eurobonds. Institutional investors are now the biggest buyers of Eurobonds, but since they are bearer bonds wealthy individual investors are also attracted to Eurobonds, often for tax avoidance reasons. For many governments and multinational firms, Eurobonds have become a favored means of raising capital. However, only big, well-known firms with excellent credit ratings can borrow in this market.

Foreign Bonds

The other major opportunity for long-term financing in offshore financial markets is provided by foreign bond issues. Unlike Eurobonds, foreign bonds are issued by foreign borrowers in a single national capital market and are denominated in the currency of the lending country. (A bond denominated in Swiss francs and issued in Switzerland by an American firm is an example of such an issue.) Many governments strictly control the ability of foreigners to raise bond financing in their domestic capital market. Partly because of tough regulations and disclosure requirements, the foreign bond market has not expanded as rapidly as has the Eurobond market. Countries in which significant amounts of foreign bond financing have been raised include Switzerland, the United States, Britain, Japan, the Netherlands, and West Germany. In 1986, foreign bond issues increased to $38.4 billion.

International Aid Flows

Significant international capital transfers are accounted for by the flow of aid from the rich to the poor countries. Aid has been defined as consisting of "the donation of financial or real resources by one country to another without the expectation of an equivalent payment in return."[11] Grants and subsidized loans account for most aid flows.

OECD estimates show that in 1985 official flows of aid to the developing countries amounted to some $41 billion, a 17 percent increase over aid transfers of $35 billion in 1981. Nearly $30 billion of this aid was provided by the OECD countries who increased their assistance by 23 percent to $37 billion in 1986. COMECON and OPEC provided some $3 billion each in 1985. Despite a United Nations target of 0.7 percent of GNP, the 1985 OECD average of aid as a proportion of GNP was only 0.35 percent. COMECON's performance was even worse, at 0.21 percent. However, as is evident from Figure 4-3, some countries are much more generous than others.

In 1986, aid accounted for 66 percent of total financial flows to LDCs as compared to only 35 percent in 1980.[12] The greater relative importance of aid flows is mainly the result of a collapse in net flows of private investment and bank loans to LDCs. Private investment and loans fell from $74 billion in 1981 to just $29 billion in 1985. The result is that the total net flow of funds to the LDCs was only some $80 billion in 1985 as compared to $139 billion in 1981.[13] This decline is a serious problem for LDCs and is symptomatic of a lack of interest by Western firms in business opportunities in these countries.

Capital flight is also a major problem in many LDCs. In 1976–1985, nearly $200 billion of capital was moved out of 18 LDCs, equal to around 50 percent of total borrowings of those countries in this period.[14] Many of these funds were transferred legally by firms and wealthy individuals; however, illegal transfers are also common. Illegal transfer methods include smuggling cash; sending funds through banks, lawyers, and holding companies in tax havens; manipulating import and export invoices and transfer prices; and currency swaps. Most such illegal flows occur in reaction to economic and political turmoil and typically end up in the United States or Switzerland.

Multilateral aid to the developing world is channeled through a number of development finance institutions. The World Bank, described earlier, plays a dominant role in providing long-term finance for development projects. A number of other institutions, such as the regional development banks, the United Nation's International Fund for Agricultural Development, and the Islamic Fund for Economic Development, are also significant channels for development aid.

Current Problems

We have seen that the effectiveness of the international financial markets in enabling borrowers to find funds and lenders to seek the best return for their assets has improved significantly in recent years. At the same time, the flow of official development funds from the rich to the poor countries has also increased. Despite these developments, there are still substantial barriers to capital mobility. Three major impediments may be identified.

Government-imposed *exchange controls* impede the inflow and outflow of capital. Despite the reduction in the incidence and level of such barriers noted earlier, exchange controls are still widespread. Even in the OECD group, countries

FIGURE 4-3   Official Development Assistance*

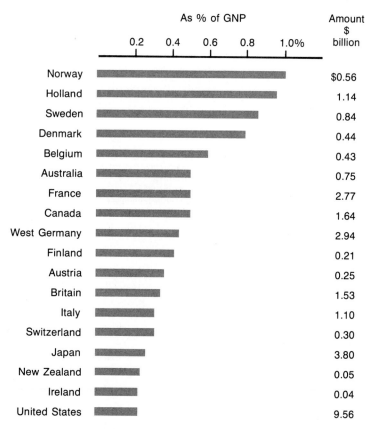

Flows of Development Assistance from the OECD countries in 1985

Country	As % of GNP	Amount $ billion
Norway		$0.56
Holland		1.14
Sweden		0.84
Denmark		0.44
Belgium		0.43
Australia		0.75
France		2.77
Canada		1.64
West Germany		2.94
Finland		0.21
Austria		0.25
Britain		1.53
Italy		1.10
Switzerland		0.30
Japan		3.80
New Zealand		0.05
Ireland		0.04
United States		9.56

*Grants and subsidized loans.

(Source: *The Economist,* July 5, 1986.)

such as the United States, Britain, Germany, and Switzerland (where controls have been substantially abolished) are still the exception rather than the rule. In centrally planned economies and in many NICs and LDCs, draconian foreign-exchange regulations are often imposed. Even where stringent control exists, ways to circumvent the rules—ranging from currency smuggling to transfer price manipulation— often generate substantial funds transfers.

In an era of flexible exchange rates, *foreign exchange risk* is an important barrier to capital mobility. The volatility of rates and the difficulty of accurate forecasting are key problems. Exchange exposure has to be compensated by higher expected rates of return.

Sovereign risk, the possibility that foreign governments will default on loans from foreign banks and agencies or impose restrictions on private debt repayment, is also a serious problem. Although outright debt repudiation is rare, five countries (Vietnam, Guyana, Liberia, Sudan, and Peru) have fallen so far behind in IMF debt repayments that they have been declared ineligible for new loans. The plight of other debtor nations, such as Brazil, Mexico, Argentina, and Nigeria (with end-1987 debts of $114 billion (bn.), $105 bn., $49 bn., and $27 bn. respectively) are also a source of great concern. (See Table 4-1.) Commercial banks are loath to lend money to risky or highly indebted nations, which are also unable to borrow large amounts in the Euromarkets. Many of the LDCs and NICs are, therefore, at very best, only marginal participants in the international capital markets.

TABLE 4-1
Highly Indebted Countries

	Total Outstanding Debt, $ bn. end 1987	Interest Payments as % of Exports
Argentina	49.4	33.1%
Brazil	114.5	30.2
Chile	20.5	29.5
Colombia	15.1	16.6
Mexico	105.0	32.7
Morocco	17.3	25.4
Nigeria	27.0	11.6
Peru	16.7	29.0
Philippines	29.0	19.0
Venezuela	33.9	22.5
Yugoslavia	21.8	7.7

Source: *The Economist,* February 6, 1988, p. 80.

THE POLITICAL ENVIRONMENT

International Political Factors

Agmon[15] claims that the most important political organization is the sovereign state because of its ability to issue a currency, to tax, and to regulate. In the international arena, very few organizations enjoy such powers. Consequently, the international political context is much less important than the national political environment. Despite this, there are some important political dimensions that supercede national boundaries and have important implications for international marketing.

The most obvious dimension is the political relationship between nations, particularly in regard to trade with central command economies. In such countries, international flows of trade and investment are directly controlled by the government's central planning apparatus, and political considerations play an important and direct role in business relationships. For example, purchases of Cuban sugar by the Soviet Union result more from political than economic factors.

In most industrial nations in the West, the ability of governments to influence international commercial relationships is more limited, and requires the passage of explicit laws. In the absence of such laws, government influence is relatively limited. From time to time, however, Western governments do pass laws that control international flows of trade and investment for political reasons. Nonetheless, the political perceptions of executives and the public do impact international business relationships. Consumer views of the political climate in foreign countries may, for example, shape perceptions of products made in that market. Feelings of political harmony and congruity of interest encourage bilateral business.

There are also important political dimensions to regional economic integration. This is particularly the case for more ambitious arrangements such as a common market. In the EC, member countries negotiate as a bloc on trade issues and try to coordinate their foreign policy on issues of common interest. Thus, in the case of South African sanctions, the EC's foreign ministers agreed to a common package of measures following intensive consultations and negotiation. Another example of the political implications of economic union is provided by the Andean Pact. A key element in the pact is the imposition of common conditions for incoming foreign direct investment. The pact aims to ensure that the member nations present a common front to the MNCs, preventing any playing off of one country against another in order to achieve optimum entry terms.

International organizations also play an important role in the development and implementation of policies that express the political will of member countries. The policies of the IMF and World Bank, discussed earlier, are strongly influenced by the views of the major industrial countries, who play a major role in financing these organizations. In the case of countries in the developing world, the United Nations Conference on Trade and Development (UNCTAD) reflects their political aspirations for a new international economic order. Understanding their demands is essential to anyone interested in doing business in the developing world.

The United Nations Conference on Trade and Development

Formed in 1964 to promote the development of the LDCs, UNCTAD has been called the third world's pressure group, and its emergence was due to the dis-satisfaction felt by many LDCs with the current economic framework, which is seen to favor the rich at the expense of the poor.

At periodic UNCTAD conferences, the developing countries have presented a variety of demands designed to improve their economic performance and bring about a significant transfer of resources from the rich. Their program calls for increased aid and low-interest loans to the LDCs; relief from debt repayment burdens; commodity agreements guaranteeing the LDCs markets and higher, more stable prices for their commodity exports; and an end to discriminatory import controls that limit LDC exports of agricultural, processed, and manufactured goods such as textiles. In support of these demands, LDCs point to a continuing deterioration in their terms of trade (the ratio of their export to import prices), which they blame for their balance of payments problems; the need to borrow large amounts from overseas; and a resulting crippling repayment burden in many countries.

To date, little progress has been made on many of the concerns forwarded by the LDCs at the UNCTAD meetings. Many of the demands are considered unrealistic by the industrial countries. There has also been an unwillingess to provide increased assistance to countries that have developed economic systems—often characterized by a high level of state control—considered inherently inefficient by many economists.

To an increasing degree, there is a tendency for rich donor countries and some international organizations to make increased loans and aid conditional upon economic reforms in recipient countries. In the case of many LDCs in Africa, for example, typical conditions are a call for a higher priority on agricultural development, lessened dependence on imports, reduced state regulation, and currency devaluation. Although resented by some LDCs, there is evidence that many African countries accept a need for change and have been adopting many of these recommendations.

UNCTAD conferences are held every four years. The seventh meeting was held in Geneva in 1987. At this meeting, progress was made on a plan to establish a Common Fund for Commodities (CFC). The objective of the CFC is to finance commodity buffer stock operations that would stabilize the prices of primary agricultural commodities. The plan is not supported by the United States and, despite the progress made in Geneva, its future is uncertain.

The LDCs hope that pressures they exert will succeed in the same way as the initiative that led to the successful creation of the Generalized System of Preference (GSP). The GSP requires that the developed countries grant preferential tariff treatment to imports of manufactured and semimanufactured products produced in LDCs. The first GSP scheme was adopted by the EC in 1971. The United States implemented the scheme in 1976, and duty-free entry terms are now granted to many products from over 130 LDCs.

THE INTERNATIONAL LEGAL ENVIRONMENT

The traditional thrust of international law has been to establish a legal framework to regulate interaction between nation states. Classic issues dealt with include the law of the sea, nationality, and boundary line disputes. With regard to economic matters, the development of international law has been heavily influenced by laissez-faire philosophies, the legal regulation of economic activities being traditionally viewed as largely the responsibility of national law.

As a result of these factors, classic international law has had limited impact on international business. There are bodies of law other than public international law that have a significant impact on the international operating environment. These include the legal implications of bilateral and multilateral treaties and conventions, regional law, and the extraterritorial impact claimed for some national laws by some countries.

Bilateral Treaties

Bilateral treaties regulating commercial relations between two countries are commonplace. For example, the United States has signed over 130 treaties of Friendship, Commerce, and Navigation (FCN) since the eighteenth century. Typically, FCNs deal with the rights of citizens from the two countries to trade and invest in the foreign country, and they generally guarantee nondiscriminatory treatment on a reciprocal basis. Bilateral tax treaties are also commonly entered into by the United States and other industrial nations. Usually these treaties attack problems of double or overlapping taxation.

Treaties also deal with many other commercial issues. The United States and Britain have, for example, signed a treaty aimed at increasing cooperation to regulate the evolving global markets in commodities and securities. Particular goals include controlling market participants and uncovering insider trading and other securities fraud. Both countries plan to negotiate additional treaties with other interested countries.

Multilateral Treaties

Multilateral treaties also have had an important impact. The 1947 GATT agreement, for example, established rules of conduct in international trade and provided for a resolution process for trade disputes. Although the GATT has had a major impact, it also suffers from weaknesses common to many international treaties. A number of safeguards in the agreement allow many countries to back out of their GATT obligations when convenient. In addition, widely used methods of protectionism, such as voluntary import restrictions, are not covered in the treaty. Also, in the absence of a strong central policing authority, GATT members breaking the convention are not exposed to significant sanctions other than retaliation from other GATT members.

An area where international marketers have a strong interest in legal protection concerns intellectual property rights such as patents and trademarks. Multilateral treaties regulating this area include the International Convention for the Protection of Industrial Property, popularly known as the Paris Union, and the Madrid Arrangement for International Registration of Trademarks. (These treaties are discussed in more detail in Chapter 13.)

Regional cooperation and economic integration are generally based upon a multilateral treaty, such as the Treaty of Rome in the case of the EC. In the EC, not only is the Treaty of Rome very important, but there has also been established a process for developing a common body of regional law relating to certain commercial and social issues. In the case of international business, movement toward the development of common product standards and antitrust laws are particularly interesting. Other areas where there has been discussion on common

EC regulations concern the obligations of MNCs to consult labor unions, product liability standards, and worker representation on company boards.

Dispute Resolution

The resolution of legal disagreements involving parties from different countries poses a number of special questions. The most obvious are "Which body of law is to be applied?" and "In which courts is litigation to be pursued?" Commonly the international firm will seek to specify that their domestic law and domestic courts will be used to resolve disputes. Foreign parties will tend to press for the jurisdiction of their local law and courts.

Rather than leave these issues to chance, many firms insert a clause into a contract to cover jurisdictional matters. Alternatively, the parties to the contract may agree to settle any disputes by means of a specified arbitration process rather than resorting to litigation. This is often desirable, since arbitration is usually less expensive, takes less time, and is less harmful to future relations between the parties than is litigation. Arbitration provides an opportunity for mediation by experts, occurs in secrecy and is, generally, nonconfrontational. However, in cases where the validity of the contract itself is in dispute, recourse to litigation is necessary.

In cases of international arbitration, the International Chamber of Commerce based in Paris is quite extensively used, though it has no compulsory jurisdiction and makes no use of case law. It makes most of its decisions on the basis of equity, and its effectiveness derives largely from the expertise of the arbitrators used. Other options include the London Court of Arbitration, and the American Arbitration Association.

In cases of investment disputes, a World Bank sponsored body provides a little used facility, the International Center for Settlement of Investment Disputes, for the arbitration of disputes between MNCs and host governments. The International Court of Justice also provides a channel for resolving intergovernmental investment disputes. Nations may also agree to form ad hoc tribunals to resolve commercial disputes. The United States and Iran, for example, agreed to participate in a special tribunal set up in 1981 at the Hague to resolve United States–Iranian business claims that accrued in the period following the Iranian revolution.

Extraterritoriality

Some nations have claimed an extraterritorial jurisdiction for elements of their domestic law. In the case of the United States, extraterritorial impact has been claimed for a number of laws, including the export administration and antitrust regulations. Such claims have sometimes resulted in situations in which United States subsidiaries overseas have been ordered, following United States government pressure, by the parent firm not to contravene United States law by undertaking an overseas business transaction that is legal according to the local law.

A good example concerns the 1982 dispute over Soviet gas pipeline exports. In this case the United States government attempted to embargo the export of gas turbines that European firms intended to sell to the Russians for their oil and gas distribution pipelines. It was argued by the United States that these turbines contained United States-made parts and, in several instances, were made by licensees of United States firms, and that the products were therefore subject to United States export control laws. Foreign subsidiaries of United States companies were also instructed not to participate in this project. The validity of this extraterritorial application of United States law was not accepted by the European governments concerned, and most of the European companies involved ignored the United States' attempt to impose its export controls overseas.

It is apparent that the notion of extraterritorial jurisdiction of domestic laws is a very sensitive issue. It raises the possibility of intergovernmental disputes and can sometimes place firms, particularly the overseas subsidiaries of American MNCs, in a difficult bind—facing conflicting pressure from the United States and host governments.

SUMMARY

The international environment is made up of international institutions, agreements, and systems that impact on flows of trade, investment, and know-how across national boundaries and also affect market conditions in individual countries.

In the post-war period, the international trading environment has been liberalized as many barriers to trade have been removed or reduced. GATT, an international organization dedicated to reducing trade barriers, has played a major role in this process. Protectionist tendencies still remain strong in many countries, and GATT has not been able to deal effectively with barriers to agricultural trade and nontariff barriers. Measures such as voluntary export restrictions have become common. As a result of this new protectionism there are still severe limits to free trade in important industries. The Uruguay Round of GATT negotiations, begun in 1987, will address some of these problems and also focuses on the extension of GATT rules to trade in agricultural products and services, better observance of current GATT rules, and the protection of intellectual property rights.

Commodity prices are generally established in key markets that reflect the interplay of international movements in demand and supply. Because of factors making for inelasticity on the demand and supply side for many commodities, there has been interest in developing special arrangements regulating commodity trade. Commodity agreements bring together producers and consumers. Their aim is to reduce price volatility by such measures as buffer-stock arrangements and controls over supply. Producer agreements, where commodity exporters form cartels in an effort to unilaterally control price setting, are an alternative approach. However, with the exception of OPEC, the impact of both producer and commodity agreement has been limited.

The OECD, made up of the rich industrial nations, provides a useful forum for discussion, consultation, and analysis and is an important source of economic, social, and financial data, and economic reports.

International economic integration has had an important impact in Europe, as manifested in a major common-market arrangement, the European Community, and a less important free-trade agreement, the EFTA. Outside Europe, the economic integration movement has had limited success. Although many schemes have been implemented, most have not been very successful. Intractable problems have often resulted from limited trust and consensus between participants and a fear of unequal division of the benefits from union.

The IMF and the World Bank are two key international financial institutions. The IMF operates as a forum for discussion and negotiation on international financial issues, lends to governments with balance-of-payments problems, and helps regulate the international monetary system. Its role as a lender has been criticized by many LDCs. The World Bank is less controversial. It has traditionally operated as a development bank, mainly financing infrastructure-related projects in the developing countries. Recently there has been pressure, notably from the United States, for the bank to encourage borrowers to move toward more market-based economic policies.

In the postwar period up to 1972, the Bretton Woods system, based upon fixed exchange rates, enjoyed a good deal of success in promoting stability and efficiency in international monetary relations. However, failing confidence in the dollar caused the system to collapse, and by 1973 most major trading countries had moved to a system of floating exchange rates. Under current arrangements the United States dollar still has a pivotal role, but there are no generally agreed rules regarding exchange rates and international reserves, and most currencies float or are pegged. There is disagreement about the effectiveness of this more flexible arrangement, but—despite the problems arising from increased foreign exchange risk—there is little prospect at present of a more structured international monetary system being established.

In the international capital markets important trends over the last decade include the dramatic growth of the Euromarkets, movement toward deregulation of financial markets, and fewer currency controls in rich Western countries. As a result, international capital mobility and international financing have been facilitated and international financial markets are more integrated than formerly. The basic reason for the development of the Euromarkets is that they are highly efficient markets largely free from government regulation.

Significant capital transfers are accounted for by the flow of aid from the rich to the poor countries. However, the flow of aid has not increased greatly in recent years. This development, along with a collapse in the flow of private investment and bank loans to the developing world, has resulted in a decline in the net flow of funds to LDCs.

Despite the increased effectiveness of international financial markets, serious barriers to capital mobility are posed by exchange controls in many countries. Foreign exchange and sovereign risk also inhibit international capital flows.

Political relationships among nation states can have an important impact on international business relationships. This is particularly true in trade with central-command economies. Economic integration can have political implications as members coordinate policy and present a common front in negotiations.

UNCTAD promotes economic development in the developing world. Major demands forwarded at periodic UNCTAD conferences include more aid and low-interest loans to the LDCs; relief from debt repayment burdens; commodity agreements with higher, more stable prices; and easier access to markets in the developed countries. To date, little progress has been made on most of these demands, and many potential suppliers of aid in the West are pressing for basic economic reforms, designed to promote free market forces, as a condition for increased aid.

Classic international law has had limited impact on international business. Other bodies of law do have a significant effect on the international operating environment. These include the legal implications of bilateral and multilateral treaties and conventions, regional law, and the extraterritorial impact claimed for some national laws.

DISCUSSION QUESTIONS

1. Why do many LDCs feel that the current international economic order discriminates against them? What measures do they promote to rectify this situation?
2. Distinguish between the *trade creation* and *trade diversification* impact of transnational economic integration.

3. Why have flows of aid accounted for an increasing proportion of financial inflows in many LDCs during the 1980s?
4. Comment on the following statement: "Nontariff barriers to international trade are currently the most serious threat to free trade.
5. In what ways have the international marketing activities of United States firms been affected by the formation of the European Community?
6. "Floating exchange rates cause serious problems for international marketers and it is desirable to return to the exchange rate stability enjoyed under the Bretton Woods system." Do you agree?
7. The GATT agreement suffers from important weaknesses common to many multilateral treaties. What are these weaknesses and why has it been difficult for GATT to control protectionist initiatives adopted in many countries during the 1980s?

ADDITIONAL READING

Bouchet, M. H., *The Political Economy of International Debt* (Westport, CT: Quorum Books, 1987).

Choate, P., and J. Luner, "Tailored Trade: Dealing with the World as It Is" *Harvard Business Review,* January–February 1988.

Folks, W. R., and R. Aggarwal, *International Dimensions of Financial Management* (Boston: Kent, 1988).

Kline, J. M., *International Codes and Multinational Business* (Westport, CT: Quorum Books, 1987).

Litka, M., *International Dimensions of the Legal Environment of Business* (Boston: Kent, 1988).

Malloch, T. R., *Issues in International Trade and Development Policy* (New York: Praeger, 1987).

Moran, T. H., *Multinational Corporations—The Political Economy of Foreign Direct Investment* (Lexington, Mass.: Lexington Books, 1985).

Stern, R. M., *United States Trade Policies in a Changing World Economy* (Cambridge, Mass.: MIT Press, 1987).

Williamson, J., *The Open Economy and the World Economy* (New York: Basic Books, 1983).

ENDNOTES

1. See "GATT Knows Who the Trade Sinners Are," *The Wall Street Journal,* January 2, 1986, p. 1.
2. See *The Economist,* July 18, 1987, p. 70.
3. See "The Icy Trade Winds," *The Economist,* August 9, 1986, pp. 49–50.
4. See *The Wall Street Journal,* March 6, 1987.
5. Hodgson, J. S. and M. G. Herander, *International Economic Relations* (Englewood Ciffs, NJ: Prentice-Hall, 1983).
6. "Evolution of the European Community," *Finance and Development,* September 1986, pp. 30–31.
7. See "The Currency Carousel," *The Economist,* August 23, 1986, p. 64.
8. See "London's Euroboom," *The Economist,* August 23, 1986, pp. 60–61.
9. Morgan Guaranty Trust, *World Financial Markets,* November–December 1987.
10. Ibid.
11. Williamson, J. *The Open Economy and the World Economy* (New York: Basic Books, 1983).
12. See "Spaghetti Rations," *The Economist,* February 6, 1988, p. 67.
13. See "Less Money for More People," *The Economist,* July 5, 1986, p. 32.
14. See *The Wall Street Journal,* May 27, 1986, p. 2.
15. Agmon, T. *Political Economy and Risk in World Financial Markets* (Lexington, Mass.: Lexington Books, 1985).

PART ONE CASES

1. Widget Wars

Industrial widgets are made and used in the production of small machines throughout the world. The U.S. is the major market. Recent closures of smaller widget companies in the U.S., ostensibly due to foreign competition, have triggered the U.S. government to consider quotas on widget imports. How would such quotas affect each of the companies below?

Company A is the major U.S. widget manufacturer. Except for some minor exports to Canada, all sales are in the U.S.

Company B is a major U.S. sewing machine manufacturer that uses significant amounts of widgets in production.

Company C is the second largest widget company in the United States. (Sales = 75 percent of company A's.) Two-thirds of its sales are in the United States and one-third overseas. All production is in the United States.

Company D is the third largest U.S.-based widget company. (Sales = 50 percent of company A's.) Half of its sales are in the United States and half are overseas. All overseas sales are supplied

by local subsidiary production. Various overseas subsidiaries also supply half the sales made in the United States.

Company E is a major U.S. manufacturer of consumer electrical products. Widgets account for 30 percent of its manufacturing costs. Ten years ago, a shortage of widgets inspired the company to begin producing them for its own consumption. Currently, it consumes 50 percent of its widget production and sells the other 50 percent on the U.S. market. Its position in the widget market is miniscule compared to that of the major U.S. producers.

Company F is a large Japanese manufacturer of widgets. Its sales are equal to company A's. All production is in Japan. Exports account for 75 percent of all sales. The U.S. market accounts for 25 percent of total sales.

Company G is a major European manufacturer of widgets. Half of its widgets are produced and subsequently sold in Europe. The other half are produced and sold in the U.S.

Company H is a major Korean electrical fixture company. (Sales = company E's.) Forty percent of its sales is in the U.S. It is currently buying widgets from company C, but no purchasing contract exists between the two companies.

This case was prepared by Kate Gillespie, University of Texas at Austin, for classroom discussion.

2. Nitrofix Ghana

Craig Michael Lee, the project advisor to the vice-president of the international division of Nitrofix,

Prepared by William A. Stoever, Keating Crawford Professor of International Business, Seton Hall University, and Marla Gottlieb, Rutgers Graduate School of Management. The authors acknowledge their inspiration from the Ghana Fertilizers case prepared by John M. Stopford, which appears in Vernon and Wells, *Manager in the International Economy,* 3rd ed.

Inc., had a long meeting in mid-1982 with Bawol Cabiri, the commercial consul at the Ghana Trade and Investment Office in New York City. Lee hoped that the talk would enable him to decide whether it might be worthwhile to pursue an investment opportunity in Ghana.

A Ghanaian government representative had first approached Nitrofix about establishing a fertilizer plant in 1981, two years after Dr. Hilla Limann became the country's first democratically elected president in over a decade. The Limann government was actively seeking foreign investment, reversing previous governments' socialist practices and antipathy to private investment. However, Nitrofix was hesitant to enter an agreement because of Ghana's past political instability and economic chaos, and negotiations had proceeded fitfully. Then the Limann government was overthrown in a military coup on December 31, 1981. Lee had assumed that was the end of the matter until the Ghana Trade and Investment Office contacted him again in mid-1982 and mentioned that some very favorable terms might now be possible for the investment. His recent meeting with Cabiri focused on the possibility that Nitrofix might invest in a plant in Ghana to be operated as a joint venture with either private Ghanaian entrepreneurs or with the government. A tentative name was agreed upon: Nitrofix (Ghana) Ltd. Lee had been impressed by Cabiri's knowledge and understanding and by the potential profitability of the project. However, he knew that he had to evaluate a number of issues of vital importance including:

- ☐ the condition of the Ghanaian economy,
- ☐ the political climate in Ghana and West Africa,
- ☐ the existence of a Ghanaian and/or African market for fertilizer,
- ☐ Ghana's policies toward foreign investment, and
- ☐ the financial arrangements.

He also knew that if his company decided to follow up on the possibility, it would have to prepare for negotiations on a wide range of matters.

NITROFIX, INC.

Nitrofix was a medium-sized U.S. manufacturer of nitrogenous fertilizers that had made a specialization of setting up plants to serve the local markets in smaller countries overseas. In the 1960s, their first international ventures had gone into the smaller countries of Western Europe, but in the 1970s they had expanded into friendly Third World countries such as the Philippines, Indonesia, Thailand, and Venezuela. The company thoroughly analyzed its overseas investments, and they had generally panned

out well, contributing most of Nitrofix's growth in sales and profits for two decades. In the 1960s Nitrofix had usually insisted on 100 percent ownership of each overseas subsidiary, but in the 1970s they had come to recognize both the necessity and the desirability of entering into joint ventures with local partners when terms and conditions were suitable.

THE POLITICAL ECONOMY OF GHANA

After a day of library research, Lee pieced together the following information about Ghana's political and economic situation. The country had received independence from Great Britain in 1957, the first black colony in Africa to become independent. Its first prime minister (later president) was Dr. Kwame Nkrumah, an eloquent spokesman and leader for the emerging aspirations of Africa. Thanks largely to its position as the world's largest cocoa exporter, Ghana was the richest country in Africa at the time of independence. Continuing a British colonial tradition, the new government invested a substantial part of its revenues in education at all levels from primary school through university. As a result Ghana had a high level of literacy and more college graduates than the country could absorb. But economic policy moved from one disaster to the next. The Nkrumah government embarked on a series of expensive projects such as grandiose industrialization schemes and public buildings that drained the country's coffers while contributing little to its growth. The government's policies toward private enterprise (both Ghanaian and foreign) reflected a basic ambiguity that has persisted for two decades. On one hand, the Ghanaians recognized their need for the capital, entrepreneurial initiative, managerial know-how, and technology that domestic and foreign companies could supply; but on the other hand, they were impressed with the socialist, state-directed model of development and were concerned that private capitalists, if left unchecked, would accumulate most of the country's wealth and benefits of development for themselves. Nkrumah's solution was to attempt to channel and control private investment by establishing four categories of enterprises:

1. State enterprises—wholly government owned, supposed to include most large businesses;
2. Private enterprises—owned by Ghanaians or foreign investors or joint Ghanaian–foreign ventures;
3. Joint state/private enterprises—partnerships, generally between the government and foreign investors;
4. Cooperatives.

A government agency was to supervise domestic and foreign investments to ensure that they complied with the requirements of their assigned categories.

A Capital Investments Act was passed in 1963. It set up a scheme of priorities and incentives to attract foreign investment, provided such investment conformed to the conditions set down by the government. Initially a fair amount of investment was attracted, but a lot of it went into capital-intensive, high-technology plants that were inefficient and expensive producers for the small Ghanaian market. Meanwhile agricultural development was neglected.

Nkrumah was overthrown by military coup in 1966. The military regime attempted to liberalize the economy, reduce import and currency controls, increase the role of the market in allocating resources, and create a more attractive climate for foreign investment. In spite of their efforts, however, the economy remained largely stagnant.

The military stepped aside as promised in 1969, and a former university professor, Dr. Kofi Busia, was elected president. Buoyed by a boom in cocoa prices during his first year in office, Busia initiated an expansionary program intended to increase the rates of domestic savings and investment. But imports of consumer items swelled, world cocoa prices fell, inflation heated up, and the balance-of-payments deficit worsened.

Another military coup was staged in January 1972, bringing to power a group calling itself the National Reconciliation Council (NRC). This group set out to undo the liberalizations of the previous five and a half years. They clamped on wage, price, and rent controls; vastly increased import and currency controls; reasserted the program of state enterprises; nationalized 55 percent of most of the larger domestic- and foreign-owned businesses; and held down prices paid to cocoa farmers in an attempt to increase the state share of agricultural revenues. The consequences were disastrous. Cocoa production fell off, and farmers began smuggling their crops to neighboring Ivory Coast and Togo, where they could obtain much higher prices. Once one of the most abundant food producers in Africa, the country now had to import canned goods and staples from Europe and the United States, and it was caught in the vise of spiraling oil prices. Inflation, the government deficit, the money supply, and the balance-of-payments deficit ballooned. Corruption and mismanagement in the government machinery and the state enterprises were rampant. Skilled and educated people fled to jobs in Nigeria, England, and the United States. The cumbersome administrative procedures prevented the government from utilizing even the foreign aid that was given to it. Some factories were operating at less than 25 percent of capacity because the shortage of foreign exchange made it impossible to import necessary raw materials and spare parts. Foreign companies faced a proliferation of controls and hindrances; for example, one company applied in 1972 for permission to repatriate a dividend and was still waiting in 1979 for the foreign-exchange allocation to come through. Some foreign companies pulled out, and virtually no new investment came into the country. Meanwhile, the military rulers divided into factions and struggled among themselves for control of the government, with the result of paralysis and continuous crisis in the country's political leadership.

In June 1979 a group of junior Air Force officers overthrew the NRC regime and installed as president flight lieutenant Jerry Rawlings, the son of a British father and a Ghanaian mother. Rawlings stepped aside three months later, after the election of Hilla Limann, a former diplomat and economist, as president. In spite of his lack of political experience, Limann proved to be an adept politician. He neutralized some potential coup-makers in the military and lined up enough support in the newly reconstituted Parliament to institute a program of economic reforms. His government imposed severe austerity measures, enabling the country to meet its obligations on its foreign debts for the first time in five years and to regain a measure of international creditworthiness. Prices paid to cocoa farmers were trebled, reversing the declining production figures and reducing the amount of smuggling. Many problems remained, however. The inflation rate was still above 50 percent a year, shortages of food and spare parts continued, and the country's best managers continued deserting the inefficient state industries in favor of higher-paying jobs abroad. The government hesitated to take one of the most necessary but politically risky steps, devaluation of the Ghanaian currency, the cedi. The IMF tried to impose devaluation as a condition for the granting of further credits, but Limann feared that such a move might trigger another coup, and the IMF relented somewhat. In spite of an increase in cocoa production, the country's export revenues declined because of a steep fall in the world price.

President Limann made clear his intention to seek new foreign investment for Ghana. His government enacted a new Investment Code designed to

> ... encourage foreign investments in Ghana by the provision of incentives, to promote the development of Ghanaian entrepreneurs, to indicate enterprises in which the State and Ghanaians are required to participate in any investment and the extent of such participation, to make provision for the registration of technology transfer contracts ...

The Code assured foreign investors of "protection" and a fair return on their investment. It specifically eliminated any restrictions on transfers out of Ghana of fees, charges, capital, and profits to the investor's country of origin. It established a Ghana Investing Centre chaired by the vice-president of Ghana to dismantle regulatory and administrative barriers to investment and to review investment projects; the Centre could decide which projects should qualify for special incentives. All approved enterprises were to receive five-year exemptions from customs duties for machinery and equipment imported for use in the enterprises, three years' customs exemption for spare parts, guaranteed manufacturing or establishment licenses, guaranteed immigration of necessary expatriate personnel, and certain tax exemptions and remittance guarantees for such personnel. In the manufacturing sector, the government sought industries in which the country had a raw material advantage, underutilized existing plant capacity, or the capacity to conserve and/or earn foreign exchange. Projects qualifying for investment included agro-based industries, those processing raw materials originating in Ghana, animal feed, and fertilizer, among others. Companies in the export sector could be exempted from company income tax during an initial period, provided they declared no dividends during that period.

Evidently the new Investment Code made a favorable impression on at least a few potential investors, because Lee recalled seeing a couple of items in the newspapers during 1981 mentioning that a few U.S. and European companies were exploring possibilities for new investments in Ghana. Lee himself was attracted by the country's advantages—rich soil, adequate rainfall, an educated and energetic population, potential mineral wealth, and the beginnings of a national development program. Lee thought it would be very desirable for Nitrofix to be the first fertilizer producer in Ghana and thus secure an entrenched position in what could become a very prosperous market. But he knew that many problems remained. The country was still deeply in debt, its currency vastly overvalued, its foreign exchange reserves close to zero, its economy dependent on the vagaries of the world cocoa market, its borrowing power from the IMF and private lenders essentially exhausted, and its record of economic mismanagement still needing much improvement. If only they could get their act together.

On New Year's Day 1982 Lee was shocked to learn that the Limann government had been overthrown in yet another military coup, Ghana's fifth in fifteen years. This one too was led by Jerry Rawlings, then 34 years old. In radio broadcasts Rawlings claimed that Limann had been incapable of solving Ghana's economic problems, and he announced his intention to retain the presidency "as long as necessary." It soon became apparent, however, that he did not enjoy much popular support and did not have many ideas on how to improve the country's economic situation. Ghana appeared to have suffered another political and economic setback, at least temporarily.

Table 1 gives the most recent statistics Lee could find on the Ghanaian economy. Tables 2, 3, and 4 give some statistics on the world production, consumption, and price of cocoa. Table 5 shows

TABLE 1
Statistics on Ghanaian Economy

	1974	1975	1976	1977	1978	1979	1980	1981
Total export	840	929	952	1,106	1,645	1,201	—	—
Exports of cacao	496	551	516	680	1,033	—	—	—
Imports	944	909	969	1,176	1,653	1,299	—	—
Foreign debt (claims on government)	574	881	1,513	2,527	4,287	4,413	5,724	9,494
Official reserves	92	149	203	162	288	300	216	196

above figures in millions of cedis at official exchange rate

	1974	1975	1976	1977	1978	1979	1980	1981
Official exchange rate	.8696	.8696	.8696	.8696	.3636	.3636	.3636	.3636
*Black market exchange rate	.65	.52	.23	.13	.10	.07	.04	.02

above figures in United States dollars per cedi

	1974	1975	1976	1977	1978	1979	1980	1981
Consumer price index	77.0	100.0	156.1	337.8	584.8	903.0	1355.4	2934

1975 = 100

* *Pick's Currency Yearbook, 1977–79.*

Sources: *International Financial Statistics,* except where noted otherwise; 1980 and 1981 rates from current news articles.

TABLE 2
World Production of Cocoa Beans in Principal Exporting Countries

(in thousands of metric tons)

Crop Year	Brazil	Ghana	Ivory Coast	Nigeria	World Total
1967–68	145	422	147	239	1,352
1968–69	165	339	145	192	1,242
1969–70	201	416	181	223	1,435
1970–71	182	392	180	308	1,499
1971–72	167	464	226	255	1,583
1972–73	162	418	181	241	1,398
1973–74	246	350	209	215	1,448
1974–75	273	377	242	214	1,549
1975–76	258	397	231	216	1,509
1976–77	234	320	230	165	1,340
1977–78	283	268	304	205	1,502
1978–79	314	250	312	137	1,480
1979–80	294	290	373	169	1,617
1980–81	350	255	352	165	1,584

Source: *1981 Commodity Yearbook, p. 85.*

**TABLE 3
Consumption of
Cocoa**

*(in thousands of
metric tons)*

Year	World total
1967	1,366
1968	1,410
1969	1,353
1970	1,355
1971	1,438
1972	1,565
1973	1,556
1974	1,478
1975	1,462
1976	1,525
1977	1,367
1978	1,391
1979	1,437
1980	1,468

[handwritten: Tourly by slight increments]

**TABLE 4
Spot Cocoa Bean Prices**

*(yearly/monthly average,
New York)*

Year	In U.S. cents per pound
1975	75.9
1976	109.2
1977	214.4
1978	174.2
1979	160.4
1980	135.4
1981	108.5
1982 Jan	116.0
Feb	107.0
Mar	102.0
Apr	99.0
May	94.0

[handwritten: low, high, form to something else]

Sources: Figures for 1967–1980 from
Commodity Yearbook, 1981; figures for
1981–1982 from *Survey of Current
Business.*

the consumption of fertilizer in Ghana and other
countries.

MARKET FOR FERTILIZER

Agriculture is a way of life for the people of Ghana,
employing 60 percent of the labor force and producing 42 percent of the gross domestic product
in 1980. However, out of the 23 million hectares
suitable for farming, only 3 million hectares, or
13 percent, were under cultivation. Methods of
cultivation were divided into two general categories:
traditional (or subsistence) and new, improved
practices. Traditional methods were characterized
by the use of simple tools; they relied almost entirely
on human labor, resulting in inefficient processing
and storage methods and low crop yields. The new
methods stressed the use of chemicals (fertilizers
and pesticides) as well as farm machinery and
implements.

Over 90 percent of farming was undertaken
by subsistence-level private farmers cultivating small
plots of land, generally between 3 and 4 hectares.
Soil fertility on these farms was generally maintained
by crop rotation and burning of vegetation cover;
the latter practice returned potash and some minerals to the soil, but it caused the loss of important
organic matter and other minerals. Burning was
especially damaging if done too frequently or at
the wrong season, conditions likely to result as
land use intensified.

While the cultivation of tree crops (cocoa,
coffee, rubber, and palm oil) was labor-intensive,
mechanization was introduced in the cultivation
of field crops such as maize and rice. Mechanical
cultivation would lead to rapid deterioration of
the organic matter in the soil and the depletion
of soil nutrients. Therefore, fertilizers were used
to replenish lost minerals, or else crop yields would
decline.

The Limann government declared that agriculture would be the number one priority for
development and investment. The government encouraged the development of large-scale commercial farming, which required the use of modern
techniques. In order to boost overall productivity
and expand agricultural output, the government
supplied many inputs including hoes, seed rice,
and groundnuts (peanuts). It also distributed over

TABLE 5
World Fertilizer Usage

	(kilograms of inorganic fertilizers* per hectare of land under arable cultivation and permanent crops)			
	1961–1965 (yearly average)	1967	1972	1977
World	27.9	39.9	54.3	68.0
Africa	4.7	6.3	10.0	12.4
N. & C. America	41.2	61.3	69.7	83.2
S. America	8.4	11.2	24.7	38.8
Asia	11.8	18.5	31.0	45.4
Europe	103.9	139.6	188.7	210.3
Oceania	34.0	34.1	37.4	36.2
USSR	18.0	33.7	53.2	77.6
Selected Countries				
Africa				
Egypt	109.9	100.2	146.7	187.5
Ghana	0.6	0.5	1.7	10.9
Kenya	9.6	17.2	24.9	22.7
Nigeria	0.1	0.3	0.8	3.1
South Africa	23.4	32.9	47.6	59.6
Sudan	3.7	6.3	8.0	4.3
Uganda	0.7	0.8	1.5	0.5
Zaire	0.2	0.5	0.7	1.4
N. & C. America				
Canada	12.4	20.4	23.2	34.3
Cuba	94.0	169.3	76.2	132.7
Mexico	11.3	18.5	29.3	46.0
United States	52.2	77.4	86.2	99.5
S. America				
Argentina	0.9	2.2	2.5	2.2
Brazil	9.1	13.8	45.2	77.4
Asia				
Bangladesh	4.4	10.6	20.0	37.1
China	13.2	24.1	45.5	74.3
India	3.7	7.1	16.7	25.3
Indonesia	8.4	8.6	28.9	35.0
Japan	305.2	387.4	389.5	428.1
Thailand	2.2	7.7	10.8	15.6
Turkey	3.9	10.6	22.4	46.5
Europe				
France	133.9	191.6	284.5	277.6
Netherlands	534.9	626.2	719.5	737.3
Hungary	52.9	91.3	182.7	278.7
Italy	60.2	73.8	125.3	140.9
Poland	65.2	117.9	201.1	241.0
Romania	7.8	27.4	40.1	54.2
United Kingdom	198.9	254.2	240.0	287.6
Oceania				
Australia	24.5	26.6	26.1	24.5
New Zealand	737.6	720.3	1319.5	1296.3

* Inorganic nitrogenous, phosphatic, and potash fertilizers.
Source: *The World Food Book* (1981), pp. 214–215.

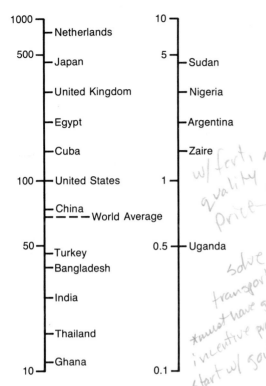

TABLE 5a
Kilograms of Inorganic Fertilizers Per Hectare of Land under Arable Cultivation and Permanent Crops (Log Scale), 1977

one million bags of fertilizer to small producers, commercial farms, and para-state organizations.

These steps alone would not be sufficient to improve productivity or increase the usage of fertilizers, however; raising the educational level of the farm population would be a fundamental necessity to boost the understanding and acceptance of fertilizers. Such an educational program would require a massive effort by the government. But the more energetic and literate younger generation who might be more amenable to adopting new practices have been leaving the countryside for the cities. Furthermore, the archaic land tenure system is based on traditions and customs that discourage innovation and thus constitute a formidable obstacle to the acceptance of fertilizer by small farmers.

Cocoa is raised both by small farmers who

convert a portion of their subsistence holdings to production of the cash crop and by larger plantations and state farms. The cocoa industry is the main source of Ghana's foreign exchange earnings, accounting for approximately 65 percent in an average year. It employs 11 percent of the nation's labor force and is believed to account for a large part of its fertilizer usage. However, cocoa production has declined steadily since the early 1960s, and by 1980 Ghana had fallen from first to third place among the world's major exporters. The factors responsible for the decline in output include low producer prices, poor maintenance of cocoa farms, aging of cocoa trees and cocoa farmers, scarcity of farm labor in the major producing areas, and ineffective control of pests and diseases. Poor transportation and a lack of infrastructure are problems, as well as smuggling to neighboring countries where better prices are obtainable. Storage facilities have also deteriorated.

After reviewing the preceding information, Lee concluded that there would be many imponderables in any effort to estimate the growth potential of the Ghanaian fertilizer market. So much would depend on noneconomic factors such as the effort and expense the government might decide to put into promoting the use of fertilizer and the pace at which Ghanaian farmers would accept it. Lee did find some tables apparently indicating that the use of fertilizers was growing in Ghana and enabling comparisons to other countries. (See Tables 5 and 5a.) However, he also found another source that said that Ghanaian consumption of nitrogenous fertilizers had peaked at 11.0 thousand metric tons in 1975–76 and had declined somewhat for several years thereafter. Consumption of potash and phosphate fertilizers had also decreased since 1975–76.

Lee also wondered whether some Ghanaian fertilizer production might be exportable to other West African countries. Ghana had joined the Economic Community of West African States (ECOWAS) at its inception in 1975. This community had a total of sixteen member states,* many of which were even smaller and poorer than Ghana. It was

---

*Benin, Cape Verde, The Gambia, Ghana, Guinea, Guinea-Bissau, Ivory Coast, Liberia, Mali, Mauritania, Niger, Nigeria, Senegal, Sierra Leone, Togo, and Upper Volta (now Burkina Faso).

supposed to become a common market with the elimination of trade barriers among its members and a common external tariff. Its members were supposed to work cooperatively for agricultural development, the construction of infrastructure to improve regional transportation and communications, and industrial growth. However, most of the members could not afford to lower their own tariff barriers or to take any concrete steps to implement the regional integration plans. Furthermore, Nigeria, with its oil wealth and naptha feedstocks, would be likely to grab the lead as the dominant nitrogenous fertilizer exporter in the region.

PLANT TYPE AND SIZE

Lee knew that the technical and economic factors involved in the choice of plant size and production methods for nitrogenous fertilizers were very complex and were subject to change depending on the price of the primary input, naptha, a petroleum derivative. Nonetheless, he knew that Nitrofix had three basic choices of technology and that significant economies of scale could be achieved in both construction and per-unit production costs as plants were made larger and more advanced. He obtained some ballpark figures from one of the company engineers:

and production costs had a way of soaring when plants were put into developing countries because of shortages of materials and the added costs and inefficiencies of trying to train and use unskilled manpower. The steam-reforming production technique was outdated and inefficient, but it had the advantages of being easier to learn and using equipment that could be obtained used from other LDCs.

Another alternative was for the Ghanaians to import U.S. or European ammonium nitrate. The world price was rather volatile, fluctuating between $50 and $90 per ton during the previous five years. Lee estimated a good average would be $65 per ton (the equivalent of paying $130 per ton of ammonia). In all likelihood, importing fertilizer would be cheaper than trying to produce it in Ghana because of the added expenses and hassles of operating in a faraway LDC. (Lee figured that transportation costs would approximately even out regardless whether unprocessed naptha or processed ammonium nitrate was shipped to Ghana.) By producing it themselves, however, the Ghanaians *might* save some foreign exchange, raise the skills and industrial experience of some workers, and add to the foundation for the country's industrial development. A shiny new plant would also make the government leaders look good.

Annual production capacity (tons)	Production technology	Factor proportions	Construction cost (U.S.)	Production cost per ton of ammonia
20,000	steam-reforming	relatively labor-intensive	$20 million	$130
80,000	reciprocating compressor	relatively capital-intensive	$60 million	$120
160,000	centrifugal compressor	capital-intensive	$90 million	$100

The ammonia (from whatever source) would then be converted into ammonium nitrate—the actual fertilizer—in a technologically simple process. This diluted the value of the ammonia by about 50 percent: one ton of ammonia made two tons of ammonium nitrate. Lee was aware that construction

THE FINANCIAL AND OWNERSHIP ARRANGEMENTS

The Investment Code required that any foreign investment in fertilizer be a joint venture, 55 percent Ghanaian and 45 percent foreign. All other things being equal, Nitrofix might have preferred 100 percent ownership and control, but they also knew that there were some advantages to having a local partner. Lee noted that in spite of the apparent rigidity of the Code, the 1979 Constitution allowed some room for further negotiations. If the enterprise was cast as a joint venture, he assumed that each partner would put in equity capital proportional to its percentage ownership. This was not a rule cast in stone, however, and considerable flexibility might be achieved by negotiating the valuation of whatever machinery Nitrofix contributed, the rate at which contributions in cedis were valued, and the mixture of equity and debt contributed by each partner.

If the partners agreed to go with the 20,000-ton plant employing steam-reforming technology, it would be ideal from Nitrofix's point of view to make its entire contribution in the form of used equipment. The valuation of such equipment would be quite arbitrary: its value as scrap might be $100,000, but it might produce several million dollars worth of output per year for somebody who could keep it running. Lee suspected the Ghanaians were too sophisticated to accept such outdated technology or at least to give it a very high valuation, however.

As to choice of partner, Nitrofix would probably have preferred a private investor or group, but Lee doubted that private citizens would be capable of raising that kind of money in Ghana, and Nitrofix was most reluctant to take on a partner that didn't contribute a fair share of the risk capital. Realistically, therefore, they would probably have to go with the government.

Another question was the matter of debt versus equity. In order to minimize their exposure in a country like Ghana, Nitrofix would have preferred to put in a relatively small amount of its own capital as equity and to obtain most of the financing in the form of loans. On a $20 million project, for example, Lee wondered whether Nitrofix could put in as little as $4.5 million, the Ghanaian partner $5.5 million, and the remaining $10 million come from outside lenders. However, it was questionable whether outside lenders would put up this large a percentage on such a risky venture, and Nitrofix might end up having to pay for a much higher percentage of a much larger project. What's more,

interest rates in the Eurodollar market were then running about 15 percent, which would make them think carefully about taking on a hard-currency debt. And there wasn't a lot of money available for soft loans at this time, either.

Cabiri said the government would help arrange local financing for plant construction and local supplies and would try to help obtain hard-currency financing for necessary imports. It might offer to guarantee any borrowings from international banks, for example. But in view of the country's desperate financial straits, Lee seriously doubted whether the banks would give much weight to such guarantees. Furthermore, he was most reluctant to have Nitrofix bear the entire foreign-exchange risk of the project; the Ghanaians were going to have to come up with a decent share of the dollars.

Overhead expenses and taxes were other imponderables. Lee made the optimistic assumption that overhead expenses might run only 10 percent of gross sales, although he was aware that red tape, delays, and corruption often ate up a much larger percent of the profits in LDCs. Ghana imposed a 50 percent tax on corporate income, but Lee assumed Nitrofix could get a holiday from all taxes for at least the first five years of production, and maybe for ten. However, he knew the Bank of Ghana and the Ministry of Finance would object if the tax abatement was too generous.

It was obvious from all these considerations that the problems of financing and risk might be enough to discourage Nitrofix from the venture. However, Lee's preliminary calculations suggested the possibility of some very handsome returns if everything went right. Nitrofix would of course seek tariff protection against fertilizer imports. If they got a 100-percent tariff, they might be able to sell their Ghanaian production for as much as $260 per ton. He recognized that the higher the tariff, the less the net economic benefit to the host country would be. But he calculated that if they went ahead with the 160,000-ton plan *and* obtained 50 percent financing at 15 percent *and* were able to sell their entire output at $260 per ton *and* were able to hold their overhead costs to 10 percent of sales *and* could get a complete tax holiday, Nitrofix, Inc., might earn $6.6 million per year on a $20 million investment—a handsome return. And the returns could be even higher if they could get

take on more. go have gov't agree to persuade people – starter programs

subsidized loans, a subsidized plant site, payments for training workers, etc. Perhaps if they waited a year or two they could get a lower rate on their hard-currency borrowings. On the other hand, the returns would be lower as soon as the tax holiday ran out or was cancelled, or if they decided to go with the 80,000-ton plant, or if Lee's assumptions regarding the size of the market or the low amount of overhead did not pan out. (Lee also calculated that they would need at least 22 percent tariff protection in order for the plant to break even if all his optimistic assumptions held true.)

In some ways the 20,000-ton plant seemed the most attractive for both Nitrofix and Ghana, despite its badly outdated technology. Lee wondered if Nitrofix Inc. could get a 45 percent stake in exchange for some obsolescent steam-reforming equipment from their Greek or Philippine subsidiaries plus a promise to provide technical assistance and train Ghanaians to run the plant. The Ghanaian partner would get 55 percent in exchange for supplying 15 million cedis ($5.5 million at the official exchange rate); this money would pay local expenses for setting up the plant. They would seek a $10 million Eurodollar loan to cover the hard-currency expenses. With a 100-percent tariff, this plant should produce a pre-tax profit of $580,000 if everything went right. Nitrofix's share would be $261,000—not bad considering that it would be an essentially costless investment for them.

Another factor that could help make the investment more attractive would be if Nitrofix could find a way of reducing some of the risks. Lee wondered whether they could bargain the Ghanaians into giving Nitrofix's shares a priority claim to dividends, for example. Maybe Nitrofix could cast part of its compensation in the form of a management fee or licensing payment off the top—say 1 or 2 percent of gross revenues. They might be able to obtain insurance from the Overseas Private Investment Corporation (OPIC) against the risks of expropriation, war, and currency inconvertibility; the premiums on such insurance could run up to 1.5 percent of the amount of coverage (0.6 percent for expropriation, 0.6 percent for war, revolution or insurrection, and 0.3 percent for currency inconvertibility, if Nitrofix elected to take the full coverage).

Reviewing all of the above information, Lee realized that he faced a daunting task in trying to evaluate it and formulate a decision. But he also looked forward to it as an interesting challenge.

Part II
Analyzing
Global Market
Opportunities

Knowledge of a foreign market's size, structure, growth, and other key characteristics is essential for the design of successful local marketing programs. Without a detailed understanding of a market's basic demographics and socio-cultural features and their implications for marketing, the selection of target markets and design of foreign marketing programs remains mere speculation. Accordingly, in this part we examine these demographic and socio-cultural aspects of foreign markets and then examine the problems and approaches to gathering relevant data.

Chapter 5: examines the economic environment of foreign markets. Global marketing managers need a basic understanding of the structure of their foreign markets and of how to assess the economic forces interacting in and affecting local markets. The chapter identifies and discusses several of the variables used to make such assessments and the limitations of these variables.

Chapter 6: examines socio-cultural influences on buyer behavior. To make effective decisions, global marketing managers must acquire an understanding of their foreign customers' behavior, especially their buyer behavior. The chapter therefore identifies and discusses germane cultural and social elements and presents a model for analyzing their effects on buyer behavior.

Chapter 7: discusses the various problems and issues confronting a global marketing manager conducting marketing research in and across foreign markets. It also discusses research design issues, problems associated with the use of secondary and primary data, and organizing marketing research efforts.

Chapter 8: looks at techniques commonly used to assess marketing opportunities and examines the various factors, problems, and issues a manager needs to address when making market entry or market expansion decisions.

Case Studies: Niagra Electronics
U.S. Agricultural Tractors

Chapter 5
The Structure and Demographics of Global Markets

INTRODUCTION

A major task in researching foreign markets is accurately estimating their current and future size. Key company decisions depend on these estimates, for example, deciding which markets to enter, or whether to expand or withdraw. Such estimates also assist in the optimal allocation of budgets among established foreign markets and product lines.

A basic yet detailed understanding of the size, structure, and dynamics of each country's economic activities underlies and helps ensure that market estimates are correctly prepared and reliable. These estimates generally involve analysis of secondary data on each country's economic activities and are based on such demographic and structural variables as population, income patterns, and manufacturing output. Solid data offer the researcher economies of time and cost.

The chapter is divided into four parts, the first of which describes three levels of economic activity of particular interest to international marketers. The next two parts look at some common quantitative indicators of the economic activity and relative attractiveness of foreign markets. The fourth part briefly discusses typical problems encountered in comparisons of secondary data on two or more national economies.

MEASURES OF ECONOMIC ACTIVITY

As part of ongoing planning, companies prepare a large number of market-size estimates. Each type of demand measurement serves a specific purpose. One marketing scholar, for example, has identified ninety different types of demand estimates; these range from long-range forecasts of world demand to more specific short-range forecasts for individual product items.[1] Fundamental to the accuracy and reliability of demand estimates is a sound understanding of the economic forces that stimulate and mold demand and how they change. To rank countries according to their relative short- and long-term market attractiveness, international marketers should periodically conduct cross-national assessments of relevant demand-creating factors.

The National Economy

Whether a company should enter, remain, or withdraw from a country is partly a function of the host country's economic activities and the rate at which these activities are changing. A rough but useful estimate of these activities and how they are changing can be obtained by carefully studying selected demographic data and interpreting them within local economic, social, cultural, political, and legal contexts.

Many demographic indicators can be used to measure a country's economic activities and concomitant attractiveness. These include measurements of population, population distribution, income, income distribution, and so on. The indicators used and their relative importance depend on several factors. China, for example, has a very large population, but relatively few Chinese have the income needed for high-priced products such as refrigerators and automobiles. Switzerland, with its smaller but richer population, may be more attractive for some companies. Some countries may have both the population and the income to make them attractive, but socio-cultural influences may make certain products unattractive to them. In addition, the governments of some countries may hinder, restrict, or even forbid the importation of some products, even those not produced locally.

Specific Measures of Market Activity

For a company to flourish in the near term it needs more than demographic data and assessments of product attractiveness. It must also understand the size, structure, and dynamics of its immediate market. Ultimately, companies are interested in determining the relative attractiveness of either a country's *consumer market,* its *industrial market,* or both. Any meaningful assessment requires that the indicators used to measure economic activity reflect as closely as possible the demand for the products or services to be offered. Managers must therefore obtain market attractiveness measures that focus on buyers (actual and potential) who have an *interest* in economic exchanges, the *income* to purchase products or services, and *access* to the types of products or services to be offered.

For example, in the United States, the bulk of Coca-Cola sold is consumed by teenagers and young adults. Thus, Coca-Cola should know not only the size and growth rate of the country's population between the ages of 14 and 30 but also its location and accessibility. On the other hand, a manufacturer of textile equipment would be interested in the size and structure of a country's textile industry, its rate of modernization, and its location.

THE STRUCTURE AND DYNAMICS OF NATIONAL MARKETS _____

Estimating the market attractiveness of a particular country involves more than the use of demographic data (that is, population, population distribution, income, income distribution, number of households, and the like). It also requires a fundamental understanding of how these data reflect the dynamics of a particular market situation. Interpreting and combining national demographic data meaningfully requires some knowledge of the country's stage of economic development, its marketing infrastructure, and the rules and regulations governing its commerce.

Indicators of National Economic Activity

There is a substantial body of secondary data and information available describing economic dimensions of most countries. International organizations such as the United Nations, the World Bank, and most governments publish many documents containing information of value to marketers interested in evaluating the relative attractiveness of foreign markets. The United Nation's *Statistical Yearbook* and several other of its compendiums contain global data on agriculture, mining, manufacturing, construction, energy consumption, rail and air transportation, wages, prices, housing, education, media, and consumption expenditures. In general, complete economic data are available for the industrial countries but not for the developing countries. LDC data are less complete and often out of date. Nevertheless, any marketer's initial problem in assessment is more one of abundance of data than absence of data. This chapter discusses the most salient indicators of economic activity.

Global Population Patterns

The most basic information required to estimate a country's market potential is its population. For low-priced products such as soft beverages and many food staples, population may be more important than income. Even for high-priced products the size of the market expressed as potential users is of critical importance. Regardless of standard of living among buyers, managers must ask the three following questions: (1) Which markets are to be served? (2) How they are to be served? (3) How is the marketing budget to be allocated?

In 1800, the world's population was about 1 billion people. By 1987, it was 5 billion people. By 2000, it is expected to be 6.1 billion. An increasing portion of the world's population will be located in the developing countries. In 1950, about two-thirds of the world's population was found in the developing countries. By 1983, this had increased to about 75 percent and by 2000 it is expected to exceed 80 percent.[2] The 1986 edition of *The World Bank Atlas* lists data for 184 countries and territories. Of these, 128 had populations of one million people or more. However, the number of countries that are "worthwhile" markets will vary from company to company. I.B.M. and Singer market their products in more than 130 and 180 countries and territories, respectively. However, most firms limit their overseas activities to a much smaller group of countries.

Distribution of the World's Population

Table 5-1 lists the 30 most populous countries in the world. One striking feature of the data is the heavy concentration of the world's population in a very few countries. In 1983, 82 percent of the world's population of 4.7 billion people were citizens of just 30 countries; the remaining 18 percent was distributed among 154 countries and territories not listed on the table. Furthermore, the concentration of population is skewed even within the top 30. The five largest countries accounted for 51.4 percent of the world's population; the next five, an additional 11.4 percent; and the following five, 6.6 percent. Thus, if population were the major criterion for determining market potential, a firm need concentrate its marketing effort only in a handful of countries to have the potential for serving the bulk of the world's people.

Although international marketers are concerned primarily with serving national markets, regional population patterns are important. This is especially true for companies supplying several foreign markets from strategically located production facilities in just a few countries.

In 1983, Asia was home to about 2,071 million people, with India and China accounting for 1,752 million. The total population of the densely populated European Community was considerably less, only 310.4 million. Four of the 12 EC members had populations over 50 million. South and Central America, with a more thinly populated but larger land area, had a total population of 360.4 million, with the

TABLE 5-1
The World's 30 Largest Countries by Population: 1983*

Country	Population (millions)	Country	Population (millions)
1. China	1,019	16. France	55
2. India	733	17. Philippines	52
3. USSR	273	18. Thailand	49
4. USA	234	19. Turkey	47
5. Indonesia	156	20. Egypt	45
6. Brazil	130	21. Iran	43
7. Japan	119	22. Ethiopia	41
8. Bangladesh	95	23. South Korea	40
9. Nigeria	94	24. Spain	38
10. Pakistan	90	25. Poland	37
11. Mexico	75	26. Burma	35
12. West Germany	61	27. South Africa	32
13. Viet Nam	59	28. Zaire	30
14. Italy	57	29. Argentina	30
15. United Kingdom	56	30. Colombia	28

* Numbers have been rounded to nearest million.
Source: *The World Bank Atlas* (Washington, D.C.: World Bank, 1986), pp. 6–9.

largest populations concentrated in Brazil and Mexico. North America's population totaled 259.4 million people and Africa's, 234 million.

Global Population Growth Rates

The growth rate of a particular country's population is also of interest to marketers when planning future activities. Population trends are of major consequence to some companies. For example, Gerber, Coca-Cola, and companies selling educational materials or birth control devices depend on relatively young populations. On the other hand, the insurance and medical supply industries have more at stake in countries with mature or aged populations.

While a high growth rate can indicate economic growth for some countries, it can portend economic troubles for others. A telling indicator is the country's ability to balance population growth with corresponding increases in economic activity. Should West Germany's population and economic activities continue to grow at their current rates, by 2024 Germans will be 40 percent better off than they are today. On the other hand, Kenyans will probably be poorer. To keep up with its current population growth, the Kenyan economy would have to grow 6.2 percent annually, something that has not occurred since 1978.[3]

With the exception of East Germany and Hungary, countries with populations of greater than one million are expected to increase between 1980 and 2000. Their rate of population growth, however, now ranges from a low of 0.0 percent in Denmark to a high of 4.0 percent in Jordan and Libya. The populations of East Germany and Hungary are projected to decline at about 0.1 percent over the same period.

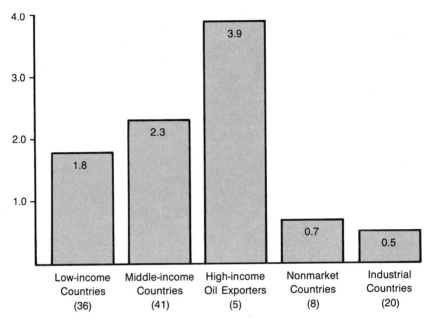

FIGURE 5-1 **Annual Population Growth Rates by Economic Group: 1985–1990** (Source: *World Development Report 1986* [World Bank, New York: Oxford, 1986] Table A.1, p. 154.)

That there is a roughly direct correlation between population growth rates and economic activity is suggested by the data in Figure 5-1. The population growth rates of low-income countries are lower than those of middle-income countries, which in turn are lower than those of the high-income oil exporting countries. However, the rate of growth of the industrial countries is considerably lower than for all other groups. There are obvious reasons for this seeming disparity. Reasons for an increase in population growth rates in middle income countries include increased prosperity, and improved medical care. Reasons for less rapid growth rates in the industrial countries include the desire for a better standard of living and the wide use of birth control.

As with most averages, there are exceptions. For example, the projected population growth rates for the high-income countries of Australia (1.1 percent) and Ireland (1.0 percent) are very similar to those for middle-income South Korea (1.2 percent) and Singapore, and low-income China (1.2 percent).

Characteristics of the Population

Any study of population demographics involves more than the counting of heads. Marketers' understanding of population and its implications is enriched when they factor in information on education, occupation characteristics, income distribution, and consumption patterns.

Age Distribution of the Population. The distribution of the U.S. population by age has proven a useful segmenting variable. There is indeed a correlation between age and consumers' wants. For example, in the United States, young couples with babies and young single adults have different needs. (The same is generally true in other countries.) But age and life-cycle variables can be tricky, especially when applied to foreign markets. When American children reach adulthood, they generally leave home and establish their own households. This is not so generally the case in other countries. In many Asian countries, male children remain with their parents; their brides come to live with them. The number of households thus remains somewhat stable. However, the size of the households varies. In Chinese households it is not uncommon to have three or even four generations living under one roof.

Many developing countries are experiencing a population explosion. Some 90 percent of the global population growth is occurring in the LDCs. Because of the short life expectancy in LDCs, a major segment of their populations are concentrated in the economically inactive under-15 age group. As Table 5-2 data indicate, over 40 percent of the populations of many low- and middle-income African, Asian, and Latin American countries fall into this category. This amount is double that of the industrial countries of Asia, North America, and Europe (just over 20 percent).

Age distributions within countries at the same economic level also vary. While the European countries have approximately the same number of people over 59 as they do under 15, Canada and the United States tend to have more people in the latter category. Similar differences can be noted between India and Bangladesh on the one hand and Argentina and South Korea on the other hand.

Education of the Population. The general level of education of the population is also of considerable interest. As in the United States, education can be an important indicator of market attractiveness. For example, educated people tend to read more books and magazines, travel more frequently, and demand higher quality products than their less-educated counterparts.

In 1983, 56 percent of the U.S. population between the ages of 20 and 24 was enrolled in institutions of higher education. In Canada and West Germany, the percentages were respectively 42 and 30 percent. In sharp contrast, we find Brazil and Chile at 11 percent, Mexico at 15 percent, and Venezuela at 22 percent. In low-income Bangladesh, India, and Kenya, the rates were 4 percent, 9 percent, and 1 percent, respectively.

In general, level of education corresponds closely with a country's stage of economic development. In 1983, the average percentage of the populations of the industrial countries enrolled in higher education was 37 percent; in secondary education, 85 percent; and in primary education, 100 percent.[4] In middle-income countries the percentages for the same levels of education were 12 percent, 47 percent, and 100 percent. In low-income countries only 4 percent of the population was enrolled in higher education, 31 percent in secondary education, and 91 percent in primary education.

Labor Force. Data on a country's labor force also contribute to a deeper understanding of market attractiveness. Labor force statistics provide some rough but useful indicators of a country's economically active population: its location, occupations, and interests. This is especially true if data are available on the

TABLE 5-2
Age Structure of Population by Economic Group and Selected Countries

Country/Group	Life Expectancy (1984)	Average Percentage of Population by Age Group (1975–1984)					
		Under 15	15–29	30–44	45–59	Over 59	Total 15–59
Industrial countries	76						
Belgium	75	20	24	19	19	19	61
Canada	76	22	27	22	15	15	64
France	77	22	23	20	17	17	60
West Germany	75	17	24	21	13	20	58
Japan	77	23	21	16	19	14	56
Sweden	77	19	21	22	16	23	59
United Kingdom	74	20	23	20	17	21	60
United States	76	22	26	21	14	16	61
Middle-income countries	61						
Argentina	70	30	24	19	15	12	58
Brazil	64	38	29	17	10	6	56
Indonesia	55	40	28	17	11	5	54
Mexico	66	46	27	14	8	5	49
Philippines	63	41	29	16	9	5	54
South Korea	68	32	31	19	12	6	62
Low-income countries	60						
Bangladesh	50	46	26	15	9	5	49
India	56	39	28	17	10	6	55
Kenya	54	51	25	13	7	3	45
Sri Lanka	70	35	30	18	11	7	50
Nonmarket economies	68						
Bulgaria	71	22	21	20	20	16	62
Czechoslovakia	70	24	22	21	17	16	60
Romania	71	27	21	19	19	14	59
USSR	67	not available					

Source: World Development Report 1986 (World Bank, New York: Oxford, 1986), p. 180 (life expectancy data), and *Demographic Yearbook* (New York: United Nations, 1984), p. 188, Table 7 (age structure data).

distribution of the labor force among the major economic sectors (agriculture, industry, and services). For example, the needs and wants of agricultural workers tend to vary with their lifestyles. These workers' product preferences differ from those of industrial and service workers, who tend to have higher incomes and who are more easily reached by advertisers than are agricultural workers.

The distribution of a labor force is strongly correlated with stage of economic development. In 1984, about 70 percent of the labor force of low-income countries was employed in agriculture, the remaining 30 percent being equally divided between industry and services. In middle-income countries, 44 percent of the labor force was in agriculture, 22 percent in industry, and the remaining 34 percent in services. In industrial countries, these percentages were 36 percent in agriculture, 21 percent in industry, and 44 percent in services.

Between 1965 and 1984, there has been a general global trend toward a reduction in the agricultural labor force with corresponding increases in the industry and service sectors. This shift to a service-oriented labor force has been most pronounced among middle-income and industrial countries. The labor force in the service sectors of the industrial countries grew from 25 percent in 1965 to 44 percent in 1984 and from 26 percent to 34 percent in middle-income countries.

Global Income Patterns

As noted earlier, markets are made up of actual and potential buyers who have not only the interest but also the ability to enter into economic exchanges. Thus a country's income and how it is distributed among its population are of critical importance to the international marketer.

Distribution of the World's Income. There are several common measures for estimating a country's ability to purchase the products and services needed or wanted by its population. These include *gross national product* (GNP) and *gross domestic product* (GDP), expressed in total and per capita terms. When data on the distribution of income among a country's population and industrial sectors are added, additional insights can be gained.

Which measurements should be used to determine a country's potential attractiveness is heavily influenced by the types of products or services under consideration. Generally, a country's GNP and GDP—expressed in absolute terms or industry proportions—are better indicators of total demand for industrial goods and capital equipment than are per capita income figures. However per capita income or even population figures may be good indicators of demand for many consumer products, such as soaps or detergents, ball-point pens, and food staples.

Gross National Product. Ranking countries according to GNP provides a useful starting point for understanding a country's relative attractiveness. It is apparent that global income is highly concentrated among a few countries. The aggregate GNP of the 30 countries listed in Table 5-3 represents 83.5 percent of the world's GNP. Put differently, the remaining 154 countries and territories account for a mere 16.5 percent of global GNP. This high degree of concentration becomes even more striking when we consider that, in 1983, 61.8 percent of the world's GNP was concentrated in just five countries.

When the information presented in Tables 5-1 and 5-3 is considered together, it is easy to understand why the United States, Japan, West Germany, and the United Kingdom are considered key markets by many international companies. Each country represents a relatively large market with considerable capacity to fulfill its own economic needs.

Another way to look at the distribution of global GNP is regionally. As the data presented in Table 5-4 show, 35.4 percent of the global GNP is concentrated in Canada and the U.S. An additional 26.2 percent is concentrated in the 12 countries making up the European Community (EC). The European Free Trade

TABLE 5-3
The Fifteen Major Markets of the World: GNP and GNP/Capita (1983)

		Market Size: GNP (U.S. $ millions)				Market Size: GNP/Capita (U.S. $)	
Rank	Country	GNP	Percent of World GNP	Rank	Country	GNP Per Capita	Percent of World GNP
1.	United States	3,300,560	32.4	1.	United Arab Emirates	23,770	0.3
2.	Japan	1,204,330	11.8	2.	Switzerland	16,250	1.0
3.	West Germany	700,450	6.9	3.	Kuwait	16,200	0.3
4.	France	572,610	5.6	4.	United States	14,080	32.4
5.	United Kingdom	517,110	5.1	5.	Norway	13,990	0.6
6.	Italy	363,100	3.6	6.	Sweden	12,440	1.0
7.	China	306,060	3.0	7.	Canada	12,280	3.0
8.	Canada	305,940	3.0	8.	Saudi Arabia	12,220	1.3
9.	Brazil	241,910	2.4	9.	Denmark	11,540	0.6
10.	India	192,940	1.9	10.	Australia	11,460	1.7
11.	Spain	182,350	1.8	11.	West Germany	11,400	6.9
12.	Australia	176,170	1.7	12.	Finland	10,710	0.5
13.	Mexico	163,510	1.6	13.	France	10,480	5.6
14.	Netherlands	141,730	1.4	14.	Japan	10,100	11.8
15.	Saudi Arabia	127,330	1.3	15.	Netherlands	9,870	1.4
	Percent of world GNP*		83.5				68.4

* **Note:** The data excludes 31 countries for which data is not available. Except for Yugoslavia and China, these 31 countries include the centrally planned economies.
Source: *The World Bank Atlas* (Washington, D.C.: The World Bank, 1986), pp. 6–9.

Association (EFTA), comprised of six countries with relatively small populations, account for 3.8 percent of the global GNP. By contrast, the 163 countries and territories not listed in Table 5-4 account for only 21 percent of the world's income.

Per Capita Distribution of GNP. The relative attractiveness of a country's market may not be adequately expressed when measured by total population or GNP. Consequently, the statistic most frequently used to measure a country's economic attractiveness is *per capita income.* This measurement is widely accepted as an indicator of a country's degree of modernization and the quality of its consumer and industrial markets. However, as noted in Chapter 3, there are problems with per capita income data. Among the industrial countries, Japan, West Germany, and Belgium have relatively equal distributions of income with the upper 20 percent of households earning about five times as much as the households in the lower 20 percent. In contrast, the upper 20 percent of Canadian, French, and U.S. households earn about eight times the income of the lower 20 percent. Differences in the incomes of households of middle- and low-income countries are even more pronounced. The upper 20 percent of households in Brazil and Kenya earn about twelve times that of the lower 20 percent.

Table 5-4 gives some indication of the wide range of per capita income among countries and regions. Among the industrial countries of North America and

TABLE 5-4
Global Distribution of GNP and GNP/Capita by Region and Country: 1983*

Region/Country	GNP (U.S. $ millions)	GNP by Region (U.S. $ millions)	Percent of World GNP	GNP/capita (U.S. $)
North America:				
Canada	305,940			12,280
United States	3,300,560	3,606,500	35.4	14,080
European Community:				
Belgium	89,970			9,130
Denmark	59,020			11,540
France	572,610			10,480
West Germany	700,450			11,400
Ireland	17,490			4,990
Italy	363,100			6,390
Luxembourg	5,330			14,620
Netherlands	141,730			9,870
Portugal	22,490			2,230
Spain	182,350			4,770
United Kingdom	517,110	2,671,650	26.2	9,180
European Free Trade Association:				
Austria	69,660			9,230
Finland	52,090			10,770
Iceland	2,430			10,240
Norway	57,820			13,990
Sweden	103,640			12,440
Switzerland	105,300	390,940	3.8	16,250
Other Regions/Countries:				
Australia	176,170			11,460
Japan	1,204,330	1,380,500	13.6	10,100
Rest of world	2,133,390	2,133,398	21.0	852
Total world	10,182,980		100.0	3,238

*Note: The data excludes 32 countries for which data is not available. Except for Yugoslavia, these 32 countries include the centrally planned economies.
Source: *The World Bank Atlas 1986* (Washington, D.C.: World Bank, 1986), pp. 6–9.

Europe, Portugal is the poorest. Luxembourg is the richest. However, a high degree of poverty prevails in most nations; the average per capita income of the rest of the world is under $1000. Thus on the basis of per capita income it appears that most countries do not have very attractive markets.

Distribution of GDP by Economic Sector. Yet another way of understanding the potential size and dynamics of a market is to look at the distribution and changes in distribution of income among major economic sectors. Table 5-5 presents data on the distribution of GDP among the agricultural, industrial, and service sectors of the world's major country groups in 1984. There has been a widespread recent shift from agriculture to industry and services, and these data provide additional support for asserting a correlation between the distribution of

TABLE 5-5
GDP Structure of Production: Agriculture, Industry, and Services (1984)

Country Group	Share of GDP by:		
	Agriculture	Industry	Services
Developing countries*	21	37	42
Low-income countries	36	35	29
Africa	38	16	46
Asia:	36	36	28
India	35	27	38
China	36	44	20
Middle-income countries	14	39	47
Oil exporters	15	39	46
Oil importers	14	37	49
Major exporters			
of manufactures	12	38	50
High-income oil exporters	2	62	36
Industrial market economies	3	37	60
World, excluding nonmarket			
industrial economies	10	38	52

* **Note:** Developing countries are divided into low-income countries with 1984 GNP per capita incomes of less than $400, and middle-income countries with GNP per capita incomes of $400 or more. Data for developing countries are based on a sample of ninety countries.
Source: *World Development Report 1986* (World Bank, New York: Oxford, 1986), Table A.5, p. 156.

income among economic sectors and the stage of economic development. Compared to middle-income and industrial countries, low-income countries generally generate considerably more of their income from agriculture. In industrial countries, the service sector is an increasingly important source of national income.

Market shifts present many opportunities for international marketers. With the shift from an agriculture-based to a manufacturing- and services-based economy, there comes a general increase in demands for capital-intensive farming, construction, and power-generating equipment, machinery, and other industry and service-related products. The shift also results in changes in the location and occupations of the country's labor force. With movement from rural to urban locations, the need for manufactured consumer products becomes more widespread.

Conditions Affecting National Economic Activity

Although an overall appreciation of the size and growth in economic activities can be gained from a study of demographic variables, such data do not alone provide the insights on which to judge the relative attractiveness of a particular market. The well-informed marketing manager is more interested in learning about the likely composition of these activities and the constraints that will be imposed once marketing operations are underway. Such knowledge can be gained only by analyzing the demographic measurements within country-specific contexts. Three factors critically affecting the market attractiveness of a particular country are (1) its stage of economic development, (2) its marketing infrastructure, and (3) the role played by government in commerce.

The Stage of Economic Development

Several theories have been advanced to explain economic development. One widely heeded theory is attributed to Walter Rostow.[5] After studying the history of economic growth, Rostow concluded that nations pass through five distinct economic stages:

☐ The traditional society,

☐ preconditions for takeoff,

☐ the take-off,

☐ the drive to maturity, and

☐ high mass consumption.

In the *traditional stage,* a country's economy is primarily agrarian, and most manufacturing is in the form of family-based cottage industries. If a middle class exists, it is quite small. Also, there is very little upward social movement. For a traditional society to enter the second stage, three *preconditions* are required: an entrepreneur class must emerge; the government must become committed to modernization and be willing to spend public funds on education and the development of an infrastructure to service industry (transportation, communication, and electrical power); and one sector of the country's economy (generally agriculture or mining) must be capable of generating sufficient income (foreign exchange and domestic savings) to finance a drive to modernize.

In the *takeoff stage,* manufacturing becomes the leading growth sector; political, social, and commercial institutions are modified to help sustain growth. This stage is eventually replaced by a *drive-to-maturity.* During this fourth stage, manufacturing aggressively acquires the most advanced technology available and becomes capable of producing a widening variety of products. During the fifth and last stage, *mass consumption,* emphasis shifts to the manufacture of consumer durables and the development of the services needed to help the population attain a relatively high standard of living. Let us see how Rostow's paradigm applies today.

One characteristic of developing countries is that they initially specialize in the production and export of a small number of commodities. Typically, such production is labor intensive and uses a large proportion of the land. For example, over 70 percent of Bolivian and Colombian exports are tin and coffee, respectively. As countries evolve, however, the variety of exports expands to include an increasing number of manufactured products. Cases in point: in addition to coffee, Brazil exports shoes, clothing, and other light manufactures; the exports of Argentina and Mexico are also now more diverse, with no single commodity capturing more than 25 percent of exports.

In their early stages of economic development, most countries establish industrial policies and incentives that concentrate on light manufactures for export. Frequently, these activities are located in export zones separate from the country's indigenous industry. The industrial structure of many developing countries thus has a certain duality. While a country's export zone may be characterized as modern, its domestic industries may be antiquated or poorly developed. Such distinctions can easily be overlooked when using aggregate data to evaluate a country's industrial activities.

The development of the domestic sector may require considerable government support, the infusion of capital, new equipment, and the development of the country's infrastructure. Such developments provide considerable opportunities for foreign companies. However, because of scarce resources, modernization efforts are heavily skewed in favor of a few primary industries that have the inputs required to develop them.

In addition, fundamental prerequisites for development are investments in infrastructure facilities such as electric power, water supply, waste disposal, railroad and road systems, and other commercial facilitators. Most LDCs assign top priority to their development and often provide major opportunities for foreign companies willing to work with local authorities in building an appropriate infrastructure.

South Korea exemplifies the stages through which developing countries pass. The transformation of its manufacturing sector has been very rapid and has followed a predictable sequence. Initially, emphasis was placed on the development of a light manufacturing sector (clothing). This stage was followed by the development of an intermediate manufacturing sector (assembly of automobiles and electronic appliances). Emphasis is currently on developing manufacturing (steel, electronics, automobiles). Concurrently, South Korea has stressed education, the development of its infrastructure, and the aggressive acquisition of current technology to ensure the competitiveness of its industrial and service sectors.

Rostow's theory has met with considerable criticism. Many countries, particularly the European countries, did not "take off"; instead, they evolved gradually. Also, in real life, it is often difficult to distinguish among the five stages. However, the usefulness of Rostow's theory should not be dismissed. For the international marketer, it does provide useful guidelines for grouping countries. Each stage does indeed offer new marketing opportunities for the aggressive international marketer and a different competitive environment. The paradigm also provides some indication of the types of government regulations to be expected and the kinds of incentives provided foreign investors.

One method for deciding the stage in which a particular country is situated is to study the composition and trends of its productive activities. The pattern of distribution of employment and GNP between secondary, tertiary, and services activities discussed in Chapter 3 is often very helpful.[6] Primary activities include agriculture and extractive industries. Secondary activities include manufacturing, processing, and construction. Tertiary activities include wholesaling and retailing, transportation, and the communication industries. Service activities include government, professional, and miscellaneous services.

A comparison of the employment composition of three industrial countries and three developing countries is presented in Figure 5-2. Pairs of countries were selected on the basis of population and land area size in order to increase the reliability of the comparisons (that is, differences between industrialized and developing countries).

Additional insights can be gained by studying the composition of the country's exports and imports. As already noted, a country in the early stages of development generally exports unprocessed commodities (such as iron ore, bauxite, tin, coffee), and imports consumer products for the wealthy sectors of their populations. As

Three Examples of Industrial Countries

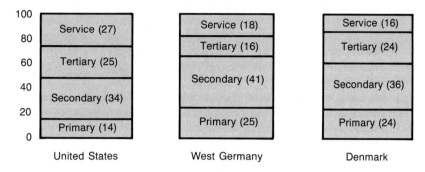

United States   West Germany   Denmark

Three Examples of Developing Countries

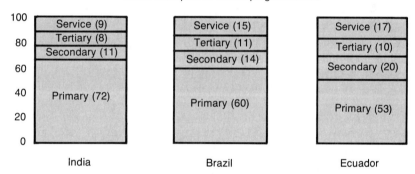

India   Brazil   Ecuador

FIGURE 5-2   **Composition of Productive Activities Based on Sector Employment** (Source: From Endel-Jakob Kolde, *Environment of International Business*, 2nd ed. [Boston: Kent Publishing Co., 1985], p. 153. © by Wadsworth, Inc. Reprinted by permission of PWS-KENT Publishing Company, a division of Wadsworth, Inc.)

the country advances, its manufactured exports become more dominant and more diverse. The composition of imports also changes. Initially, heavy emphasis is on the acquisition of plant and equipment and on component parts for assembly and reshipment as finished exports. Eventually imports become more diverse. A considerable portion of trade in manufacturers between industrial countries is in similar product categories and is the result of product differentiation.

The Marketing Infrastructure

As a country develops economically, marketing typically takes on increased importance. This occurs partly in response to an increase in the width and depth of product offerings made available by competing companies. To be successful, companies find it necessary to position themselves in increasingly specialized markets, to develop brands and brand loyalty, and to improve on such activities as marketing research, advertising effectiveness, and customer service.

As it gains in importance, the country's marketing infrastructure evolves and becomes more sophisticated. For example, marketing research agencies begin to appear and become increasingly sophisticated in the types of services they offer. The country's distribution, retailing, and media infrastructures become more comparable to those of the industralized countries.

The importance of such developments cannot be overstated for the international marketer accustomed to purchasing a sophisticated array of marketing services. Manufacturing companies from most developed countries rely on a network of services and facilities provided by independent channel members, advertising agencies, market research agencies, banks, and other financial institutions. Until such support facilities and services are provided, firms have to either modify their marketing activities or to forgo the market entirely.

Three infrastructures are of particular importance: (1) the transportation infrastructure, (2) the communication infrastructure, and (3) the commercial infrastructure. Information on these infrastructures can be obtained from various sources, among which are commercial attachés, banks, accounting firms, and advertising agencies.

The Transportation Infrastructure

Two aspects of a country's transportation infrastructure of particular interest to the international marketer when evaluating the potential attractiveness of a foreign market are the country's internal transportation infrastructures and its transportation linkage to other countries. The significance of the internal transportation infrastructure is significantly affected by the geographical dispersement and density of the country's markets and local suppliers. The importance of the external transportation infrastructure is a function of the company's transnational flows of finished products, component parts, and raw materials between parent company, foreign affiliates, foreign customers and foreign suppliers.

The Internal Transportation Infrastructure. The transportation infrastructures of countries vary considerably. For example, in the United States agricultural products can be harvested and packaged in California and delivered to supermarkets on the east coast in about three days with very little damage or loss. In contrast, it has been estimated that in Colombia more than 40 percent of locally grown foodstuffs is lost in transit because of poor refrigeration, bad roads, or the use of antiquated storage and distribution methods.

Some appreciation of internal national transport capabilities can be gained from a study of data on the number of registered motor vehicles (commercial, private, mass transit), volume of surface freight (road and rail), and miles of paved and unpaved roads. Interesting international comparisons can be made on the basis of these and similar statistics. Consider automobile ownership data. Automobile ownership varies considerably within and between economic groups of countries. While the number of persons per car is 1.8 in the United States, it is 2.3 in Canada, 3.4 in the United Kingdom, and 4.6 in Japan. Weigh these data against 8.2 persons per car in Argentina, 13 in Brazil, 14 in Mexico, 135 in South Korea, and 785 in India. The same degree of variation also pertains when comparing the number of persons per mass transit and commercial vehicles. In the United States, there are 431 persons per mass transit vehicle but only 6.8 persons per commercial vehicle. In West Germany the figures are 866 and 47.4, respectively, in Brazil, 1,086 and 139; in India, 6,492 and 2,198.

The External Transportation Infrastructure. Considerable trade between countries may also be part of the requirements of an international company. In these cases, it is also necessary to evaluate the country's accessibility by sea, air, road and rail. This can be done by studying a country's port facilities, frequency of merchant shipping and commercial air, road and rail travel, and volume of trade. Remember, however, also to check on the points of entry stipulated by the local government: In the early 1980s, to discourage imports of electronic appliances from the Far East, France designated a poorly equipped and landlocked city, Orleans, as the point of entry for such appliances.

The Communications Infrastructure

In addition to being able to move goods within and between countries, the company must also be able to communicate with its targeted markets, its suppliers, other foreign affiliates, and its home office. Ability to communicate effectively depends heavily on the host country's internal communication infrastructure and its communication linkages with other countries.

Internal Communication Infrastructure. A preliminary assessment of this infrastructure can be gained from studying the country's media in absolute and relative terms. For example, data grouped by incomes is presented in Table 5-6 for telephones, newspaper circulation, and television and radio ownership. In 1981, the United States had 78.9 telephones per 100 people compared to 48.8 telephones in West Germany, 7.2 telephones in Brazil, and 0.5 telephones in India. Just as important for the marketer is the mix of media. In the United States, television and radio are relatively more widespread than newspaper circulation when compared to other industrial countries such as Finland, West Germany and Japan. Daily newspaper circulation in the United States in 1981 was 282 per thousand population compared with 480 in Finland, 423 in West Germany and 569 in Japan. However, when television and radio ownership per thousand population are compared, the results are quite different. In the United States, the number of television and radio receivers per thousand population is 631 and 2,110, respectively; in Finland, 414 and 875; in West Germany, 348 and 383; and in Japan, 551 and 688.

External Communication Infrastructure. The ability to communicate with headquarters or another affiliate of the company can be of crucial importance. Obviously, the speed and reliability of the various forms of communication need to be investigated by the would-be marketer. In some countries, the most reliable form of communication may be by telex. Mail and telephone systems may be unreliable, antiquated, or prone to breakdowns. Mail delivery, even by airmail, may be unprofitably slow. For example, in 1988 it took as much as three weeks to deliver a letter from the United States to Brazil, some parts of Canada, and Mexico. Some companies accordingly make heavy use of embassy mail pouches or have employees act as couriers for important documents and reports transported internationally.

TABLE 5-6
Indicators of the Communication Infrastructures of Selected Countries

Economic Group/ Country	Telephones per 100 population (1981)	Daily newspaper circulation, copies per 1000 population (1979)	Television sets per 1000 population (1981)	Radio sets per 1000 population (1981)
Industrial countries:				
Belgium	38.7	228	300	466
Canada	69.3	241	489	1149
France	49.8	205	361	927
West Germany	48.8	423	348	383
Japan	47.9	569	551	688
Sweden	82.8	526	387	847
United Kingdom	49.7	n.a.	411	963
United States	78.9	282	631	2110
Middle-income countries:				
Argentina	9.8	n.a.	197	748
Brazil	7.2	44	122	308
Indonesia	0.4	n.a.	21	120
Mexico	7.7	n.a.	111	288
Philippines	1.5	n.a.	22	44
South Korea	7.7	197	175	413
Low-income countries:				
Bangladesh	0.1	5	1	8
India	0.5	20	2	59
Kenya	1.3	10	4	33
Sri Lanka	0.7	n.a.	3	107
Nonmarket economies:				
Bulgaria	17.0	234	187	238
Czechoslovakia	21.0	304	281	316
Romania	n.a.	181	170	143
USSR	9.3	396	306	504

n.a.: Data not available.
Source: *Statistical Abstract of the United States 1985* (Washington, D.C.: U.S. Department of Commerce, 1986), p. 849.

The Commercial Infrastructure

Also vital to a firm is the host country's commercial infrastructure; that is, the availability and quality of such supporting services as banks and financial institutions, advertising agencies, distribution channels, and marketing research agencies. Companies heavily dependent on institutions such as these for domestic marketing activities often find considerable variations in the effectiveness, efficiency, and the services offered in foreign markets.

An evaluation of a country's commercial infrastructure cannot be made solely on the basis of the presence of commercial institutions. As will be discussed in later chapters, a relatively intimate understanding of local business practices, sociocultural factors, and government regulations is mandatory.

The Role of Government

The role played by governments in the regulation of commercial activities is somewhat conditioned by a country's stage of economic development. Many developing countries develop five-year economic plans that have a profound influence on current and future economic activities. Targeted industries may receive special fiscal and financial incentives to encourage development or modernization. Such incentives typically include tax credits on customs duties, reduced turnover taxes, low interest rates on loans, and deductions on corporate taxes. In some cases, local industries are also given protection from foreign competition.

As will be discussed in later chapters, there are also considerable differences in the regulations and laws imposed on commercial activities and transactions. Areas affected include labeling laws, media use regulations, health and safety standards, and pricing regulations. Considerable variation exists also among patent, copyright, and trademark laws. Countries may also regulate and/or discriminate against foreign investments. These constraints limit marketing activities and other policy options in overseas markets.

THE ATTRACTIVENESS OF CONSUMER AND INDUSTRIAL MARKETS

That a comparative study of national economic activities is an essential part of long-term marketing planning is a given. However, the international marketer must also make near-term decisions on the scope and level of effort of marketing programs within and across foreign markets. Potentially attractive target markets must be selected, marketing mixes developed, and market budgeting undertaken. When making these critical decisions, an international manager needs accurate and comparable measures of the size, structure, and dynamics of the specific potential markets.

Indicators of Market Attractiveness

To provide a framework for studying the size, structure, and dynamics of a country's specific markets, we will briefly discuss three consumer and three industry market measures. Consumer market indicators to be discussed are (1) urbanization patterns, (2) household income patterns, and (3) consumption patterns. The industry market indicators are (1) industry structure patterns, (2) industry specialization patterns, and (3) industry expenditure patterns. These six measures have been chosen for illustrative purposes only; any final choice of variables is strongly influenced by specific product offerings.

The Measurement of Consumer Markets

Although two countries may have similar population sizes, current and future per capita incomes, marketing infrastructures, and commercial laws and regulations, their relative attractiveness for international firms may be quite different. The final choice depends on an analysis of each country's consumer markets using traditional segmenting variables such as geographic, demographic, psychographic, and product-related consumer characteristics. To reduce the time and effort expended on these activities, the investigating analyst needs to reduce the number of countries to a manageable number. A necessary but preliminary step is to study the overall size and composition of each country's consumer markets, their accessibility, and their expenditures on relevant products and/or services.

Urbanization Patterns

The long-term movement of people from rural to urban areas is critical to an understanding of the current and future attractiveness of national markets, particularly consumer markets. Urban populations tend to be more educated, are certainly more accessible, and are more heavily dependent on the purchase of manufactured goods. They also tend to be relatively more sophisticated buyers of products and services and generally enjoy a wide choice of competing products and services.

The communication media are most developed and effective in cities; urban populations depend heavily on these media for the information needed to make product and service decisions. Rural populations generally depend more heavily on word of mouth for product and service information. While modern transportation and communication systems have greatly reduced the differences between urban and rural populations in the industrial countries, significant differences between these two populations still remain in the developing countries.

The data on the rate of urbanization presented in Table 5-7 illustrate the wide variations found among various countries. It is worth stressing that urbanization patterns tend to vary according to a country's economic situation and stage of development. In general, developed countries are relatively more urbanized than developing countries. Nonetheless, rapid urbanization is occurring in many developing countries.

Since the early 1960s, many developing countries have experienced considerable urbanization; rural populations have sought employment in higher-paying activities generally found in urban centers. This shift from the farms to the cities is not unprecedented. Most of the developed countries experienced similar population movements as they industrialized. What is unprecedented is the speed at which this movement has occurred. In many countries, such as Brazil, Mexico, and Thailand, rapid movement of rural populations to urban centers has resulted in large unemployed or underemployed urban populations, overcrowding, poor housing, and inadequate water supplies, sewerage disposal, and mass transit and communication systems. To reduce problems such as these, Mexico and Thailand have implemented industry development policies designed to redistribute their populations away from the major population centers.

Because of high levels of poverty, urban markets in LDCs are not as attractive as in more developed countries. The rural populations of developing countries may also be less attractive for several reasons. Their incomes are generally quite low; the markets are difficult to reach; rural populations tend to be more conservative and tradition-oriented than their urban counterparts.

Dividing a market solely on the basis of geography tends to be risky. Canada is the second largest country in the world in terms of land area, but the majority

TABLE 5-7
Rate of Urbanization in Selected Countries: 1965–1984

Country	Urban Population				Average annual population growth
	As percentage of total population		Average annual growth rate (percent)		
	1965	1984	1965–73	1973–84	1973–84
Industrial market economies:					
Belgium	86	89	0.9	1.2	0.1
Canada	73	75	1.9	1.2	1.2
France	67	81	2.0	1.2	0.5
West Germany	79	86	1.2	0.3	−0.1
Japan	67	76	2.4	1.4	0.9
Sweden	77	86	1.6	0.7	0.2
United Kingdom	87	92	0.7	0.2	0.0
United States	72	74	1.6	1.3	1.0
Middle-income countries:					
Argentina	76	84	2.1	2.1	1.6
Brazil	51	72	4.5	4.0	2.3
Costa Rica	38	45	3.8	3.3	2.9
Hong Kong	89	93	2.1	2.6	2.4
Indonesia	16	25	4.1	4.5	2.3
Mexico	55	69	4.8	4.0	2.9
Philippines	32	39	4.0	3.7	2.7
South Korea	32	64	6.5	4.6	1.5
Turkey	32	46	4.9	4.0	2.2
Venezuela	72	85	4.8	4.3	3.3
Low-income countries:					
Bangladesh	6	18	6.6	7.7	2.5
India	19	25	4.0	4.2	2.3
Kenya	9	18	7.3	7.9	4.0
Sri Lanka	20	21	3.4	3.5	1.8

Note: Developing countries are divided into low-income countries with 1984 GNP per capita incomes of less than $400, and middle-income countries with GNP per capita incomes of $400 or more.
Source: *World Development Report 1986* (World Bank, New York: Oxford, 1986), Table 31, pp. 240–241, and Table 25, pp. 228–229.

of its 25 million people are concentrated in a narrow band along its U.S. border. Most of the country is very thinly populated. Also, the heavily populated band includes both English- and French-speaking people with diverse product preferences and lifestyles. Thus, to gain a viable estimate of Canada's market attractiveness, international marketers who use geographic variables should also use other segmenting variables such as household income and consumption patterns.

Household Income Patterns

Household buying power affects people's ability to buy, the types and quality of products they buy, and where they buy. As shown in Table 5-8, such buying power is not evenly distributed within and across countries. In the United States, the richest 20 percent of the population receives nearly 40 percent of the country's total money income. In Brazil, the figure is nearly 67 percent, and in Kenya it is just over 60 percent. At the other end of the spectrum, the poorest 20 percent of these populations receive, respectively, about 5 percent, 2 percent, and 3 percent of their total money incomes.

Additional variation in the income received by the population of a particular country is noted if the populations are segmented along ethnic, religious, and regional lines. In the United States, the average income received by black households is less than that received by white households, and households in the Northeast have more buying power than households in the Southeast. Another aspect of buying power strongly influenced by sociocultural differences (not captured in the data presented in Table 5-8) is the use of consumer credit. Europeans and

TABLE 5-8
Distribution of Household Income for Selected Countries

Country	Percentage share of household income by percentile groups of households					
	Lowest 20%	Second quintile	Third quintile	Fourth quintile	Highest 20%	Highest 10%
Industrial market economies:						
Belgium (1978)	7.9	13.7	18.6	23.8	36.0	21.5
Canada (1981)	5.3	11.8	18.0	24.9	40.0	23.8
France (1975)	5.3	11.1	16.0	21.8	45.8	30.5
West Germany (1978)	7.9	12.5	17.0	23.1	39.5	24.0
Japan (1979)	8.7	13.2	17.5	23.1	37.5	22.4
Sweden (1981)	7.4	13.1	16.8	21.0	41.7	28.1
United Kingdom (1979)	7.0	11.5	17.0	24.8	39.7	23.4
United States (1980)	5.3	11.9	17.9	25.0	39.9	23.3
Middle-income countries:						
Argentina (1970)	4.4	9.7	14.1	21.5	50.3	35.2
Brazil (1972)	2.0	5.0	9.4	17.0	66.6	50.6
Costa Rica (1971)	3.3	8.7	13.3	19.9	54.8	39.5
Hong Kong (1980)	5.4	10.8	15.2	21.6	47.0	31.3
Indonesia (1976)	6.6	7.8	12.6	23.6	49.4	34.0
Mexico (1977)	2.9	7.0	12.0	20.4	57.7	40.6
Philippines (1970)	5.2	9.0	12.8	19.0	54.0	38.5
South Korea (1976)	5.7	11.2	15.4	22.4	45.3	27.5
Turkey (1973)	3.5	8.0	12.5	19.5	56.5	40.7
Venezuela (1970)	3.0	7.3	12.9	22.8	54.0	35.7
Low-income countries:						
Bangladesh (1976)	6.2	10.9	15.0	21.0	46.9	32.0
India (1975)	7.0	9.2	13.9	20.5	49.4	33.6
Kenya (1976)	2.6	6.3	11.5	19.2	60.4	45.8
Sri Lanka (1969)	7.5	11.7	15.7	21.7	43.4	28.2

Note: Developing countries are divided into low-income countries with 1984 GNP per capita incomes of less than $400, and middle-income countries with GNP per capita incomes of $400 or more.

Source: *World Development Report 1986* (World Bank, New York: Oxford, 1986), Table 24, pp. 226–227.

Japanese are much less likely to purchase durable consumer products on credit than are most Americans.

Consumption Patterns

Study of a country's overall level of consumption also provides valuable insights into the relative attractiveness of national markets. It is also important to have some understanding of the composition of consumption.

Table 5-9 presents data on consumption expenditures for several countries. A useful theory to explain the structural differences among household expenditures in industrial countries and those of the middle- and lower-income countries is the law of consumption advanced by Ernst Engel. Engel's law states that as family income rises (1) the percentage spent on food declines, (2) the percentage spent on housing and household activities remains constant, and (3) the percentage spent on other categories (such as clothing, transportation, recreation, education) increases.

There are also significant differences within countries between the consumption patterns of rural and urban markets. In general, rural populations spend a larger percentage of their income on food, than on housing and other categories.

The Measurement of Industrial Markets

Like consumer products companies, manufacturers of industrial goods also need a wide variety of information on foreign markets before they can accurately rank markets by relative attractiveness. Analysis of national demographic variables on the size and composition of each country's industrial sectors, their relative importance, and their current and future plans is essential.

Industry Structure Patterns

A study of national production activities is essential for three reasons. It indicates the types of products that can be produced locally. These data can be used as proxies for measuring market opportunities and the probable level of import competition. In addition, it provides some indication of the industrial base of the country and its ability to supply locally the inputs for the manufacture of consumer and industrial goods. Third, identified trends in manufacturing production can be used to indicate current and future needs for various types of capital equipment.

Table 5-10 presents data on the distribution of industrial activities of a number of countries grouped according to per capita income. As can be expected, the production activities of countries in the early stages of growth (when per capita income is low) are centered on such necessities as food and clothing. As incomes grow, these industries decline in relative importance and are replaced in importance by such industrial activities as machinery, chemicals, and "other manufacturing."

As an extreme example, 59 percent of Sri Lanka's industrial activities concentrate on the production of food and clothing. The production of machinery and chemicals only adds 11 percent to Sri Lanka's income. Conversely, in Sweden, food and clothing production contribute only 12 percent; machinery and chemicals contribute 49 percent.

TABLE 5-9
Consumption Expenditures of Selected Countries

Country	Food and Beverage	Clothing and Footwear	Housing and Operations	Household Furnishings	Medical Care and Health	Transportation	Recreation	Other*
Industrial market economies:								
Belgium	24.5	6.6	16.8	13.2	9.6	12.4	5.0	11.9
Canada	18.1	9.4	19.9	8.4	3.5	15.7	11.5	13.1
France	21.0	6.7	16.3	9.5	15.0	12.7	7.9	11.0
West Germany	26.4	8.6	18.3	11.2	2.9	15.7	8.4	8.6
Japan	25.0	6.6	17.8	7.0	9.9	8.6	10.3	15.1
Sweden	24.3	7.9	25.8	7.0	2.5	15.6	10.3	6.7
United Kingdom	20.6	8.3	18.5	7.6	1.1	17.1	9.7	17.2
United States	16.7	8.3	19.8	6.2	11.2	15.5	9.6	12.8
Middle-income countries:								
Mexico	38.4	10.7	11.2	11.7	5.0	9.3	4.9	8.9
Philippines	54.6	6.2	12.1	7.0	2.9	3.3	4.3	9.8
South Korea	45.5	7.2	9.7	4.7	4.3	10.3	9.4	9.0
Low-income countries:								
Bangladesh	n.a.							
India	62.3	9.5	7.0	4.2	2.5	7.9	3.0	3.6
Kenya	49.2	7.7	12.6	9.4	2.2	8.4	4.1	6.4
Sri Lanka	58.2	12.2	4.3	4.5	1.6	12.3	3.9	3.2

* *Other* includes expenditures for personal care, restaurants, and hotels.

n.a.: data not available.

Note: For the following countries expenditures are expressed as percentages of total consumption in constant prices: Base year for Belgium, Sweden, and the United Kingdom is 1980; Canada, 1981; France, 1970; West Germany and the United States, 1975. The expenditures for the remaining countries are expressed in current prices: Mexico, 1970; Philippines, 1982; South Korea, 1980; India, 1970; Kenya, 1980; and Sri Lanka, 1975.

Source: *National Accounts Statistics: Main Aggregates and Detailed Tables 1983* (New York: United Nations, 1986), Table 2.6.

TABLE 5-10
Industry Structure by Selected Countries

Economic Group/ Country	Distribution of manufacturing value added (percent, 1980 prices)					Degree of Specialization	
	Food and Agriculture	Textiles and Clothing	Machinery and Transport Equipment	Chemicals	Other Manufacturing	1975	1983
Industrial countries:							
Belgium	19	9	25	12	25	12.6	13.7
Canada	14	7	22	7	49	10.4	11.0
France	16	7	34	8	34	12.7	13.4
West Germany	10	5	41	9	34	13.7	15.2
Japan	10	6	38	7	40	12.1	15.2
Sweden	9	3	32	7	50	16.5	17.5
United Kingdom	14	6	33	10	36	11.5	11.7
United States	10	6	33	9	42	11.4	11.5
Middle-income countries:							
Argentina	22	10	16	9	42	11.8	13.3
Brazil	21	11	17	11	40	12.3	11.5
Indonesia	21	7	7	6	60	29.1	28.2
Mexico	28	13	12	13	35	11.1	12.0
Philippines	44	14	8	7	28	21.8	24.0
South Korea	10	19	24	12	36	10.0	11.0
Low-income countries:							
Bangladesh	18	40	6	22	14	35.4	33.3
India	13	27	18	11	32	15.9	14.8
Kenya	37	12	15	8	29	18.3	15.9
Sri Lanka	44	15	4	7	32	26.2	26.8
Nonmarket economies:							
Bulgaria	20	14	20	7	39	11.4	11.1
Czechoslovakia	8	10	39	8	35	15.3	17.3
Romania	16	9	34	11	30	n.a.	n.a.
USSR	22	15	29	6	28	18.3	18.7

Note: If the value added of all sectors of the economy are equal, the degree of specialization equals zero. If only one sector exists, the value is 100.

Source: *World Development Report* (World Bank, New York: Oxford, 1986), and *Industry and Development: Global Report 1986* (New York: United Nations, 1986) Statistic Annex, various pages.

Degree of Industrial Specialization

Additional insight into the relative attractiveness of foreign consumer and industrial markets can be gained from looking at demographic variables that measure the depth of a country's industrial base. One such measure, presented in Table 5-10, is the degree of industrial specialization. The higher the value of this variable, the more concentrated the production base of the country. For example, Canada's industrial specialization value of 11.0, indicates that its industrial base is relatively more varied than those of Sweden and Indonesia, with their respective values of 17.5 and 28.2. These figures imply that Canada is probably better able to supply more completely the needs of its consumer and industrial markets than are Sweden and Indonesia. Competition from local producers is therefore probably more intense in Canada. Sweden and Indonesia present more varied opportunities for foreign companies and competition is relatively more intense among importers than between them and local producers.

Industry Expenditures

Although helpful in providing an overall assessment of market opportunities for industrial goods, figures on the distribution and scope of a country's production activities are not sufficiently revealing to provide a true measure of product demand. A more accurate assessment, one requiring neither extensive time nor effort, can be gained by studying capital equipment and input expenditures by the industrial sector. Sufficiently detailed information for a preliminary assessment can be obtained from various sources, including the United Nations, the World Bank, and national accounts.

In developing countries in the early stages of their economic development, capital equipment expenditures are heavily skewed in favor of equipment and plant. In the industrialized countries, these expenditures are, on a per capita basis, generally smaller, and they are for the maintenance and modernization of already existing industrial sectors. This is especially true of industries experiencing little technological advancement.

Conditions Affecting Market Potential

While secondary data on population and income characteristics provide insight into the economic activities of countries, they do not provide enough details to estimate accurately the demand for a particular consumer or industrial product or service. Data are needed on potential customers and on the company's ability to compete effectively in each country.

Fortunately, when conducting preliminary evaluations of relative attractiveness, it is not necessary to collect information and data on all aspects of a country's environment and markets. (Doing so is extremely costly and frustrating.) The choice of variables and the depth of detail required is determined and limited by the purpose of the assessment. The marketing analyst should examine only the most relevant indicators. A manufacturer of home furnishings, such as carpeting, drapes, and bedding, needs to look carefully at the formation of households and the division between housing ownership and rental. A processed-food manufacturer needs to isolate price and sales trends of nonprocessed and processed foodstuffs.

Considerable care needs to be exercised in the choice of market indicators. While universal indicators are of value, others are often needed to accurately reflect the specific situation in a given country.

CROSS-NATIONAL COMPARISON PROBLEMS

To rank countries according to their relative attractiveness, allocate marketing resources, and develop synchronized marketing programs for more than two countries, the international marketer frequently finds it necessary to compare markets. However, before applying secondary data to a particular marketing problem, the analyst must determine the comparability, equivalence, and reliability of data. In many cases, he or she must convert national statistics to some common unit of measurement. These requirements present unique and challenging problems for international marketers, as has already been indicated when discussing per capita GNP data in Chaper 3.

The Comparability and Equivalence Issue

Considerable difficulties are likely to be encountered when establishing the comparability and equivalence of secondary data from different countries. These difficulties are particularly marked for LCDs. Although less marked for industrialized countries, comparability and equivalence problems also exist. The problems most frequently encountered when attempting to compare measurements of a particular demographic variable across countries are (1) disagreements over which items are included in the measurement, (2) disagreements over the class classification systems used, and (3) differences in the figures themselves. The first two problems arise because there are no universally accepted systems for measuring population, industry activity, and national accounts. The third problem exists because socio-cultural, political, and other environmental factors have a direct bearing on how data are interpreted. (As we will see in Chapter 6, we tend to evaluate situations in light of our own experiences and socio-cultural backgrounds.)

Different Measurement Systems

The lack of universally accepted macroeconomic measurement systems magnifies problems of comparability and equivalence encountered when using secondary data. Discrepancies can sometimes be observed in macroeconomic data such as population, GNP, motor vehicle registrations, and consumer durables. These discrepancies may result from differences in the way the variables are defined. For example, some countries consider refugees part of the population of their country of origin; others include them in the census. Likewise, the GNP may or may not include the income of nationals working or residing in foreign countries. Television sets may be classified as recreational items (West Germany) or as home furnishings (United States). Automobiles may be classified as commercial vehicles even though they are used extensively for personal transportation.

Problems of Interpretation

Another limitation when using national figures is the lack of comparability of the figures themselves. In the case of profit data, adjustments may be needed to take into account variations in the tax structures of the countries under review. In some countries, taxes collected on inputs are rebated if the final products are exported. Also, the tax rates applied to corporate income vary considerably by country. In general, interpretation problems are most acute in comparisons of data for developed and developing countries.

Under normal conditions, per capita income statistics are the best single indicators of the potential attractiveness of markets. However, as was seen in Chapter 3 such data is often not directly comparable.

Consumer expenditures vary in terms of the amounts spent on food, housing, recreation, and so forth, but the distribution of household incomes does not provide the marketer with an accurate measure of potential attractiveness for particular types of products or services. Often there is considerable variation in expenditures within each category among countries. In the United States, a relatively large portion of the population own their homes. Thus data on the formation of households is a relatively reliable proxy for measuring the demand for home furnishings (drapes, carpeting, gardening equipment, and related products) and do-it-yourself products. In other countries, this variable may not be so reliable. As noted earlier, the populations of some countries are declining. Food expenditures are also significantly influenced by socio-cultural factors and they vary considerably. In Mexico and Brazil, fresh vegetables are in great demand. In more industrialized countries, where both spouses work outside the home, labor-saving and time-saving processed foods are increasingly preferred. Leisure and recreational activities also vary, partly because of socio-cultural factors and partly because of climatic and geographical factors. (A framework for capturing many of these variations is presented in Chapter 6.) Similar problems of interpretation abound when attempting to compare the composition of industrial activities across countries and their marketing implications.

The Reliability Issue

Reliability generally refers to the extent to which the data used are free of error. There are many reasons to doubt that secondary data published by various sources are uniformly reliable across countries. Two sets of factors that contribute significantly to this problem are (1) the data collection process, and (2) the reasons for the collection and publication of secondary data.

The Data Collection Process

Secondary data published by industrialized countries are likely to be more accurate than data published by developing countries. This level of accuracy is due largely to the mechanisms used to collect the data. In many industrialized countries, relatively reliable and sophisticated collection procedures are used to collect data on their populations and industrial activities. Elsewhere, in countries where large portions of the populations are illiterate, such data may be based on estimates or on rudimentary procedures incorporating a high degree of measurement error. All developing countries, however, must not be lumped together. For instance, South Korea and India collect generally reliable data.

Other Problems with Secondary Data

The reasons underlying collection and publication of secondary data must also be scrutinized when investigating national markets. Official statistics are sometimes overly optimistic, in part because of national pride and a need to impress sources of foreign private and public loans. According to statistics compiled by a government agency, Colombia's exports of clothing grew from about $9 million to about $77 million (an increase of $68 million) between 1972 and 1974, seemingly evidence of a rosy export performance. On closer investigation, a consultant to the World Bank discovered in 1979 that actual exports grew only $46 million during the period. The $22 million difference was attributed to a discrepancy between registered exports (goods to be exported) and manifested exports (goods actually exported).[7] In another situation, a U.S. team was able to confirm that 60 million frozen chickens had been shipped to Saudi Arabia in 1975, even though official figures claimed that only 10 million chickens had been imported.[8] Whether errors such as these are intentional, the result of poor record keeping or misuse of data is not always clear.

National statistics may also be systematically unreliable because those asked to divulge information (such as households and companies) may deliberately, or unintentionally distort their responses to surveys. The desire for anonymity for socio-cultural, competitive, or tax reasons is also quite pervasive. Tax evasion is more rife in some countries than others.[9] Thus, reported household incomes and business profits may be understated.

The Conversion Issue

Conversion problems arise because national measurements of value, such as GNP, household incomes, and manufacturing value-added, are initially expressed in local currencies. To be of use to a foreign marketer, these statistics often have to be converted to some common unit of measurement. Frequently, conversion involves the use of the United States dollar, or some other hard currency.

When conversion is required, a key decision is the selection of an appropriate exchange rate. In most cases, official exchange rates are used. However, there are several major problems with using an official exchange rate (or any other exchange rate) to convert national currency figures to a common currency. Since exchange rates are influenced by supply and demand conditions for foreign exchange, and government fiat, they may not reflect the relative domestic purchasing power of two currencies. That is, one U.S. dollar may not purchase the same basket of goods in the United States and another country when the dollar is converted into local currency.

Some governments regulate official exchange rates very closely, others allow considerable variations to occur before they intervene in foreign exchange markets by buying and selling currencies. The role governments play in the manipulation of their currencies vis-à-vis other currencies is partly a function of the international monetary system, and partly a function of their perceptions concerning the economic and political well-being of their countries. A government interested in developing demand for its products in other countries may intervene in foreign exchange markets in an attempt to lower the value of its currency.

Even if governments do not intervene in foreign exchange markets, foreign exchange rates still do not necessarily reflect the relative domestic purchasing power of currencies. The supply and demand of foreign currencies fluctuate in response to many factors and at any particular time, the external value of a currency may be quite different from its domestic value.

SUMMARY

In order to make foreign market choices, develop appropriate marketing programs, and judiciously allocate marketing resources across a number of markets, marketing managers need information on each market's size and structure, and how salient economic forces dynamically interact and affect future trends. In addition, the information collected and analyzed for each country must be presented in a way that permits managers to rank countries by relative attractiveness.

A preliminary yet essential part of such assessment involves a study of secondary data describing the major economic dimensions of each country's macroenvironment and its consumer and industrial markets. This chapter looked at several of the indicators commonly used to measure the size and structure of foreign markets: the size and distribution of a country's population and income, its consumption expenditures, and the degree of specialization of its industrial base. We noted, however, that the final choice of indicators, especially those used to gain an initial assessment of a country's consumer and industrial markets, is determined by the company's market offerings.

The chapter identified two types of problems associated with the use of secondary data. First, to identify correctly the market and marketing implications of data, it must be interpreted within the environmental context in which they were measured. This requires an understanding of the country's stage of economic development, the extent to which its marketing infrastructure has been developed, and the significance of the rules and regulations imposed on marketing activities by a country's government.

Second, the comparability, equivalence, and reliability of data must be initially viewed with some skepticism. As with all secondary data, there are questions concerning the comparability and equivalence of the units of measurement and the class classifications used. These problems tend to be magnified when attempting to make international comparisons. Given the lack of international agreement on measurement systems, there is considerable variation among countries on factors included in a particular variable and on the classifications employed. The reliability and accuracy of the data published by various authorities must also be questioned. The relative reliability and sophistication of the collection mechanisms varies considerably, as do the motivations underlying the collection and publication of the data. Desire for anonymity by those participating in surveys may also cause unreliability.

Finally, the problem of currency conversion must also be addressed. A key decision to be made is the selection of an appropriate exchange rate, for official and unofficial exchange rates rarely reflect the relative domestic purchasing power of the currencies involved.

DISCUSSION QUESTIONS

1. Distinguish between national economic and national market activities. Then explain the relevance of each to the international marketing manager.

2. Discuss at least three potential problems in using secondary data.

3. What are the limitations of per capita income data in evaluating a foreign market's potential for a consumer products company and an industrial products company?

4. A European manufacturer of glass bottles and jars is interested in estimating the potential attractiveness of Indonesia for its products. Identify the sources and the types of data the company will need in order to obtain a preliminary estimate. Defend your recommendations.

5. What is meant by the words *comparability* and *equivalence* when referring to secondary data? Give examples of each.

6. What limitations can a country's infrastructure impose on the marketing effort of a foreign company? Will these limitations be of equal concern to a consumer products company and an industrial products company?

7. For what kinds of products might a country's total GNP and total population be reasonable proxies for market potential? In the two cases you selected, what other data might be required?

ADDITIONAL READING

Henzler, Herbert, "Shaping an International Investment Strategy," *The McKinsey Quarterly,* Spring 1981.

Huszagh, Sandra M., "Third World Markets Demand Household Data for Successful Consumer Goods Marketing: Mexico as a Case Example," *International Marketing Review,* Vol. 1, Spring–Summer 1984.

Kaynak, Erdener, and Ronald Savitt, eds., *Comparative Marketing Systems* (New York: Praeger, 1984).

Marketing in Developing Countries, edited by S., Kindra (New York: St. Martin's, 1984).

Lasserre, Philippe, "The New Industrializing Countries of Asia—Perspectives and Opportunities," *Long Range Planning,* June 1981.

Sherbini, A. A., "Import-Export Marketing Mechanisms," *MSU Business Topics,* Spring 1968.

ENDNOTES

1. Philip Kotler, *Marketing Management: Analysis, Planning, and Control,* 5th edition (Englewood Cliffs, N.J.: Prentice-Hall, 1984), p. 225.
2. *The World Bank Atlas 1986* (Washington, D.C.: The World Bank), p. 12.
3. "World Population," *The Economist,* June 3, 1987, p. 51.
4. The data on education is from *World Development Report 1986* (Washington, D.C.: The World Bank). Percentages greater than 100 indicate that enrollment exceeds the enrollment for the normal age group.
5. Walter W. Rostow, *The Stages of Economic Growth* (New York: Cambridge Univ. Press, 1960).
6. See E. J. Kolde, *Environment of International Business* (Boston: Kent 1985), Chapter 8, for a more complete discussion of this approach.
7. David Morawetz, *Why the Emperor's New Clothes Are Not Made in Colombia* (Washington, D.C.: World Bank, 1980).
8. John F. Maloney, "In Saudi Arabia, Sands, Statistics Can Be Shifty," *Marketing News,* July 2, 1976, p. 6.
9. Susan P. Douglas and C. Samuel Craig, *International Marketing Research* (Englewood Cliffs, N.J.: Prentice-Hall, Inc., 1983), p. 79.

Chapter 6
Culture and Global
Buyer Behavior

INTRODUCTION

In Chapter 5, we looked at national markets in terms of size, stage of economic development, infrastructure, and purchasing power. However, market needs and opportunities cannot be determined solely on the basis of economic data. Markets and market behavior are strongly affected by cultural factors. In this chapter, we therefore focus on the cultural dimension of buyer behavior.

This chapter is divided into five major parts. In the first part, we review some of the issues and problems confronting marketing managers when attempting to use buyer behavior concepts and models in different cultural settings. Then we define culture and discuss the impact it has on buyer behavior. Ten elements of culture are identified and discussed to illustrate how culture affects what, why, when, where, and how buyers purchase products and services. In the third part, we introduce a cross-cultural buyer behavior model that combines cultural, social, and economic dimensions of the marketplace. The fourth part briefly discusses the relative cultural sensitivity of industrial and consumer markets. The fifth and final part presents an approach for the cross-cultural analysis of consumer behavior.

INTERNATIONAL MARKETING AND BUYER BEHAVIOR

An understanding of buyer behavior is central to successful marketing. To develop effective marketing programs, the marketing manager must have knowledge of the needs and wants of potential buyers, how they arise, and how and where they are likely to be satisfied.

Culture and Buyer Behavior Concepts

Buyer behavior is affected by many factors. Class, education, age, and psychological traits are just four of the many factors useful in distinguishing different buyer groups. Considerable effort has been invested in researching the relationships that exist between the marketing-mix variables and buyer needs and response. From this effort have evolved many buyer behavior models, concepts, and techniques. Although these models, concepts, and techniques can be used in other countries, their *application* may differ substantially from country to country, as will the *interpretations* given particular data or information about consumers.

For example, social classes exhibit distinct product and brand preferences for such things as clothing, automobiles, furniture, and leisure activities. Since virtually all societies exhibit social stratification, it would appear reasonable to assume that the social class concept has virtually universal validity. However, caution is advised. India, for example, has some 3,000 distinct castes and subcastes, each of which may be suitable for a particular marketing effort.[1] Some marketers have segmented the United States into six distinct classes.[2] In societies such as Sweden and the Netherlands, class differences are less marked, and there may be fewer distinct "class" groupings.

Family buyer behavior and the family life cycle must also be examined with caution. Although these concepts may have universal validity, their application will vary from society to society. In the United States, family members often exercise a strong collective influence on buyer behavior. Although the decision maker may be the husband, wife, or child—depending on the product under review—other family members frequently play crucial influencing roles. This is not the case in other societies. In China and the United Kingdom, for example, children play a smaller role in family decisions.

The family life-cycle concept assumes that people pass through stages in their lives and that these stages can be used to segment the market. That is, each life stage is associated with a somewhat different set of wants, incomes, and consumption patterns that differ from that in other stages. The family life-cycle concept has been used successfully by marketers in many different national settings, but the stages the life cycle is divided into vary from culture to culture and within cultures over time. For example, in the United States, the traditional family life cycle is divided into nine stages: bachelor, newly married, full nest I, full nest II, and so on.[3] However, a more recent approach that takes into account the high divorce rate and the decision by many couples to delay or to not have children divides the family life cycle into six stages and several substages. These stages are young single, young married without children, other young, middle-aged, and so on.[4] These two examples demonstrate that the stages researchers use must (1) reflect the lifestyles of the targeted market as they affect wants, incomes, and consumption patterns and (2) be reevaluated periodically. The frequency of the reevaluation depends on the rate at which the marketing-relevant socio-cultural characteristics are changing. Countries in earlier stages of economic development tend to be socio-culturally more stable than countries in advanced stages of development.

Apparent similarities such as language can also hide subtle but important differences between markets. International marketers have often shown a higher propensity to misinterpret a marketing situation when the cultural and economic environments of the foreign market are apparently the same as their own.[5] For example, Philip Morris lost a considerable amount of money when it tried to introduce a U.S. cigarette to the Canadian market. Management was under the erroneous impression that Canadians and Americans had similar smoking habits because they spoke the same language, had similar cultural heritages, dressed more or less the same, and watched many of the same television programs.

As described in Exhibit 6-1, Campbell Soups lost $30 million in Europe before it accepted the idea that British and U.S. soup consumers were different in three important ways. First, British soup consumers have different taste preferences. Campbell Soups made no attempt to modify the taste of their soups for the British palate. Second, British soup consumers had not been educated to the condensed soup product concept. Because of the smaller can size, they thought they were being asked to pay twice as much as they were accustomed to pay for canned soup. Third, British soup consumers did not respond the same way to U.S. advertising as did U.S. soup consumers. The reaction to freckled-faced children telling their parents what they wanted to eat was quite negative. British children, according to the adage, are to be seen, not heard. In the United States, children are more frequently asked what they would like to eat, what they want to wear, and even what they would like to learn.

EXHIBIT 6-1 _____

The Campbell Soup Experience _____

Oscar Wilde once noted that the United States and England were two great nations separated by the same language, for—in spite of many similarities—there are vast differences in nuances and emphasis. David Dutton, a one-time managing director of one of Britain's largest advertising agencies, once explained the impact that these differences have on American businesspeople: "It is perhaps understandable that Americans tend to enter the United Kingdom with a bit too much self-assurance. They feel at home here and are bound to make mistakes." The following is an example of such a mistake.

Notwithstanding its vast resources and marketing expertise, Campbell Soups made a major blunder when entering the British market in 1959. As a result of this mistake, it only secured about 15 percent of the British market between 1959 and 1966. H. J. Heinz, which could boast of about only 5 percent of the U.S. market., was the dominant force in the British soup market with about 60 percent market share. In fact, Heinz had been in Britain so long and had established itself so well that many Britons thought of it as a domestic company.

The first mistake Campbell made was to assume that the British consumer was familiar with its condensed soup concept. It made no effort to educate the consumer. The British consumer, accustomed to the ready-to-eat Heinz soups, was unaware of Campbell's product form. Since it had not been explained to them, Campbell's soups were at some disadvantage on the retail shelf because of their smaller size. In spite of an avalanche of advice, it took Campbell two years to embark on the necessary educational advertising and promotion programs to sell the British on the idea of condensed soups.

Campbell further compounded its problems by initially refusing to tailor its flavors in soups to foreign tastes. For example, the British were unaccustomed to the taste of Campbell's original tomato soup. It was too sweet. The taste of well-established and branded local varieties, such as those offered by Heinz, were so different from Campbell's flavors that it was not until Campbell had made significant changes in its soups' flavors that sales perked up.

Campbell also erred in its advertising. The British consumer, not so strongly influenced by a "youth culture" as the American consumer, found many of the firm's initial advertising efforts too youthful and fanciful. For example, it is not customary for children to tell their parents what they want to eat.

_____

Source: Brian Toyne, "Home Products, Inc." *Consumer Behavior Dynamics: A Casebook,* Wayne Delozier, ed. (Columbus, Ohio: Charles E. Merrill, 1977), pp. 225–226.

Buyer Behavior in a Global Setting

A major task for the international marketer is to discover how similarities and differences between consumers in overseas markets affect behavior in the marketplace. These questions must be answered if appropriate *target markets* are to be selected and effective *marketing programs* developed.

To understand foreign buyer behavior, the international marketer is required to perform the same four basic tasks required of the domestic marketer, but within and across foreign markets: (1) identify relevant similarities and differences in the market under review; (2) select buyer behavior models, concepts, and techniques that are valid for the market under review; (3) modify their application to meet the markets' characteristics; and (4) interpret the results within the context of these markets. These four tasks are highly interrelated. Information gathered for one task is required by the others and will eventually affect all the tasks. Although the logical sequence of these tasks is to move from *identification* to *selection* to *modification* and finally to *interpretation,* the conclusions reached and the decisions made as a result of each task may have to be reevaluated. Thus, the tasks are shown in Figure 6-1 in a circular format.

THE ROLE OF CULTURE

Particular cultural contexts lie at the root of most market differences. Culture conditions most of our actions and feelings. We live our lives using prevalent norms, values, and attitudes. Our tastes, the types of clothing we wear, and the foods we eat are culture bound. Even the way we walk, what we "see," and how we feel are determined, at least in part, by our surroundings. The way we behave toward others, what we expect from others, what we view as achievement and success, how we react, and how we solve problems are also largely conditioned responses.

Cultural and social behavior patterns are not innate; they are learned. We begin indoctrination shortly after we are born, and it lasts our whole life. Even if we are uprooted and spend considerable portions of our lives in other cultures, we continue to be influenced by earlier cultural and social experiences.

Since a large proportion of consumption behavior is determined by cultural heritage, international marketers need to know which elements in a particular culture have the greatest influence on specific buyer behavior. They need this

FIGURE 6-1   International Marketing's Four Buyer Behavior Tasks

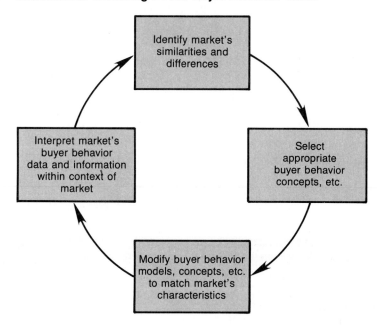

knowledge to determine the extent to which these elements vary across cultures and are changing within cultures.

What is Culture?

One authority identified 164 definitions of culture.[6] Fortunately, we are not interested in most of them. They either refer to phenomena outside the scope of this book or are too specialized and so of little value to the marketing manager. Marketing managers are primarily interested in those elements of culture that will help them understand the buyer. They need to know both which factors influence a consumer's needs and wants and how they go about satisfying these needs and wants.

For our purposes, we will define culture as follows:

Culture is the learned ways of group living and the group's responses to various stimuli.

Harris and Moran suggest that culture can be divided into ten distinctive categories: communication and language, beliefs and attitudes, values and norms, sense of self and space, relationships, time and time consciousness, mental process and learning, rewards and recognitions, dress and appearance, and food and eating habits.[7] These categories are not exhaustive. Terpstra, for example, has identified eight categories: language, religion, values and attitudes, education, social organization, technology and material culture, politics, and law.[8] Regardless of the categories we use, we need to select them on the basis of their relevance to the product or service being marketed. Each category cannot be treated as mutually exclusive, for they are highly interdependent. Because an African or an Arab uses a product developed by a Western culture, such as a radio or a bus, does not mean he or she has accepted the manufacturer's culture or other products from that culture.

The ten categories identified by Harris and Moran will be used in this chapter. They are sufficiently broad to provide a good idea of the influence culture has on buyer behavior. They directly affect buyer behavior and provide additional insight into such factors as reference groups, occupation, and beliefs traditionally used for understanding buyer behavior and segmenting markets as shown in Figure 6-2.

Several examples of the pitfalls unwary marketers have fallen into are described in Exhibit 6-2. The examples are identified according to the cultural dimensions discussed next.

Communication and Language

Language is the primary means of communication. It is the medium we all use to interpret our environment, give meaning to specific events, and convey thoughts and feelings. It embodies the philosophy of the culture and conditions the user to look at the world and interpret experience in a special, even unique, way.

At least two aspects of language are of critical importance to marketers, language as a *communication tool* and the *heterogeneity* of languages. The first deals with the relevance of the explicit and implicit parts of all communications—the spoken and silent parts of communication. The second deals with the number of languages spoken in one country or by a group of countries.

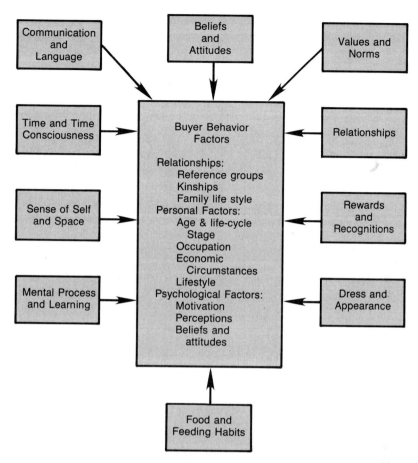

FIGURE 6-2 **The Socio-Cultural Dimensions of Buyer Behavior**

Language as a Communication Tool. According to Edward T. Hall, a professor of anthropology, language has two major components.[9] There is a *silent language* and a *spoken language*. Both are always used to communicate thoughts and feelings. Even when communicating by telephone, a pause or the tone of voice may change the meaning of the words being spoken. Both components are important when developing advertising themes using visual aids such as for print, T.V., or cinema. *The way people stand and the gestures they use are as important as what they say or do.*

We will use the following definition of silent language.

Silent language is nonverbal communication involving gestures, grimaces, posture, color, and distance.

We can tell when people are happy or angry by their facial color or expressions, by the way they walk, stand, sit, or hold their hands. Unfortunately, "body language" is frequently conditioned by culture. For example, people in the United States stand approximately 18 inches apart when talking to one another. In Latin countries,

EXHIBIT 6-2 _____
Examples of Cultural Blunders Made by International Marketers _____

Language	A U.S. toothpaste manufacturer promised its customers that they would be more "interesting" if they used the firm's toothpaste. What the advertising coordinators did not realize, however, was that in Latin American countries "interesting" is another euphemism for "pregnant."	*Religion*	England's East India Company once caused a revolt when it did not modify a product. In 1857, bullets were often encased in pig wax, and the tops had to be bitten off before the bullets could be fired. The Indian soldiers revolted since it was against their religion to eat pork. Hundreds of people were killed before order was restored.
Food	Chase and Sanborn met resistance when it tried to introduce its instant coffee in France. In the home, the consumption of coffee plays more of a ceremonial role than in the English home. The preparation of "real" coffee is a touchstone in the life of the French housewife, so she will generally reject instant coffee because its casual characteristics do not "fit" into the French eating habits.	*Social Norms and Time*	A telephone company tried to incorporate a Latin flavor in its commercials by employing Puerto Rican actors. In the ad, the wife said to her husband, "Run and phone Mary. Tell her we'll be a little late." This commercial has two major cultural errors. Latin wives seldom dare order their husbands around, and almost no Latin would feel it necessary to phone to warn of tardiness since it is expected.
Values	In 1963, Dow Breweries introduced a new beer in Québec, Canada, called "Kebec." The promotion incorporated the Canadian flag and attempted to evoke nationalistic pride. The strategy backfired when major local groups protested the "profane" use of "sacred" symbols.		

Source: Adapted from David A. Ricks, *Big Business Blunders: Mistakes in Multinational Marketing* (Homewood, Ill.: Dow Jones-Irwin, 1983).

the distance is about 12 inches. It is even less in Arabic countries. In the United States, a person expresses approval by nodding his or her head up and down. In the Philippines, however, "A jerk of the head downwards means no, while a jerk upwards means yes."[10]

Hand movements also differ from country to country. Throughout most of Western Europe, Brazil, and the United States, a raised thumb is used as a signal of approval. But in Greece, this hand sign is a gross insult. There are three categories of expressive hand movements: mimic signals, symbolic gestures, and baton gestures.[11] They are as follows:

Mimic signals attempt to mimic the object or activity being communicated, such as drinking from an imaginary glass or running a finger across the throat to signal death or to stop whatever a person is doing. Although these gestures vary from culture to culture, they are more likely to be understood than the other two categories of gestures.

Symbolic gestures are arbitrary and possess no obvious relationship to the meaning communicated. These gestures tend to be culturally distinctive, such as the way one nods approval or uses the thumb to indicate approval or an insult. Consequently, they often result in serious misunderstandings when people of different cultures meet.

Baton gestures are hand movements that accompany speech. They are used as a means of assisting and emphasizing speech and vary by culture. For example, the British place little importance on hand movements. In contrast, they are an integral part of communicating for Italians and most Latin Americans.

There are about 3,000 languages, and if language is the mirror of a culture, there are about 3,000 different cultures in the world.[12] Spoken language is defined as:

Spoken language is communication involving vocal sounds in meaningful patterns and, when they exist, written symbols.

Since there are some 184 countries and territories, this means many countries have more than one language *and more than one culture.* For example, French and Flemish are the languages of Belgium. English, French, and several North American Indian languages are used in Canada. Even in the United States, Spanish is the only language spoken by many Hispanics (for example, Cubans, Mexicans, and Puerto Ricans).

Besides the major languages, there are dialects, accents, slang, jargon, and variations such as idioms. Even a grunt, hiss, or sigh can be variously interpreted, for they tend to be manifestations of subcultures. So although the major language of a country may be English or Spanish, it may be composed of several subcultures of significance to the marketer. Furthermore, some subcultures, such as the military, have terminology and signals that cut across national boundaries.

A major difficulty confronting the international marketer is the translation of a concept (product, advertising theme) from one language to another, even from one dialect to another. For example, United Airlines, on acquiring Pan Am's Pacific routes in 1985, used the Australian film star, Paul Hogan on the cover of its in-flight magazine with the caption "camping it up." The backdrop was the Australian outback. United was quickly informed by Hogan's lawyers that, in Australia, the caption implied acting in an effeminate fashion. *The nuances associated with words may vary from language to language and within languages; therefore, a literal translation may not be possible.* This is particularly true of colloquialisms and slang.

Even within major languages like English and Spanish, the meaning of words and expressions varies from country to country. These differences need to be considered when developing manuals and advertising scripts and when communications occur between a company and its foreign affiliates. For example, in Argentina the word for butter is *manteca.* In most other Spanish-speaking countries, it is *mantequilla.* Different words are also used by different English-speaking countries. The following pairs of words are used to express the same physical items in the United Kingdom and the United States (the first word is generally used in the United Kingdom, the second in the United States): *drawing pin* and *thumbtack, elevator* and *lift, lorry* and *truck.* Other differences exist. The Canadian and English gallon is approximately 13 percent larger than the U.S. gallon, and 1 billion is 100 million in the United Kingdom and 1,000 million in the United States.

Choice of words, accent, dialect, and the pattern of speech are indicators of the person's social standing (class). Manual workers, white collar workers, managers, and the social elites use different vocabularies, dialects, or accents. These differences also need to be taken into account when developing print and audio promotional messages, especially when these messages are for a particular segment of the market.

Beliefs and Attitudes

People in all cultures have a concern for the supernatural. This is evident in their religions, religious practices, and superstitions. Religion provides meaning and motivation beyond the material aspects of life. It gives meaning to such things as life, what is right and wrong, and what is good and bad. It gives rise to values and attitudes that, in turn, shape the practices or behavior of the culture's members. As such, religion (or its traces) is central to a culture. Educational systems, economic systems, political organizations, and social relations are partly or largely determined by religion. Even in the Soviet Union, where the Communist party has officially adopted atheism, many people still practice their religions, and its society is still strongly influenced by the rituals and sacraments of a begone era.

There are many religions, and Terpstra suggests that each nation can be considered to have a unique religious profile.[13] Many examples of the influence religion has on buyer behavior—such as on values and norms, time, and sense of self—can be identified.

Holidays. Every religion has its holy days, which vary in number and significance. For example, Colombia and the United States are both Christian countries, yet Colombia recognizes more than 30 religious holidays; the United States recognizes considerably fewer. These holidays have a varying impact on marketing and consumption.

For many Christian countries, the Christmas season has a significant effect on production, advertising efforts, and retail sales. Retailers begin ordering and accumulating inventory several weeks, even months, before the season starts. For Muslims, the holy month of Ramadan—with its fasting and prayer—negatively affects retail sales and production.

Taboos and Consumption Patterns. In most countries, religion affects consumption patterns by restricting the consumption of certain foods and beverages. For example, pork is not eaten by Jews and Muslims, and beef is not eaten by Hindus. Further, smoking and drinking alcoholic beverages are both frowned on—if not forbidden—by strict Muslims and Protestants. Religious taboos also extend beyond food to include acceptable and unacceptable desires and behavior patterns. Acceptable clothing for women in Islamic countries and the role of machinery among the Amish are examples of the effects religion may have on the consumption patterns of markets.

Economic Development and Materialism. Each religion places a different emphasis on the material and spiritual lives of individuals. This, in turn, fosters beliefs, attitudes, and practices that influence the economic activities and life styles of individuals, even countries. Many studies on religion and economic activity suggest that religion has a major influence on economic development through its effect on individual attitudes towards material possessions, work, achievement, and so on.

For example, Hinduism (India), Buddhism (generally Asian countries), and Islam (generally Middle Eastern and some African countries) are all associated with countries at the lower end of the economic development scale. The countries and regions at the upper end of the scale are generally Protestant (such as Scandinavia, North America, and West Germany). Catholic countries tend to be between these extremes (France, Italy, Spain).

The influence that various religions have on the economic behavior of individuals can be highlighted with a few examples. The Four Noble Truths of Buddhism state that (1) human suffering is omnipresent and an integral part of nature; (2) it is caused by desire for material possessions and self-seeking enjoyment; (3) it can cease only when desire ceases; and (4) cessation of suffering can be obtained only by freeing oneself from lust, ill will, untruthfulness, killing, stealing, and so on. Buddhism has been described as the striving for a state of "wantlessness" and contemplation. Its world-denying orientation is considered by many an obstacle to economic development.[14] However, Lester points out that the Buddhist community of monks has maintained an academic tradition for more than 2,000 years, a tradition that has allowed Buddhists to take up Western education with relatively more ease than in regions with nonliterate religious traditions.[15] As noted by Terpstra and David, Mahayana Buddhism is an important part of the religious scene of such countries as Japan, South Korea, Singapore, and Taiwan[16] and these countries are among the fastest-growing countries in the world at this time.

Islam includes both a belief system and a minutely detailed, legalistic way of life embracing every aspect of life. It is also fatalistic. That is, the Sharia, or the law of Islam, details every aspect of life; everything that occurs is seen as the result of divine will. Except for oil-producing countries like Saudi Arabia, Kuwait, and Libya, Muslim nations are at the lower end of the economic development scale. Thus, it is not too surprising to find that many scholars and government officials inside and outside Islam consider religion a deterrent to change and economic development. For example, a former Malaysian Prime Minister, Tunku Abdul Rahman, organized a conference of Islamic countries to consider how the prophet's teachings could be accommodated in a changing world.[17]

The beliefs and practices that flow from Catholicism and Protestantism, two major branches of Christianity, also appear to have differing influences on economic activity and, consequently, economic development. Protestantism, for example, resulted in the downgrading of the Church and the rise of individualism. It also facilitated the development of a work ethic. To work hard was a religious duty, and its rewards (increased productivity and income) were signs of God's approval. At one time, Protestantism also emphasized asceticism. Accordingly, hardworking and thrifty Methodists, Puritans, and Quakers became exemplary capitalists.[18] Catholicism, on the other hand, has traditionally made a sharp distinction between the secular life and the religious life. It still fosters the belief that salvation can be obtained only through the Church. Consequently, the Church has a strong influence on secular activities, and secular institutions are not viewed as negatively by Catholics as by Protestants.

Though there is some correlation between a country's religion and its economic development, it is at best a weak relationship. For example, in 1983, a sample of Protestant countries had per capita GNP incomes ranging from $7,710 to $16,250; a sample of Catholic countries had incomes ranging from $750 to $10,480; excluding oil-exporting countries, a sample of Muslim countries had incomes ranging from $690 to $2,320, and Japan, a Shinto-Buddhist country, had a per capita income of $10,100.[19]

All cultural dimensions of a society and individuals are subject to change. For example, there are no "pure" Catholic or Protestant economies. Even when countries adopt state religions, as have the United Kingdom, Spain, and Italy, the religious context of the country is not necessarily monolithic or all pervasive. Further, most religions, including Islam, Hindu, Buddhism, Catholicism, and Protestantism, comprise many sects or denominations, each of which stresses particular beliefs and practices. This can result in buyer behavior differences within countries and among countries dominated by one religion.

Values and Norms[20]

From its value system, a culture sets norms of behavior for the society. These standards may range from the work ethic to the position of women in society. People in different cultures are pleased, concerned, annoyed, or embarrassed about different things because they perceive situations differently. The norms at work strongly influence consumption patterns. In one country, it may be acceptable to spend discretionary income on material things for one's self or one's family; in another, discretionary income must be used to help kin. In Japan and Germany, thrift is emphasized. In the United States, consumption is emphasized. In France and the United States, an overt display of success is acceptable. But in the United Kingdom, such a display would be considered vulgar and in bad taste.

Compared with other societies, Brazil and the United States place considerable emphasis on youth. This has resulted in the development of a youth culture, products and services that emphasize youthful appearance and lifestyles. In contrast, some Arab, Asian, and African countries venerate age. In these countries, persons do not fear getting old and thus do not place much importance on products and services that emphasize youthful appearance and lifestyles.

Sense of Self and Space[21]

The comfort one has with self is influenced by culture. Self-identity, self-worth, and self-appreciation can be manifested by a humble or modest bearing in one place (Japan, China), whereas another calls for an aggressive or macho behavior (United States, Latin America); a sense of independence, assertiveness, and creativity in one culture (United States) is countered by group cooperation, harmony, and conformity in another (Japan). Cultures may also be structured and formal or flexible and informal. In India, for example, the caste system determines a person's place in society at birth. In the United States, social mobility is largely determined by a person's education, ability, and economic success.

As we noted earlier, some cultures require more physical distance between the individual and others, whereas others desire closer contact. In Latin American countries, physical contact is encouraged. In the United Kingdom and the Scandinavian countries, physical contact is generally avoided except between close family members. Insensitivity to such basic differences can result in misunderstandings. For example, many Europeans use what Americans consider weak handshake. To Europeans, however, a North American's strong handshake is offensive. North Americans interpret the handshake as reflecting a person's character; the stronger the handshake, the stronger the character. Europeans tend to use other signals, such as language, dress, and social position.

Relationships

Cultures establish human and organizational relationships in many ways. Key factors include age, sex, wealth, power, and wisdom. The family unit is the most common expression of such factors. The family unit ranges from the small to the large. In the United States, the nuclear family—parents and children—is the norm. But in a Hindu household, the family includes mother, father, children, parents, uncles, aunts, and cousins—all under one roof. In many cultures, the authoritarian figure in the family is the oldest male. However, male responsibilities differ. In the Middle East, the oldest male is responsible for many household decisions. In other cultures, such as Thailand, females manage the household and its finances. In China, the elderly hold positions of high honor and are considered wise. In other cultures, they may be considered burdensome or foolish and ignored.

Time and Time Consciousness

In the more industrialized countries, time tends to be viewed as linear (events and opportunities occur only once) and thus is important and valuable. The saying "time is money" exemplifies this view. In more traditional and agricultural societies, time is viewed as circular. Thus, events and opportunities will be repeated, just as the seasons are repeated. These differing views of time affect business in many ways. Time-saving devices, punctuality, and rewards for being on time are expressions of a linear sense of time.

Views on time are broadly significant. Most middle-class North Americans are oriented to the future. Many Europeans, particularly the British and French, often focus on the past. Thus, tradition and a sense of history play much more significant roles in the buyer behavior of Europeans than of North Americans. This translates into a greater resistance to change, and product innovation is therefore more difficult in such societies.

Sense of time differs by culture. Generally, North Americans, Germans, and the English are precise about the clock, whereas Latins are casual. In much of Africa, time is not so rigidly adhered to as in the United States, and people can arrive several hours late for a meeting. Lateness does not mean, as it would in the United States or Germany, that the person lacks interest in the meeting or is lazy.

In Britain and North America, a person may be 5 minutes late for a business appointment. In Latin America, 30 minutes is acceptable and expected. At social functions, it is not polite to arrive at a party at the designated time; in fact, a Latin American host or hostess may be annoyed if you arrive on time.

Time, in the sense of the year, varies by culture, even subculture. In some areas of the world, such as Europe and the northern part of the United States, people think in terms of the four seasons. In other parts of the world, such as Brazil, Colombia, and California, the seasons tend to be ignored. The year is simply divided into wet and dry seasons. Differences like these affect the seasonality of product offerings, promotional campaigns, and so on.

Mental Process and Learning

A person can also observe striking differences in the way people think and learn. Kolde has suggested that the Arabic and British cultures emphasize *particularistic* and *pragmatic* thinking modes.[22] In these and similar cultures, data, material objects, and other individuals are viewed in terms of a particular goal or result. Thus, considerable attention is paid to detail, procedures, and circumstantial factors rather than general principles or abstract concepts. The French, on the other hand, are conditioned to place general principles ahead of practical considerations. The German culture emphasizes a systems orientation and systematic processes. Since thinking precedes and conditions behavior, differences such as these result in different behavioral patterns.

Different thinking modes can result in misunderstandings in communications, especially when people from different cultures are required to work together in solving problems. For example, if a Frenchman, an Englishman, and a German were working together in formulating an advertising campaign, their different thinking modes could cause misunderstandings. The Frenchman would likely seek to understand the general principles involved; the Englishman would be interested in identifying the factors impacting on the problem; the typical German would be concerned with the problem's impact on other aspects of the operation. Similar misunderstandings could arise in the minds of the targeted customers. Their interpretation of the message would be strongly influenced by their culturally determined ways of analyzing information.

Rewards and Recognition

Another way of observing a culture is to note the *manner and method of offering praise* for superior performance and accomplishment. Testimonial dinners, expense accounts, titles, and monetary rewards are used differently according to the cultural context. In the United States, the size of the office and its location are symbols of authority. Even office equipment such as the desk, telephone, and calendar can have significance. In other cultures, for example, some Arab and European countries, no such outward recognition is given to a position in an organization.

The status given particular occupations varies by cultures. In India, economists, doctors, and engineers are held in high regard and are of the Brahman class. Among the educated, there is an abundance of people trained in these occupations.

The same is true of several African countries. In Latin America, considerable status is given to poets and authors. In the United States, lawyers, doctors, and executives are held in high regard. The implications of such differences are important when developing advertising campaigns.

Motivation is also different from culture to culture; the members of different cultures pursue different goals and are gratified by different rewards. For example, in Australia, assertive behavior is approved and rewarded. This form of behavior is viewed positively and associated with go-getters and achievement. In China, submissiveness is valued and rewarded. In the United States, work and initiative are valued and rewarded. In other cultures, people expect to be rewarded for their social position, family, or clan ties.

Dress and Appearance

The clothes and jewelry we wear and the body decorations we use all tend to be culturally distinctive. Most of us are aware of major differences in outerwear, such as the Japanese kimono, the African headdress, the Polynesian sarong, and the American Indian headband. However, we are not often aware of or sensitive to more subtle differences, such as the waisted suit of the Frenchman, the loose cut of the American's suit, and the disapproval of short-shorts in French-speaking Canada. Customs and tradition determine acceptable modes of dress and length of hair. Even colors and color combinations are culturally determined. In the United States and Europe, black is worn for mourning. White is used for mourning in China and the Middle East. Differences like these cannot be overlooked when developing promotional materials and selecting colors to be used for products and packaging. They are even important when selecting the adornments to be worn by personnel who will come in contact with the public. For example, United Airlines ordered its flight and desk attendants to wear white carnations during the inauguration of its Pacific routes. It was not aware that white was associated with funerals in most Asian countries.

In Latin American countries, Italy, and France, men may carry shoulder or hand purses in which they keep their wallets, money, checkbooks, and other items traditionally carried by other Europeans and North Americans in the pockets of their trousers and jackets. This is in part because of a preference for tight-fitting clothing and in part because of climate. In many Latin American countries, a purse is used to protect against pickpockets.

Food and Feeding Habits

The manner in which food is selected, prepared, presented, and eaten often differs by culture. In Europe, delicacies include brains, lungs, the heart, and other internal organs; in the United States, these are generally used for dog food. In the United States, corn is a favorite vegetable for many people, but in Europe, it is considered feed for cattle.

There are also significant differences in table manners and eating habits. The seating arrangement at the table is important in Japan and Europe; it is more casual in the United States. North Americans and Europeans can be distinguished by how they use the knife and fork. The American will switch the fork back and forth from one hand to the other; the European will not.

The ten elements described provide a simple framework for assessing a particular culture, but they do not include every aspect of culture. What needs to be remembered is that all aspects of culture are interrelated; to change one part is to change the whole. *It is the interaction of various elements that results in cultural distinctiveness.* Thus, in trying to compartmentalize a complex concept like culture, there is the danger of losing a sense of its wholeness. The following section describes several ways of comparing "total" or "macro" cultures.

Classifying Cultures

Although each culture is unique, cultures are not mutually exclusive. They tend to exhibit similarities. Terpstra has proposed that cultures can be described along five dimensions: cultural variability, cultural complexity, cultural hostility, cultural heterogeneity, and cultural interdependence.[23] They are shown in Figure 6-3. The first three occur within cultures; the other two can be observed among cultures.[24]

Cultural Variability

Cultures vary in terms of their stability and rate of change. Some cultures are very stable; others are unstable. Some change slowly; others change more rapidly. *The greater the cultural variability, the more unpredictable cultures are for business operations in general and international operations in particular.* Under conditions of high variability, greater local autonomy is probably advisable, if not necessary. This translates into greater local control over the marketing function, approaches, and programs, particularly for companies whose products and services are sensitive to socio-cultural factors and changes in these factors.

Cultural Complexity

Cultures differ widely in terms of whether unspoken, unformulated, and implicit rules govern behavior.[25] Hall suggested that cultures can be classified according to their contextural expression.[26] *Low-context cultures* (such as those associated with Switzerland, West Germany, and the United States) are characterized by overt or explicit behavior. Information is coded, messages are transmitted formally, fewer distinctions are made between outsiders and insiders, and change is easy and rapid. *High-context* cultures (such as those associated with Britain, Japan, and China) are characterized by more covert behaviors. Information is implicit in the physical context or is internalized within people; relational bonds

FIGURE 6-3   **Five Ways of Classifying Cultures** (*Source:* Vern Terpstra, *The Cultural Environment of International Business.* Cincinnati, Ohio: South-Western Publishing Co., 1978, p. xviii.)

	DIMENSION	(LOW)	(HIGH)
Within Cultures	Cultural Variability	low & stable change rate . . . high & unstable change rate	
	Cultural Complexity	simple (low context) . . . . complex (high context)	
	Cultural Hostility	munificent (benign) . . . . malevolent (illiberal)	
Among Cultures	Cultural Heterogeneity	homogeneous . . . . heterogeneous	
	Cultural Interdependence	independent . . . . interdependent	

tend to be strong; greater distinctions are made between those outside and inside the culture; and cultural patterns are long-lived and resistant to change.

In low-context cultures, written contracts and communications tend to be more important than verbal agreements. When disputes arise, the outcome will depend on what has been agreed to in writing. Introductions and other formalities are quickly dispensed with when business is conducted. In high-context cultures, the need to know more about the business associates is crucial. Business relationships, as with personal relationships, depend on mutual trust. When a Japanese executive makes a commitment for his company, he shares personally in this commitment.

Cultural Hostility

Cultures and subcultures exhibit varying degrees of hostility toward other cultures. Some cultures can be considered tolerant (even highly receptive), but others can be opposed (even malicious) in their attitudes toward foreign products, foreign companies, foreign managers, and so on. For example, as a group, Americans openly seek foreign products and services, attaching considerable prestige and status to their acquisition (BMWs, Gucci shoes, Cartier watches). Other cultures view the purchase of foreign products and services as unpatriotic and foreign companies and their activities as threatening their way of life. Thus, there can be considerable resistance to things foreign, and the international firm may have to use local brands and become identified with the country's business community.

Cultural Heterogeneity

Cultural heterogeneity refers to the degree to which cultures are dissimilar. This dimension occupies much of the attention of most international marketers. It is not just a question of the diversity in the individual elements (the ten variables discussed earlier) that makes up cultures but also the overt expression of their interaction, such as their variability, complexity, and hostility. The greater the heterogeneity among cultures, the more individualized the marketing approach needed or the better the segmentation must be. The greater the homogeneity, the greater the opportunities for marketing program and process uniformity.

Studies suggest that there is often as much cultural heterogeneity within countries as between countries. The United States is culturally more heterogeneous than Japan. Although the U.S. macroculture stresses certain underlying values such as achievement, success, activity, efficiency, progress, material comfort, individualism, and youthfulness and the term *melting pot* suggests homogeneity, distinct subcultures do exist. These ethnic, religious, racial, and regional groups each have distinctive lifestyles that influence their buying behavior. Other countries have even more marked diversity. For example, Nigeria's several distinct tribes cannot be grouped when mounting marketing campaigns. But other subcultures are less easily targeted because demographic and geographic segmenting variables are difficult to establish (as in the case of the Sunni and Shiite Islamic sects of Iran). Further, some countries were created by Western powers during the colonial period. Colonializing powers ignored historical and cultural heritages and created countries that are not culturally distinct from others in the region. In such cases, different countries can be grouped into larger, culturally homogeneous groups of people.

Cultural Interdependence

Cultural interdependence refers to the degree of sensitivity of a culture to respond to conditions and developments in other cultures. Cultural interdependence is fostered by advances in communications and transportation, changes in personal mobility, and regional and international agreements and institutions. For example, television shows, movies, and international travel promote a greater awareness of cultural differences and may lead to the modification of cultural and social patterns over time.

Factors that influence *cultural interdependence* include the culture's variability, complexity, and hostility. Although the Japanese have been involved in international trade and business for several decades—economic interdependence—they have been slow to change their cultural and social patterns. The same is true of the member countries of the European Community. The Germans are still Germans, the French still French, and so on.

The adoption of another society's products does not mean the cultural and social patterns of the other society have been adopted. Because Colombians and Englishmen drink Coca-Cola and use pocket calculators does not necessarily mean they have aligned their cultural and social lifestyles more closely to that of the United States. The material culture of a society is only one element of its macroculture.

A CROSS-CULTURAL BUYER BEHAVIOR MODEL

A major task of the international marketer is to identify relevant similarities and differences among the global company's various national target markets. This task is not easy and is made even more complicated because experts and business people disagree over whether buyer behavior is converging or diverging globally.

Some experts, such as Levitt, argue that as countries industrialize, basic human needs and behaviors become similar and that—except for minor changes to adjust for peculiar circumstances—essentially the same products can be sold with similar promotional appeals in all overseas markets.[27] Other experts argue that all societies are culturally unique and thus pose unique sets of marketing problems that keep changing over time. This group argues that there cannot be any single unified approach and that the marketing mix must be adjusted to satisfy for local conditions.

Neither argument is entirely true. The first argument emphasizes identifying cultural similarities across markets and assumes universal traits exist. This approach is of particular value to those firms interested in using *global strategies*. A marketing goal of such companies is to identify market segments that ignore national boundaries. Essentially, these market segments have needs or wants that can be satisfied with the same product. Regardless of nationality, they respond in a similar fashion to a marketing program. The other perspective highlights *distinctive* cultural traits. This approach tends to be the focus of firms using *national strategies*. These companies seek to satisfy some uniquely national need or want.

Ideally, international marketers attempt to develop marketing programs that are sensitive to both similarities and differences. But in practice, they are strongly influenced, if not entirely constrained, by the company's corporate strategy, the approach used to service particular foreign markets, and the budget allocated to these markets.

Figure 6-4 presents a simplified cross-cultural stimulus–response model of buyer behavior. It is based on a more comprehensive model proposed by Sheth and Sethi.[28] The model is descriptive; it simply identifies factors that stimulate and condition buyer behavior in different cultures. Its purpose is to help managers identify and understand the underlying cultural, social, and economic influences on buyer behavior. (More intensive discussion of the implications these factors have for international marketing can be found in later chapters, particularly those dealing with marketing strategy and the marketing-mix elements.)

Response-producing stimuli and *response-conditioning* forces enter the buyer's "black box", the brain and other human processing devices, and produce certain responses. The response-producing stimuli consist of the factors shown on the left of Figure 6-4: nature of innovation, product factors, channels of communication, and sources of communication. The response-conditioning forces consist of the major forces in the buyer's environment: economic, cultural, and social. The response-producing stimuli and the response-conditioning forces interact with the buyer's *propensity to change* and *personal factors* to produce the buyer

FIGURE 6-4 **A Cross-Cultural Model of Buyer Behavior** (*Source:* Loosely based on the Sheth-Sethi model presented in Jagdish N. Sheth and S. Prakash Sethi, "A Review of Cross-Cultural Buyer Behavior." A paper presented at the "Symposium on Consumer and Industrial Buying Behavior," University of South Carolina, March, 1976.)

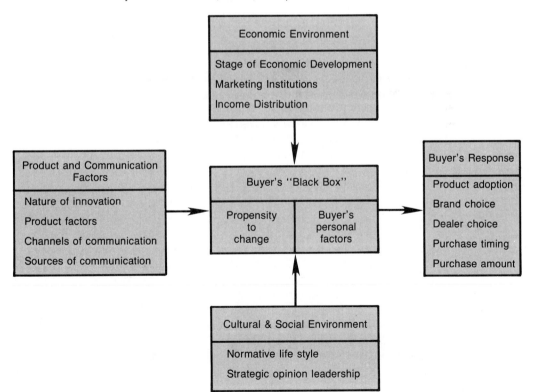

responses shown on the right: product adoption, brand choice, dealer choice, purchase timing, and purchase amount.

Propensity to Change

The *propensity to change* is central to the model.[29] It refers to the willingness of a society in general, a market segment and individual consumers in particular to change present consumption patterns. For example, the United States appears to have a higher propensity to change than do other industrialized countries. And industrialized countries appear to have higher propensities to change than do the traditional agricultural societies. At the same time, however, certain products, like Coca-Cola, also seem to be readily adopted by many cultures. The reason for these differences will become clear as we discuss the model.

Sheth and Sethi propose that the propensity to change can be measured on two scales: the degree of dissatisfaction with existing alternatives in a product class and the aspiration of a culture to improve itself with respect to the product class.[30] At any particular point in time, some cultures have a higher propensity to change from one product to another, whereas others are resistant to such change. A Third World country may be receptive to change from bicycles to automobiles because of its economic development; an industrialized country may seek to change from automobiles to some other form of transportation because of pollution and traffic congestion.

Individual Buyer Behavior

A high propensity to change does not mean a particular innovation will be adopted. The actual adoption of an innovation depends on the interaction effect of the buyer's personal factors and the market's propensity to change. The international marketer is primarily interested in the likelihood that a sufficient number of buyers will change. Evaluating such a likelihood requires a broad understanding of the market's propensity to change and its interactive effect with the buyer's personal factors. This information is needed as background information for analyzing and interpreting buyer behavior using the traditional but modified buyer behavior models and concepts suggested by factors identified in Figure 6-5.

Product and Communication Factors

Except for collectors, a buyer rarely if ever acquires a product—particularly a new or innovative product—merely to possess it. Purchase is inextricably connected to the buyer's view of self in relation to what he or she wants to be and to how the product might help him or her achieve this. Factors that stimulate interest in a new product include the relative newness of the product and the company's ability to communicate relevant information about the product and its attributes.

Nature of Innovation

Sheth and Sethi propose a system of categorizing innovations as perceived by buyers within their personality–cultural setting: consumption substitution in-

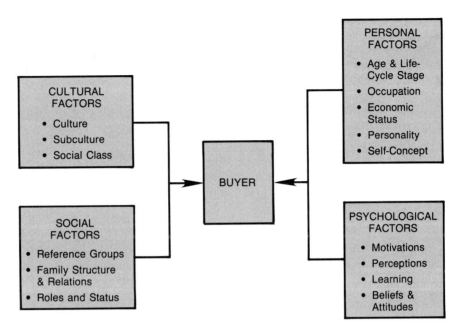

FIGURE 6-5: Examples of Personal Traits Affecting Buyer Behavior

novations, new want-creating innovations, and income-adding innovations.[31] By classifying potential customers according to these or similar categories, the marketer is better able to decide on the kinds of marketing programs required to gain acceptance of the company's product.

Consumption substitution innovations are not actually innovations. The buyer is familiar with the generic product and its attributes. "Substitution" implies that the buyer has either grown tired of the present product and is seeking variety or is seeking to improve the quality of the product. In either case, the marketing program would probably emphasize brand switching or brand positioning using culturally defined cues.

New want-creating innovations are of three kinds: complementary products, new contingency products, and culturally neutral products. Complementary products are purchased to improve on the use of an existing product (new software for a personal computer) or to increase the satisfaction derived from a product the buyer already possesses or consumes (new type of steak sauce). New contingency products are purchased because a new need has arisen, such as a change in the social status or occupation of the buyer (a larger house, a fur coat). Culturally neutral products are new to the market, thus no socio-cultural framework exists within which to evaluate their attributes (the introduction of chewing gum or lipstick where nothing similar previousy existed). Products new to a society are generally neutral but eventually become culturally, socially, and economically positioned. Chewing gum in Britain has social class connotations. Middle-class and upper-class adults generally view gum chewing negatively. Until this "social (status) sorting out" has occurred, the product is socially and culturally neutral. That is, the product is eventually accepted or rejected by appropriate groups within the society, such as elites, experts, or peers.

Income-adding innovations include products that may have a positive effect on the buyer's income. However, even in these cases, cultural and social implications are involved in adoption decisions. For example, some buyers will be concerned with the social-image implications of the new product, others with the effect the additional income will have on their social standing.[32]

Product Factors

The *characteristics of the product affect its rate of adoption*. Because of certain characteristics, some products quickly gain acceptance and are adopted (digital watches and pocket calculators in the United States). Others take a long time to gain acceptance and may never be widely adopted. For example, dishwashers were slow to be adopted because it was believed they did not clean dishes as effectively as by hand. Rogers has identified five product-related characteristics that appear to be especially important in influencing the rate of adoption: (1) relative advantage, (2) compatibility, (3) complexity, (4) trialability, and (5) observability.[33]

Relative advantage is the degree to which the new product is *perceived* to be superior to existing products. The greater the perceived advantage over currently used products, the more quickly the new product will be adopted. For example, without testing the product, the pocket calculator was perceived by most people in the United States as being both more accurate and quicker and simpler to use than was the slide rule. However, the product's advantage in one culture may not be viewed as an advantage in another culture. A labor-saving or time-saving attribute of a household appliance may be viewed as important advantages in the United States but of little value in Peru.

Compatibility is the degree to which the new product matches the values and experiences of the potential user. For example, a U.S. company's introduction of cake mixes to the British market initially failed for several reasons. First, the British prefer a cake similar to poundcake or sponge cake. Why? Unlike Americans, who eat cake with a fork, the British eat it with their fingers. Second, the British housewife saw her family role diminish in importance because of the reduction in the time it took to prepare food for her family. Another example was the introduction in the United States of an aspirin that could be chewed. It did not require water and apparently failed because the use of water is part of the ritual for curing a headache.

Complexity is the degree to which the new product is relatively difficult to understand or use. Compared to the slide rule, the pocket calculator is relatively simple to understand and use. Consequently, it was quickly adopted. This factor depends on the technological sophistication of the potential buyers. People in the United States generally are quite adept technologically; people in less developed countries are generally not so exposed to technologically advanced products and are less likely to possess the same degree of technological sophistication.

Trialability is the degree to which the new product can be tried or tested on a limited basis. Some products such as hair shampoos, detergents, and toothpastes can be easily divided into smaller amounts and distributed as samples. Automobiles cannot, so demonstrators must fulfill this requirement. Pocket calculators can be tested at a retail store.

Observability is the degree to which the results of the use of the new product are observable or describable to others. Since the results of using a pocket calculator can readily be demonstrated and easily understood, the calculator has been widely adopted in many countries.

In Chapter 12, we cover the issues and problems concerned with the diffusion and adoption of products in foreign markets and the impact that these processes have on product policy.

Communication Channels

The channels through which communication flows and the channels through which it must flow if an innovation or new product is to be accepted vary by culture and even subculture. Each culture accepts or rejects particular channels of communication by attaching different social and cultural connotations to them. Thus, mail-order catalogs may be acceptable in the United States for introducing new products but unacceptable in West Germany. In addition, the introduction of a new channel of communication, such as television advertising, must also be socially and culturally accepted before it can become useful to the marketer. In some European countries, television advertising is viewed partly as entertainment and has less influence on buyer behavior.

Sheth and Sethi suggest that channels of communication be dichotomized initially as *significative* or *symbolic.*[34]

Significative Communication is communication about the new product or innovation through its physical attributes. The channels for such communication are free samples, demonstrations, store displays, trade fairs, and so on. The advantage of these channels is that the potential buyer is able to use his or her five senses in evaluating the product. These channels also tend to be least subject to social and cultural misinterpretation. The disadvantage of depending too heavily on significative channels is that they may not be available, or they may be subject to legal restrictions.

Symbolic Communication is limited to linguistic and pictorial representation and relies on only two of the five senses, the eyes and ears. The channels for such communication include mass media, direct mail, billboards, and packaging. Two types of problems are associated with symbolic communication. The first relates to the technological, legal, moral, and economic differences among countries that limit the availability of these channels. For example, the United Kingdom does not permit advertising on public television. In Colombia and Venezuela, most of the population does not own television sets. And in many Third World countries, illiteracy is quite high; accordingly, the use of printed materials may have limited value.

The second and perhaps more important problem is that the cultural and social milieu is an important determinant of buyer behavior and an individual's pattern of communication. Each audience perceives and interprets the message in a particular cultural framework. For example, the choice of spokesperson becomes critical. A female cannot be used in most Muslim countries, and an expert may have little meaning in a traditional or agricultural country ruled by elites. In Brazil and Colombia, where most affluent households have maids, the use of the housewife to sell detergents is an anomaly. The Brazilian housewife is shown giving instructions to her maid; the U.S. housewife touts the product herself.

Communication Sources. The sources of communication are of three types: *commercial sources* such as the company, *neutral sources* such as government reports and noncommercial press releases, and *social sources* such as friends and relatives. In general, social sources have been found to be the most credible, and commercial sources the least. However, there are exceptions. Studies indicate that the degree of advertising saturation of the commercial source has an impact on the message's credibility. In many developing countries, advertising and promotion are novel and thus considered highly entertaining and without bias.

In most societies, a small group of individuals (strategic opinion leaders) acts as a primary force in the diffusion and adoption process. Strategic opinion leadership has been found to have a direct influence on a society's propensity to change and on the success or failure of new products and product classes. Furthermore, its composition changes in relation to a country's stage of economic development. In traditional societies and newly industrializing societies (such as many Arab countries), the *strategic opinion leadership* is generally made up of the society's social elite. These leaders tend to fear external forces because they may create a middle class or threaten the existing social structure. Their opinions are reinforced in traditional societies by the acceptance of the hierarchical structure and social relationships.[35]

In industrialized and affluent societies, the *strategic opinion leadership* generally comprises experts who gain their ability to influence as a result of their achievements and expertise (health foods and athletes, automobiles and car racers). For example, Sears, Roebuck contracted with Johnny Miller, a well-known professional golfer, to advertise its line of menswear. Unfortunately for Sears, Miller's golf game hit a slump that lasted several years.

Cultural Lifestyles

The propensity of change and the buyer behavior of individuals is conditioned by a society's economic, cultural, and social environments. The interaction of these three environments results in differing cultural lifestyles. For our purposes, it is profitable to divide cultural lifestyles into two broad categories: normative and personal.[36]

Normative Lifestyle

The term, *normative lifestyle* describes those cultural expectations imposed on individuals by their society and refers to the economic and consumption value system of a society. As previously identified, this value system comprises the individual and combined effects of the society's religion, its values and attitudes, its stage of economic development, its laws, relationships, and so on. All impose certain consumption expectations on each individual in a society, culture, or subculture. These expectations are not limited to overt behavior but extend to the cognitive areas of interest and opinion.

To correctly interpret buyer behavior using models and concepts developed in other cultures, the international marketer needs to have a clear understanding of the *normative lifestyle* of the culture under review. Sheth and Sethi suggest that the *normative lifestyle* of a society, culture, or subculture is in fact the sum of six buyer behavior effects:[37]

1. The influence of culture on the physical and motor development of individuals (nimbleness, dexterity);

2. The influence of culture on the information-processing mechanisms (cognition, perception, and logical thought);

3. The nature of symbolic thought and expression (myths, beliefs, and ritual practices);

4. The influence of culture on role expectations and the socialization of individuals (husband role, parent role, work role);

5. The influence of culture on social change and innovation as related to personality (social risk attached to adopting an innovation);

6. The influence of culture on conformity, deviancy, and mental health.

Personal Lifestyle

Personal lifestyle refers to the beliefs of individuals about the consumption activities of individuals in their society, culture, or subculture. Such things as shopping behavior, price consciousness, and home involvement in the buying process are manifested as a result of *personal lifestyle.* The factors that affect these personal beliefs include education, personality, psychological traits, experience, specific economic and social circumstances, physical environment, and other factors shown in Figure 6-5.

Although the *propensity to change* may be high and sufficient buyers may be willing to adopt the new product or innovation to provide a profitable target market, adoption also depends on other environmental factors not covered in this model. For example, eventual commercial success depends on the existence of adequate marketing institutions, such as distributors, retailers, and media.

THE CULTURAL SENSITIVITY OF MARKETS

Firms implicitly or explicitly adopt a *global-market strategy* or a *national-market strategy* when marketing in overseas markets. To some extent, the choice is the result of a tradeoff between the needs to compete with other companies in its industry and to address the needs or wants of the marketplace. Some companies choose to emphasize one or the other. Caterpillar and Komatsu, for example, tend to emphasize the industry, and Pillsbury and Benetton tend to emphasis the marketplace. Other companies, such as Philips and General Electric, must be responsive to both industry and market conditions.

As Porter has noted, *industry imperatives* include such factors as the structuring of the industry, entry barriers, the cost behavior of the industry, and the bargaining power of buyers and sellers.[38] For example, in highly concentrated industries with few competitors competing for market share within and across national markets, a firm must always be aware of its competitors' actions and be ready to respond. This might involve seeking increased efficiency in the production of products, the introduction of new, competitor-induced products, aggressive price cutting, predatory and retalitory advertising campaigns, and attempts to dominate channels of distribution. *Marketplace imperatives* deal specifically with the market and can be broadly divided into economic and socio-cultural imperatives. Some markets are more susceptible to cultural and social influences than others, such as buying habits, tastes, and product styles. Others are generally more sensitive to economic forces, such as the purchasing power and size of the purchasing unit. Although no rigid guidelines can be given, some general observations can be made.

Markets can be divided into *consumer markets* and *industrial markets.* Consumer markets can be further subdivided into durable goods markets and nondurable goods markets. A further profitable distinction in the international marketplace is to divide durable goods into technological products and nontechnological products.

Industrial Markets

The main distinction between industrial markets and consumer markets is that industrial buyers are interested in solving problems. Generally, these problems are to reduce costs, to increase production and administrative efficiency, to produce a particular type of product, or to effect a combination of these goals. Consequently, industrial buyers tend to be rational and emphasize economic goals. Cultural and social considerations play a relatively less important role in the purchase decision. To some extent, industrial markets can be viewed as global markets. There are, however, differences that need to be considered when selecting the products to be marketed and the marketing programs to be used. Government regulations, the size and sophistication of the potential buyer's operations, and the context within which the product or service is to be used all have an impact on the marketing effort.

Consumer Markets

Consumer markets consist of buyers interested in satisfying a personal need or want. They are generally more susceptible to cultural and social forces than are industrial buyers. The influence of socio-cultural factors is most apparent in the purchase of nondurable products such as clothing, foods, body adornments, and cosmetics. It is less apparent in the purchase of durable goods, such as television sets, radios, and small and large household appliances.

There are exceptions, however, which makes the international marketer's task more interesting and challenging. The purchase of refrigerators, for example, is sensitive to both spatial and social factors, such as room size and shopping habits. Europeans tend to live in smaller homes and purchase smaller refrigerators than Americans. They shop for food more frequently and in smaller amounts than

Americans. The reasons for this include the social function of meeting friends, lack of an automobile and inadequate parking facilities. On the other hand, Mexicans frequently purchase large refrigerators because of their large families and for status. Examples like these, and there are many of them, suggest that it is important to understand the social and cultural factors influencing buyer behavior.

CULTURAL ANALYSIS OF GLOBAL MARKETS

Whether a firm is pursuing a national-market or global-market strategy, it is interested in increasing the effectiveness and efficiency of its marketing programs within and across foreign markets. It must therefore know to what degree it can use the same product, pricing, promotion, and distribution strategies in more than one market.

Unfortunately, the dual goals of program effectiveness and efficiency are in conflict. Market effectiveness is achieved by adapting marketing programs to marketing characteristics and conditions within markets. While doing so incurs additional marketing and production costs, the firm strengthens its market competitiveness by being more responsive to the needs of the marketplace. Efficiency, on the other hand, is achieved by minimizing marketing program changes across markets. Thus, the firm minimizes marketing and production costs and strengthens its competitiveness vis-à-vis its competitors. The economic and competitive implications of both goals need to be taken into account when making program adaptation decisions.

Both goals depend on understanding the cultural context of each market and the degree to which they are culturally similar. Thus, global companies need to develop a capability to conduct cross-cultural analysis of buyer behavior. Such a capability can help these companies optimally balance the competitive benefits to be derived from effectiveness and efficiency.

Cross-Cultural Analysis

"Cross-cultural analysis is the systematic comparison of similarities and differences in the material and behavioral aspects of cultures."[39] In marketing, cross-cultural analysis is used to gain an understanding of market segments within and across national boundaries. The purpose of this analysis is to determine whether the marketing program, or elements of the program, can be used in more than one foreign market or must be modified to meet local conditions.

The approaches used to gain this understanding draw on the methods developed by such social sciences as anthropology, linguistics, and sociology.[40] Standard marketing research techniques, such as multiattribute and psychographic techniques can be used. For example, Berger, Stern, and Johansson used a multiattribute method to study Japanese and American car buyers, and Boote used a psychographic approach to study the segmentation of the European Community.[41]

In marketing, cross-cultural analysis most often involves identifying the effects culture may have on family purchasing roles, product function, product design, sales and promotion activities, channel systems, and pricing. One approach suggested by Engel, Blackwell, and Miniard to the study of the effects of culture on buyer behavior, and thus on the marketing-mix elements, is presented in Exhibit 6-3. This involves answering a comprehensive list of questions, although these are neither exhaustive nor specific. For example, a manufacturer of processed foods would be interested in knowing the impact that culture has on such things as taste, purchasing habits, and eating habits. A manufacturer of household appliances,

EXHIBIT 6-3

A Framework for Cross-Cultural Analysis of Buyer Behavior

Determine Relevant Motivations in the Culture:

☐ What needs are fulfilled with this product in the minds of members of the culture?
☐ How are these needs presently fulfilled?
☐ Do members of this culture readily recognize these needs?

Determine Characteristic Behavior Patterns:

☐ What patterns are characteritstic of purchasing behavior?
☐ What forms of division of labor exist within the family structure?
☐ How frequently are products of this type purchased?
☐ What sizes of packages are normally purchased?
☐ Do any of these characteristic behaviors conflict with behavior expected for this product?
☐ How strongly ingrained are the behavior patterns that conflict with those needed for distribution of this product?

Determine What Broad Cultural Values Are Relevant to This Product:

☐ Are there strong values about work, morality, religion, family relations, and so on, that relate to this product?
☐ Does this product connote attributes that are in conflict with these cultural values?
☐ Can conflicts with values be avoided by changing the product?
☐ Are there positive values in this culture with which the product might be identified?

Determine Characteristic Forms of Decision Making:

☐ Do members of the culture display a studied approach or an impulsive approach to decisions concerning innovations?
☐ What is the form of the decision process?
☐ Upon what information sources do members of the culture rely?
☐ Do members of the culture tend to be rigid or flexible in the acceptance of new ideas?
☐ What criteria do they use in evaluating alternatives?

Evaluate Promotion Methods Appropriate to the Culture:

☐ What roles does advertising occupy in the culture?
☐ What themes, words, or illustrations are taboo?
☐ What language problems exist in present markets that cannot be translated into this culture?
☐ What types of salespersons are accepted by members of the culture?
☐ Are such salespersons available?

on the other hand, would be particularly interested in how potential buyers view a product's reliability, durability, and repairability.

Misinterpreting Cross-Cultural Assessments

A major problem confronting international marketers when conducting cross-cultural studies is the reduction—if not the elimination—of cultural bias. In this regard, marketers need to be constantly sensitive to the influence that their own cultures have on their interpretation of given events, behavior, and information. A major difficulty is in recognizing that our experiences and the way we interpret these experiences are culturally defined and affect how we perceive things. We are often unaware of the influence that culture has had in our lives, on our behavior, and on the decisions we make. For example, an Italian observing two people standing close to each other and gesticulating energetically might well assume that the people were discussing something of mutual interest; an American would probably assume that the two were in a heated argument.

Sources of Cultural Misinterpretation

Although a list of questions similar to those in Exhibit 6-3 can be developed with relative ease, the way they are to be presented and the interpretation of responses require considerable cultural sensitivity. Adler identifies three sources of cross-cultural misinterpretation: (1) subconscious cultural blinders, (2) lack of cultural self-awareness, and (3) projected similarity and parochialism.[42]

Subconscious cultural blinders are tendencies to make subconscious, culturally based assumptions about events, people, and behavior. The Italian and the American deriving differing conclusions regarding the behavior of two people is an example of the subconscious influence of culture. Sensitivity to this type of misinterpretation is particularly important when developing advertising material, whether visual or verbal. For example, it has been determined that English-speaking Canadians are more message oriented than French-speaking Canadians.[43] The latter react more to the source of the advertisement. Differences such as these need to be taken into account if the effectiveness of an advertising campaign is not to be suboptimal.

Lack of cultural self-awareness refers to our lack of awareness of our own cultural characteristics. Americans are often surprised by the way foreigners see them. For example, Indians see Americans as being in a perpetual hurry; Kenyans see them as distant, even with fellow Americans; Colombians see them as being entirely work oriented; and Japanese consider them rude.[44] Our inability to see ourselves as others see us, and our lack of understanding concerning how our cultures influence our behavior and our decisions can easily result in misunderstandings. The situation described in Exhibit 6-4 illustrates how easily misunderstandings can arise if we are insensitive to the influence that our own cultures have on our expectations of others. Exhibit 6-4 describes a situation in which an American supervisor who favors employee participation interacts with a Greek subordinate who favors an autocratic supervisor. It demonstrates the attribution process—the process by which we seek to give meaning to the behavior and words of others. We tend to interpret the actions of others in terms of our own cultural framework.

Projected similarity and parochialism refer to our tendency to assume that

EXHIBIT 6-4
An Example of Cross-Cultural Communication Failure

	Behavior		*Attribution*
American:	How long will it take you to finish this report?	**American:** **Greek:**	I asked him to participate. His behavior makes no sense. He is the boss. Why doesn't he tell me?
Greek:	I don't know. How long should it take?	**American:** **Greek:**	He refuses to take responsibility. I asked for an order.
American:	You are in the best position to analyze time requirements.	**American:** **Greek:**	I press him to take responsibility for his actions. What nonsense: I'd better give him an answer.
Greek:	10 days.	**American:**	He lacks the ability to estimate time; this time estimate is totally inadequate.
American:	Take 15. Is it agreed? You will do it in 15 days?	**American:** **Greek:**	I offer a contract. These are my orders: 15 days.

In fact, the report needed 30 days of regular work. So the Greek worked day and night, but at the end of the 15th day, he still needed to do one more day's work.

American:	Where is the report?	**American:** **Greek:**	I am making sure he fulfills his contract. He is asking for the report. (Both attribute that it is not ready.)
Greek: **American:**	It will be ready tomorrow. But we had agreed it would be ready today.	**American:** **Greek:**	I must teach him to fulfill a contract. The stupid, incompetent boss! Not only did he give me the wrong orders, but he doesn't even appreciate that I did a 30-day job in 16 days.
The **Greek** hands in his resignation.		The **American** is surprised. **Greek:**	I can't work for such a man.

Source: Simcha Ronen, *Comparative and Multinational Management* (New York: John Wiley & Sons, 1986), pp. 101–102.

people from other cultures (or situations in other cultures) are similar to those found in our own cultures. Exhibit 6-4 illustrates not only a lack of cultural self-awareness but also the tendency to project cultural characteristics onto others. Both the American and the Greek unconsciously assumed that the behavior of the other was culturally similar to his own.

The Self-Reference Criterion

Lee has suggested that the root cause of most international business problems is the result of the *self-reference criterion* (SRC), the unconscious tendency to refer to one's own cultural values when evaluating situations in other cultural environments.[45] Lee further noted that a conscious effort must be made to minimize this tendency if errors in judgment or interpretation are to be avoided. He proposed the following four-step, cross-cultural approach for identifying and correcting for SRC:[46]

1. Define the business problem or goal in terms of your own cultural traits, habits, or norms.

2. Define the business problem or goal in terms of the foreign cultural traits, habits, or norms. Make no value judgments.

3. Isolate the SRC influence in the problem, and examine it carefully to see how it complicates the problem.

4. Redefine the problem without the SRC influence, and solve for the optimum business goal situation.

The ability to use this framework depends on an intimate knowledge of other cultures as well as one's own culture. Essentially, the cross-cultural analysis of markets requires:

1. Cultural empathy or an ability to understand the inner logic and coherence of other ways of life, and

2. An ability to be nonjudgmental about the values underpinning buyer behavior in other cultures.

The first capability can be developed only as a result of exposure to other cultures, sensitivity training, and a conscious effort to see the world as others see it. The second capability is also the result of a conscious effort; it requires an understanding of our own culture and an ability to overcome a natural tendency to make judgments based on this culture. Marketers are more likely to be successful when they seek to understand buyer behavior within a specific cultural context and adapt company's marketing strategies to that culture rather than attempting to change it.

SUMMARY

In this chapter, we looked at a central problem facing international marketers, understanding foreign buyer behavior. Before marketers can identify appropriate target markets and develop effective marketing programs, they need to know what, why, when, where, and how customers select and purchase products and services.

Although many models, concepts, and techniques have been developed to analyze buyer behavior, not all are necessarily appropriate for all foreign markets. Certainly, none can be applied without thought. In most cases, buyer-behavior models and concepts must be selected, modified, and applied differently, and the results must be interpreted in the context of the local market. These adjustments are primarily the result of economic, cultural, and social differences among markets. To be successful, the international marketer must be sensitive to and have an understanding of the socio-cultural and economic dimensions of each market and must be sensitive to how they work individually and together to affect buyer behavior.

Each market is a socio-culturally unique

mix of elements. Markets differ in terms of their language and method of communication, beliefs and attitudes, values and norms, sense of self and space, relationships, time and time consciousness, mental processes and learning, rewards and recognition, dress and appearance, and food and eating habits. All markets possess characteristics in common and are not mutually exclusive to other markets. They also possess characteristics that make them unique. Consequently, buyer behavior in each market is both similar to and different from buyer behavior in other markets.

The buyer's behavior is influenced by four major factors: the product's diffusion and adoption characteristics, the market's propensity to change, the market's normative lifestyle, and the buyer's personal lifestyle. An understanding of each of these factors and their interactive effect on buyer response provides the international marketer with the information necessary to accurately select, modify, apply, and interpret buyer behavior models and concepts.

A major problem confronting the international marketer is the natural tendency to misinterpret situations, events, people, and behavior in other cultures because of subconscious cultural blinders, lack of cultural self-awareness, and projected similarities. These three sources of cultural misinterpretation are examples of our tendency to use a self-reference criterion (SRC) when faced with new situations.

DISCUSSION QUESTIONS

1. What elements of culture are most relevant to marketing? Defend your answers.
2. How might a lack of cultural self-awareness affect a marketer's decisions concerning the four elements of the marketing mix?
3. Describe six forms of nonverbal communication that you use. Do you believe that they would have the same meaning in another culture? Why or why not?
4. Why should a marketer be interested in the study of comparative culture?

5. Prepare an outline of a cross-cultural analysis for the sale of (1) a soft beverage, (2) a toaster oven, and (3) machine tools.
6. Define *self-reference criterion*. How might it interfere in the development of an international marketing program?
7. Give three marketing-related examples of cultural misinterpretation due to cultural blinders and projected similarities.

ADDITIONAL READING

Brislin, Richard W., *Cross-Cultural Encounters* (New York: Pergamon, 1981).

Douglas, Susan P., and Bernard Dubois, "Looking at the Cultural Environment for International Marketing Opportunities," *Columbia Journal of World Business,* Vol. 12, Winter 1977.

Hofstede, Geert, *Culture's Consequences: International Differences in Work-Related Values* (Beverly Hills, Calif.: Sage, 1980).

Managing in Different Cultures. Edited by P. Joynt and M. Warner. Universitetsforlaget, AS, Oslo, Norway, 1985.

Muller, Thomas E., and Christopher Bolger, "Search Behaviour of French and English Canadians in Automobile Purchase," *International Marketing Review,* Vol. 2, Winter 1985.

Redding, S. G., "Cultural Effects on the Marketing Process in Southeast Asia," *Journal of Market Research Society,* April 1982.

Thorelli, Hans B., "Comparative Consumer and Industrial Buying Psychology," *International Marketing Review,* Vol. 2, Winter 1985.

ENDNOTES

1. Vern Terpstra, *The Cultural Environment of International Business* (Cincinnati, Ohio: South-Western, 1978), p. 39.
2. James F. Engel and Roger D. Blackwell, *Consumer Behavior,* 4th ed. (New York: Dryden, 1982), p. 129.
3. William D. Wells and George Grubar, "Life Cycle Concepts in Marketing Research," *Journal of Marketing Research,* November 1966.
4. Patrick E. Murphy and William A. Staples, "A Modernized Family Life Cycle," *Journal of Consumer Research,* June 1979.
5. David A. Ricks, Y. C. Fu, and J. S. Arpan, *International Business Blunders* (Columbus, Ohio: Grid, 1974).
6. Vern Terpstra, *The Cultural Environment of International Business* (Cincinnati, Ohio: South-Western, 1978), p. xii.

7. Philip R. Harris and Robert T. Moran, *Managing Cultural Differences* (Houston, Tex.: Gulf, 1985), pp. 58–61.

8. Terpstra, *Cultural Environment,* p. xiii.

9. Edward T. Hall, *The Silent Language* (New York: Doubleday, 1959). This author has two other books that should also be read by anyone interested in doing business in another culture: *Beyond Culture* (New York: Doubleday Anchor, 1977); and *The Hidden Dimension* (New York: Doubleday, 1966).

10. Harris and Moran, *Managing Cultural Differences,* p. 419.

11. Peter Collett, "Meetings and Misunderstandings," *Cultures in Contact,* Stephen Bochner ed. (New York: Pergamon, 1982), p. 83.

12. Terpstra, *Cultural Environment,* p. 3.

13. Ibid., p. 31.

14. Ibid., p. 44.

15. Robert C. Lester, *Theravada Buddhism in Southeast Asia* (Ann Arbor, Mich.: University of Michigan, 1972).

16. Vern Terpstra and Kenneth Davis, *The Cultural Environment of International Business,* 2nd ed. (Cincinnati, Ohio: South-Western, 1985), p. 97.

17. Ibid., p. 101.

18. Ibid., *in re* Quakers.

19. Included in the Protestant group are Australia, Canada, Denmark, Federal Republic of Germany, Finland, New Zealand, Norway, Switzerland, the United Kingdom, and the United States. Countries in the Catholic group are Argentina, Austria, Belgium, the Dominican Republic, France, Mexico, the Philippines, and Spain. Those in the Muslim group are Algeria, Egypt, Jordan, Morocco, Syria, and Turkey. The data are from *The World Bank Atlas 1986* (Washington, D.C.: World Bank, 1986).

20. Draws heavily from Harris and Moran, *Managing,* p. 60.

21. Ibid., p. 61.

22. Endel-Jakob Kolde, *Environment of International Business,* 2nd ed. (Boston: Kent, 1985), p. 423.

23. Terpstra, *Cultural Environment,* p. xvii.

24. Ibid.

25. Edward T. Hall, *Beyond Culture* (New York: Doubleday Anchor, 1977).

26. Edward T. Hall, "Learning the Arab's Silent Language," *Psychology Today,* August 1979, pp. 45–53.

27. T. Levitt, "The Globalization of Markets," *Harvard Business Review,* May–June 1983, pp. 92–102.

28. Jagdish N. Sheth and S. Prakash Sethi, "A Review of Cross-Cultural Buyer Behavior," paper presented at the Symposium on Consumer and Industrial Buying Behavior, University of South Carolina, March 1976.

29. Ibid., p. 15.

30. Ibid., p. 16.

31. This section draws heavily from Sheth and Sethi, "Review," pp. 32–36.

32. Ibid., p. 35.

33. Everett M. Rogers and F. Floyd Shoemaker, *Communications of Innovation* (New York: Free Press, 1971), pp. 22–23.

34. Sheth and Sethi, "Review," p. 24.

35. Ibid., pp. 21–22.

36. The division of cultural life style into normative and personal life styles was suggested by Sheth and Sethi, "Review," p. 20.

37. Ibid., p. 18.

38. M. E. Porter, *Competitive Strategy: Techniques for Analyzing Industries and Competitors* (New York: Free Press, 1980).

39. James F. Engel, Roger D. Blackwell, and Paul W. Miniard, *Consumer Behavior,* 5th ed. (New York: Dryden, 1986), p. 397.

40. See, for example, R. W. Brislin, W. J. Lonner, and R. M. Thorndike, *Cross-Cultural Research Methods* (New York: John Wiley & Sons, 1973).

41. K. A. Berger, B. B. Stern, and J. K. Johansson, "Strategic Implications of a Cross-Cultural Comparison of Attribute Importance: Automobiles in Japan and the United States," in Proceedings of the American Marketing Association Educator's Conference (Chicago: American Marketing Association, 1983), pp. 327–332, and A. S. Boote, "Psychographic Segmentation in Europe," *Journal of Advertising Research,* Vol. 22 (December 1982), pp. 19–25.

42. N. J. Adler, *International Dimensions of Organizational Behavior* (Boston: Kent Publishing Company, 1986) p. 61.

43. Robert Tamilia, "Cross-Cultural Advertising Research: A Review and Suggested Framework," in Ronald C. Curhan, ed., 1974 Combined Proceedings of the AMA, "French Canada," pp. 131–134.

44. John P. Feig and G. Blair, *There is a Difference,* 2nd. ed. (Washington, D.C.: Meridian House, 1980).

45. J. A. Lee, "Cultural Analysis in Overseas Operations," *Harvard Business Review,* March–April 1966, pp. 106–114.

46. Ibid., p. 110.

Chapter 7
Global Marketing Research: Conceptual Issues, Techniques, and Organization

The collection, analysis, and dissemination of information is increasingly a key element in a firm's domestic and international success. Managers cannot make sound business decisions without reliable data. A host of decisions depends on such data—which national markets to enter, what national strategies and plans to pursue, what products to add or drop, what advertising theme to use, what price to charge, and what distribution channels to use, just for starters. Sound information is also needed for evaluating the effectiveness of the company's primary strategies and plans in each of its markets and to assess the performance of its operations. Finally, reliable information is essential for monitoring the economic, political, and legal trends in each market so that necessary changes can be made in local operations, resource allocations, and marketing programs.

Three basic types of research provide both domestic and international companies with vital information: (1) industry research, (2) market research, and (3) marketing research. In some companies, these research activities are formalized; in others, they are informal and carried out in an ad hoc manner. The three types of research may also be distinct activities or treated as one comprehensive activity.

Industry research is undertaken to provide information to decision makers interested in formulating, modifying, or radically altering *corporate* and *business* strategies. Its primary focus is on the *competitive environment* in the *industry* or industries in which the company competes. That is, it is concerned with the factors that have a bearing on the intensity of competition (technology, size, and number of competitors).

Market research is undertaken to provide information to decision makers interested in formulating, modifying, or radically altering the *business* strategies of the company. The primary focus of this type of research is on the *markets* in which the various divisions or business units of the company competes. That is, it is concerned with analyzing the present and future action of its competitors *in specific markets* and the factors that influence market trends (demand and supply trends, market share, market position, sales analysis, and forecasts).

Marketing research is undertaken to provide information to those decision makers responsible for the efficient and effective operation of the company's *marketing* function and activities. The primary focus of this type of research is on *the users* and *potential users* of the *company's products* and the factors that influence their decision to purchase. Basically, this means analyzing those factors that have an influence on product, price, promotion, and distribution decisions.

Examples of the types of research problems studied are listed in Exhibit-1. This list is not exhaustive; it simply provides some idea of the pervasive need for research.

Research activities involving investigations within or between foreign countries must not be considered mere extensions of domestic research. As soon as the

EXHIBIT 7-1
Examples of Research Activities Undertaken
by Companies

Corporate Responsibility or Enterprise Strategy Research

1. Consumers' right to know studies
2. Ecological impact studies
3. Social values and policies studies
4. Cross-national managerial practices studies

Industry or Corporate Strategy Research

1. Corporate and business unit portfolio studies
2. Manufacturing cost studies: economies of scale, learning curve
3. Strength of channel relationships
4. Shared costs or activities of business units
5. Resource studies: financial, depth of management
6. Labor force climate
7. Economic and political trend analyses
8. Competitor studies: strengths and weaknesses

Market Research

1. Market potential studies
2. Market share analysis
3. Market characteristics studies
4. Distribution channel studies
5. Sales analyses: products, territories, sales force
6. Competitive product studies

Marketing Research

1. Buyer behavior studies
2. Product testing
3. Packaging studies
4. Price elasticity studies
5. Buyer motivation studies
6. Media research
7. Copy research

decision is made to conduct research in another national market or across several national markets, myriad problems arise that often are not encountered in the conduct of purely domestic research. At best, the failure to recognize these problems results in findings that are of no value to the decision maker. At worst, it results in decisions that may prove extremely costly for the firm.

The purpose of this chapter is to provide direction in conducting international research with particular emphasis on international marketing research. We will identify and explain the major methodological considerations in cross-national and foreign-country research. Understanding these issues and their implications is crucial to the conduct of international marketing research.[1]

THE INTERNATIONAL RESEARCH PROCESS

The international research process is identical to the domestic process. It consists of a number of sequential activities as shown in Figure 7-1: (1) identification and definition of the research problem, (2) selection of an appropriate research design and samples, (3) collection of relevant data and information, (4) analysis and interpretation of the data and information collected, and (5) dissemination of the resulting problem-specific information.[2]

Although the processes used in domestic and international market research are the same, international research differs from domestic research in at least five ways. First, the research focus may be on a single national situation or be global (cross-national) in scope. Second, because the company is operating in more than one country, the problems investigated may be unique (or at least more complex). Third, research methods may need to be modified for each country or culture because of peculiar local differences. Fourth, unique problems

FIGURE 7-1   The Research Process Stages and Associated International Issues and Problems

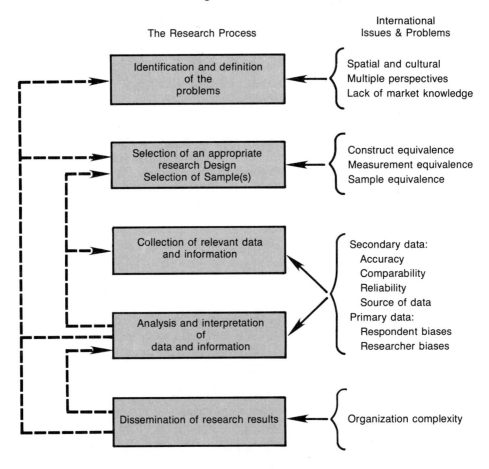

are associated with the collection, analysis, and interpretation of secondary and primary data. Last, the dissemination of market-related information is more complex than on the home front.

In international marketing, the chance of introducing potential *research errors* at each stage of the research process is compounded. Introduction of errors must be minimized whenever possible. (They can never be eliminated completely.) Unfortunately, many of the errors in international research are problem specific.

We will now discuss general issues in research and how these issues affect research activities.

PROBLEM FORMULATION ISSUES

Boyd, Westfall, and Stasch[3] identify four steps in the problem-formulation stage that are of universal concern to researchers: (1) who the decision makers are, the environment in which they are functioning, and the resources they control; (2) the objectives or goals of the research; (3) the possible courses of action available for solving the problem under review; and (4) the consequences of each alternative course of action. Although the need to clearly define a problem and courses of action available for its solution are universal, the four steps pose different and sometimes unique problems for the international researcher.

Spatial and Cultural Separation

Those charged with research and decision making often are geographically separated or have different cultural backgrounds and experiences. This hinders the researcher's ability to arrive at a well-defined understanding of the research problem, and the courses of action available to the decision maker. Face-to-face meetings to discuss a problem situation are often costly and time consuming because of geographic distance. Communication problems can also arise, even when both can communicate in the same language and have access to telecommunication devices such as telex machines, telephones, or even closed-circuit television.

Multiple Perspectives

Marketing on an international or global scale poses many problems that are considerably more complex than those encountered domestically. For example, the company's marketing presence may vary considerably from market to market; it may be exporting to Mexico and Saudi Arabia, have a limited number of personnel operating out of sales offices in France and Italy, and have complete marketing staffs, including marketing researchers, in Brazil and West Germany. Marketing objectives and goals may be quite different for each of these countries. In addition, the socio-cultural, economic, legal, and political dimensions of market situations may vary considerably, and the resources available to the decision maker in each market may be quite different. Consequently, the factors influencing the need for research, particularly cross-national research, may vary considerably.

The Need for Exploratory Research

Understanding of a problem often requires an appreciation of background factors such as the reasons for the decision maker's interest in the issue. Frequently, these underlying factors have to be unearthed in a preliminary *situational study* which require studying company records and appropriate external sources and, possibly, interviewing persons within and outside the company. Exploratory-research may also be needed because the decision maker, researcher, or both may be unfamiliar with a particular foreign situation. However, such a study becomes problematic when undertaken in an international setting because of the problems discussed above.

RESEARCH DESIGN ISSUES

A *research design* is simply the framework or plan adopted to study a particular research problem. It is the blueprint followed when collecting and analyzing data. Its dual purpose is to ensure that the study is relevant to the problem and that it employs economic, effective procedures.

Regardless of the basic research design selected—exploratory, descriptive, or causal—several considerations are of basic concern to researchers conducting foreign or cross-country research. An understanding of these considerations is crucial because in many instances the findings will be rendered useless if they are not anticipated in the research design.

Three issues critical to research design are: (1) construct equivalence, (2) measurement equivalence, and (3) sample equivalence. *Construct equivalence* is concerned with the question "Are we studying the same phenomenon in countries X and Y?"; *measurement equivalence* with "Are the phenomena in countries X and Y measured the same way?"; *sample equivalence* with "Are the samples used in countries X and Y equivalent?" Although these issues are interrelated, for the purpose of discussion, we consider them separately. Further, we assume that the researcher is conducting research on a phenomenon in one or more foreign countries (a United States or Brazilian researcher might, for example, study an advertising theme in France or across a number of European countries).

Construct Equivalence

Construct equivalence deals with how both the researcher and the subjects of the research and others involved see, understand, and code a particular phenomenon. The problem confronting the international researcher is that—because of socio-cultural, economic and political differences—perspectives may be neither identical nor equivalent. The international researcher is constantly faced with the self-reference criterion problem and the implications it has in the formulation of a research design.

Five aspects of construct equivalence are of major concern when conducting foreign or cross-country research: functional equivalence, conceptual equivalence, definitional equivalence, temporal equivalence, and market structure equivalence.[4] Examples of the types of problems each aspect may pose are presented in Exhibit 7-2.

EXHIBIT 7-2

Examples of Construct Equivalence Problems

Functional Equivalence

In England, Germany, and Scandinavia, beer is generally perceived as an alcoholic beverage. In Mediterranean lands, however, beer is considered akin to soft drinks. Therefore, a study of the competitive status of beer in Northern Europe would have to build in questions on wine and liquor. In Italy, Spain, or Greece, the comparison would have to be with soft drinks.

In Italy, it's common for children to have a bar of chocolate between two slices of bread as a snack. In France, bar chocolate is often used in cooking. But a West German housewife would be revolted by either practice.

A third of all German and Dutch businessmen take their wives with them on business trips, as opposed to only 15 percent of their English and French counterparts. As a study for one hotel delicately put it, the criteria each group uses in judging hotels and the services they offer clearly are likely to be different.

Conceptual Equivalence

Were a researcher to use the concepts "outgroup" and "ingroup" in the United States and Greece, two different groups would be included. In the United States, the ingroup includes people from one's own country and the outgroup includes foreigners. In Greece, the outgroup includes countrymen with whom the person is not closely associated.

Personality traits such as aggressiveness, or assertiveness may not be relevant in all countries or cultures. The concept may be absent from the culture and language, or takes on an entirely different meaning. For example, when Athenians were asked to help fellow Greeks and foreigners mail letters, the Greeks received worse treatment than the foreigners.

As a final example, the Japanese and Western concepts of decision-making differ considerably. Whereas the Western sees decision-making as a discrete event, the Japanese cannot make that distinction.

Definitional Equivalence

In France, fragrance is measured on a hot-cold continuum. In the United States and the United Kingdom, this is not an attribute assigned to fragrances. That is, the attribute used to categorize product classes may vary from one country or culture to another.

The beer example cited under functional equivalence provides another example of the problems in achieving definitional equivalence. In the United Kingdom beer would be classified as an alcoholic drink. In Mediterranean cultures it should be classified as a soft drink.

Source: Functional equivalence examples are taken from Lee Adler, "Special Wrinkles in International Marketing Research," *Sales & Marketing Management.* Copyright © 1976. Conceptual equivalence examples are taken from Richard Brislin, Walter J. Lonner, and Robert M. Thorndike, *Cross-Cultural Research Methods* (New York: John Wiley & Sons, 1973), p. 7.

Functional Equivalence

Functional equivalence deals with the *activity-function* relationship of human behavior *as perceived by the actor(s).* For example, what function is being served when someone offers you a cup of coffee? In the United States, such a gesture is merely one of politeness; it can be safely refused. In Saudi Arabia, such a gesture may have social implications; the refusal may be considered an affront.[5]

Three aspects of functional equivalence need to be considered in any research: the function served by the activity, the object (if any) used in the activity, and the name or term given to the activity.

For example, cycling in the United States is primarily a recreational activity, not so in the Netherlands and China, where it is used primarily for transportation. Consequently, the object or bicycle is viewed as a recreational device in the United States and a transportation device in the other two countries. Competing products in the United States would be other recreational products. In the Netherlands and China, competing products would include other forms of transportation, such as buses and trains. The words *cycling and bicycle* would conjure up different meanings in the minds of American and Dutch or Chinese consumers.

Shopping for food is another example of an activity fulfilling different functions. In the United States, shopping for food is generally perceived as a chore. In France and some other countries, this activity has a significant social dimension. The French housewife's interaction with local shopkeepers and neighbors during her shopping activity is an integral part of her daily social life. The marketing implications of this *activity–function* difference are many and varied. For example, the French housewife shops for food more frequently, purchases smaller amounts, and therefore has relatively less need for a large refrigerator than does the American housewife.

Conceptual Equivalence

In contrast to functional equivalence, conceptual equivalence is primarily concerned with the concepts *used by the researcher* to identify the activity–function relationships in countries under investigation. Many concepts are culture bound and therefore inappropriate for use in other countries or for cross-national studies. Conceptual equivalence can also be at issue in the selection of the terms or words used to measure certain items. (This particular problem will be discussed later in conjunction with translation equivalence.)

As suggested in Chapter 6, problems in conceptual equivalence can arise when selecting United States consumer behavior models, concepts, or constructs for use in overseas consumer research. We do not mean to imply that consumer behavior models and concepts developed in one country should not be used in another country or that specific models should not be developed. Rather, we stress that researchers need to be aware of the possible need to modify a particular concept or to select one more appropriate to the consumers under study. For example, a bicycle study may well focus on the issue of "reliablity". However a Chinese consumers definition of a reliable cycle may be very different from that of American cyclists.

Research that is basically exploratory or descriptive does not need to establish conceptual equivalence in the research design stage. However, conceptual equivalence is required when interpreting any *differences* uncovered during research. It is essential to remember that no matter how *obvious* a concept is in one culture, that concept may not exist in another culture. If it does, it may take on a different meaning. *The researcher cannot assume that a particular model, concept, or construct is transferable.*

Definitional Equivalence

A third type of construct equivalence relates to the categories used by the researcher to group data. Relevant product classes, family roles, occupations, and so on differ from country to country. For example, "dessert" in Great Britain and France may include fresh fruit and different types of cheese; in China, sweet items do not generally form part of the meal. Beer, as described in Exhibit 7-2, may likewise be variously categorized. Occupations and the social status given to particular occupations also vary from one country or culture to another. In the United States, the social status of the businessperson is considerably higher than it is in those African countries where the commercial activity is often left to Indians.

An even more fundamental example of definitional equivalence problems is offered by Mayer:[6]

> An attempt to standardize age groupings on an international basis had to be abandoned. It was found that persons in the same age groups in different cultures were at different stages in their life and family cycles. Hence, defining age groups that were chronologically identical did not in fact create comparable groups.

Temporal Equivalence[7]

Research in two or more countries or cultures can be conducted simultaneously, sequentially, or independently. As a consequence, the possibility of *temporal error* is introduced into international research. (Such errors are not generally of importance to the domestic researcher). To assume that a temporal error can be eliminated by taking simultaneous measurements of a phenomenon in the countries of interest can be erroneous. Seasonal, cultural, political, and economic factors may be such that the measurements are not equivalent. Since Argentina and Australia are in the southern hemisphere, their seasons are opposite to those in the United States and Europe at any given time of year. Moreover, the purchase of gifts for Christmas primarily occurs only in countries with a Christian heritage. Further, the product or service marketed by an international company may not be in the same stage of the product life cycle in all the countries studied. A product might be in the mature stage of its cycle in the United States market, in its growth stage in Europe, and in its introduction stage in Latin America. Because of such differences, conducting the same research simultaneously in different countries will neither guarantee nor necessarily provide comparable data.

Market Structure Equivalence

A final source of construct error of particular concern to the international researcher deals with market similarity, which can be divided into two parts—market characteristics and marketing institutions. For example, consumption patterns and market response rates are affected both by product awareness and product availability. These variables, in turn, are affected by the availability of adequate channels of distribution, advertising coverage, product substitutes, and competitive intensity.

Measurement Equivalence

Measurement equivalence deals with the methods and procedures used by the researcher to collect and categorize essential data and information. Construct and measurement equivalence are highly interrelated. Measurement is the operationalization of the constructs to be used. However, the achievement of construct equivalence does not automatically guarantee measurement equivalence. As Green and White explain:[8]

> ... consider this problem with respect to the cross-national measurement of affection, an idea frequently expressed in promotional campaigns. While the concept of affection is probably universal, and while the function affection performs is probably similar across nations, the exact form which affection takes in each society differs considerably. Therefore, cross-national instruments that employ the identical measures of such phenomena may not provide data which permit reliable comparisons to be made.

Emic and Etic Measures

International researchers may use one of two general types of measures in their studies, *emic* or *etic*.[9] Emic instruments are designed to study a phenomenon within only a single country or culture. Etic instruments are culture free and can be employed in several countries or cultures.

Both types of measurement have advantages and disadvantages. When the emic approach is adopted, country-specific instruments have to be developed for each country or culture involved in the study in order to ensure comparability of results. When the etic approach is adopted, each measurement in the instrument has to be tested to ensure that it is culture free or, at least, culture unbiased.

In practice, etic instruments are often very difficult to develop and the emic approach is used more. Research instruments are altered to account for differences among the countries or cultures of interest. When developing emic instruments to measure the same phenomenon across several countries or cultures, the international researcher must be concerned with obtaining *gradation, translation,* and *scale equivalences.*

Gradation Equivalence

Gradation equivalence deals with equivalence in the units of measurement used. The need for equivalence with regard to monetary measurements and such physical measurements such as weights, volume, and distance is obvious. Not so obvious is the need to have equivalence in such things as product grades, quality, and safety standards and procedures. These vary from country to country.

More subtle differences in the gradation of research instruments involve perceptual cues (color, form, or shape) and other nonverbal stimuli.[10] As Ricks observed:[11]

> ... green, a popular color in many Moslem countries, is often associated with disease in countries with dense, green jungles. It is associated with cosmetics by the French, Dutch, and Swedes... To most of the world, blue is thought to be a masculine color, but it is not as manly as red in the United Kingdom or France ...
> Red is felt to be blasphemous in some African countries but is generally considered to be a color reflecting wealth or luxury elsewhere.

In the case of color perceptions the problem is actually more complex than just interpreting the meanings attached to different colors. Heider and others claim that Western subjects perceive more color classes than some African subjects.[12] For example, some African tribes do not discriminate between blue and green.

Translation Equivalence

As we noted in Chapter 6, language is both verbal and nonverbal. Both aspects of language have to be considered when using a research instrument in different countries with different languages or when using secondary data sources. Though the need to translate verbalized questions or statements is superficially obvious, the need to translate what nonverbal stimuli connote is sometimes overlooked. Both "translation" requirements are central to the establishment of construct validity and are therefore potential sources of error.

Verbal Translation. Several recognized methods are available for translating questions from one language to another. A brief description of four frequently used methods follows:[13]

Back Translation Back translation involves having the source questions translated from one language to the targeted language by one translator and then having the translated questions translated back to the source language by another translator. This process is repeated until the originator of the questions is satisfied that the translated questions are representative of the source questions.

Parallel Blind Translation The parallel blind translation involves having several translators translate the source questions independently. The results are then compared and any discrepancies resolved by the translators.

Committee Translation As the name implies, the source questions are translated by a group of translators. The major difference between this approach and the previous is that the translators discuss the translations during the translation process, not afterward.

The Random Probe Method. This procedure requires the placing of probes at random both in the source and the translated questionnaires during the pretesting stage of the research to determine whether the respondents understand the questions in the same way.

Translation techniques can be very time consuming and costly, but none is sufficiently rigorous to ensure total linguistic equivalence. Mayer, in fact, suggests that linguistic comparability may be fundamentally unobtainable.[14] For example, a product concept, such as Campbell's condensed soups or Carnation's instant breakfasts, may not exist in certain languages or may have no meaning in certain cultures.

Marketing researchers must recognize that source questionnaires may need modifying. They can do so by using *decentering.*[15]

> In this process both the source and the target language versions are viewed as open to modification. If translation problems are recognized within the source

document, it is modified to be more easily translatable. Through this process, the source questionnaire itself becomes clearer and more precise.

Nonverbal Translation. Translation of nonverbal aspects of a research instrument requires establishing equivalence in any perceptual cues used, such as colors, shapes, and symbols. As Douglas and Craig succinctly describe:[16]

> Translation of nonverbal stimuli requires attention to how perceptual cues are interpreted in each research context. Misunderstanding may arise because the respondent is not familiar with a product or other stimulus, for example, with an electrical appliance, or with the way in which it is depicted. Alternatively, respondents may misinterpret stimuli because the associations evoked by the stimuli differ from one country or culture to another.

Secondary Data Source Translation. Although translation equivalence is of particular importance when developing instruments to collect primary data, it is also important when translating secondary data documents. For example, when translating from English English to American English, we often assume that the words and symbols used have the same meaning and connotations. They may not. In the United States, a *billion* is a 1,000 million; in the United Kingdom, it is a 100 million. We encounter the same problem when using secondary-source documents from Latin American countries. Although they have a common language, Spanish, they may use different words and symbols or ascribe different meanings and connotations to particular words. In Puerto Rico, the decimal part of a number is separated from the rest of the number by a period; in the rest of Latin America, a comma is used (101.10 and 101,10 respectively). When evaluating and comparing taxonomies of secondary data across national boundaries translation problems may also arise. For example, a publicly held company in Columbia may be legally and operationally different from firms classified under the same label in the United States.

Scale Equivalence

A final concern for the international researcher when developing an instrument for collecting primary data or evaluating the results presented in a secondary data source document is the scoring, or scalar, equivalence of the measure used. For example, a five- or seven-point scale is normally used in the United States to measure such things as preferences or attitudes. In other countries ten- or twenty-point scales may be common.[17] The use of an uncommon scale can result initially in uncertainty and frustration and eventually in unintentional response errors.

A second scale equivalence problem deals with the weight, or relative importance, assigned to respondent scores. The researcher cannot safely assume that the distribution of responses to a particular question is identical for different countries or cultures. The relative importance respondents place on the various scale values may differ, as may the interpretation of ascribed values.

Instrument validity presents a third problem. This is important for image studies, where the focus of comparison may be stores, products, even countries (stereotypes), and it is necessary to compare the results of one study with those of another study. In a five-country study, Davis, Douglas, and Silk determined that three types of measurements commonly used in consumer research (demographic and other characteristics, involvement in household tasks and decisions, and lifestyle variables) resulted in significant between sample reliability differentials.[18] The technique used to achieve linguistic and conceptual equivalence in the measurements employed was routine back translation procedures. The authors concluded that the differentials were the result of the measures used, not the nationality or language of the samples.

Sampling Equivalence

Researchers generally collect information on or about a portion of a population. That is, a sample is taken from a larger group, or population and the data and information collected is used to infer something about that population. The ability to make inferences about the larger group depends partly on the method used to select the sample. Because of socio-cultural, economic, and political differences among or between countries, the international researcher faces two problems not encountered by the domestic researcher: (1) identifying and operationalizing comparable populations, and (2) selecting samples that are simultaneously representative of their populations and comparable across countries.

Definition of the Population

Populations can be defined using either externally imposed criteria or internally dictated traits. That is, a population can be expressed in terms of location, income, age, and educational characteristics or in terms inherent in the subjects themselves, such as psychological and personality characteristics. Each technique poses problems for the international researcher interested in cross-national comparability.

For example, an externally imposed definition, such as income classification, ignores the fact that particular income groups may have different lifestyles and family styles in different countries and cultures. Internally generated definitions may include subjects that in one culture or country may have a high interest in the product offering of the company, and in another a low interest. Further, because of cultural and social differences, the behavior of individuals may vary across cultures. For example, status is overtly expressed in the United States through the acquisition and display of material possessions. In the United Kingdom, it is expressed more by position in the community or family. The international researcher thus cannot assume that externally imposed or internally generated population definitions are comparable.

The problem of defining a family unit or a household has already been discussed in Chapter 6. To generalize this definition so that it has comparable meaning across cultures is extremely difficult. Comparable meaning can indeed be achieved, but each definition entails implicit assumptions about the family or household. For example, those persons at a particular address can be used to define household. But does such a definition imply similar marketing behavior when the husband has more than one wife, each of whom lives in a separate dwelling? Such may be the case in cultures where polygamy is accepted.

Scope and Representativeness of the Sample

To reduce the possibility of alternative explanations of results, the researcher needs to select comparable samples from each population. However, because of the problems just discussed, doing so is not always possible. It can also be difficult, costly, and time consuming. Some markets do not have sufficient potential for the company to warrant the expense of obtaining truly representative samples. Moreover, representative samples from each population may exhibit such extreme variations as to make cross-national comparisons difficult, if not impossible.

A commonly employed sampling technique in cross-national studies is to restrict the scope (domain of inclusion) within the sample. Segments of the population assumed to be of little interest would be excluded. For example, in their comparison of French and United States shoppers, Green and Langeard restricted the scope of their French sample to ensure that it had the same relationship to the French population as did the United States sample and population.[19] That is, they used the same demographic variables (age, income, education, and employment) in both countries. As a result, they sacrificed representativeness, but enhanced the possibility for comparability in terms of the selected demographic variables.

SECONDARY AND PRIMARY DATA ISSUES

Secondary data are pre-existing statistics or information gathered for a purpose other than that of the immediate study. *Primary data* are compiled by the researcher expressly for the immediate investigation. If General Motors were to collect demographic data on automobile purchasers for the purpose of determining who buys the various types and sizes of cars sold in Brazil, the data so collected would be primary data. If it were to obtain the same information from documents published by a market-research organization like Nielsen or from internal records gathered for some other purpose, that information would be secondary data.

The issues surrounding the collection and use of foreign secondary and primary data cannot be easily separated. The researcher must be as meticulous when analyzing or using secondary data as when analyzing or using primary data. This is particularly true of internal secondary data. For example, the findings of a study on the effectiveness of particular advertising themes in Venezuela cannot be blindly accepted as relevant for Colombia. Although the following discussions have been loosely divided into secondary and primary data issues for ease of presentation, the reader needs to remember that no such separation truly exists.

Secondary Data Issues

Although secondary data have many advantages, their use pose problems for international researchers. The problems arise primarily from a need to be extra-sensitive to the inherent disadvantages associated with the use of secondary data. In the following sections, we highlight some of the major advantages, disadvantages, and problems when using secondary data for international research. They involve questions concerned with (1) accuracy, (2) comparability, (3) reliability, and (4) source of data.

Accuracy

Different sources often report different values for variables such as GNP, households, vehicle registrations, and the number of retail outlets. There are five main reasons for the discrepancies. One is that the *definitions* used by various sources for a particular statistic may differ. For example, in Colombia, export statistics are based on registered exports and manifested exports. Registered exports are for the purpose of getting an export license and may never materialize as exports. Manifested exports are actual exports. The two statistics seldom agree.

A second possible reason for differences is the *purpose* for which the statistics were collected. For example, in Italy, Mexico, and Peru, production data are often inaccurate since they are frequently used by the government to collect taxes. As a result, some companies keep two sets of books, one for public use and the other for internal use. A third reason is that *timeframes* used for collecting the data differ. *Adjustments* may also be made to the collected data before they are published. As noted earlier, GNP and trade data may be overstated or understated by governments for political reasons. Finally, the *mechanisms* used to collect data may vary from one country or agency to another. In many countries where a substantial portion of the population is illiterate or the government's infrastructure inadequate, population census may be based on estimates.

Clearly, these situations cast doubt on the accuracy of the data and their appropriateness for research. In general, it is desirable to understand how a specific statistic is defined in each of the countries included in the study and which statistics are best suited for the research at hand.

Comparability

The comparability of data varies from one country or agency to another. A population census may not only be inaccurate but may also vary in terms of frequency taken. In the United States, a comprehensive population census is conducted every ten years. In Saudi Arabia, the first census was conducted in 1974. Consequently, population data are often based on *estimates* of population growth. Measurement units may also vary from one country or agency to another. In many Latin American and European countries, workers are paid a "thirteenth month" as an automatic bonus sometime during the year. These payments are included as part of the workers' income.

Reliability

Still another problem is the reliability of secondary data. Will the same result be obtained when measurement is repeated in a different context, fashion, or time? Portes views this problem as having two parts, *data stability* and *data internal consistency*.[20] Data stability refers to the consistency of the data on a particular variable over time. Data internal consistency refers to the consistency of the variable's definition for the period of interest. The items included as part of the variable, the base-comparison periods, and the methods used for evaluating and presenting data change from time to time. Data reliability varies from one country to another and from one period to another.

Primary and Secondary Sources of Secondary Data

A *primary source* of secondary data is the source that originated the data. A *secondary source* is a source that obtained the data from an original source. *The cardinal rule in using secondary data is to always use the primary source when available.* Why? The quality and appropriateness of the secondary data needs to be evaluated in terms of the immediate research, and primary sources are typically more accurate and complete than are secondary sources.

For example, the *Statistical Abstract of the United States* is a secondary source. The data it contains are from other government and trade sources. Consequently, the researcher using only the *Statistical Abstract* would be violating the cardinal rule in the use of secondary data. He or she would be making assumptions about research design, instruments used, the analysis and interpretation of the data, and the presentation of the findings that may be incorrect. Such assumptions cannot be made safely about foreign secondary sources. However, the primary source may not be available.

A substantial amount of information needed to answer questions on foreign markets can be obtained from five basic sources: international organizations, governments, banks, international consulting firms, and company documents. In addition to providing documentary information, many organizations involved in producing these data provide primary research services.

International Organizations. Six important sources of data and information are the United Nations (UN), the United Nations Industrial Development Organization (UNIDO), the Organization for Economic Cooperation and Development (OECD), the International Monetary Fund (IMF), the General Agreement on Tariffs and Trade (GATT), and the World Bank. The UN is the major source of world economic data. In addition to publishing aggregate data on the economic development of the world (*Statistical Yearbook of the United Nations*), the organization publishes regional reviews (*Economic Survey of Europe* and *Economic Survey of Asia and the Far East*) covering developments on such topics as agriculture, industry, foreign trade, balance of payments, and logistics. The *World Economic Survey* provides an overview of current economic issues, whereas the *World Trade Annual* provides data from the principle trading nations by commodity and country.

The primary objectives of UNIDO are the acceleration of industrialization of the developing countries and the fostering of industrial cooperation between different regions and countries. As part of this effort, it publishes many reports and documents of interest to international companies. It s annual report, *Industry and Development: Global Report,* presents a review of and short-term forecasts for the level of output in 28 branches of industry in different regions and in as many countries as possible.

The OECD conducts economic studies on the performance of its 24 member countries. The *OECD Economic Outlook* provides a semiannual survey of trends in the member countries. The *OECD Economic Surveys* contain information on the economic standing of each member country.

The IMF provides information on many national economic and financial indicators. It publishes biweekly the *International Monetary Fund Survey,* which focuses on global economic trends. The IMF also publishes the monthly financial status of 104 countries in *International Financial Statistics.*

GATT makes available various guidebooks and directories that are of help to the international marketer, for example, *Guide to Sources of Information of Foreign Trade Regulations* and *World Directory of Industry and Trade Associations.*

The World Bank's *World Tables* summarizes data on living patterns using such indicators as radio, television, telephone, and car ownership per thousand households. It also publishes annually *The World Bank Atlas,* which presents information on population, gross national product, life expectancy, infant mortality, and education for the world's various countries and territories.

Governments. The international marketer's own government and the governments of the countries in which he or she is interested are also valuable sources for information on markets. For example, the United States government publishes continually a series of publications focusing on foreign market opportunities. *Global Market Surveys* include in-depth reports for specific United States products and industries with export growth possibilities in selected foreign countries. *Country Sectoral Surveys* report on selected countries with the most promising opportunities for United States firms. *Overseas Business Reports* provide basic marketing background information on many countries. *Foreign Economic Trend Reports* give in-depth reviews of current business conditions and short-term prospects country by country. These reports include information on gross national product, foreign trade, wage and price indices, unemployment rates, and construction starts.

Governments also have commercial attachés and counselors at their foreign embassies and consulates who are generally good sources of information on the local commercial environment. In many cases, they can also provide commercial leads and introductions. If they do not have the required information, they can generally guide the researcher to the right source.

Banks and Other Financial Institutions. The international departments of banks also provide many services for their customers through their foreign branches and affiliates. These services include locating overseas markets for products and services; foreign sources of supply, locating potential foreign investors, distributors, and agents; and obtaining specific information concerning current economic and political conditions and foreign-exchange regulations. Large United States, British, and German banks, for instance, have worldwide networks of branches and affiliates from which they glean local information.

International Consulting Firms. A number of companies gather, organize, and make available information of value to international marketers. Dun and Bradstreet, for example, provides financial and marketing information as well as credit information. Its foreign counterparts may be reached through the Foreign Credit Interchange Bureau (FCIB) of the National Association of Credit Men and provide credit information and a worldwide collection service.

The large advertising agencies through their overseas offices provide their clients specific guidance in marketing products in various markets. Many of them will also provide marketing research services on request. Large accounting firms, such as Price Waterhouse, Ernst and Whinney, and Deloitte, Haskins and Sells offer advisory services and publish materials for international marketers.

Major research companies like Burke and A. C. Nielson, have overseas offices that provide market information and intelligence services. Business International and the Economist Intelligence Unit (associated with the *Economist*) publish newsletters and reports on political and economic conditions and specific industry situations. The latter also conducts studies for individual companies. In addition, many data bases can be purchased.

Company Documents. Another source for information on foreign markets is company records. The company's experience in other markets and the results of previous marketing studies often provide valuable insights into possible customer reactions and marketing problems.

Primary Data Issues

When there are no adequate sources of secondary data, the researcher must collect primary data. Of particular concern for the international marketing researcher collecting such data are the inherent respondent and researcher biases involved. These biases differ from those in domestic research only in degree.

Respondent Biases

The researcher needs to be alert to the possibility of three types of respondent biases: (1) social bias, (2) nonresponse bias, and (3) researcher–respondent interaction bias.

Social Bias. Douglas and Craig identify three types of social bias that may be present when collecting primary data: social acquiescence or courtesy bias, social desirability bias, and topic bias.[21] The first deals with the tendency in some cultures to provide the researcher with answers that the subject feels are desired. *Courtesy bias* is relatively more common in Asian and Middle-Eastern countries. For example, Triandis and Triandis found that United States subjects were not so acquiescent as Greek subjects.[22] And the Japanese culture imputes a strong sense of obligation to ensure that another person is not distressed or offended.

Social desirability bias deals with the social desirability of the items under study, even the questions used. For example, the response of some subjects may be an attempt to give answers that they believe reflect a particular social status, educational level, and so on. This bias is particularly marked among well-educated urban subjects, or upper-level social classes across countries.

Topic bias deals with the social sensitivity of particular topics in different countries or cultures. As we noted in the previous chapter, each culture has its own taboos. For example, discussion of sex tends to be taboo in India, and the open display of affection between persons of the opposite sex is frowned on in Thailand.

The response styles of cultural groups have been found to be different. For example, Mitchell noted that Indians were more likely to be yea-sayers than the Chinese.[23] In addition, cultural groups vary in the degree of accuracy of their statements. Japanese may understate the value of their assets or properties, whereas Middle-East respondents may exaggerate. Different cultural groups might also respond differently to open-ended questions.

A final example of the biased response problem deals with the sex of the respondent. During a five-country study, Almond and Verba discovered in Mexico that 64 percent of the respondents were female although they made up only 52 percent of the population.[24] In contrast, in different studies in India, 80 percent of the respondents were male. This particular response-bias problem can also be viewed as a nonresponse-bias problem because some segments of the population are inaccessible to researchers.

Nonresponse Bias. There are also obvious cultural patterns of nonresponse. Almond and Verba also noted during their five-country study that the response rates in the various countries varied from 17 to 41 percent. In addition, individual item nonresponse may vary significantly among countries. United Kingdom respondents tend to be more reluctant to answer personal questions than United States respondents, and Indians, as stated earlier, are hesitant to answer questions with a sexual connotation.

Researcher–Respondent Interaction Bias. Many primary research studies require interaction between the researcher and the respondent. Unfortunately, the interaction of researcher and respondent can have a strong and differential impact on the responses obtained from subjects in different countries and cultures. Two aspects of this problem need careful consideration by the researcher, the *location of the interaction* and *the relative social status* of the researcher and respondent (that is, "class").

The location in which the interaction takes place and the presence of others can have a strong impact on the responses obtained. For example, the subject might look to the others present for the "appropriate" response. This, of course, is not unique to foreign countries and cultures. However, in cultures such as in Islamic countries, it is almost impossible to interview the homemaker alone.

Many more cultural aspects need to be considered when interviewing subjects in foreign cultures or countries than when interviewing subjects from one's own culture. Subtleties of class distinction vary considerably and frequently have significant meaning in other cultures. As we suggested in Chapter 6, the choice of words and phrases, clothing, and gestures reflect status. These, in turn, can influence the responses of the subject. For example, the answers of lower-class subjects may be biased if the interviewer is from the upper class.

A similar situation can arise if the interviewer is a foreigner. In some cultures, inquisitive foreigners (even cultural outsiders such as someone from another social class) are automatically viewed with mistrust. Consequently, misinterpretation of the study's intent can easily occur and the responses accordingly contaminated. The criteria used to select interviewers must take into account such biases.

Researcher Biases

The biases above have been viewed from the perspective of the respondent; similar biases are present in the researcher. As noted earlier, a foreign researcher is constantly burdened with a self-reference criterion problem. This is particularly true when the researcher is directly involved in interviewing the subjects using tools such as structured interview guides and open-ended questions.

ORGANIZATION OF INTERNATIONAL RESEARCH

At the start of this chapter, we noted that research data is required by different managerial levels on many different topics. This suggests that several questions need to be answered concerning the structure and organization of international research. Of primary importance are the following concerns:

1. How much research should be done by the corporate staff, the regional staff, and the local staff, and how much should be delegated to external research organizations?
2. How should the research be controlled and administrated when initiated, conducted, and reported?
3. What kind of information should be collected, and what budget should be allocated for the task?

Several factors influence the answers to these questions. The most important include (1) the type of decision for which the research is being conducted, (2) the company's organizational structure, and (3) the form of its market presence in the country or countries to be included in the study. Other factors might also be considered, such as whether the company is pursuing a global-segmentation strategy or a national-segmentation strategy. Although all three factors are highly interrelated, they will be discussed separately for ease of presentation.

Types of Decision and the Research Activity

The decisions made by various managerial levels can be classified as *strategic* and *operational*. Establishing the relationship between the information requirements for these decisions and the research organization and its focus also involves decision making.

Research and Strategic Decisions

Global strategic decisions are made primarily at the corporate level, regardless of whether the company is pursuing a *global-segmentation strategy* or a *national-segmentation strategy*. These decisions are concerned with such things as the company's codes of conduct, market expansion and development strategies, and market selection and entry strategies. Decisions also have to be made on such topics as the degree of marketing or product standardization to be adopted across markets and the position to be taken in each market.

Strategic decisions require information on the overall global position of the company so that available and future resources can be optimally allocated across its business units, among countries and among product markets. As we noted earlier, these decisions require information inputs from all the functional areas such as marketing, finance, production, personnel, and logistics. They also entail decisions related to capital budgeting, production scheduling and anticipated market activities.

The potential for economies of scale and experience and the exploitation of the other competitive advantages inherent to the global company (and discussed in Chapter 10) suggest the need for an integrated perspective in all research. Since many research decisions need to be made recurringly, portions of the research activity can be routinized. Much of the information needed by the company's strategic decision makers on salient external and internal factors can be routinely collected and forwarded to some central point for analysis and thus made part of a computerized international data bank.

Research and Operational Decisions

Operational decisions are made primarily at the business unit, regional or local levels, and are concerned with day-to-day operations and the implementation and measurement of the strategic decisions. The location of the research activity providing the information needed to support these decision-making activities depends on several factors, among which are (1) whether the company has a global or national focus, (2) the organization structure of the company, (3) the functional area making the decision, and (4) the nature of the problem.

For marketing, these factors are closely linked to target-market and marketing-program decisions. For example, companies marketing to global-market segments are interested in identifying universal attributes across national markets. This implies a more centrally coordinated and administered research activity. On the other hand, companies marketing to national-market segments generally focus on identifying and satisfying local needs or wants. A national focus implies a more decentralized and closely administered research activity. These companies, can also benefit from the research undertaken in their different national markets. Consequently, there is still a need for the results of the various marketing research activities to be made available to other subsidiaries.

Organizational Structure and the Research Activity

In broad terms, a company's research activity can be centrally or decentrally organized. As we just explained, the approach adopted by a particular company is strongly influenced by its dominant international strategy. There are advantages and disadvantages to both approaches.[25]

Centralized Research Structures

Centralized research activity has the advantage of facilitating uniform research processes in international markets. Comparability across national markets in terms of constructs, measurement, and sampling is thus more easily controlled. The centralized approach also provides a broader, more global perspective to the research activity, and it reduces the possibility of internal coordination problems and duplication. Another advantage is the enhanced ability of the company to hire and train research personnel.

A centralized research approach facilitates the development of cross-national buyer behavior models, the identification of universals, and the standardization of marketing programs based on the comparison of multiple market research studies. Development of an integrated global-marketing information system and an international information bank is also made easier. Finally, economies of scale may be gained. For example, data coding, data interpretation, and data presentation for several countries or projects can be handled by the same personnel.

There are serious disadvantages to the centralized research approach. Primarily, in-depth knowledge of specific national markets may be lacking due to insufficient local input in the research process and the utilization of inappropriate methods.

Decentralized Research Structures

Decentralized research has the major advantage of market proximity. This, in turn, provides greater market familiarity in such things as local economic and political conditions, buyer habits, and attitudes. Further, access to local secondary data and sources is enhanced and possibly incurs less expense. Communication with local decision makers is also enhanced when the research is decentralized.

Conflict over the objectives and significance of the research for corporate or regional managements may frequently occur. The coordination and cross-national comparison and interpretation of specific research undertakings is complicated (for example, construct, measurement, and sampling equivalence), and become more difficult and problematic. And the task of developing an international in-formation bank and the dissemination of information become managerially more complex.

Market Presence and the Research Activity

To some extent, the difficulties encountered in the collection of secondary and primary data depend on the nature of the firm's market presence in a particular national market. In cases where the company has a limited operational presences (exporting, independent distributors), many additional problems are present. Are the agents familiar with the company's objectives and research methods? Can equivalence in the critical aspects of the research be achieved? What proprietary information can be disclosed? How much control is possible?

SUMMARY

In this chapter, we looked at many of the issues and problems confronting the international researcher. It was pointed out that the five-stage international research process is identical to its domestic counterpart. That is, both are concerned with providing decision makers with the information necessary to make decisions. However, it was noted that the international researcher is faced with unique and more problems. Further, these problems introduce potential research errors at each stage of the research process.

For example, spatial and cultural separation of decision maker and researcher, the multiple perspectives inherent in global business, and the lack of familiarity with each national situation heighten the potential for misunderstandings during the problem formulation stage of the research. Additionally, the need to achieve comparability in research design, data analysis, and data interpretation—especially when more than one country is being studied—introduces unique equivalence problems. Not only must there be equivalence in the constructs being employed across national markets, there must also be equivalence in the measures used and the samples employed.

The use of secondary and primary data also poses special problems for the international researcher. When using secondary data the international researcher must pay particular attention to the accuracy, comparability, and reliability of the data and their source. When collecting and analyzing primary data the major sources for error are the biases introduced by the subjects and the researcher. Since these biases are primarily the result of socio-cultural differences, the researcher must be very sensitive to the implications of differences when collecting, analyzing, and interpreting primary data from foreign markets.

Finally, we noted that the organization and focus of international research is strongly influenced by the company's global strategic focus, the types of decisions being made, and the company's market presence in the countries under study. For example, global-market companies tend to use a more centralized approach to international research than do national-market companies. However, since each approach provides a company with certain advantages and disadvantages, both approaches may be used. That is, some research activities may be highly centralized, whereas others may be decentralized.

that need to be accounted for when deciding whether research should be centralized or decentralized.

ADDITIONAL READING

Cosmas, Stephen C. and Jagdish N. Sheth, "Identification of Opinion Leaders Across Cultures: An Assessment for Use in the Diffusion of Innovation and Ideas," *Journal of International Business Studies,* Vol. 11, Spring–Summer 1980.

Green, Robert T. and Isabella C. M. Cunningham, "Family Purchasing Roles in Two Countries," *Journal of International Business Studies,* Vol. 11, Spring–Summer 1980.

Khanna, Sri Ram, "Asian Companies and the Country Stereotype Paradox: An Empirical Study," *Columbia Journal of World Business,* Vol. 21, Summer 1986.

Ofir, Chezy, and Donald R. Lehman, "Measuring Images of Foreign Products," *Columbia Journal of World Business,* Vol. 21, Summer 1986.

Research in Marketing, Vol. 7, Jagdish N. Sheth, ed. (Greenwich, Conn.: JAI Press, 1984).

DISCUSSION QUESTIONS

1. Identify and describe the three aspects of construct equivalence that need to be considered when developing a marketing research instrument for a foreign market.

2. What are some of the major additional complexities that are usually encountered when doing marketing research in a foreign country that are not experienced when doing research in one's own country?

3. Differentiate between the emic and etic research approaches by explaining when and how each should be used.

4. Explain what is meant by *measurement equivalence* and how the problems inherent in it can be handled when conducting marketing research in several national markets.

5. Explain how a company's strategic focus (global market versus national market) will affect its foreign marketing research activities.

6. Identify and discuss the major considerations

ENDNOTES

1. For a more extensive discussion of international research problems and issues see Susan P. Douglas and C. Samuel Craig, *International Marketing Research* (Englewood Cliffs, N.J.: Prentice-Hall, 1983).

2. Some authors make a distinction between research design and the identification of information sources. In this chapter, we do not.

3. Harper W. Boyd, et al., *Marketing Research* (Homewood, IL: Richard D. Irwin, 1977), p. 206.

4. See Charles S. Mayer, "Multinational Marketing Research: The Magnifying Glass of Methodological Problems," *European Research,* Vol. 6, (March 1978), pp. 77–83.

5. David A. Ricks, *Big Business Blunders* (Homewood, IL: Dow Jones-Irwin, 1983), p. 9.

6. Ibid., p. 80.

7. The discussion on temporal equivalence and market structure equivalence draws heavily from Mayer's "Multinational Marketing . . . Methodological Problems."

8. Robert T. Green and Phillip D. White, "Methodological Considerations in Cross-National Consumer Research," in *International Marketing: Managerial Perspectives,* S. C. Jain and L. R. Tucker, Jr. (Boston: Kent, 1979), pp. 170–171.

9. The terms *emic* and *etic* come from the words *phonemics* and *phonetics*. Phonemics is the study of sounds in language. Phonetics attempts to generalize universal principles about such sounds.

10. Douglas and Craig, *International Marketing*, p. 140.

11. Ricks, op. cit., p. 33.

12. For an example of the literature on this subject, see E. R. Heider, "Focal Color Areas and the Development of Color Names," *Developmental Psychology*, 4 (1971), pp. 447–455.

13. Mayer, "Multinational Marketing," p. 81.

14. Ibid., p. 81.

15. Ibid.

16. Douglas and Craig, op. cit., p. 141.

17. Susan P. Douglas and Patrick LeMaire, "Improving the Quality and Efficiency of Life-Style Research," in *The Challenges Facing Marketing Research: How Do We Meet Them*, XXV ESCOMAR Congress, pp. 555–570.

18. Harry L. Davis, Susan P. Douglas, and Alvin J. Silk, "Measure Unreliability: A Hidden Threat to Cross-National Marketing Research," *Journal of Marketing*, Vol. 45 (Spring 1981), pp. 98–109.

19. Robert T. Green and Eric Langeard, "A Cross-National Comparison of Consumer Habits and Innovator Characteristics," *Journal of Marketing*, Vol. 39 (July 1975), pp. 34–41.

20. Alejandro Portes, "Sociology and the Use of Secondary Data," in *Quantitative Social Science Research in Latin America*, Robert S. Byars and Joseph L. Love eds. (University of Illinois Press, 1973), pp. 211–212.

21. Douglas and Craig, op. cit., pp. 190–191.

22. Harry C. Triandis and Leigh M. Triandis, *A Cross-Cultural Study of Social Distance* (Washington, D.C.: American Psychological Association, 1962).

23. Robert E. Mitchell, "Survey Materials Collected in Developing Countries: Sampling Measurement and Interviewing: Obstacles to Intra- and Inter-National Comparisons," *International Social Science Journal*, 17 (1965), p. 4.

24. G. Almond and S. Verba, *The Civil Culture: Political Attitudes and Democracy in Five Nations* (Princeton, N.J.: Princeton University, 1965).

25. This section draws heavily from Flemming Hansen, "Managerial Implications of Cross-Cultural Studies of Buyer Behavior," in *Consumer and Industrial Buying Behavior*, Arch G. Woodside, Jagdish N. Sheth, and Peter D. Bennett, eds. (New York: North-Holland, 1977).

Chapter 8
Assessment of Global Marketing Opportunities

A core requirement for companies using a strategic approach to manage their businesses is the capability to generate and effectively use two types of information. Such firms need systematically and periodically collected information in order to control and evaluate current activities and to best allocate resources in order to achieve corporate objectives. The source for this information is the firm's planning information system. Firms also occasionally need information in order to evaluate possible changes or additions to current activities. This assessment activity may use the company's regular information system and be incorporated as part of planning activity. More often it is an event that occurs on an ad hoc, irregular basis.

X

The **assessment process** consists of identifying, analyzing, and selecting additional marketing opportunities that meet the firm's strategic objectives and match its competitive advantages and provides informational assistance for the development of marketing objectives and strategies, the planning of marketing tactics, and the implementation and control of the marketing effort.

The assessment process used by a global firm is more complex than that for a national firm. Not only must it include the scanning and evaluating of a number of countries for marketing opportunities, but it must also provide information helpful for determining the most appropriate *market-presence–marketing-effort* combination possible under the limitations imposed by international and national environments and the company's own objectives and resources. In this chapter, we present an overview of: (1) the types of assessments made; (2) the techniques used; (3) the problems that may arise; and (4) the methods that have been developed to ensure that the outputs of the assessment process are part of the international firm's investment, resource allocation, and marketing decisions.

THE SCOPE AND NATURE OF THE ASSESSMENT TASK _____

Types of Assessments

Two basic types of assessments may be undertaken by the marketing staff of an international firm at any particular point in time: a *market-entry assessment* and a *marketplace assessment*. A third type of assessment that may involve the marketing staff is the *noneconomic environment assessment*. A brief description of each type of asssessment follows.

paper

Market-Entry Assessment

The first (and actually the least encountered) type of assessment is undertaken to identify and select marketing opportunities in national markets not previously serviced and to provide informational assistance for the development of an appropriate market presence and marketing effort.

The stimulation for market-entry assessment can be from the parent office, a regional office, or a local affiliate, and may be the result of such things as

220

unsolicited foreign orders, actions of competitors, or previous experience. For example, a company that has been successful in exporting its products to Japan might become interested in Hong Kong, South Korea, Taiwan, or some other Asian country as a possible additional market. Although the stimulation to investigate the potentials of other markets may occur at different organizational levels in the company, the actual decision to enter a particular national market is generally made at corporate headquarters. A firm investigating a new market for the first time is said to be involved in a market-entry assessment.

Marketplace Assessment

The second type of assessment involves two important aspects of an ongoing foreign operation: (1) whether to change the *market presence* of the firm (that is, to increase or decrease the firm's level of involvement) and (2) whether to introduce a *new product* to a particular foreign market (to transfer a product from an established market to a new market) or change some other element of the firm's strategy.

The impetus for this marketplace assessment may come from the parent, region, or local affiliate and, unlike the market-entry decision, the decision for a change in market presence or the introduction of a new product may be made at any of these levels. Deciding factors include the resources required and the firm's objectives and operating procedures.

Neither the market-entry nor the marketplace assessment should be confused with routine planning undertaken by the firm. The last activity deals with the resource allocation and control system utilized by both national and international firms to determine the focus of and future commitment to current activities. The market-entry and marketplace assessments are used to determine what changes, if any, need to be made to current international activities. As a result of both assessments, the firm may make fundamental changes to the way it operates *internationally:* the number of countries it operates in, the way it operates in a particular country, or the product line it may offer in a particular country.

Noneconomic Environment Assessment

The third type of assessment generally involves the evaluation of social and political environments of those countries within which the international firm is already active or is planning to become active. The purpose of noneconomic environment assessment is to determine the effects that the politics, law, and culture might have on the company's operations. The stimulation for such an assessment is either some internal event (such as a market-entry or marketplace assessment) or the result of some external event (such as a change in government or a change in government policies toward foreign firms).

The location and responsibility for this third type of assessment depends on whether the process has been formalized. Those companies with a formalized process generally conduct the assessment at corporate headquarters. However, Kobrin and others have found that the responsibility for the assessment can range from a junior staff analyst with part-time responsibilities to a group of five or more professionals charged with developing and implementing formal assessment on a continuous basis.[1] When the assessment has not been formalized top management is likely to bear responsibility for it. If the firm has an international division, the responsibility generally lies there.

Two Assessment Approaches[2]

The selection of marketing opportunities is heavily influenced by the nature of the firm's definition of its market. The market can be defined in terms of the customers to be served (government, education, business, households), customer functions (measurement, material handling, gift giving), geographic boundaries (state or province, country, region), technologies employed (oil heat, coal heat, electric heat), and so on. Each definition may have profound implications for strategy. The situation is further complicated by the analytical approach adopted.

Two distinct analytical approaches to assessment have evolved: a *top-down* approach and a *bottom-up* approach. Significant differences between these approaches influence the manager's views of the marketing opportunities under review.

The top-down approach reflects the need of management to understand the capacity of the firm to compete and to apply resources to secure a sustainable competitive advantage. Management wants answers to the following questions:

1. What will be the *scope* of the business activity? A narrow definition of the market limits the firm's competitive involvement. For example, a company could limit its scope in a new market to supplying one product to a narrow market segment. A broader definition recognizes that the company is in the business of meeting the needs of several market segments with a complete product line.

2. What is the *basis for selection* of an opportunity? In particular, do currently served markets reflect the presence of significant cost discontinuities between different segments of the market, and does the marketing opportunity under review also exhibit these discontinuities? For example, are the costs of marketing to one segment considerably higher than to another segment?

3. What is the current and forecast *performance* within the market under review? Can present competitors find better ways to satisfy market needs or achieve cost advantages? Can potential competitors enter from other geographic areas or offer substitute technologies?

4. What will be the broad *strategic thrust* in the market, and what does that thrust imply for resource requirements or contributions? Answers rely on forecasts of market share and market growth and stage of product life-cycle analysis.

5. What are the *opportunities* for growth in the market that can best utilize the firms experiences? That is, what is the most attractive growth sector?

The bottom-up approach is usually employed by marketing management and emphasizes product changes, advertising themes, promotional efforts, and price strategies. Use of this approach implies a narrower tactical perspective. Thus, the bottom-up approach emphasizes such specific concerns as:

1. What is the current and forecast *performance* within the market under review? Elements of this analysis deal with specific areas of vulnerability to competition and the company's ability to satisfy evolving market needs.

2. How can the *efficiency* of current marketing programs be improved? That is, what elements of the marketing mix can be refined (better targeting of advertising, improving distribution coverage, and so on)?

3. What opportunities exist for improving *profitability* within a particular market by changing the operation's marketing presence, repositioning, product enhancement, and the addition or deletion of items from the product line?

When conducting market-entry or market-presence assessments, managers need to use both approaches. When conducting a new-product assessment for an ongoing operation, only the bottom-up approach need be employed.

Motivation for the Assessment

The reasons for undertaking a particular type of assessment can be neither easily nor quickly summarized. However, they can be grouped under five general types of pressures, either domestic or foreign: (1) competitive pressures, (2) political pressures, (3) economic pressures, (4) internal (firm) pressures, and (5) international pressures.

Depending on the type of pressure, the firm may seek to expand or contract its foreign marketing activities. Examples of these pressures are listed in Table 8-1. It is important to note that not all pressures are the result of marketplace changes, nor do they necessarily affect the marketing activity initially. However,

TABLE 8-1
Possible Motivations for an Assessment

Motivations	Domestic	Foreign
Competitive environment	To avoid larger competitors To extend a product's life cycle To follow competitors or clients To benefit from proprietary information and products Respond to an unsolicited order Access to foreign technology	Less competition Local or international competitors appear Foreign firm seeks a joint venture, or a licensing agreement Expansion of market
Political environment	Changes in domestic regulations (e.g., taxes, labor laws) Take advantage of incentives (generally export incentives)	Change in government Government invitation Change in government policies towards foreign firms
Economic environment	Reduce seasonal effect on production or sales Expand market base Labor costs increase	Change in economic stability Change in fiscal or monetary policies
Internal (firm's) environment	To reduce production costs To increase experience effect To reduce surplus capacity Reorganization of international operations Change in management (attitudes) Change in portfolio (result of change in corporate mission or strategies)	Request from HQ, regional office, or subsidiary Change in local management
International environment	Change in regulations related to overseas investments Changes in regional agreements Change in governmental policies with other countries	Change in tariff or non-tariff barriers Change in repatriation policies Change in foreign exchange regulations

marketing activity eventually will be affected. An example of the influence a number of pressures may exert in one situation is presented in Exhibit 8-1.

Elements of the Assessment

Regardless of whether the assessment undertaken is a market-entry or marketplace assessment, each is characterized by the following needs:

☐   The need to identify market opportunities, their potentials, and their success

---

EXHIBIT 8-1 _____
The Campbell Soup Experience in Japan _____

A good example of the pressures that may affect a company and result in a change in market presence is the experience of Campbell Soups in Japan.

Type of Pressure	Situation	Action Taken
Market control	Campbell Soups entered the Japanese market more than twenty years ago through a Hong Kong trading company called Dodwell. In turn, Dodwell distributed Campbell Soups products through Mitsui and Co. To gain better control over distribution, Dodwell was subsequently dropped and Mitsui became the importer.	Eliminated a middleman
Competitive threat and political action	By the mid-1970s, local companies began entering the market, and the Japanese government erected tougher import barriers. As a result of these changes, Campbell Soups entered into a joint venture with Toyo Suisan. In May 1976, Campbell Toyo Ltd. was formed with Campbell Soups owning 51 percent. The joint venture began blending and canning operations in 1977 using imported frozen ingredients purchased from Campbell Soups through Mitsui.	Negotiated a joint venture
Competitive threat continued	However, the joint venture ran into some major problems. Competition intensified, and the Campbell brand name was not well known outside the major urban centers. By 1982, Campbell Soups had decided that a centralized coordinated marketing effort was required.	
Reorganization	Around the same time, Campbell Soups also restructured its international division. The new president of the international division began a major review of Campbell Soups' overseas activities. Analysis of the Japanese operation suggested that the two partners had different strategy philosophies, and that the joint venture should be dissolved by buying out its Japanese partner. This was completed in August 1983. Mitsui assumed all distribution activities for *Campbell Japan Inc.*, the new company.	Joint venture dissolved and wholly owned subsidiary formed

Source: "Campbell Soups Up Its Japan Operations After Liquidating JV," *Business Asia*, January 27, 1984.

requirements; the national and international barriers that hinder attaining the estimated potential; and the characteristics of potential competitors.

☐ The need to determine the types of marketing activities required to successfully compete for the selected marketing opportunities;

☐ The need to determine the type of market presence required to effectively and efficiently support the various types of marketing activities being considered;

☐ The need to determine the level of resource commitment required for each market presence-marketing effort alternative considered;

☐ The need to complete a noneconomic environment assessment if an entry or market presence change is under review; and

☐ The need to determine whether other activities or opportunities provide better possibilities for achieving corporate objectives. (For example, since corporate resources are limited, an opportunity cost analysis is required to ensure the firm is making the best use of its opportunities, resources, and competitive advantages.)

Factors Affecting the Assessment

Five main factors affect the value of any assessment: (1) who conducts the assessment, (2) the accuracy of the assessment's information base, (3) the use and misuse of data and information, (4) the cost-benefit ratio of the assessment, and (5) the implementation risks.

Who Conducts the Assessment

A firm conducting an assessment may call on its employees to undertake the collection, analysis, and presentation of the recommendations; it may use the services of an outside market research service or consultant, or it may use a combination of internal and external resources. Further, assessment may be undertaken at corporate headquarters, a regional office, a local affiliate, or a combination of all three. Each style has its advantages and disadvantages, as Table 8-2 shows.

A major problem confronting the firm is how to reduce researcher bias in the interpretation of data and information. A local market research service or the local staff of an ongoing operation is more likely to correctly interpret local political, legal, economic, and sociocultural trends and nuances than is a regional or headquarters staff. Local assessors are not as likely to make self-reference criterion mistakes, are more likely to have access to needed data and information sources, and can more quickly and less expensively obtain the assistance of local experts. Local experts, however, may not have a comprehensive understanding of the firm's global strategy and objectives and may be blind to opportunities that a stranger to their culture might see.

In the early 1980s, for example, the Palanpur Jains of India realized that the beginnings of an entirely new market for diamonds in the United States was being overlooked by the traditional diamond merchants, the Israelis and the Belgians. Yet there was a slowly growing demand for small, low-priced stones. The Jains began to supply this market; by mid-1987, they had become the world's biggest exporters of small polished diamonds.[3]

TABLE 8-2
Some Advantages and Disadvantages of Internal and External Assessment

Location of Activity	Advantages	Disadvantages
Internal assessments		
Local staff:	1. Access to primary data 2. Closer to market 3. Helps develop local expertise 4. Knowledge of market and local culture 5. Less expensive than other types of activities	1. Lack of necessary skills 2. Lack of necessary resources 3. Communication problems with headquarters
Headquarters staff	1. Access to needed skills and resources 2. Acquires direct knowledge of market 3. Direct knowledge of company's objectives, policies, and products	1. Susceptible to self-reference mistakes 2. Misinterpretation of data 3. Access to data and information more difficult 4. Expensive
External assessments		
Local branch of international research agency	1. Better for small markets 2. Objectivity 3. Local market knowledge 4. Better for one-time studies 5. Local cultural expertise 6. Access to primary data and information	1. Communication problems 2. May not be available 3. Lacks knowledge of company's objectives, policies, and products 4. Expensive

Accuracy of the Data and Information

Accuracy of an assessment also depends on a firm's ability to obtain reliable and comparable data. In general, the types of information necessary for a marketplace assessment are more readily available than that needed for a market-entry assessment. When a firm is already operating in a country, its local marketing staff can collect both the secondary and primary data required to analyze potential marketing opportunities. Because of cost constraints, an initial market-entry assessment generally precludes use of primary data, depending instead primarily on secondary sources.

The single most important source of information for firms already involved internationally is their overseas managers and those with international experience stationed at corporate headquarters. Other sources include banks and the public press, local government agencies and libraries.

Uses and Misuses of Data and Information

Lack of specific market knowledge or experience may result in the misapplication of reliable data and information. Consider the use of import data. Although import data can be used to identify and estimate demand for particular products, such data must be used carefully when generalizing. For example, an analyst needs to know whether the imported product is viewed as a luxury item (jeans in parts of Europe), whether it capitalizes on a "foreign" label (foreign cars and beers), and whether a national distribution system exists for the product.[4]

Cost-Benefit Ratio of Assessments

The world's income is not distributed uniformly. In 1983, the top five countries generated 61.8 percent of the world's GNP; the top ten, 75.7 percent; and the top fifteen, 83.5 percent.[5] These disparities demonstrate that very frequently a firm can justify only a modest market-research expenditure for most of the world's countries. In other words, the firm must use only those assessment techniques and methods that are cost-to-profit effective.

Implementation Risk

Of the three assessment decisions identified, a firm's resources are exposed to the greatest uncertainty during the market-entry phase. The market-entry assessment is plagued with greater data and information problems, the need to use less costly techniques and methods, and a greater probability of misinterpretation by the assessment staff. Additionally, the market-entry *decision* is also accompanied by a considerable allocation of corporate resources (capital outlays and managerial attention). Accordingly, the firm is exposed to a higher degree of risk when implementing a market-entry recommendation than when implementing a marketplace assessment recommendation. It foregoes other opportunities and is exposed to actual losses if the new market proves to be unprofitable. To offset this greater risk, the investigating firm generally requires a high initial return on its investments.

MARKET-ENTRY ASSESSMENTS

The purpose of the market-entry assessment is to answer the general question: Should we market overseas and if so, where and how?; and more specifically, Should we enter a particular country and if so, how? Since there are as many as 184 potential national markets to select from, the assessment used to answer the first question generally involves a four-step analysis. The assessment used to answer the second involves a two-step analysis. These steps are shown in Figure 8-1.

The first step screens out markets because of *domestic regulations* (Trading with the Enemy Act) and *management preference* (top management may decide that Europe is the only region to be reviewed). The second step screens out economically unattractive markets. The third provides an advanced, or in-depth, analysis of the remaining marketing opportunities. The fourth step involves a tradeoff analysis that compares the remaining marketing opportunities with the company's objectives, current activities, and resources.

Before a market-entry decision can be made, eleven questions related to the market and the firm's operations must be answered. The initial market-entry assessment answers the first three questions. The advanced market-entry assessment answers the remaining eight (once attractive marketing opportunities have been found). All 11 questions are shown in Exhibit 8-2.

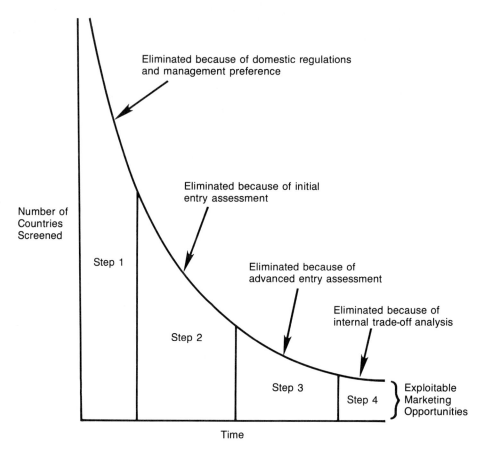

Number of
Countries
Screened

Eliminated because of domestic regulations
and management preference

Eliminated because of initial
entry assessment

Eliminated because of
advanced entry assessment

Eliminated because of
internal trade-off analysis

Step 1

Step 2

Step 3

Step 4

} Exploitable
Marketing
Opportunities

Time

FIGURE 8-1   A Four-Step Entry Assessment Procedure

Initial Assessment of Market Opportunities

To reduce the large number of potential national markets to a number suitable for more in-depth and more costly analyses, techniques have been developed to screen out economically unattractive prospects. The techniques can be divided into two groups: those used to identify *incipient* or *latent* market demand and those used to identify *existing* market demand.[6]

Incipient market demand is future demand. A demand will exist in the future, but conditions have not yet changed sufficiently for the need or want to manifest itself (the population may be aware of a particular need or want, but their income is insufficient to satisfy it, or the country has not yet reached a higher level of development where a particular need or want generally appears).

Latent market demand is untapped demand. A demand exists for a particular product or service, but no one has yet offered a product or service to satisfy the need or want.

EXHIBIT 8-2
Eleven Critical Entry Questions

1. **What domestic regulations prohibit the sale of products and/or services to specific countries?** U.S. citizens are subject to United States laws regardless of the nation within which they conduct business. They are also subject to U.S. government embargos (such as the Trading with the Enemy Act), subject to U.S. antitrust laws, and prohibited from participating in unauthorized boycotts of friendly nations. It is therefore necessary to check *domestic* trading regulations and laws concerning the countries under review before undertaking lengthy and frequently costly assessment of marketing opportunities.

2. **What is the nature and potential size of the market?** Is there an existing, latent, or incipient demand? If existing, what is its stage in the product lifecycle?

3. **What are the political and social environments like?** Does the local government encourage foreign companies to invest in its country? Do the regulations and policies toward foreign companies reduce their ability to maximize their competitive advantages? Is there social unrest?

4. **What is the competitive environment like, and what barriers are there to the market?** What political, legal, and competitive barriers exist that may affect the firm's ability to serve the market in a way that meets corporate objectives and policies?

5. **What are the major (generic) response characteristics of the market in terms of the marketing mix?** Is the market responsive to mass-communication methods? Is the market responsive to price or is it more concerned with nonprice features of the mix? Is the market responsive to new ways of distributing the product or service? Is the market responsive to minor style or feature changes?

6. **What are the major characteristics of potential competitors?** Do our competitive advantages provide us with a competitive edge?

7. **What company demand can we expect?** That is, given the determinants of market demand and competition, what marketing effort must be expended to gain a satisfactory market share?

8. **What are the international logistical requirements necessary to serve the market?** (These requirements are not to be confused with the local distribution system)

9. **What types of market presence are permitted and which are optimum for the firm?** (exporting? sales branch? joint venture? wholly owned subsidiary?)

10. **What are the resource requirements?** Do they necessitate changes and/or additions to our current resources? Will a redeployment of present resources be necessary?

11. **Does the market under review meet the company's objectives and goals and match its competitive advantages?**

Existing market demand is current potential demand. It is not to be confused with current consumption. Current consumption is the sum of local production, inventory, and imports less exports. Current potential demand is current consumption plus unsatisfied demand for currently available products.

Although latent or existing demand may indicate an immediate marketing opportunity, incipient demand should not be ignored. Coca-Cola, for example, promotes its name in many markets where its products are not yet sold by helping in the construction of clinics and schools. Though this is partly altruistic, the company's image and brand awareness are also being developed and heightened preparatory to entering these markets. General Foods, on the other hand, developed a pasta product, its *Golden Elbow* macaroni specifically aimed at satisfying the latent demand of the nutritionally disadvantaged in the United States and the Third World. The product, which had more than seven times the protein of traditional macaroni and required no special storage conditions, helped alleviate nutritional problems in Peru and Brazil.[7]

Existing demand denied foreign companies should not be ignored. Colgate-Palmolive (India) Ltd., a wholly owned affiliate of the U.S. company, is not permitted to expand its production of toothpaste or to diversify into related lines, such as toothbrushes. Yet in 1986, with an eye on future lifting of these retrictions, the company invested heavily in such activities as team sports, coaching camps, and community dental health checkups to create a favorable public image.[8]

Identifying Latent and Incipient Market Demand

The estimation of latent and incipient market demand necessitates the forecasting of future demand for products or services not currently available. Further, incipient demand forecasts must also provide some approximation of when that demand can be expected to become latent. In both cases, however, specific historical data are lacking; thus alternative means of forecasting demand are needed. Fortunately, several methods are available using minimum information to assess a local market's potential demand. Success of these methods depends on finding meaningful substitute, or proxy, variables for any missing information. The following six methods have gained widespread acceptance: (1) demand pattern analysis, (2) international product life cycle, (3) income elasticity measurements, (4) analysis by analogy, (5) proxy and multiple factor indexes, (6) input–output analysis.[9]

Demand Pattern Analysis. A country's manufacturing production can be consumed locally, exported, or added to inventory. It can also be supplemented by imports. Therefore, by analyzing local production, inventory, and patterns of international trade for a country, it is possible to estimate consumption trends and marketing opportunities. When categorized by industry, demand pattern analysis can indicate market potential not only for end-product usage but also for the industry's supply needs (plant, equipment, construction equipment). Further, the share of total production by specific industries provides an indication of the country's stage of economic development. During the early stages—when income per capita is low—local manufacturing supplies the necessities of life (food, clothing, beverages). As incomes grow, initially prominent industries decline in relative importance and are replaced by other more capital-intensive and higher-skill industries (metal products, machinery, chemicals). The typical demand patterns shown in Figure 8-2 suggest that, generally, the share of income spent on food and textiles declines and the demand for chemicals and metal products increases as income per capita increases.

International Product Life Cycle. The international product life cycle concept can also be used as a basis for identifying potentially attractive markets. By estimating

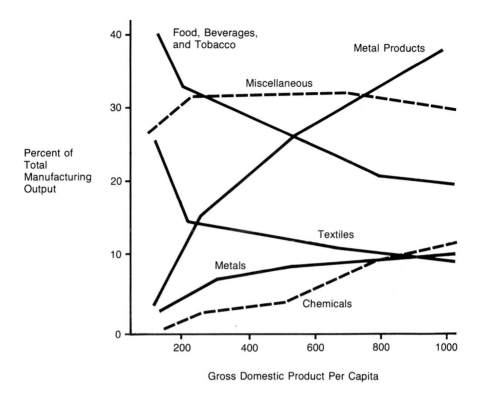

Based on time series analysis for selected years, 1899–1957, for seven to ten countries depending on commodity.

FIGURE 8-2 **Typical Demand Patterns in Industrializing Countries** (*Source:* Reprinted from Reed Moyer, "International Marketing Analysis," *Journal of Marketing Research*, November 1968, pp. 353–360 published by the American Marketing Association.)

the regional time lags between the introduction of a product (similar to the one the firm wishes to market overseas) in one market and then another, managers can obtain improved and more specific estimates than they can by using demand pattern analysis. This approach also provides useful information on the possible sequential attractiveness of markets as well as on when local competition may appear.

Income Elasticity Measurements. This relationship, which measures the percentage change in demand for a product divided by the percentage change in income over a given period, can be used as a basis for predicting changes in the quantity demanded of a particular *generic* product. For example, an analysis of the income elasticity of demand often reveals the following:

□ As income increases market potential is greater for goods with high elasticity coefficients than for those with low ones.

- Necessities, such as food and clothing, tend to be income inelastic (although income increases, the absolute amount spent on these necessities will remain more or less the same).

- Demand for durable consumer goods tends to be income elastic (the amount spent on these types of products increase as income increases).

- Capital goods tend to be income elastic and will therefore increase as income increases.

Care needs to be taken when using income elasticity measurements. The slope and location of the demand curve are a function of not only income. Other relevant determinants of the demand curve include taste, socio-cultural, economic, and legal factors. As shown in Figure 8-3, we cannot assume that the location and

FIGURE 8-3   Demand Curves for the Same Product in Two Countries

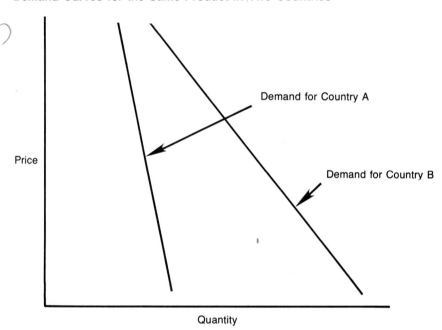

Factors influencing location and slope of demand curves:

Market size differences
Stage of the product life cycle
Stage of industrialization
Income distribution differences
Cultural and social differences
Legal differences
Distribution channel differences
Media differences
Availability of and preferences for
    alternative products (substitutes)
Competitor prices

slope (elasticity) of the demand curve in one country will be exactly the same as that in another.

Proxy and Multiple Factor Indexes. Indirect variables may be substituted when information is not available. A single factor index measures potential market demand by using a proxy variable that is intuitively or statistically correlated with the demand being estimated. For example, a sucker rod manufacturer evaluating Venezuela as a potential market found no product-specific market information. However, sucker rods are used in the extraction of oil to connect the pumping unit on the surface to the submerged pump in the well. By correlating drilling rig activity with sucker rod consumption, the manufacturer was able to arrive at a reasonable estimate.

There are, of course, many indicators to select from that provide some idea of the stage of development of a market. A few of the ones selected by various experts in comparative marketing are shown in Exhibit 8-3. The indicators used actually depends on the company's products or services.

A multiple factor index uses two or more proxy variables believed to be correlated with demand for the product under review, to measure potential market demand.

Estimation by Analogy. Estimation of market potential by analogy is based on the transfer of the market demand experienced in one country to another

---

EXHIBIT 8-3
Stage of Market Development Indicators

1. Per capita GNP
2. Ability to imitate and absorb other countries' production methods
3. Radio receivers per 1,000 population
4. Newspaper circulation per 1,000 population
5. Percentage of adult population literate
6. Total volume of trade (imports and exports) in U.S. dollars
7. Motor vehicles per 1,000 population
8. Percent of GNP originating from tertiary sector
9. Percent of population in cities of 20,000 or more
10. Character of legal system
11. Degree of Westernization
12. Percent of GNP accounted for by wholesaling and retailing
13. Road kilometers per 100 square kilometers

14. Domestic trade, wholesale and retail, as a percentage of GNP
15. Industrial output/workers
16. Road density
17. Character of legal system
18. Total population
19. Food expenditures/private consumption
20. Agricultural population/total population
21. Secondary and university school enrollment
22. Character of bureaucracy
23. Number of households
24. Railroad density
25. Life expectancy
26. Average household size
27. Annual rate of population growth
28. Exports/Gross National Product
29. Manufacturing workers/labor force
30. Constitutional status of present regime

Source: Vern Terpstra, *Comparative Analysis for International Marketing* (Boston: Allyn & Bacon, 1967), p. 146. The indicators are ranked according to the bearing they have on the marketing system of a particular country. The values of many of these indicators can be found in the *Statistical Yearbook of the United Nations.*

using one of two assumptions. The first assumes that the two countries under review are comparable at the same point in time. The second assumes that the demand for a product develops in much the same way in many countries at comparable stages of economic development.

Under the first assumption, the potential market demand for country B is estimated by obtaining a macroeconomic indicator from both countries (countries A and B, where country A is chosen based on availability of market data). This indicator is then used as an estimate of the consumption or demand of the country being evaluated.

Suppose that the demand for autos in Argentina (DA) is found to be highly correlated with income (IA). Then the demand for autos in Bolivia (DB) would be assumed to be:

$$\frac{DB}{IB} = \frac{DA}{IA} \therefore DB = \frac{DA \cdot IB}{IA}$$

where: IB = income in Bolivia is known, as are DA and IA.

Under the second assumption, the product usage or market development moves through comparable cycles as countries industrialize. Consequently, the market demand in country A at industrial stage n is a basis for estimating the market demand in country B, when it reaches industrial stage n.

If we assume that Mexico's stage of industrialization is comparable to that of the United States in 1920, the demand for autos in Mexico would be equivalent to United States demand in 1920. Possible adjustments to the estimate would include population differences and income differences using 1920 data for the United States and current data for Mexico.

Both techniques assume that the consumption functions for the two countries are comparable. This is not usually the case. The techniques are less applicable when the consumption functions are nonlinear, and cultural preferences are divergent. In the Bolivia auto case, adjustments need to be made for different driving habits, availability and use of mass transit systems, and so on. Another problem is to correctly identify comparable stages of development of the two countries under review. Moreover, the expectations of consumers in developing countries are being affected by the dramatic developments in worldwide communications and by movies and TV shows originating from developed countries. Nonetheless, when data are limited, the techniques above can prove very useful, especially if combined with one of the other techniques discussed in this chapter.

Identifying Existing Demand

When estimating existing demand, use can be made of marketing experience and available historical data. The techniques employed are similar to those used domestically. However, they need to be cost-to-benefit effective. Three techniques that provide sufficient information to determine whether a more rigorous analysis is worthwhile are (1) single and multiple regression analysis, (2) input–output analysis, and (3) expert opinion.[10]

Single and Multiple Regression Analysis. Regression analysis provides two general techniques for estimation in the international setting. When historical data are available, single or multiple factors associated with a particular demand can be analyzed to develop a forecasting model. When data are not available, analogy can be used to derive demand estimates. In this case, the single or multiple factor demand model developed for country A is transferred to the country under review. Its advantage over the analogy approach is to provide a more statistically verifiable estimate in terms of significance.

The regression technique should only be used with considerable care. The same limitations are applicable as for the analogy approach.

Input–Output Analysis. Input–output analysis is basically a tabulation of trans-. actions among the various producing sectors of an economy. As shown in Table 8-3, purchases in one sector are the sales of others. When using this approach for forecasting demand, the procedure is to assume a change in final demand and then use past relationships among interindustry flows to trace the effect on the particular demand being analyzed. By modifying the initial assumptions used, several scenarios can be developed and the resulting outcomes analyzed. For example, different levels of government expenditures, purchases by consumers, imports, and economic conditions can be assumed and their impact on demand determined.

The accuracy of the approach is highly dependent on the correlations developed between products or industries; it is useful only to the degree that these correlations are valid. Managers must recognize that the correlations are affected by production levels and over time.

Expert Opinion. Forecasts can often be obtained by turning for assistance to local experts such as distributors, trade associations, and suppliers. In addition, economic and industry forecasts from well-known market research and consulting firms like A. C. Nielsen and Kurt Salmon can be purchased for many countries, both developed and developing. In those cases when the firm is already operating internationally, it is also possible to draw on the experience of its personnel located in countries similar to the one under investigation. These advisors can provide valuable insight into factors that may influence demand and into those that may differ from domestic factors. One approach that frequently uses experts is the *Delphi* technique. In this technique, elements or factors affecting a particular situation are identified. Then, a panel of experts are asked to rank the importance of these factors. The ranked factors are then frequently assembled into an overall measure or index.

Noneconomic Environment Assessments

When making the decision to enter a new market, market potential is a critical factor. It is, however, not the only factor. Consideration must also be given to noneconomic environmental aspects of the countries under review. These may include the political stability of the country, its investment climate, its profit remittance and exchange controls, its taxation and expropriation policies, the attitudes of its political parties toward foreign investors, labor strikes and unrest,

TABLE 8-3
Example of an Input–Output Table

Country A—Transactions, 1960

	Agriculture	Food processing	Coal	Electric energy	Plastic products	Apparel
Agriculture	—	30	—	—	—	—
Food processing	25	—	—	—	—	—
Coal	—	10	—	50	10	8
Electric energy	10	30	5	—	25	5
Plastic products	—	10	—	5	—	5
Apparel	—	—	—	—	—	—
Wages and salaries	80	50	40	30	100	70
Imports (total)	35	20	15	25	40	75
Agricultural chemicals	20	—	—	—	—	—
Paint and varnishes	5	—	—	5	10	—
Textiles	5	—	—	—	—	60
Iron castings	5	—	5	5	—	—
Other	—	20	10	15	30	15
Profits, interest, depreciation, taxes	30	30	40	40	75	40
Total output	200	200	100	150	250	200

Country A—Production Coefficients, 1960

	Agriculture	Food processing	Coal	Electric energy	Plastic products	Apparel
Agriculture	—	0.250	—	—	—	—
Food processing	0.125	—	—	—	—	—
Coal	—	0.050	—	0.333	0.040	0.025
Electric energy	0.050	0.150	0.050	—	0.100	0.025
Plastic products	—	0.050	—	0.033	—	0.025
Apparel	—	—	—	—	—	—
Wages and salaries	0.400	0.250	0.400	0.200	0.400	0.350
Imports (total)	0.175	0.100	0.150	0.167	0.160	0.375
Agricultural chemicals	0.100	—	—	—	—	—
Paints and varnishes	0.025	—	—	0.033	0.040	—
Textiles	0.025	—	—	—	—	0.300
Iron castings	0.025	—	0.050	0.033	—	—
Other	—	0.100	0.100	0.100	0.120	0.075
Profits, interest, depreciation, taxes	0.250	0.150	0.400	0.267	0.300	0.200
Total output	1.000	1.000	1.000	1.000	1.000	1.000

Source: Reprinted, by permission of the publisher, from AMA MANAGEMENT REPORT No. 53, © 1960 American Management Association, New York. All rights reserved.

administrative procedures, and public sector industrial activities. For example, the political stability or investment climate of a country may have a strong bearing on the form of market presence the firm will adopt. If the situation is highly volatile, the firm may decide that a legal presence is not advisable and that the

		Country A—Transactions, 1960 (cont.)			
		Final demand			
Consumer expenditures	**Government operations**	**Exports**	**Investment**	**Total final demand**	**Total output**
100	—	50	—	150	200
150	—	25	—	175	200
15	5	—	5	25	100
35	10	—	30	75	130
10	—	220	—	230	250
30	—	150	—	200	200
—	20	—	100	120	490
150	10	—	175	335	545
—	—	—	—	—	—
5	—	—	15	—	—
15	—	—	—	—	—
—	—	—	10	—	—
130	10	—	130	—	—
—	—	—	50	50	325
510	45	445	360	1,360	2,460

operating presence should take the form of an offshore operation (that is, all sales, service, and other support personnel are stationed in some other country). This could occur even when potential market demand would warrant and support a total marketing effort.

The Checklist Approach. Measurements of the noneconomic aspects of a country's environment still tend to be relatively unsophisticated and unstructured. Subjective and often ethnocentric techniques, in which variables considered risk factors are rated for each country being reviewed, are widely used. An example of one U.S.-based multinational company's investment climate rating scale is shown in Table 8-4. Points are assigned to each of eight categories that defines the firm's investment climate. The assigned points are then added, and the country is classified on a good-to-poor continuum. For poor climates, either a higher return on investment or a limited form of market presence is indicated.

A simple checklist approach like the one just described is best suited for initial entry assessment. It is simple, and data on the various factors included are available for many countries from sources such as *IL&T: Investing, Licensing & Trading Conditions Abroad,* published by Business International. Business International also publishes reports on conditions in many countries by region. These are *Business Asia, Business America, Business Europe,* and *Business Latin America.*

As companies become increasingly dependent on foreign revenues to support domestic and foreign strategies, internal pressures arise for a more formalized, periodic, and systematic type of assessment. For example, a major petrochemical company conducts daily assessments of its markets overseas by examining some

TABLE 8-4
Corporate Rating Scale for Determining a Country's Investment Climate

	Number of Points	
Item	Individual subcategory	Range of category
Capital repatriation		
No restrictions	12	0–12
Restrictions based only on time	8	
Restrictions on capital	6	
Restrictions on capital and income	4	
Heavy restrictions	2	
No repatriations possible	0	
Foreign ownership allowed		
100% allowed and welcomed	12	0–12
100% allowed, not welcomed	10	
Majority allowed	8	
50% maximum	6	
Minority only	4	
Less than 30%	2	
No foreign ownership allowed	0	
Discrimination and controls, foreign vs. domestic businesses		
Foreign treated same as local	12	0–12
Minor restrictions on foreigners, no controls	10	
No restrictions on foreigners, some controls	8	
Restrictions and controls on foreigners	6	
Some restrictions and heavy controls on foreigners	4	
Severe restrictions and controls on foreigners	2	
Foreigners not allowed to invest	0	

TABLE 8-4 (cont.)

	Number of Points	
Item	Individual subcategory	Range of category
Currency stability		
Freely convertible	20	4–20
Less than 10% open/black market differential	18	
10% to 40% open/black market differential	14	
40% to 100% open/black market differential	8	
Over 100% open/black market differential	4	
Political stability		
Stable long term	12	0–12
Stable, but dependent on key person	10	
Internal factions, but government in control	8	
Strong external and/or internal pressures that affect policies	4	
Possibility of coup (external and internal) or other radical change	2	
Instability, real possibility of coup or change	0	
Willingness to grant tariff protection		
Extensive protection granted	8	2–8
Considerable protection granted, especially to new major industries	6	
Some protection granted, mainly to new industries	4	
Little or no protection granted	2	
Availability of local capital		
Developed capital market, open stock exchange	10	0–10
Some local capital available, speculative stock market	8	
Limited capital market, some outside funds (IBRD, AID) available	6	
Capital scarce, short term	4	
Rigid controls over capital	2	
Active capital flight unchecked	0	
Annual inflation for last 5 years		
Less than 1%	14	2–14
1%–3%	12	
3%–7%	10	
7%–10%	8	
10%–15%	6	
15%–35%	4	
Over 35%	2	
Total		8–100

Source: Reprinted by permission of the *Harvard Business Review.* An exhibit from "How to Analyze Foreign Investment Climates" by Robert B. Stobaugh, Jr. (September/October 1969). Copyright © by the President and Fellows of Harvard College; all rights reserved.

400 separate variables.[11] Variables included in reviews such as these are measurements of local instability (riots, purges, government crises), foreign conflicts (diplomatic expulsions, military violence), political climate (role of military, influence of particular legislators), and economic climate (GNP, inflation, external debt levels). The assessments are frequently judgmental and can utilize techniques like Delphi.

Advanced Assessment of Marketing Opportunities

Having looked at several ways to identify a few marketing opportunities in a large number of countries, we are now ready to examine the remaining countries in more detail. The advanced entry assessment is designed to answer questions 4-11 of Exhibit 8-2. Since this stage does not depart substantially from domestic practices, we will highlight only those areas and considerations unique to the international context. The advanced entry assessment involves the seven steps indicated by the headings of the following sections.

The Operating Environment

A company evaluating a country for the first time is involved in a three-part environmental assessment. It must first obtain an overview of the economic, technological, political, legal, cultural, and social structural dimensions of the country; their relationships; and their individual and joint effects on the key components of the company's competitive environment (markets, customers, competitors, distributors and dealers, suppliers, facilitators, and publics). Environmental elements requiring analysis are shown in Exhibit 8-4. Second, the firm needs information on the current conditions and trends of these environmental dimensions. This part of the assessment is comparable to the environmental forecast undertaken domestically when planning the firm's activities for the following year. The major difference is the importance placed on the various elements of the environment and their dynamic relationships. Assessment must be done within the structural context of each country's environment. Finally, the firm needs information on the various barriers to access to the market so that it may determine their effect on the company's competitive advantages and ways of doing business.

Structural and Trend Analyses

The task of simultaneously analyzing the environmental dimensions of several countries with widely varying characteristics may appear formidable. Fortunately, the task can be reduced to manageable proportions by judiciously selecting only those aspects of the environment for analysis that are of competitive importance to the firm. For example, the marketing staff of a producer of consumer goods will emphasize disposable income, distribution of wealth, family lifestyle, rate of family formation, and the availability of distribution systems and media. The marketing staffs of producers of industrial goods will be more concerned with the technological development of the market, the number and location of industrial buyers, their cost structures (wage rates, costs of inputs), and the availability of sales personnel. An example of one company's choice of criteria for selecting Latin American marketing opportunities is shown in Exhibit 8-5.

In addition to carefully selecting the environmental elements to be studied, the analysis of marketing opportunities can be simplified to some extent by clustering them according to criteria that have been found to be of value to the firm. Three criteria frequently used to cluster countries are geographic proximity, level of income or stage of economic development, and social and cultural characteristics. These criteria can be used individually or combined. The choice will

EXHIBIT 8-4

Possible Components of the General and Industry Environmental Assessment

Many variables that can be measured are not included in the following list. Variables chosen depend on the nature of the business and the marketing presence to be adopted. In addition to obtaining information on the current status of the variables, it is necessary to obtain information on trends, and make forecasts.

Demographic
1. Characteristics of population: size, age, family units, and so on
2. Geographic distribution of population
3. Urbanization

Education
1. Literacy level
2. Specialized vocational training
3. Higher education
4. Special management training
5. Attitude toward education
6. Educational match with company requirements

Economic
1. General economic framework including the following:
2. Central banking system
3. Monetary and fiscal policies
4. Factor endowment: capital, labor, land
5. Social overhead: energy base, communication system, transportation system
6. External dependency
7. Balance of Payments
8. Labor climate

Political/Legal
1. Political organization
2. Foreign policy
3. "Rules of the game"
4. Flexibility of law and legal changes
5. Government attitude toward business
6. Government attitude toward foreign businesses

Cultural/Social
1. Public attitude toward business
2. Public attitude toward business people
3. Public attitude toward foreign business and managers
4. Business attitude toward public and work force
5. Business attitude toward government
6. Business attitude toward foreign business
7. Public attitude toward achievement and work
8. Attitude toward wealth and material gain
9. Attitude toward risk taking
10. Attitude toward time
11. Attitude toward change
12. Class structure and social mobility

Technology
1. Level of technological sophistication
2. Source of technology
3. Absorptive capabilities

Industry
1. Number, size, and location of competitors
2. Number, size, and location of suppliers
3. Bargaining power of suppliers
4. Bargaining power of buyers
5. Entry and exit barriers

EXHIBIT 8-5
Opportunity Screening Variables Used by Pillsbury for Latin American Markets

As companies become more experienced in operating internationally, they often develop criteria to help them identify promising opportunities. Such is the case of Pillsbury. The following is an example of the criteria used by this company for its Latin American markets. All ten criteria are equally important; they are not ranked sequentially or according to importance.

Criterion	Explanation
Size and scale of market	Since food processing companies deploy significant fixed assets, they need a critical market mass that will allow efficient use of resources and assets. Consequently, Pillsbury generally seeks markets that combine market size and disposable income.
Government attitude toward foreign investments	Because of the large investments needed in fixed assets, Pillsbury seeks markets whose governments hold positive attitudes toward such investments.
Human resources	Pillsbury's local personnel policies are based on the belief that companies such as theirs ultimately will be run by local management teams. Consequently, they prefer markets that already have developed managerial pools from which to draw personnel.
Foreign exchange rate outlook	Since most Latin American countries have "soft" currency problems, Pillsbury is particularly interested in demonstrating a decent return on investments once local earnings are converted into U.S. dollars (using forecasted exchange rates).
Repatriation of dividends	Pillsbury's policy is that dividends can be delayed and profits reinvested in profitable local businesses (expansion or acquisitions).
Political and economic stability	Pillsbury feels comfortable with markets that have consistent political and economic histories, since consistency is an important aspect of predictability. This criterion is very qualitative; it involves management judgment.
Export capability	For two reasons, Pillsbury likes to get involved in markets where it can satisfy local needs and export. Exporting gains the support of local government; the company obtains hard currencies (most exports are in U.S. dollars).
Institutions	Since food processing companies are generally subject to numerous local regulations, Pillsbury is interested in knowing what bureaucracies exist, what permits and approvals are needed, and so on.
Partners	Pillsbury has a clear-cut policy of sharing market risks and rewards with local partners. It therefore is interested in knowing the availability of partners, their solvency, their track records, and what they can bring to a partnership.
Evaluation of opportunities	Markets are also selected or eliminated on the basis of their competitive intensity. If the state of the industry is so advanced that Pillsbury does not believe a sustainable competitive position can be achieved, the opportunity is rejected—even if the other nine criteria can be met.

Source: Speech given by a Pillsbury representative to the International Business Conference, College of Business Administration, University of South Carolina, March 1984.

depend on the types of products the firm markets and such internal considerations as the firm's international organization and location of production facilities.[12]

What Are the Market Barriers?

International companies are faced with two unique sets of barriers and one set of barriers that may differ substantially from those encountered domestically; that is, they are faced with *exit barriers, entry barriers,* and *marketplace barriers.* They must deal with any exit barriers that their own governments have erected (trade and foreign investment restrictions), and they must contend with any barriers that foreign governments have erected (profit remission policies, licensing requirements, tariffs, quotas). At the same time, marketplace barriers, arising from local nationalism and other pressures on foreign firms, can be substantially different from those encountered domestically or in other foreign markets. Companies contemplating foreign marketing opportunities for the first time need to familiarize themselves with a comprehensive list of barriers, such as shown in Exhibit 8-6. Companies experienced in international trade or business will concentrate primarily on the more specific, market-related barriers. The impact that such entry and market barriers may have on a company's strategy is presented in Exhibit 8-7.

What Is the Generic Demand?

The approach used to estimate generic demand depends on whether the demand is existing or latent. If existing, current and future demand can be estimated using historical data and a technique such as regression analysis. It is easier to determine market potential for a continuous innovation, particularly if the market under review is similar in critical characteristics to those of another country in which the company operates. Market-size determination becomes easiest when the product is a line extension. For discontinuous innovations or latent demand conditions, estimates of market size are less reliable. There are no historical data; proxies must be used.

Regardless of the nature of the demand, the firm assessing a marketing opportunity in another country for the first time *must* obtain sufficient information to answer several important product and consumer-behavior questions. That is, analysis must follow the traditional approaches developed for the introduction of a new product. Typical questions to ask in this stage include the following:

1. What functional use does the product serve? What basic need does the product serve? The basic need relates to the inherent qualities of the product as contrasted to modifications designed to appeal to particular customer groups.

2. How is this functional use currently being satisfied, under what conditions, and how will this affect market potential?

3. Where and how are current products designed to satisfy this functional use purchased? Through what types of outlets?

4. How does the proposed product compare to current products in terms of features, price, quality, warranties, servicing, and maintenance?

5. If dealing with existing demand, what is the market's stage in the product life cycle? If dealing with latent demand, are the attributes of the product compatible with the market's socio-cultural and technological dimensions?

EXHIBIT 8-6 _____
Possible Exit, Entry, and Marketplace Barriers _____

> **Exit barriers (domestic & foreign)**
> Export restrictions
> Foreign exchange controls
> Profit, royalties, and capital remission controls
> Taxation of remissions
> Transfer of people controls
> Transfer of technology controls
> Limitations of foreign risk insurance
> Foreign investment restrictions
>
> **Entry barriers (foreign)**
> Tariffs
> Quotas
> Transfer of people controls
> Transfer of property and trade-name rights
> Government policies for investments
> Prohibitions or limits on foreign ownership
> Natural resource extraction prohibitions
> Prohibitions on acquisitions
> Import deposits
> Local content, and policies for employment and production
> Customs and other delays
>
> **Marketplace barriers (foreign)**
> Access to warehousing facilities
> Access to salesforce personnel
> Access to management personnel
> Access to production personnel
> Access to capital markets
> Access to media; media regulations
> Access to suppliers
> Access to channels and channel captains
> Size, resources, and products of established competitors
> Price controls, price maintenance regulations
> Local safety and environmental regulations
> Distrust of foreigners

Traditional techniques, such as product positioning, are useful in this stage of the analysis.[13] Product positioning maps can be used to identify potential opportunities and develop competitive strategies by identifying areas where no product is meeting a perceived need. Maps also help identify the firm's potential competitors. Johansson and Thorelli, for example, used this technique to position domestic and foreign automobiles according to the perceptions of U.S. respondents.[14] Caution must be used, however, when selecting a map's coordinates. For example, a U.S. company selling industrial products might use buyer size as one of its market criteria. If it has standardized the dimension and categorizes buyers as large, medium, and small, a problem arises. A large company in the United States is not necessarily the same as a large company in Ecuador. The latter may use technologies and management practices that differ from its U.S. counterpart and geographically serve a limited market.

EXHIBIT 8-7

Overcoming Barriers the Levi Strauss Way

When entering Mexico, Levi Strauss was faced with stiff barriers and considerable marketplace uncertainty. To reduce its investment risk, it used a *stepwise* entry strategy. This strategy provided flexibility in use of resources. The firm could withdraw from the market if warranted, or depending on market developments, it could penetrate still further. The situation facing Levi Strauss and the actions it took are described below:

Factors	*Situation*	*Action Taken*
Trade barriers	High trade barriers precluded the exporting of denim clothing to Mexico.	Decided to produce locally to overcome barriers.
Market uncertainty	The market was a source of considerable uncertainty. The firm did not know whether suitable denim fabric could be purchased locally, whether local apparel producers were capable of stitching the apparel effectively, and whether there was sufficient demand.	Firm subcontracted the production of denim and the production of apparel to local firms.

Source: "Levi Strauss Step-by-Step Approach to Lucrative Mexican Market," *Business Latin America,* November 25, 1971.

Once the questions above have been answered, additional information may be sought to determine whether the market can be subdivided into major segments on the basis of cost discontinuities and customer dimensions. These types of information will be useful later (1) to determine probable responses of the market or market segment to various marketing mix alternatives (2) and to answer questions related to corporate strategies.

Who Are the Competitors?[15]

Once the generic demand for the company's product line, latent or existing, has been determined, managers must analyze the firm's potential competitors and their possible reaction to the company's presence in the market. Competitive analysis is normally defined as an examination of the strengths and weaknesses of the firm relative to its competitors. In an international setting, this analysis implies at least two tasks. First, it is advisable to categorize competitors as *international* (whether foreign or national) and *national.* This is because the competitive advantages of each group are substantially different. International competitors have the potential to develop the unique advantages, or leverages, discussed elsewhere. But national competitors may have more experience in the marketplace and be able to develop stronger relationships with local institutions (preferential treatment by various government agencies, distributors). Second, it is necessary to analyze the marketing activities of each group of competitors and the various forms of market presence adopted by foreign competitors.

In general, the following questions should be raised and answered for each marketing opportunity under review:

1. How many competitors and potential competitors are there, who are they, and how should they be classified?

2. What are the strengths and weaknesses of potential competitors in terms of market presence, product lines, access to distribution channels, access to suppliers, access to capital requirements, economies of scale, experience effect, proprietary technology, access to favorable market and production locations, access to government subsidies and preferential treatment?

3. What reaction can be expected from competitors, and how long will it take them to react? Foreign competitors may have different goals and views of the world.

Estimating Company Demand

Company demand is the company's share of market demand; it depends on the company's marketing effort relative to the marketing efforts of its competitors and many other factors. Since information from subsequent steps in an assessment is needed to arrive at an estimate of what the firm's actual marketing effort will be, the assessment from this point on is iterative. That is, the company first decides what market share it would like. Then it determines the effort required in terms of market presence-marketing mix alternatives and the likely responses of its competitors, all within the constraints imposed by the various barriers and the company's objectives and resources. Standard techniques such as those found in most traditional marketing textbooks can be used to estimate company demand.[16]

The extent of the analysis undertaken will depend on the estimated potential of the market. If the demand is latent, for example, it might be sufficient to determine the contribution (that is, price less landed cost of goods) and how this contribution should be used to obtain the desired quantity of sales. If the demand is existing, is of sufficient size and the marketing efforts of competitors can be determined, a more elaborate analysis may be desirable. Such an analysis usually reviews the relative quality of the product, its price, advertising and promotion costs, sales force costs, and relative effectiveness.

Can We Deliver and From Where?

If the firm intends to deliver finished products, parts, or other inputs to the market under review, it needs to review its sourcing and delivery alternatives.

Sourcing Alternatives. Companies with two or more production locations need to determine which location should be used to source the potential market. Among the factors that need to be considered are product characteristics, such as the weight and volume of anticipated shipments. These factors may result in tranportation costs that eliminate all or a good portion of the advantages gained through economies of scale, or lower-cost sites. Other factors include proximity of the production location to the market, differences in tariff and nontariff barriers because of product origin (shirts made in Hong Kong destined for the United States are limited by quota, but shirts made in Jamaica are not subject to U.S.

quotas), and the desire to keep particular production sites busy (a company may be under governmental or labor pressures to keep a particular plant open). Considerations like these need to be analyzed for marketing effectiveness and logistical efficiency.[17]

Delivery Alternatives. Companies must also select an appropriate delivery system. This will depend on such considerations as desired delivery time, costs and the availability of various forms of transportation and their infrastructures. For example, fashion-sensitive and perishable goods require faster delivery than staple or nonperishable goods, and the additional costs involved in using, say, air freight. Moreover, the time delays in clearing customs at a port facility may suggest an alternate transportation mode is needed. Such is the case for fashion-sensitive apparel and cut flowers being shipped to the United States by air rather than by sea because of normal delays in customs. Further, transportation infrastructures vary considerably from country to country. This is not always a matter of the country's stage of industrialization. Though somewhat limited transportation infrastructures can be expected in developing countries, topographical features may limit the usefulness of a particular type of transportation the firm traditionally uses, such as railroads or trucking.

In addition, delivery assessment cannot stop at the port of entry. Because of considerable differences in the transportation infrastructures of markets, it needs to include an analysis of delivery alternatives from the port to the firm's warehousing facilities.

What Market Presence Should Be Adopted?

Managers must also evaluate each opportunity in terms of the impact the various market-presence alternatives will have on marketing and its ability to compete for market share. Possible questions that need answering in terms of the marketing-mix elements are listed in Table 8-5. Once information has been collected, the various market-presence alternatives need to be compared to determine which are the most suitable. However, the final decision concerning the form of market presence also depends on other factors, such as the firm's resources, the impact that these marketing opportunities will have on other activities, and the firm's objectives and long-range strategy.

A possible method that helps promote a systematic appraisal of the alternatives is the weighted index method shown in Table 8-6. The first column lists factors the firm's marketing management consider important for the successful marketing of the firm's products in that particular country. In the second column, the weights assigned to these factors reflect their relative importance in terms of the firm's competitive advantages, the market's success requirements, and the competitor's competitive advantages. The various market-presence alternatives under review for each factor are rated on a scale from 0.0 to 1.0. Then, to obtain an overall rating, the importance of each success factor is multiplied by the rating given each alternative.

This rating device is used only to demonstrate how a more systematic evaluation of market-presence alternatives can be developed. It is not designed to make decisions for management. Rather, it provides information useful for analyzing the benefits and costs (in terms of competitiveness in the marketplace) of the alternatives under review.

TABLE 8-5
Possible Questions Relating Marketing Strategy and Market Presence

Marketing Strategy Elements	Marketing Presence Questions
Overall marketing strategy	Is the presence appropriate for achieving the marketing strategy's objectives? That is, does the presence provide for: ☐ the achievement of market share objective? ☐ consistency with the stage of product life cycle? ☐ meeting competitor's strategies? ☐ sufficient flexibility to take advantage of future market growth?
Target market	Is the presence appropriate for achieving target market objectives? That is, does the presence provide for: ☐ the acquisition of desired market knowledge (market feedback)? ☐ the achievement of company image objective? ☐ the achievement of desired market positioning objective? ☐ the achievement of market segmentation objectives?
Product	Is the presence appropriate for achieving product-line objectives? That is, does the presence provide for: ☐ the achievement of brand identity and loyalty objectives? ☐ the desired warranty and service support? ☐ sufficient flexibility for product-line extension?
Price	Is the presence appropriate for achieving pricing objectives? That is, does the presence provide for: ☐ the achievement of ROI or payback objectives? ☐ the achievement of channel and end-user pricing objectives? ☐ sufficient flexibility to meet market or competitor changes?
Promotion	Is the presence appropriate for achieving promotion objectives? That is, does the presence provide for: ☐ the achievement of advertising objectives? ☐ the desired media coverage? ☐ the achievement of company demand objectives? ☐ the desired salesforce activity levels?
Place (distribution)	Is the presence appropriate for achieving place objectives? That is, does the presence provide for: ☐ the achievement of coverage and service objectives? ☐ sufficient flexibility to change channels by adding to, or eliminating, channel members? ☐ the desired inventory levels in products and spare parts?

Is the Opportunity Profitable?

Once the market's potential, the company's share of this potential, and the market-presence–marketing-effort alternatives have been identified, it is possible to determine the types of resources required (human, material, and financial)

TABLE 8-6
A Possible Rating Scale for Market Presence Selection*

Market success requirements†	Relative weight (A)	Ability of market presence option to match market requirements (B)											Rating (A/B)
		0.0	0.1	0.2	0.3	0.4	0.5	0.6	0.7	0.8	0.9	1.0	
Company identity	0.00												
Brand identity	0.15												
Delivery time	0.15												
Warranties	0.05												
Postsale service	0.10												
Inventory control	0.10												
Price control: Channel members	0.05												
End users	0.10												
Channel control	0.05												
National distribution	0.10												
Salesforce control	0.05												
Advertising control	0.10												
Total	1.0												

* Ranking to be done for each market presence alternative and each marketing opportunity.
† Success requirements may vary by market, the products or services provided by the company, and the company's objectives and generic strategies.

and to estimate start-up costs, operating costs, profit streams, and the rate of return on the investment for each year in the plan. If the initial entry is part of a step-by-step development of the marketing opportunity, like that used by Levi Strauss in Mexico, the anticipated changes in the company's market presence and marketing effort need to be included. That is, various future scenarios can be developed and their profitability calculated using techniques such as the *range of estimates* or *risk analysis.*

Range of Estimates.[18] This technique begins with the identification of factors that have the potential to affect profitability. Estimates are then made of the values of these factors over an appropriate time horizon, and a cash flow projection is made for the investment. Next comes a sensitivity analysis to determine the impact on profitability if a change should occur in any factor. Once the factors that substantially impact on profitability have been identified, iterations utilizing multiple value assumptions within reasonable ranges can be made and a range of likely cash flows from the investment projected. Factors affecting profitability may include sales, costs of labor, inflation rates, tax rates, depreciation allowances, interest rates, tariffs, and foreign-exchange rates.

Risk Analysis.[19] Risk analysis is a sophisticated application of probability theory. As in the range of estimates technique, critical variables are identified and probabilities are estimated on the outcome of each variable. A simulation model is then used to obtain a distribution of probable profits. The value of this approach is that it provides explicit estimates of the probable effects of changes in individual factors in a country's investment climate.

Which Marketing Opportunities Match Corporate Needs?

Even if the identified marketing opportunity is found to be economically attractive, it is still necessary to determine its appropriateness for the company. That is, does it match the company's objectives, global strategies, and resources? Figure 8-4 shows a set of questions that should be put to each marketing opportunity. If the opportunity does not satisfy these questions within the limits imposed by the company, it should be dropped from further consideration.

MARKETPLACE ASSESSMENTS ————————————————————

The purpose of the marketplace assessment is to help management answer one of two key questions: (1) Should we change our market presence in a particular country and, if so, how? (2) Should we add a new product to our line or drop an old one and, if so, what should be added or dropped and how? Both questions can be answered using the advanced entry-assessment approach discussed in the previous section. Further, the company has information and experience in the market under review, and it can draw on local personnel. However, the goals underlying a marketplace assessment are sufficiently different from those of an entry assessment to warrant further comment.

Market-Presence Assessment

A major difference between the market-presence assessment and the market-entry assessment is that the latter assessment always involves a potential expansion of the firm's international involvement. The market-presence assessment, on the other hand, is used to help determine whether the firm should *expand, contract,* or *eliminate* operations in a particular country.

The reasons for initiating the assessment are quite varied, but are generally the result of some change in the firm's external or internal environments. External reasons include changes in such things as a market's tariff and nontariff barriers, competitive environment, and political and legal environments. Internal reasons include changes in such things as the firm's objectives, organization structure, and resources. Whether the reason is internal or external, each has an important bearing on the market-presence alternatives investigated.

For example, Venezuela recently liberalized its investment rules and incentives to develop its agricultural sector. In response to this liberalization, many foreign companies altered their positions in the country.[20] Espalsa, a local Nestlé affiliate, purchased a pasta manufacturer. The Savoy Group, the local affiliate of Beatrice, acquired Taoro, a local baked goods company. Other companies responded by integrating backward into crop production and livestock raising.

When the Brazilian government recently decided to restrict access to its informatics market, foreign companies responded in three different ways.[21] IBM entered into a minority joint venture with Gerdau, a local steel group with little experience in the industry. Although IBM has only a 30 percent equity position

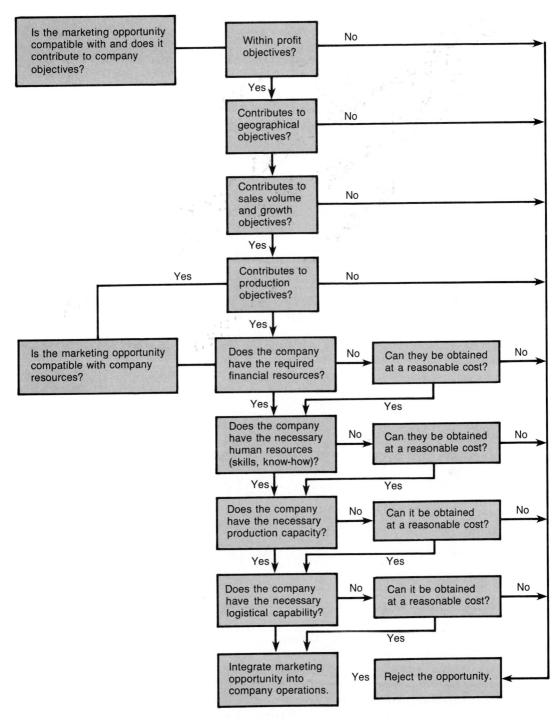

FIGURE 8-4 **Evaluating Marketing Opportunities in Terms of Company Objectives, Strategies, and Resources**

in the joint venture, it plans to be the effective leader because of its technological dominance. In contrast, Hewlett-Packard opted for a joint venture with Iochpe, a local group experienced in informatics. Facit, a Swedish electronics office equipment firm, sold its Brazilian operation to a local group; this same group also purchased Philco Semiconductores from Ford do Brasil.

Expansion of Operations. When the market-presence assessment is undertaken with the idea of expanding the firm's operations in a particular market, management's focus must be on determining which market-presence alternative best enhances the company's competitive strength, increases its market share, and better serves its export markets.

Contraction or Elimination of Operations. When the market-presence assessment is undertaken with a view to either reducing the size of the company's presence or eliminating it, management's focus must be two-pronged, how to best minimize the competitive threats that such a change may have in the marketplace (loss of marketing effectiveness), and what impact will the change have on the company's operations in other markets (plant utilization, revenues, logistics).

New Product Assessment

The focus of the new product assessment depends largely on the *origin* of the new product and the *source* of the assessment request. If the new product was developed locally to meet the needs of the local market or to improve the competitive strength of the subsidiary, the focus of new-product assessment will be strongly, if not totally, operational and will use the bottom-up approach described earlier.

However, there are two other sources for new-product: the company's home market and one of its other markets. The decision to introduce one of these products into the market under review can be made at corporate headquarters, at regional headquarters, or by the local management.

If the request comes from corporate or regional headquarters, the assessment will be strongly, if not totally, strategic and combine the top-down and bottom-up approaches. That is, the assessment must provide information useful for both strategic and operational decisions. If the request is from the local management, assessment focus will be primarily operational.

THE INFORMATION SYSTEM AND THE ASSESSMENT PROCESS _____

For a company starting to internationalize its operations, the three types of assessments described in this chapter are often isolated events. However, as dependency on foreign activities increases, internal pressures eventually result in various aspects of these assessments being integrated into the company's information system. First, the company experiences a growing need for information to help safeguard its foreign investments. Second, it experiences a growing need for more sophisticated assessment approaches to ensure that future marketing opportunities and marketplace changes are consistent with its objectives and overall strategies and can be integrated into current activities. To meet these needs, the company develops international *monitoring* and *search* capabilities.

These capabilities are conceptually the same for national and international companies, but two major operational differences exist: (1) monitoring and search activities must cover more than one country, each with unique competitive and environmental attributes, and (2) the information generated by these capabilities needs to *match* the informational requirements of several levels of management with differing perspectives. For example, corporate-level managers need information with which to make strategic and control decisions. Subsidiary or country-level managers need information for operational and functional decisions.

The Monitoring Activity

The purpose of the *monitoring* activity is to anticipate those changes in the company's national markets and international environment that may affect its operations and to ensure that information on these changes and their potential impact are transmitted to appropriate management levels. These changes can be sudden or gradual in nature, external or internal in origin, and strategic or operational in importance.

Examples of a sudden external change requiring immediate management attention include the overthrow of a government, a change in government policy toward foreign companies, a major devaluation, and the market entry of a major competitor. These changes have both strategic and operational implications. An example of a sudden internal change also needing immediate management attention is a shortage of components for products manufactured at several plants around the world and sold in even more markets. Although this shortage is primarily operational (resulting in possible delivery delays and customer and revenue losses), it could have strategic implications if the part is used in products manufactured and sold by several divisions with profit and loss responsibilities.

To obtain warning sufficient to trigger corrective action, a firm needs to monitor variables critical to its strategic position and operations in each of its markets. However, it must take care when selecting those variables.

Kotler identifies four ways that companies can monitor their environments:[22]

Undirected viewing General exposure to information where the manager has no specific purpose in mind.

Conditioned viewing Directed exposure, not involving active search, to a more or less clearly identified area or type of information.

Informal search A relatively limited and unstructured effort to obtain specific information or information for a specific purpose.

Formal search A deliberate effort—usually following a preestablished plan, procedure, or methodology—to secure specific information or information relating to a specific issue.

In well-run companies, all four ways are used to maximize the advantages of each while minimizing their weaknesses. For example, at one extreme, undirected viewing provides flexibility in the collection of pertinent data and information; it does not ensure that relevant information reaches appropriate decision makers. At the other extreme, formal search tends to be inflexible, but it does ensure that the information collected reaches appropriate decision makers.

Although it is possible to develop basic data-based and decision-based informational models that ensure that particular types of information and data are collected, analyzed, and passed on to the appropriate management levels, models need to be tailored to the particular environmental attributes of each market, and their importance to the company's overall operations. The types of management structure used locally and internationally require that these models be improved over time.

Though the types of variables monitored can be divided into the five major categories shown in Table 8-7, the variables actually monitored vary from company to company.

TABLE 8-7
Information Categories for an International Monitoring System

Category	Major Components	Examples of Variables Monitored*
Competitive environment Major environmental forces affecting company's ability to compete in a national market	Markets	☐ Market size and growth trends ☐ Changes in market institutions ☐ Changes in types of media and coverage ☐ Demographic changes ☐ Needs and tastes of customers
	Competitors	☐ New entrants ☐ Market presence changes ☐ Product-line changes ☐ Advertising and salesforce changes
	Suppliers	☐ Substitute product introductions ☐ Forward integration plans ☐ New entrants
	Capital markets	☐ Working capital market changes ☐ Investment capital market changes
	Technology	☐ Product technology changes ☐ Manufacturing technology changes
	Legal	☐ Product regulations and law changes ☐ Pricing regulations and law changes ☐ Promotion regulations and law changes ☐ Distribution regulations and law changes
Political environment Major forces affecting company's ability to be in national market	Political parties	☐ Changes in government ☐ Changes in political figures ☐ Changes in political philosophies
	Government policies	☐ Changes in policies toward foreign companies
	Public opinion	☐ Changes in attitude toward foreign companies ☐ Social unrest, demonstrations

TABLE 8-7 (cont.)

Category	Major Components	Examples of Variables Monitored*
Economic environment Major forces affecting company's level of activity in a national market	Population	☐ Income distribution trends ☐ Urbanization changes ☐ Growth trends
	Infrastructure	☐ Electrification trends ☐ Communication trends ☐ Transportation trends ☐ Education trends
	Government	☐ Economic policy changes ☐ Fiscal and monetary policy changes ☐ Foreign company discrimination trends
	Economic conditions	☐ Inflation rate trends ☐ External dependency changes ☐ Business cycle trends
Internal (firm's) environment Major forces affecting company's ability to operate in a national market	Intracompany supplies	☐ Inventory levels ☐ Transportation network changes ☐ Changes in external dependency ☐ Available resources
	Intracompany transfers	☐ Changes in ability to transfer personnel ☐ Liquidity changes and availability of financial resources
	Intracompany dependency	☐ Changes in production schedules due to stoppages at key plants ☐ Delays in the introduction of announced products
International environment Major forces affecting company's ability to exit and enter a national market and operate between markets	External economic relations	☐ Tariff and nontariff changes ☐ BOP trends ☐ Changes in foreign exchange controls ☐ Changes in external trading incentives
	External political relations	☐ Changes in treaties and agreements and their interpretation ☐ Changes in military policies
	External legal relations	☐ Changes in policies toward foreign personnel ☐ Changes in policies toward foreign resource transfers ☐ Changes in foreign tax agreements and property rights

Note:
* The listed variables are provided as an indication of the complexity and scope of the monitoring activity. The choice of variables to be monitored will depend on the company's strategies and operations. For example, a textile company would be interested in the availability of water; a food processor would be interested in agricultural developments; an office equipment manufacturer would be interested in changes in regulations covering warranties and copyright laws. These variables are not listed above.

The Search Activity

Three basic search activities are undertaken by international companies: (1) the search for new marketing opportunities consistent with its objectives, strategies, and resources; (2) investigation of environmental changes identified by the company's monitoring activity; and (3) an internal search for information on previous activities that would be of benefit in the formulation of future strategies.

Identifying and selecting new marketing opportunities has been described in detail above. However, as the company acquires international experience, there is pressure to standardize at least some elements of the assessment. To be of value, an assessment must provide the kinds of information useful in weighing the *relative* merits of each opportunity. For example, if one of the company's generic strategies is to be the cost leader in its industry, it may prefer those opportunities that permit the use of standarized products or parts. Consequently, the company needs data and information that can be compared across national markets or market segments. Some companies, such as Nestlé, have adopted procedures that are significantly standardized.[23] However, there are inherent dangers in a standardized approach. There is the possibility of overlooking unique market features and using the procedure without being aware of the assumptions underpinning it and their implications for the company.

Investigating environmental changes involves two types of activities, the investigation of critical environmental variables and the investigation of abrupt changes. The first involves tracking the relevant demographic, economic, political, and legal dimensions of the market and estimating the impact that related changes might have on the firm's local and international operations and strategies. The second investigation typically involves assigning individuals or ad hoc teams to explore the ramifications of any change on the company and to suggest what can be done in the short term to reduce its impact on corporate performance.

The internal search, involves searching the various organizational units of the firm for relevant data and information on previous or ongoing operations, information that would help in the formulation of future business or functional strategies. To aid in this internal search, some companies have created centralized international data and information banks. Coca-Cola, for example, has created a data bank of marketing strategies used in its many foreign markets. The bank includes reasons for the success or failure of such strategies. Such data banks give the country-level marketing manager the ability to systematically draw upon previous experience when evaluating marketing strategies.

The Matching Activity

The timely matching of information and decision-making responsibilities is always a problem; it becomes even more so for the international firm. The international company is operating in more than one country, each with its own particular attributes and evolving political, economic, and social situations. As a result, data proliferates; and there is a tendency to pass on too much data and information. To reduce confusion and information overload, decision makers need systems that screen out noncritical data and information. (Deciding what information is critical and how it should be presented has its own sets of problems.) Each management level within an international company has different information needs. Thus any information system also needs to provide for and ensure that the information deemed critical flows up, down, and across divisional and country levels. One solution to the overload and distribution problems is to build *escalation points* into the information system. At various levels in the organization, key persons are assigned to decide whether the information reaching them is to be *escalated* to a higher management level, returned to a lower level, or passed on to an appropriate manager at the same level.

SUMMARY

In this chapter, we concentrated on the three main types of assessments undertaken by an international company: market-entry assessment, marketplace assessment, and noneconomic assessment. By definition, market-entry assessments includes all assessments designed to help a company identify and select marketing opportunities in countries not previously serviced and to develop appropriate market presence-marketing efforts.

A comprehensive market-entry assessment generally involves two phases: an initial market-entry assessment and an advanced market-entry assessment. The initial market-entry assessment involves two steps. The first eliminates markets because of domestic regulations and management preference. The second eliminates those markets that are either economically or competitively unattractive. The advanced market assessment also involves two steps. The first step is an in-depth analysis of the remaining marketing opportunities. This includes an evaluation of competitive environments and market barriers and a more advanced and detailed estimation of each market's demand. The second step involves a tradeoff analysis that compares the remaining marketing opportunities with the company's objectives, current activities, and resources to determine the validity of market expansion.

Marketplace assessment involves two important aspects of an ongoing operation in a foreign market, whether to change the market presence of the firm and whether to introduce a new product to a particular foreign market.

More accurate assessments are normally possible when the company has information and experience in the market under review, and it can draw on local personnel for assistance.

Noneconomic assessment involves an analysis of the social and political environments of those countries in which the company is either active or planning to become active. The purpose of this form of assessment is to determine the effects that the political, legal, and social factors may have on the firm's operations. The assessment often involves evaluating changes in a host country's political stability, investment climate, profit remittance and exchange controls, and taxation and expropriation policies. The attitudes of a country's political parties toward foreign investors and any changes in these attitudes are also of interest to the company.

Also reviewed were two assessment approaches often used by international companies, the top-down approach and the bottom-up approach. We noted that the top-down approach places considerable emphasis on the strategic decision needs of the company. In contrast, the bottom-up approach emphasizes the operational decision needs of the company.

Finally, we reviewed the information system's role in assessment. Like the national company, the international company develops international monitoring and search capabilities to meet information needs. Unlike the national company, the international firm must conduct monitoring and search activities over more than one country, each with its peculiar competitive and environmental attributes. It must also disseminate information to various management groups with differing geographical and strategic perspectives. Corporate-level managers, for example, need information with which to make strategic and control decisions. Subsidiary or country-level managers need information to make operational and functional decisions. The potential for information overload is especially great in international firms and requires considerable powers of selectivity from its managers.

DISCUSSION QUESTIONS

1. Identify and discuss three reasons (pressures) for undertaking a foreign market assessment. Explain how each pressure may affect the scope and content of the assessment.

2. Explain what a *market-entry* assessment is and how it may differ from a *marketplace* assessment.

3. What is a noneconomic environmental assessment, and when is this type of assessment likely to be undertaken?

4. Contrast the bottom-up and top-down assessment approaches. Is a company likely to use both? Why or why not?

5. Identify the basic elements common to both the market-entry and the marketplace assessments. Will there be any differences in how these elements are treated by the marketing researcher?

6. Identify and discuss the advantages and disadvantages of three major sources for secondary data on overseas markets.

7. Discuss three factors affecting the value of an overseas assessment.

8. What are some of the problems an international marketing manager can expect to encounter when creating a centralized marketing information bank? How can these problems be solved?

ADDITIONAL READING

Douglas, Susan P., C. Samuel Craig, and Warren J. Keegan, "Approaches to Assessing International Marketing Opportunities for Small and Medium-Sized Companies," *Columbia Journal of World Business,* Vol. 17, Fall 1982.

Goldstein, Elisabeth, and Jan Vanous, "Country Risk Analysis: Pitfalls of Comparing Eastern Bloc Countries Without the Rest of the World," *Columbia Journal of World Business,* Vol. 18 Winter 1983.

Johansson, Johny K., and Ikujuro Nonaka, "Market Research the Japanese Way," *Harvard Business Review,* May–June 1987.

Kaynak, Erdener, and A. Coskun Samli, "Eastern European Marketing Systems and Western Marketing Research Voids: A Research Agenda," *Journal of Business Research,* Vol. 14, April 1986.

Wijnholds, Heiko de B., "Market Forecasting for Dual Economies: The Application and Accuracy of Income Elasticities," *Journal of International Business Studies,* Vol. 12, Winter 1981.

ENDNOTES

1. For a discussion of the noneconomic assessment, see Stephen J. Kobrin, et al., "The Assessment and Evaluation of Noneconomic Environments by American Firms: A Preliminary Report," *Journal of International Business Studies,* Vol. 11, No. 1, Spring–Summer 1980, pp. 32–47.
2. George S. Day, "Strategic Market Analysis and Definition, an Integrated Approach," *Strategic Management Journal,* Vol. 2 (1981), pp. 281–299.
3. "The Big Money in Cheap Rocks," *Forbes,* August 10, 1987, pp. 64–68.
4. A. A. Sherbini, "Marketing in the Industrialization of Underdeveloped Countries." *Journal of Marketing,* Vol. 29, January 1965, pp. 28–32.
5. *World Bank Atlas 1986* (Washington, D.C.: World Bank).
6. H. Igor Ansoff, *Corporate Strategy* (New York: McGraw-Hill, 1965), p. 191.
7. For more details on the General Food example, see Louis Turner, *Multinational Companies and the Third World* (New York: Hill and Wang, 1973), pp. 159–160.
8. "How Colgate-Palmolive Handles the Expanding, Restrictive India Market," *Business Asia,* May 19, 1986, p. 155.
9. For a more detailed explanation of these techniques, see Reed Moyer, "International Market Analysis," *Journal of Marketing Research,* Vol. 5, (November 1968), pp. 353–360.
10. Ibid.
11. R. J. Rummel and David A. Heenan, "How Multinationals Analyze Political Risk," *Harvard Business Review,* January–February 1978, p. 72.
12. See, for example, S. Prakash Sethi, "Comparative

Cluster Analysis for World Markets," *Journal of Marketing Research,* Vol. 8, (August 1971), pp. 348–354.

13. See, for example, A. Ries and J. Trout, *Positioning: The Battle for Your Mind* (New York, N.Y.: McGraw-Hill, 1981).

14. J. K. Johansson and H. B. Thorelli, "International Product Positioning," *Journal of International Business Studies,* Vol. 16, No. 3, (Fall 1985), pp. 57–75.

15. For a detailed discussion of competitor analysis, see Michael E. Porter, *Competitive Strategy: Techniques for Analyzing Industries and Competitors* (New York: Free Press, 1980).

16. Philip Kotler, *Marketing Management: Analysis, Planning, and Control,* 5th ed. (Englewood Cliffs, N.J.: Prentice-Hall, 1984), pp. 230–232.

17. John Fayerweather and Ashok Kapoor, *Strategy and Negotiation for the International Corporation* (Cambridge, Mass.: 1976), pp. 13–14.

18. Robert B., Stobaugh, "How to Analyze Foreign Investment Climates," *Harvard Business Review,* September–October 1969, pp. 100–108.

19. Ibid.

20. "MNCs Respond Cautiously to Venezuela's New Push to Develop Agriculture," *Business Latin America,* February 24, 1986, pp. 52–53.

21. "Brazil's Informatics MNCs Turn to Joint Ventures to Survive Market Reserve, *Business Latin America,* October 27, 1986.

22. Kotler, op. cit., p. 192.

23. Ralph Z. Sorenson and Ulrich E. Wiechmann, "How Multinationals View Marketing Standardization," *Harvard Business Review,* May–June 1975, pp. 54ff.

PART TWO CASES

3. Niagra Electronics

Although Richard Kilman had been in the African nation of Niagra for only six months, he was beginning to feel as though he had been there forever. In part, this was because the initial excitement of living in a new and very different country had worn off. More importantly, it reflected a growing number of problems that Richard was facing in his job as manager of manufacturing operations in Niagra Electronics Ltd., a subsidiary of Boston Global Electronics (BGE), a large U.S. multinational corporation based in Charlotte, North Carolina.

Prior to coming to Niagra, Kilman had been in charge of production operations at a BGE plant in Texas. Although he was only twenty-nine, he had over six years experience in manufacturing and been promoted rapidly to increasingly more responsible positions. He had been offered the job in Niagra because of his strong track record. The fact he was a bachelor was also important; BGE did not have the expense of moving and supporting a family in Niagra.

Kilman had been eager to accept the overseas post. The factory in Niagra was a large and important facility that sourced not only local demand but also exported to other markets in Africa. He was also confident that he could do a good job and his performance in this high-profile position would be noticed. His confidence stemmed from his belief that manufacturing was essentially a technical problem and that he was an expert in the appropriate technology. Prior to his move to Niagra, Kilman was put through a one-day training session on BGE's activities and priorities in Niagra and the essentials of everyday life there.

Although this seminar was useful, it did not fully prepare Kilman, who had never been outside the United States before, for his new situation. Initially, however, the novelty of living in an exotic and challenging environment was both exciting and stimulating. He had been particularly energized

---

This case was prepared by Peter Walters.

by the chance to rectify what he perceived to be shortcomings in the manufacturing system. During the first months of his assignment, therefore, Richard was fully occupied settling in and planning the introduction of the changes he felt necessary.

The changes in work practices envisaged by Kilman were—in his view—not very sweeping. Essentially, they involved the introduction of productivity-related payments, rather than the old flat rate system. Preliminary estimates indicated that the pay of the typical worker would increase by around 5 percent and that productivity would, on average, grow by 18 percent. However, the pay of less effective workers would fall substantially, by as much as 20 percent in some cases. This fall would be counterbalanced by much larger than average increases for the most efficient workers, most of whom were relatively young.

Niagra Electronics had a tradition of paternalism. Although all workers belonged to a trade union, this was a company union that had been established by management. Kilman had consulted with the local personnel manager, Johnson Ezembakwe, a Niagran citizen who was a graduate in management from the local university. Ezembakwe had expressed some skepticism about the new system and had argued for detailed consultation with the workers. Kilman's view was that the prospect of extra pay would silence opposition to his plan. However, he did agree to meet with the trade union's executive committee a week before the planned introduction of the new system. Kilman thought that the meeting had gone very well. He had emphasized the benefits of the new system, and Ezembakwe had explained how it would work. Although the committee had not expressed support for the change, no overt opposition was evident.

The following day after work, a noisy meeting of the workers took place at which they voted 61 percent to 39 percent to oppose the plan. (Most support for the new system came from the younger workers who were most likely to benefit from the changes.) A delegation of worker representatives, many of whom were not members of the union committee, met with Ezembakwe the following day. Their message was that the proposed changes ran counter to important Niagran traditions of solidarity equality, and respecting and taking care of the aged. Supporters of the new scheme were labelled as sell-outs who had let greed overcome their native traditions. Furthermore, the representatives stated that any attempt to implement the new system would be resisted by a strike and that the company union would, in the event of a strike, seek affiliation with an outside trade union.

Richard Kilman was shocked by the opposition to his plan and believed that firm action was needed to deal with the opponents to the scheme. In his view, the technological and cost arguments for the system were so strong that to compromise would be a disaster. He believed that an example should be made of the "troublemakers," who should be summarily dismissed. Any other workers joining a strike should also be fired and be replaced with younger workers. (These were in plentiful supply owing to high local unemployment.) Kilman argued that although replacements would be expensive in the short-term, the long-run benefits would greatly outweigh any costs.

Johnson Ezembakwe called for a more conciliatory approach. He pointed out that the new system did indeed run counter to important local traditions and that serious trouble was likely in the event of a strike. He proposed that the new system should be dropped and that negotiations on less radical changes should be entered into with the worker delegation. Ezembakwe confirmed that it would probably be possible to replace striking workers with recruits from the large pool of unemployed. However, he also asserted that the fired workers would be unlikely to take such action lying down.

As if the strike threat was not enough, Kilman was also faced with three other problems that demanded immediate action. Two of these problems concerned questionable payments. One situation was fairly straightforward. Important spare parts were needed to repair a machine that was inoperable and had accordingly caused a 7 percent reduction in output. The necessary parts had already arrived in Niagra and were awaiting customs clearance. However, due to a lack of customs officials

and unofficial policy, clearance was unlikely in less than six weeks. It was, however, possible to jump the line by making a payment of around $500 to the local customs supervisor.

The other payments situation was more complex and dealt with environmental standards that were due to come into effect in six months. Meeting the new standards would demand investment of some $170,000 in pollution-control equipment. Conversations with colleagues and contacts in locally owned firms had made very clear that many local competitors were not planning to invest in the equipment needed to meet the new standards. A Niagran friend of Kilman's had explained that the government did not expect most firms to comply, and this would not be a problem so long as a substantial payment were made to the campaign funds of the ruling party, which was firmly entrenched in power.

When Kilman raised these problems with the Managing Director of Niagra Ltd., he was told to go and discuss the situation with the firm's local auditors. At this meeting, Kilman was told that officials in this firm would take care of the necessary payoffs, obtaining the required funds by inflating their auditing fees. Payment to the customs official could be made immediately. However, more care would be needed regarding the payment to the party. Negotiations on the size of the "contribution" would be needed; it was indicated that a payment of some $20,000 would be required.

The third problem dealt with the appointment of a new production engineer as Kilman's assistant. Kilman wanted to appoint Jane Moses, a Niagran citizen with an engineering degree from Georgia Tech. Moses had worked as an intern in the plant he had managed in Texas. Moses had impressed him as capable and very hardworking and he knew that she wished to return to Niagra when her internship finished in two months. However, Ezembakwe adamantly opposed her appointment. His initial argument was that she would be too expensive and that there were plenty of local engineers available. When further pressed, however, he admitted that his main objection was that her appointment was contrary to local custom; males in Niagra would not accept leadership from a female.

Conversations with other Niagrans confirmed the validity of Ezembakwe's statement. Kilman was in a real quandary regarding this appointment. No other candidate with Jane Moses's ability had applied for the position. On the other hand, the new assistant would have to work with and supervise male staff members.

4. U.S. Agricultural Tractors _____

Tom Madison, Director of Market Research at U.S. Agricultural Tractor (USAT), has just come from an important meeting at which it had been decided to initiate a study of export opportunities for the firm's tractors. Since he had no experience in international market research, he was rather concerned about how best to approach this task.

United States demand for tractors had stagnated due to a recession in the farming industry. Because of pent up demand for its big, high-performance machines, USAT had weathered the recent recession better than had some of its larger competitors. However, during the past year, the order backlog had been completed and there was an urgent need for new business. It was this situation that had provided the impetus for considering export opportunities, and Tom had been asked to come up with a short list of the most attractive overseas markets. These are to be reviewed at a meeting in one week. Time was short since work was already well advanced on the 1988 marketing plan.

Because of time constraints, Tom decided to split the analytical work between his staff on a regional basis. Mary Collier was accordingly asked to evaluate a group of countries in the Asia-Pacific area. These markets were Australia, Hong Kong, India, Indonesia, Japan, Malaysia, New Zealand, China, Taiwan, and South Korea.

In order to provide a common framework for comparative analysis, Madison felt that it was important to identify a list of critical variables. He therefore decided to meet with his staff to discuss possible decision criteria.

At this meeting it was determined that three variables would be considered during the preliminary screening work prior to the forthcoming

_____
This case was prepared by Peter Walters.

meeting. Since most agricultural output is required to meet domestic food needs, it was decided to use data on the *population* in each country as a criterion. USAT's tractors are large, high-performance machines and are consequently expensive. A measure of ability to purchase is provided by *Gross Domestic Product per capita;* this was used as the second variable. Finally, *the number of tractors in a country* was used as an indicator of overall historic demand for tractors. Tom was not entirely satisfied with these three measures, but he believed they were the best available at such short notice.

An additional theme taken up at the meeting was the need to pursue more detailed evaluation of the "short list' markets initially identified. Tom instructed each member of his staff to consider this issue over the next week. He was particularly interested in two kinds of feedback. The first concerned the *type of information* that needed to be acquired. Perhaps of even greater significance, was the question of *how to go about* reviewing the most interesting markets in depth.

Tom anticipated that, during the detailed evaluation phase of the research, it would be probably necessary to acquire primary data on the markets of greatest interest. Since USAT had neither experience nor physical presence in overseas markets, he wondered whether his own staff should attempt the required research. This would necessitate travel and research overseas and this firsthand learning might be very valuable.

An alternative would be to use an outside market research bureau. If an external agency were to be used, Tom preferred to use USAT's regular United States agency. However, the firm did not have any overseas offices. Tom wondered if they would be able to do the work; if they were unable to help, he was anxious to receive feedback on other options.

QUESTIONS

1. What is your opinion of the *inital screening* criteria? Suggest additional measures that could be used during initial screening.
2. Using the three screeening criteria decided upon, evaluate the Asian-Pacific markets that Mary Collier has been asked to analyze. Be sure to score each country on each of these factors. (*The United Nations Statistical Yearbook* is a useful reference source.) Using this data—and any other *initial screening* measures that you feel to be relevant and for which you are able to obtain data—recommend three Asian-Pacific markets for more detailed analysis.

3. What advice would you give Tom Madison concerning the *detailed evaluation* of the *short-list markets*?
4. How should Tom approach the task of collecting *primary data* on the short-list markets?

Part III
Corporate Dimensions
of the Global Marketing
Effort

Part II focused on gathering information on and analyzing foreign markets. It also showed that market diversity complicates the process of selecting foreign marketing opportunities. Those opportunities selected must support the company's strategic objectives and goals. Thus, a basic understanding of the company's global strategies and the impact that they have on the marketing effort is essential for managers. Accordingly, Part III deals with international strategic marketing planning, the problems encountered when extending the marketing effort to include foreign markets, and the various marketing strategies and marketing-mix policies adopted for overseas markets.

Chapter 9: examines the basic strategy concepts and strategic planning techiques necessary for an understanding of the relationship between a company's corporate strategy, its corporate planning process, and its marketing effort. It also examines variables used to analyze the competitive environment and some of the techniques used by managers when deciding how resources should be allocated among markets.

Chapter 10: focuses on the issues and problems confronting a company developing global marketing objectives and strategies. In doing so, it examines four generic strategies, the two geographic expansion strategy options available to global companies, and the factors influencing the forms of market presence or entry mode to be employed in individual countries.

Chapter 11: concludes the discussion on the relationship between corporate strategy and the global marketing effort by focusing on the company's global marketing mission and its core marketing strategy options. The choice of marketing strategy and the characteristics of the company's foreign national markets are also examined.

Case Studies: KNP Papier N.V.
Cairo Barclays International Bank
Fishing Industries

Chapter 9
Corporate
Strategy and
Global Marketing

INTRODUCTION

Successful companies look beyond present activities and implicitly or explicitly develop "game plans" to achieve future objectives and goals. These game plans are designed to provide companies with the capabilities, skills, resources and organizational structure for meeting competitive challenges and taking advantage of future opportunities. The plans are based on assessments of the firm's past and present competitive strengths and weaknesses and its competitive position in the industry or industries in which it competes.

Five corporate game plans are presented in Exhibit 9-1. Each plan reflects the competitive competencies of a company and its planned reaction to changes in the competitive environment, and each is a strategy that is the result of formal or informal planning.

The terms *corporate planning, strategic planning,* and *business planning* are used variously to describe this planning process.[1] Underlying the planning activity is the belief that much planning results in a better coordination of the various activities of the company; provides a corporatewide focus, purpose, and cohesion; and enhances chances of success.

Marketing plays a critical role in the planning process since it is the link between a firm and its markets. It is also one of the key means by which a company achieves its objectives. The marketing staff assists in the identification, analysis, and selection of environmental opportunities and is responsible for developing and implementing plans to exploit these opportunities.

In this chapter, we therefore consider the strategic planning process and the role marketing plays in this process. This will provide us with the necessary platform for the more detailed discussion of the international dimensions of strategy in Chapters 10 and 11. First, we discuss the terms *strategy, plan,* and *planning process:* What do they mean? What roles do they play in company activities? Second, we discuss some of the factors critical to the formulation of strategies and plans. Third, we present some of the techniques used when developing particular strategies and plans. A discussion of three generic strategic approaches available to marketing concludes the chapter. There, we identify and briefly explore the implications of operating internationally.

FOUR PRIMARY STRATEGIES

Considerable confusion surrounds the terms *strategy, plan,* and *strategic planning.* Some writers use *strategy* and *plan* interchangeably; others, *strategy* and *strategic planning.*[2] To reduce confusion, many companies adopt their own definitions. To IBM, a plan connotes a design to ensure that near-term departmental tasks fit together to advance the company's long-range objectives. *Corporate strategy* is seen as a summary of a number of functional and product-line strategies.[3]

The modern company consists of four primary organizational levels—the *enterprise, corporate, business,* and *functional* levels. For a company to effectively pursue its goals and objectives, the present and future activities of these four levels must be internally consistent, mutually supportive, and unified in responses

EXHIBIT 9-1
Five Corporate Game Plans—1984

Alcan Aluminum, Ltd.

In 1984, many North American manufacturers were in the initial stages of developing markets abroad to offset stagnating domestic growth. Alcan Aluminum, Ltd., a Canadian company, then operated in 33 nations with 57 percent of its sales outside North America. Alcan's president and chief executive, David M. Culver, viewed current restructuring of the aluminum industry as a unique opportunity for the strategic repositioning of the company. Alcan sought additional capacity through an aggressive *acquisition strategy* designed to exploit Alcan's low-cost producer status and its position in international markets. Its goal: to compete more directly with competitors, especially the U.S. giant Alcoa.

Lucky-Goldstar Group

The South Korean company Lucky-Goldstar Group was responsible for 10 percent of South Korea's GNP. Sales had nearly doubled in five years. To maintain this explosive growth, Lucky began expanding into other fast-growing fields through a *joint-ventures strategy* with foreign firms, particularly U.S. companies. These joint ventures were designed to gain an edge over rivals at home and to push Lucky into new overseas markets and technologies. In addition, Lucky centralized its R&D staff and doubled its R&D budget.

Burlington

Burlington, the world's largest textile manufacturer, actively sought out specialized, high-margin *market niches* to bolster profits. A departure from Burlington's traditional approach of producing mainly commodity products, this strategy represented more of a marketing concept. President and CEO Frank S. Greenberg

noted that "the environment has changed." As the U.S. economy has rebounded, consumers have become more fashion conscious. Burlington has also invested heavily in ultramodern textile machinery to provide capacity and flexibility to respond to these high-end market niches.

3M Co.

In an effort to balance the cyclical nature of its business, 3M Co. decided to aggressively pursue lucrative consumer markets. 3M set up a separate marketing group with responsibilities for 5,000 consumer products and placed a renewed emphasis on traditional marketing, particularly advertising and promotion. 3M's goal was not to compete directly with other marketing giants. Instead, it would continue (1) to promote older products by introducing existing products into new markets and (2) to develop new products for consumers by adapting existing commercially successful products and technologies.

Cooper Industries, Inc.

In 1984, Cooper Industries, Inc., was comprised of three divisions: compression and drilling equipment, tools and hardware, and electrical and electronic products. The latter two divisions were the result of acquisitions in 1981 and were the company's salvation during the slump in the oil and gas industry. Recognizing the contributions made by these acquisitions, Cooper continued to pursue a *growth strategy* by acquiring additional basic manufacturing operations, ones countercyclical to existing businesses. It backed these acquisitions by aggressively investing in capital outlays for efficiency improvements and by disciplining manufacturing operations to bolster profitability.

Sources: "Corporate Strategies," *BusinessWeek,* July 9, 16, 23 and August 13, 27, 1984 issues.

to competitive changes in the external environment. This cross-level match is illustrated in Figure 9-1. The common objective of the four primary strategies is to match the current and future activities of the four company levels to four specific aspects of the operating environment. The combination of the objectives, goals, and strategies form the company's *master strategy*.

The company's corporate management generally develops the enterprise and corporate strategies. These guide the company into future profitable activities and provide decision rules for the sequential allocation of resources among business units. In turn, each business unit is reponsible for developing a business strategy to guide it toward the goals set forth in the corporate strategy. The functional areas (manufacturing, finance, marketing, and personnel) are required to develop functional strategies that achieve the objectives and goals contained in the business

FIGURE 9-1   Four Primary Strategies: The Company–Environment Match

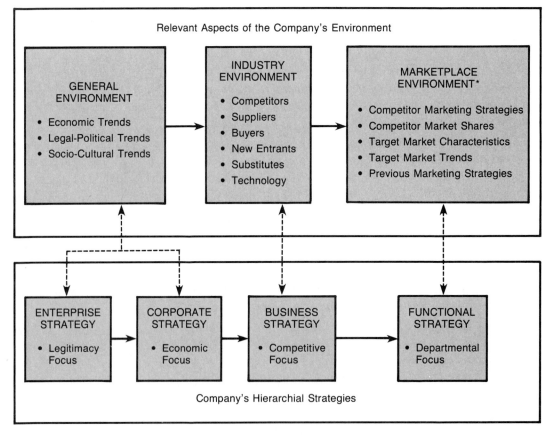

*The elements of the marketplace environment will depend of which functional area is being considered. The elements listed are examples of those considered when developing a marketing strategy.

strategy. In each case, the strategies affect the allocation of resources necessary to simultaneously achieve the objectives of the four organizational levels.[4]

Enterprise Strategy[5]

An *enterprise strategy* attempts to define the role the firm will play in the everyday affairs of society. Increasingly, companies recognize that they have obligations toward their shareholders, employees, customers, and communities. Commonly accepted obligations include dividends for shareholders, safe working conditions and job security, products of high quality, and the role of good citizen within the community. Not so clear or commonly accepted is the scope and nature of these obligations, especially when other countries are involved. What is an adequate dividend? What is job security? What is a high-quality product? What is a good citizen? The scope and nature of a company's obligations are dynamic and, it is essential to note, vary from one country to another.

> An **enterprise strategy** is a statement of a company's social-legitimacy concerns, what it sees as its social responsibilties, and what business practices are to be followed.

This particular aspect of a global company's master strategy is of growing importance to home and host governments alike. Domestic and foreign governments, labor unions, and the societies they represent, are increasingly concerned about the economic, political, socio-cultural, and environmental effects global companies have on society. Governments and labor unions are also increasingly concerned about companies' business practices.

The chief executive of a global company can be confronted with situations that defy easy decisions. For example, the Henkel Group of West Germany and Procter & Gamble of the United States may sincerely want to be good citizens of host countries. However, the very fact that the companies operate simultaneously in several countries can result in situations that give rise to conflicting social, political, and economic responses.

How, for example, can a U.S.-based company be a good citizen of both the United States and Argentina when both countries are facing balance-of-payment problems? The U.S. government would like to have large dividends repatriated from Argentina. Argentina, on the other hand, would like no dividends remitted to the United States. Similarly, a company like RCA would like to manufacture components and assemble products in low-wage countries. Doing so would result in less expensive television sets in the United States and increased employment for workers abroad. However, it might also result in a loss of employment in the United States. A U.S. pharmaceutical company might be permitted to market a drug in a European or Latin American country but, because of different testing prodedures, be denied the same right in the United States. In this last case, the decision to market or not to market abroad is partly an ethical one; it is contingent on the company's evaluation of the testing procedures used in the various countries and on its ultimate concern and responsibility for the health of the consumer.

Problems like those itemized above are serious. Some companies face these issues squarely and develop codes of business conduct. Others do not. The problems will not go away; they are of growing concern in the international business community. Since the mid-1970s, the United Nations and other international organizations have been actively trying to develop guidelines for company behavior.

Corporate Strategy

Corporate strategy addresses a key economic question: *What business or businesses should a company be in?* In the case of multibusiness companies, it also focuses on ways to integrate these businesses into an effective portfolio of activities.

> A **corporate strategy** is a statement of a company's purpose, growth direction(s), and long-range objectives.

Decisions have to be made about which business units should receive additional resources, which should be used to supply required financial resources, and which should be eliminated or divested. Economic, political, and socio-cultural issues are all relevant to corporate planning. Their combined influence on the future success of the industry or industries in which the company has decided to compete is significant.

A company's corporate strategy is based on an analysis of and decisions about the projected interaction of the company with its general environment and about the most appropriate approach(es) to be used to achieve long-range objectives. As such, a corporate strategy provides a comprehensive set of rules and guidelines for pursuing short-range objectives. That is, it identifies the industry or industries in which the company will compete, the foreign markets and market segments, the level of support each business unit is to receive, and the goals these units are to achieve.

Abell and Hammond divide a company's *corporate strategy* into two parts, *definition* and *mission*.[6] The *definition* broadly outlines the company's product and market scope (which customer groups and customer functions are to be satisfied and by what technology). The corporate definition also establishes geographic scope. The corporate *mission* consists of the company's performance expectations for each business unit (sales growth, market share, return on investment, net income). It may include statements concerning each unit's international activities.

Business Strategy

Business strategy deals with these three questions:

1. How should a company compete in its various businesses?
2. What competitive position should each business unit assume to reach its corporate-specified goals?
3. How should the corporation allocate its resources to achieve the desired competitive position?

In addition to addressing these three broad questions, a business strategy should integrate the business unit's functional areas into a coordinated and cohesive effort. The business planning environment consists of those elements of the environment that directly effect competition within the business unit's industry (competitors, suppliers, buyers, new entrants, substitute products, and technological trends in manufacture and products).

A **business strategy** is a detailed statement of the business unit's definition, mission, objectives, and the approaches to be used to achieve the company's long-range objectives.

A *business strategy* is based on an analysis of and decisions about the near-term interaction of a company's business unit with its industry (or competitive) environment. It includes statements about the unit's product, and market scope, and performance expectations. These unit-level definition and mission statements need to be consistent with the corporate definition and mission statements. That is, they need to support the corporation's long-range objectives, specified competitive position, geographic reach, and allocation of resources.

As we will discuss in detail in Chapter 10, the geographic environment of business units with international activities depends on whether the industry is *global* or *national*. When a company competes in a global industry (such as agricultural equipment, automobiles, cameras, chemicals, earth-moving equipment, and medical products), a business unit's competitive environment crosses national boundaries. For companies competing in essentially national industries (such as apparel, processed foods, and household products), the competitive environment is defined mostly by national boundaries.

Functional Strategy

A *functional strategy* addresses two issues: the response of the functional area policy to the operating environment and the coordination of the various functional policies. First, it is designed to "match" functional area policies, objectives and plans with changes in the functional area's relevant environment. This environment is identified as the marketplace environment in Figure 9-1 and consists of those elements that affect a particular function's operations. For example, monetary and fiscal policies, interest rates, and so on affect the financial function's strategy. Competitor product offerings, services, prices, and advertising campaigns affect the marketing function's strategy. The functional strategy also integrates the various activities of the functional area into a cohesive and focused effort. Marketing operations such as sales, distribution, marketing research, and advertising need to be coordinated and focused on achieving previously specified objectives and goals in the targeted marketplace. Marketing programs must be developed that obtain a response from the targeted market consistent with the marketing function's goals *and* those of the other functional areas.

A **functional strategy** is a detailed statement of the short-range objectives and method(s) to be used by a functional area to achieve its business unit's short-term goals and the company's long-range objectives.

In the case of a company involved in international marketing activities, the geographic extent of the functional strategies depends on whether its business units are serving *global markets* or *national markets*. For example, Corning Glass operates several business units internationally.[7] Its Television Products Group supplies a relatively small group of original equipment manufacturers located in Asia, Europe, and North America. Its technology is mature; its products are more or less homogeneous; and, regardless of the customer's nationality, success depends on costs, delivery, and quality. Thus, the essential dimensions of this business unit's marketing strategy are more or less impervious to local market differences. In contrast, its Consumer Products Group caters to the cookware needs of mass markets in many countries. Although confronted by some large global competitors such as Noritake of Japan, most of its competitors are either regional or local. Moreover, its markets are reached through retailers. Thus, the essential dimensions of this business unit's marketng strategy are sensitive to local differences such as variations in distribution channels, advertising, and product substitution.

The Strategy Hierarchy

The hierarchial relationship among the four primary strategies implies a spiral of constraints. The move from an enterprise strategy to a functional strategy represents a move *down* the organizational hierarchy and increasing *closeness* to the marketplace. At the same time, constraints *increase*. Each primary strategy constrains every other primary strategy. This is particularly true for the lower-level strategies. Higher-level strategies supply the objectives, goals, and decision rules that lower-level plans must respond to.

Plans and Strategy

A *plan* is the strategy of a lower organizational level. It is an explicit statement of the methods prescribed for achieving the strategy of a higher organizational level.

Marketing and the Primary Strategies

The relationship between marketing management and the four primary strategies is shown in Figure 9-2. On the one hand, the marketing staff acts as a source for information and recommendations on the firm's present and future marketplace activities. On the other hand, marketing is responsible for obtaining a desired response from each market in which the company is active.

Marketing provides corporate planners with information and recommendations that are used in plotting the future direction of the company. Marketing fulfills this role by:

1. Identifying and making recommendations about future trends and opportunities in the markets where the company is already active;

2. Identifying and making recommediations about new market opportunities;

3. Providing estimates of the marketing resources (budget and staff) needed to exploit these opportunities.

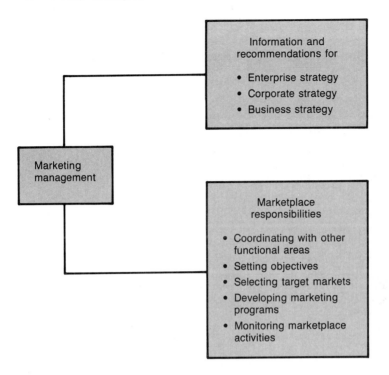

FIGURE 9-2 Marketing Management Strategic Planning Process

Marketing-supplied information is used in the formulation of corporate and business strategies. As a result, marketing plays a key and influential role in deciding the final configuration these strategies take.

In addition, the marketing staff is responsible for developing and implementing *marketing strategies* that simultaneously meet the following four conditions:

1. They must be designed to achieve the objectives and goals set forth by the company and each business unit;

2. They must be synchronized with the objectives and goals of each business unit's other functional strategies (production, finance, personnel);

3. They must be within budgeted resources;

4. They must obtain a predetermined response from the marketplace.

Figure 9-3, which represents a single business unit with four foreign operations, illustrates the complexity of the constraints imposed on the international-marketing function. Since many global companies (for example, Canon, Ford, and Philips), operate in a large number of countries, the managerial complexity of meeting the four conditions listed above cannot be overstated. (How the marketing staff attempts to meet these basic conditions is covered extensively in later chapters.)

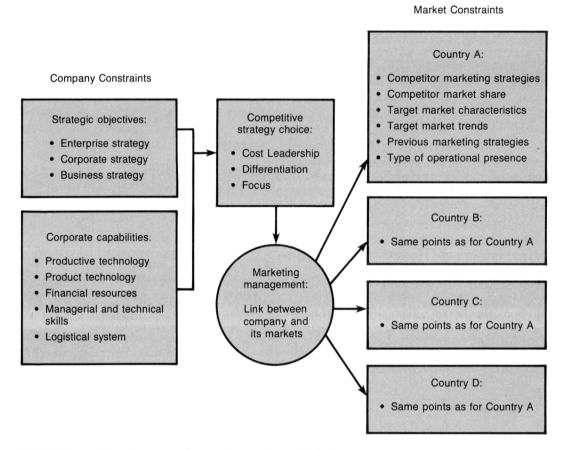

FIGURE 9-3   The Company–International Market Relationship

THE STRATEGIC PLANNING PROCESS

The process used to arrive at a strategy or plan is the *strategy planning process.* It is circular, systematic, and periodic. The process can be started when and where desired, involves a specified number of activities and decisions, and occurs at specific time intervals.

Each company that adopts a strategic planning approach develops a planning process to meet its particular needs. Since the purpose of planning is to map a course of action custom-tailored to the needs of a company, the planning process reflects the company's particular resources, history, philosophy, and previous decision making practices.

Some companies use a continuous process; others use an annual planning cycle. Some start the process at the top of the organization and move down; others start from the bottom and move up. Some use a three-year planning horizon; others, a six- or even a ten-year horizon. Whatever the case, the process is strongly influenced by the parent company's home-country socio-cultural and economic environments. For example, U.S. fabric producers generally use an annual planning cycle with a three-year planning horizon. They tend to believe that fabrics, even technological changes in manufacturing, have three-year cycles. Asian and European fabric producers generally use an annual planning cycle with a ten-year planning horizon. They believe in focusing on long-range industry trends.[8] Neither example typifies most Latin American plans. Because of widespread economic and political volatility, many Latin American companies tend to use a shorter planning cycle. Even so, certain elements are common to most strategic planning processes.

> The **strategic planning process** consists of those functions and organizational units responsible for the development of primary strategies. As such, its purpose is to identify and develop a corporate purpose, objectives, goals, and the planning of programs of action that effectively relate the company, its businesses, and functional areas to their relevant environments and that enables the company to successfully exploit future marketplace opportunities in which it is likely to enjoy a differential or competitive advantage.

An example of one strategic planning process is shown in Figure 9-4. The process is characterized by eight sequential steps (activities). These eight activities are undertaken whether the end result is a corporate, business, or functional strategy. The diagram assumes, as does most management literature, that a successful company is one that develops an appropriate strategy to reach its objectives, builds an appropriate organizational structure, cultivates a "culture" to carry out this strategy, and assigns the appropriate human and material resources to get the job done. In such an approach, strategy—not organizational structure—is the starting point; the organization and the distribution of the human and material resources within the organization become the means to achieve company objectives and goals.

COMPETITIVE ANALYSIS AND STRATEGY

The strategies developed and implemented by marketing management are directly linked to and constrained by the company's corporate and business strategies. For example, if a hypothetical conglomerate decides to develop its building systems division potential by using the profits generated by its industrial products division, the industrial products division's role might be to maintain its market position at minimum cost. Accordingly, new product development and aggressive promotional activities might be curtailed. In contrast, the marketing activities undertaken by the building system division will expand and be aimed at building market share and market position.

The development of a strategy can be divided into two broad yet linked activities, *competitive (or external) analysis* and *resource allocation (or internal) analysis.* Regardless of the type of primary strategy under review, both types of analysis are essential. For example, the decision by the conglomerate above to concentrate resources on its building systems division and to use the profits from

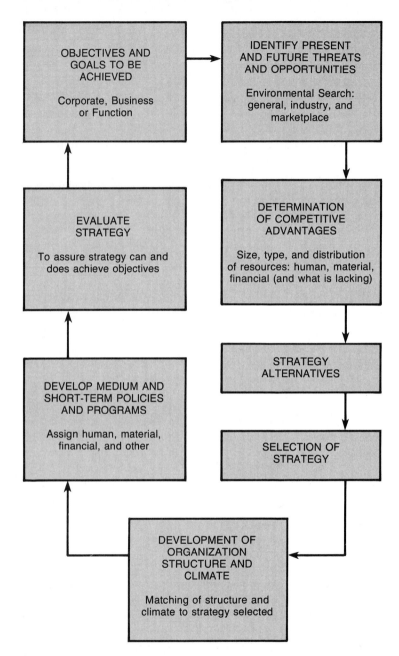

FIGURE 9-4   The Strategy Planning Process

the industrial products division to finance a competitive thrust would most likely be the result both of an evaluation of the company's and divisions' external environments and the competitive implications of the required reallocation of resources for the company, the two divisions singled out for attention, *and* the company's other divisions.

Competitive Analysis

The purpose of a *competitive analysis* is to provide insights into a company's competitive position vis-à-vis competitors and environmental trends in order to develop the four primary strategies discussed earlier. There are two dimensions to such an analysis, (1) an analysis of external factors and (2) an analysis of internal factors.

External Factors

External factors that directly influence a company's primary strategies include customers, suppliers, current competitors, future competitors, substitute products, environmental trends, market characteristics, and industry cost behavior.

Customer Analysis and Segmentation

Customers are a key consideration in the formulation of strategy. Their bargaining power and needs have to be studied at the corporate, business, and functional levels.

Customer Bargaining Power. Customers can influence prices and bargain for higher quality or more services. They can also play one competitor against another. This bargaining power of buyers may affect the ability of a company to develop and implement strategy.

An analysis of the buyer side of the market should include:

1. An assessment of the present and future *buyer structure* (their concentration, the company's dependency on particular buyer groups);
2. A description of the *buyers' characteristics* (alternative ways of gaining satisfaction, dependency on particular product characteristics, and access to information);
3. An analysis of the buyer factors that affect their *price behavior.*

Internationally, buyers can be classified two general ways: as either global, regional, or national; and as either concentrated or diffused. The implications for marketing are different for each of the resulting six types of buyer groups.

An example of *concentrated national buyers* are local government agencies responsible for the purchase of communications, electrical power, and transportation infrastructure systems. To cater to the needs of these buyers, companies such as GTE, Boeing, and Westinghouse have highly focused marketing activities. They must be not only capable of satisfying local specifications and conditions but also sensitive to any political considerations involved in the decision process. *Diffused national buyers* are buyers of consumer products such as household supplies and foodstuffs. These buyer groups are nationally defined because their needs are strongly influenced by local socio-cultural and economic factors. In this case, a company such as CPC International is interested in responding to the expressed needs of an aggregated group of local buyers more effectively than their competitors. International companies buying products and services are an example of *concentrated global buyers*. To cater to the needs of these buyers, international banks and advertising agencies such as Chase Manhattan and Dentsu of Japan, respectively, have to be highly focused in their marketing activities. They must be not only capable of satisfying the local needs of their customers but also capable of satisfying their global coordination and integration needs. *Diffused global buyers* are buyers of electrical appliances such as television sets, VCRs, and automobiles. These buyer groups are globally defined because their needs are not strongly influenced by local socio-cultural and economic factors. A company such as Sony of Japan, for example, is interested in responding to the needs of a fairly homogeneous cross-national group of buyers. Like their national counterparts, these buyers express their bargaining power as a group rather than as individual buyers.

Customer Needs and Segmentation. As suggested above, customers are not homogeneous in their need for a particular product or service. By segmenting customers into subgroups with similar needs, companies can better choose which groups to serve. Market segmentation is key to strategic planning at the corporate and business levels. When done effectively, segmentation results in the division of the market into subparts that are (1) identifiable, (2) accessible and responsive to specific marketing approaches, (3) of sufficient size to be profitable, and (4) defendable against competition. At the corporate level, segmentation is one of several parameters used to divide the company into business units. At the business-unit level, it is one of several parameters used to focus the unit's marketing activities.

Segments may be described either in terms of benefits sought or in terms of the identity (characteristics) of the customers in the segments. Benefits sought include such physical aspects of the product as quality and type of service provided and price. Customer characteristics include such things as geographic location, income, and family status. (These features of market segmentation will be covered more intensively in later chapters as they relate to the formulation of marketing strategies.)

Broad market segmentation decisions are made at the corporate level. These decisions, in turn, have a direct bearing on a company's competitive advantage and marketing activities. Further, competitors who identify new market segments have a distinct advantage over competitors who merely react; changes in segmentation often have significant implications for doing business. For example, a redefining of the market may impact on a company's marketing, production, finance, engineering, and the skill requirements of its personnel.

Examples of the questions marketers should ask about market segments are listed in Table 9-1. They only suggest the scope of essential questions, and they are not necessarily ranked according to importance. The questions that need to be raised and the weight given those questions depend on the reasons for asking them. For example, the formulation of corporate, business, and functional strategies involves different objectives and goals with different time horizons. When asking "*Where* are the customers located?" corporate planners are interested in the general geographic location of the firm's various markets. On the other hand, when developing a marketing strategy the focus is on the specific location of potential customers within one market and their interest in a particular product or product line. Furthermore, the significance of the answers also differ. What does the location of national markets mean for logistics, production strategy, profit repatriation? For the marketing manager, the answer has implications for channel strategy, advertising strategy, and packaging strategy.

TABLE 9-1
Components of Customer Audit for Strategy Development

A. What?	1. What benefits does the customer seek? 2. What factors influence demand? 3. What functions does the product perform for the customer? 4. What are the important buying criteria? 5. What are the criteria used for comparing products? 6. What services do the customers expect?
B. How?	1. How do customers buy? 2. How long does the buying process last? 3. How do various elements of the marketing program (mix) influence customers at each stage of the process? 4. How do customers use the product? 5. How does the product fit into their lifestyle or operations? 6. How much are they willing to spend? 7. How much do they pay?
C. Where?	1. Where is the decision made to buy? 2. Where do customers seek information about the product? 3. Where do customers buy the product?
D. When?	1. When is the first decision to buy made? 2. When is the product repurchased?
E. Why?	1. Why do customers buy? 2. Why do customers choose one brand as opposed to another?
F. Who?	1. Who are the occupants of segments identified by previous questions? 2. Who buys our products? Why? 3. Who buys our competitors' products? Why?

Source: Adapted from Derek F. Abell/John S. Hammond, STRATEGIC MARKET PLANNING: Problems and Analytical Approaches, © 1979, pp. 49–50, 185. Reprinted by permission of Prentice-Hall, Inc., Englewood Cliffs, New Jersey.

Competitor Analysis

Analyzing competitors is useful for two reasons. As Abell and Hammond suggest, competitor analysis reinforces the customer analysis undertaken by the company.[9] By understanding a competitor's corporate, business, and functional strategies, managers gain additional insight into how buyer behavior is interpreted by competitors. Competitor analysis also provides a yardstick for estimating how a particular competitor may react to changes in the company's corporate, business, or functional strategies, or to future changes in the marketplace.[10] Understanding a competitor's weaknesses, strengths, and the strategies it uses deepens understanding of potential competitive actions.

Competitor analysis can be divided into two broad classes of questions:

1. Who are the present and potential competitors?

2. How do they compete?

Identification of Competitors Present competitors can be grouped according to how they define their activities: Thus competitors can be categorized by the *customer group* served, the *customer function* satisfied, or the product's *technology* base. In terms of customer groups, for example, Campbell Soups sells extensively in the United States and the United Kingdom consumer markets. Heinz sells similar products to the institutional market in the United States but to the consumer market in the United Kingdom. In terms of functions served, Apple sells personal computers primarily to individuals and competes with IBM, which sells complete systems that include personal computers. Finally, companies selling fabrics made from natural fibers or components made from plastic compete with companies selling fabrics made from synthetic fibers or components made from metal.

In addition to identifying competitors' market approaches, managers need to subdivide them according to how they define their activities. That is, do the company's direct competitors serve approximately the same *customer groups,* seek to satisfy the same *customer function,* and use the same *technologies?* For example, General Foods and Nestlé are competitors in processed coffee on a worldwide basis. In contrast, Campbell Soups and Heinz are not direct competitors in the United States, but they do compete directly with each other in the United Kingdom.

Potential entrants to the market also need to be identified. As shown in Figure 9-5, newcomers may enter the market from one of four directions. These directions may be defined as follows:

1. **Product Expansion** Potential competitors may already be selling products to the company's customers and are expanding their participation by adding directly competitive products (for example, they initially sold computer hardware and decide to expand into software).

FIGURE 9-5   Sources of New Competitors

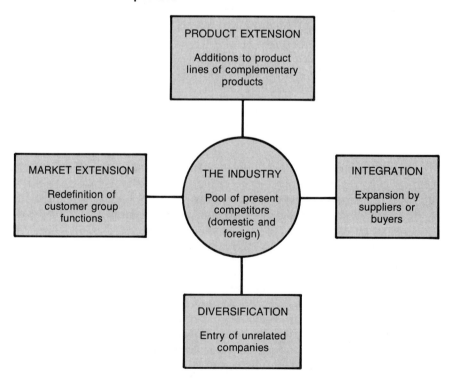

2. **Market Expansion** Potential competitors may already be satisfying one segment of the market served by the company and are expanding their participation into the company's segment of the market (for example, Heinz expanding into the consumer soup market in the U.S.).

3. **Integrative Expansion** Potential competitors may be the company's present suppliers or buyers, expanding into the company's market through forward or backward integration (for example, Riegel, a fabric producer, entered the apparel industry).

4. **Diversification Expansion** Potential competitors may be from unrelated industries, entering the market as a result of a desire to reduce or offset undesirable environmental trends in their industries. (For example, to reduce the economic impact that the aging of the U.S. population was predicted to have on its economic performance, Coca-Cola purchased a movie company and a winery.)

Competitor Evaluation Each competitor's competitive capabilities should be evaluated separately. To lump them together does not provide the kinds of information needed to assess competitive threats or opportunities nor to project competitive reactions. These individual assessments need to include at least the four areas discussed in detail below):

1. What is the competitor's current strategy?
2. How is the competitor performing financially and in the marketplace?
3. What are the competitor's strengths and weaknesses?
4. What proactive and reactive competitive actions can be expected in the future?

Competitive Strategies Competitor's primary strategies need to be evaluated. How does each one define customer groups, customer functions, and technologies at each level of the organization? How does each business unit segment the market, which segments are being pursued, and where?

Determining the *mission* that each business unit has in the competitor's overall portfolio is also important. Is it being managed for sales, growth, market share, net income, ROI, cash? What appear to be the goals for each major segment of each busines unit, in aggregate and geographically?

Finally, each competitor's operational policies and budget need to be examined. For example, each competitor's marketing mix, manufacturing, R&D, purchasing, and physical distribution policies need to be evaluated. So, too, do the size and the allocation of the budget among the various business units.

Competitor Performance The actual performance of each competitor must be determined (or estimated). Such things as sales, growth, market share, profits, margins, net income, ROI, and cash flow are essential information. Any analysis should also take into account the competitor's performance on a regional or even country-by-country basis when appropriate.

Competitor Strengths and Weaknesses An analysis of each competitor's strengths and weaknesses includes a comparative assessment of *at least* the following factors:

☐   Products and product qualities,

☐   Distribution channels and the competitor's position relative to dealers, wholesalers, and retailers,

☐ Marketing and selling capabilities and flexibility,

☐ Operations and physical distribution capabilities,

☐ Financial capabilities and flexibility,

☐ Management and human resources (skills, experience, and flexibility),

☐ Costs and how they are changing,

☐ Dependency on suppliers and buyers.

When companies are involved in foreign activities, assessments should be done on a regional or country basis. Moreover, the effectiveness of the competitor's coordination and integration activities should also be assessed.

Competitor Reaction An analysis should project how each competitor is likely to react to (1) changes in the industry and the marketplace and (2) any specific competitive moves that the company or another competitor might make. How is each competitor likely to use the resources at its disposal? How is it likely to try to reduce or offset any weaknesses?

This analysis depends on the information obtained as a result of strategy, performance, and strengths and weaknesses assessments. More important, the conclusions so arrived at depend on the accuracy and soundness of data used and assumptions made. To minimize the possibilities of arriving at erroneous conclusions, all possible sources of information need to be used. In the case of U.S. companies, these sources include published financial reports and reports to the Securities and Exchange Commission. Less obvious sources include suppliers serving a firm and its competitors, buyers who purchase competitors' products, security analysts' reports, and competitors' speeches and news releases. Patent files should also be searched.

Supplier Bargaining Power

Suppliers can exert bargaining power over companies in a particular industry by threatening to raise prices, reducing the quality of the products or services offered, or rationing supplies among various customers. Firms overdependent upon a particular supplier or group of suppliers and the market situation, are particularly exposed to increasing supplier costs that cannot be passed on to the consumer.

Any analysis of supply-side market economics should include:

1. An assessment of present and future *supply structure* (supplier concentration, product differentiation, and entry barriers);

2. A description of the *character of competition* in the supplier industries, both present and future;

3. An analysis of the *cost structure* and *cost behavior* of supplier industries.

This analysis will provide the company with an enhanced understanding of its present and future vulnerability to supplier pressures.

Product Substitutes

All companies in a particular industry are competing, in a broad sense, with companies in other industries producing substitute products that satisfy the same *customer function.* For example, in developing countries such as Brazil and Thailand, automatic washing machines compete with manually washed clothes, fresh vegetables compete with packaged vegetables, and buses compete with bicycles.

The most competitive substitute products are those that are price–benefit competitive or produced by high-profit industries. For example, introducing costly large mainframe computers in a market where wages for bookkeepers are very low may be very difficult. The price of the computer coupled with the rapid technological changes occurring in the computer industry may prove insurmountable barriers to substituting them for manually maintained accounting systems. The personal computer, on the other hand, may have a better price–benefit ratio.

High-profit industry substitute products may pose a potential threat since opportunities for significant price reduction are present. In the temporary secretarial help industry, for example, word-processing systems represent a potential threat. The inevitable cost escalation of labor-intensive secretarial support renders word-processing systems increasingly more attractive. A possible response by temporary help companies is to offer product packages consisting of both secretaries and word-processing systems.

Analysis of Environmental Trends

Environmental analysis involves the careful study of economic, social, political, and technological changes. Such changes continually mold consumer behavior and, therefore, competitive strategies. The level of analysis undertaken depends on the type of primary strategy under review.

As noted earlier, changes in the general environment are of concern when formulating corporate strategy. The industry environment is the main focus when formulating business strategy and the marketplace is the main concern when formulating functional strategies. Each level of environmental analysis is closely related to the other levels of analysis and should not be done in isolation.

Market Characteristics

Separate analyses of buyers, competitors, suppliers, or environmental trends are insufficient bases for formulating strategy. One must also analyze how these factors interact, the structure of facilitating organizations such as channel members and media, and the forecasting of demand. Three areas of particular concern are (1) changes in market boundaries, (2) the availability and nature of the marketing infrastructure, and (3) demand forecasting.

Market boundaries generally change because of the introduction of new product technologies, the diffusion of innovations, competitor initiatives, or the changing needs or wants of buyers. Market redefinition can occur in one of three ways:[11]

1. **New Product Technology** New technology can replace existing technology. For example, the watch market was redefined with the introduction of digital watches; the entertainment market was redefined first with the introduction of television and subsequently with the introduction of video players and recorders.

2. **Market Extension** Market boundaries also are redefined as a result of the extension of a particular product technology to new customer groups. This is part of the normal process of *diffusion*. For example, the chip used in computers has been extended to household appliances such as ovens, dish-washers, clothes washers, and temperature-control systems.

3. **Consumer Functions** Market boundaries can also be changed by changing the functions served by a product. For example, the introduction of automatic tellers to the banking industry expanded customer services. The same is also true of the stand alone personal computers converted into a computer system through the use of peripherals.

The marketing infrastructure is critical to the marketing success of a company. As we discussed in Chapter 5, the marketing infrastructure comprises several elements that change as a country develops its industrial and service sectors. In addition to the environmental factors already discussed, there are three market-specific factors that need careful evaluation: marketing intermediaries, media, and transportation. These factors directly affect a company's ability to promote, sell, and distribute goods to the final consumer. Since these factors vary considerably from one country to another, they are of particular concern to the global company interested in a new foreign market.

Demand forecasts are used to guide a company when making resource and budget allocations. In the case of foreign markets, the company is interested not only in knowing the level of demand for its products but also in their demand elasticities. Because of socio-cultural and economic variations, the slope of the demand curve can vary significantly from market to market.

Industry Cost Behavior

There are two aspects to an analysis of an industry's cost behavior. Both are influenced by the productive technologies used. They are (1) scale effects and (2) experience effects. Although both effects are always present, they vary considerably by industry.

Scale effects denote the behavior of variable costs and fixed costs with production volume. There are two types of production scale effects. *Short-run* economies of scale occur as the quantity produced by a particular plant increases. *Long-run* economies are economies of size. They are obtained by using larger plants. In addition to saving building costs, larger plants also tend to have lower operating costs per unit of output. There are other types of scale effects. Economies can also be realized with purchased items (raw materials and shipping) or obtained in such activities as marketing, sales, distribution, administration, and R&D.

It is evident that companies should consciously pursue strategies designed to maximize the scale effects of their operations. A company that concentrates its marketing and sales activities in large urban areas will probably have higher economies in distribution, advertising, and selling than one that scatters these activities over large and relatively sparsely populated areas.

Experience effects denote the behavior of costs as output is accumulated. Studies on a wide range of industries indicate that as industries gain experience (or accumulate output), the cost per unit of output declines.

The difference between the experience effect and the scale effect is illustrated in Figure 9-6. In the case of scale, variable costs decline to a certain point as output increases. Beyond this point, increases in output result in increasing costs. In the case of experience, total costs decline at a *measurable and predictable* rate as output is accumulated. Total costs include administrative, sales, marketing, and so on, in addition to manufacturing costs.

The rate at which total costs decline for every doubling of accumulated output

FIGURE 9-6   Industry Cost Behavior: Scale and Experience Effects

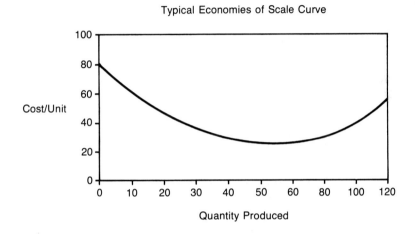

Typical Economies of Scale Curve

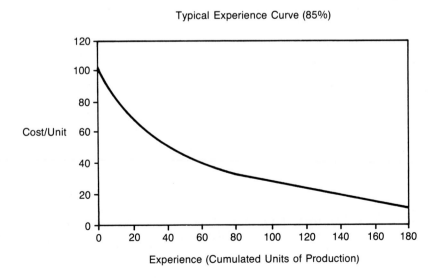

Typical Experience Curve (85%)

is the *learning rate.* As mentioned earlier, the experience effect is different for each industry. For example, between 1957 and 1974, the manufacture of 3-ton split-system air conditioners had an 80 percent learning curve. On the other hand, for the manufacture of viscose rayon between 1930 and 1966, total costs declined 31 percent for every doubling of output.[12]

Internal Factors

A company's competitive strategies cannot be based solely on an evaluation of the environment, customers, suppliers, present and potential competitors, and substitute products. The external analysis has as its objective the identification of *opportunities,* and the requirements for successfully exploiting them.

The company must also undertake an internal assessment to determine whether it has the *distinctive competencies* and resources required to take advantage of a particular opportunity. This assessment includes an analysis of its method of doing buisness, its resources, its organization structure and "climate," and its technical and managerial skills. The purpose of the assessment is to determine whether the company has the competences necessary for success. For example, Procter & Gamble is a leader in marketing and merchandising skills, and DuPont possesses considerable expertise in developing high-density optical disks.

Although each company has a unique set of capabilities, most fall into a limited number of categories, each with particular strategy implications. These capabilities can be broadly divided into four categories: (1) skills, (2) capital, (3) delivery, and (4) inputs.

The ability of a company to cope with continually changing market opportunities and competitive threats depends in part on the *technical* (product innovation and production) and *managerial* (marketing, finance) skills possessed by its personnel. The types of skills possessed by the company and competitors, and those required to be successful need to be crosschecked.

The emphasis to be placed on technical and managerial skills and the areas of expertise in each depend on the industry or industries in which a company competes. For example, companies competing in consumer products generally need to emphasize marketing skills and require particular expertise in consumer-behavior research, mass communications, and distribution. Companies competing in high-tech products need to have strong capabilities in those technical skills necessary for innovative technology.

The company's other capabilities also need to be evaluated. For example, success may depend on an ability to obtain capital from external sources (financial markets) and internal sources (profits) to finance the particular type of strategy decided on. In some cases, the logistical or physical distribution capabilities of the company may play a critical role in its success. Finally, the ability to develop and to maintain secure sources of vital inputs, such as raw materials and components, can be of central importance.

The *transferability* and *controllability* of these capabilities also need to be evaluated. Can capabilities be easily transferred to and absorbed in other national markets? Can they be controlled?

STRATEGIC MARKET PLANNING TECHNIQUES[13]

Once a company has developed a clear idea of the primary strategies it wishes to pursue, it needs to review its current portfolio of markets to determine the roles they should play. Identifying which business activities should be emphasized, which should be maintained at present levels, and which should be reduced or eliminated are major tasks in strategic planning.

Strategic market planning for companies with multiple products, multiple markets, or both, is a particularly complex problem. In the last decade, several business-portfolio techniques have been developed to help companies evaluate their current activities. We now discuss two of the better-known techniques, growth-share matrix and market-attractiveness–business-position assessment.

Growth–Share Matrix

The objective of the growth–share matrix technique is to assist managers in determining the strategic roles for each *business unit* or *product* of a company on the basis of (1) its market growth rate and market share relative to competition and (2) its cash-flow potential. A typical growth–share matrix chart is shown in Figure 9-7. Each circle represents a product with sales equivalent to the area of the circle. The product's vertical position on the chart is determined by the market's growth rate (in units or value corrected for inflation). Its horizontal position is determined by its market share relative to the company's largest competitor.

Specifically, the *market growth rate* is the annual growth rate of the market in which the product competes. In Figure 9-7, it ranges from 0 to 20 percent, with the 10 percent growth rate arbitrarily used to separate markets into high- and low-growth markets.

FIGURE 9-7   Example of a Growth-Share Chart

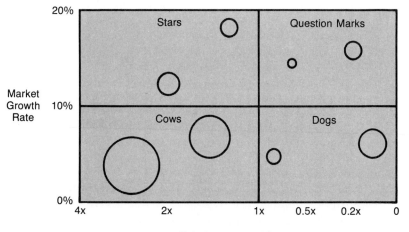

Relative Market Share

Relative market share is the ratio of the company's unit or dollar sales of a particular product to the unit or dollar sales of the same product by the company's largest competitor. A ratio of 0.20 means the company's sales are 20 percent of the leader's share. A ratio of 2.00 means the company's sales are twice those of its largest competitor.

Four basic strategies can be pursued with a given product: *build share, hold share, harvest,* or *withdraw.* The strategy selected depends on the product's present market and cost position, the product's life-cycle stage (measured in terms of the market growth rate), the company's resources relative to the major competitors, its time horizon, its other products, and the likely reactions of its competitors. A simplified example of possible strategy alternatives in terms of market position and the product's life-cycle stage is shown in Table 9-2. Many other factors need to be considered before a decision is reached. For example, a follower may decide not to attempt to increase share if more experience is required to catch up with the leader.

The strategic alternatives suggested by the *growth–share matrix* address three of the key elements to strategic market planning. A great deal of additional information must be evaluated before deciding on the basic strategies for each business unit or product. The additional information includes such important factors as barriers to market entry, technological changes, social/legal/political

TABLE 9-2
Basic Strategies for the Product Life Cycle and Market Position

Market Position	Product Life-Cycle Stage		
	Growth	**Maturity**	**Decline**
Leader **(High share)**	*Build* share by reducing prices to discourage new competitive capacity.	*Hold* share by improving quality, increasing sales effort, and advertising.	*Harvest:* Maximize cash flow by reducing investment and advertising, development, etc. (Market share will decline.)
	Utilize own capacity fully, adding in anticipation of needs.		
Follower **(Low share)**	Invest to increase share.	Either *withdraw* or *hold* share by keeping prices and costs below those of the market leaders.	*Withdraw* from market.
	Concentrate on a segment that can be dominated. (Become a nicher.)		

Source: Adapted from Derek F. Abell/John S. Hammond, STRATEGIC MARKET PLANNING: Problems and Analytical Approaches, © 1979, pp. 49–50, 185. Reprinted by permission of Prentice-Hall, Inc., Englewood Cliffs, New Jersey.

pressures, unions, management capabilities, and so on. Although these considerations cannot be included on the growth–share charts, they must be included in any strategy analysis.

Market-Attractiveness–Business-Position Assessment

The growth–share matrix provides valuable insights into the relationships that exist among a company's businesses or products and internal cash flows, market shares, and projected growth directions vis-à-vis competitors. However, the insights provided by this technique are often insufficient to make investment decisions affecting the mission of a business unit. For example, the ability to generate a positive cash flow may be viewed as less important than ROI when comparing the attractiveness of investing in one business or product rather than another. Further, the growth–share technique provides only partial insights into how one business unit might be compared with another in terms of investment and competitiveness.

Concern for these issues resulted in the development of the *market-attractiveness–business-position assessment,* technique shown in Figure 9-8. As with the previous analysis, a two-dimensional chart is used. In this case, the sales of a business unit are shown on the chart as a circle whose area is proportional to the business unit's total sales. The vertical and horizontal axes are labeled market attractiveness and business position, respectively.

The two axes are multifactor measurements. For example, the attractiveness

FIGURE 9-8   Example of a Market Attractiveness–Business Position Chart

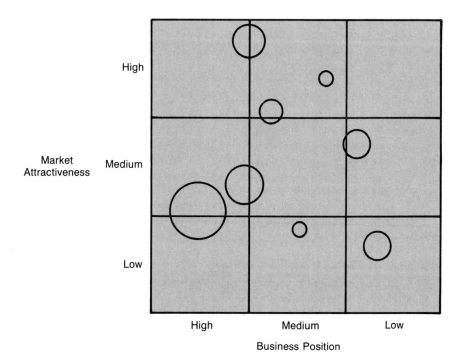

of a particular market could be a weighted combination of its growth rate, profit margin potential, and the degree of government regulation. Moreover, a company's position in the market could be a weighted combination of its technological leadership, manufacturing costs, and market share. What makes a market attractive or a business position in a market strong depend partly on company objectives. A possible method for arriving at the coordinates to be used to plot market–business combinations is illustrated in Table 9-3. The weights and rating scales actually used are decided on by a company's management.

Market-attractiveness–business-position analysis generally involves three distinct stages. First, assessments are made of the market's current attractiveness and the company's business position in the market. Second, the analysis is repeated, using anticipated changes in the market. Third, implications of alternative strategic changes on the company's business position are explored. The focus of this analysis is on the ROI potential of alternative strategies. As such, it complements the growth–share analysis, which is primarily concerned with cash flow implications.

International Implications[14]

The use of portfolio techniques internationally is considerably more complex than in a domestic context. This complexity arises because the company must be simultaneously sensitive to different market, company, and industry conditions in each of the countries it is competing in. A global company operating in two or more national markets is faced with different competitive environments, economic and political risks, market barriers, and market potentials. It may also be operating in these markets for different strategic reasons using different operational modes.

International portfolio techniques should provide guidelines for allocating resources across several countries, target markets, product lines, and marketing activities. Further, the industry, market, and company factors included in market attractiveness and business position measurements need to take into account variations in these factors across national markets.

General Electric, for example, uses a five-level portfolio approach: (1) product (2) product line, (3) market segment, (4) business unit, and (5) business sector. This multilevel approach can be extended across national markets as illustrated in Table 9-4. Particular attention needs to be given to the linkage among the various strategic levels within and across national markets as well as to the costs, potential economies of scale and experience, and economic and political risks involved. (These and other factors and their implications for strategy are discussed more fully in Chapter 10, where a market-attractiveness–business-position approach used by Ford is described.)

STRATEGY CHOICES[15] _____

A company can select from three generic strategies: (1) overall cost leadership, (2) differentiation, and (3) focus. More than one strategy may be simultaneously pursued. The same strategy need not be used for all business units of a company or for its product lines. If the company operates in more than one national market,

TABLE 9-3
Examples of Multifactor Market Attractiveness and Business Position Measurements

	Factor	Score* (A)	Weighting (B)	Ranking (A)(B)
	Market size	.5	10	5.0
	Size of key market segments	.5	5	2.5
	Annual market growth rate (units)			
	Total	1.0	5	5.0
	Segments	1.0	10	10.0
	Buyer concentration	1.0	15	15.0
Market Attractiveness	Seasonality	0.0	5	0.0
	Price elasticity	1.0	10	10.0
	Types of competitors	0.5	5	2.5
	Competitor intensity	0.5	15	7.5
	Capacity utilization	0.0	10	0.0
	Maturity of technology	0.5	10	5.0
	Social attitudes	Must be acceptable		
	Government influence	Must be acceptable		
			100	62.5
	Market share (in equivalent terms)	1.0	5	5.0
	Share of key segments	0.5	10	5.0
	Annual growth rate:			
	Total market	1.0	5	5.0
Business Position	Market segments	1.0	15	15.0
	Vulnerability to new technology	0.0	5	0.0
	Brand reputation	1.0	15	15.0
	Margins	0.5	5	2.5
	Scale and experience	1.0	10	10.0
	Capacity utilization	0.5	5	2.5
	Ability to cope with government regulations	1.0	10	10.0
	Ability to cope with social change	1.0	10	10.0
	Management skills	1.0	5	5.0
			100	85.0

*High = 1.0
Medium = 0.5
Low = 0.0

Source: Adapted from Derek F. Abell/John S. Hammond, STRATEGIC MARKET PLANNING: Problems and Analytical Approaches, © 1979, pp. 49–50, 185. Reprinted by permission of Prentice-Hall, Inc., Englewood Cliffs, New Jersey.

TABLE 9-4
Possible Levels and Units of International Portfolio Analysis

Level of Analysis (Type of Strategy)	Unit of Analysis						
	Single Country				Multiple Countries (Clustering Factors)		
	Country	Type of operation	Market segments	Product lines	Countries by type of operation	Countries by type of operation by market segment	Countries by type of operation by market segment by product line
Corporate							
Business unit							
Market segment							
Product line							
Product							

Source: Adapted from Yoram Wind and Susan Douglas, "International Portfolio Analysis and Strategy: The Challenge of the 80s," *Journal of International Business Studies,* Fall 1981, p. 71.

it may select different strategies or combinations of strategies for each of its markets.

Cost Leadership

A cost leadership strategy is based on the *scale and experience effects* discussed earlier. A company achieves cost leadership in an industry by pursuing a set of coordinated functional strategies emphasizing scale economies, the rapid accumulation of experience, or both.

Several strategic implications are associated with both effects. Their appropriateness depends on (1) the industry's cost behavior, (2) the market's stage of development, and (3) the market's rate of growth. Although the following discussion concentrates on the experience effect, similar implications exist for the scale effect.

First, in industries where a significant portion of total costs can be explained in terms of the experience effect, important cost advantages accrue to companies pursuing aggressive marketing strategies geared to accumulating experience faster than competitors. The benefits accruing to the cost leader include accepting competitor prices and benefiting from larger margins or setting prices that will drive out smaller, less cost-efficient competitors.

Experience can be obtained using one of four strategic alternatives:

1. Accumulate output by gaining market share in one market,
2. Accumulate output by accumulating market share across several markets,
3. Combine the first two alternatives,
4. Introduce other products using the technology or components that benefit from experience.

The alternative selected depends on the company's resources, the competitive situation in the market or markets, and the desirability of head-on competition.

Generally, cost leadership is best gained during the initial phases of a new market. As shown in Figure 9-6, the cost reductions in monetary terms are greatest at the start. However, the risks are generally greater with such a strategy. Why? The market's potential is difficult to judge, strategies designed to gain market share are costly in the short run, and competitor reaction cannot be predicted with any degree of accuracy. A company could end up using considerable resources in a market with very little potential.

In fast-growing markets, a company can often gain experience and grow rapidly with limited direct competition. However, this strategy is costly in the short run because of the need to reduce margins, advertise heavily, and develop new products.

In no-growth or slowly growing markets, experience can be gained only by taking market share from competitors or seeking markets elsewhere. To take market share from established competitors is generally difficult, costly, and time consuming. To avoid direct competition with well-established competitors, companies often expand into other national markets.

Differentiation

The second strategy is to differentiate the company's product or service offerings. That is, the company attempts to create a product or service that is perceived as unique. The differentiation may be "unique" in terms of a physical feature or quality, a particular type of service, or a dealer network. For example, a competitive strength of Sears, Roebuck is its national network of service centers. This strength is especially important in a highly mobile society. Also, IBM and Caterpillar Tractor hold differentiated positions in computers and farm equipment on a global scale because of their strengths in R&D, quality control, and marketing.

Focus

A *focus strategy* is really a special case of the differentiation strategy. It involves concentrating on a particular market segment, product segment, or geographic area. The company pursuing a focus strategy is not competing on an industrywide basis. Rather, it focuses its resources and marketing efforts on serving a particular customer group or customer function very well. The company opts for serving these segments better than competitors attempting to operate in a larger number of segments. At the same time, the firm may pursue a cost leadership or a differentiation strategy. Such companies include Black and Decker in hand tools and MicroPro International in personal computer software.

SUMMARY

It is management's responsibility to identify market needs and translate them into profitable need-satisfying activities. To do so, managers develop four primary types of strategies as the output of the strategic planning process.

Marketing management plays a key role in both the development of the strategies and the planning process. It is responsible for providing information on and recommendations about market opportunities and trends. This information and these recommendations are used by corporate management in the formulation of an enterprise strategy, a corporate strategy, and one or more business strategies. At the same time, the marketing staff is responsible for developing, implementing, and monitoring marketing strategies designed to achieve the objectives and goals set for it by the corporate staff in each market.

The main purpose underlying the four primary strategies is to profitably match the future activities of a company with its operating environments. The strategies are statements that define the company's overall objectives and goals and the means by which these objectives and goals are to be achieved. They are guidelines used by the company, its business units, and functional areas to ensure that their various near-term activities and the resources allocated to these activities lead to the company's long-range objectives and goals.

To assist management when developing strategies and allocating resources, several portfolio techniques have been developed. The growth–share technique is used to identify the implications that the internally generated cash flow has on strategy decisions. The market-attractiveness–business-position analysis is used to better understand the strategic implications of investment decisions.

A global company must develop primary strategies for each of the national markets it competes in. Doing so is an extremely complex task. Not only must the strategic planning process be extended to include two or more countries, the portfolio planning techniques developed to assist management in this task need to be modified to include the particular conditions encountered internationally. For example, the global company competes in markets with different competitive environments, risks, entry barriers, and market potentials. Each country may also impose demands on its business community that are different from those imposed by other countries.

DISCUSSION QUESTIONS

1. Distinguish among a corporate strategy, a business unit strategy, and a functional strategy by comparing what you believe would be examples of their *definition* and *mission* statements.

2. What are the major problems confronting a company competing in two or more countries when formulating (a) business unit strategies, and (b) marketing strategies? What problems do you anticipate might arise when attempting to coordinate these two levels of strategy?

3. Select a multibusiness company with which you are familiar. Identify the business units and distinguish between each unit's competitive pressures by contrasting their market and competitive conditions. Will these differences have an impact on the marketing strategies of each unit? Will one unit be more sensitive to local conditions than another unit? Explain your answers.

4. A global company competing in three global industries wants to use the growth–share matrix to assess the strategic role of each of its business units. What are the problems it will face in determining (a) the market growth rate for each business unit and (b) its relative market share ratio? Identify and discuss some of the other factors that need to be taken into account to determine the strategic role of each business unit.

5. Identify the major dimensions used to analyze a competitor's strength and weaknesses. Do local, regional, and global competitors need to be analyzed separately? Explain your answer.

ADDITIONAL READING

Carapellotti, Lawrence R., and Saeed Samiee, "The Use of Portfolio Models in Production Rationalization in Multinational Firms," *International Marketing Review,* Vol. 1, Spring–Summer 1984.

Ohmae, Kenichi, "Becoming a Triad Power: The New Global Corporation," *International Marketing Review,* Vol. 3, Autumn 1986.

Oliva, Terence A., Diana L. Day, and Wayne S. DeSarbo, "Selecting Competitive Tactics: Try a Strategy Map," *Sloan Management Review,* Vol. 28, Spring 1987.

Porter, Michael E., "Changing Patterns of International Competition," *California Management Review,* Vol. 28, Winter 1986.

Takeuchi, Hirotaka, and Michael E. Porter, "Three Roles of International Marketing in Global Strategy," in *Competition in Global Industries,* Michael E. Porter, ed. (Boston: Harvard Business School, 1986).

Watson, Craig, M., "Counter-Competition Abroad to Protect Home Markets," *Harvard Business Review,* January–February 1982.

ENDNOTES

1. We shall use *corporate planning* and *strategic planning* interchangeably. The term *business planning* will be restricted to mean the planning process and the plans that result from it at the business unit level of the organization.

2. John H. Grant and William R. King, in *The Logic of Strategic Planning,* (Boston: Little, Brown and Company, 1982), p. 4, define strategy as a "timed sequence of internally consistent and conditional resource allocation decisions that are designed to fulfill an organization's objectives."

3. *The I.B.M. Finance and Planning Staffs* (Armonk, NY: IBM), p. 13.

4. Grant and King, *Logic,* p. 4.

5. See Dan E. Schendel and Charles W. Hofer, *Strategic Management: A New View of Business Policy and Planning* (Boston: 1979), for a more detailed discussion of the legitimacy strategy issue. Also see Thomas Donaldson, *Corporations and Morality* (Englewood Cliffs, NJ: Prentice-Hall, 1982).

6. See, for example, Derek F. Abell and John S. Hammond, *Strategic Market Planning* (Englewood Cliffs, NJ: Prentice-Hall, 1979), pp. 9–10.

7. This example is based on information presented in C.K. Prahalad and Y. L. Doz, *The Multinational Mission: Balancing Local Demands and Global Vision* (New York: Free Press, 1987), pp. 16–24.

8. Brian Toyne et al., *The Global Textile Industry* (London: George Allen and Unwin, 1983).
9. Abell and Hammond, *Strategic Market,* p. 51.
10. Ibid.
11. Abell and Hammond, op. cit., p. 56.
12. Ibid., pp. 110–111.
13. This section draws heavily from Abell and Hammond, *Strategic Market.*
14. See, for example, Yoram Wind and Vijay Mahajan, "Designing Product and Business Portfolios," *Harvard Business Review,* January–February 1981, pp. 155–165, and Yoram Wind and Susan Douglas, "International Portfolio Analysis and Strategy: The Challenge of the 80s," *Journal of International Business Studies,* Fall 1981, pp. 69–82.
15. See Michael E. Porter, *Competitive Strategy: Techniques for Analyzing Industries and Competitors* (New York: Free Press, 1980), pp. 35–40.

Chapter 10
Global Strategy
and Global
Marketing Management

_____

Conceptually, the formulation of strategy is the same for national and global companies. Both use four levels of strategy to coordinate, integrate, and focus their activities at a common set of goals: enterprise, corporate, business, or functional. However, the *strategies* and the *strategy formulation process* used by global companies are more complicated than those for national companies. The major reason for this is that the global company operates in two or more national environments and is therefore subject to unique competitive and environmental pressures.

The global company's management has *attitudes* toward doing business overseas that bear directly on the strategy formulation process used and the strategies developed. For example, does the management view its overseas business as secondary to or as an integral part of its domestic activities? The company must also balance conflicting requirements for a *cohesive corporate strategy* with a need to be *responsive to local national environments*. That is, each national environment in which the firm operates exerts economic, competitive, political, legal, and social pressures that may require different strategic responses. At the same time, the company faces internal and competitive pressures to harmonize local strategies across national markets to ensure that its mission and objectives are achieved and that its resources and capabilities are optimally utilized.

Many companies have the potential to develop *competitive advantages* not available to companies operating in only one national market. The global company must also determine how it intends to compete in each of its foreign markets by selecting an appropriate *market presence*. The interplay of these complications and advantages is shown schematically in Figure 10-1. These complications and advantages have a direct impact on international marketing management. They impose constraints on which market opportunities can be pursued and which worldwide and local marketing strategies can be adopted and implemented.

MANAGEMENT ATTITUDES AND INTERNATIONAL STRATEGY _____

A company's international objectives, strategies, allocation of resources, and operating approach are strongly influenced by the attitudes its management has toward doing business overseas. Perlmutter identifies four general types of attitudes, popularly known as *ethnocentric* (home-country oriented), *polycentric* (host-country oriented), *regiocentric* (regional oriented), and *geocentric* (world oriented).[1] Though these attitudes do not appear in companies in their pure form, they are clearly distinguishable and useful for classification purposes. These attitudes reflect the goals and philosophies of the company and lead to different strategies, planning procedures, and operations. Elements of each type of attitude appear in all firms.

Ethnocentric Orientation An ethnocentric attitude assumes that home-country nationals are superior to foreigners, and are more trustworthy, and reliable. Management practices and experience are seen to have universal

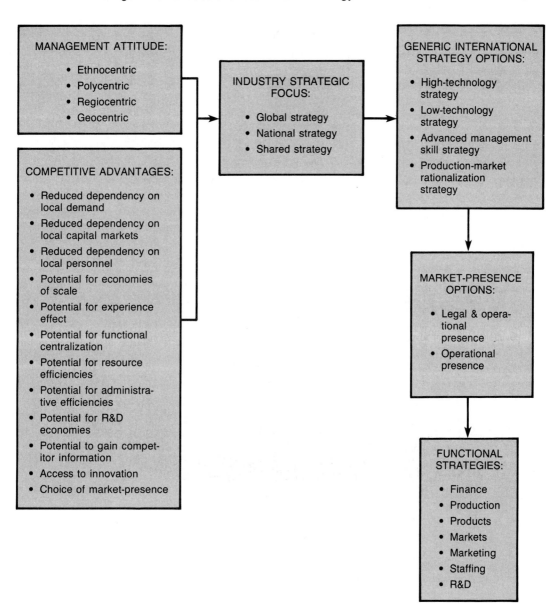

FIGURE 10-1   Corporate International Strategy

validity and home-country practices and experiences are viewed as superior to foreign-country practices and experience and *are believed to be transferable.*

Polycentric Orientation A polycentric attitude is the opposite of an ethnocentric one. Host-country cultures are viewed as very different and difficult to understand. Foreign-country nationals know what is best for them, and their management practices and experience are superior, in the host country, to home-country management practices, and experience. This orientation assumes that *home-country management practices and experiences are not transferable*

Regiocentric Orientation A regiocentric attitude assumes that countries can be geographically grouped since they have commonality in culture, management practices, and experiences. *These practices and experiences are assumed to be transferable within each regional group.*

Geocentric Orientation A geocentric attitude assumes that there are both similarities and unique differences in terms of home-country and foreign-country nationals, their management practices and experience, and the operating environment. Superiority is not equated with nationality. The ultimate goal of this orientation is the development of a worldwide approach within the entire organization (headquarters and subsidiaries) that builds on the strengths of its many parts and that uses the best person for the job, regardless of nationality.

Attitudes have been found to change as a company becomes more internationally experienced. The direction of change is generally from ethnocentrism to polycentrism to regiocentrism, and finally to geocentrism. However, geocentrism is not inevitable. Some companies encountering operational problems during an advanced stage may revert to a previous stage. Perlmutter likened this movement as an evolutionary, or learning, process. Attitudes—especially ethnocentric, polycentric, and regiocentric attitudes—reflect beliefs held consciously or unconsciously by management about other cultures. *They do not necessarily reflect actual conditions and may overlook key elements of the competitive nature and structure of foreign markets.*

Examples of the pervasive influence that these attitudes have on the management of overseas operations are presented in Table 10-1. As illustrated by the marketing function, these attitudes affect every aspect of the company's operations.

COMPETITIVE ADVANTAGES OF GLOBAL COMPANIES

Companies operating in two or more national markets have the potential to develop several competitive advantages unavailable to national companies. Which of these *potential competitive advantages* is developed, however, depends on environmental, marketplace, and firm-related factors. The following two sections identify several potential competitive advantages and discuss factors that may impede or enhance their development.

Potential Competitive Advantages

Twelve examples of the potential competitive advantages inherent in companies operating in two or more national markets are presented in Exhibit 10-1. There are many others, some of which will be discussed in later chapters.

Companies cannot develop these potential advantages without taking into account the environments in which they operate, their strategic plans, and the resources on which they can call. As a consequence, the managers of these companies are also limited in the types of functional strategies they can develop and implement.

Limitations on Realizing Competitive Advantages

Three sets of factors limit a company's ability to fully develop the above competitive advantages: (1) firm-related factors, (2) environmental factors, and (3) marketplace factors. Companies thus tend to optimize rather than maximize these advantages. Table 10-2 lists some of these limiting factors. Since the influence they have on a company's ability or desire to develop the competitive advantages listed above is complex, only advantages have been identified. The reader may find it helpful to refer to this diagram after we have completed our discussion on market presence alternatives and to complete it for a specific company and country.

Selecting which advantages to pursue on a global or national basis is extremely complicated. Environmental and market factors cannot be controlled by the company. A company must decide which factors are sufficiently similar to be treated on a global basis and which are so unique that they must be handled locally. At the same time, the costs and benefits of each advantage must be weighed against the company's global objectives, strategies, and resources. Although the problems associated with developing these advantages will become clearer in the later sections, we present here three examples using the three sets of factors identified above.

1. **Management Attitude** A *polycentric attitude* works against most advantages that benefit from a global perspective. That is, a decentralized or nationally fragmented approach toward international operations is reinforced. Opportunities to accumulate experience, gain economies of scale, exploit resource cost differences, and gain from the centralization and transfer of experience from one market to another are forfeited. At the same time, this attitude reinforces a high degree of responsiveness to local market and environmental conditions. Conversely, an *ethnocentric attitude* tends to work blindly toward the achievement of most of the advantages that benefit from a global perspective. For example, the opportunity to gain economies of scale is reinforced. However, such a company is not responsive to local market and environmental conditions.

2. **Host Government Policy** Governments are very mindful of the politics and economics of a variety of issues, such as employment, devaluations, national defense, and dependency on foreign countries. The result is that they may bring pressure to bear on foreign companies to manufacture and establish R&D facilities locally, and employ local managerial personnel. Restrictions such as these may reduce the company's ability to fully develop the advantages identified above.

3. **Consumer Needs and Wants.** The needs or wants of local customers will quite often vary sufficiently from country to country to warrant local attention. This will reduce the company's ability to develop and implement standardized marketing programs. However, it is still possible for the company to benefit from the transfer of its marketing system, or marketing approach. Market size also plays an important role in the ability of the company to develop a globally

TABLE 10-1
Management Attitudes and International Operations

Organization Activity	Ethnocentric	Polycentric	Regiocentric	Geocentric
General activities				
Complexity of organization	Complex in home country, simple in other countries	Varied and independent	Increasingly complex, and regionally interdependent	Highly complex, and worldwide interdependent
Decision making authority	High in headquarters	Relatively low in headquarters	Aim for a collaborative approach on a regional basis between headquarters and regional headquarters, and region and subsidiaries	Aim for a collaborative approach on a worldwide basis between headquarters and subsidiaries
Evaluation and control	Home standards applied for persons and performance in all national markets	Determined locally	Find standards which are regional (multicountry) and local	Find standards which are universal and local
Rewards and punishment incentives	High in headquarters and low in subsidiaries	Wide variation; can be high or low rewards for subsidiary performance	Regional and local executives rewarded for reaching regional and local objectives	International and local executives rewarded for reaching local and worldwide objectives
Communication: information flow	High volume to subsidiaries of orders, commands, advice	Little to and from headquarters and little between subsidiaries	Both ways and between headquarters and regions; regional heads part of management team	Both ways and between subsidiaries; subsidiary heads part of management team
Perpetuation (recruiting, staffing, development)	Recruit and develop people of home country for key positions everywhere in the world	Recruit and develop people of local nationality for key positions in their own country	Recruit and develop from region for key positions in countries of region regardless of nationality	Recruit and develop people regardless of nationality for key positions everywhere in the world

Marketing activity				
Markets	Foreign markets are secondary to home market and primarily viewed as a means to dispose "surplus" domestic output	Each market independent of all other markets	Each region viewed as one market regardless of national boundaries	Entire world viewed as a potential market, regardless of national boundaries
Needs and wants of markets	Viewed as universal	Viewed as different	Viewed as basically the same within regions	Viewed as segmented
Policies and procedures	Identical to those employed domestically	Developed independently for each market	Developed for each region	Developed on a world wide basis, yet recognizing difference of submarkets
Market programs	Identical to domestic programs; no major changes made to product-lines, and other elements of marketing mix	Individualized for each market; separate product lines developed for each market, and domestic products adapted to local needs and wants	Developed regionally; standardized product lines are developed for each region, and domestic products adapted depending on the uniformity of needs and wants of region	Developed on a world wide or submarket basis depending on uniformity of needs and wants among submarkets
Marketing research	No systematic research conducted overseas	Conducted independently in each market	Conducted on a regional basis, and shared within region	Conducted on a worldwide basis and shared with subsidiaries

Source: Adapted from Howard V. Perlmutter, "The Tortuous Evolution of the Multinational Corporation," *Columbia Journal of World Business*, January–February 1969, p. 12, and Yoram Wind, Susan P. Douglas, and Howard V. Perlmutter, "Guidelines for Developing Marketing Strategies," *Journal of Marketing*, Vol. 37, April 1973, pp. 14–23.

EXHIBIT 10-1 _____

Examples of the Potential Competitive Advantages Firms Marketing in Two or More Countries Have Over National Firms _____

Reduced Dependency on Local Demand Companies operating in two or more national markets are not as dependent on the economic conditions of one market as are national companies. Consequently, the impact of local business conditions on the generation of revenue and profits are lessened. For example, for two years in a row, Ford's losses in its U.S. market were more than offset by its international earnings. This enables companies with international operations to frequently weather economic downturns better than do their national competitors. In addition, they may not be as dependent on market share in any particular market as are their national competitors.

Reduced Dependency on Local Capital Markets Global companies are also better able to circumvent local monetary policies and shortages of local funds and to benefit from differential interest rates. National competitors generally lack the experience and resources to "tap" foreign financial markets.

Reduced Dependency on Local Personnel The focus of the educational system varies from country to country. This often means that labor and management personnel with needed technical skills and experience are in short supply. The global company can overcome this deficiency by transferring personnel. National competitors are forced to delay possible activities while local personnel are trained, or are restricted as to the strategies they can undertake.

Potential for Economies of Scale Global companies also have an advantage because the demand from several markets can be aggregated to provide economies of scale in the manufacture of products or component parts, providing them with a comparative cost-leadership advantage over national companies.

Potential for the Rapid Accumulation of Experience Because of its potentially larger market base, the global company also can accumulate experience more rapidly and thus move down its experience curve ahead of national competitors. This provides it with an additional advantage over and above that provided by economies of scale.

Potential Economies from the Centralization and Transfer of Functional Experience The global company has the potential to reduce duplication of effort and bring together a variety of

uniform approach. Some markets are just too small to support the company's usual marketing approach.

INDUSTRY STRATEGIC FOCUS[2] _____

In recent years, there has emerged a growing need for some companies to develop and implement global strategies. This pressure results from national industries becoming global industries. The chemical, construction equipment, pharmaceutical, electronic, and automobile industries exemplify a few of the industries that are now considered global. Firms within these industries must be aware of and responsive to global competitive trends. Companies such as Caterpillar, Dow, Ford, Komatsu, Pfizer, Philips, and Toyota must coordinate their worldwide activities to compete successfully. Still, there are industries that have not faced similar globalization pressures. Firms within these industries tend to compete on a national level. Beatrice Foods, Brown Boveri, GTE, ITT, Nestlé, and CPC International are examples of companies within such industries. Although both types of companies

EXHIBIT 10-1 *(continued)* _____

national market experiences for use by its functional areas when developing, testing, and implementing future strategies.

Potential to Gain from Resource Cost Differences Costs of labor, management, and other resources vary from country to country. The global company can take advantage of these differences to reduce manufacturing and administrative costs, thereby developing a competitive advantage over national competitors.

Potential to Increase Administrative Efficiency The global company can develop and utilize more efficient administrative systems (accounting, finance, marketing, and personnel) than can national competitors and introduce these systems into its new markets.

Potential to Spread R&D Costs Across Several Markets In addition to gaining economies of scale in manufacturing, the global company is also able to spread its R&D costs across several national markets, thus reducing its dependency on one market (which would then have to carry the cost burden for the development of products). The resulting cost reduction per unit can be passed on to the customer, thus providing the global company with an additional advantage over na-

tional competitors, or it can more easily recover R&D costs within a short payback period.

Potential to Gain Competitor Information Companies operating in the domestic markets of their foreign competitors are better able to understand the strategies and practices of these competitors. For example, foreign competitors who establish operations in the United States have the opportunity to evaluate their U.S. competitors *and* to gain competitive experience from competing with large companies in a large, geographically dispersed national market.

Access to Innovation By operating in national markets that are the sources of technological improvements and product innovations, the global company is in a better position to acquire this information as it becomes available. It thus achieves a competitive edge over those competitors that are strictly national in scope and that must wait for these improvements and innovations to be made public.

Flexibility in Choice of Market Presence to be Used While a local company must develop a total operation, regardless of the market's potential, a global company can minimize its investment in the market by exporting, establishing a sales branch, or entering into a joint venture.

are "global" (in that they view the world's markets as legitimate competitive arenas and attempt to exploit their competitive advantages across national markets), we will refer to the former as *global-industry* companies, and the latter as *national-industry* companies.[3]

A **global-industry company** is a firm whose strategic position in national markets is fundamentally affected by its industry's economics and competitive situation in other regional or national markets. Because of its industry's global characteristics, a global-industry company must compete on a worldwide basis, coordinating particular aspects of its operations, such as manufacturing, logistics, product lines, and marketing, or it will face strategic disadvantages. To be competitively successful, global firms must develop most of the competitive advantages identified in the previous section to their optimal potential.

A **national-industry company** is a firm whose strategic position in national markets is not affected by its industry's economics and competitive situation in other regional or national markets. That is, the national-industry company's

TABLE 10-2
Possible Factors Influencing the Potential Development of Competitive Advantages

Potential Competitive Advantages	Firm-Specific Factors										
	EPRG	*Resources available*	*Global horizon*	*Information*	*Technology*	*Manufacturing complexity*	*Administrative complexity*	*Rate of change in technology*	*Marketing complexity*	*Value-to-weight ratio of product*	*Attitude toward risk*
1. Reduced dependency on local demand											
2. Reduced dependency on local capital markets											
3. Reduced dependency on local personnel											
4. Potential for economies of scale											
5. Potential for experience effect											
6. Potential for functional centralization											
7. Potential for administrative efficiencies											
9. Potential for R&D economies											
10. Potential to gain competitor information											
11. Access to innovation											
12. Choice of market presence											

industry lacks essential global characteristics; the company can compete on a country-by-country basis without loss of strategic advantage. Even this type of company benefits by selectively developing some of the advantages identified previously (the centralization and transfer of functional experience; increased administrative efficiency).

Companies do, of course, fall between these groups; they find it necessary to compete on both levels and attempt to balance the benefits derived from being responsive at the national and global levels. In some areas, such companies attempt to exploit the advantages of centralization; in others, they seek to gain from decentralization. Companies pursuing this approach will be classified as *multifocal* companies.[4]

A major difference between global-industry and national-industry companies

TABLE 10-2 *(cont.)*

Environment-Specific Factors								Market-Specific Factors						
Economic structure and stability	*Legal structure and laws*	*Political structure and stability*	*Government policies*	*Social and cultural system*	*Trade barriers*	*Trade agreements*	*Foreign exchange laws and risks*	*Market size*	*Market location*	*Marketing institutions*	*Socio-cultural factors*	*Competition*	*Product regulations*	*Advertising regulations*

is the relative emphasis placed on industry and marketplace factors and local government regulations. Some of the factors that differentiate these groups' strategies are shown in Table 10-3.

Companies like Philips have additional coordination and strategy problems when compared to companies like Beatrice Foods. As illustrated in Figure 10-2, the various businesses of Philips are not subject to the same internal and external pressures as those of Beatrice Foods. Its semiconductor and telecommunications businesses (units 1 and 2 in Figure 10-2) may benefit from a strategic emphasis on industry factors, but its small domestic appliance business (unit 6) may benefit from an emphasis on marketplace factors. Beatrice Foods businesses, on the other hand, all tend to benefit from an emphasis on marketplace factors. The diversity of strategy alternatives across businesses within Philips results in considerable management complexity.

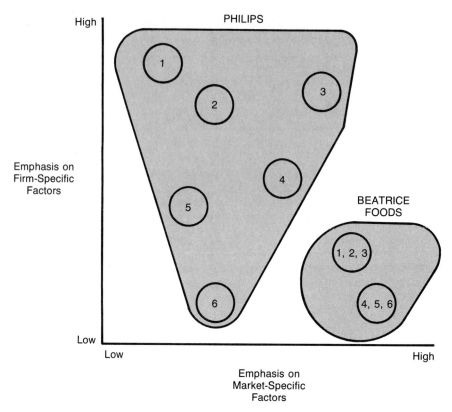

FIGURE 10-2   Industry Strategy Focus: Firm-Specific and Market-Specific Factors (*Source:* Adapted from Gary Hamel and C. K. Prahalad, "Managing Strategic Responsibilities in the MNC," *Strategic Management Journal,* Vol. 4, (1983), pp. 341–351.)

Advantages and Disadvantages of the Company's Industry Strategic Focus[5]

Because of industry and marketplace forces, a company is not entirely free to select which *industry strategic focus* it will adopt. To be successful, a company generally must be responsive to the competitive forces of its industry. This results in the adoption of a global-industry or national-industry focus, either explicitly or implicitly. An example of a company that changed its focus from national to global in response to competitive changes was General Motors when it introduced the *world car* concept. This innovation is described in Exhibit 10-2. Notice that, as a result of this reorientation, the company stressed many of the benefits discussed earlier as competitive advantages.

Each industry's strategic focus involves significant costs and benefits. A company with a global-industry focus has a worldwide perspective on opportunities and threats. It develops an excellent strategic control system for its foreign operations. That is, its foreign operations are centrally coordinated to achieve the company's global objectives. At the same time, it tends to be less sensitive to local conditions

TABLE 10-3
Possible Factors Differentiating between a Global or National Strategy

Factors	Global Strategy	National Strategy
Firm-specific factors		
1. Manufacturing economies	The economical output level of a single plant transcends the needs of a single national market, thus forcing coordination across markets.	The economical output level of a single plant satisfies the needs of the single national market.
2. Experience effect	The manufacturing technology employed is subject to significant cost declines as a result of cumulative volume, thus providing an economical incentive to standardize the output across markets.	The manufacturing technology employed is not subject to significant cost declines as a result of cumulative volume. There is no incentive to standardize output across markets.
3. R&D economies	The R&D effort has scale economies, thus providing an incentive to centralize the activity to achieve a cost advantage.	The R&D effort lacks scale economies. Thus, there is no incentive to centralize the activity.
4. Asset and investment intensity	Investments in plant and equipment are of such a magnitude that they can be recouped only in a number of national markets; thus, resource allocations and technology transfers need to be centrally coordinated.	Investments in plant and equipment can be recouped in single national markets.
5. Management resources (skills and experience)	Economies of scale may exist that exceed the size of national markets for some functional areas, such as marketing and finance (the selling activity associated with heavy construction, aircraft, and computers). The company can spread these costs across several national markets.	Management resources and experience, such as marketing and finance, while transferable, cannot be spread across national markets.
6. Logistical system	If the logistical system used by the company involves fixed costs in equipment, these can be spread across many national markets, thus providing an incentive for cost saving by central coordination.	Little external sourcing is required, such as for the food processing industry.

and strategically less mobile and responsive. A company with a *national-industry* focus benefits from a high degree of national market sensitivity and strategic responsiveness to local conditions. The costs incurred for this sensitivity and responsiveness are the potential lack of a worldwide perspective and of strategic control of operations abroad. That is, the foreign operations of a national-industry company may not be coordinated to achieve global objectives.

To reduce the costs and enhance the benefits associated with both types of focus, some companies develop a *shared* or *coordinated planning approach*. This

TABLE 10-3 *(cont.)*

Factors	Global Strategy	National Strategy
7. Proprietary technology	The acquisition of some proprietary technology as a result of R&D is so costly that many national markets are required to recoup costs. Computers, aircraft, and turbines are examples.	The cost of acquiring proprietary product innovations can be recouped from a single national market.
Market-specific factors		
1. Stage of product life cycle	An advanced stage in the international product life cycle of some products provides multiple replacement markets for second and third generation products. Globally coordinated production and marketing activities provide considerable competitive advantages.	In early stages of the international product life cycle of a product the company's ability to develop or use a global strategy is limited. The lack of market knowledge and its potential is a strong incentive for a national focus.
2. Needs or wants of target market	A predominance of multinational customers who demand a standardized product, prices, and services across national markets (heavy earth-moving equipment, computers, and telecommunication systems), or have "universal" needs or wants (soft drinks, appliances) forces or provides opportunities for the coordination of production and marketing across national boundaries.	The lack of "universal" customer needs or wants because of sociocultural differences forces product adaptation by markets.
3. Product substitutes	The characteristics of local product substitutes are such that they do not impede the introduction of standardized products.	The availability of product substitutes may require a level of local responsiveness that impedes the implementation of a global strategy in production or marketing.
4. Local competition	A small and identifiable group of global strategy competitors in most of the company's markets forces a global approach on the company.	A large number of local or national strategy competitors forces a local responsiveness to individual national markets.

approach is warranted when responsiveness to both global and national forces need to be emphasized. The penalty for this approach, however, is an increase in conflict, ambiguity, and administrative costs.

Marketing and the Company's Industry Strategic Focus

Although the implications of the company's industry strategic focus for the international marketing function and its management will be detailed in later chapters, some general observations are in order at this point. The *target market* selected and the *marketing programs* used in each national market are strongly influenced by a company's industry strategic focus.

TABLE 10-3 *(cont.)*

Factors	Global Strategy	National Strategy
Environment-Specific Factors:		
National factors		

1. Host-country government policies:
  a. Foreign company discrimination
  b. Economic development planning
  c. Industrial policies
	Local governments provide incentives to attract companies because of the contributions they can make, such as technology transfers, employment and access to other markets. These incentives may be in the form of protected markets, tax holidays, freedom to pursue global strategies, and so on.	Local content laws, local procurement laws, and other discriminatory laws reduce the economic viability of a multicountry coordinated strategy and forces a more national strategy focus. Also, governments may insist on local production as part of their economic development and industrialization plans.

2. Economic framework
  a. Infrastructure
  b. Availability of resources
  c. Availability of marketing institutions
		The infrastructure and availability of such things as marketing institutions may require sufficient modification to require a national focus.

International factors		
1. Regional agreements and treaties	Regional agreements such as the European Community's permitting the free flow of goods between member nations provide incentives for centralizing production and marketing activities.	

2. Trade barriers
  a. Tariff barriers
  b. Nontariff barriers
		Tariffs, duties, and quotas have the same effect as transportation costs. They may eliminate, or at least reduce, the benefits of economies of scale in production and marketing.

Note: For a discussion of some of these items, see Gary Hamel and C. K. Prahalad, "Managing Strategic Responsibility in the MNC," *Strategic Management Journal*, Vol. 4 (1983), pp. 341–351, and Michael E. Porter, *Competitive Strategy: Techniques for Analyzing Industries and Competitors* (New York: Free Press, 1980), Chapter 13.

The Target Market

Global-industry companies seek similar target markets in the national markets in which they operate. These companies are interested in identifying target markets that have similar needs or wants and that respond similarly to particular marketing programs, especially to standardized products. The Japanese watch company Seiko, for example, targets its marketing activities at a particular segment of the watch market—regardless of nationality. Its segmenting variables are price and style. Unisys, a U.S. computer company, also seeks the same target market in each of its national markets; its target markets consist of businesses and institutions with similar information-processing needs. Pepsi-Cola also looks for a particular target market regardless of nationality; it is interested in satisfying thirst with a soft beverage under similar use conditions. What is common to all three companies is the need to identify target markets with a *universal* need or want that can be satisfied under similar use conditions. *These companies are satisfying a need or*

EXHIBIT 10-2 _____
The World Car and Its Challenges: The Development of a
Global Perspective _____

In 1981, General Motors noted consumers and competition were global in scope. The manufacture and sale of automobiles was not "compartmentalized by country." In reaction to this reality, General Motors developed the *world car* concept. It was one way for General Motors to achieve the efficiencies necessary to compete on a global basis. The following [chart] highlights the key elements of the concept and some of the benefits General Motors believed would accrue to the company.

Key Elements of the World Car Concept

The term *world car* denoted a business concept rather than any one specific vehicle. It has two key elements:

□ An advanced basic design concept leading to vehicle designs that meet critical worldwide stan dards and that can be modified to meet customer demands and tastes and the requirements of national governments.

□ The sourcing of components worldwide wherever possible.

Benefits to General Motors

The world car is actually a family of cars of similar external dimensions produced in different countries. The concept had a number of advantages for General Motors' international operations:

□ These cars can be adapted to use a number of similar or interchangeable parts and compo- nents. Further, putting the world car concept into effect was to ensure that the best talents and resources of GM's worldwide organization were available to each unit. Versions of GM's fuel- efficient, front-wheel drive subcompact J car were to be produced in the United States, Canada, the Federal Republic of Germany, the United Kingdom, Belgium, Australia, Brazil, South Africa, and Japan. . . . The J car product lineup was to offer a range of models tailored to the needs and desires of customers in each of those countries.

□ Designing a family of vehicles was also to provide General Motors with sufficient flexibility among source plants to allow incorporation of any engineering changes needed to meet local customer demands and governmental regulations.

□ Vehicles were to be produced in volumes to achieve economies of scale. These cars would be sold in countries where they were manufactured and assembled, as well as in countries with similar market requirements.

□ Components could be produced in several different geographic locations at economical vol- umes. Export of these components was to generate foreign exchange for the country and im- port credits for General Motors.

Thus, an integrated global approach was to improve engineering effectiveness, reduce tooling and production costs, provide economies of scale for both components and finished products, and increase manufacturing and supply flexibility. Together, these benefits were to enable GM to compete more effectively, not only in the United States, but around the world.

_____
Source: Adapted from *1981 General Motors Public Interest Report*, p. 18.

want not strongly affected by socio-cultural factors. In many cases, such companies are durable goods manufacturers, but not always. British Petroleum and Gillette, both nondurable goods manufacturers, also use this marketing approach.

National-industry companies (Pillsbury and Goodyear), on the other hand, seek to satisfy needs or wants that are either strongly influenced by socio-cultural factors or by local government regulations. For these companies, the market's nationality is an important segmenting variable.

Market-Mix Elements

Since the global-industry company seeks to satisfy a universal need or want, its marketing activity is both relatively uncomplicated and transferable. It can generally develop a standardized marketing program that has as its core either a standardized product or a product line that uses standardized parts. To ensure that it will benefit from economies of scale in production and move rapidly down its experience curve, it tends to centralize its product development and design activity, its market and marketing research activity, and the coordination of its marketing operations. For example, it feels considerable pressure to simultaneously introduce new products or innovations the world over.

In contrast, the marketing activity of the national-industry company is not easily transferable. Such a company generally adopts a decentralized approach for its product development and design activity, its marketing research activity, and the development and implementation of its marketing programs. It too may benefit from economies of scale, but not for the same reason as a global-industry company. Although a global-industry company can aggregate unit sales across several markets to obtain experience and economies of scale in manufacturing, a national-industry company generally acquires sufficient market share within single markets to achieve such economies.

FOUR GENERIC INTERNATIONAL STRATEGIES ───────────────────

Four international corporate strategies have evolved over the years. They are briefly described in Table 10-4. They seldom appear in companies in a pure form; and companies may use more than one strategy. Each strategy has certain *internal (or firm) success requirements.* Consequently, the choice of strategy is strongly influenced by the company's industry strategic focus.

Fayerweather and Kapoor find that companies operating in two or more countries emphasize one or more of the following strategies because of environmental pressures, competition, and corporate capabilities:[6]

1. **Dynamic High-Technology Strategy.** In certain industries, companies can become market leaders by developing a distinctive competence in technological innovation. At the same time, this places them in a strong bargaining position with local governments. The acquisition of advanced technology is seen by most governments as critical to the future of their countries.

2. **Low or Stable Technology Strategy.** Although some companies are in industries with low or stable technological innovation, they become market leaders by developing distinctive competence in other competitive areas (such as brand identity, manufacturing know-how). However, since their technology

TABLE 10-4
Four Generic International Strategy Alternatives

Generic Strategy	Global Company Capabilities	Company's Economic Return System	Operating Structure Requirements	Company's Bargaining Power with Host Country
Dynamic high-technology strategy	Continuing flow of technically significant new products	Steady flow of payments in royalties or from sales margins (R&D "uplift")	Sustained high-quality R&D program. Reasonable control of application of technology abroad	Strong bargaining power based on desire of host country for future technological innovations
Low or stable technology strategy	Useful technological skill, but low sophistication or slow rate of change	Full income realized in a short period	A short-term transfer arrangement: sale or turnkey installation. Sufficient control to assure income payment	Relatively weak bargaining power dependent on technology and competition
Advanced management skill strategy	High competence in marketing or other management fields	Steady flow of dividends from ongoing operations	Continuing integrated operations in fields with management skill competitively effective	Weak bargaining power due to low priority placed on management skills by host country
Production-market rationalization strategy	High value-to-weight or volume ratio; high labor intensity in production; strong global or regional marketing system	Regular flow of dividends from either production units or marketing system	Low-cost production sites; strong global marketing organization; standardized products; highly integrated control of operations; full ownership preferred	Strong bargaining power due high priority for exports or employment in producing countries, and weak in importing countries

Source: Adapted from J. Fayerweather and Ashok Kapoor, *Strategy and Negotiation for the International Corporation* (Cambridge, Mass.: Ballinger, 1976), p. 19.

is widely held, they are not in as strong a bargaining position with local governments as are dynamic high-technology companies.

3. **Advanced Management Skill Strategy.** Companies can also become market leaders by developing a distinctive management skill such as marketing or coordination. The bargaining position of these companies with local governments is mixed. The governments of developing countries give low priority to these skills compared to technological skills and knowledge. There is greater acceptance among the governments of more advanced countries.

4. **Production-Market Rationalization Strategy.** Companies can also become market leaders in their industries by producing products at low-cost locations and shipping the output to global markets. The bargaining position of these companies is strong with the host governments of countries where production occurs, but the firm has much less leverage in other markets where the product is only imported.

The bargaining power that the various strategies provide the company when negotiating with the governments of host-countries is considerable. In some cases, bargaining power can determine whether a company will enter or remain in a national market. Recently, a well-known U.S. pharmaceutical company was planning to withdraw from a Latin American country. The collapse of the country's currency and the resulting foreign-exchange controls imposed by the government had turned a profitable market into an unprofitable one. However, the government placed a high value on the company's health-care products, and a preferential exchange rate was successfully negotiated. The company remained in the country. Similarly, in 1981, General Motors negotiated successfully with the Australian government. (See Exhibit 10-3.) In GM's case, the company was able to negotiate a mutually satisfactory trade agreement.

EXHIBIT 10-3
General Motors and Australia's Local-Content Regulation

Although the *world car* concept outlined in Exhibit 10-2 is relatively simple, its implementation is not. Tariff and nontariff barriers such as local-content requirements, national or regional safety and environmental standards, local test procedures, and local inspection requirements are major obstacles. Australia's 85 percent local-content regulation is but one example of the obstacles General Motors encountered when implementing its *world car* strategy.

The solution was an agreement under which Australia revised its local-content regulation to allow for "complementation." That is, instead of locally producing a high percentage of each car, as required by the regulation, General Motors–Holden's Limited agreed to produce about 300,000 engines in Australia each year and to export at least 200,000 of them. In return, Holden was permitted to import into Australia an equivalent value of transmissions and axles. Thus, as many as 100,000 engines were to be produced for the Australian market at a 300,000-unit-volume cost. Australia would lose no production or foreign exchange, and GM would achieve necessary economies of scale...

This agreement demonstrates how flexibility and innovation in negotiation are invaluable to solving trade and economic problems for host countries and global companies.

Source: Adapted from *1981 General Motors Public Interest Report*, p. 20.

Dynamic High-Technology Strategy

IBM (U.S.), ICI (U.K.), and Siemans (West Germany), three computer companies, are examples of global companies that use dynamic high-technology strategies. They are also global-industry, durable-goods companies. To be successful, these companies must generate a continuous flow of innovative products as well as a continuous demand for these products. To meet both goals, two crucial requirements must be satisfied. First, these companies must support strong R&D programs. (IBM, for example, allocates more than 8 percent of its earnings each year to R&D activities.) Second, sufficient demand for standardized products must be found to generate the revenue required to support these R&D activities. That is, the basic products must satisfy a universal need.

Generally, dynamic high-technology strategy companies face few national competitors. Because of high investment and technology barriers, most of their competitors are global. There are exceptions. Some countries, such as Brazil, are fostering indigenous high-tech companies by restricting markets and subsidizing local R&D activities.

When dynamic high-tech companies establish overseas manufacturing subsidiaries, full control—including ownership—is often sought to ensure against the loss of proprietary information essential to economic security. During negotiations with the Mexican government in the mid-1980s, IBM insisted on 100-percent ownership of its Mexican facility, even though Mexican law required foreign companies to enter into minority joint ventures with Mexicans. IBM was successful partly because it agreed to export 90 percent of its Mexican output, thus generating foreign exchange. It also provided employment for Mexicans.

In recent years, many dynamic high-tech companies are creating *strategic partnerships* with other firms in the same industry to remain competitive across a number of activities.[7] AT&T has marketing agreements with Olivetti and Philips in small computers and communications, respectively. Siemens has marketing agreements with Xerox in peripherals and with Fujitsu in large computers. Strategic partnerships are also being created in low- or stable-technology industries such as the automotive industry. In most cases, however, the partnerships are formed to provide complementary activities; one company will focus on R&D and manufacturing while the other handles distribution and marketing. Companies do not generally exchange information and know-how on key competencies.[8]

Low or Stable Technology Strategy

Examples of global companies that use low or stable technology include Caterpillar (U.S.) and Komatsu (Japan), two earth-moving equipment giants, and John Deere (U.S.), and Massey-Ferguson (Canada), two agricultural-equipment companies. Companies such as these tend to be global-industry, durable-goods companies. The major corporate strengths required for this, a low- or stable-technology strategy, are reputation, manufacturing know-how, economies of scale, and the ability to produce standardized products and interchangable parts on a global basis. Since investment barriers vary from industry to industry, there may be few or many national competitors. For example, John Deere and Massey-Ferguson's major competitors in the manufacture and marketing of large tractors are other global companies. This contrasts with the small-tractor market, where local competitors exist in many national markets.

Advanced Management Skill Strategy

Both national- and global-industry companies use this type of strategy. Procter and Gamble, Colgate and Quaker Oats are examples. The major corporate strengths required include high managerial competence in planning, marketing, finance, and organization, plus the ability to transfer these distinctive managerial competences through administrative systems and personnel to foreign countries. Because of the need for these transfers, operating control of foreign subsidiaries is generally sought by the company. In the case of national-industry companies, local competition may be strong because of investment barriers and needs or wants that are socio-culturally defined.

The Production-Market Rationalization Strategy

A company adopting this strategy must satisfy four crucial requirements: (1) The product should have a relatively high value-to-weight or volume ratio to offset the costs of shipping it from the place of manufacture to the place of consumption. (2) Parts of the production process should be labor intensive and separable from the rest of the production process in order to locate these labor-intensive activities in low labor-cost countries. (3) Control over the production process is essential to ensure coordination of the various production units and maintenance of the standards and quality of the finished product. (4) The company needs tightly coordinated international marketing and logistics organizations with access to one or more large national markets. For example, control (or at least influence) over channel members and price is often achieved through well-known brands. Companies that have successfully used this strategy can be found in most industries. Diverse examples include Lanier (office equipment), Ford (automobiles), and Oxford Industries (apparel).

SELECTION OF FOREIGN MARKETS

A company attempting to expand its international operations must decide on the number of countries it will compete in, the markets and market segments it will serve, the form its market presence will take, and how best to allocate its marketing effort. All these considerations have an impact on the company's marketing activities across and within national markets.

The number of countries to compete in, the choice of markets and market segments, and the form of market presence are contingent on many factors. Choices are affected by the role the market is to play in the company's network of foreign activities, the market's attractiveness, the company's competitive strengths, and the company's expansion strategy. Examples of how these factors impact choices of countries, markets, market presence, and the types of techniques used to aid management in making these decisions are presented below.

The Company's Expansion Strategy

Ayal and Zif present a framework for selecting, planning, and evaluating a company's multinational expansion.[9] It is based on such variables as the market's sales response function, product characteristics, and the company's decision criteria, and it leads to the adoption of a *geographic diversification or concentration strategy*. The adoption of one of these two strategies determines a company's rate of entry into new markets and the allocation of the marketing effort among markets. The Ayal–Zif framework can be used on a global, regional, or national scale. Our discussion is centered on the major variables listed in Table 10-5, variables that are considered important in the selection of a particular expansion strategy.

The Sales Response Function

The term *sales response function* refers to the relationship between marketing expenditures and the amount of sales these expenditures generate. This relationship is often used by marketing managers when allocating resources among markets, market segments, product groups, and even products. If, for example, sale of a particular product is growing rapidly for every additional dollar spent and more slowly for another product, the marketing manager will probably allocate proportionately greater marketing resources to the first product. This assumes that all other factors are held constant.

The sales response function can also be used to determine whether a company should enter many or few foreign markets. If the marketing management believes it faces a sales response situation that is concave, showing a strong response for every additional expenditure in most markets, it has strong motivation to follow a diversification strategy. If, on the other hand, the sales response function is

TABLE 10-5
Important Factors Influencing the Choice between Market Expansion Strategies: Diversification and Concentration

Factors	Prefer Diversification if:	Prefer Concentration if:
Sales response function	Concave	S-shape
Growth rate of each market	Low	High
Demand stability in each market	Low	High
Competitive lead time	Short	Long
Spill-over effect	High	Low
Need for product adaptation	Low	High
Need for communication adaptation	Low	High
Economies of scale in distribution	Low	High
Program control requirements	Low	High
Extent of constraints	Low	High

Source: Adapted from Igal Ayal and Jehiel Zif, "Marketing Expansion Strategies in Multinational Marketing," *Journal of Marketing*, Vol. 3, Spring 1979, p. 89 published by the American Marketing Association.

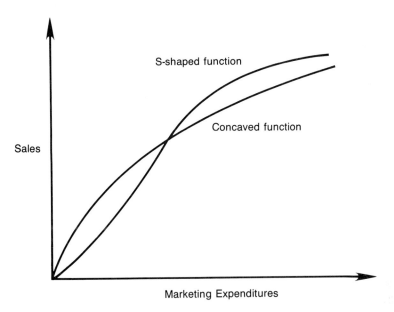

FIGURE 10-3 **Alternative Sales Response Functions for a Market, Market Segment, Product Group, or Product** (*Source:* Based on Igal Ayal and Jehiel Zif, "Marketing Expansion Strategies in Multinational Marketing," *Journal of Marketing*, Vol. 3, Spring 1979, p. 89.)

believed to be generally **S**-shape, as shown in Figure 10-3, a market concentration strategy is generally preferable. In the first situation, it makes sense to spread marketing effort internationally. This is not the case for **S**-shape response functions. The concave response function is frequently generated by a unique product or marketing program. The **S**-shape response function is likely for products that are widely available from different sources, or companies, and that do not enjoy a distinct advantage over competing products.

Growth Rate of Each Market

The rate of growth of demand in each market also influences management's decision to diversify or to concentrate its marketing effort. When the growth rate is high, it is often better to concentrate the effort on a few markets (to ensure that market share is maintained and exploited as a result of lower manufacturing costs and rapid gains in accumulated experience). Additional markets can be penetrated by relying on independent distributors and licensing arrangements. When the market growth rate is slower, it is better to adopt a diversification strategy to tap as many markets as possible (to gain economies of scale in production and accumulated experience). The lower production costs that result can be passed on to the customer, thus providing the company the opportunity to exploit a competitive advantage.

Demand Stability in Each Market

The stability of demand in each country impacts directly on the company's profitability performance. The more stable sales and profits are in each country, the less need there is for diversification. A company can concentrate on strengthening its market position in each of its foreign markets. Diversification can be used to reduce the overall risks associated with unstable demand situations.[10]

Competitive Lead Time

For innovative companies following high-technology strategies, market lead time over competitors and potential imitators is critical. When the competitive lead time is short and the timing of the introduction of a new or modified product is critical to market success, companies have a strong motivation to diversify. The company will be faced with a favorable sales response function for only a short time, and its competitive advantage frequently depends on achieving economies of scale and accumulated sales in order to move down the industry's experience curve more rapidly than competitors. Companies that have a long lead time or no innovative advantage experience fewer pressures to adopt a diversification strategy.

The Spillover Effect

The term *spillover effect* denotes situations in which the market in one country becomes aware of a product as a result of a marketing program in another country. This can occur, for example, when a communication medium (radio or television) is heard or viewed in more than one country. In such a situation, pursuit of a diversification strategy can be quite beneficial. Additional markets can be tapped with limited additional promotional expense, and the marketing effort can be aided by the promotional experience in the initial market.

The Need for Product and Communication Adaptation

The adaptation of one or both of these marketing-mix elements is often costly and resource consuming. Therefore, it may lead to the adoption of a concentration strategy. For example, major product modifications to meet local governmental and market requirements in a number of markets can reduce a company's ability to benefit from accumulated experience in production. If communication modification requires sizable outputs for consumer research and advertising, the benefits of following a diversification strategy are diminished.

Program-Control Requirements

The greater the need to control marketing programs in foreign markets—as is often the case for custom-tailored products, the establishment of a regional or worldwide identity, and consistency in after-sales services—the greater the motivation for a concentration strategy. Control takes management effort, time, and resources. The greater the diversity of its markets and the more geographically dispersed a company's efforts, the more difficult it is to tightly control activities.

The Extent of Constraints

As mentioned above, there are many internal and external constraints on a company's foreign activities. *External constraints* include trade and travel impediments and government restrictions. *Internal constraints* include financial-resource limitations, production-capacity restrictions, and personnel limitations. The more severe these constraints, the more likely it is that a company will be restricted to a concentration strategy.

The Country-Attractiveness–Company-Strength Matrix

To help marketing managers in their decision making, Harrell and Kiefer propose a framework based on the portfolio approach touched on in Chapter 9.[11] This framework, used by Ford's tractor operations, has been devised to help marketing managers compare alternative countries and markets and classify them according to potential. When combined with the concentration–diversification method suggested by Ayal and Zif, it provides a sound basis for the selection and classification of countries, markets, and the form of market presences to be used. Both methods can also be used to make marketing-resource allocations. Remember, however, that other considerations are equally important. The overall strategic plans the company has for its divisions, its logistical capabilities, and its financial resources are just a few of the other considerations that enter into final decisions.

The Harrell–Kiefer framework is based on the construction of the two-dimensional matrix shown in Figure 10-4. Two scales are used to position the analyzed countries according to their attractiveness and the company's relative competitive strength for a given product or product line. Each scale is a linear combination of several weighted factors. The factors used by *Ford Tractor* are listed and described in Exhibit 10-4. Each is measured on a 10-point scale. Other factors, such as those listed in Table 10-5 could be added or substituted for the one in Exhibit 10-4. One's choice depends on the particular situation for which the matrix is to be used. Many factors cannot be easily quantified and must be

FIGURE 10-4 **Country Attractiveness-Company Strength Matrix** (*Source:* Gilbert D. Harrell and Richard O. Kiefer, "Multinational Strategic Market Portfolio," *MSU Business Topics*, Winter 1981, pp. 5–15.)

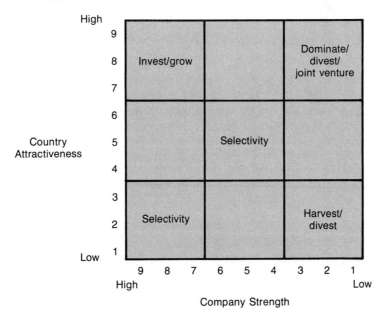

EXHIBIT 10-4

Examples of the Types of Factors to Be Used in a Country Attractiveness–Competitive Strength Matrix

Country Attractiveness Factors

☐ *Market Size* Market size is measured according to projected average annual sales. It can be in value or unit terms. Ford uses a three-year average of unit sales to avoid demand fluctuations resulting from economic conditions, such as business down turns, strikes, and so on. This factor is critical because of the impact it has on economies of scale, technical assistance requirements, training, and after-sales support.

☐ *Market Growth* A critical consideration in estimating the rate of growth of the market is the time period used. In Ford's case, an annually compounded percentage increase in sales for a ten-year period was used. The actual period used can be the one used for the domestic market, or a more conservative one if the risks involved warrant the use of a longer period.

☐ *Government Controls* The factors used to measure government controls depend on the purpose of the analysis. Ford uses three factors: price controls, homologation requirements, (nontariff barriers such as local safety and product standards, regulatory red tape, and regulations governing local content and compensatory exports). The purpose behind using these particular factors is to measure the impact that government has on market entry, protection of local industry, and price regulations.

☐ *Economic and Political Stability* As with government controls, many factors can be used to measure economic and political stability. Examples of the more easily determined economic stability include the rate of inflation and trade balance. Both impact on cross-border intracompany transfers, currency, and capital flow controls.

determined subjectively. Generally, the weights used when combining the factors will also be subjectively arrived at, reflecting the decision maker's impressions on the relative importance of each factor in defining country attractiveness and the competitive strength required to excel in the marketplace.

Countries falling into the upper left-hand corner of the matrix are considered prime candidates for new investments or additional funding. These countries have the highest attractiveness rating and the company has the greatest competitive capabilities to exploit the opportunities. Countries falling into the upper right-hand corner of the matrix are also highly attractive, but the company lacks the necessary competitive strengths to successfully exploit opportunities. It might attempt to correct the situation by selectively developing the strengths needed or by gaining them through an acquisition or a joint-venture arrangement. If none of these options is feasible, the company should reduce its market presence, cut back on its marketing effort, or retreat from the market entirely. Countries falling into the lower right-hand corner of the matrix are prime candidates for "harvesting." That is, the company's market presence would be systematically reduced while the cash flow generated from the business is maximized. Not only are such countries not attractive, but the company lacks the competitive strengths to maintain a market position. In other areas of the matrix, the situations are more complex, and a company will need to analyze each case carefully to determine its approach.

EXHIBIT 10-4 *(continued)* _____

Competitive Strength Factors

☐ *Market Share* Market share is generally critical because of its impact on both economies of scale and experience in production. Ford uses two factors: total share of the market and the number of major competitors in the market.

☐ *Product–Market Fit* Many factors are available for measuring the degree to which an existing product meets a particular market's need. Factors used by Ford could be horsepower classes and unique features. The closer the fit, the more likely the company could enjoy nonprice competitive advantages without having to alter their product.

☐ *Contribution Margin* The contribution margin is generally expressed as either gross profit per unit, or profit as a percentage of dealer cost. Higher margins may indicate greater control over prices. Lower margins may indicate inefficiencies in the local operation, competitive pressures and government price controls. A higher contribution margin provides additional funds to support marketing activities such as promotional campaigns, technical services, and channel discounts.

☐ *Market Support* Marketing support attempts to measure such things as the quality of the foreign marketing personnel, distribution facilities and capabilities, technical services support, and promotional capabilities. In the case of Ford, two factors are used to measure market support: the general image of the company in the foreign market and a composite indicator of its marketing support capabilities made up of the factors shown above.

Source: Compiled from Gilbert D. Harrell and Richard O. Kiefer, "Multinational Strategic Market Portfolios," *MSU Business Topics*, Winter 1981, pp. 5–15.

CHOICE OF MARKET PRESENCE _____

A company operating in two or more countries participates in foreign-market activities through one of four basic mechanisms: (1) licensing, (2) export, (3) foreign direct investment, or (4) contract manufacturing. An experienced company with a global perspective will generally use one or more of these mechanisms, selecting them on the basis of specific criteria. Global firms are often best positioned to discriminate between these market presence options since a national company must develop a total operation, regardless of the market's characteristics and potential.

Figure 10-5 identifies the major forms of *market presence*, and the primary factors that have a bearing on the form to be used in a particular foreign market. The company's choice of market presence is influenced by many factors.

A company's market presence is defined as follows:

Market presence is the legal and tangible operational method used by a company to exploit a marketing opportunity in a foreign market.

When establishing or expanding its *market presence* in a foreign market, a company must decide what its *legal presence* and *operational presence* will be.

Both decisions have a direct impact on the company's marketing activity in foreign markets.

Legal presence is the legal status of the company's presence in the foreign market.

Legal factors have a major impact on how a company is organized. To gain access to a particular country, a company must comply with all applicable legal provisions. Since laws are never identical from country to country, the legal aspects of establishing a foreign entity must *always* be handled as special cases.

The form the company's *legal presence* takes determines the company's legal responsibilities and situation. Thus the legal presence determines whether the company is to be treated as a foreign citizen or a local citizen; what laws, regulations, and taxes are to be applied; and the location of any necessary litigation.[12] Each form of legal presence also has implications for the company's operations in another country. These implications are covered in the next section.

Operational Presence is the actual form and nature of the firm's activities in a foreign market. This presence may be either physical or by proxy.

The form a company's operational presence takes determines the extent of its marketing and manufacturing effort in a foreign market. In the case of licensing, for example, the firm may have no physical presence in the market and little control over its licensees' activities. Foreign direct investment, on the other hand, unifies physical presence and provides significant direct control.

Types of Market Presence

Factors affecting the two basic market presence categories—legal and operational presence—are identified in Figure 10-5. Global companies use these forms strategically; They need not use a single market-presence strategy. For example, IBM uses both types of market presence and several of the subforms within each category.

We define the various market presence forms below, beginning our discussion with the legal aspects of each form in the host country. When the parent company is a U.S. company, the company's overseas operations are generally viewed as extensions of the company and subject to U.S. laws and regulations. The governments of most other countries do not agree with the U.S. practice of claiming such *extraterritorial rights*. In fact, in *1983*, the British government ordered four British companies to defy the U.S. trade embargo against supplying the Soviet pipeline project.[13]

In the next two sections, we discuss operational advantages and disadvantages of the main market presence options and the factors that influence their selection.

Legal-Operational Presence

Three basic market presence forms imply both a legal presence and an operational presence: (1) foreign branch, (2) a foreign subsidiary and (3) joint venture. These forms of market presence are frequently called *foreign-based affiliates*. Establishment of such affiliates nearly always requires foreign direct investment.

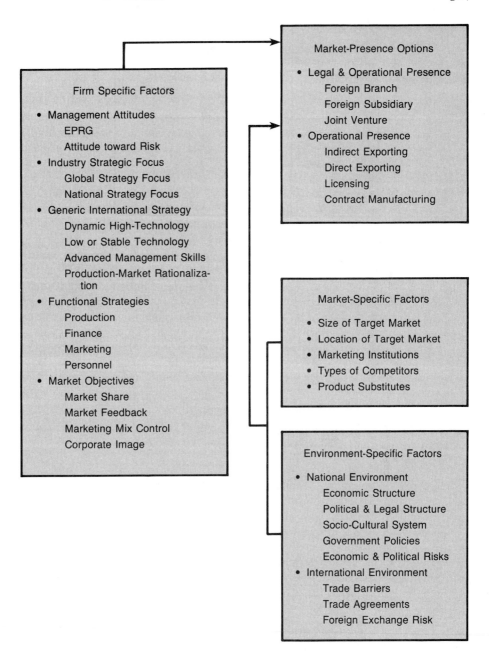

FIGURE 10-5 **Possible Factors Affecting Market-Presence Selection**

Foreign Branch

A **foreign branch** is an offshoot or extension of the company in a foreign market. It is a separately located unit of the company, directly responsible for fulfilling whatever operational duties are assigned to it by corporate management regarding sales, customer service, physical distribution, etc.

A branch is legally a part of the company. When the branch is located in the same country as the company, the company is responsible for any legal action taken either by or against the branch. When the branch is located in another country, such an arrangement often becomes legally intolerable for the host government. This is, because the party legally responsible, the company, is outside the local country's jurisdiction. Many host governments only permit branch operations to nonresident companies if the branch agrees to be "domesticated" by becoming a citizen of the country in which it operates. Such an agreement creates subtle problems.

Business licenses are often required when establishing branch status overseas. They are frequently of short duration, and renewals involve considerable expense and uncertainty. Also, the liabilities of the company are not restricted to the assets of a given branch. For example, Pan Ams' branch in Guatemala was sued for alleged infractions in Nicaragua. This action was possible since there is no legal separation of branches from the company.[14] A branch may also be so defined that the total profits of the company, not just the branch's local earnings are locally taxable. For reasons such as these, branches are rarely used by global manufacturing companies. A more frequently used form is the foreign subsidiary.

Foreign Subsidiary

A **foreign subsidiary** is a local company owned and operated by a foreign company under the laws of the host country.

Although the trend today is for legal forms of enterprise (partnerships, corporations) to become relatively similar, significant differences still exist. A most important organizational form is one that does not legally separate the company from its owners; that is, the owners' liabilities are equal to their investments in the enterprise and this is the key feature of the foreign subsidiary. Examples of this form of company are the *limited liability companies* found in many countries: in the United Kingdom (PLC), West Germany (G.m.b.H.). and the U.S. corporation. Despite similarities in many cases, this form of enterprise also exhibits significant differences. These forms limit the liabilities of the subsidiary to the assets of the subsidiary and not the whole company.

The foreign subsidiary is not free of legal problems. For example, to qualify for status as a legal enterprise in most countries, companies must *by law* fill a portion of the directorship or key positions in the firm with local nationals. The intent of this mandate is to reduce the parent company's control, something that is often perceived as undesirable by the management of the foreign affiliate. To be competitively successful, for example, a global-oriented company using a dynamic high-technology strategy, needs to have a high degree of managerial control over its manufacturing activities and technology. To safeguard itself, the parent company often fills overseas positions with people of unquestionable loyalty or it restricts their official powers by asking the persons filling these positions to contractually delegate operational responsibilities to individuals appointed by the company.[15]

In recent years, questions of the geographic extent of a foreign subsidiary's liabilities have been raised. For example, cases against the foreign subsidiaries of Raytheon in Italy and Swift in Argentina extended liabilities beyond the subsidiaries' assets.[16] This is a major concern since a key advantage of establishing a foreign subsidiary has been that liability is limited to the assets of just the subsidiary and not the whole firm. The question of the parent company's liabilities was also raised in the tragic case involving Union Carbide in Bhopal, India, in 1984, when an estimated 2,500 persons died as a result of a leakage of isocyanate.[17] An unsuccessful attempt was made to have the case tried in the United States under U.S. law.

Joint Venture A frequently encountered condition for incorporation is that a specified portion of the equity be held by local citizens. Mexico, India, and the Andean Pact countries (Colombia, Ecuador, Peru, and Venezuela) are examples of countries that require, or have required, joint ventures or partial-ownership arrangements.

> A **joint venture** is a company in which two or more economic entities participate on a permanent basis. Participation can consist of equity capital, manufacturing processes, patents, trademarks, or other operationally essential factors.

The joint venture is a partnership between two or more parties. In international joint ventures these parties will be based in different countries, and this obviously complicates the management of this arrangement. Joint ventures are an important form of business organization in the developing countries, widely used in developed countries, and often preferred over wholly owned subsidiaries, regardless of local requirements.[18] The international joint venture has become increasingly popular in the 1980s as global companies forge strategic partnerships. A sampling of U.S.–Japanese joint ventures include Bendix and Murata Manufacturing Company (machine tools), Boeing and Mitsubishi Heavy Industries (aircraft), General Motors and Fujitsu (machine tools), Chrysler and Mitsubishi Heavy Industries (automobiles), and Allen Bradley and Nippondenso (programmable controllers and sensors).[19]

Legally, the joint venture falls under local company or corporation law when participation is in the form of equity. When one or more of the partners make no equity contribution, the joint venture is based on contract law. Operationally, the joint venture provides advantages unavailable to the foreign subsidiary. It also has many disadvantages, which will be covered shortly.

Operational Presence

Foreign direct investment implies the establishment of one of the forms of legal-operational presence reviewed above. However, four basic market-presence forms have no legal presence implications and are thus considered only as an operational presence: (1) indirect exporting, (2) direct exporting, (3) licensing, and (4) contract manufacturing. No physical presence may be involved. *Some aspect of the company, such as its name, product, service or trademark, is always present in the foreign market.* We now examine these four forms of operational presence.

Indirect Exporting

Indirect exporting involves the sale of a company's products or services in a foreign market without the manufacturer undertaking the necessary export marketing and distribution activities. These are either carried out by the overseas customer or external intermediaries such as an export management company or export merchant.

In indirect exporting, the company treats the sale of its products or services to an overseas buyer like a domestic sale. Such sales may be the result of unsolicited orders from foreign buyers or due to the activities of an export intermediary. However, no overseas marketing effort is undertaken by the company; it is simply fulfilling an order that results in eventual sale to a foreign end-user.

Direct Exporting

Direct exporting involves the establishment of an "in-house" exporting capability. The sale of a company's products or services in a foreign market are the direct result of this capability.

When involved in direct exporting, the company or a foreign affiliate assumes responsibility for identifying suitable foreign buyers, establishing working relationships with them, conducting market research, arranging physical distribution, handling export documentation, handling payments, and so on. These exporting tasks are carried out within the firm, usually in an export department. Intracompany sales that cross national boundaries are also considered as direct export sales. Although the buyer is a foreign affiliate or branch the normal tasks must still be performed by an export department.

Licensing

Licensing involves a contractual agreement wherein the licensor makes available to the licensee (a foreign company or individual) knowledge, which is often embodied in intangible industrial property such as a patent, a manufacturing process, or a trademark, in return for revenue which usually takes the form of royalties based on output and sales, and the licensee's commitment to specified conditions (product quality, confidentiality, cross-licensing).

The licensing agreement should *always* be formalized in a written document. Some of the conditions usually found in the agreement include: a description of the knowledge and proprietary rights transferred; the terms of the royalties to be paid; where and how the rights are to be used and for how long; the territory covered by the agreement; methods of control; the performance required of the licensee, such as its marketing effort; the country in which disputes are to be handled; and if necessary, the method of arbitration. Included in this type of involvement are management contracts and turn-key projects.

Contract Manufacturing

Contract manufacturing involves the manufacture of a firm's product(s) or components by a foreign producer.

The company or a foreign affiliate enters into an agreement with a foreign producer who agrees to produce the products or components stipulated by the contract. Except for the royalty and marketing clauses, the conditions usually included in the contract are similar to those for a licensing agreement. Payment by the company or foreign affiliate to the contractee is generally on a per unit basis, and quality and specification requirements are extremely important. Marketing of the product is handled by the contractor. The product can be sold by the contractor in the country of manufacture, its home country, or some other foreign market.

This form of business organization is quite common in particular industries. For example, Benetton, a successful Italian apparel manufacturer, relies heavily on a contractual network of small overseas apparel manufacturers. Approximately 12 percent of all U.S. imports of apparel are contracted for by U.S. apparel manufacturers using lower-cost foreign producers. It is also used by electronics firms such as Lanier and IBM who depend on contract manufacturing for some of their parts or finished products.

The Advantages and Disadvantages of Market-Presence Alternatives

Each market-presence alternative can be used as a strategic tool for achieving a company's objectives in a particular national market. Like most tools, however, each is not equally appropriate for all situations. The choice of market presence depends on company, environmental, and market circumstances at a particular point in time, and on the company's future global and local plans.

A company with a global-strategy focus and pursuing a dynamic high-technology strategy would probably like to have full ownership and control over its production facilities around the world and full operational control over its standardized marketing activities. Yet, governmental policies and other environmental factors may work against these coordination needs in a particular national market. If the market is considered commercially desirable, the company must arrive at a market-presence solution that meets its internal and competitive needs as well as those imposed by the local environment and market. The solution can be quite unexpected, as in the case of IBM in Yugoslavia. In this particular instance, the U.S. company helped the Yugoslavian government set up a government-owned distributorship. The distributor's personnel are trained in the company's products and sales and in customer-service procedures, and the distributorship must adhere to carefully developed performance standards. The arrangement is equivalent to a *marketing joint venture*. A similar approach was adopted by Hewlett-Packard in 1986 in Brazil, where market access is restricted by the Brazilian government to local companies.

The advantages and disadvantages of each market-presence alternative should be evaluated and contrasted with other viable alternatives. Some of the major advantages and disadvantages of each market presence are presented in Table 10-6.

Legal-Operational Presence

A major difference between the three market-presence forms that include a legal presence and the four that provide only an operational presence is that the former require a tangible resource commitment in another country. Thus, some of the company's assets are exposed to overseas political and economic risks. However, a legal-operational presence provides the company with more direct control over production and marketing activity.

Of the three forms of legal-operational presence, the joint venture is the most complicated. The foreign branch and foreign subsidiary are clearly under the operating control of the parent company. Control is not so clear in the case of the joint venture. The following discussion centers on the joint venture. The advantages and disadvantages of the other two forms are summarized in Table 10-6.

The Advantages of a Joint Venture. The advantages to be gained from a joint venture fall into three areas: *political considerations, financial advantages,*[20] and *operational advantages.* We consider each in turn.

The quickening expansion of joint-venture companies is partially the result of governments' attitudes toward foreign ownership of business. In general, government attitude, especially among Third-World and industrializing countries, has shifted from favoring wholly owned subsidiaries to joint ventures. Many countries are closing their borders to foreign companies unless they are willing to accept local partners.

Such joint-venture policies are defended on several grounds. First, joint ventures permit local capital to participate in profitable and productive undertakings and reduce the flow of profits and the repatriation of capital to the parent company. Second, technology and management know-how are more efficiently and rapidly transferred. Third, joint ventures reduce the economic domination of particular industries by foreign enterprise, and lessen "improper" political influence. By complying with the joint-venture policies of a country, a foreign company gains governmental approval and reduces the risk of expropriation or other governmental actions. It may also benefit from more favorable interpretations of local regulations and laws.

Financial considerations are also important. By sharing the capitalization of a company with local partners, a foreign company with limited financial resources can enter into more national markets than would otherwise be possible. Because of the lower investment, a joint venture reduces financial and expropriation risks. Because of the lack of capital markets in many developing countries, joint ventures may be the only way to obtain local equity financing.

A number of operational advantages are also relevant. The joint venture may provide the foreign company with an ability to enter a potentially profitable market when it lacks experience in a particular national market or when it needs to respond quickly because of competitive threats. The local partner may provide the foreign company with needed managerial, technological, or productive resources

TABLE 10-6
Possible Advantages and Disadvantages of Various Forms of Market Presence

Type of Market Presence	Advantages	Disadvantages
Legal-Operational		
1. Foreign branch	Minimum commitment of assets Full control of operation Acquire market contacts Acquire market knowledge directly No dilution of profits	Uncertain future Taxation problems Assets in other markets vulnerable Assume all market risks Investments exposed to political and economic risks
2. Foreign subsidiary	Full control of operation Acquire market contacts Acquire market knowledge directly No dilution of profits Limited liability	Investment required Commitment of other resources and assets Investments exposed to political and economic risks Assume all market risks

3. Joint venture	Shared market risk
	Reduced political risk and discrimination
	Access to market knowledge
	Access to technology, products, trademarks, and so on
	Access to marketing network
	Reduced investment requirements
	Access to experienced labor force
	Access to suppliers
	Tax advantages
		Loss of control, which may result in:
		  Conflicts over dividends objectives
		  Conflicts over marketing objectives
		  Conflicts over production objectives
		  Conflicts over financial objectives
		  Conflicts over personnel objectives
		  Conflicts over supplier objectives
		  Conflicts over transfer prices
		  Conflicts over R&D efforts and costs
		Limitations on profits
		Contributions to joint venture can become disproportionate

Operational-Presence		
1. Indirect exporting	No investment required No other resources required No experience required No market or political risk	No market knowledge acquired No control over marketing mix elements other than product
2. Direct exporting	Market knowledge acquired More control over marketing mix	Some domestic investment required Allocation of output may be required Little control over market price because of tariffs and lack of distribution control
3. Licensing	No investment required No market or political risk Provides a return on R&D investments Revenue from untapped markets Protection from patent infringement Avoids high tariffs and other import restrictions Obtain reciprocal benefits	Creates potential competitors Relatively low return on sales Can restrict or delay long-term plans High taxes levied on royalties in some countries Limits expansion of national markets Seldom results in the development of product or service to fullest potential
4. Contract manufacturing	No investment required Obtain lower labor costs Obtain "made in" label for local market Reduce political risk in local market	Some loss of control over quality Increased complexity in administration of production and logistics Transfer of production know-how Potential for local competitor

at substantial savings of time and money. It may also provide a local distribution system, a local supplier network, knowledge of the local market and marketing institutions and high level business and political contacts. Benefits such as these were the reasons a large number of U.S. companies originally entered Europe in the 1950s and 1960s via joint ventures.[21] The same reasons underly the forming of strategic joint ventures in the 1980s.

The Disadvantages of a Joint Venture. Joint ventures can be short-lived. In some cases, foreign companies seek local joint-venture partners to gain experience and quick access to a foreign market. Once these objectives have been achieved, the joint venture is terminated. Joint venture partnerships may also be short-lived if the local partner is either small or unable to make continuing contributions. For example, the larger partner may not consider a particular market opportunity attractive because its potential is too small. The smaller partner might disagree.

Although there are considerable advantages for entering into joint ventures with local partners, many global companies prefer to establish *foreign subsidiaries.* In fact, some companies refuse to invest in joint ventures. Table 10-6 spells out four reasons for a foreign subsidiary bias. Most of these disadvantages work against a global company's desire to develop some or all of the *competitive advantages* described earlier. Moreover, the *global industry* company, because of its need to coordinate activities on a global rather than a national scale, experiences considerable internal pressure to avoid joint ventures whenever possible.

The disadvantages of the joint venture can be grouped under: (1) risk of loss of operational control, (2) risk of disclosure of proprietary information, and (3) the dilution of earnings. In most cases, it is not the joint venture that is the problem; the basic motivations of the partners simply are not congruent.[22]

Loss of Operational Control. Joint ventures may result in a *loss of operational control.* A joint venture is generally a partnership between a global company and a local company or group of individuals. Increasingly, however, it may be between two global companies of different nationalities. Regardless of who the parties are to a joint venture, their reasons for entering into the agreement will probably differ and may eventually result in conflicts of interest. When the joint venture is between a global company and a local company, these conflicts of interest generally arise from differences in market perspective. The global company has a multimarket perspective and the local partner a national-market perspective. That is, the global company may view local production and marketing activities as only a small yet integral part of a much broader spectrum of activities. The local partners, on the other hand, may view these same activities as the joint venture's primary activities. Typical conflicts include disputes over the reinvestment of earnings, the level of production assigned the joint venture by the global company, the level and type of R&D undertaken locally, and the transfer prices charged by the global company for various inputs.

Other disadvantages include the possibility of problems with the global company's home government over such issues as restraint of trade, the introduction of a local management whose desire for autonomy may be supported by local governments, the introduction of management practices that differ from those of the global company, and even the export markets to be served by the joint venture.

When the joint venture involves two global companies, conflicts still occur. In the case of the original Chrysler–Mitsubishi joint venture, Mitsubishi was to provide Chrysler with technology for the manufacture of small automobiles and entry into Japan. In return, Mitsubishi was to receive access to Chrysler's distribution system in the United States and other countries in which Chrysler operated. Conflicts arose. Mitsubishi did not believe Chrysler was marketing the joint venture's automobiles aggressively enough, and Chrysler was disappointed with the sale of Chrysler products in Japan. At the root of the problem were the disparate reasons for the two companies to join forces. Chrysler wanted temporarily to fill a gap in its product line, and Mitsubishi wanted access to the large U.S. market in order to compete more economically with other Japanese automobile manufacturers.

The need for *disclosure of proprietary information* also presents problems for partners in a joint venture. For a joint venture to work, there needs to be a free flow of information between partners. However, many of the practices used by global companies to avoid or defer taxes and to protect themselves against foreign exchange losses are not appropriate or feasible when there are local partners or shareholders.[23] This is because of the greater danger that these practices will be disclosed, and also because their use is often not in the interest of the local joint venture partner. Even more important is another type of operational problem: the local partner may gain access to the global company's technology or other distinctive competences. In fact, the transfer of some types of information to the joint venture could result in the local partner becoming a viable competitor at some future date. This, of course, is also true in the case of other forms of strategic partnerships between two global companies licensing and contractual arrangements.

Dilution of earnings is often cited as another joint venture problem. Brooke and Remmers suggest that perhaps the most compelling reason global companies "are reluctant to enter into joint ventures is an unwillingness to share the earnings of a subsidiary which they have developed."[24] For example, companies with a competitive technological advantage obtained as a result of in-house R&D activities do not see why they should share the results with local partners who have not taken any of the risk.

Operational Presence

The four forms of *operational presence* also offer advantages and disadvantages. Although the company may not have a legal or physical presence in the market, it can still benefit from a foreign market using one of these forms of market presence.

Exporting When viewed as strategic tools, *indirect* and *direct exporting* provide the global company with three major types of advantages: (1) limited asset exposure, (2) market flexibility, and (3) operational flexibility. We now discuss each in turn.

A major advantage of exporting is that no overseas investments are necessary. Thus, the company does not expose its assets to the political and economic risks inherent in the legal-operational forms of market presence. Moreover, it can quickly withdraw from the market should it prove unattractive. These risks are carried by intermediaries. Exporting is especially advantageous when the market is politically or economically unstable.

Another important advantage of exporting is the avoidance of financial and other resource commitments in a foreign market that may eventually prove to be unprofitable or smaller than estimated. Accordingly, the company can use exporting to test the market's potential and to learn about its characteristics *before* establishing a legal-operational presence.

Depending on its corporate strategy, a company can use exporting to augment domestic demand, rid itself of surplus inventory, offset declining or seasonal domestic demand, and gain access to markets too small to support more sophisticated and costly marketing activities. In such instances, the company can use its productive capability more efficiently and gain economies of scale and, possibly, experience. In addition, when using an indirect exporting approach, a company can avoid the expenses of an export department. Finally, the global company can use exporting to rationalize production, gain from labor-cost differences, and serve several geographically clustered national markets from strategically located production sites.

However, exporting is not without potential disadvantages. Both the indirect and the direct exporter often have little control over the prices established for its products in foreign markets. Tariffs and duties are certainly beyond the company's control, and its ability to control channel markups may be limited. In addition, other key marketing mix elements, such as the quality and level of the sales activity, customer service, and advertising, may also be beyond company control. In the case of indirect exporting, the company depends on intermediaries for its export sales, and does not learn much about exporting. Contacts are not established in the markets in which its products are sold, and it accumulates no knowledge about its customers, and the (overseas) operating environment.

Licensing. Many of the advantages inherent to exporting and joint ventures also apply to licensing arrangements. The licensor conserves capital and management resources and avoids many of the political, legal, and economic risks associated with wholly owned subsidiaries or branches. Like joint ventures, licensing generally benefits from a favorable attitude on the part of the local government. In addition, the licensor benefits in four other areas: (1) additional revenue, (2) market development, (3) protection of intangible industrial property, and (4) reciprocal rights.[25]

A company can gain *additional revenues* by licensing industrial property rights in unexploited overseas markets. These revenues can be used to offset research expenses or to increase returns from research. For example, Milliken, a large U.S. textile company, regularly licenses to foreign companies fabric-formation and related know-how developed through its intensive R&D program. In this way, Milliken recoups some of its R&D costs as royalties. Philip Morris, the makers of Marlboro cigarettes, has licensed the brand name Marlboro to a sports apparel manufacturer in Colombia. Since Morris had no interest in entering the apparel business, it was willing to let one of its brand names be used to generate additional revenue.

Licensing can also be used by companies in *market development*—to build brand awareness and product acceptance in foreign markets. As awareness develops, foreign customers may demand other products manufactured by the home company. Licensing can also be used to test a market's potential without incurring risks and when the market is protected by protectionist trade barriers,

Licensing aids in the *protection of intangibles.* In some countries, a tradename, brand, or even a patent is protected only if it is in use. In such situations, licensing can be used simultaneously to avoid piracy and to generate royalties.

Under a *reciprocal-rights* arrangement, two companies agree to exchange rights to new technology and products. Such an agreement may be included in the original licensing agreement or linked to it as a parallel agreement. Both practices are quite widespread, particularly between and among U.S., European, and Japanese companies seeking strategic partnerships. As noted by Kolde, "some companies report that such reciprocal rights are of greater value than the royalty payments received under the licensing arrangement, since the foreign research talent is obtained at a comparatively low cost."[26]

A major disadvantage of licensing is that it may inadvertently restrict the company's long-term strategic plans. Licensees are interested in using the license for their own goals, not those of the licensors. A licensee may not be willing to make the financial and managerial commitments necessary to develop the market's potential according to the licensor's desires and may become a competitor. It is also difficult to drop licensees and this limits short-term flexibility.

One very real obstacle is the licensee's middle position between the licensing company and its customers. Customers may identify more strongly with the licensee than with the licensor. Other reasons advanced for not licensing include limits on profits, problems over quality control, the high taxes levied on royalties by some countries, and the difficulties inherent in changing the conditions of the licensing arrangement to mirror changes in the company's competitive position, resources, and objectives.

Three examples of licensing problems and issues are presented in Exhibit 10-5. Notice that these include experiences companies have had because they did *not* license or were not aware of the implications that licensing might have on market-development plans and profit potential.

Contract Manufacturing The advantages of contract manufacturing can be used by both national and global companies. For example, many U.S. apparel producers and retailers use overseas contract manufacturing to increase their price competitiveness in the U.S. apparel market. Contract manufacturing is also a viable approach for those global companies with large national markets and distinctive competencies in marketing or logistics.

The major advantages of the approach can be grouped under three headings: (1) political considerations, (2) economic considerations, and (3) barriers to trade. These advantages are discussed briefly below.

Many governments view contract manufacturing favorably and it thus has political benefits. For example, Mexico and Colombia have passed laws encouraging such undertakings. They provide employment and encourage local businessmen to become internationally oriented. These laws permit local and foreign companies to import, free of tariffs, materials and other inputs for assembly in their countries

EXHIBIT 10-5 _____

When to License: Examples of Problems to Watch For _____

The following examples illustrate just three of the problems involved in the licensing decision. As will be seen, the decision *not* to license can be as traumatic as the decision *to* license.

Protecting Industrial Property Rights

Shortly after World War II, parts "specifically for the use in" equipment manufactured by the Caterpillar Tractor Company began surfacing for sale in various markets. These products had neither been approved nor manufactured by the Caterpillar Company. The firm, however, was unable to establish any legal claims. If the company had initially sought out a local partner, the demand for these similar parts most assuredly would have benefited Caterpillar. As it turned out, the local manufacturers of the parts saw no reason to avoid competing with the totally foreign-owned Caterpillar Tractor Company. *A licensing agreement with a local manufacturer would have provided the company with some protection.*

The Loss of Markets

In one case, a U.S. manufacturer not only licensed the manufacturer and sale of its products to an English firm but also granted the firm the exclusive right to sublicense the U.S. expertise to other countries. At the time the decision was made, the company was not interested in expanding overseas. The firm believed that it was best to simply collect the royalties and thus eliminate the need to provide additional investment money. Within a few years, worldwide markets for the firm's products developed. Naturally, the company greatly regretted its earlier decision permitting exclusive licensing.

The Loss of Potential Profits

A U.S. pharmaceutical firm licensed its manufacturing techniques to an Asian company. The Asian company, heavily promoting the products, enjoyed great success. As a result of the licensing agreement terms, however, almost all of the tremendous profits were reaped by the Asian company. If the U.S. firm had committed to a more direct form of involvement, such as equity participation, it could have earned greater profits. In this instance, the company's failure to carefully study the market and product opportunities eventually resulted in its loss of profits.

Source: David A. Ricks, *Big Business Blunders: Mistakes in Multinational Marketing* (Homewood, Ill.: Dow Jones-Irwin, 1983), pp. 104–105.

provided that the output is exported. The benefits of these provisions for the foreign company are access to inexpensive labor and lower capital investment.

Benefits of an economic nature accruing to users of contract manufacture include access to lower labor costs, and avoidance of local labor laws, regulations and other problems stemming from inexperience in manufacturing overseas. The company also gains the advantage of being able to place a "made in" label on products sold in the country of manufacture. An important advantage to the company wishing to market its products in the country of a contract-manufacturing operation is the circumvention of international trade restrictions imposed by the local government. Contract manufacturing can also eliminate transportation costs and major documentation problems.

As with the other methods discussed above, contract manufacturing is not without drawbacks. If the manufacturing process adds most of the value added, the *contract manufacturer* may end up with the larger portion of the profits. If marketing is the major activity, the contracting company will benefit more. Another potential problem is finding qualified local manufacturers that can meet the quality and specifications required for the product. It may take several years to train a local producer; such training involves proximity and a considerable amount of executive time and effort. The contractor may also have to share proprietary production and production know-how and may be training a future competitor. In addition, contract manufacturing increases the complexity of administering the company's logistical and inventory systems.

Marketing and the Market-Presence Choice

Many factors influence the *market presence* a company selects for a particular national market. Some are peculiar to the company (plans for the market, availability of human and other resources, lack of market experience), some are imposed by the environment (political uncertainty), and some are required by the market (reliable post-sale service).

Because of the interplay of all these forces, the market presence finally selected may not be the one indicated by the economic potential of the market or even the one most suitable to "tap" this potential. The important thing to remember is that the imperatives of local markets and competition must be balanced against the strategic imperatives of the company; these tradeoffs are within the control of the company.

The various forms of market presence are strategic tools, means by which the company can achieve its objectives in a particular market, and can be changed as market conditions and environmental forces warrant and as the company's objectives, strategies, and resources change. For example, a company may sequentially develop a foreign market, first by using local distributors, then through a joint venture, and, finally, with a foreign subsidiary. This stepwise entry strategy was used by Campbell Soups in Japan and Levi Strauss in Mexico, and effectively balances each company's investments in a market with its experience and the market's potential.

Three sets of factors, or needs, have to be addressed when making a market-presence choice. They can be considered as questions:

1. What does the company need to achieve its global and local objectives?
2. What constraints does the local environment impose on the market-presence decision?
3. What form of market presence is required to achieve the company's local market objectives?

These needs are briefly discussed below.

Meeting Company Needs

All the forms of market presence discussed so far may be appropriate at some point or for a particular situation, regardless of the global-company's industry strategic focus and generic international strategy. The choice of form depends on the company's strategic objectives and resources. The company's industry strategic focus and generic strategy determines the conditions that need to be met. For example, a company following a dynamic high-technology strategy may still use a contract manufacturer in another country to manufacture low-tech components. A company following an advanced management-skill strategy may use a foreign distributor if the market is too small to support its usual marketing approach. The degree of flexibility and innovativeness demonstrated by a company in the use of the various market-presence forms can be critical to its success.

Meeting Environmental Constraints

Not all market-presence forms are appropriate for each national market the company may be interested in. The political, economic, and social environments of a market strongly affect the form of market presence used, as may domestic laws and regulations. In fact, the home and local environmental constraints may be such that the company may retreat, even when there is an attractive market potential. Some of the factors that need to be addressed when making a market-presence decision follow:

Home-Country Considerations Many countries impose constraints on the international activities of their companies. The U.S. government has often placed restrictions on foreign investments in certain parts of the world. The United States also has laws that forbid companies from trading with other countries and boycotts have been imposed on trade with certain countries, as in the case of the Soviet gas pipeline. Restraints such as these have a direct impact on where and how companies can do business.

Host-Country Considerations Two major factors affecting the choice of market presence are political and economic risk. What is the *predictability* of a national market's political and economic environments? How changeable is the local government's attitude toward foreign enterprise in general? What is the nature of the laws and regulations that govern its behavior? Will the company's ability to repatriate earnings and capital change? Will its ability to import needed inputs change? Will its ability to freely transfer managerial and technical personnel be restricted? The questions are many, and all must be answered. The less predictable the political and economic environments, the more flexibility a company needs.

Other concerns that need to be addressed include the stage of economic development of the country, the attitude the general public has toward foreign companies, the availability and sophistication of needed infrastructure support and the economic potential of the intended market. These and similar factors determine the kinds of marketing efforts required and have a direct impact on the effort a company is willing to expend.

Meeting Market Needs

The target market's characteristics have an important bearing on the market presence selected. The market's potential, its sophistication, the type and level of competition it fosters, and the company's experience with the local market or similar markets will individually and collectively influence choice.

EXHIBIT 10-6
The Learning Stages of a Global Company

Stage 1

Many companies begin the internationalization process by extending their business activities *nationally*. Companies operating in geographically large markets such as the United States, Australia, and Canada have the opportunity to accumulate experience and capabilities necessary to control and operate widely dispersed manufacturing and marketing activities. That is, they develop the policies and procedures necessary to efficiently and effectively communicate with and operate branches and subsidiaries that are geographically separated. This provides them with some of the capabilities necessary for international business. Other companies, such as those located in geographically small markets like Switzerland, must gain this experience and capability mainly in the international arena.

Stage 2

The first international business experience for many firms is indirect exporting. Many companies do not take even this initial step because of preconceived ideas about risks and costs. Studies indicate that U.S. nonexporters are reluctant to enter into exporting because they do not trust foreigners, know little about documentation requirements, are afraid of language problems, know nothing about the market, know nothing about foreign currencies and how to handle them, and are unwilling to make the initial effort necessary to establish contacts. Most also believe exporting is more expensive, and the returns less than what can be obtained domestically. The initial exporting activity is generally through an independent distributor or the result of unsolicited orders.

If the company successfully overcomes its inexperience and its foreign sales begin to increase, it will generally establish an export department to provide itself with control over these activities. It may also start to add production capacity to serve its overseas customers. The company has now made a commitment to international activities.

Stage 3

This stage involves the company's first overseas investment operation. It might be the establishment of a marketing subsidiary or even a manufacturing subsidiary. The motivation is again control over its foreign markets and stepping over trade barriers. The initial overseas operation is strongly influenced by the management's attitude. If polycentric, the operation will have a high degree of autonomy. If ethnocentric, it will be controlled tightly by the parent company. As the company gains experience the attitude may shift to regiocentric. At the same time, the company also accumulates knowledge about its competition and becomes more dependent on its overseas earnings. This will result in the creation of an international division to control and coordinate international activities with domestic activities.

Stage 4

At stage four, the company has integrated its international and domestic activities. It no longer views the international and domestic arenas as separate when setting annual objectives and allocating resources: one feeds the other. Nor are foreign marketing opportunities arbitrarily overlooked. The selection of marketing opportunities is soundly grounded in strategic, economic, and political rationales.

In addition to these factors, others need to be considered. Three examples follow:

☐ **Penetration and Development of the Market** If the market is economically attractive, the company will want to be assured that the market will be penetrated or developed in accordance with its potential. That is, the company will want a form of market presence that provides sufficient control to ensure that an appropriate market position is attained.

☐ **Market Communication** If the market is characterized by intensive competition and volatility, or if it requires close monitoring for other reasons, the company must select a form of market presence that will ensure that it is kept directly in touch with the market. Although a legal-operational presence will provide a more direct communication link with the parent company, some of the operational-presence forms can be made to serve the same purpose.

☐ **Acquisition of Experience** If the market potential warrants, the company may also need to be assured that it will develop sufficient market expertise to become directly involved at some later time. Since market potential is not always easily determined, the choice of market presence needs to allow for gaining experience. That is, future market-presence forms should never be ruled out if they look at all promising (a stepwise entry strategy should always be considered).

CORPORATE LEARNING AND GLOBAL STRATEGY

Our discussion so far has assumed that the company is experienced in international activities or can acquire such experience. Companies must learn how to operate internationally; the learning experience can at times be quite painful.

The learning experience that global companies go through can be divided into four distinct stages which most "global" pass through (see Exhibit 10-6).

SUMMARY

In this chapter, we looked at several of the company-related issues and factors affecting the formulation and implementation of marketing strategy abroad. Included were the attitudes of the company's managers; the company's industry focus; and its choice of generic strategy, geographic expansion strategy, and market presence.

The attitude of management toward doing business overseas will influence the strategies, planning procedures, and operations adopted by a company for those overseas activities. We classified these attitudes as either ethnocentric, polycentric, regiocentric, or geocentric. Their influence on foreign marketing activities and strategies was also examined.

Companies operating in two or more national markets have the opportunity to develop competitive advantages not available to national companies. Many of these potential competitive advantages are associated with the company's foreign marketing effort. However, which advantages are stressed and developed depends on several factors, some of which are not under the control of the company. For example, each national market exerts economic, competitive, political, legal, and social pressures that may require different strategic responses. These must be considered carefully even though the company may simultaneously want to harmonize local strategies across national markets (to ensure that its mission and objectives are achieved and its resources and capabilities optimally utilized).

The particular industry competitive and regulatory conditions are a major factor influencing a company's foreign marketing activities. Global-industry companies need to be responsive to global competitive conditions and trends and will be subjected to strong pressures to coordinate and integrate their marketing activities on a worldwide basis. In contrast, national-industry companies need to be responsive to local competitive conditions and trends, and will tend to use marketing programs tailored to local needs or wants.

Four generic strategies where identified: dynamic high-technology strategy, low- or stable-technology strategy, advanced management-skill strategy, and production-market rationalization strategy. The generic strategies adopted by a global company for its overseas activities impact the types of marketing strategies used within and across national markets. Important to each of these four generic strategies is the relative bargaining strength of a company when negotiating with local governments. In some cases, the company's bargaining power determines whether it will enter or remain in a national market.

A company's foreign marketing activities are also directly affected by the geographic expansion strategy adopted. That is, a company will, implicitly or explicitly, select a geographic concentration strategy or a geographic diversification strategy. The strategy adopted will determine the rate at which new markets are added and will influence the level of the marketing effort undertaken in each foreign market. Moreover, it will exert influence on the

company's market-presence decisions. For each foreign market it plans to compete in, the company must make two decisions about its market presence. It will have to decide on its legal presence and its operational presence. These decisions are determined partly by the salient dimensions of the market's competitive environment and partly by the strategic needs of the company. The final form of the market presence has a significant impact on the company's marketing activities, both across and within national markets.

A company eventually becomes "global" only as a result of a learning experience that often follows four distinct stages. Not all companies become global companies; many are quite satisfied with their international performance as, say, international or multinational companies. They lack the competitive, profit, or growth motives necessary to become truly global. In addition, not all global companies have evolved in the incremental manner indicated.

DISCUSSION QUESTIONS

1. Distinguish between an ethnocentric and a polycentric attitude; explain how these contrasting attitudes might affect the product policy of a consumer products company.
2. Select two conflicting potential competitive advantages and discuss how government regulations and cultural differences might either inhibit or enhance their development.
3. First, identify a company that can be classified as a global-industry company; explain your choice. Then, identify two competitive advantages your company might be interested in developing; explain why.
4. Which of the four generic strategies would a national-industry company be likely to adopt? Explain your reasoning.
5. Distinguish between geographic diversification and geographic concentration strategies. What are the factors that will influence a company's selection of one of these strategies? Will all divisions within a multibusiness company adopt the same strategy? Why or why not?
6. Is it always necessary to treat the legal- and

operational-presence dimensions of a company's market presence separately? Why or why not?

ADDITIONAL READING

Alden, Vernon R., "Who Says You Can't Crack Japanese Markets," *Harvard Business Review*, January–February 1987.

Atac, Osman A., "International Experience Theory and Global Strategy," *International Marketing Review,* Vol. 3, Winter 1986.

Bartlett, Christopher A. and Sumantra Ghoshal, "Managing across Borders: New Strategic Requirements," *Sloan Management Review*, Vol. 28, Summer 1987.

Charavarthy, Balaji S., and Howard V. Perlmutter, "Strategic Planning for a Global Business," *Columbia Journal of World Business*, Vol. 20, Summer 1985.

Daniels, John D., "Bridging National and Global Marketing Strategies through Regional Operations," *International Marketing Review*, Vol. 4, Autumn 1987.

Denis, Jean-Emile and Daniel Depelteau, "Market Knowledge, Diversification and Export Expansion," *Journal of International Business Studies*, Vol. 16, Fall 1985.

Hamel, Gary, and C. K. Prahalad, "Do You Really Have a Global Strategy?" *Harvard Business Review*, July–August 1985.

Reich, Robert B., and Eric D. Mankin, "Joint Ventures with Japan Give Away our Future," *Harvard Business Review*, March–April 1986.

Jatusripitak, Somkid, Liam Fahey, and Philip Kotler, "Strategic Global Marketing: Lessons from the Japanese," *Columbia Journal of World Business*, Vol. 20, Spring 1985.

Keegan, Warren J., "Strategic Marketing Planning: The Japanese Approach," *International Marketing Review*, Vol. 1, Autumn 1983.

Perlmutter, Howard V., and David A. Heenan, "Co-operate to Compete Globally," *Harvard Business Review*, March–April 1986.

Simmonds, Kenneth, "Global Strategy: Achieving the Geocentric Ideal, *International Marketing Review*, Vol. 2, Spring 1985.

Sims, J. Taylor, "Japanese Market Entry Strategy at Work: Komatsu vs. Caterpillar," *International Marketing Review*, Vol. 3, Autumn 1986.

ENDNOTES

1. Howard V. Perlmutter, "The Tortuous Evolution of the Multinational Corporation," *Columbia Journal of World Business*, January–February 1969, pp. 9–18. Also see Yoram Wind, Susan P. Douglas, and Howard V. Perlmutter, "Guidelines for Developing International Marketing Strategies," *Journal of Marketing*, Vol. 37, April 1973, pp. 14–23.

2. For a more detailed discussion of the implications of market and firm factors on strategy formulation, see Gary Hamel and C. K. Prahalad, "Managing Strategic Responsibility in the MNC," *Strategic Management Journal*, Vol. 4, (1983), pp. 341–351, and Michael E. Porter, *Competitive Strategy: Techniques for Analyzing Industries and Competitors* (New York: The Free Press, 1980), Chapter 13.

3. For a detailed discussion on global and national responsive firms, see Yves L. Doz, *Strategic Management in Multinational Companies* (New York: Pergamon, 1986), Chapters 7 and 8.

4. The term "multifocal" is borrowed from Doz, *Strategic Management.*

5. This section is based on William H. Davidson, *Global Strategic Management* (New York: John Wiley & Sons, 1982), p. 318.

6. This section is based on the four strategy models suggested by John Fayerweather and Ashok Kapoor, *Strategy and Negotiation for the International Corporation: Guidelines and Cases* (Cambridge, Mass.: Ballinger, 1976), pp. 18–24.

7. See C. K. Prahalad and Yves L. Doz, *The Multinational Mission* (New York: The Free Press, 1987), pp. 48–50, and H. V. Perlmutter and D. A. Heenan, "Co-operate to compete globally," *Harvard Business Review*, March–April 1986, pp. 136–152.

8. Doz, *Strategic Management.*

9. Igal Ayal and Jehiel Zif, "Market Expansion Strategies in Multinational Marketing," *Journal of Marketing*, Spring 1979.

10. Seev Hirsch and Baruch Lev, "Sales Stabilization Through Export Diversification," *The Review of Economics and Statistics*, August 1971.

11. Gilbert D. Harrell and Richard O. Kiefer, "Multinational Strategic Market Portfolios," *MSU Business Topics*, Winter 1981, pp. 3–15.

12. Endel-Jakob Kolde, *International Business Enterprise*, 2nd. ed. (Englewood Cliffs, N.J.: Prentice-Hall, 1968), pp. 185–190, and John D. Daniels, Ernest W. Ogram, Jr., and Lee H. Radebaugh, *International Business: Environments and Operations*, 3rd. ed. (Reading, Mass.: Addison-Wesley, 1983), pp. 488–490, present some interesting insights into the legal and operational aspects of the various market-presence forms discussed in this section.

13. "Britain Orders 4 Firms to Defy U.S. Pipeline Ban," *Wall Street Journal*, August 3, 1983, p. 30.

14. Daniels, Ogram, and Radebaugh, *International Business*, p. 489.

15. Kolde, op. cit., p. 187.

16. Detlev Vagts, "A Local Economic Disaster: Can the

U.S. Parent Walk Away Scot-Free?" *Worldwide Projects and Installations*, November–December 1973, pp. 38–40.

17. "Union Carbide Fights for Its Life," *Business Week*, December 24, 1984, pp. 52–61.

18. See Paul W. Beamish and John C. Banks, "Equity Joint Ventures and the Theory of the Multinational Enterprise," *Journal of International Business Studies*, Vol. 28, No. 2 (Summer 1987), pp. 1–16.

19. Robert B. Reich and Eric D. Mankin, "Joint ventures with Japan give away our future," *Harvard Business Review* March–April 1986, pp. 78–86.

20. See Michael Z. Brooke and H. Lee Remmers, *The Strategy of Multinational Enterprise*, 2nd ed. (London: Pitman, 1978), pp. 206–208, for a more detailed discussion of the financial advantages of a joint venture.

21. Lawrence G. Franko, "Joint-Venture Divorce in the Multinational Company," *Columbia Journal of World Business*, May–June 1971, pp. 20–21.

22. Prahalad and Doz, *The Multinational Mission*, p. 165.

23. Brooke and Remmers, *Strategy* p. 220.

24. Ibid., p. 221.

25. Kolde, op. cit., pp. 214–215.

26. Ibid., p. 215.

Chapter 11
The Dimensions of Global Marketing Strategy

INTRODUCTION

DEFINING THE GLOBAL MARKETING MISSION

The Global Segmentation Strategy: Global-Market Segments; National-Market Segments; Mixed-Market Segments. The Global Marketing Approach: The Competitive-Market Positioning Strategy; The Core Marketing-Mix Strategy; Corporate Global Marketing Strategy Practices.

FOREIGN MARKETS AND GLOBAL MARKETING STRATEGY

Classifying Foreign Markets. Global Portfolio Assessment. Foreign-Market Assessment: Competition; Market Characteristics; Market-Decision Effects. Foreign-Market Categories: Integrated National Markets; Critical National Markets.

GLOBAL MARKETING-MIX POLICIES

Marketing-Mix Policies and the Global Segmentation Strategy: Global-Market Companies; National-Market Companies. Marketing-Mix Policies and the Geographic Expansion Strategy. Misjudging Market Segments.

SUMMARY

DISCUSSION QUESTIONS

ADDITIONAL READING

ENDNOTES

_____

The purpose of marketing strategies, domestic or global, is to influence the level, composition, and timing of demand in one or more target markets in order to help the company achieve its objectives.[1] Domestic and global marketing strategies attempt to match the company's changing objectives, resources, and capabilities to the changing conditions of the targeted markets at a particular point in time. This is accomplished in three major steps: (1) selecting competitive market positions in the target markets; (2) deftly combining the marketing-mix elements of product, price, distribution, and promotion to support these market positions; and (3) effectively allocating marketing resources to the various target markets.

Notwithstanding similarities, the development, implementation, and control of global marketing strategies are considerably more complicated than the same for domestic markets. Complications arise from the following four sources:

1. Global marketing strategy decisions need to take into account the changing international environment and the changing national environments in which the company is competing.

2. Global marketing strategy decisions must also take into account variations in the size, degree of market sophistication, stage of development, sales response characteristics, and competitive conditions in many overseas markets concurrently.

3. Global marketing strategy decisions also need to take into account the strategic role assigned each foreign market in the overall plans of the company.

4. Global marketing strategy decisions need to harmonize the sale responses from the foreign markets in such a way that, when aggregated, they support the company's overall strategic objectives and are within the company's regional or corporate capabilities and resources.

The first two complications are external to the company and concern the environment within which the company competes. The second two are internal to the company and concern the constraints imposed by the company on the marketing strategy decisions of the global marketing management team. These internal constraints frame which global marketing strategy decisions are made and govern how the external considerations are handled.

In this chapter, we will discuss the corporate framework within which global marketing strategies are formulated. Our discussion will be concerned primarily with those corporate decisions that influence the choice of target markets, the competitive position to be taken in the target markets, and the blending and emphasis placed on the marketing-mix elements. These corporate decisions are listed on the left-hand side of Figure 11–1 and will be discussed shortly.

During our discussions of corporate decision making, it is important to keep in mind the critical, even vital, role that environmental factors play in the selection of the target market and the development of the marketing mix. No element of the marketing strategy can be treated entirely in isolation. The influence that the external factors may have on marketing-mix decisions will be discussed in considerable detail in Chapters 12–16. The influence that external factors have on

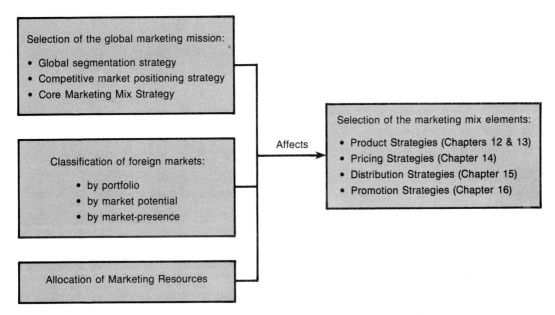

FIGURE 11-1   Comprehensive Global Marketing Strategy Formulation System

the selection of the target market and the position taken in each foreign market will be covered in this chapter.

DEFINING THE GLOBAL MARKETING MISSION

A company relies on its marketing management team to monitor opportunities and to develop marketing objectives and plans that are consistent with its business strategies and that contribute to its business objectives. Together, the company's business strategies and objectives define the role played by its marketing management team and provide the team with a set of comprehensive rules and guidelines for decision making. To some degree, this role distinguishes the company from its competitors and identifies the scope and content of its marketing activities. It reflects the company's marketing philosophy and strategic purpose, and it indicates the principal markets and the primary customer needs it will attempt to satisfy. We call this overall marketing role the company's *corporate marketing mission* and define it as follows:

> **The corporate marketing mission** prescribes the scope and nature of the company's competitive interaction with its target markets by broadly defining the major markets the company is interested in satisfying, the way these markets will be segmented and satisfied, and the competitive position taken in particular market segments.

By broadly defining the major markets it is interested in satisfying, the way these markets are to be segmented and satisfied, and the competitive position to be taken, the company lays down the general parameters within which marketing strategy decisions are made. Within this general framework, marketing's tasks are to select specific target markets, define market positions, develop and implement marketing mixes, and establish marketing expenditure levels.

The company's international corporate marketing mission is particularly important because it establishes the basis for foreign marketing activities. Global companies recognize that they cannot serve all customers on a global scale. The customers are too numerous, too widely scattered, and too heterogeneous in needs and wants. Instead of competing everywhere, often at a competitive disadvantage, companies choose to compete in those foreign-market segments that they can serve most effectively. The way these segments are selected and satisfied and the role they play in the company's overall marketing activities are strongly influenced by the corporate marketing mission.

The company's *global marketing mission* is predicated on its corporate marketing mission and broadly defines its global segmentation strategy, its global marketing approach, and its foreign-market expenditure levels. In combination, these three components of the global marketing mission determine the structure and content of the company's core marketing strategy and the degree to which that strategy and its elements may or may not be modified to handle national differences.

The Global Segmentation Strategy

A company marketing in several foreign markets can choose to serve the same market segments on a global basis, the same market segments on a national basis, or a combination of global and national segments. The three segmentation alternatives, called *global-market segments, national-market segments* and *mixed-market segments,* are illustrated in Figure 11–2. The circles represent the *geographic extent* of each market segment. In the first example, the company has three business units, each of which is involved in serving markets in the United States and one or more foreign markets. In the second example, the company is serving different markets that are nationally distinct. The third example is a combination of the other two examples.

Global-Market Segments

Examples of companies that market to *global-market segments* include Coca-Cola and Pepsi-Cola (soft beverages), Canon and Minolta (cameras), Seiko and Citizen (watches), and Fiat and Daimler-Benz (automobiles). These companies, although competing in different industries and serving different markets, approach the task of segmenting their markets similarly. Essentially, they concentrate on segmenting markets according to a set of segmenting variables (such as demographics, buying practices, preferences, and benefits sought) that ignore national boundaries. These companies also seek to identify and serve market segments whose needs cannot be divided into distinct cultural groups of buyers. They concentrate on identifying what is common in the needs of customers across foreign-market segments rather than on what is different in those segments. Soft beverages, for example, serve basically the same core purpose and are used in essentially the

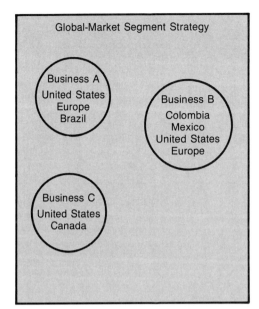

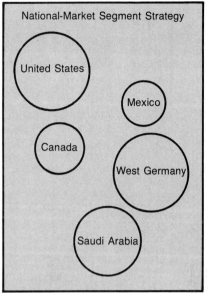

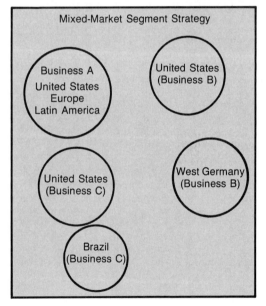

FIGURE 11-2 **Three Global Segmentation Strategies** (Examples are for U.S.-based companies)

same way, regardless of cultural and national differences of buyers. The same is true for cameras, watches, and automobiles.

There are many marketing strategy implications that need to be understood when adopting a global-market segmentation strategy. Several are presented in Table 11–1.

TABLE 11-1
Examples of Marketing Strategy Implications of Global- and National-Market Segmentation Strategies

	Global-Market Segmentation Strategy	National-Market Segmentation Strategy
Selection of major markets	□ Selection on the basis of business unit portfolio decisions and the global competitive positioning of the company □ Emphasis on identifying universal needs and requirements that can be satisfied by standardized products □ Other marketing-mix elements used to reduce or offset differences in market needs and requirements (heavy promotion, price adjustments, reliable delivery)	□ Selection of foreign markets on the basis potential and local competitive conditions □ Emphasis on identifying and satisfying local needs and requirements
Major global customers	□ Centrally processed and coordinated sales to major global customers	□ None exist
Role of markets in company's activities	□ Individual foreign markets treated as an integral part of a business unit's portfolio of activities	□ Individual foreign markets treated as separate business investments
Product decisions	□ Product development and product-line decisions centrally coordinated and managed to gain from experience and economies of scale □ Development of global brands and trademarks □ Global product-marketing positioning	□ Product development, and product-line decisions made locally. Economies of scale more important than cumulated experience □ Emphasis on the use of local brands and trademarks □ Emphasis on local product–market positioning
Product sourcing decisions	□ Product sourcing for foreign markets from global network of production facilities centrally coordinated and managed	□ Primary sourcing of foreign markets in form of inputs, except for products developed for narrowly defined regional markets
Pricing decisions	□ Foreign-market pricing decisions centrally coordinated and managed and strongly influenced by business-unit portfolio decisions □ Intracompany transfer pricing centrally coordinated and managed	□ Foreign-market pricing decisions made locally and determined by local market and competitive conditions □ Intracompany transfer pricing regionally coordinated
Channel and distribution decisions	□ Emphasis on using similar channels and outlets in foreign markets	□ Channel and outlet decisions made locally and on the basis of local market conditions
Promotional decisions	□ Emphasis on developing global-brands and trademark recognition	□ Emphasis on developing local brand and trademark recognition
After-sales services	□ Global service standards and procedures used by company and independent dealers	□ Global service standards and procedures modified for local conditions

Undifferentiated Marketing. A global-market segment strategy is not necessarily the same as an undifferentiated marketing strategy. Companies using a global-market segment strategy use market segmentation and targeting techniques and offer a product designed to meet the needs of a particular group of customers on a global basis. An undifferentiated marketing strategy ignores market segment differences. In the international arena, the undifferentiated marketing strategy is basically ethnocentric, and it is undertaken without regard to competitive conditions within and across foreign markets.

Another distinction is that companies using global-market segment strategies know that they are competing in global industries and that their major competitors are probably other global companies. To be successful under such circumstances, these companies find it necessary to develop global competitive advantages such as worldwide brand names, worldwide product positions, universal after-sales service standards and procedures, and globally coordinated pricing strategies.[2] In recent years, Coca-Cola has been busy pursuing a two-pronged global marketing strategy (1) the development of what it terms "megabrands" and (2) the development of a global marketing mix that emphasizes *availability, affordability,* and *acceptability.*[3] Megabrands consist of those products sold in all foreign markets under the same brand names. Currently, Coca-Cola has seven megabrands: Coca-Cola, Coca-Cola Classic, Diet Coke, Cherry Coke, Diet Cherry Coke, Caffeine-free Coke, and Caffein-free Diet Coke.

On the other hand, companies using an undifferentiated marketing strategy may or may not be competing in global industries. Benefits obtained from an undifferentiated marketing strategy are that it minimizes marketing research, product development, production, inventory, and transportation costs. However, this policy of cost minimization is achieved without regard to local and global competition, local demand conditions, and the differentiated needs of the market. Many small exporting companies and companies in the first stages of internationalizing marketing activities adopt this strategy. They lack the resources or foreign-market knowledge to undertake a more comprehensive and targeted approach.

Marketing Strategy Decisions. A company pursuing a global-market segmentation strategy recognizes that its marketing strategy is not developed solely for the purpose of maximizing customer satisfaction in a particular foreign market. Rather, it is simply one of the means by which the firm competes globally. Thus, competing globally demands a marketing approach that allows for:[4]

1. Foreign markets to be selected and classified according to their contribution to the overall global competitive position of the company.
2. Foreign markets to be treated as an integral part of an overall *business portfolio* to be increased or decreased depending on the profitability of the business and its position within the company's overall strategic plans.
3. Products and product lines are designed for global not local market performance.
4. Products and product lines are priced for global not local market reasons.
5. Foreign markets to be supplied from strategically positioned production facilities and through standardized channels and outlets.

To satisfy these five requirements, the formulation of marketing strategy must be centralized and controlled. Although local market conditions and trade barriers are important, they are not as important as maintaining a regional or global competitive position vis-à-vis global competitors. In such cases, to maximize global competitive advantages, marketing strategy focuses on developing regional or global brand names, standardized products, standardized warranties, standardized packaging, standardized channels, and standardized after-sales services. On the other hand, pricing is often used competitively to stop, for example, competitors entering particular markets.

Moreover, because of their importance to cash flow and as potential competitive threats, major foreign markets and large customers are often singled out for special attention.

A good example is a British company, BSR, the world's largest producer of automatic record changers. In the 1970s, when Japanese exports of audio equipment were growing rapidly, BSR recognized that it could lose its market base in the United States and Europe if the Japanese began marketing record changers. BSR redesigned its products to Japanese specifications and offered distributors aggressive price discounts and inventory support. The Japanese could not justify expanding their own capacity. BSR not only stalled the entry of the Japanese into the record-changer market but it also moved ahead of its existing competitor, Garrard.[5]

In addition to meeting internal needs, the global-market segmentation strategy also provides potential customers with certain advantages, especially if they cross national borders. For example, global brand names, standardized products, outlets, and after-sales services help foreign customers identify products they are accustomed to buying and give them assurance that their quality and servicing requirements will be met.

National-Market Segments

Companies serving the same market segments in multiple markets but on a national basis are marketing to *national-market segments*. Essentially, these companies seek to satisfy the needs of market segments that are *within national boundaries*. Thus, geographic location is the first variable used to differentiate markets. Other segmenting variables are then used to identify market segments with similar needs within each foreign market that the company wants to satisfy. For example, Pillsbury sells its food products in many countries, but the products it sells in one country many differ substantially from the products sold in other countries (in form, packaging, taste, and the way the food is prepared). Accordingly, it recently developed for its U.S. market a unique line of food products for preparation in microwave ovens.

A company using a national-market segmentation strategy is competing at a local level with domestic competitors and, possibly, global competitors using similar strategies. The competitive advantage this type of global company has over its competitors depends largely on the effective integration of two factors, marketing strategy flexibility and the global marketing support infrastructure.

Marketing Strategy Flexibility. To be locally successful, the company needs in-depth knowledge about each foreign market it is competing in, and a local capability to exploit this knowledge in order to serve and respond to unique national-market needs or requirements. Thus, target market selection, product development, product testing, marketing research, and the formulation of marketing mixes, such as brand names, packaging design, pricing, distribution, after-sales services, and promotion, tend to be handled locally.

Global Marketing Support Infrastructure. To be successful at the global level and to enhance its competitiveness at the local level, a company using a national-market segmentation strategy supports local marketing activities by providing assistance (when requested) on such matters as marketing research approaches and methods, product development and testing procedures, and the transfer of experience gained in other markets. That is, the company develops a global marketing support infrastructure. A key element of this infrastructure is the *marketing information system.*

The marketing goal of companies using a national-market segmentation strategy is to satisfy the needs and requirements of local target markets more efficiently and effectively than its global and local competitors. In contrast to companies pursuing global-market segmentation strategies, these companies require an overall marketing approach that allows for:

1. Foreign markets to be selected on the basis of their individual potentials.
2. Foreign markets to be treated independently as elements of an overall foreign-market portfolio to be increased or decreased depending on individual profitability.
3. Products and product lines to be tailored to the particular needs and requirements of local markets.
4. Products and product lines to be priced according to local demand and competitive conditions.
5. Channels to be developed according to local competitive conditions and market circumstances.
6. Promotional themes and campaigns to be developed according to local competitive conditions and market circumstances.

In the case of nationally focused companies, similarities in market-mix decisions across foreign markets are more the result of using similar marketing techniques, procedures, and methods than of underlying global objectives. Cross-sharing of marketing experience may also result in the adoption of similar products, packaging, pricing, and promotional strategies. However, local market acceptance and market conditions are the key criteria used when transferring marketing programs from one market to another.

Mixed-Market Segments

Strict adherence to either a global- or national-market segment strategy is rare. Most global companies, especially as they gain experience and become established in a number of foreign markets, use a combination of global and national segments. Companies such as Coca-Cola, General Foods, and Pillsbury have found that some national market segments are sufficiently large and attractive to warrant individualized attention. They have also discovered that other foreign markets are so small that it is not economical to treat them individually. Therefore, these small markets are grouped together as *market clusters.*

For example, Coca-Cola sells Kin mineral water in Argentina, Sprite Light in Switzerland, and Fanta Fruit Punch in Japan. General Foods sells its packaged grocery products, coffee, and processed meats globally, but it has restricted its food-service industry activities to the United States, the United Kingdom, West Germany, and Canada. In addition, many companies, such as Pillsbury, find it beneficial to *regionalize* some marketing programs. For example, Pillsbury sells its ice-cream products primarily through supermarkets in the United States but through ice-cream parlors in Singapore, Hong Kong, Japan, and Puerto Rico—in effect, satisfying different market segments with the same product. It also has Burger King operations in Canada, Puerto Rico, Europe, and Australia, but it confines its Steak and Ale and Bennigan's operations to the United States.[6]

The Global Marketing Approach

In addition to deciding on a global, national, or mixed-market segment strategy, the global company must also decide on the approach it will take to satisfy its customers while meeting the company's objectives. Doing so involves two major steps. The first step is formulating a *competitive-market positioning strategy.* The second step is deciding on which element(s) of the marketing mix to emphasize. These two decisions are largely shaped by the company's history, the current preferences of the management and owners, its resources, and its distinctive competences. It is also strongly influenced by global and local competitive conditions.

The Competitive-Market Positioning Strategy

A global company can attempt to take one of four competitive positions in each of its foreign markets. Using the classification system popularized by Kotler, it can seek to be the *market-leader,* a *market challenger,* a *market follower,* or a *market nicher.*[7] These four competitive positions, along with a description of their attributes and the types of marketing strategies they entail, are presented in Table 11-2.

If one of these competitive positions becomes the basis for all the foreign markets it competes in, the company is using a *global competitive positioning strategy.* For example, Coca-Cola's stated objective is to be the undisputed market leader in "the soft drink business" in all the countries it does business in.[8] As recently as 1985, it claimed to have more than a 40 percent average sales share of soft drink sales in the 155 countries it marketed in. Even stronger positions were held in markets that had been identified as major. Moreover, it plans to maintain or expand its dominance by capitalizing on its trademarks, marketing and distribution system, significant financial resources, knowledge of business conditions around the world, and heritage of excellence.

Most large global companies do not have the resources, inclination, or entry capabilities to assume the same position in all of their foreign markets. They are more interested in their overall, global competitive positions within their strategically defined businesses. General Motors, Toyota, Polaroid, Procter & Gamble, and many other large global companies pursue a *mixed competitive positioning strategy.*

TABLE 11-2
Four Competitive Market Positioning Strategies

	Market Leader	Market Challenger	Market Follower	Market Nicher
Attributes				
Market position	☐ Firm with the largest market share*	☐ Firm with the next largest share*	☐ Firm with the third largest market share*	☐ Remaining firms
Competitive intent	☐ Interested in maintaining competitive position	☐ Interested in increasing market share, and/or taking market leader position	☐ Interested in maintaining present market share and competitive position	☐ Interested in serving market segments not of interest to larger companies
Typical Market and Marketing Strategies*	☐ *Expansion of total market* — attract new users — increase usage rates — find new markets (overseas) ☐ *Protection of market share* — product innovation — exchange of threat — brand extension — heavy advertising ☐ *Expansion of market share in existing market* — market penetration — cost leadership — service leadership	☐ *Expansion of market share in existing markets* — product innovation — product proliferation — improve services — heavy advertising ☐ *Expansion into other markets* — find new markets (overseas) — follow the leader (overseas) — distribution innovation — cost reduction	☐ *Maintain market share in existing markets* — brand reinforcement — marketing mix emulation — maintain product quality — maintain service levels ☐ *Expansion into other markets* — follow the leader selectively — follow the leader closely — follow the leader at a distance — avoidance of competitors	☐ *Maintain market share in existing markets* — specialized product features — specialized product lines — customer specialists — quality/price specialists — service specialists ☐ *Expansion into other markets* — geographic specialists — narrow product lines — superior service — premium quality and prices — avoidance of competitors

* Philip Kotler used 40%, 30%, 20%, and 10% market shares in his taxonomy of the four competitive market positioning strategies. These percentages, however, vary considerably by industry and country, and are strongly influenced by industry concentration. A better (but more difficult classification to measure) is by the company's *competitive intent.*

** Many of the marketing strategies are similar, especially among market leaders and market challengers.

Source: Adapted from Philip Kotler, *Marketing Management: Analysis, Planning, and Control,* 5th ed. (Englewood Cliffs, N.J., Prentice-Hall, 1984), Chapter 12, pp. 383–413.

For example, General Motors is the market leader in the United States, a market follower in Europe, and a market nicher in Japan. This is partly the result of the relationship between the company and its foreign subsidiaries. The subsidiaries are highly autonomous, and thus have considerable control over local marketing decisions. It is also partly the result of local market conditions, trade barriers, and government regulations.

Campbell Soups is another example of a company that pursues a mixed competitive positioning strategy. It is the market leader in the U.S. consumer soup market, but a market nicher in the United Kingdom. Heinz, on the other hand, is the market leader in the U.K. consumer soup market, and a market nicher in the United States. In this case, Campbell Soups has not been successful in developing a product and marketing-mix strategy capable of dislodging its competitors in its European markets. However, it may not be Campbell Soups' purpose to dislodge Heinz in Europe. Hamel and Prahalad have argued that a dominant position is not required in all foreign markets.[9] For example, a market share of 5 percent in a particular country is quite adequate if it enables the firm to influence the behavior of key global competitors.

As described in Table 11-2, the competitive position taken in a foreign market has a strong influence on the marketing-mix strategies developed and implemented by the company. A company selecting a market-leader position is confronted with the need to develop marketing strategies designed to expand total demand, to protect market share, to expand market share, or to effect some combination of these goals. A market nicher, on the other hand, is interested in developing marketing strategies geared to the specialized needs or requirements of narrowly defined markets. In both these and the other two cases, the marketing strategy choices are also strongly influenced by portfolio decisions: business portfolio decisions in the case of global-market segments and foreign-market portfolio decisions in the case of national-market segments.

The Core Marketing-Mix Strategy

The emphasis placed on a particular product or element of the marketing mix is often decided at the corporate or regional level of the organization. For example, Canon maintains strict control over its copiers and brand name, but gives its local marketing subsidiaries quite a bit of latitude in developing their supporting and positioning marketing mixes. Xerox, on the other hand, tends to retain centralized control over the Xerox brand, marketing approach, and servicing procedures, even in the case of joint-venture arrangements.[10]

The degree of latitude given marketing managers to make marketing-mix decisions is partly a function of the company's segmentation strategy, partly a function of its competitive positioning strategy, and partly a function of its product decisions. Considering segmentation and product at this time—as well as the fact that the target market is implicitly included—four general marketing strategy alternatives are available. These four alternatives are shown in Figure 11-3, which charts the global marketing strategy matrix.

Pure Global Marketing Strategy. The ideal global marketing strategy is to market a standard product to a global-market segment using marketing programs

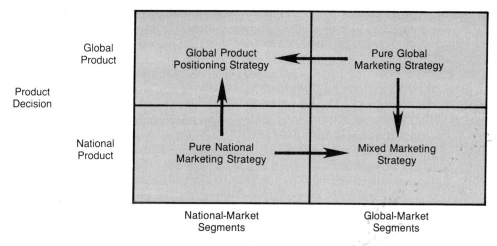

FIGURE 11-3   **The Global Marketing Strategy Matrix**

that exhibit a high degree of uniformity. Many companies seek to use this strategy, but none pursues it totally. Coca-Cola, IBM, Procter & Gamble, and Xerox are examples of companies that attempt to use pure global marketing strategies.

Despite the obvious economies and efficiencies, the pure global marketing strategy is more an ideal than a reality. Its limitations are primarily market induced. From a company viewpoint, the pure global marketing strategy is probably economically and competitively preferable if it is competing in a global industry and its competitive advantages are based on global brand-name recognition, cost-leadership, or product technology strategies. All these conditions can be found among a large number of industries and companies.

From a market perspective, the pure global marketing strategy is feasible only if market conditions are virtually identical *across* markets. For example, a company would have to have the same competitive position in all foreign markets, and the features, benefits, market position, and use conditions of its products would have to be identical across foreign markets. The foreign markets would also have to be in the same stage of the product life cycle, have identical marketing demand situations, response characteristics, infrastructures, and be protected by similar tariff and nontariff barriers.

Since market conditions vary across foreign markets, there is no such thing as a pure global marketing strategy. Instead, there are many different global strategies. Although these strategies have many of the attributes of a pure global marketing strategy, they also have some of the attributes of the global product positioning strategy, or the mixed marketing strategy. Coca-Cola, for example, is the market leader in all the markets in which it competes; however, because of its emphasis on availability, it has had to modify its channel strategy to handle differences in market conditions. To some extent, it is pursuing a global product positioning strategy; and to support its global competitive positioning strategy in some markets, it has found it necessary to increase its product offerings. Thus it is pursuing either a national marketing strategy in particular markets or a mixed marketing strategy across several markets.

The value of the global marketing strategy lies in the framework it provides for establishing the objectives, standards, and procedures to be used worldwide. It is the standard toward which the company strives and the basis for marketing policies.

Pure National Marketing Strategy. A company offering a product designed to meet the unique needs of a national target market and using a marketing mix specifically tailored to meet local market and competitive conditions is understood to be using a pure national marketing strategy. This strategy is more likely to be employed by domestic companies and global companies in their domestic and major foreign markets. If a national marketing strategy is successful, the tendency among global companies is to use either a *global product positioning strategy* or a *mixed marketing strategy* in other markets. That is, the product—or some element of the marketing mix—becomes the basis, or core element, for marketing strategies implemented in other markets.

There are many examples of pure national marketing strategies and their eventual extension to other markets. A few are presented in the following paragraphs.

Global Product Positioning Strategy. The core element in this strategy is a standardized product developed by the company for its home market or one of its larger foreign markets. What is important is the position that the product occupies in a specific national-market segment. Since this market segment position is determined largely by consumer perceptions, the task of the marketing management team is to use the marketing-mix elements to develop, alter, or reinforce the product's position in the consumer's mind. This can be done in several traditional ways, such as emphasizing the product's features, benefits, use patterns, or even other products.[11]

For example, Johnson & Johnson's Reach toothbrush was developed for the U.S. market but subsequently made available to its foreign marketing subsidiaries to more quickly recoup R&D and testing expenditures. Except for the brand name, the subsidiaries were given considerable latitude in deciding on the local marketing mix. The reason for this was that it was felt that local customer preferences, usage patterns, and factors such as competing products, varied sufficiently among markets to warrant a nationally focused approach.

In general, the global product positioning strategy is the result either of modifying a pure global marketing strategy (in order to handle significant differences in the market conditions of major markets) or of the extension of a core product designed as part of a pure national marketing strategy. From a corporate perspective, this strategy makes sense when economies of scale or cumulated experience are present and when high product development costs are involved. From a market perspective, the strategy makes sense if the product serves a need that is mostly culture free but requires perceptual positioning to ensure a favorable reception. For example, the act of shaving is culture free; the habit of shaving may indeed be culturally defined. Thus to create demand, a razor-blade manufacturer might attempt to modify the shaving habits of a local market through the use of persuasive advertising and aggressive channel positioning.[12]

Mixed Marketing Strategy. The mixed marketing strategy can be based on either a particular product or one of the marketing-mix elements considered instrumental in the company's success. In both cases, the product (or marketing-mix element) is used as the basis of a marketing program in a global-market segment. That is, the company attempts to exploit a market-tested element of its strategy across several national markets. The other elements of the strategy are used to handle differences in the company's competitive market position and variations in local market conditions.

Exxon's tiger in the tank theme is a classic example of a company using an advertising theme designed for one market in a global-market segment.[13] Polaroid's instant camera exemplifies the extension of a U.S.-oriented product concept to a global-market segment. In the case of Polaroid, however, market conditions and its competitive market position vary considerably across foreign markets.

Corporate Global Marketing Strategy Practices

Business International recently found that companies may define their market strategy as either global or national although it incorporates elements of both.[14] Brand names, packaging, and physical characteristics of product may be standardized to gain a competitive advantage, as may a basic advertising message. But pricing (based on local manufacturing costs, competitive pricing, taxes, and so on), sales techniques, nuances in advertising copy, and the selection of channel intermediaries may be differentiated by market.

In addition, some of the companies surveyed found a two-step approach useful. The first step typically involves the development of a systematic corporatewide approach to product, pricing, distribution and sales policies, and the role of central marketing research. The resulting policies, which provide the basic framework within which local marketing decisions are made, are reviewed periodically and updated as required. The second step involves tailoring the core marketing strategy elements to meet local needs in order to optimize marketing success. That is, the surveyed companies used a core marketing strategy coupled with a *global product positioning strategy,* a *mixed marketing strategy,* or both.

An earlier survey by Sorenson and Wiechmann supports the Business International survey.[15] They interviewed 100 executives from 27 global companies in the food, soft drink, soap-detergent-toiletries, and cosmetics industries. As shown in Figure 11-4, the marketing program and its elements exhibited a high, but not overwhelming, propensity to be standardized across foreign markets.

Although the Sorenson and Wiechmann survey was concerned only with the European and U.S. operations of such companies as Coca-Cola, General Foods, Nestlé, Procter & Gamble, and Revlon, its findings are still of value; they indicate that some accommodation is made for local conditions. The marketing-mix elements most susceptible to local conditions are price, creative expression, sales promotion, media allocations, and size of outlets. Significantly, the study determined that many decisions that deviate from a standardized approach were made in order to meet local mandatory requirements of the market, such as government laws. Further, standardization was found to be more the result of the marketing management process than of any benefits to be gained in the marketplace. That is, a company's goals and the way its marketing activity was structured and controlled

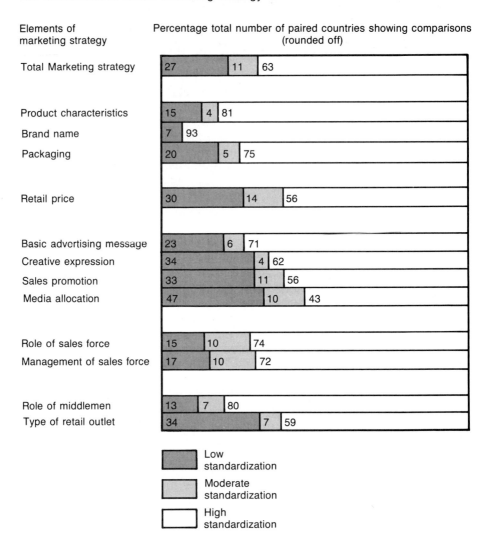

Elements of marketing strategy	Percentage total number of paired countries showing comparisons (rounded off)
Total Marketing strategy	27 / 11 / 63
Product characteristics	15 / 4 / 81
Brand name	7 / 93
Packaging	20 / 5 / 75
Retail price	30 / 14 / 56
Basic advertising message	23 / 6 / 71
Creative expression	34 / 4 / 62
Sales promotion	33 / 11 / 56
Media allocation	47 / 10 / 43
Role of sales force	15 / 10 / 74
Management of sales force	17 / 10 / 72
Role of middlemen	13 / 7 / 80
Type of retail outlet	34 / 7 / 59

Low standardization

Moderate standardization

High standardization

FIGURE 11-4   Standardization of Marketing Strategy Elements (Source: Reprinted by permission of the *Harvard Business Review*. An exhibit from "How Multinationals View Marketing Standardization" by Ralph Z. Sorenson and Ulrich E. Wiechmann [May/June 1975]. Copyright © by the President and Fellows of Harvard College; all rights reserved.)

tended to have a greater influence on marketing decisions than did the market characteristics.

FOREIGN MARKETS AND THE GLOBAL MARKETING STRATEGY _____

The way a company classifies its foreign markets has an important bearing on marketing strategy decisions. How foreign markets are classified indicates their strategic importance to the company and the role they are to play in achieving corporate objectives. Thus, the foreign market's classification reflects the marketing resources that will be allocated to it and the degree of corporate control exercised in the formulation and implementation of marketing strategies. To some extent, how the foreign market is classified also determines the degree to which elements of the marketing mix may be modified.

Classifying Foreign Markets

Three major assessments are involved in classifying foreign markets: (1) a portfolio assessment, (2) an assessment of the market's potential, and (3) a market-presence assessment. We discuss these in the order listed. However, this order does not necessarily imply a sequential decision process. The decisions are highly interdependent and may occur simultaneously.

Global Portfolio Assessment

As already mentioned, global companies using a global-market segment strategy view their foreign markets somewhat differently from companies pursuing a national-market segment strategy. The difference is most pronounced in how these two types of global companies classify foreign markets when using the portfolio techniques discussed in Chapter 9.

In the case of global-market companies, the portfolio techniques are used as aids in evaluating business units across foreign markets. The foreign markets are primarily treated as elements of a particular business unit's activities; therefore, they are not looked at individually at this stage of the strategic assessment. In the case of national-market companies, the portfolio techniques are used to evaluate the strategic merits of each foreign market. The two perspectives are illustrated in Figure 11-5 using the growth–share matrix.

A global-market company would probably use global industry growth rate and relative global market share as proxies for determining the competitive positions of its various business units and the cash-flow requirements to operate these units. Three major assumptions support this approach. First, the industries in which the company's business units are competing are sensitive to the cumulated experience effect. Thus, the company with the largest relative share is assumed to be the lowest cost producer. Second, the foreign markets are supplied from strategically located production facilities. Third, foreign-market sales are included in computing overall global market shares, and are therefore integral parts of the business unit's global competitiveness.

Following the logic of the growth–share matrix in Figure 11-5, cash cows—including home and foreign market operations—would be used to finance the activities of stars and those question marks identified as having future potential. Question marks not chosen for additional investment would be managed to generate short-term cash flow. Dogs would be either divested or harvested.

The implications for marketing are obvious but quite general. The central objective underlying the marketing strategies used by business units designated as cash cows is to *maintain* market share in order to continue generating large positive cash flows. The objective of the marketing strategies used by star business

Portfolio for a Global-Market Company

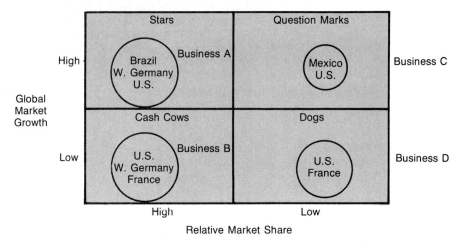

Relative Market Share

Portfolio for a National-Market Company

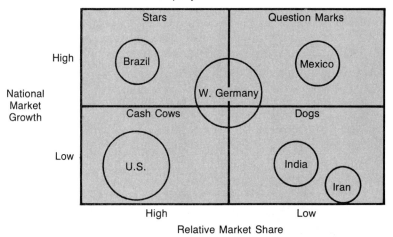

Relative Market Share

FIGURE 11-5   Foreign Market Portfolio Assessment: Global-Market and National-Market Companies (Example is for U.S.-based companies)

units is to *build* market share, thereby strengthening the company's competitive position. Increasing market share and strengthening competitive position are also appropriate strategies for question-mark units, whose shares must grow if they are to become stars. The objective of the marketing strategies used by business units classified as dogs and retained by management to be *harvested,* is to generate short-term cash flows, regardless of long-term market effects.

A *national-market* company would use the national industry growth rate and the relative national market share to arrive at an assessment of its competitive position and the cash flow required to operate in each foreign market. Three major assumptions and one exception underlie this approach. First, the industries in which the company is competing are national in scope and are probably more sensitive to economies of scale than to cumulated experience. Second, the market is supplied by local production facilities. Third, market share estimates are based strictly on national sales, so each foreign market is treated as a separate business. The exception to this rule occurs when a strategically located production facility is used to supply a number of nearby markets, *provided they have similar market characteristics and thus can be treated as one market.*

The marketing strategy implications are the same as for global-market companies, except that they deal with foreign markets rather than global business units. The marketing objectives of building, maintaining, and harvesting markets underpin local marketing strategy decisions.

The various portfolio techniques available to help management make strategic choices about their business units or foreign markets provide some direction in formulating marketing strategy. However, since they are of limited value, they do not exhaust the issue of classifying foreign markets. For example, they do not include other factors that may play a more decisive role in the formulation of marketing strategies. Further, profitability depends on more than just market share, and market share is not always a good proxy for competitive position.[16] And the techniques do not take into account coordination and integration requirements and certainly do not provide detailed information.

Foreign-Market Assessment

The assessment of foreign markets is a recurring activity used to rank current *and* future markets in order to effectively allocate scarce resources *within* the broad guidelines laid down in the portfolio assessment. Three categories of factors are present in all foreign-market assessments: (1) competition, (2) market characteristics, and (3) market decision effects.[17] Each set of factors has implications for the company's marketing effort. These implications are in addition to those stemming from the company's portfolio assessment.

Competition

When evaluating competition, the company will make a distinction between local and global competitors since it may respond differently to their competitive threats. Global competitors are highly visible, generally are larger and better resourced than local competitors, and need to be reacted to, possibly on a global scale. Three competitive strategies are often used: *follow the leader, exchange of threat,* or *avoidance.*[18]

The first two strategies are quite prevalent among companies competing in global industries and involve either the addition of new markets or the expansion of in-place marketing activities. In the *follow-the-leader* strategy, the company will either invest in the same countries as its major competitors or in other countries to ensure that it maintains a similar global position. The strategies used in either case are aimed at maintaining a relative competitive position similar to that in the home market.

In the *exchange-of-threat* strategy, a company domiciled in one country establishes a market presence or increases its marketing activities in either the home market or a major foreign market of its global competitor. An example of this type of strategy would be the increased marketing activity by General Foods in Europe in retaliation to Nestlé's increased activities in the United States. The purpose underlying this strategy is to reestablish competitive stability between competitors. Another example of the strategy is Goodyear's response to Michelin's entry into the U.S. market in the 1970s.[19] In the early 1970s, Michelin used its strong European profit base to enter the U.S. market. Goodyear responded to the competitive threat in Europe, not in the United States. Had Goodyear responded entirely in the United States, it would have gained nothing in the way of new market share.

The follow-the-leader and exchange-of-threat strategies are basically *confrontation* strategies. Their use depends on a careful assessment of the company's ability to maintain or improve on its competitive position, the costs involved in entering new markets or mounting an aggressive marketing campaign in an existing market, and the likely reactions of competitors. The marketing strategies generally used in supporting these corporate-level strategies are aimed at developing a market position, penetrating a market, or challenging the market position of the competitor.

The *avoidance* strategy is often used by companies in the first stages of international expansion or by companies that lack the resources to directly challenge their competitors. Foreign markets that do not pose a threat to the company's major global competitors are selected and then developed. Davidson cites Control Data as an example.[20] This company's first foreign markets were Israel and Hong Kong. It subsequently entered Yugoslavia and other Eastern bloc countries, countries believed to be of only secondary importance to its major competitors.

Local competitors pose yet another type of competitive threat since they are confined to one foreign market. They are intimately knowledgeable of local conditions, may be protected to some extent by government regulations, and may have a competitive position with local suppliers and channels of distribution. They may also have a perceptual advantage in that they are viewed as "national" companies. In the absence of global competitors, the company can, and probably should, concentrate its marketing efforts on establishing a firm footing in the market, developing a competitive position, and building market share. These objectives involve a high degree of management commitment, corporate resources, localized marketing strategies, and time. National-market companies are more likely to face this type of situation than are global-market companies. Also, because of the high degree of commitment required, geographic concentration (discussed in Chapter 10) is probably preferable to geographic diversification. Finally, the global company must possess competitive strengths that local competitors lack and must be able to transfer these strengths to the foreign market. Therefore, the company is likely to emphasize the *advanced management skill strategy* (also discussed in Chapter 10). In terms of the marketing effort, the company must make use of its standardized marketing process, the experience gained in similar market situations, and the core elements of marketing programs developed for and proved successful in other markets.

Market Characteristics

The analysis of foreign markets involves two interdependent evaluations: an evaluation of the *market's environment* and an evaluation of the *market's potential*. Since these activities and related techniques were covered extensively in Chapter 8, we will look only at broad parameters. These assessments focus on the market's current situation and near-term trends.

The market-potential assessment is done to determine the foreign market's current and future status in the company's global plans. New foreign-market opportunities and established foreign-market operations are treated separately. The new market assessment is done to determine if it should be added to the company's current portfolio of activities. The assessment of current operations is done to determine whether these operations should be maintained at their current levels of activity or changed and, if changed, how. In both cases, however, two broad questions must be answered by the assessment:

1. How does the market fit in with the company's marketing activities in size, growth rate, stage of development, nature of demand, response characteristics, product offerings?

2. What is required of the company's resources, product offerings, type of market presence, and so on to establish a competitive market position, to gain, or to expand on its market share?

The common purpose of the first question is to provide information useful for estimating a market's future attractiveness. These estimates include revenue and cost predictions and an appraisal of the resources needed to establish a desired competitive position and market presence. For example, the size and growth rate of the market can be used to roughly estimate the foreign market's potential for generating near-term revenue. However, the market's stage of development (income distribution, size and number of buyers, size and number of suppliers, and the market's infrastructure) and the nature of its demand (latent, irregular, full) are needed to arrive at a more accurate estimate. Further, knowledge of the market's location in the country and its response characteristics are also needed. These have direct bearing on such things as channel selection, pricing, and promotional activities. Thus, they affect operational budget requirements. Finally, the current product offering, including both company and competitor products, directly affects the company's product strategy and sourcing decisions.

The second question provides information needed to evaluate the impact that various forms of market presence will have on the company's ability to establish a competitive position and generate a desired level of income. Unlike domestic companies, global companies must effectively utilize their products, marketing skills, and resources on a global basis. Thus, they will seek a competitive position and use a form of market presence that meets local needs and market conditions while remaining optimal for the company. Campbell Soup's penetration of the Japanese market and Levi's penetration of the Mexican market (described in Chapter 10) are examples of companies changing their forms of market presence as they gained a competitive position in a foreign market, more accurately estimated a market's potential, and developed a working knowledge of its environment.

The purpose of the environmental assessment is to determine the market's economic, legal, political, and social structure and prevailing conditions. For example, the degree of stability or *uncertainty* in the economic and political dimensions of an environment has a direct bearing on the form of market presence established if the market is a new one, or how it should be changed if it is an existing one. The economic and political stability of the market largely determines the company's long-term ability to generate a steady flow of revenue. It also determines the degree of risk its assets may be exposed to. The legal and social dimensions, on the other hand, provide useful information concerning the competitive "rules of the game," the business climate, and some indication of market trends. The information collected on these four environmental dimensions is used when making decisions about additional capital expenditures, and the allocation of operating funds. Examples of the kinds of information thus collected are presented in Exhibit 11-1.

Market-Decision Effects[21]

Of particular concern to global-market companies and to national-market companies serving a cluster of markets from a centrally located production facility are the problems associated with supplying—or withdrawing from—markets. These problems can be broken down into three groups: *market-entry effects, sourcing effects,* and *administrative effects.* The local marketing effort of the company is directly affected by all three sets of problems. They impact on a variety of decisions, such as the company's presence and its local inventory, distribution, and pricing policies.

EXHIBIT 11-1 _____

Examples of Market Environmental Measures _____

Economic Measurements

Rate of growth
Manufacturing output/GNP
Rate of inflation
Unemployment
Balance of payments
Industry structure
Disposable income
Foreign investment restrictions

Political Measurements

Type of government structure
Age of political system
Number of political parties
Foreign relations and policies
Industrial policy
Monetary and fiscal policy
Government role in economy

Legal Measurements

Property rights
Patent and copyright protection
Consumer legislation
Labor legislation
Commercial codes
Repatriation (profits and investments) restrictions

Social Measurements

Population trends
Life-expectancy trends
Education (type and level)
Income distribution
Rural and urbanization trends
Literacy trends

Market-Entry Effects. The decision to add a new market or expand or contract activities in an existing market may affect the composition of the company's global activities; it certainly affects capital expenditure plans. For example, a company may have to make some extensive changes in its global strategy, as was the case when IBM decided in the mid-1980s to source Central and South American markets from Mexico. IBM's ability to serve the large Mexican market was contingent on its agreement with the Mexican government to export 90 percent of its output.

Any decision to add a new market or to expand activities in an existing market requires changes in a company's capital expenditures and staffing plans. Managers may have to be reassigned and local personnel hired, trained, or fired. Changes such as these incur large one-time costs and may impact on the timing of the market-entry decision.

Sourcing Effects. Decisions must also be made concerning which production facilities will be used to supply a new or expanded market and which will suffer because of a contraction. In both cases, the sourcing decision cannot be made in isolation. Since production-capacity utilization rates will be changed, other markets supplied from the same sources will be affected as a result of changes in production costs and delivery schedules. The former may affect local prices; the latter, inventory policies. Since the volume of the shipments is affected, sourcing decisions may also impact on delivery costs.

Administrative Effects. Administrative effects include those changes that impact operational decisions. They include, among other things, the ongoing administrative costs associated with operating in a foreign market. Thus, they have an effect on operational budgeting plans. For example, the decision to add or expand a market can have a negative impact on operations in other foreign markets, especially during the initial market-development stages when a negative cash flow typically exists. Administrative costs may exceed revenues for quite some time. These administrative costs include such things as local salaries, hiring costs, and the support of financial, accounting and industrial relations staffs necessary to meet government regulations. They may also include higher-than-normal marketing expenditures needed to establish a market position, develop channels of distribution, and create or expand an after-sales service facility.

Foreign-Market Categories

Companies often classify their foreign markets using terms that give some idea of their strategic importance and the way they are to be treated. A foreign market's classification indicates, to some extent, the types of marketing decisions that need to be made, and the levels of management (corporate, regional, local) included in the marketing strategy decision-making process.

For example, one company classifies its markets as either *agent markets* or *fully integrated markets.*[22] An agent market is a market in which the company has a licensee, a contract manufacturer, or a distributor. A fully integrated market is a market with a manufacturing and marketing subsidiary. In this particular case, agent markets are handled from a regional office, and fully integrated markets are run by a general manager (president), under whom are a financial director, production director, and marketing manager. Though marketing decisions (such as the introduction of a new product to a fully integrated market) need approval from regional headquarters, in most cases, headquarters merely "rubber-stamps" local decisions. In the case of agent markets, however, all marketing-strategy decisions are made by the regional marketing staff.

One useful way to classify foreign markets is according to operational characteristics, as *export markets, partially integrated markets,* or *fully integrated markets.* Another way is to classify foreign markets explicitly on the basis of strategic importance; the resulting continuum ranges from *noncritical national markets* to *critical national markets.* When both approaches are used, management is better able to simultaneously understand the relative operational and strategic merits of each of its foreign markets.

Integrated National Markets

Export Markets. Of the three types of markets, export markets are customarily the least controlled and developed. Many export markets are of low importance to a firm because of their limited potential or economic and political risk and are served from one or more production facilities located in other countries. However, there are exceptions. For example, Boeing, Lockheed, and McDonnell Douglas, can be classified as global-market companies, yet do most of their overseas sales in the form of exports. The characteristics and price of their commercial and military aircraft permit them to serve overseas markets from one, or just a few, production locations. Reasons of economics, such as the need for highly concentrated and large capital investments and large, highly skilled labor forces, reinforce the need for centralized production. Moreover, for many medium- and small-sized companies, the only form of international business is through exports. In all these cases, foreign markets are extremely important.

In many cases, export markets are not closely controlled by the company. Because of the need to use agents and independent distributors, the company has little control over end-market prices, the level of the sales effort, the level of the promotional effort, and the quality of the after-sales services provided the customer. Unless their products have some unique or distinctive advantage, companies have a hard time developing the competitive position they might otherwise desire. (Some of the measures that can be taken to reduce these disadvantages will be discussed in later chapters.)

Partially Integrated Markets. The company has both a legal and an operational presence in the markets included in this classification. But this presence is either a sales branch or a sales subsidiary. Although these markets are served from one or more production facilities located in other countries, the company considers the markets sufficiently important to warrant close control. The company's motivation for this form of market presence might be the desire to maintain or expand market share or to strengthen its competitive position. For example, Cica Trade, the trading arm of Cica, a large multibusiness Brazilian company, has a sales subsidiary in Hong Kong that is responsible for the coordination of marketing activities in neighboring Asian markets.

By having a market presence, the company is in a better position to control implementation of its marketing strategy and can exercise more control over the end-market pricing of its products, the selection of channel intermediaries and outlets, sales force activities, media and advertising-theme selection, levels of promotional expenditures, and after-sales services. At the same time, however, the sales branches and subsidiaries may depend on a central or a regional marketing staff for marketing research, promotional materials, and other services.

Fully Integrated Markets. This designation is generally reserved for major foreign markets and involves a manufacturing and marketing presence in the country. Because they are strategically important, the company has decided to devote considerable resources to these markets in order to establish strong competitive positions. In many ways, these markets are treated like domestic markets. They may be used as product-development sites, and the local market may be used to test-market new products and new marketing campaigns.

Critical National Markets

Most global companies implicitly or explicitly classify their foreign markets in terms of their strategic importance. The criteria used varies by company, as does the relative importance placed on each factor. However, as Hamel and Prahalad suggest, global companies must distinguish between the following five objectives:[23]

1. Low-cost sourcing (a foreign country may be critical because of labor costs, not sales);

2. Minimum scale (a foreign country may be critical because it serves several other markets in the region);

3. A national profit base (the market's sales contributes significantly to the company's cash flow);

4. Retaliation against a global competitor (the market has been selected primarily to balance a threatening move by a key competitor); and

5. Benchmarking products and technology in a state-of-the-art market (the United States is believed to be key market in terms of product innovations).

Since a foreign market's strategic importance depends on multiple factors, affiliate performance measurements and resource allocation criteria will vary across markets. For example, profitability expectations may have to be set relatively low if the market has been selected primarily as a retaliation market.

GLOBAL MARKETING-MIX POLICIES

Given a general understanding of the framework within which foreign marketing strategy decisions are made, we are now ready to examine the implications of this framework for the various marketing-mix policies used to guide the local marketing effort. Our discussion at this point will be brief.

Marketing-Mix Policies and the Global Segmentation Strategy

The *product, pricing, distribution,* and *promotion* policies guiding a global company's marketing effort are strongly influenced by its global segmentation strategy. In turn, marketing-mix policies establish the degree of flexibility local marketing managers have when fine-tuning marketing strategies to meet local market and competitive conditions. Examples of the areas over which global companies often want consistency in decision making include intercorporate pricing, brands and trademarks, after-sales service standards, and the selection of advertising agencies.

Global-Market Companies

Although it is too sweeping a statement to say that global-market companies establish global marketing-mix policies, there are strong internal pressures for marketing-mix policies to be centrally developed, coordinated, and modified. Since these companies are competing with other global companies in global-market segments, there are strong competitive pressures to develop and market products in a *consistent* and *cost-effective* manner across foreign markets. That is, the internal tendency is to produce and market standardized products through similar channels and outlets, using global brands and trademarks, similar advertising messages, and uniform pricing strategies. There may also be pressures to provide global product warranties and (standardized) after-sales services and to use global advertising agencies. Since these companies tend to concentrate their productive capabilities in just a few countries for economic and political reasons, international sourcing (logistics) and intracompany pricing of products are critical; they are also generally centralized and tightly controlled.

In most cases, external pressures interfere with these strong internal needs, as illustrated earlier in Figure 11-4. These pressures are basically of three types: industry practices, government regulations, and market conditions.

Industry Practices. Although some industries can be classified as global for the reasons given in Chapter 10, local industry practices vary and differentially affect the company's desire and ability to implement global marketing-mix policies. A good example is the effect that national industry practices may have on a company's product warranty policy. For example, in the 1960s, Chrysler offered a five-year, 50,000-mile warranty on its Simca cars in the United States but only a two-year warranty in Europe. The reason for warranty differences was the desire to match U.S. and European industry practices at that time.[24] Significantly, Chrysler also avoided unnecessary expenses in Europe by offering a two-year warranty.

Care needs to be exercised when deciding to match or to deviate from local industry practices. For example, when the warranty covering a product is traditionally limited to basic performance, it is generally extended to all markets the products are sold in. Allis-Chalmers, Caterpillar, and Parker Pens are example of companies that offer the same basic warranty in all of their markets.[25] In these cases, the products serve the same function and are used in basically the same way and under similar conditions in all markets. Minolta, on the other hand, is an example of a company that offer the same basic warranty only in markets where its cameras are officially sold. In Minolta's case, the motivation for limiting the warranty was to reduce the flow of its cameras through unofficial channels that were taking advantage of foreign-market price differences.

Government Regulations. Government regulations can affect all marketing-mix policies. In some cases, if the company wants to be in a particular foreign market, it may have to alter its product(s) to meet local safety and health regulations and product specifications. For example, British lawnmower manufacturers did not enter the West German market because they felt the cost of meeting local noise requirements was prohibitive.[26]

Global-market companies also have to comply with local pricing and advertising requirements. Price controls are frequently used by governments in countries experiencing high inflation and in some countries for social welfare reasons. Further, the attitude of governments toward the social value of advertising varies from country to country and is reflected accordingly in local advertising laws. For example, comparative advertising—a common practice in the United States—is not permitted in West Germany, thus affecting a U.S. company's ability to use universal advertising messages based on comparative statements. Access to certain types of media, such as television, found competitively useful in some countries may be severely limited or entirely forbidden in other countries, as is the case in Denmark, Norway, and Sweden.

Market Conditions. As we will see in later chapters, local market conditions can have a pervasive influence on marketing-mix policies and decisions. For example, conditions of local use may vary considerably from country to country and therefore need to be taken into account when making product adaptation and warranty decisions. Air conditioners may be used much more heavily in some countries than in others. Outboard motors may be used for commercial fishing in some countries and recreational fishing in others.

The ability to provide a prescribed level of after-sales service may also be difficult. It depends not only on a company's market presence, but also on its ability to find suitable servicing facilities in export markets and in those places where it lacks such facilities.

These are but a few examples of the types of problems encountered when attempting to establish global marketing-mix policies. (These problems are explored intensively in Chapters 12–16.)

National-Market Companies

A national-market company faces a different set of problems and pressures than a global-market company. In this case, marketing-mix policies need to be quite flexible in order to permit local marketing managers to respond to unique national-market conditions and opportunities. At the same time, however, the policies need to encourage local managers to draw on the experience, resources, and capabilities that provide this type of global company with major competitive advantages. Thus, the marketing-mix policies developed by a national-market company tend to be used more as guidelines than as directives.

In national-market companies, local marketing managers tend to have considerable authority over product-development decisions, product-line decisions, brand and trademark decisions, pricing decisions, advertising decisions, and channel and servicing decisions. As we mentioned, Pillsbury uses many national brand names. Even Coca-Cola has developed fruit-flavored soft drinks for some national markets. As mentioned earlier, the types of outlets used also vary by market.

Although local marketing managers are given considerable latitude in their decision-making authority, the company is still interested in maintaining consistency in the standards used by local managers. The role of marketing-mix policies is to seek compatability and consistency in these decisions. For example, local marketing managers are often required to follow certain procedures when making marketing-mix decisions, and they may be restricted to adding those products that fall within limits established by the corporate or regional marketing staffs. They may also be required to meet stipulated product specifications, such as the quality and grades of the ingredients used, and to meet certain standards in their advertising and servicing of products.

Market-Mix Policies and the Geographic Expansion Strategy

A global company's geographic expansion strategy affects market-presence and resource allocation decisions. For example, a company pursuing a concentration strategy is interested in fully developing the potential of each national market it enters. It will, as a result, devote considerable management time and resources to establishing a competitive market presence in the market. This implies heavy promotional outlays, strong control of channels and outlets and, in some cases, the use of a penetration pricing strategy. On the other hand, a company pursuing a diversification strategy will limit the resources and management time used to establish a market presence in any particular country. This generally implies less promotional expenditures, greater reliance on independent distributors, and a tendency to use a skimming price strategy.

The choice of market presence largely determines which marketing-mix elements will be stressed and controlled locally. For example, export markets are often treated differently from markets in which the company has at least a sales branch or subsidiary. In export markets, the company generally forfeits direct control over channel management, end-market pricing, promotional activities and decisions, after-sales servicing standards, and so on. At the same time, however, it retains control over product decisions and often markets a standardized (or minimally modified) product and attempts to influence local decisions by persuasion.

Resource allocation decisions, on the other hand, have a strong influence on the *level* of the marketing effort in a particular market. Local advertising expenditures, sales promotion expenditures, channel discounts, sales force activities, and many other expenditures and activities are directly affected by resource allocation decisions.

Misjudging Market Segments

Because of sharp contrasts in the needs and requirements of global-market and national-market segments, considerable care needs to be taken in determining whether the company is serving global or national-market segments. Doing so is much more difficult in practice than in theory since company experience and management attitudes intervene. There are many examples of companies that have misjudged the type of markets they are serving.

The misidentification of market segments and the subsequent rejection of a company's core product have resulted in companies withdrawing from potentially lucrative markets. Such were the withdrawals of Campbell Soups and Gerber from the Brazilian market. Both companies were unable to change the habits and beliefs of Brazilian cooks and mothers concerning the preparation and nutritional benefits of their products.[27] Campbell Soups' decision to withdraw came after three years and an advertising campaign costing $2 million. The companies were unable, or unwilling, to add products to their product lines that were more culturally suitable for the Brazilian market. They possibly placed too much faith in their abilities to change behavior as a result of persuasive advertising. Because of their success in other markets with their core products (condensed soups and bottled baby foods), they also may have decided they were dealing with global-market segments instead of national-market segments and thus misinterpreted marketing research findings, ignored market research findings, or failed to ask the right questions.

SUMMARY

Domestic and global marketing strategies are essentially similar in that they consist of a target market and a marketing-mix designed to match the company's changing objectives, resources, and capabilities to the changing conditions in the targeted market at a specific point in time. The purpose of marketing strategies is to influence the level, composition, and timing of demand from one or more target markets in order to help the company achieve its objectives. There are, however, important differences between domestic and global marketing strategies.

The factors that distinguish global marketing strategies from domestic marketing strategies can be divided into four groups. First, global marketing strategies need to be responsive to differences in the competitive environments of the foreign markets. Second, they must be responsive to differences in the needs and requirements of these markets. Third, the responses obtained from foreign markets must be in line with and supportive of the strategic roles of those markets in the company's portfolio of foreign activities. Fourth, they must accentuate the company's competitive advantages within and across foreign markets.

The company's global marketing mission broadly defines the parameters within which global marketing strategy decisions are made. It defines the company's global segmentation strategy, the marketing approach to be used, and the method to be used for allocating foreign-market expenditure levels. These, in turn, specify the type of marketing strategy to be used in a particular foreign market.

Companies marketing to one or more foreign markets can opt to serve the same market segments in all countries using one marketing strategy, the same market segments but with different marketing strategies, or some combination of strategies. The choice of market segmentation strategy depends on many factors, among them the company's previous international experience, its products and technologies, and management preferences. Most important, of course, are the needs and requirements of the target markets and whether they are universally or nationally defined. This is strongly influenced by the types of products the company markets. At the same time, however, companies that have been successful in marketing to one or more foreign markets tend to try to replicate their experience in other foreign markets without changing or adapting their domestic marketing strategy. Moreover, companies dominated by an ethnocentric management tend to use a global-market segmentation strategy; those dominated by a polycentric management, a national-market segmentation strategy.

The global company can seek either to use the same marketing approach in all its foreign markets or to vary the approach according to competitive and market conditions. Competition with other global companies has a strong influence on which foreign markets are considered important and which peripheral. This, in turn, sequentially affects decisions and (1) the competitive position to be taken in, (2) the resources to be allocated to, and (3) the marketing strategies to be used in, specific foreign markets.

DISCUSSION QUESTIONS

1. Explain what is meant by *global marketing mission* and how this mission could affect the marketing activity of a U.S. company in South America.
2. Distinguish between a global-market segment and a national-market segment. What are the marketing implications for a company serving national-market segments on a worldwide basis?
3. Distinguish between a global-market segment strategy and an undifferentiated marketing strategy.
4. Contrast a "pure" global marketing strategy and a "pure" national marketing strategy. What conditions would need to prevail for the former strategy to be feasible?
5. What are the major groups of factors that must be taken into account when conducting a foreign-market assessment? Include examples of each group of factors in your answer.
6. Discuss the implications that the company's geographic expansion strategy may have on the ability of a local marketing manager of a

foreign subsidiary to develop and implement marketing programs.

ADDITIONAL READING

Hallen, Lars, and Jan Johanson, "Industrial Marketing Strategies and Different National Environments," *Journal of Business Research,* Vol. 13, December 1985.

Johansson, Johny K., and Hans B. Thorelli, "International Product Positioning," *Journal of International Business Studies,* Vol. 16, Fall 1985.

Keegan, Warren J., Richard R. Still, and John S. Hill, "Transferability and Adaptability of Products and Promotion Themes in Multinational Marketing—MNCs in LDCs," *Journal of Global Marketing,* Vol. 1, Fall–Winter 1987.

Levitt, Theodore, "The Globalization of Markets," *Harvard Business Review,* May–June 1983.

Marr, Norman E., "Understanding Customer Service for Increased Competitiveness," *International Marketing Review,* Vol. 4, Autumn 1987.

Martenson, Rita, "Is Standardization of Marketing Feasible in Culture-Bound Industries? A European Case Study," *International Marketing Review,* Vol. 4, Autumn 1986.

Quelch, John A, and Edward J. Hoff, "Customizing Global Marketing," *Harvard Business Review,* May–June 1986.

Van Mesdag, Martin, "Winging It in Foreign Marketing," *Harvard Business Review,* January–February 1987.

Walters, Peter G. P., "International Marketing Policy: A Discussion of the Standardization Construct and Its Relevance for Corporate Policy," *Journal of International Business Studies,* Vol. 17, Summer 1986.

ENDNOTES

1. Philip Kotler, *Marketing Management: Analysis, Planning, and Control* (Englewood Cliffs, N.J.: Prentice-Hall, 1984), p. 15.
2. For a good discussion of global strategy implications, see Michael E. Porter, "Changing Patterns of International Competition," *California Management Review,* Vol. 28 (Winter 1986), pp. 9–40.
3. The Coca-Cola Corporation, 1985 Annual Report.
4. For a discussion of some of these points, see Thomas Hout, Michael E. Porter, and Eileen Rudden, "How

Global Companies Win Out," *Harvard Business Review,* September–October 1981.

5. Ibid.

6. The Pillsbury Company, 1985 Annual Report.

7. The four competitive market positions used in this chapter were adopted from Philip Kotler, *Marketing Management,* Chapter 12.

8. The Coca-Cola Corporation, 1985 Annual Report.

9. Gary Hamel and C. K. Prahalad, "Do you really have a global strategy?" *Harvard Business Review,* July–August, 1985, pp. 139–146.

10. Michael E. Porter, "Changing Patterns of International Competition," p. 20.

11. Yoram J. Wind, *Product Policy: Concepts, Methods, and Strategy,* (Reading, Mass.: Addison-Wesley, 1982), pp. 79–81.

12. For an interesting example of this particular problem, see the case study "Gillete Industries Ltd. (F)," ICCH 9MIF, Harvard Business School.

13. John K. Ryans, Jr., "Is It Too Soon to Put a Tiger in Every Tank?" *Columbia Journal of World Business,* March–April 1969, pp. 69–75.

14. *161 More Checklists: Decision Making in International Operations,* (New York: Business International Corporation, 1985, p. 92).

15. Ralph Z. Sorenson and Ulrich E. Weichmann, "How Multinationals view Marketing Standardization," *Harvard Business Review,* May–June 1975, pp. 38ff.

16. Michael E. Porter, *Competitive Strategy: Techniques for Analyzing Industries and Competitors* (New York: Free Press, 1980), pp. 363–367.

17. For additional discussion and another way of grouping the factors used in assessing foreign markets, see William H. Davidson, *Global Strategic Management* (New York: John Wiley & Sons, 1982), Chapter 3.

18. The names attached to the three strategies and the discussion draw heavily from Davidson, pp. 85–94.

19. Hamel and Prahalad, op. cit., p. 146.

20. Davidson, op. cit., p. 94.

21. For a fuller discussion, from which this one draws heavily, see Davidson, pp. 109–114.

22. *Designing the International Corporation Organization* (New York: Business International Corporation, 1976), p. 92.

23. Hamel and Prahalad, op. cit., p. 146.

24. Vern Terpstra, *American Marketing in the Common Market* (New York: Praeger, 1967), p. 80.

25. Subhash C. Jain, *International Marketing Management* (Boston: Kent, 1984), pp. 375–376.

26. Vern Terpstra, *International Dimensions of Marketing* (Boston: Kent, 1982), p. 89.

27. "Campbell Soup Fails to Make It to the Table," *Business Week,* October 12, 1981, p. 66, and "Gerber Abandons a Baby-Food Market," *Business Week,* February 8, 1982, p. 45.

PART THREE CASES
5. KNP Papier N.V.

Koninklijke-Nederlandse Paperfabrieken N.V. (KNP), or Royal Dutch Papermills, specializes in the production and sale of paper and paperboard products to serve the printing and packaging industries throughout the world. The firm originated in 1850 as a small papermill on the Maas River in the province of Limburg in the Netherlands, and this location in the city of Maastricht continues to be the site of one of the three modern Dutch papermaking mills operated by the firm. Another papermill containing two papermaking machines is located across the Maas in Belgium, while the firm also produces packaging materials at various European locations and has investments in paper merchant operations in a number of countries.

These activities reflect a progressive expansion of the firm, and the corporate headquarters for the management of the domestic and international activities of the firm occupies a modern office building located at Erasmusdomein 50, in a newer portion of the ancient and historic city of Maastricht. It is here that Herr Wilmer Zetteler, the Commercial Director of KNP België, considers his response to an interviewer's questions concerning the emerging international business strategy of KNP and the decisions that will be necessary to meet the challenges faced by the firm he represents. Mr. Zetteler appreciates that any reply he might make must be understood in the context of the emerging position of his firm in the paper industry and the European Community.

KNP AND THE WORLD PAPER INDUSTRY

The evolution of the papermaking industry and the emergence of the modern European economic

This case was prepared by Alan D. Bauerschmidt, Professor of Management, University of South Carolina, and Daniel Sullivan, Tulane University.
Copyright © 1988 by Alan D. Bauerschmidt and Daniel Sullivan.

system has shaped the development of KNP. In the year immediately following World War II, the relatively undamaged but depreciated plant at Maastricht produced only 10,000 tons of paper, but by 1950 the firm had begun its pioneering effort in the production of coated paper and became the first European producer of such papers, using technology obtained under a license from the Consolidated Paper Company in the United States. A companion plant, also producing the top grade coated paper used in the printing of brochures, art books, and catalogues is located at Nijmegen on the Waal River. Another mill at Meerssen, a town outside the city limits of Maastricht, produces uncoated papers that are world renowned in the markets for colored and watermarked paper, although the overall demand for such traditional forms of paper remains small and the capacity of the three papermaking machines at this plant totals only 27,000 tons per year.

The oil price shock of 1973 led the firm to reconsider its fundamental strategy and further specialize in the production of high-grade coated papers to gain prominence in international markets. This is a field of activity in which the firm was already a world leader, and it has expanded that position in the specialized grades of paper it now produces. A mill was constructed at Lanaken, across the Maas in Belgium, to further advance this niche strategy in the area of lightweight coated paper. The products of this plant, incorporated as KNP België, are used mainly in the printing of magazines, brochures, catalogues, and promotional material. This plant became the site for the addition of a second papermaking machine in 1986, increasing the capacity of the plant by 175,000 tons of paper each year. The original Fourdrinier machine at this location has an annual capacity of 115,000 tons, and the combined capacity of the four mills operated by KNP in the two countries is approximately 700,000 tons per year, with a total of seven papermaking machines in addition to the three small machines at the Meerssen plant.

The separate packaging division of KNP has nine plants that produce various forms of paper and paperboard for the packaging industry and other industrial applications. These products include solid, folding, corrugated, and other board products for the converted manufacture of boxes. In addition, the plants at Oude Pekela and Sappemeer produce a greyboard used in the manufacture of files, jigsaw puzzles, books, and various types of deluxe packaging. This product of KNP's Verpakkingsgroep is exported to manufacturers in 35 countries under the Kappa board trade name, and the firm is the world's largest manufacturer of this product.

The plant at Oude Pekela in the Netherlands' northern province of Groningen also produces the solid paperboard that is used in the manufacture of boxes that are necessary for the export of packaged products, as well as some typical products such as flowers, vegetables, and fruit. This paperboard product is manufactured on machines similar to those used in the manufacture of paper, but the paperboard machines of KNP use purchased waste paper, rather than virgin pulp, as a raw material in the manufacturing process. The firm owns and operates eight waste-paper collection firms that have a capacity to provide 250,000 tons of this raw material each year. Some 30,000 tons of this capacity was added during 1986 with the acquisition of two firms.

A factory in the Dutch town of Eerbeek produces folding box board. This product consists of thin layers of board used mainly for boxes and packaging, and the pharmaceutical and food industries create a heavy demand for this product of KNP. Again, as with all the paperboard manufacturing conducted by KNP, waste paper is the raw material used in the manufacture of this product. Overall, KNP processes 500,000 tons of waste paper in the course of a year's operation, and there is strong price competition from nearby firms in West Germany for this essential raw material.

In 1986, KNP acquired the German firm of Herzberger Papierfabrik Ludwig Osthushenrich GmbH that manufactures boxes in four locations in West Germany. The Oberstrot plant gained in the Herzberger acquisition also produces liner and corrugated board used in the manufacture of boxes and other packaging applications. The Herzberg and Oberau plants that were acquired also produce the corrugated materials used in box converting operations, while the Herzberg location joins the Eerbeek plant in the Netherlands in producing the folding board used in the manufacture of boxes. These acquisitions increased the capacity of the packaging division of KNP by 60 percent, and the Herzberger plants draw on the paperboard stocks of KNP for a portion of their required raw materials. It might be noted that the Herzberger operations convert 70 percent of their board output into boxes.

In addition to the four German packaging plants gained in this recent acquisition, KNP has ownership positions in boxmaking operations in the Netherlands, Italy, and Spain; each of these is supplied with paper and paperboard stock manufactured by other divisions of the firm. KNP is also a partner in a joint venture with Buhrmann-Tetterode N.V. in the operation of a mill at Roermond (on the Maas River just north of Maastricht), which is capable of producing 350,000 tons of packaging paper used in the manufacture of corrugated containers. With the addition of a fourth machine at the mill in 1986, this joint venture has become one of the principal suppliers of packaging paper for the European market.

The third organizational component of KNP resulted from a series of acquisitions of paper merchants beginning in the late 1970s that served to complete the forward integration of the value chain associated with papermaking, converting, and distribution. Each of these acquisitions involved a defensive strategy to prevent competitors from capturing existing channels of distribution for KNP products. At the present time, KNP conducts paper merchant operations in Belgium, France, and the United Kingdom that complement the distribution operations of Scaldia Papier B.V., a wholly owned subsidiary of the firm at Nijmegen in the Netherlands. In addition, the firm owns an approximate 35 percent interest in Proost en Brandt, the largest paper merchant in the Netherlands, located in Amsterdam.

Exhibit 1 displays the group structure of KNP, while Exhibits 4 and 5 summarize the plant capacity of the principle divisions of the company. Exhibits 2 and 3 provide a financial summary of the activities of the firm as drawn from the current annual reports.

EXHIBIT 1
KNP Papier N.V.
Group and Divisional Organization

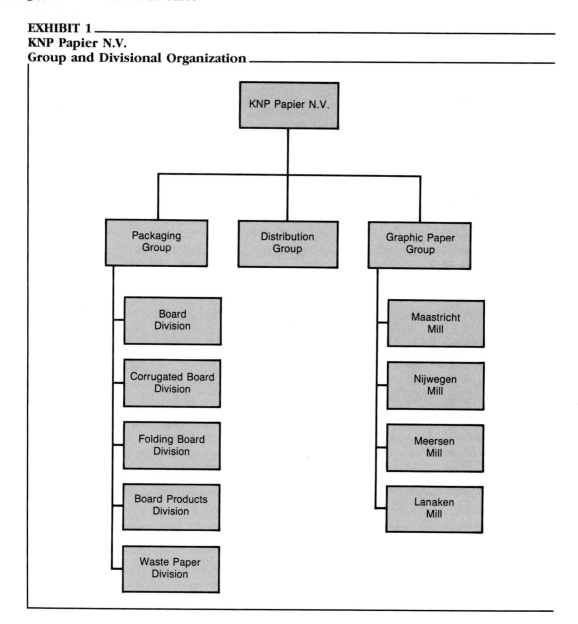

Internationalization of the Firm

The extension of KNP's activities outside of its home country is not surprising; along with most other Dutch manufacturers, the firm has always been an exporter and maintained an international perspective. The market for paper in the Netherlands is insufficient to support a plant dedicated to that market, and any firm manufacturing paper in the Netherlands must visualize a market that extends beyond the borders of its home country. Europe is KNP's principal market, and in 1986, 75 percent of its paper products and 45 percent of its packaging materials were sold outside the Netherlands.

In fact, all of the products produced by the firm are manufactured for the larger European market, as there is no distinct market for paper in

EXHIBIT 2
KNP PAPIER N.V.
BALANCE SHEET
(Figures in Thousands of Dutch Guilders)

	1986	1985	1984	1983	1982	1981	1980	1979	1978	1977
ASSETS										
Tangible Fixed Assets	1156529	606237	433024	397588	384692	382035	341651	332083	323274	334550
Financial Fixed Assets	51848	55252	43826	7337	17752	20067	18603	19720	43716	54239
Inventories	289363	201059	203194	182381	178384	185376	163377	157340	130188	117327
Accounts Receivable	418355	260556	267031	227434	203701	199923	162865	162105	123938	116868
Cash	185307	195864	10938	8311					5471	9572
	2101402	1318968	958013	823051	784529	787401	686496	671248	626587	632556
LIABILITIES AND EQUITY										
Issued Share Capital	82810	74180	70943	70943	59185	56909	56909	56909	56909	56909
Share Premium Account	103691	58784	41644	41644	31420	33696	33696	33696	33696	33696
Other Reserves	421543	330634	255009	206545	173966	168820	165382	165322	168871	164501
Shareholders Equity	608044	463598	367596	319132	264571	259425	255987	255927	259476	255106
Minority Interests in Group Companies	104918	70786	2215	123	123	140	106	103	103	103
Equalization Fund (Subsidiaries)	180434	70858	61451	47677	39464	34135	22325	1037	3894	
Group Equity	893396	605242	431262	366932	304158	293700	278418	266067	263473	255209
Provisions	198743	102802	105403	92809	118259	117348	109842	114348	112826	118911
Long-Term Liabilities	535398	271398	137988	147820	166002	147535	110017	121448	130684	108578
Current Liabilities	473865	339526	283360	215490	196110	228854	188219	169385	119604	149858
	2101402	1318968	958013	823051	784529	787437	686496	671248	626587	632556

EXHIBIT 3
KNP PAPIER N.V.
PROFIT AND LOSS STATEMENT
(Figures in Thousands of Dutch Guilders)

	1986	1985	1984	1983	1982	1981	1980	1979	1978	1977
Net Sales	1581491	1616344	1496887	1213461	1174308	1164384	1065293	950886	816592	717514
Changes in Inventories	4079	11301	3587	−9165	8870	8387	4326	11504	5439	2762
Own Work Capitalized	7191	6573	4077	5274	5609	5782	5214	3573	2879	1263
Other Operating Income	8672	2583	475	796	2241	1331	652	2318	1949	529
	1601433	1636801	1505026	1210366	1191028	1179804	1075485	968281	826859	722068
Raw Materials and Consumables	855784	917468	944217	717926	722904	742812	627443	524025	419638	411239
Work Subcontracted and Other External Costs	89073	82489	63485	59173	52316	51036	53421	50912	42925	33238
Labor Costs	316833	314731	288278	283633	290399	287311	289270	273932	250956	205788
Depreciation of Tangible Fixed Assets	74809	71547	55113	54758	52836	51524	51290	50132	47685	44675
Other Operating Costs	69786	59666	49572	42649	30245	39891	39842	36867	32136	25563
Total Operating Costs	1406285	1445901	1400665	1158139	1156700	1172574	1061266	935868	793340	720503
Operating Results	195148	190900	104361	52227	34328	7310	14219	32413	33519	1565
Profit on Financial Fixed Assets	131	167	201	0	0	0	0	0	0	900
Interest Income	5101	11558	3437	2139	2609	2527	1478	1351	1297	784
Interest Expense	13871	27624	18443	17603	22236	19854	15716	14200	12226	6564
Results on Ordinary Operations Before Taxes	186509	175001	89556	36763	14701	−10017	−19	19564	22590	−3315
Taxes Thereon	68720	66140	27643	10457	4014	−5959	−143	10284	9637	−3245
	117789	108861	61913	26306	10687	−4058	124	9280	12953	−70
Share on Results of Partly owned companies	15103	8397	1481	−1672	−2070	−2128	55	1813	920	1446
Results on Ordinary Operations after Taxes	132892	117258	63394	24634	8617	−6186	179	11093	13873	1376
Extraordinary Income	0	0	0	11764	−97	0	−14443	0	0	0
Companies Net	132892	117258	63394	36398	8520	−6186	−14264	11093	13873	1376
Minority Interests	297	−21	−16	0	0	0	0	0	0	0
	132595	117279	63410	36398	8520	−6186	−14264	11093	13873	1376

EXHIBIT 4
KNP Papier N.V.
Plant Capacities of Packaging Group

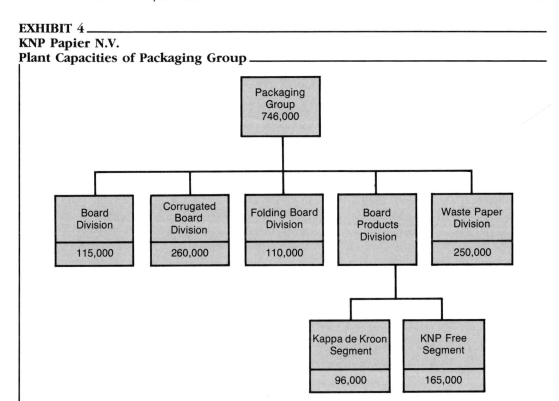

Capacity figures are in tons per annum.

EXHIBIT 5
KNP Papier N.V.
Plant Capacities of Graphic Paper Group

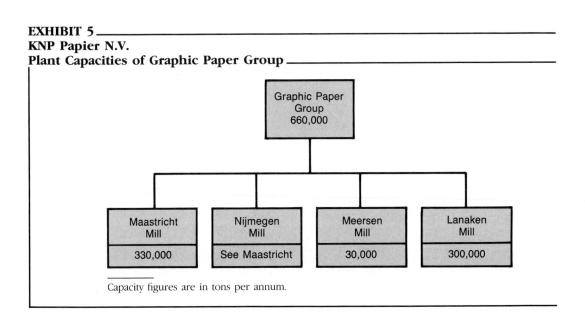

Capacity figures are in tons per annum.

the Netherlands. The portion of the total output of the firm sold outside the European market consisted of products similar to that produced for the primary market, although the firm is willing to meet the specifications of purchasers in every market that is within its capability. Therefore, it is impossible for anyone in the firm to recall the first sale overseas; however, the location of the original mill on the Maas between Belgium and Germany would suggest that sales of paper products to printers in these nations must date from the origin of the firm.

The portion of Belgium immediately adjacent to the province of Limburg is included in the Belgian province of Limburg, and the people of that province are largely Flemish, with close ethnic and cultural ties to the Dutch. A similar situation exists to the east, where there are relatively strong cultural links with the inhabitants of those portions of Germany adjacent to the Dutch border, as no natural barriers divide the two nations in this portion of the Rhine lowlands fringing on the Ardennes. The history of these two portions of Europe include a strong common link that is connected with the defensive positions held by the Romans on the Rhine and Charlemagne's capital in Aachen, immediately to the east of Maastricht.

Because of these demographic and geographic features, KNP identifies Europe and the European Community as its principal international market. The modern manufacture of paper products depends upon sufficient demand to permit capacity operation of large-volume paper machines. Each of the paper machines operated by KNP reflects state-of-the-art technology, and the firm has made a great effort and investment in the greenfield development of modern plants (the rebuilding of existing machinery to permit it to effectively compete in its specialized niches). The Netherlands has a population of approximately 15 million, and this is a woefully inadequate number to provide the demand that would absorb the capacity of a single modern paper machine manufacturing lightweight coated paper for the printing trades that is the premier product of the firm. On the other hand, the European Community has a population of over 300 million and a modern economy that can easily support a number of competing firms manufacturing the types of paper products produced by KNP.

It should be understood that in most European countries paper is traditionally marketed through paper merchants who serve to distribute the various products of paper mills to converters and printers. These merchants serve national or subnational markets. Although the original relationship of KNP with a foreign market is lost in history, its typical pattern of market development has been to establish a relationship with paper merchants in the various national markets it chooses to serve.

Sometimes this pattern of market development is not quite as straightforward. When the demand for light-weight mechanical machine coated paper in the United States emerged, KNP already maintained a relationship with a paper merchant on each coast to serve the United States market for the other products of the firm, but the lightweight coated product required a more direct approach to the printing customer. KNP skirted the traditional distributors and developed an exclusive relationship with the Wilcox-Walter-Furlong Paper Company, a paper merchant in Philadelphia, to stock and sell KNP's product in the eastern portion of the United States. The firm followed a somewhat different but equally effective route to the burgeoning market for lightweight coated paper in the western portions of the United States; there it markets the product to printers through the offices of MacMillan Bloedel, a firm that holds a major stock interest in KNP, and whose chairman and director of international operations both serve on the Supervisory Board of KNP.

The firm has progressively increased the capacity of its plants to meet increased demand in its committed markets. KNP makes a commitment to a market when it contains the potential for a continuing demand for the specialized products of the firm. Such demand can exist only in a nation or an integrated group of nations with a modern and sophisticated economy. The European Community is an example of such a market, and the emergence of the Community in the years following World War II paralleled the development of KNP's international ventures.

The foreign activities of KNP can be divided into basically two segments and two stages. The first stage included a segment that existed since the beginnings of the firm in the nineteenth century with the transport of the products of the firm to immediately adjacent localities that by force of political circumstances happened to be in other nations. At the same time, the special products of the firm were entering into the more extensive foreign trade that is historically typical of firms in the Netherlands. There is no clear separation of these two segments of the initial foreign trade of this firm.

The second stage of the international business activity of the firm was a simple elaboration of the trade conducted across national political boundaries. This was the broader cross-national trade permitted by the development of the European Community. Thus the international business activity of KNP can be divided into a pre- and post-World War II period, with the more worldwide export activity of the firm overlapping these two periods.

As indicated above, the establishment of the European Community appears as the most important factor in the development of KNP. The history of growth and development of KNP following World War II is not atypical of other manufacturers throughout the various industries of Europe. However, this apparent motivation for the expansion of international activity does not account for the management knowledge and skill that had to be present to permit the firm to grasp the opportunity provided by the reconstruction of the European economy under the new economic confederation.

The operating capacity of modern papermaking mills is the key factor in the extension of markets. The trend has been toward larger and larger capacity as the technology of papermaking has evolved. One can only speculate as to the course of actions that firms would take if technological developments advanced an opportunity for mini-mills such as has occurred in the steel industry. Papermaking is only one example of an industry that requires a highly developed economy to absorb efficient production.

The European Community is a unique design to overcome the various barriers that prevent the extension of economic activity to permit efficient production. As the Community emerged, firms in the paper industry—among others—used skilled sales agents who were proficient in dealing with the new market. At the same time, firms that were extending their activities throughout the growing market became expert in meeting the different needs of the various component national economies. Language provides no barrier to a firm such as KNP, where executives typically speak a number of the European languages. It is also apparent that residual differences in the cultures of the various nations that make up the European Community provide a negligible barrier to the international business of firms in the papermaking industry.

As far as the extracontinental trade of KNP is concerned, it exported its specialized products to South Africa and the Middle East initially. After the beginning of the present decade, it began exporting its products to Australia and the Far East, along with an emerging export activity to the United States and Canada. These new locations for trade presented no special problems and the penetration of new markets depends more on the level of economic development of the country than any other factor. For example, language barriers are unimportant, as managers in the firm have the necessary language skills, and the firm has been accustomed from its earliest days to the language necessities and cultural appreciations associated with foreign export.

The inclusion of the United Kingdom in the European Community provides insight on the way in which KNP goes about extending its international market. The firm considered its traditional markets as including France and Germany, in addition to the Benelux countries, and it was committed to this combination of markets. It then began to develop a similar long-term commitment to the paper market in the United Kingdom, which began with the unusual measure of first working through a sales agent to reach the outlets to the printing trades. At a later point, the firm establishing a more permanent position in the United Kingdom by having Contract Papers Limited, the largest of the English paper merchants, distribute its paper products. KNP now owns a 45 percent interest in this company and has an option to acquire 55 percent of the outstanding capital shares of the firm.

As indicated previously, KNP moved to the acquisition of paper merchants in many of its committed markets under the pressure of competitive actions that threaten to control such channels of distribution. This has occurred in the Netherlands, Belgium, France, and the United Kingdom. It has not taken place in Germany, which represents the other major national market of KNP in the European Community. While competitive pressures have not induced such an extension of the firm in the German market, KNP is monitoring this situation very carefully. The firm is also continuing to evaluate the possibility of extensions of its marketing effort through sales offices that would operate as adjuncts to its traditional paper merchant approach to the printing trades in each of its committed markets and to rely on sales agents to market residual output in noncommitted or developing markets.

KNP is now one of Europe's largest producers of coated paper as well as a leading producer of board. Both of these activities are highly specialized and internationally oriented fields, and it should be noted that the Netherlands imports over half its total paper requirement while exporting 60 percent of its total paper and board production. This notice is reinforced by an examination of KNP's *1986 Annual Report,* which shows that 31 percent of sales were in the Netherlands, 55 percent elsewhere in the European Community, and 14 percent elsewhere in the world.

Globalization of the Firm

KNP has not reached a stage of globalization characterized by intermediate production in various localities and final production in the specific markets served. This is more the result of the technology of paper production rather than the character of the particular strategy of KNP. While the specialized paper products of KNP are global products, their manufacture does not lend itself to a global integrated strategy. Therefore, KNP would be best described as following a multifocal international business strategy.

Following the theoretical distinction made between the concepts of internationalization and globalization, it might be noted that the paper industries in Europe and North America have different configurations. American firms tend to be more fully integrated vertically and horizontally in respect to the full range of forest products. European firms, with the exception of the Scandinavians, have little opportunity to integrate backward and acquire extensive woodlands in their home countries. Because North American firms can command woodlands adequate to supply the

raw materials for paper production and have a large domestic or regional market for their products, globalization of production is generally a moot point and of only theoretical interest in strategic planning. Because European paper manufacturers lack a wider forest-products orientation there is little inclination to consider the opportunities to exploit comparative advantage in many global manufacturing locations. Globalization, therefore, is oriented toward forward integration of distribution activities. The Swedes and Finns, on the other hand have forest resources but are handicapped by lack of a domestic market for finished paper products and face firm competitors in the markets for paper products in developed nations where high value-added products might be sold.

KNP appears among those European firms on the leading edge of globalization of distribution activities in the paper industry. As indicated previously, KNP has seen fit to acquire foreign paper merchants that are involved in the warehousing of paper products for sale to converters and printers in various domestic markets. At present KNP owns Paperteries Libert S.A. in Paris; the firm also has a 51 percent interest in Scaldia Papier N.V. in Wilrijk, Belgium, and a 45 percent interest in Contract Papers (Holdings) Ltd. in London. At home the firm holds a 32 percent interest in Proost en Brandt, N.V. in Amsterdam, acquired in the early 1970s, and a 51 percent interest in Scaldia Papier B.V. in Nijmegen.

These acquisitions took place during 1978 and 1979 as a defensive move to protect vital channels of distribution in the European Community from competitors, and Mr. Zetteler denies that the firm was principally interested in capturing profits from distribution or promoting growth through constraints on channels. Competitors began acquiring paper merchants that sold KNP products and threatened to promote the stock of goods manufactured by their own firms. The paper merchants acquired by KNP continue to stock a full range of goods, including those produced by competitors.

Paper merchants are the traditional extension of the distribution system in the paper and paperboard industry. Paper manufacturers receive orders from paper merchants for the range of common products that are intermediate goods used by final producers. They also may enter into various forms of cutting and sheeting operations as an

EXHIBIT 6
KNP Plant Locations

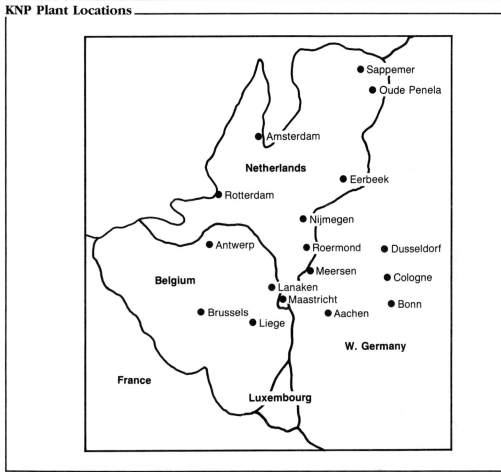

adjunct to distribution. Occasionally, a paper manufacture will sell directly to the larger printing and converting firms, but the operation of direct sales offices can be considered as the more modern development. Nevertheless, all three of these arrangements are extant and viable methods of distribution.

Paper merchants serve national markets through a fleet of trucks that transport the warehoused products to printers and manufacturers of converted paper products, who either distribute products to final consumers or supply manufacturers producing products with a paper or board component. Generally, paper merchants cater to the needs of users in their own country, and KNP's paper merchants are each national firms with wide distribution in their respective nations.

No distinct figures exist in published reports as to the results of KNP's foreign ventures in distribution channels. Overall, distribution provided 7.9 percent of operation revenues of the firm and 2.0 percent of operating profits, while the paper group provided 62.9 percent of operating revenues and 71.7 percent of operating profits, and the packaging group produced 29.2 percent of operating revenue and 26.3 percent of operating profits. These figures ignore the influence of internal transfers, which made up 8.2 percent of the total operating activity of the firm and may have had an important part to play in the reported results in respect to distribution.

Other Aspects of Globalization

While the acquisition of an ownership position in paper merchant operations is a major thrust of the international marketing strategy of KNP, it does not mark the initial globalization of the activities of the firm. The purchase of shares in Celupal S.A., a manufacturer of paper products for the packaging industry in Spain, took place some 20 years ago. The global connotations associated with the construction of the Lanaken plant can also be debated.

In many respects the creation of KNP België fN.V. in Lanaken is a prime example of the establishment of a greenfield manufacturing operation in a foreign country. The Lanaken paper manufacturing operation was established at the point when the business strategy of the firm shifted toward the production of special grades of coated paper for the printing trades. This decision was the result of the energy crisis in the early 1970s that led the firm to exploit those grades of specialty paper that had a higher value added in manufacture. It was largely distinct from the move to acquire paper merchant operations outside the country, although the two strategic moves took place during the same decade and generally support the strategy of focusing on a segment of the overall line of products in the paper industry. The creation of the greenfield operation at Lanaken was in support of an offensive European niche strategy, while the acquisition of paper merchants in France, Belgium, and the United Kingdom was a defensive maneuver to prevent erosion of existing channels of distribution that supported the more extensive range of products produced by KNP.

Some portion of the lightweight coated paper produced at Lanaken is shipped to the Netherlands: however, it is obvious that the Lanaken plant was established to serve the European market that is the principal focus of the firm. Nevertheless, it is clear that the plant might have served the same purpose if located in the Netherlands, and although the Belgian government did provide certain assistance and cooperation during the establishment of the plant this was not a prime consideration in the location of the new mill.

It can be supposed that the plant that was finally constructed at Lanaken would have had to be located somewhere in the heavy industrial triangle of northwest Europe to minimize the transportation costs of final distribution to key European markets. The Liege-Limburg-Aachen area is close to the heart of this triangle and is well served by the infrastructure necessary for paper production. The location of Lanaken (adjacent to the Albert Canal) provides direct access to the facilities of the port of Antwerp and pulp shipments from worldwide sources. It therefore is likely that any other decision to locate this plant would have been close to the actual location, which is quite ideal. The Lanaken plant does draw a small portion of its coating material requirements from the Maastricht plant, producing some economies of scale in this aspect of the operation, but otherwise the papermaking plants are self-sufficient and completely independent.

The situation is somewhat different in respect to the packaging materials operations of KNP in Germany, Italy, and Spain. The packaging converters of the firm draw on the packaging paper and paperboard manufactured by KNP in the Netherlands and Germany to fulfill or supplement their raw material requirements, and economies of scale in the production of packaging paper and board are the principal reasons for the production of these intermediate products at central locations. It is necessary that such locations be strategically situated to minimize transportation costs, and the firm is contemplating some restructuring of activities at a later point in time to rationalize production at the acquired packaging plants.

Although the paper production facilities of KNP are largely freestanding in each of the two national operations, distribution of paper products remains in part dependent on owned paper merchants and sales offices in host country locations. The packaging material production facilities of KNP depend upon multinational operations of specialized components of the manufacturing value chain. The company therefore provides an illustration of the use of two types of global strategy.

Future Globalization of Activities

Given the past strategic development of KNP, it is obvious that the firm will adopt the form of global production and distribution strategy dictated by the present state-of-the-art at any point in time. The firm is somewhat more judgmental about the degree to which it would internationalize its activity. For example, KNP will not seek to enter the American market on a short term basis simply because a temporary shortfall in supply exists in this market and existing capacity of the firm is temporary underutilized. It must be ready to make a long-term commitment of capacity to this market before it would consider exporting any product.

It also appears that KNP has no intention of locating production stages in various parts of the world to capture the benefits of comparative advantage, but this is more likely the result of the nature of the integrated operation of paper manufacturing; the industry is limited in the amount of global specialization that can be practiced. On the other hand, the firm does specialize in the production of paper and paperboard and its conversion into packaging materials in separate national locations.

A more important question is whether KNP would ever consider entering into the upstream, extractive portion of the paper business that would provide for the globalization of the firm, given the limited opportunity to manufacture pulp in the Netherlands. American observers have the example of the major papermakers in their countries being integrated backward into the extractive portion of the business and consider it a competitive advantage. Some American and Japanese firms have been enticed into participation with foreign governments in the development and harvest of forest resources to obtain sure sources of supply for pulp.

Theorists suggest from empirical evidence provided by certain industries that the evolution of globalization and internationalization includes the backward and forward integration of the firm into global arrangements. The previous example of some American and Japanese firms integrating backward into the forests of less developed nations to gain assured sources of cheap raw materials for paper manufacture is one instance of an evolutionary development in globalization. Another example of globalization is the shipping of antiquated paper machines or converting equipment to less developed countries where they can be operated in a

somewhat economic fashion with low-cost labor or energy resources.

FUTURE STRATEGIC DEVELOPMENTS

There is no doubt that the top management team of KNP is aware of these developing features of the worldwide paper industry, and it is evident that Mr. Zetteler will take these features into account as he contributes to the decisions that will shape the future of KNP. It is already apparent within his own division of the firm that technological developments at hand will shortly begin to modify the marketing and production strategies of the firm and the industry. For example, the firm plans to bring a 70,000 ton capacity chemi-thermomechanical pulp line into integrated operation with the new Paper Machine 8 at the Lanaken mill during May of 1987. This will mark the first integrated paper production operation for KNP, using hardwoods drawn from the Ardennes and replacing the chemical pulp purchased in the international commodity markets. The firm contemplates doubling this integrated capacity with a second pulp line in the next couple of years. It is rumored that chemical-thermomechanical pulp (CTMP) operations of this sort have the potential to permit reduction of the minimal efficient scale (MES) of production of high value-added paper products such as lightweight machine coated papers that are produced in bulk in the around-the-clock operation of high-speed paper machines.

The emergence of KNP and firms that follow its lead as an integrated European producer of special papers for the printing trades would undoubtedly enhance the opportunity to compete in various world markets. The United States has already witnessed the penetration of its domestic markets for printing papers as a result of a strong dollar in the early 1980's, and the superior quality of certain paper products that has been the result of innovations in production by European firms. However, any firm that wishes to make a committed entry into the U.S. market would have to consider the costs of transportation of finished paper goods and the comparative advantage of U.S. producers resulting from available forest resources.

6. Cairo Barclays International Bank_____

In the early 1980s, management at Barclays Bank International (BBI) was considering whether to expand business in Egypt—then limited to an offshore banking joint venture—to include onshore banking as well. A move to onshore banking represented an opportunity for increased profits, but management foresaw various problems and risks associated with such a move. Cairo Barclays International Bank (CBIB) was a 50/50 joint venture between U.K.-based BBI and an Egyptian state-owned bank, the Banque du Caïre. Any change in current policy would need the approval of both parent companies as well as the approval of the investment authority of the Egyptian government.

COMPANY BACKGROUND

CBIB was a joint venture between two major banks. Barclays Banks International Limited was a wholly owned subsidiary of Barclays Bank Limited, head-quartered in the United Kingdom. The Barclays Group had total assets exceeding $30 billion (U.S. dollars) and approximately 5,000 offices in seventy countries. BBI itself was Britain's largest international bank, with over 1,700 offices. The bank engaged in commercial banking, merchant banking, development financing, insurance, leasing, and trust management. Banque du Caïre, on the other hand was one of the four state-owned commercial banks in the Arab Republic of Egypt. As of December 31, 1976, the bank's total assets amounted to 919 million L.E. (approximately $1,300,000,000). Banque du Caïre was active in the fields of foreign trade, tourism, shipping, and construction. The bank's branch network consisted of branches and agencies. It was the only Egyptian bank with joint ventures in Saudi Arabia, Abu Dhabi, Bahrain, and Sharjah.

Barclays had operated independently in Egypt

from 1864 through 1956. It had played a significant role in financing the cotton crop in Egypt during World War II and had been important bankers to the Allied Forces in North Africa. By the mid-1950s Barclays' presence in Egypt amounted to 44 branches controlled by a local board in Alexandria. In the wake of the 1956 Suez Crisis, during which Britain, France, and Israel attacked Egypt, Barclays was nationalized along with other British and French properties in Egypt. The branches of the nationalized company became the Bank of Alexandria.

By the mid-1970s, however, Egypt had a new president, Anwar Sadat, and conditions had changed enough to suggest that some form of reconciliation was possible. After fifteen years of "socialism" and the virtual exclusion of all foreign investment, Egypt had passed new legislation, Law 43, encouraging the return of foreign investment. Law 43 offered a number of incentives to potential investors, including a five-year tax holiday. However, the Egypt government retained the right to approve or reject proposed investments.

The economic situation in Egypt at the time apparently demanded a radical change in government attitudes towards private business—both foreign and local. For years, Egypt had experienced a negative balance of trade and had accumulated a large international debt. Almost all industry in Egypt was state owned, inefficient, and unable to compete in world markets. Private investment, especially foreign investment, was expected to supply much-needed capital, management know-how, and technology to help Egyptian industry become more competitive. Foreign banks were encouraged to enter (or re-enter) the market in order to facilitate the financing of this endeavor. Like most developing countries, Egypt depended heavily on the banking system to promote growth in industry and other businesses since capital markets (stock markets) were nonexistent or underdeveloped.

Concurrently in London, BBI had identified the Middle East as a priority area into which to expand. In early 1974, a senior management team from BBI toured the Middle East. When in Egypt,

---

This case was prepared by Kate Gillespie, University of Texas at Austin, for classroom discussion.

they spoke with representatives of the Central Bank. The Central Bank at that time informed BBI that Egypt was about to embark on its open-door policy and suggested a possible joint venture between BBI and Banque du Caïre. When the open-door policy—enacted through Law 43 of 1974—came into effect in June, BBI considered its incentives, including the five-year income tax holiday, favorable enough to begin serious negotiations with Banque du Caïre concerning an offshore joint venture. An offshore venture would involve transactions in convertible foreign currencies only. The venture would not take deposits or make loans in the local currency, Egyptian pounds.

In March 1975, certain members of BBI management were wondering whether opting simply for an offshore joint venture was the correct manner in which to enter the Egyptian market. An onshore project would allow dealings in both foreign currency and Egyptian pounds. Nonetheless, since the statutes for CBIB had been already submitted to the Egyptian authorities for approval, they considered that it was too late to change. In the meantime, Banque du Caïre was endeavoring to form an onshore bank with several other foreign banks. It was agreed that should one of the major American banks in the negotiations drop out BBI would assume its share. This project, however, did not come to fruition. The Presidential Decree ratifying the establishment of the CBIB offshore project was passed on June 25, 1975, and the company was fully incorporated by autumn of that year.

Still, the governor of the Central Bank had given BBI approval in principle to extend its partnership with the Banque du Caïre to cover an operation in local currency. By January 1976, BBI had drawn up a Shareholders Agreement and statutes for the proposed new joint venture for discussion with Banque du Caire. Banque du Caïre, however, was reluctant to go ahead with an onshore joint venture until BBI's status vis-à-vis the Arab Boycott List was clarified. Barlcays was put on the list because of certain business connections with Israel—connections it was attempting to sever. Although BBI was struck off the boycott list 18 months later, the onshore project was essentially shelved for the next few years as CBIB's offshore project found itself in a successful period of profits and growth. In the meantime, Banque du Caïre formed

two onshore joint ventures; one with French interests, the other with Arab and Far East interests.

THE ONSHORE DECISION

Like most banks, CBIB made money by attracting deposits, then loaning out these funds less a reserve amount determined by the government. The differential between the interest rates paid on loans and those paid on deposits contributed to the bank's profits and overhead. In Egypt, interest rates were regulated by the government.

Although CBIB was established to take advantage of President Sadat's open-door policy and the consequent flow of foreign investment into Egypt, the number of foreign investment projects was lower than anticipated. Nonetheless, investment in Egypt was increasing, and CBIB's medium-term loan portfolio covered a score of projects with a total investment of nearly $150 million, including hotels, office development, hospitals, aluminum extrusion, marble tile and slab manufacture, furniture, corrugated paper boxes, oil services industries, textiles, and the production of agricultural chemicals.

Like most other Law 43 banks, however, most of CBIB's business was financing foreign trade. While industrial exports remained stagnant during the late 1970s and early 1980s, Egypt was acquiring foreign exchange from nontraditional sources. Although Egyptian petroleum reserves were limited, the country was benefiting from increasing oil sales. The reopening of the Suez Canal and increasing tourism to Egypt also contributed to the nation's foreign exchange earnings. Furthermore, Egyptians working in the oil rich Arab Gulf states sent home remittances either to their families in Egypt or to their own bank accounts in the country. (See Exhibit 1.) In late 1976, to further encourage remittances, Egyptians were allowed to open checking and savings account in foreign currencies without going through cumbersome red tape. Concurrently, the government radically loosened its strict control on imports. Pent-up consumer demand in Egypt resulted in soaring imports of consumer durables and nondurables.

In addition to making loans to projects in Egypt and financing the increased trade, CBIB de-

EXHIBIT 1 _____

Foreign Exchange Earnings From Nontraditional Sources
(in Millions of U.S. dollars) _____

	1974	*1975*	*1976*	*1977*	*1978*
Petroleum	186.4	315.1	643.3	724.7	880.5
Remittances	217.6	342.0	559.1	885.2	1773.2
Suez Canal	—	84.6	310.3	426.8	512.6
Tourism	100.5	102.2	208.8	339.6	570.4
Total	504.5	843.9	1721.5	3275.8	3727.8

Source: National Bank of Egypt statistics.

posited a proportion of its own deposits in Eurodollar accounts in Europe where they would earn higher interest rates than they could in Egypt.[1]

A move to onshore operations, however, would likely result in considerably more absolute profits due to increased business. (See Exhibits 2 and 3 for CBIB's Balance Sheet and Profit and Loss Account.) In addition, the mandatory margin between the deposit and lending rate in Egyptian pounds compared favorably with narrower margins on foreign currency lendings. An analysis of several competitors in the market suggested that onshore operations might also be advantageous. (See Exhibits 4–9). Furthermore, dealing with both local and foreign currencies would enable CBIB to better serve its corporate clients, who necessarily required Egyptian pounds as well as foreign currency. Management also believed that the bank could gain better control over its loans. At that time, CBIB had to send its customers to other Egyptian banks for their local currency needs (such as working capital for salaries and expenses accrued locally). Sometimes CBIB would arrange for the customer to use the facilities provided by Banque du Caïre. Nonetheless, management believed that the customer found dealing with two banks a nuisance.

Despite the advantages of an onshore operation, BBI management recognized that there were considerable disadvantages to such a move as well. By law, BBI could enter such a venture only as a

minority partner; that is, it could hold up to only 49 percent of equity. However, CBIB then operated under a management clause requiring 75 percent board agreement on loans and questions of policy. Therefore, BBI management was uncertain as to the extent of their possible loss of power in a decreased equity position.

Furthermore, management projected that original capital and customer deposits would give the bank enough Egyptian pounds for its first year of operation. Thereafter, it would need to locate new sources of Egyptian pounds. Banque du Caïre could possibly make pounds available, but there was no guarantee of this from month to month. Also, borrowing from the Banque would be far more expensive than simply paying interest on customers' deposits. In order to deal in domestic currency, therefore, CBIB might need to establish a fairly extensive branch system throughout Egypt to attract deposits in Egyptian pounds. Other onshore banks had needed to do this; banks with foreign partners had been highly successful in attracting customers from state-owned banks in the localities where they had opened. The step to commercial banking would require greater overhead costs—more real estate and staff requirements—whereas one of the attractions of offshore banking had been the relatively low overheads involved. Most offshore banking operated out of Cairo alone. In addition to increased overheads, there would now also be increased reporting requirements to the Central Bank.

If BBI decided to try to move on shore, it would need a local Egyptian partner to offer the 49 percent foreign equity participation. Management

_____

[1]Eurodollars refer to U.S. dollar accounts held in banks outside the United States.

EXHIBIT 2
Cairo Barclays International Bank
Balance Sheet

(As of 31st December in U.S. $)	1980	1979	1978
LIABILITIES			
Share Capital (fully paid)	10,000,000	10,000,000	10,000,000
Legal Reserve	515,240	286,540	152,440
General Reserve	2,680,000	2,380,000	1,180,000
Retained Profits	2,593,196	193,099	125,458
Shareholders Funds	15,788,436	12,859,639	11,457,898
Current & Deposit Amounts	117,219,182	61,835,088	36,351,476
Other Liabilities	4,550,275	5,141,086	1,136,678
Dividend Proposed	1,500,000	1,200,000	800,000
	139,057,893	81,035,813	49,746,052
ASSETS			
Cash at Banks*	14,349,625	18,897,145	7,305,930
Time Deposits with Banks*	32,762,780	21,478,000	16,855,550
Loans, Advances, and Other Accounts maturing within one year	77,242,870	26,414,629	14,785,360
	124,355,275	66,789,774	38,946,840
Loans, Advances, and Other Accounts maturing over one year	12,064,558	11,551,277	8,504,782
Investment at Cost	1,900,000	1,900,000	1,900,000
Fixed Assets less Depreciation	738,060	794,762	394,340
	139,057,893	81,035,813	49,746,052

* Includes deposits in Eurodollar accounts overseas

therefore had three basic options. (1) They could simply apply to have their current joint venture turned into an onshore operation. This would require BBI to relinquish its current 50 percent equity position in favor of a minority holding. (2) BBI and Banque de Caïre could form a second joint venture, one separate from their current operation. (3) BBI could look for other Egyptian partners for the new venture. At first, Law 43 banks (like CBIB) had been joint ventures between foreign concerns

EXHIBIT 3
Cairo Barclays International Bank
Profit and Loss Account

For the Year Ended 31st December, in U.S.$	1980	1979	1978
INCOME			
Interest and Commissions Received	17,664,715	9,483,844	4,416,448
EXPENSES			
Interest and Commission Paid	10,712,553	5,315,420	1,762,932
General, Administrative Expenses and Provisions	2,234,111	1,364,604	1,124,566
Depreciation	144,284	123,141	76,976
	13,090,948	6,803,165	2,964,474
Net Profit	4,573,767	2,680,679	1,451,974

and one of four state-owned Egyptian banks. More recently, however, banks established by private Egyptian citizens had been allowed to enter the market under Law 43. Therefore, a number of private interests in Egypt were likely to be interested in a joint venture with BBI. In fact, one of the new private Egyptian banks had already expressed an interest in such a partnership. In any case, BBI would need approval from the Egyptian government before undertaking any of three options. Although the Central Bank had tentatively approved the idea in the mid-1970s, it could not be sure that the government would not change its mind.

Of the alternatives, BBI preferred to keep Banque du Caïre as a partner in a move to onshore operations by changing CBIB from an offshore to onshore bank. The major reason for this was the existence of a solid base of customers who would also borrow in Egyptian pounds. Banque du Caïre's interest in such a venture, however, had fluctuated in the recent past. Banque du Caïre possiby stood to lose some of their own current customers to a new joint venture. On the other hand, a new joint venture might bring in new customers. At the moment, management at CBIB suspected that the Banque was committed up to its lending limits and might therefore look favorably upon beginning an onshore venture with BBI. However, the question of conflict of interest between Banque du Caïre and an onshore joint venture between it and BBI could become a problem. Different managers' views on the onshore issue illustrate the complexity of the issue.

> CBIB is profitable and highly respected the way it is. The problems involving organization and staffing in Egypt are significant. We were fortunate that we were able to hire back a number of employees who had worked for Barclays back in the 1950s. It's hard to predict what we'll be like if we try to double the size of the bank.
>
> We're doing well the way we are—but what about the future? Right now almost everyone in banking in Cairo is doing well. Every year more banks enter the market. Where will growth come from?

> Cairo's turned into a boom town in the last few years, and the banks have profited from it. But Egypt is still a country full of poor people; and the population growth rate is very high. Under the late President Nasser, conspicuous consumption was kept to a minimum. The differences between the haves and the have-nots is much more apparent today. Some people characterize Law 43 as bringing in "foreign banks, soft-drink factories, and real-estate speculators." There has been no overnight miracle in turning around Egyptian industry; but that's unrealistic to expect. Still, most of our customers think President Sadat's liberalizing moves have been beneficial and will bring greater prosperity to Egypt. If we move on shore we will be in a position to take advantage of this new prosperity.

> It's true that Egypt will consider foreign investment proposals for onshore banking. Still, no country feels good about foreigners taking over their banking systems. As long as foreigners deal only in foreign currencies, bad feelings can be kept to a minimum.

> Offshore banking might just be a fad of the 1970s. It seemed the ideal path for international banks—relatively low overheads and relatively little involvement in domestic affairs of the host country. Now the international banking community is taking a second look at onshore business.

QUESTIONS

1. How do you make a buck (or a pound) in the Egyptian banking business?
2. Evaluate BBI's decision to enter the market as it did.
3. Evaluate BBI's options to expand its product line in Egypt.
4. What role does the Egyptian government play in the market? How might government actions or attitudes affect BBI's options?
5. What course of action would you recommend to management at BBI?

EXHIBIT 4

Cairo Barclays International Bank

Profits (U.S.$ Millions) of Major Law 43 Banks

Name	1976	1977	1978	1979	Position
Onshore Banks					
Chase National Bank	2.78	3.96	5.4	7.1	2
Egyptian American	—	1.5	3.3	5.0	3
Suez Canal Bank[1]		(1st accounting year to 31.12.79)		7.62	1
Off-shore Banks					
CBIB	0.5	1.1	1.45	2.68	5
Misr Iran Development Bank	1.7	2.1	2.6	3.92	4
Société Arabe International de Banque	—	0.48	1.3	2.16	6

[1] The Suez Canal Bank was the only one of these major six Law 43 banks that was not a joint venture with a substantial overseas concern. Most stockholders in the Suez Canal Bank were private Egyptians, some very influential in government circles.

EXHIBIT 5

Percentage Return on Equity[2] of Major Law 43 Banks

Name	1976	1977	1978	1979	Position
Onshore Banks					
Chase National Bank	78	77	53.3	62.5	1
Egyptian American	—	53	45.62	33.6	3
Suez Canal Bank		(1st accounting year to 31.12.79)		53	2
Offshore Banks					
CBIB	5.1	9.7	11.57	21.28	4
Misr Iran Development Bank	8.6	9.7	12.84	13.9	6
Société Arabe International de Banque	—	8	12.6	19.17	5

[2] Share capital and retained profits

EXHIBIT 6

Cairo Barclays International Bank

Deposits (U.S.$ Millions) in Major Law 43 Banks

Name	1976	1977	1978	1979	Position
Onshore Banks					
Chase National Bank	83.2	124.5	140.7	194.2	2
Egyptian American	—	69	72.2	121.3	3
Suez Canal Bank		(1st accounting year to 31.12.79)		201	1
Offshore Banks					
CBIB	5.05	22.3	36.3	61.8	5
Misr Iran Development Bank	30	48	53.1	60	6
Société Arabe International de Banque	—	8.4	21.1	97.4	4

EXHIBIT 7
Loans (U.S.$ Millions) of Major Law 43 Banks

Name	1976	1977	1978	1979	Position
Onshore Banks					
Chase National Bank	20	46.5	55.8	74.2	2
Egyptian American	—	21	48.5	71.27	3
Suez Canal Bank	(1st accounting year to 31.12.79)			145.6	1
Offshore Banks					
CBIB	5.4	11.2	23.3	36.4	4
Misr Iran Development Bank	—	3.2	9	20	6
Société Arabe International de Banque	—	4.1	21.5	30	5

EXHIBIT 8
Cairo Barclays International Bank
Percentage Return on Total Assets of Major Law 43 Banks

Name	1976	1977	1978	1979	Position
Onshore Banks					
Chase National Bank	2.47	2.37	2.8	3.13	3
Egyptian American	—	1.76	2.9	2.98	4
Suez Canal Bank	(1st accounting year to 31.12.79)			3.7	1
Offshore Banks					
CBIB	3.46	3.08	2.91	3.30	2
Misr Iran Development Bank	3.38	2.16	2.08	2.21	5
Société Arabe International de Banque	—	0.62	1.2	1.94	6

EXHIBIT 9
Cairo Barclays International Bank
Percentage Growth in Total Assets of Major Law 43 Banks

Name	1976	1977	1978	1979	Position
Onshore Banks					
Chase National Bank	—	47.8	12.6	21.77	4
Egyptian American	—	—	33	46.2	2
Suez Canal Bank	(1st accounting year to 31.12.79)				
Offshore Banks					
CBIB	—	118	45.4	62.8	1
Misr Iran Development Bank	—	83	33.6	39.2	3
Société Arabe International de Banque	—	—	42	6.9	5

7. Fishing Industry

Fishing Industry Ltd. (FI) is a small Norwegian company owned by Ole Pedersen and his family. The company has for many years been exporting to Western Europe and Latin America, and occasionally to China (PRC) and other countries in the Far East. The company produces and installs equipment for land-based fish industry processing plants. Many of the physical products supplied are produced by subcontractors and FI commonly has primary responsibility for the necessary engineering, installation, and start-up work in the customer's factory.

The marketing department is headed by Petter Haag, who has direct responsibility only for Scandinavian sales. Ole Pedersen takes care of all other exports himself. The export markets are mainly serviced by agents (Europe) and trading houses (distant markets). China, however, has been serviced by FI directly. Although Ole Pedersen acts as the company's export manager, all the "paper work" in connection with exports is handled by Petter Haag's department.

Key data regarding FI's recent performance and situation are shown below.

within the equipment industry, a kind of gentlemen's agreement, that each company should concentrate on its own established markets and compete only in the more marginal markets. Thus, FI has not entered markets in the United States, Canada, and Japan. This agreement was no longer being respected and the competition—especially from Japanese, Italian, and Canadian firms—is now much keener in the markets that Pedersen regarded as "his own."

Despite offering a higher quality product than the competition, FI's activities are suffering from the stiffer competition, which has recently resulted in downward pressure on prices, stagnant sales, and lower profits. Major competitors are shown in Exhibit 2.

More than a decade ago, Pedersen had realized that the markets in the developed, Western countries were saturated and offered little growth potential. His view is supported by the recent sales data on projected 1985 sales shown in Exhibit 3.

Because of his gloomy assessment of opportunities in traditional markets, Pedersen had, during the 1970s, started paying more attention to pos-

EXHIBIT 1

	1980	1981	1982	1983
Net Sales [Nkr. million]	45	53	51	53
Home Market	9	7	12	12
Scandinavia	8	7	8	7
Europe	15	18	17	16
Latin America	8	9	8	9
Far East	2	10	5	6
Other	3	2	1	3
Operating Profits [Nkr. m]	3.1	5.2	2.9	2.8
Interest Costs [Nkr. m]	(2.3)	(2.0)	(3.0)	(3.1)
People Employed	75	83	84	85

Looking at these figures, Mr. Pedersen and Mr. Berg are not very optimistic about the future. Historically, there has been a global understanding

This case was prepared by Carl-Arthur Solberg, Norweigan School of Management, Oslo, Norway.

sibilities in developing countries. Southeast Asia and China, in particular, looked promising, so Pedersen signed up for the trade delegation tour to China arranged by the Norwegian Export Council in 1974. The Chinese visited Norway in 1975, and negotiations for a trial order started. After two

EXHIBIT 2

	World Sales in 1983 [Nkr. million]
Nippon Fish Equipment Ltd., Osaka	130
Canequip Corp., Fishing Division	100
Fishing Industry Ltd.	55
Italpescara	40
Other (4 Europe, 1 South Korea, 2 Latin America)	125
Nkr. 7 = U.S. $1	450

more trips to China and many frustrations, FI finally received an order for one small factory in 1976 valued at Nkr. 350,000. Mr. Pedersen later learned why it took two years: the Chinese had gathered information from other suppliers, and competitors in Denmark, Japan, and Canada had received similar trial orders.

The contract was fulfilled in 1977; nothing more was heard from China for more than a year. Pedersen tried to keep contact, but it was difficult to reach the persons who actually evaluated equipment and who decided what to buy. After several attempts to reestablish contact, Pedersen received an invitation to come to China in 1979. He took Mr. Andresen and Mr. Skog with him, and after two weeks he returned with a Nkr. 17 million contract for equipment for 25 factories to be delivered in 1981, 1982, and 1983.

In November 1983, the Chinese invited Pedersen and Andresen to China in order to discuss possible joint-venture operations in China. In Beijing they were presented with the outline of an agreement of cooperation with the following main features:

1. Fishing Industry Ltd. and China National Fishing Corp. would start a 49/51 joint-venture company in one of the new Special Economic Zones (SEZ) in Guangdong province, with the Chinese having majority ownership. The company would produce equipment on license from Norway and would supply the Chinese market as well as other markets in Southeast Asia and Latin America.

2. The annual sales were projected at Nkr. 100 million.

3. Fishing Industry Ltd. would be in charge of all export operations, while China National Fishing Corp. would take care of the Chinese market. China would receive about 30 percent of the annual production of the joint-venture company.

4. Total investment: Nkr. 25 million to be shared 49/51.

The Chinese suggestion seemed tempting to Ole Pedersen. FI was obviously a preferred partner for the Chinese, and the investment in China might provide a solid platform for further export operations in Asia.

However, Pedersen had also looked at other possibilities in the area. The company had for a long time been exporting to the Philippines through a Swedish trading house, but it had never achieved a good foothold in the market, mainly due to the high cost of producing in Norway. A joint-venture agreement with Philippine interests had already been considered—before the Chinese proposition was presented. With the Philippines as a base, FI could be more competitive in the (ASEAN) area.

Two important factors had to be considered:

1. The Philippines engagment might well torpedo the joint venture with China.

2. The investment required for the Philippines project was only Nkr. 8–10 million, and the financing of the project was very favorable. The project was initiated by the Asian Development Bank, which would also grant the joint-venture company a low-rate loan. FI's share of the project would be 40 percent.

Ole Pedersen concluded that the short-term return (3–4 years) on investment for the Philippines project will be substantially higher than that for

EXHIBIT 3 _____

	Sales [Nkr. m]		
	1975	*1980*	*1985**
Western Europe	110	105	110
Eastern Europe	50	50	55
United States/Canada	90	95	110
Latin America	30	40	50
Far East	40	55	75
Africa	15	20	25
Other	35	40	40
	370	405	465

*Forecast

the Chinese venture. On the other hand, long term considerations seemed to favor the project in China.

Mr. Pedersen is well aware that his company is in a difficult situation and there is a lot of uncertainty within the organization as to what steps should be taken. Two possible projects are at hand—and a whole continent (North America) has not been explored at all. The Board of Directors has not yet been directly involved, but has expressed some concern about the magnitude of the projects.

EXHIBIT 4 _____
Cash Flow Analysis: China
(Figures in Million Nkr.) _____

Year	1	2	3	4	5	6
Investment costs[1]	(13.)	(12.0)				
Working Capital		(1.0)	(2.0)	(2.0)	(3.0)	(2.5)
Sales						
China	—	—	8.0	15.0	30.0	35.0
Export	—	8.0	20.0	30.0	45.0	55.0
	—	8.0	28.0	45.0	75.0	90.0
Operating Cost						
Training	1	0.5	—	—	—	—
Operations						
Salaries	1.5	4	6.5	7.5	8.5	8.5
Materials	—	3	13.0	20.0	35.0	40.0
Export cost and overhead	1	1.5	4.0	5.0	7.0	8.0
	(4)	(9.0)	(23.5)	(32.5)	(50.5)	(56.5)
Cash Flow before debt servicing	(17.0)	(14.0)	2.5	10.5	21.5	31

[1]49 percent of the investment is to be financed by Fishing Industry (FI). These may be financed by loans from the Norwegian EXIM Bank and FI equity. Required investment of Nkr. 12.2 million. With 100 percent loan, 3 years grace, 10 years payback, and 11 percent interest, FI will have the debt servicing burden depicted below:

Year	1	2	3	4	5	6
Payback	—	—	—	1.2	1.2	1.2
Interest	0.6	1.5	1.8	1.7	1.5	1.3
Total	0.6	1.5	1.8	2.9	2.7	2.5

EXHIBIT 5

Cash Flow Analysis: Philippines
[Figures in Million Nkr.]

Year	1	2	3	4	5	6
Investment Cost	(6)	(3)				
Equity	2	1.8				
Loan	4	1.2				
Working Capital	—	(0.6)	(1.2)	(1.8)	(1.7)	—
Sales	—	5.0	14.0	25.0	35	35
Costs:						
Training	0.5	0.5	—	—	—	—
Operations						
Salaries	1.	2.0	2.5	3.0	3.0	3.0
Materials	—	2.0	5.5	11.0	16.5	16.5
Marketing and						
Other overhead	0.5	1.0	2.0	4.0	6.0	6.0
	(2.0)	(5.5)	(10.0)	(18.0)	(25.5)	(25.5)
Debt servicing:						
Payback	—	—	—	(0.5)	(0.5)	(0.5)
Interest	(0.2)	(0.5)	(0.6)	(0.5)	(0.5)	(0.4)
Cash Flow	(2.2)	(1.6)	2.2	4.2	6.8	8.6

EXHIBIT 6
Market Size and Competitive Situation in Western
Europe and Asia, 1985

	Market Size mill. Nkr.	Yearly Growth 85–90*	Estimated Market Shares (%)					
			Danfish	FI	IP	CE	Pescado Portugues	Others
Norway	15	+2%	20%	75%	—	—	5%	—
Denmark	6	+3%	50	30	15	—	—	5
Sweden	6	+10%	10	55	20	—	10	5
Iceland	8	+2%	20	50	—	30	—	—
Finland	2	—	—	50	20	—	—	50
United Kingdom	15	+5%	5	40	20	15	10	—
Germany	11	+0	40	10	20	—	—	—
Benelux	7	+0	15	20	30	15	—	20
France	5	+10%	—	10	50	—	—	—
Italy	10	+12%	—	30	40	10	20	—
Spain	7	+20%	—	5	35	—	35	25
Portugal	21	+6%	5	·15	25	—	40	15
Other	2	—	—	—	—	—	50	50
Total W. Europe (mill.)	110		13	35	23	6	16	17
			Nippon	FI	IP	CE	Korea	
India	15	+10%	35%	—	30%	20%	15%	
Japan	25	+2%	85	—	—	—	15	
ASEAN	10	+20%	35	10	25	20	10	
Republic of China [PRC]	NA	NA	NA	NA	NA	NA	NA	
Other	25	+15%	60	—	5	15	20	
Total Asia	75		52	1	8	9	12	

FI — Fishing Industry
IP — Italpescara
CE — Canequip Corp.

* Forecast

EXHIBIT 7
Details of Chinese Joint-Venture Proposal

1. Pricing, Profit and Remittance Issues

During the negotiations, the Chinese have had some problems in understanding Western marketing and pricing philosophies. FI uses some 20–25 percent of turnover on marketing activities. The Chinese were suspicious about the claim that marketing was that difficult. Such cultural differences on this particular issue may prove to be a problem when prices and profits are calculated. The Chinese desire for majority shareholding and the right to designate the Chairman of the Board emphasize the acuteness of this factor. Ole Pedersen concludes that the accounting principles, and thereby the basis for profits and dividends, eventually are to be decided on by the Chinese. He is also concerned about the possibilities for repatriating the dividends and other earnings due (royalties, management fees and so on). Although the rules state that the investor has the right to repatriate earnings, the bureaucrats in the Chinese public agencies still stuck to their old habits of excessive and zealous controls, thus considerably delaying transfers.

2. Staffing and Equal Pay

Another problem is the staffing of the Chinese plant. FI could provide only four persons to train the Chinese and run the plant. It would also be necessary to train some Chinese workers in Norway, thus taxing the already scarce resources of the company. The Chinese usually emphasize this part of the technology transfer because their ultimate aim is to increase their technological skills. In addition, the Chinese are expected to require the use of the so-called "equality salary system," implying that Chinese personnel occupying similar positions as their Western counterparts in the joint-venture company should have the same salary. Most Western companies find this requirement quite unfair and onerous. Experience shows that Chinese staff—both clerical and blue collar—are not as productive and do not deserve equal pay.

3. Equity Capital

The Chinese normally insist that all the investment be in the form of equity. FI will therefore have to borrow over 10 million Nkr. Pedersen doubts his bankers will support that kind

EXHIBIT 7 (*continued*) _____

of money, given the poor operating results of the last several years. He therefore decides that a key issue during the negotiations should be alternative ways of financing the venture. It is obvious that the financial package is of utmost importance for the project. Some of the Board members have already indicated mixed feelings concerning the whole project, so the financial burden should be minimized.

4. Political Risks

Pedersen is a bit apprehensive about the political risks involved. The Chinese appear to favor foreign investment and technology, but recent reshufflings in the politbureau are perhaps a warning of harder times to come. However, his Chinese counterparts show little sign of concern and promise "business as usual."

5. SWETRADE

The Swedish trading company, SWETRADE, that acted as an agent for FI in some Asian markets, is very concerned about the Chinese proposal. Their managing director, Svante Ekstroem, regards the China joint venture as a threat to existing business in Southeast Asia. Even if they are invited to participate in the Chinese venture, which is unlikely since the Chinese are reluctant to involve third-party investors, he is apprehensive about the project. The limited experience of SWETRADE in doing business with the Chinese has been rather negative. Ekstroem therefore doubts that SWETRADE should get inovlved.

However, their FI-related business in Southeast Asia amounts to 2 million Nkr., and with increasing demand being forecast over the next five years, Ekstroem believes he should push the Philippino project. In a phone call to Pedersen, he suggests that SWETRADE be willing to invest in 50 percent of the non-Philippino part of the project. He also airs the possibility of taking charge of the marketing activities from China, if that project materializes.

Part IV
Dimensions of
Global Marketing
Strategy

The first five chapters in this section build on the knowledge, concepts, and techniques discussed in the first three parts by focusing on the product, price, distribution, and promotion elements of the global marketing mix. The sixth chapter discusses the issues and problems associated with export operations.

Chapter 12: focuses on the processes of product development, diffusion, and adoption in global markets. These activities are of central importance for successful product innovation in global markets.

Chapter 13: presents a detailed discussion of the fundamental components of an international product program. Managing an international product line and the crucial standardization issue are also reviewed in detail.

Chapter 14: examines a number of pricing issues that are of special concern for international marketers. A general framework for international pricing decisions is presented, and key problems facing decision makers in the international price-setting process are reviewed.

Chapter 15: inspects the three parts of the distribution strategies developed and implemented by the global marketing manager. The chapter also examines various internal and external influences on channel development and the issues and problems that the diversity of national distribution systems pose for global marketing managers faced with coordinating and integrating distribution activities across national markets.

Chapter 16: examines the role that promotion plays in global marketing. This is principally accomplished by reviewing the promotional elements to be managed, and the influence that ethical, social, and regulatory differences have on the development of national and global promotion strategies. Also discussed are within and cross-national promotion problems encountered by management.

Chapter 17: concludes with a review of issues and problems in the management of export operations. Importing is also discussed.

Case Studies: RXR Computers Ltd.
HSK Medical Supplies Company
Technologies CI, SA
Norstar Plastics
Makhteshim Chemical Works
Prima Diapers
General Consumer Products, Inc. (A)

Chapter 12
Dimensions of Global Product Policy I: Managing Product Development, Diffusion, and Adoption

Product policy decisions are of fundamental importance and deserve the most careful attention possible of international marketing executives. The products or services that a firm chooses to sell overseas form a foundation for the firm's international marketing mix and will often limit viable options in related areas of marketing policy. The product presentation, in terms of its design, performance features, and brand name, also constitutes a very visible presence in the international marketplace and will have a major impact on consumer perceptions of the firm.

The range of the decisions that need to be made in the area of product policy is considerable. A summary of the scope of the international product manager's task has been provided by Wind, who describes this role as follows:

> To determine the number, range and type of products to be sold throughout the world, what new products should be developed for which markets and countries; what products should be added, modified, and deleted from the overall product line in each national market and when; what brand names should be used, how products should be packaged and what post sales services should be provided in each of the markets in which the company operates throughout the world. Clearly, a formidable task![1]

In this chapter, we focus on international product innovation. This requires discussing the processes of product development, diffusion, and adoption in global markets. In Chapter 13, we switch our attention to a detailed discussion of the fundamental elements of the international product program and international product line and product strategy issues.

Product innovation may be defined as *successful* new product ideas and is commonly measured by the propensity of targeted consumers to adopt a product. Success is unlikely unless managers are sensitive to the interdependencies between idea creation, product development, diffusion, and adoption.

These linkages are illustrated by Minolta's successful introduction of the Maxxum 35 mm camera into world markets in 1985. In the early 1980s, after several years of rapid growth, sales of advanced cameras leveled off. Minolta recognized that some form of heavily promoted technical innovation was necessary to stimulate demand. The most attractive new product concept was automatic focusing, and after four years of development work, the computerized Maxxum was introduced. The camera was a technological triumph with its auto-focus capability.

Minolta realized, however, that new technology was insufficient for product innovation. It gave careful attention to making the camera widely available and developed an intensive promotional campaign aimed at persuading convenience-minded, affluent consumers to buy the product. In the United States, the advertising budget was increased 50 percent to $15 million, and a catchy slogan—"Only the human eye focuses faster"—was developed. This combination of a good idea, careful product development, and heavy promotion was very effective. Despite its premium price, the Maxxum has been a major success in world markets.

Product Concepts

To avoid ambiguity in the discussion in Chapters 12 and 13, several basic product concepts are defined in Exhibit 12-1.

EXHIBIT 12-1
Basic Product Concepts*

Product

Anything that can be offered to a market for attention, acquisition, use, or consumption that might satisfy a want or need. Products may be conceptualized on three levels: The *core* benefit or service they provide; the *tangible* product, that is, quality level, styling, features, packaging, and brand name; and the *augmented* product, that is, delivery and credit, warranty, after-sales service, and installation.

Product Class

A group of products within the product family that are recognized as having a certain functional coherence.

Product Mix

A set of all product lines and items that a particular seller offers for sale to buyers. The *width* of the product mix indicates the number of different product lines carried; the *length* is the total number of items in the product mix; the *depth* is the number of variants offered for each product; and *consistency* is the degree of relationship among product lines in terms of given criteria (end use, production requirements, and so on).

Product Line

A group of closely related products that function similarly, are sold to the same customer groups, are marketed through the same types of outlets, or fall within given price ranges.

---

*These definitions are based on those used by Philip Kotler in his well-known *Marketing Management,* (Englewood Cliffs, N.J.: Prentice-Hall, 1984), pp. 462–472.

In international markets, pressure to widen the *product mix* and enlarge the length and depth of *product lines* will often be strong. At the same time, questions concerning line modernization, pruning, and featuring will arise more frequently in international firms. This follows from the diverse and dynamic nature of the international marketplace where change, often in different directions and speeds, will usually be taking place in at least some foreign markets at any one point in time.

The problems faced by management in the development, commercialization, and control of the international product mix are thus likely to be considerable. A key issue is the problem of reconciling the pressures for widening the width, depth, and length of the international product mix with the countervailing forces arising from a desire for product mix consistency; cost minimization; and a co-ordinated, focused international marketing strategy.

The Global Product Life Cycle

The product life cycle (IPLC) theory of international trade and investment (discussed in Chapter 2) has interesting implications for product strategy. However, the theory has a number of shortcomings,[2] and the model must therefore be used with care.

The theory asserts that innovating countries, usually the developed nations, enjoy a comparative advantage in the introduction and growth phases of the IPLC. The less developed countries (LDCs) tend to become more competitive as a product moves through its life cycle and will increasingly be the favored production locations as the product becomes increasingly standardized. The model emphasizes the importance of the role of innovation, the transfer of knowledge, and a dynamic view of comparative advantage in explaining the development of patterns of trade and production for manufactured goods.

The implications of the IPLC perspective for international product policy are important. Thus, the desirability of possessing a strong portfolio of new, research-intensive products is obvious. Competitive pressures will be low, premium prices and fat profit margins will be common, and management will have significant power to influence and exploit market opportunities with minimum opposition (in short, a seller's market). Product characteristics—particularly features, design, and styling—will tend to change rapidly in the early stages of the PLC. Pressures to increase the length and depth of product lines will be relatively low at this stage and can often be resisted in the absence of alternative suppliers. Major problems will be to manage the adoption and diffusion process in diverse overseas markets and decide on the optimum rate and scope of new product introductions overseas.

As the product moves from the introduction to the growth phase of the IPLC, competition increases, prices fall, and production technology and product characteristics tend to become more stable. Attractive sales opportunities open up with the rapid growth in demand. However, costs begin to become more important with greater competition. Real advances in product features and performance become less frequent, and most changes in basic product characteristics can be classified as refinements. At the same time, management interest in differentiating the product from those of competitors increases. A search for market niches frequently leads to an expansion in the product line as its length is stretched. Line-filling policies also may be stimulated in an effort to shut out competitors by plugging holes in the product line and developing a position as a full-line company.

As the product moves into maturity and then declines, the attractions of product rejuvenation, achieved either through real improvements brought about by R&D activity or through successful product differentiation, become very apparent. The product and process technology is now increasingly standardized and readily available. Firms become price takers. Cost minimization (achieved by reducing labor costs and investment in specialized machinery) becomes crucially important. In the absence of foreign direct investment in countries with comparative advantage, the original innovators are now forced to cease production. The key dynamic in product policy, in the absence of successful product differentiation, is to make products more cost effective.

Although an understanding of the IPLC model is very useful when devising and managing product policy in global markets, this perspective must be used selectively. First, the explanatory power of the theory seems limited for many products, particularly those developed outside the United States. Second, other elements of the environment in foreign markets may override the impact of the IPLC. For example, government intervention limiting foreign firms may result in limited competition in some markets where the product is very mature. Finally, the length of the IPLC will vary greatly between products, and the impact of factors such as economies of scale may imply that some products are unlikely ever to go through the full cycle.

DEVELOPING PRODUCTS FOR GLOBAL MARKETS

Development Strategies

Two crucial questions that international marketers must ask themselves are *What products should we sell in foreign markets?* and *How should/can we develop these products?* Some firms, particularly those with limited overseas operations and experience, do not take the time to address these issues; their implicit answer to these questions is "We sell overseas what we develop and market to domestic consumers." Such a crude extension strategy is unlikely to enjoy much long-run success. However, in the introduction and early-growth phases of the IPLC, when competition is nonexistent, the developer of a new product may be temporarily able to get away with a take-it-or-leave-it attitude.

The scale and extent of new product development desired is another key issue. What kind of R&D activity does the firm plan to undertake—true innovation, product improvement and modification, or cosmetic changes in naming or packaging? The thrust of the policy pursued will also vary in regard to the emphasis placed behind "internal" development as opposed to "acquiring" products by takeovers and other means. Determining the location of responsibility for international product development and designing appropriate organizational structures will also be major policy concerns.

Product development policy should reflect a firm's international marketing philosophy and strategy. Corporate goals and business definition, management attitudes, resource availability, and the nature of the firm's international operations and organizational strategy will have a major impact on the policy followed.

Three basic orientations toward international product development may be delineated:

Market Extension: An Ethnocentric Approach

An ethnocentric approach to product development, where domestic products are projected internationally, is attractive because it helps minimize costs and maximize the speed of foreign-market entry. To meet mandatory local product standards, firms adopting this approach still must undertake modifications of products.

Such a perspective may be justified by the argument that consumer needs and market conditions are becoming more homogenous internationally. In the case of firms based in the United States or in other developed economies, it is also tempting to argue that domestic consumer needs and behavior, and the products developed to meet these wants, are likely to preview patterns of demand that will be later exhibited in less economically advanced markets.

MultiDomestic: A Polycentric Approach

The view that overseas markets differ significantly in terms of level of development, consumer needs, conditions of product use, and other important characteristics are the usual rationale for a polycentric approach to international product development. In this case, overseas subsidiaries are charged with developing new products for their particular market, and central control and coordination is kept to a minimum. The result is an inevitable proliferation in the width, length, and depth of the firm's international product mix.

Global: A Geocentric Approach

A geocentric approach to international product development implies significant centralization and coordination. Products are developed to appeal to consumers in multiple markets overseas. The ideal is to identify and service global segments of demand that are substantially homogeneous in needs and behavior. This allows for significant product uniformity in international product programs so long as the conditions of product use are also fairly similar in foreign markets.

Even when global demand segments do not exist and standardization strategies are inappropriate, a geocentric orientation has substantial benefits. Unnecessary duplication of expensive R&D is avoided, product lines are rationalized, and international product diffusion is more rapidly achieved.

In their study of foreign R&D activity undertaken by multinational firms, Behrman and Fischer[3] found that firms following a multidomestic strategy are most likely to undertake R&D overseas. This followed from a desire to fully satisfy local market needs in distinctive national markets through autonomous subsidiaries that often feel they need to do their own R&D.

In the few instances of "home market," ethnocentrically oriented firms establishing foreign R&D, this was mainly to provide technical support to their foreign operations. Geocentric, "world market" firms showed a somewhat higher propensity to carry out overseas R&D but were not primarily motivated by a need to respond to local R&D needs. They were more interested in the availability of special skills overseas that were needed for specific types of R&D. The foreign R&D units of such firms tended to have worldwide product responsibility in their particular area of activity.

Creating New Product Ideas

Much international product development activity involves modifying some basic product concept. The product prototype may have been developed for a particular market, usually the home market, or may have been derived in a more geocentric fashion. Whatever its genesis, the experience and perceptions of international marketing managers and overseas customers must be taken into account prior to product modification.

"Cross-fertilization" of product ideas between operating units at home and overseas should also be encouraged because it can be an important means of generating new product ideas. In the case of firms with limited direct experience in overseas markets, close contact should be maintained with overseas distributors and intermediaries who must be encouraged to pass on new product ideas.

Contact with intermediaries in distribution channels is important but must not limit contact with end users, who are a key source of ideas and feedback. Direct customer contact is vital, and this implies that even indirect exporters should visit overseas markets and interact with their current and potential end users.

Scanning activities are also very important, however mundane. This requires monitoring relevant journals and other media, reading patent reports, and making contact with technical experts and research institutes. All too frequently, effort in these areas is limited to the most accessible sources, usually those located at home. However, exciting research is taking place in many countries, and monitoring should also focus on developments occurring in, at least, other major industrial markets.

Formalized interaction with reputable research and academic institutes at home and overseas may also be very valuable. Not only can research contracts and contact lead to useful product ideas, but they also facilitate scanning activity and may have public-relations benefits.

Competitors are very useful sources of product information. Clearly, the product strategies, product mixes, and product innovation and development activity of competing firms should be closely monitored. This can be accomplished by scanning published information sources, attending trade fairs and conferences, and acquiring information from distributors, trade sources, and competitors' customers. Direct contact with competitors may also be helpful.

New product ideas may also be purchased from other firms by means of nonequity contractual arrangements such as licensing. The acquisition of other firms provides access to the research capability of the acquired firm, as well as their current product lines and portfolio of new product ideas and projects. However, acquisition is generally expensive and not without risks. Great care must be taken to hold onto the acquired firm's idea generators and R&D staff.

Joint-venture activity with other firms, as a means of generating and developing new products, is becoming increasingly important. Obvious benefits include cost sharing, achieving critical mass, and reducing risk.

Internal research is a major source of new product ideas. In international firms, key issues include the degree to which formal research is undertaken overseas, and the extent of central control over foreign R&D. Both these questions will be considered in more detail, along with the issue of joint-venture research, in the broader context of product development.

It should be noted that the possibilities outlined above are not mutually exclusive, and firms are likely to be pursuing many different approaches to idea generation at the same time. IBM, for example, has a well-deserved reputation for their in-house basic research skills. In recent years, scientists at an IBM laboratory in Switzerland have, for example, won two Nobel prizes. However, the firm also emphasizes contact with outside research institutions. An example is provided by a $40 million plan, announced in late 1987, to collaborate with up to seven European universities and research institutes on supercomputer research and training.[4] In return for the loan of IBM supercomputer equipment and engineers, researchers at the institutes will collaborate with IBM on advanced supercomputing research.

International Product Development

Turning new ideas into viable products and the rejuvenation of aging products involves extensive development work. Apart from idea generation, which has already been discussed, other stages in this process include idea screening, concept development and testing, development of a marketing strategy, business analysis, product development, market testing, and commercialization.[5]

A basic objective when managing this process is to draw on the firm's international resources, knowledge, and experience to develop products that lend themselves to rapid diffusion and adoption in foreign markets. If this is to occur, the development process should be organized so that the focus is firmly on international market opportunities rather than on individual markets. This orientation is most likely in firms with a geocentric approach to product development.

To achieve the international perspective desirable, a good deal of centralization of R&D and other product-related activities will need to occur in most firms. Managers with international product development responsibilities should be appointed, and appropriate organizational structures should be set up. At the same time, the danger of stifling local initiatives and ideas by excessive centralization and bureaucratization of the development process must be heeded.

In addition there are conflicting pressures for the adaptation of international product presentations and rapid international product diffusion. Pressure to customize and adapt products from market to market will increase costs and delay diffusion. At the same time, particular local needs and circumstances cannot be ignored. Very real dilemmas arise as to the appropriate level of local input in the process and the extent to which product development should occur within the context of individual national markets.

The greater the level of adaptation and testing in individual markets, the slower the rate of product diffusion. However, advocates of polycentric development strategies argue that increasing attention to local needs increases the chances of local adoption (providing that competitors do not preempt the new product introduction and that costs do not rise significantly). These latter caveats are very important, and advocates of uniformity and rapid diffusion emphasize these potential drawbacks of a multimarket development strategy.

Besides being expensive, with intensive use being made of scarce technical, engineering and management skills, the international development process is very risky. Just as at home, most new product introductions fail to make a significant impact in international markets.

Internal R&D

An in-house approach to R&D has substantial benefits. These include full control over the R&D effort, confidentiality, and no conflicts of interest. However, the traditional path of internal R&D is becoming increasingly expensive in many industries. In addition, costly R&D does not guarantee successful new products. In international markets, research is often a hit-or-miss affair, consumers are fickle, and competitive pressures are strong. Internal R&D is thus often very risky. In many high-technology areas, only the biggest and strongest firms have the resources to undertake massive research and to absorb losses resulting from unsuccessful R&D.

Consider the West German electronics firm Siemens which spent over $2.9 billion on R&D in 1986. This expenditure was 11.5 percent of sales revenue, up from 8.5 percent in 1982.[6] Despite this intensive R&D effort, there are no guarantees of success in the highly competitive, global telecommunication market, where firms such as Northern Telecom, L. M. Ericsson, and Nippon Electric Corporation are also major players.

Acquisition Strategies

A primary alternative to internal R&D is acquisition. There are three basic acquisition strategies.

Perhaps the most obvious is to purchase other firms. Unilever, a giant Anglo–Dutch multinational, paid $3.1 billion for the Chesebrough-Pond company in 1987 in order to bolster its position in the U.S. personal products market. Although Unilever has enjoyed success in the United States with some homegrown personal products (Lifebouy soap, Close Up toothpaste), the firm has faced big problems in successfully transferring many of its products to the United States. The Chesebrough acquisition doubled the size of Unilever's U.S. personal products lines and strengthened their U.S. R&D and management capability.

The acquisition of foreign firms with strong product portfolios and R&D expertise may be hindered by local government opposition in some overseas markets. Acquiring well-established, profitable product lines in this manner is expensive and it will often be difficult to integrate the products and management of takeover targets with those of the acquirer.

The results of external R&D activities may also be accessed by utilizing nonequity contractual arrangements, such as licensing. Product know-how and other proprietary rights, such as trademarks, are commonly available for sale. (The principal benefits and drawbacks of such arrangements were discussed in Chapter 10.)

The third approach to product acquisition is the so-called copycat strategy. This policy greatly reduces R&D expenditure but implies acceptance of a follower position and lays the firm open to costly litigation and fierce competitive pressures. Nevertheless, it may be a viable policy for firms with production operations in countries where patent protection is not emphasized and where productive, cheap factors inputs are available.

It is estimated, for example, that at least 20 percent of the U.S. personal computer market is sourced by Asian manufacturers supplying low-cost clones of the popular IBM personal computer.[7] Their entry is facilitated by the fact that as personal computers go through the product life cycle, the market has become much less turbulent with IBM tending to have established an industry standard in the United States. Clearly it makes sense for many firms, when developing new products for the U.S. market, to emphasize the least costly means of achieving this standard. Many manufacturers have been able to replicate this standard, either by their own efforts or by licensing a clone design, without facing legal action. This strategy is particularly attractive for manufacturers with low production costs since they are able to exploit the increasing price sensitivity of the market.

Other examples of successful copycat strategies are provided by Quick, the number-two hamburger chain in Europe, and the Thai pharmaceutical industry. Although emphasizing its European heritage, the Quick hamburger is "in reality a Big Mac in brown-and-orange sheep's clothing."[8] Many Thai pharmaceutical firms make generic versions of foreign-patented drugs. They are able to do so in Thailand because the 1979 Patent Law excludes pharmaceutical products from patent protection.

Joint-Venture Strategies

A major alternative to internal R&D and acquisition strategies is the joint-venture approach. Such agreements may encompass more than just R&D and commonly include joint-production arrangements. The advantages of a cooperative approach include the sharing of R&D expenses and risk, accessing special product and market knowledge of one's partner, and providing a platform for other joint activities. The primary disadvantages of joint ventures include a lack of full control over the R&D process, nonexclusive rights to the results of R&D work, and a requirement to share otherwise confidential know-how and information.

The auto industry provides many examples of cooperative ventures. In 1986, General Motors, for example, had joint-venture arrangements for product development and joint production with both Toyota and Suzuki in Japan, Daewoo in Korea, and San Fu in Taiwan.[9]

The Dutch consumer electronics giant N. V. Philips has undertaken a number of R&D joint ventures with Japanese competitors such as Sony and Matsushita. Their primary motive has been to encourage the establishment of common global product standards for product innovations. Apart from using its technological prowess, Philips has used its political clout within the European Community to help it establish desirable joint-venture arrangements.

An interesting example of Philip's joint-venture strategy is provided by the development of the compact disc (CD) player. CD technology, which involves use of a laser to play sounds from a compact disc, was invented by Philips. Despite heavy investment by U.S. firms such as Zenith and R.C.A., all other major CD manufacturers are now Japanese. Despite spending large sums on R&D in the early 1970s, Sony began to make real progress only once Philips offered it the chance of cooperating on R&D in 1977. Philips was interested in cooperation because it wanted to ensure that their technology would set an industrywide standard and that competitors' machines would be compatible with this standard.

The early disc players (introduced in 1982) were large and expensive, and it was in developing the popular miniplayers that Sony demonstrated its skills in translating a technological breakthrough into a major new product success. The basis for this success appears to have been a particular combination of a significant resource commitment, persistence, and an applications-oriented perspective based on a sound understanding of what the consumer wants. Although Philips was not as successful as Sony in capitalizing on its technological leadership, it did achieve its major strategic goal—a single world standard for disc players.

Decision Variables

Critical factors, when determining whether to emphasize internal R&D as opposed to acquisition or joint-venture strategies, include the level and nature of R&D activity, the cost and risk of R&D programs, resource availability, knowledge of foreign customer needs and behavior and the product use environment, the level of control desired over the development process, and the importance attached to exclusive rights to new products.

Relative ignorance of foreign conditions, limited resources, and high R&D risk and cost will tend to favor cooperative efforts or acquisition strategies. Firms with extensive resources, wide experience, and secret or sophisticated technology often favor internal R&D, but will also be interested in acquisitions.

Locating International R&D Activities

In many international companies, R&D is the most centralized of the functional activities undertaken within the firm. Even when a multidomestic strategy is being followed, it is still feasible to centralize much basic R&D.

Terpstra[10] has identified the following as major arguments for centralizing international R&D:

1. Ensuring a critical mass and economies of scale,
2. Allowing easier coordination and control,
3. Facilitating the protection of know-how,
4. Making best use of the experience and expertise in the firm,
5. Minimizing the exposure of vital R&D skills and assets to foreign government control and oversight.

The primary benefits that can accrue from decentralizing R&D activities were:

1. Facilitates technology transfer.
2. Allows access to and use of valuable, cheap, foreign R&D skills.
3. Responds to demands from subsidiary management for local involvement and sensitivity to local market needs.
4. Results in public relations benefits, particularly in response to host country government pressure.
5. Reduces time lag in introducing new products locally.

Despite the continued predominance of centralized, home-based R&D, many multinationals do conduct significant R&D activities overseas. Ronstadt's research[11] indicates that most overseas R&D investment undertaken by U.S. multinationals is aimed either at facilitating the transfer and adaptation of U.S. technology and products to local conditions or at generating new products and processes specifically for local markets. Initial investment usually concentrates on establishing technical service labs. As these labs grow, they become increasingly involved in more localized product R&D independent of the parent's R&D activities. The focus of this activity is to satisfy local needs and tastes and undertake local testing. Few firms appear to have established overseas R&D in order to develop products for global markets or for other third country markets. Basic, exploratory research is also rarely undertaken overseas.

Fischer and Behrman[12] identify four ways in which a firm can establish overseas R&D activity:

1. Permit quality control or technical service units to evolve into a R&D group.
2. Directly establish a foreign R&D group.
3. Take over a foreign firm with R&D resources.
4. Collaborate in joint-venture R&D activities.

Despite strong pressure from many host governments to "localize" R&D, most foreign R&D is undertaken in rich, developed, industrial countries. R&D is "localized" in developed countries mainly because these countries are key markets for many firms, and the resources and skills needed when setting up R&D operations are locally available. For U.S. firms, traditional centers of overseas R&D are the United Kingdom, West Germany, France, and Canada. Japan is an increasingly popular site. At the same time, however, significant R&D is occurring in Mexico, Brazil, and India.

The United States is a favorite location for foreign R&D activity undertaken by non-U.S. firms. Reasons for this popularity include the size and importance of the U.S. market, the relatively wide availability of skilled scientists and technicians, the need to monitor developments in cutting-edge technology, and the dynamic nature of the U.S. marketplace.

When a firm undertakes R&D overseas, it has good reason also to seek a high degree of centralization. Major advantages of centralization include the elimination of overlapping in projects, more efficient resource utilization, and a lowered chance of omitting necessary R&D projects.

National R&D Activities

Most modern industrial inventions have originated in Western Europe and the United States. This is partly due to high R&D expenditure. In 1969, the United States and Europe accounted for 79 percent of private R&D spending in the OECD nations. By 1981, this figure had fallen to 65 percent as Japanese expenditure has increased from 14 to 21 percent.[13] Japanese spending has continued to increase rapidly, and in 1986, Hitachi displaced General Electric as the firm receiving the most U.S. patents. Table 12.1 indicates that three other Japanese firms were included in the list of the top ten recipients of U.S. patents.

The number of patents filed by a firm is but an imperfect measure of its inventiveness. As is evident from Table 12-1, the amount spent on R&D in 1987 seems to have had a limited impact on the number of patents issued. The Japanese, for example, may have been seeking patents on products invented some time ago that are only now being introduced in the United States. West German and

TABLE 12-1
Top Ten Firms Receiving U.S. Patents in 1986

Rank 1986	Company	Number of Patents	1986 R&D ($m)	R&D as % of Sales
1	Hitachi	730	1,332.0[1]	5.9
2	General Electric	713	3,300.0	9.4
3	Toshiba	691	860.6[1]	5.6
4	IBM	597	5,200.0	10.1
5	Canon	522	139.9	9.7
6	North American Philips	503	113.5	2.5
7	RCA[2]	484	N.A.	N.A.
8	Fuji Photo	446	246.0[3]	5.8
9	Siemens	409	2,486.8	11.5
10	Westinghouse	398	918.0	8.6

[1]Year end 3,31., 86.
[2]RCA is now owned by General Electric.
[3]Year end 10.20, 86.
Source: *The Economist,* May 9, 1987, p. 82.

British firms also account for a significant proportion of U.S. patents. In 1987, the foreign share of total U.S. patents issued was 47 percent, a significant rise over the average of 24 percent exhibited in the period 1963–1972.

Data on R&D expenditure and patent applications do not tell the whole R&D story. Bright ideas do not necessarily translate into successful products. Innovation occurs only when inventiveness is complemented by management and marketing skills. Many inventions do not succeed, and as few as 10 percent of new products are truly original.

The Japanese Approach

Since World War II, the Japanese have devoted considerable resources to learning from the West. They have excelled as imitators, often producing Western-invented products more effectively than do the inventing firms. Now at the cutting edge in many technologies, the Japanese have begun to launch large numbers of original products in world markets. Their successes have stimulated interest in their approach to R&D. An article in *The Economist*[14] itemized the following lessons for Western firms interested in learning from the Japanese:

1. The importance of top managers setting specific product development objectives.
2. The establishment of teams, with both managerial and technical skills, that are given strong backing and a free hand to pursue the established developmental goals.
3. Careful planning to minimize the impact of delays in the development process on the project as a whole.
4. Ensuring that learning is transferred from team members to others within the firm.
5. Involving production engineers at an early stage in the development process.
6. Building up relations with and exchanging information with suppliers' research organizations in the development process.

THE DIFFUSION OF PRODUCTS IN INTERNATIONAL MARKETS _____

The Diffusion Process

The term *market diffusion* refers to the movement of new products (through whatever entry modes and channels) to overseas markets so that they become available to foreign customers. Patterns of product diffusion may be viewed from two perspectives, production lag and market lag. *Production lag* measures the time elapsed between initial output of a new product and the commencement of production in a specified overseas market. *Market lag* is defined as the time between the initial marketing of a new product and its introduction in a specified foreign market.

Research indicates that the nature of the product, local characteristics of overseas markets, and the firm's strategy and organization all play important roles in influencing the direction and speed of the diffusion process. Key determinants include the degree of product adaptation necessary and competitive pressures faced.

Evidence on *market* lag suggests that there are sharp differences between products. One study found that the average market lag for consumer goods was over three times longer than that for industrial products.[15] This difference was thought to be due in part to a need for more modifications to consumer goods. The extent of the novelty of product performance features was also found to be important, with market lag being six times longer for completely new products than for goods with only minor modifications. Generally, it seems that rapid diffusion results when a high level of competition in overseas markets combines with a low need to adapt the product.

Many of the factors identified (in Chapter 10) as affecting decisions about the *number* of foreign markets entered by a firm also impact on the *speed* at which new products are introduced overseas.[16] Thus the prospect of achieving fast sales growth from a limited commitment of resources, the need for limited adaptation of product policy, distribution economies, and spillover effects from marketing efforts in one country to another tend to speed the rate of market diffusion overseas.

It is also apparent that there are substantial variations in *production lags* by industry and product. LeRoy[17] found that consumer goods tend to be produced overseas more rapidly than industrial goods. Davidson and Harrigan's[18] findings suggest shorter lags for goods such as paper and chemicals, with low value to weight or volume ratios. This is not surprising since high transport costs render such products expensive to export. There has also been a dramatic fall in production lags in the postwar period. The percentage of innovations produced in a foreign market within one year of U.S. introduction increased from 5.6 percent in 1945–1950 to 38.7 percent in 1971–1975.

International patterns of diffusion are distinctly affected by the nature of a firm's process of product planning and development and its organizational structure. LeRoy indicates that the speed of product diffusion is maximized in those firms geared to developing a largely standard product that, with minimum adaptation, can be marketed globally. The adoption of organizational structures in which product managers have worldwide responsibilities is also considered important in facilitating rapid diffusion.

Those firms with a multidomestic focus who develop a product for a single market and then, if the product is successful, consider adapting it to meet foreign-market requirements typically introduce products more slowly overseas. In firms where product modification is coupled with a geographic organizational structure, such an approach is almost inevitable. Local management often enjoys significant autonomy, and there is frequently no central corporate responsibility for international product diffusion.

Anyone managing international product diffusion and adoption should also be aware of three concepts in addition to traditional measures of market attractiveness: (1) product saturation, (2) regional lag, and (3) psychic distance. We will now discuss these briefly.

Product Saturation

Product saturation is the degree to which a product class and associated product lines have achieved acceptance in a market. It can be gauged by looking at the propensity of consumers to adopt (purchase and use on a continuing basis) a product. Generally, saturation levels are measured as a percentage of potential buyers or households who own the product.

High saturation implies widespread product acceptance and adoption. For new products, and for many other products in general, saturation levels tend to increase as per capita disposable income increases. There are exceptions. For example, as incomes increase, relative expenditure on products such as food and clothing tends to fall, and saturation levels for some products may fall as consumers are able to afford alternative, more expensive products.

In those overseas markets where saturation levels are high for a particular product class, strong competitive reactions can be expected for new products. "Me too" products may therefore find market entry perilous unless they can be produced less expensively or are successfully differentiated by skillful marketing.

When new products enjoy few obvious advantages over competing products, markets similar to high saturation markets, but where product penetration levels are low, may stand out as immediate candidates for entry. When measuring similarity, the most important dimensions are likely to include the level of economic development and social and cultural factors.

However, ostensible similarity on these and other dimensions can be misleading in the search for attractive overseas market opportunities. Among the more obvious confounding factors, which can lead to sharp variations in saturation levels between similar markets, will be variations in consumer needs, taste, and behavior; the conditions of product use; and the pattern of government regulation.

For example, the low saturation levels for peanut butter and handguns in many West European countries do not indicate that there are significant market opportunities for these products in these markets. Differences in patterns of food consumption and taste inhibit peanut butter sales. Stringent laws governing the sale of handguns and unfavorable attitudes toward handgun ownership help to account for very low saturation levels of this product in Western Europe. Climate can also help set saturation levels. No one expects ice-making machines or air conditioning units to be big sellers in Scandinavia.

Comparisons of saturation levels for a given product class between markets exhibiting significant similarities can help pinpoint markets that deserve immediate investigation. The example of the U.S. wine industry illustrates the potential utility of such a comparison, however, it also serves as a warning that superficial analysis can rapidly lead to erroneous conclusions.

In the late 1960s, the saturation level for wine in the United States was much lower than levels in Western Europe. A number of firms in the industry correctly concluded that major opportunities existed in the United States and that wine sales would increase proportionately with the movement toward a more "sophisticated" lifestyle. During the 1970s, sales of table wine did in fact grow more rapidly than sales of competing beverages. However, despite a decade of more than 10 percent annual growth rates, it is estimated that only about 15 percent of the U.S. population accounts for nearly all the table wine consumed in the United States, and annual per capita consumption is still only some 10 percent of that in France and Italy.[19] More important, the growth in demand has been sluggish during most of the 1980s, and sales actually fell in 1985. Explanations vary, ranging from consumer health concerns, the popularity of wine coolers, and research indicating that many would-be consumers are intimidated by a lack of knowledge about wines and confused by the wide range of wines available.

Low saturation levels in the late 1960s did indicate an opportunity. Saturation levels are still relatively low, but opportunities for growth are now much less promising than two decades ago. It now seems unlikely that wine will become the beverage of choice of the U.S. middle class. Opportunities for growth seem greatest in wine-related areas, such as wine coolers. Coolers are more in tune with the needs and perceptions of many mainstream consumers. Thus even in markets where income levels do not constrain demand, low saturation levels may not point to market opportunity.

Regional Lead-Lag

The notion that patterns of demand in a leading country may be useful predictors of subsequent demand elsewhere is central to the idea of market lag. Clearly, there is a strong similarity in the thinking underlying this idea and the rationale for using such concepts as product saturation levels, estimation by analogy, and the IPLC theory.

The United States is commonly identified as the lead market for many new products. This is a function of high income levels and wage costs, a strong entrepreneurial tradition, and the willingness of U.S. consumers to experiment. Insofar as the "lead market" is a reliable predictor of behavior in other markets, useful insights into appropriate target markets and product diffusion strategies are provided the international marketer.

The use of historic data can be very useful in helping delineate likely patterns of product diffusion and adoption, assuming other things remain equal over time. However, history does not always repeat itself. For example, data on the evolution of household ownership of television sets in 1946–1970 indicate a lag of some six years before saturations levels in Britain caught up with those in the United States.[20] Penetration levels in Germany trailed those in the United Kingdom by another six or so years. In the 1970s and 1980s, however, these traditional time lags have had limited relevance to adoption patterns for similar classes of electronic products. Rapid economic growth in Western Europe and factors such as increased product innovation by European firms have greatly shortened time lags and reversed the relative positions of some countries. Thus, some new products achieve high penetration more rapidly in West Germany than in Britain because of higher German incomes. Other new products are adopted just as rapidly in rich European countries and Japan as in the United States. Consider the case of personal computers.

British consumers have shown a greater propensity to buy PCs than have Americans. Penetration levels in Germany have also lagged behind those achieved in Britain, probably due to cultural factors that result in slow acceptance by Germans of some new household products. German consumers are conservative and cautious and do resist some product innovations. In the case of PCs, the computer games that have been sought by British and American consumers seem to have been considered frivolous by Germans. Other "local" factors are also at work: perceptions that computers make life more complex and lonely; the late introduction of computers in the school curriculum; a shortage of high-quality German software, and a distribution system that newcomers find difficult to penetrate.[21]

In general, given the decline in U.S. dominance as a source of innovations and the narrowing of the gap in the average standard of living between much of the developed world and the United States, historic patterns of regional or country lag are likely to be less relevant today than a decade or two ago. Today, it is common to ask which countries follow the lead set by European or Japanese innovators. Even in the frequent situations where the U.S. is still the lead country, the rate and the direction of product diffusion commonly depart from historic patterns.

Measures of per capita income are widely used to determine likely lead-lag times and have been used to distinguish among the five stages of market development (that is, from preindustrial to postindustrial status).[22] The importance attached to the level of per capita income is due in part to the work of Stefan Linder (discussed in Chapter 2). In Linder's view, most products are developed for the domestic market and foreign trade is seen as an extension of domestic trade. The domestic product range is therefore the basis for the export range. It follows that the potential for trade in manufactured goods is greatest between countries with similar patterns of demand. Linder views the pattern of demand as determined primarily by the level of per capita income, with income distribution and taste contributing factors. The greater the similarities in levels of per capita income, income distribution, and tastes, the shorter the period of diffusion from one market to another.

In practice, simple taxonomies based on per capita income alone are often too crude for forecasting purposes. Additional variables must be taken into account, variables that reflect the nature of the specific product market situation. Thus such factors as the conditions of product use, import duties, government regulations and the price of substitute products will affect lead-lag relationships.

Psychic Distance

The term *psychic distance* was coined by Swedish researchers at the University of Uppsala; it is used to describe sociocultural distance between countries.[23] It is a central concept in the internationalization model detailed in Chapter 17, which discusses the importance of the acquisition and evaluation of market knowledge in reducing uncertainty about foreign markets. Barriers to information acquisition include such factors as culture, language, and level of development. Uncertainty is minimized by following strategies that direct operations to those foreign markets where prior knowledge is greatest. The implication of this perspective is that products are likely to be introduced first in those markets where the psychic distance between the home country and the overseas market is minimal. However, those markets that are closest in a psychic sense may become less attractive when measured by demand potential, the competitive environment, and product saturation levels.

THE ADOPTION PROCESS IN GLOBAL MARKETS _____

Rapid international product diffusion does not ensure successful product adoption. Roger's influential conceptualization of the adoption process posits five stages, culminating in adoption: (1) awareness, (2) interest, (3) evaluation, (4) trial, and (5) adoption. These stages are spelled out in Exhibit 12-2.

EXHIBIT 12-2 _____
A Conceptualization of the Adoption Process _____

1. **Awareness** Consumer becomes aware of new product following initial exposure to it.
2. **Interest** Consumer is sufficiently motivated to search for additional information on the product.
3. **Evaluation** Development of an attitude towards the product that will predispose the consumer either to try or not try the good.
4. **Trial** Consumer tries the product in order to assess the extent to which it meets his/her needs.
5. **Adoption** Acceptance of the product for continuing use. For less expensive goods, this implies repeat purchases.

_____

Source: Rogers, E. M., *Diffusion of Innovations,* 3rd ed. (New York: Free Press, 1983), pp. 211–38.

The propensity of consumers to change from existing patterns of consumption to something new is a key variable in the adoption process. Sheth and Sethi,[24] whose theory of cross-cultural buyer behavior is discussed in Chapter 6, argue that the propensity to change is a function of *cultural lifestyle, strategic opinion leadership,* and *communication about innovation.* Intermarket differences in these variables and the degree of change implied by adopting a product are key factors affecting the international adoption of new products.

Firms are usually unable to influence significantly two determinants of the propensity to change, namely, cultural lifestyle and the identity of strategic opinion leaders. Even when a company perceives opportunities to affect one of these factors, it must exercise great caution since these are invariably sensitive areas of concern to host governments.

There is more scope for corporate action regarding the nature of the product program and communication about the innovation. To the extent that a product is adjusted to meet local needs and conditions, then the degree of change from current consumption and the level of resistance to change is likely to be lower for most new products. When communicating about new products, firms can indeed seek to influence and control the communications mix—the source, channel, and content of product-related messages—in a manner that takes into account differing market situations. To do so, managers need to tailor the content of messages to fit those characteristics identified in research as having a major impact on the rate of adoption: relative advantage, compatibility, complexity, trialability, and communicability.[25] (These factors were detailed in Chapter 6).

When managing product diffusion and adoption, it may also be helpful to classify the innovation in terms that relate to consumer perceptions of the good. Sheth and Sethi have suggested three categories of innovations. "Consumption substitution" innovations are most common; these concern new products that are familiar but owe their attractiveness to a promise of variety and enhanced quality. "New want-creating" innovations create satisfaction by improving the performance of existing products or satisfying new customer needs. "Income adding" innovations include all products that improve the income-generating capacity of the consumer.

COUNTRY-OF-ORIGIN EFFECTS

Country-of-origin effects (COE), which have been broadly defined as "any influence, positive or negative, that the country of manufacture might have on the consumer's choice process and subsequent behavior,"[26] present international managers with both opportunities and problems during diffusion and adoption. Bilkey and Nes found that the great majority of published COE studies indicate that COE does affect product evaluations.[27] However, many COE studies are flawed. Bilkey and Nes point out that a high proportion of these studies are "one cue" studies. That is, they do not give attention to other potential influences. COE may be operating as a proxy for other variables that also have an impact on product evaluations.

Other COE problems are the definition of country of manufacture, and disentangling the impact of the brand name and the home country of the manufacturing firm. Is, for example, a Honda car assembled in the U.S. from components imported from Japan and Korea perceived as a U.S. made car? Does the consumer discriminate between the country of manufacture and the fact that Honda is a Japanese firm?

If COE is found to be an important variable, we must determine the nature of its impact. In their review, Bilkey and Nes highlighted the following patterns in research findings:

☐ COE impacts consumers in developed and developing countries and influences purchasing decisions for many different classes of products, including industrial goods.

☐ Attitudes change over time and are not consistent between countries.

☐ There is a tendency for consumers to rate domestically produced goods more favorably than do foreigners. However in some countries, mainly those in the developing world, foreign-origin products may be preferred.

☐ There is often a bias against products produced in developing countries and in Eastern Europe.

A 1982 study of the attitudes of American and French purchasing directors questioned on the COE impact for products from England, France, West Germany, Japan, and the United States illustrates some of Bilkey and Nes's points, but it also indicates that generalizations can be misleading.[28] Both French and American respondents rated "made in West Germany" most favorably and the "made in France/England" labels least favorably, a finding not in line with the notion of favoring domestic goods. (This is perhaps because the respondents were professional purchasers of industrial goods and thus less likely to be swayed by nonrational factors.) Significant differences of perception were also exhibited. Japanese products had a less favorable image with the French managers than with U.S. managers. The French managers perceived Japanese products as less reliable and technically advanced. On the other hand, the French were more impressed than were the Americans with the "made in England" label because of the French perceptions of British products as inventive and luxurious.

Although most surveys indicate that U.S. consumers prefer American-made products, the flood of imported goods during the 1980s indicates that the average consumer is unwilling to pay much extra for the "made in U.S.A." label. In overseas markets, the value of the U.S. label seems to be greatest for high-tech innovations.

There is no real consensus on what determines COE bias or the degree to which such bias reflects actual differences in product characteristics and supplier performance. Some broad generalizations can be safely made from available research.

At the national level, it seems that consumer perceptions regarding the level of economic development, political system, and cultural characteristics of a source country do reflect cultural stereotyping. In general, there appears to be a positive relationship between the level of economic development and a country's image. Perceived congruence with regard to political system and cultural context also appears likely to affect bias favorably toward the country of origin. Historic ties, like those between former colonial powers and their colonies, may also be important.

The experience of individual consumers, personality characteristics, and demographics also impact stereotyping. Thus, favorable or unfavorable experiences with products are likely to predispose consumers to a certain bias. There is also evidence that consumers exhibiting low levels of conservatism and dogmatism and older persons will tend to evaluate foreign sourced products more favorably.[29]

It is important not to exaggerate the importance of stereotyping by country. One study found that 70 percent of a sample of U.S. consumers under 35 years of age had little or no interest in determining the country of origin of their purchases.[30]

Even when COE effects are strong and negative, effective marketing strategies can succeed in overcoming consumer prejudices. Most West Germans, for example, believe that they build the world's best cars. Surveys indicate that around half of West German respondents would not even consider buying a foreign-made car. Nonetheless, Japanese manufacturers have gained a 15 percent share of the West German auto market. They did so by offering reliable cars at competitive prices and by aggressively attacking niche markets. Consumer concerns regarding reliability were met by offering high-quality service and superior warranties.

MANAGING NEW-PRODUCT DEVELOPMENT

It is apparent from the preceding discussion that management needs to take into account a wide range of variables when devising international product development policies. Particular care is necessary when weighing the relative merits and drawbacks of strategic options available. Careful evaluation of the industrial, firm, and overseas operating environments in which development activities occur is required. However, regardless of the strategy adopted, some generalizations are appropriate.

First, the development policy adopted should take its cue from and be integrated into the firm's overall international marketing strategy. Second, input and active participation from local management in foreign markets during the development process is important. Local new product initiatives should be encouraged, and a local market strategy proposal and business analysis should be solicited from all potential target markets *prior to* the initiation of full-scale new product development. Local management can be asked to evaluate business prospects for an "as is" product as compared to a more localized product. Third, an international orientation to product development should be fostered at all levels and a strong central structure for managing the development process established. Such a structure is essential to ensure the development of product lines that can be diffused rapidly, effectively, and economically into international markets.

Frequently, the establishment of international product development teams is desirable. These teams should have broad functional membership, with key roles being played by representatives from engineering, manufacturing, marketing and finance. It is often useful to place an international product manager in charge of the resulting development team in order to help counteract tendencies to a multidomestic, multiproduct orientation and to provide the driving force toward global product programs. International team membership is also very important.

Development should follow well-defined objectives. In some cases, the goal may be innovation; in other cases, product rejuvenation or modification. Success should be measured by how well one meets these concrete product goals. Bright ideas alone are not sufficient. Product innovation requires ideas to be translated into real-world products that are in demand in global markets.

A key management goal should be to reduce the time needed to develop products for international markets. Shorter development cycles enable firms to charge higher prices for their new products and allow rapid exploitation of new opportunities and niches in overseas markets.

Action to shorten development cycles is being stimulated by competitive pressures. For example, the Japanese can design and build a car in about 3.5 years. This betters U.S. auto makers by an average of 1.5 years. In response to this gap, U.S. auto makers are abandoning outdated sequential approaches to product development and are initiating "parallel engineering" programs (where many separate development activities occur concurrently). They are also emphasizing development of products that can be manufactured efficiently and economically and using more outside suppliers in the development process.

SUMMARY

Product policy decisions are of fundamental importance in forming a platform for and delimiting options in a firm's international marketing mix. This chapter has discussed the development, diffusion, and adoption of products in international markets and examined basic product concepts, the implications of the IPLC model and country-of-origin effects.

It is apparent that there is a basic tension between the forces favoring the development and diffusion of an international product mix characterized by width, depth and length and the countervailing pressures for cost control and a coordinated, focused international product policy. The IPLC theory makes clear the advantages of successful innovation and the desirability of developing a portfolio of modern, research-intensive products.

Ethnocentric product-development strategies have the attraction of being cheap and rapid. A multidomestic strategy ensures greater attention to local needs and circumstances, but it does so at the cost of a less central coordination and focus. Geocentric approaches allow for the development of a more uniform product mix for world markets and facilitate rapid product diffusion, but the international demand segments so targeted may have to be limited in size.

Product innovations may be generated internally, acquired externally, or be the result of joint R&D programs. Among critical policy determinants are the scope of a firm's international product development goals, the availability of resources, knowledge of overseas customers, the economics and risk of R&D, and environmental contexts. Internal product development is often expensive, but it maximizes control. Acquisition allows for accessing the ideas of others more familiar with local customer needs and circumstances. Joint ventures spread the costs and risks of R&D, but at the cost of nonexclusive rights to the results of R&D efforts and a need to share know-how. Copycat strategies may be viable for mature products produced in low-cost manufacturing facilities. A key point is that innovations—successful new product inventions—should be the goal; there is evidence that resource commitment, persistence, and an applications orientation can be important in the achievement of this basic objective.

Most R&D activity occurs in rich industrial countries. In many international firms, R&D is centralized so that best use is made of the firm's research expertise. Decentralization, however, also has virtues. Decentralized systems can respond quickly to local demands for R&D input, allowing the development of more customized products.

The rate of international product diffusion has increased significantly in the postwar period. Critical factors impacting the process include product and market characteristics and the firm's international marketing strategy and organization. Factors such as a low need for product modification, strong competitive pressures, and a multinational product outlook help facilitate rapid diffusion.

An understanding of product saturation, regional lead-lag, and psychic distance can assist in diffusion planning. However, these ideas need to be used with great care. Low product saturation levels do not necessarily imply significant market opportunities, and patterns of regional lead-lag often reflect historical patterns now of little significance.

Rapid international product diffusion does not ensure adoption. Great care must be given to addressing factors influencing how foreign customers adopt new products. Cultural lifestyle, strategic opinion, leadership, and communication about the innovation have been identified as such critical factors.

Country-of-origin effects may have an impact on consumer purchasing. There is no consensus on what determines bias, but such factors as consumer purchasing experience; consumers' perceptions of the source country's political, economic, and cultural situation; and links between source and consuming nations have all been identified as influential.

Managers of new product development should follow the same basic steps in the international marketplace as in the home market. However, important differences require that management carefully weigh the costs and advantages of various developmental strategies. Regardless of the policy followed, local participation is desirable, but within the context of a conscious commitment to the development of international products. Policy should be integrated into the overall international marketing strategy; centralized control over development is therefore usually appropriate.

DISCUSSION QUESTIONS

1. What implications does the product life cycle theory have for international product development strategy?

2. What factors are likely to influence Japanese consumer attitudes to the "made in U.S.A." label? Would you emphasize the country of origin of American made, high-technology exports to Japan?

3. How does the task of managing product development differ between global and domestic firms?

4. Distinguish between product diffusion and product adoption. Identify policies that will facilitate the rapid diffusion of products into overseas markets.

5. How should international firms react to pressures from host governments in developing countries for increased local R&D?

6. Why are joint venture R&D projects with overseas firms becoming more common? What issues should be addressed before entering such arrangements?

7. Identify appropriate organizational structures for managing international product develop-

ment. Discuss key features of the structure(s) suggested.

ADDITIONAL READING

Ayal, Igal, "International Product Life Cycle: A Reassessment and Product Policy Implications," *Journal of Marketing,* Fall 1981.

Bartlett, Christopher A., and Ghoshal, Sumantra, "Tap Your Subsidiaries for Global Reach," *Harvard Business Review,* November–December 1986.

Gerstenfeld, A., and Lawrence H. Wortzel, "Strategies for Innovation in Developing Countries," *Sloan Management Review,* Fall 1977.

Hill, John S., and Richard R. Still, "Adapting Products to LDC Tastes," *Harvard Business Review,* March–April 1984.

LeRoy, G., *Multinational Product Strategy* (New York: Praeger, 1976).

Ronkainen, Ilkka A., "Product Development Processes in the Multinational Firm," *International Marketing Review,* Winter 1983.

Ting, W., "The Product Development Process in NIC Multinationals," *Columbia Journal of World Business,* Spring 1982.

ENDNOTES

1. Yoram Wind, "Research for Multinational Product Policy." *Multinational Product Management,* Warren J. Keegan and C. S. Mayer, eds., (Chicago: American Marketing Association, 1977), p. 165.
2. See, for example, Ian H. Giddy, "The Demise of the Product Cycle Model in International Business Theory," *Columbia Journal of World Business,* Spring 1978, pp. 90–97.
3. Jack N. Behrman and William A. Fischer, "Transnational Corporations: Market Orientations and R&D Abroad," *Columbia Journal of World Business,* Fall 1980, pp. 55–60.
4. *The Wall Street Journal,* November 25, 1987.
5. Philip Kotler, *Marketing Management* (Englewood Cliffs, N.J.: Prentice-Hall, 1984), chapter 10.
6. *The Wall Street Journal,* February 9, 1987.
7. Ibid., January 10, 1986.
8. Ibid., June 10, 1986.
9. "Asian Carmakers," *The Economist,* May 24, 1986, p. 66.
10. Vern Terpstra, "International Product Policy: The Role of Foreign R&D," *Columbia Journal of World Business,* Winter 1977, pp. 24–32.
11. Robert Ronstadt, "The Establishment and Evolution of R&D Abroad," *Journal of International Business Studies,* Spring–Summer 1978, pp. 7–24.
12. William A. Fischer and Jack N. Behrman, "The Coordination of Foreign R&D Activities by Transnational Corporations," *Journal of International Business Studies,* Winter 1979, pp. 28–35.
13. "Keeping Up with the Japanese," *The Economist,* March 16, 1985, p. 71.
14. Ibid.
15. G. P. LeRoy, "An Innovation-Diffusion Perspective." *Multinational Product Management,* W. J. Keegan and C. S. Mayer, eds. (Chicago: American Marketing Association, 1977), pp. 35–50.
16. Igal Ayal and Jakiel Yif, "Market Expansion Strategies in Multinational Marketing," *Journal of Marketing,* Spring 1979, pp. 84–94.
17. LeRoy, op. cit.
18. William H. Davidson and Richard Harrigan, "Key Decisions in International Marketing: Introducing New Products Abroad," *Columbia Journal of World Business,* Winter 1977, pp. 15–23.
19. See "Tough Times: Wine Industry Finds It May Be Its Own Worst Enemy . . .," *The Wall Street Journal,* March 19, 1986.
20. Warren J. Keegan, *Multinational Marketing Management* (Englewood Cliffs, N.J.: Prentice-Hall, 1984), p. 236.
21. See *The Wall Street Journal,* April 17, 1986.
22. See, for example 1986 *World Bank Atlas.*
23. L. Engwall, ed., *Uppsala Contributions to Business Research,* (Uppsala: Uppsala University, 1984).
24. Jagdish N. Sheth and S. Prakash Sethi, "A Theory of Cross-Cultural Buyer Behavior," College of Business Administration, University of Illinois, 1973.
25. Everett M. Rogers and F. Floyd Shoemaker, *Communication of Innovations,* (New York: Free Press, 1971).
26. Saeed Samiee, "Customer Evaluation of Products in a Global Market," College of Business Administration, University of South Carolina, 1987.
27. Warren J. Bilkey and Erik Nes, "Country of Origin Effects on Product Evaluations," *Journal of International Business Studies,* Spring–Summer 1982, pp. 89–99.
28. P. J. Cattin et al., "A Cross-Cultural Study of 'Made-In' Concepts," *Journal of International Business Studies,* Winter 1982, pp. 131–141.
29. Bilkey and Nes, op. cit.
30. Paul S. Hugstad and Michael Durr, "A Study of Country of Manufacture Impact on Consumer Perceptions," *Developments in Marketing Science* (Proceedings, Vol. 9, Academy of Marketing Science, 1986).

Chapter 13
Dimensions of Global Product Strategy II: Managing International Product Policy

INTRODUCTION

THE STANDARDIZATION ISSUE

Defining a Standard. Developing Standard International Product Presentations: The Ethnocentric Approach, The Geocentric Approach, The Regiocentric Approach. Uniform International Product Policies: Advantages, Disadvantages and Barriers. Standardizing the International Product Presentation: Implementation Policies, Other Facilitating Policies.

THE INTERNATIONAL PRODUCT PROGRAM

Localization Policy. Adaptation Policy. Characteristics of the Product Program: Product Attributes, Packaging, Labeling, Brands and Trademarks, Service Policies, Warranties.

THE INTERNATIONAL PRODUCT MIX POLICY

Planning the International Product Mix. The Product Portfolio Approach. Managing International Product Lines.

SERVICES

Special Features of the International Market for Services: Greater Protectionism, Direct Contact in Exchange Relationships, Economies of Location. Marketing Services in Global Markets: Human Resource Policies, Strategic and Tactical Flexibility, Differentiation Strategies, Promotion, Networking Relationships.

COUNTERFEITING

Anticounterfeiting Laws. Anticounterfeiting Strategies: Lobbying Activities, Combatting Counterfeiters, Product Development, Collaboration.

SUMMARY

DISCUSSION QUESTIONS

ADDITIONAL READING

ENDNOTES

INTRODUCTION

The nature of the product program adopted in global markets is a major theme in this chapter. Products have multiple attributes, and the discussion will focus on the product's physical characteristics—design, shape, and size; performance attributes; packaging and labeling; brand name and trademarks; and service and warranty backup.

Before reviewing these various elements of product policy, a thorough analysis will be presented of the extent to which product attributes should be standardized in the international marketplace. This discussion also has relevance for other elements of the international marketing mix, most notably advertising policy.

The management of the international product mix is the other main topic reviewed in this chapter. Issues discussed include the number of product lines to be offered in international markets and the length, depth, and degree of consistency among these product lines.

Finally, attention will be given to two other important topics, service products, which are becoming increasingly important in international markets, and the problem of product counterfeiting.

STANDARDIZATION ISSUES

A central issue in international marketing is the degree to which it is necessary to modify and adapt products sold in global markets. Originally raised in the context of advertising policy,[1] the discussion was broadened by Buzzell[2] and others to include product policy and other elements of the international marketing mix.

There are sharp differences of opinion on the desirability and feasibility of standardization. Levitt,[3] for example, has argued that "companies must learn to operate as if the world were one large market—ignoring superficial regional and national differences." Sorenson and Wiechmann, on the other hand, have stated that there is often excessive standardization of international marketing programs, and they have questioned the economic benefits of program standardization. In their view, "companies already using systematic cross-border analysis have realized that marketing programs cannot often be standardized."[4]

Part of the reason for sharp disagreement is a lack of precision regarding exactly what is to be standardized and where. Is it best to seek a broad uniformity in policy? Should one concentrate more narrowly, on detailed product characteristics? Disagreement on the viability of standardization strategies also reflects varying interpretations of the environment facing the international company. Insofar as market heterogeneity overseas is seen to be either narrow or waning, standardization is attractive and feasible. Even when market variables vary significantly, debate is not necessarily invalidated. First, there is a good deal of room for debate on the significance of objective differences between markets. Second, it is possible to delineate international market segments of significant size and a high degree of uniformity.

Defining a Standard

Because of the heterogeneous nature of the international operating environment and other factors discussed later, it is only in exceptional circumstances that a detailed, uniform product program is likely to be viable in world markets.[5] Along with the rare situations in which identical, international product programs are possible, the subsequent discussion will interpret product standardization to include those strategies in which there is limited "local adaptation around a standardized core."[6] Very detailed product changes (such as modification of electrical goods to meet local voltage standards) will not be considered changes in basic product characteristics. Although small changes are necessary and important, they normally have limited impact on production costs and marketing activities. The key is the degree of uniformity needed to achieve significant cost and marketing benefits. It is standardization at this level, in terms of the strategic components of the international product program, that is worth pursuing; and it is the benefits and drawbacks of uniformity at this level that will be evaluated. In terms of the geographic scope of policy, it is frequently only viable to seek significant global uniformity in terms of a limited segment of the global market place as defined by a relevant segmentation variable.

Developing Standard International Product Presentations

The ethnocentric, polycentric, regiocentric, geocentric taxonomy developed by Perlmutter[7] and discussed in earlier chapters, is helpful in understanding the various approaches to product uniformity. The polycentric approach is essentially a national responsiveness orientation. As such, it is incompatible with significant international product uniformity. This is not so for the other three approaches: they provide a useful framework for describing alternative perspectives on standardization in the international marketplace.

The Ethnocentric Approach

In the ethnocentric firm, the standard on which uniform international product presentations are based is domestic policy. Domestic product programs are projected internationally. This approach has the advantage of being simple, rapid, and economical to implement. There is no necessity to review the international operating environment, and disruption to domestic production operations is minimal.

Such an orientation may reflect two management views: that the rest of the world is similar to the domestic market or that the programs implemented for domestic consumers represent "best practice" and should appeal to foreign buyers because of the presumed advanced nature of the home market. Linder's theory of international trade (described in Chapter 2) also provides a rationale for this approach. He argues that foreign trade is basically an extension of domestic trade and that it occurs between countries sharing similar standards of living and taste. Internationally uniform product policies, based on domestic practice, are thus appropriate.

The most obvious drawback to an ethnocentric approach is the danger that the ethnocentric product will be unacceptable overseas because it does not meet consumer needs or because it contravenes key elements of the local environment, such as regulations. Despite such problems, an ethnocentric strategy may be viable in certain situations. Facilitating factors include technological leadership, high product quality, low production cost, an advanced and dynamic home market, aggressive promotion, and a focus on those overseas markets where consumer needs and product-use conditions are congruent with conditions at home.

Coca-Cola, for example, has enjoyed great success overseas with a product that was not initially developed for international markets. In 1988, Coke sold in 155 countries, with over 50 percent of its profits being generated overseas. The company has made great efforts to maintain product uniformity; any differences in taste are due mainly to local bottlers failing to uphold quality-control standards. Occasionally, government regulations cause unavoidable changes in ingredients. In West Germany, for example, Diet Coke has to be sweetened with saccharine and fructose rather than aspartame, which has yet to be approved. This means that the beverage has about 15 calories per serving, not the one calorie found in the U.S. version. However, the Coca-Cola Company is really selling a carefully developed image rather than just a soda. Highly effective promotion, careful quality control, and the existence of an international segment of cola drinkers with broadly similar tastes have all enabled Coca-Cola to enjoy great success around the world.

The Geocentric Approach

In geocentric firms, worldwide marketing policies are developed within an avowedly global context. A high degree of international uniformity in product presentations is sought. Marketing policies are formulated accordingly.

Ideally the geocentric global firm identifies homogeneous international demand segments that can be targeted with a standard product. Alternatively, it may penetrate different market segments with the same product. For example, a product aimed at middle-class U.S. Consumers may be targeted at high-income consumers in poorer markets. Or, through promotions, the firm may attempt to create an international group of consumers for the product.

The worldwide focus of a geocentric strategy is a source both of strength and weakness. Success is contingent on careful, continuous, global market research, research that is both expensive and time consuming. Sharp differences between overseas markets can necessitate either the dropping of many markets or the abandonment of global standardization programs. The existence of international groups of consumers with similar needs, income, and taste is not sufficient for successful product standardization; differences in the conditions of product use may still pose unsurmountable barriers to significant uniformity.

An ability to achieve rapid worldwide distribution of a product that meets consumer needs and is characterized by low manufacturing costs are potent attractions of a geocentric product policy. Procter and Gamble has recently shown interest in developing global products that can be diffused rapidly into world markets. Liquid Tide, for example, was developed by a team including R&D staff from Japan and the United States, and the product was launched simultaneously in both countries. The product is standard although sold in Japan under the brand name Bonus 2000.[8] This case contrasts with Procter & Gamble's traditional incremental approach toward product internationalization. It usually develops a product specifically for a single market, usually the U.S., and then gradually introduces it into other overseas markets if it proves successful at home. Such was the approach followed for Pampers disposable diapers in the late 1970s. Although this approach provides companies time for careful market evaluation and product modification, it also provides competitors time to respond to product innovations.

The Regiocentric Approach

An alternative to geocentric policies is to seek product uniformity within subglobal groups of markets, or *market clusters*. Common criteria for delineating market clusters are geographic location, level of socioeconomic development, language, and membership in a regional organization. Criteria of a more situation specific nature, such as buying habits and lifestyle, are also used.

Once subglobal market groups have been delineated, the firm develops uniform product programs for each market cluster that it chooses to service. The degree of product heterogeneity in a regiocentric firm is a function of the number of market clusters identified and those chosen as targets.

A regiocentric strategy is a compromise between polycentric and geocentric strategies. It allows for refining responses to market differences without the cost and diffusion penalties characteristic of polycentric policies. It is particularly attractive when the level of consumer demand in market clusters is sufficient to support the establishment of world-class manufacturing facilities dedicated to sourcing demand in each market group. Cost savings can arise from mass production of standard goods. However, a regiocentric perspective will usually result in the evolution of a corporate organization and culture that slows down the rate of global diffusion of product innovations and limits the scope for leveraging corporate advantages from one market group to another.

Two corollaries of this strategy become clear. The smaller the number of market clusters, the greater the attractiveness of a regiocentric orientation. And clustering on the basis of geography is often inappropriate. Geographic proximity, although important, does not necessarily imply market similarity. For example, in such important attributes as language, culture, and taste, British consumers are likely to be more similar to Australians than to their French neighbors.

Still, many firms adopting a regiocentric approach do tend to identify market clusters on a geographic basis. Ford, for example, has allowed Ford Europe considerable autonomy and Ford's European product planning and design committee has traditionally focused on developing uniform product lines for the European market. There has been little commonality between Ford automobiles sold in Europe and those sold in North America. In recent years, however, more product cross-fertilization has occurred. Efforts were made to develop the ford Escort, primarily a European-designed car, as a global product. However, U.S. management had limited confidence in the suitability of the European design and undertook extensive reengineering of the North American Escort. This increased the production cost and weight of the U.S. version. Despite reasonable market success, the car has not been a big moneymaker for Ford in the United States.[9]

Uniform International Product Policies

Advantages

Advocates of standardization policies emphasize the impact of the forces of international market integration. Jones, for example, argued over 20 years ago for standardization:

> The development and speeding up of communications is leading very much to the "one world" idea and greater centralization. Films, radio, T.V., and international magazines are leading at once to the standardization of people's ideas and wants and making possible the worldwide promotion and distribution system to supply them. The jet airplane and the trans-oceanic telephone means we can communicate across the world in minutes and travel in hours. It is becoming easier every day to establish a marketing blueprint in New York which can be applied virtually 100% intact in any market in the world.[10]

The call for greater uniformity of international policy is thus partially based on the premise that greater and more rapid international communication and contact have combined with the forces of advancing technology to have a homogenizing effect on the needs and behavior of consumers around the world.

Levitt[11] has been a forceful advocate of this perspective, and he has argued that the foundation for competitive success in international markets is an ability to offer a product that provides superior value in terms of price, quality, reliability, and delivery. Standardization is recommended as a means of gaining such advantage, since "corporations geared to this new reality benefit from enormous economies of scale in production, distribution, marketing and management. By translating these benefits into reduced world prices, they can decimate competitors."

The global corporation, should, according to this view, see international markets as being composed of global market segments where high-quality, uniform products are sold at low prices. When market heterogeneity limits opportunity for uniformity, the firm should actively promote global convergence of market segments.

The most commonly identified advantage of standardizing international product policy is that it fosters manufacturing economies. An ability to mass produce a standard product enables economies of scale to be exploited fully. Costly disruptions to the flow of production are minimized, and the tooling and set-up costs associated with manufacturing a variety of different products are avoided. If a company increases the number of locations in which it manufactures a product, the significance of these savings tends to decline.

Uniform product presentations also enable additional cost savings by reducing inventory costs and simplifying distribution. It facilitates service backup to customers, rendering it more economical. R&D economies are also positively affected. If a largely standard product is offered worldwide, R&D efforts to develop product variations are not needed. Product uniformity, it is held, should also facilitate the development of standard promotional and communication policies the world over, which can again lead to worthwhile cost savings.

Other potential standardization advantages are that standardization enables a company to derive the maximum benefit from good product ideas and to gain rapid diffusion of new products into overseas markets. Maximum exploitation of an initial competitive advantage is thereby greatly enhanced.

The growing internationalization of life, particularly in travel and communications, may present opportunities for firms able to present a coherent and consistent image on a worldwide basis. Standard product presentations facilitate the achievement of such consistency. For instance, the foreign traveler seeing familiar products in overseas locations favors them. In other circumstances, however, the very "foreignness" of a product lends it snob appeal, which may also help to increase sales.

Relatively little hard empirical data is available on the level of potential cost savings and marketing benefits that can be generated by standardization. Sorenson and Wiechmann[12] found that only one of 27 survey companies contacted was able to offer documented evidence of specific cost savings. Despite a lack of hard data, it seems plausible that production economies are a real benefit accruing from product uniformity. In the case of the advantages derived from product commercialization and marketing, the following example is illustrated.

In the pharmaceutical industry, most companies devote a high proportion of their budgets to R&D expenditures. Instances of R&D budgets exceeding 10 percent of corporate spending are not uncommon. This has had two results. First, such companies are forced to go international because overseas sales are essential for recovering heavy R&D expenditure. Second, because of the high level of research carried out by competitors, the dangers of product obsolescence are real; it is necessary to get maximum mileage out of existing and new products as rapidly as possible. A lack of patent protection in many foreign markets also encourages rapid market entrenchment to combat competition. In essence then, the operating pressures on pharmaceutical companies are such that new product developments must be made available as widely and quickly as possible on an international basis.

The relevance of potential advantages of uniformity varies according to the particular aspect of product policy being considered. Cost-saving arguments are likely to be most significant in the context of the product's physical characteristics, performance, and packaging. Standard brand names, labeling, and warranty policies are unlikely to lead to important cost economies, but play a major role in promoting a single image in the international marketplace.

Disadvantages and Barriers

Standardization of product presentations is likely to hinder high levels of market penetration in individual markets and may result in a company being shut out from important overseas markets. Uniform products may not appeal to consumers in some markets and thus often fail to meet local regulations or product-use conditions. This problem is most likely in firms following an ethnocentric policy. However, attempts to develop products for international demand segments may also fail. For example, attempts to reconcile different needs and tastes may result in products that are too bland and appeal to no one in particular. Limiting the scope and scale of a firm's international business operations is thus the most serious drawback to adopting a standardization strategy.

An example of the way in which standardization can limit overseas business opportunities is provided by the behavior of some U.S. lumber exporters. One study found that a significant number of exporters were willing to sell only lumber cut to U.S. standards.[13] As a consequence, major export markets in Europe and Japan were closed to many exporters who restricted their overseas sales to markets where U.S. grades were commonly accepted, such as the Caribbean islands.

The implementation of standardized policies necessarily results in the concentration of power and control over marketing policy at corporate headquarters. This means a great deal depends on the abilities of a small body of executives, some of whom may be out of touch with market realities overseas. Overseas marketing executives will enjoy less autonomy, which may set back morale and motivation and stifle local creativity and innovation.

Differences in the characteristics of end users are a major barrier to product standardization in international markets. Major consumer variables include level of income, consumer needs, taste, and behavior. These variables are not alone in constraining standardization. Downham, for example, has identified eight factors that result in important European market differences and necessitate mandatory changes in marketing programs even when consumer attitudes and needs are the same.[14] His eight variables are brand-name availability, variance in distribution structure, media availability, regulations affecting product formulation, packaging, advertising content, promotion, and prices.

The common features between markets may not be sufficiently powerful to provide a basis for product uniformity. It has been argued by one commentator that:

> It is much better to have a product which appeals intensively to a minority than a product which appeals only superficially to the majority on first usage. The former is likely to give you a lasting, worthwhile business; the latter is likely to provide you with a commercial squib which flares and extinguishes very quickly.[15]

The degree and significance of consumer differences are likely to vary between products and markets. But even in the case of products such as ethical pharmaceuticals, differences in national taste and preference are important. In most countries, ethical drugs are available only by a doctor's prescription, but research indicates that the outlook and prescribing habits of doctors vary greatly. These variations have their origin in differing medical traditions and systems of education. Not only do remedies of first choice for particular illnesses vary, but even when the same drug is deemed appropriate for particular illness, the actual form in which the drug is administered often varies. The most obvious example is that of injectable or oral antibiotics. In some countries, injectables form only a small part of the market; in others, they are much more important, partly because patients in these markets have greater faith in the efficacy of a drug when it is administered by injection.

Variations in the conditions in which products are used frequently have important implications for product policy. Differences in climate, topography, infrastructures, social customs, and living conditions all have a major impact. Glass, for instance, is manufactured to specifications that vary with the local climate, the crucial factor being the number of hours of sunshine enjoyed during the year and the minimum temperature experienced. Washing-machine manufacturers have developed special slimline and compact machines for markets where limited laundry space is available in the home.

Differences in product end uses can be a significant *de*standardizing factor, especially for producer goods used for highly specific tasks. Slight changes in the nature of the task necessitate changes in design and performance characteristics of the product.

National legal regulations are one of the most comprehensive and insurmountable barriers to product standardization. Legal differences reflect variances in national concerns, values, and environments. Regulations are sometimes specifically designed to protect domestic producers and product laws may serve as protectionist measures. The food industry provides many examples of the destandardizing impact of government regulation and control. Legislative control is most marked for those food products containing artificial ingredients. Additives are used in many foodstuffs and beverages as preservatives, colorants, sweeteners and emulsifiers. These lengthen shelf life, improve product appearance, and add taste and flavor. Government attitudes toward the use of such additives differ, as do regulations governing their usage.

Variance in a variety of other features of the operating environment can pose significant barriers to product uniformity. Among the most commonly mentioned are competitive conditions, the stage of the product life cycle, and accepted local practice regarding other elements of the marketing mix, particularly distribution and pricing policy.

Again, examples abound in the food industry. In many markets, there is an accepted price range for particular foods; international marketers may need to adjust the size of the product and its packaging to come into line with consumer expectations.

The imperatives of strategic market planning also tend to work against standardization abroad. Thus the objectives, strategy, and posture of the firm may have to vary significantly from market to market. Historical patterns of corporate behavior and organizational structure may hinder the implementation of standardization policies. In companies that have devolved considerable autonomy to the marketing managers in overseas subsidiaries, rapid implementation of a uniformity strategy will be difficult to accomplish without major organizational changes.

Standardizing the International Product Presentation

Implementation Policies

In firms following an ethnocentric product strategy, overseas implementation of policy is relatively simple; the domestic product line, or elements of it, also form the international product line. In the case of firms with a geocentric or regiocentric perspective, such is not the case; the implementation problem has to be carefully considered. We now consider three basic approaches to designing uniform international product presentations along with policies that facilitate international product standardization.

The International Product Line Marketing a standard international product line (IPL), either regionally or globally, is an important managerial option. IPL's with length and depth make possible the servicing of a variety of customer requirements and market situations. However, if significant benefits from uniformity are to accrue, the number of items in the line and number of variants of each item offered need to be strictly controlled.

For example, a manufacturer of toiletry products markets a standard, premium product line that is highly uniform in product policy attributes, including branding and packaging, in overseas markets. In less affluent markets, however, a lower quality product line is sold alongside the premium product. The inexpensive product is of constant quality in all markets and has a different but standard brand name. Great care is taken to dissociate the two product lines. Different packaging is adopted for the cheaper line and the company's name does not appear on either the product or its packaging. Some flexibility in packaging policy is also evident for the cheaper lines, with smaller packages being offered in some markets.

Modular Strategies Another approach to solving the problem of meeting different market needs while maximizing the degree of product uniformity is the modular approach to product development and manufacture. This involves developing a standard range of components that are usable worldwide and can be assembled in a variety of configurations. Since standard components are produced in a single location, major manufacturing economies can be realized. The products are assembled in one or more facilities around the world. A primary goal of a modular strategy is to minimize the number of variants of each major component while maximizing the number of different products that can be assembled from these components. A product line so produced has some length and depth, is able to meet a variety of consumer needs and circumstances, and can be marketed without incurring many of the usual cost and time penalties of product diversity.

An example of a firm following a modular strategy is provided by the manufacturer of sophisticated electronic equipment that produces a limited range of standard modular units. These units can be assembled in a variety of combinations, making possible a range of systems with widely varying performance features. It is thus usually not particularly difficult or expensive to meet very specific customer requirements. Product modification is, however, sometimes necessary. For example, in some markets special motor alternator units have to be used to guard against fluctuations in the power supply. Such modifications can usually be accomplished relatively inexpensively by fitting a different or extra part without product redesign.

The Universal Product Strategy The thrust of this policy is the development of a "universal" product that can be marketed globally with minimum modifications. Four ways to implement this strategy can be identified.

The first is to design a product that meets the needs of all target buyers and is able to function effectively in all overseas markets. This is a demanding objective, one that firms are frequently unable to achieve with a single, uniform product. A closely related strategy, but one that is often more feasible, is the development of a standard product meeting the needs of the most demanding overseas customer and the most stringent product-use conditions. A product suitable for many, but not all, target buyers results.

Both approaches risk significant product redundancy. The average consumer may not need or want all the product features and performance offered. However, the cost of producing a superior, flexible alternative product is high. If many buyers are unwilling to pay a premium price for a level of product performance that is not needed, aggregate demand will be low.

Instead of seeking to develop a product which meets the needs of diverse consumers very well, a less ambitious approach is to search for and capitalize on common denominators in international target market segments. Doing so requires compromises; the resulting product will be unlikely to meet all target buyer needs in every market; and the marketer risks producing a bland product that has a limited appeal to everyone but is not highly attractive to anyone in particular. Aggressive pricing, which may be feasible because this is a cost effective policy can lessen risk.

The fourth and final way to implement a universal-product strategy is to design a uniform, "core" product which is robust and can accept a variety of standard attachments, parts, and components. From this core good, it is possible to assemble a range of products with variable performance characteristics.

The first three approaches to developing a universal product imply the highest degree of uniformity but are likely to be most viable in a regiocentric plan. Feasibility problems of a high order are common when such products are aimed at global markets.

Geocentric firms faced with market heterogeneity seem most likely to be attracted to a core product strategy. For example a manufacturer of agricultural machinery faced with important differences in climate, topography, and working habits in its overseas markets uses this approach. The basic product is thus designed to a high standard and allows the machine to operate under widely different conditions. A variety of standard attachments is available to make the product conform with market requirements. Thus, flexibility in the product presentation is combined with a considerable degree of product uniformity.

Other Facilitating Policies

Overseas Assembly Overseas assembly is frequently an important element of the operations of firms that adopt either a modular or a core-product policy. Since the product being assembled varies, the incentives for centralizing assembly in a single location are fewer than for a more uniform product. Overseas assembly allows for an economical response to particular local buyer needs and product-use conditions. Standard imported components are put together, with some modifications and attachments, to provide some customization. Such a work mode is a relatively inexpensive response to pressures for local production.

An example of successful "local assembly" is provided by a manufacturer of industrial compressors which are sensitive to differences in heat and altitude and also to considerable differences in customer requirements. The export product line is standardized and, in some markets, complemented by a core-product strategy. When operating conditions and product performance requirements are such that no product in the standard export range is suitable (and also where market opportunities are attractive) local assembly makes sense. The necessary product modifications are made locally, and there is no disruption to production operations at home. On average, around 70 percent of the value of the good is made up of standard components shipped from domestic factories. This policy has been successful because of the relative ease of assembling the product, a need for only modest investment in assembly facilities, and the ease with which the product can be modified.

Buying-Out Firms adopting product standardization strategies can avoid gaps in their coverage in markets overseas by buying-out non-standard products from external suppliers. These products are then sold under the buyer's brand name alongside in-house products.

The attractiveness of a buy-out policy depends on the importance attached to achieving better coverage overseas. The availability, price, quality of suitable products, and willingness of outside firms to supply the good on an ongoing basis are also very important considerations. This policy is generally most attractive in the case of market specific low-volume products.

An example of buying out is provided by a manufacturer of "white goods" that follows a regiocentric international product policy. Typically, such a firm seeks comprehensive coverage in target markets but manufactures only standard product with a potential for high-volume sales in subglobal markets. Gaps in market coverage are "plugged" by buying out from other manufacturers. In Europe, for example, a standard compact minimachine is bought from an external supplier and marketed under the corporate brand name. Demand for this product is concentrated in France and Belgium, where kitchen space is limited and there is thus a need for a compact product.

Conclusion

It is clear from the preceding discussion that the possibility for and attractiveness of standardization strategies is very situation specific. Key variables determining choice of strategy, include the nature of the product, the number of overseas markets entered, and the degree of market homogeneity in consumer characteristics and behavior, legal environment, and conditions of product use. Other important factors include the competitive environment and the firm's international marketing objectives, strategies, and resources.

Regardless of a firm's individual situation, standardization possibilities, particularly in the context of product and advertising policy, should be carefully evaluated. Frequently, opportunities for significant uniformity will be constrained because of a need for mandatory adaptation from market to market. Where freedom from legal and other constraints mandates product adaptation, the benefits and costs of uniformity policies need to be directly addressed.

THE INTERNATIONAL PRODUCT PROGRAM

Products exhibit multiple features—including physical attributes, packaging, labeling, brand, warranty, and service characteristics—and each merits separate consideration. First, however, we will review two approaches to developing international product policy, localization and adaptation which have not already been discussed. These and the four standardization strategies are the main choices open to the international marketer.

Localization Policy

Localization entails customization of the product program from market to market and products designed to fully satisfy local customer needs and environmental forces. It usually leads to the development of a diverse collection of product programs with a limited commonality from market to market. Localization may be necessary and desirable when customer needs, the conditions of product use, and other important factors differ significantly among overseas markets. It tends to maximize sales and may be desirable when high penetration in mass markets overseas is the firm's primary goal.

The drawbacks of a customization policy are fairly predictable. This policy generally increases the costs of doing overseas business. It requires an increase in marketing resources and greater time and effort spent on development. Production costs also rise as the number of product variants increases. Developing coordinated international marketing policies becomes difficult, and rapid international product diffusion is inhibited.

Adaptation Policy

Adaptation involves significant adaptation of a basic product program from market to market to bring it into line with varied consumer needs and market environments. The basic program may be that followed domestically or, more desirably, developed after consideration of explicit needs and overseas situations. Product programs following this approach are flexible while still conforming with the basic product strategy. Where there are important differences between markets, then adaptation is permitted. However, necessary modifications have to be made within the confines of the basic product policy framework.

The advantage of adaptation is that it allows for market differences to be taken into account at a relatively low cost. Central control and coordination should be possible, marketing cost constrained, and the economics of the production process held under control.

In practice, it is often not possible to realize all these advantages at the same time. Initial adaptation frequently becomes indistinguishable from a policy of localization. Adapting successfully within the straitjacket of an overall blueprint is not easy and may not be viable in many situations.

Characteristics of the Product Program

Product Attributes

Performance characteristics, quality, features, and styling are very tangible product charcteristics likely to be major elements in most product programs. These product attributes are dependent on such variables as consumer needs, the conditions of product use, and the ability to buy.

The major problem facing the international product planner is that the factors affecting product attributes vary significantly in the international marketplace. In the United States, for example, bicycling is primarily a recreational activity; mainstream buyers need a lightweight machine designed for rapid touring. In other countries, where incomes are lower, bicycles frequently meet a need for transportation. This difference has an important impact on the bicycle's attributes. In Nigeria, the primary demand is for a heavy and durable means of basic transport. Speed, lightness, and extra features are distinctly secondary or nonissues.

Even if a bicycle satisfies the same needs in the United States and Nigeria, we cannot safely assume that uniformity of product attributes is appropriate. In much of Nigeria, there are relatively few paved roads, the operating environment is harsher, and a strong, more durable machine is mandatory. The average Nigerian is also unable to afford to spend much on a bicycle.

Product attribute decisions need to take into account the firm's overall international strategy, marketing objectives, and operating environment. In the case of bicycles, it seems unlikely that a firm with global aspirations can expect to achieve significant uniformity except on a regiocentric basis. Highly localized product presentations would also seem unnecessary. Thus, it might be feasible to develop two basic models, one designed for recreation and the other for basic transport. Using these models as the starting point, significant adaptation may be achieved by the addition of extra features to satisfy performance and quality demands.

Government-imposed product standards have an important impact on product attributes. Although primarily aimed to protect consumers, these regulations some-times limit imports. Firms have no choice but to comply with these rules. Mandatory adaptation may also be required because of differences in operating conditions. An obvious example concerns power sources for electrical equipment. Modification is essential because of a need for compatibility with the local electrical current and voltage. Without modification, products are simply unmarketable.

Government tariffs and tax systems may have implications for product design and performance features. Not uncommonly, small local changes in product attributes are desirable to ensure that the good is classified in a low tax category. Adjustments in the horsepower of automobile engines to fall within a favorable vehicle tax bracket are an example of such product modification.

Compromising on product quality in order to deal with variances in the purchasing power, needs, and perceptions of consumers raises sensitive issues. Some firms refuse to lower quality because they do not wish to tarnish their reputation and image. (Image protection is particularly important in an age of increased international communication and travel.) Reputation explains why firms offering cheaper items of lower quality frequently disguise their association with these product lines by marketing them under different brand names devoid of any parent company identification.

Packaging

Product *protection* and *promotion* are key concerns in packaging. Regarding product protection, differences in climate, the transportation infrastructure, and distribution channels all have an impact on packaging. In hot and humid climates, for example, many products are subject to rapid deterioration unless given greater protection than is necessary in temperate regions. Export distribution is often a long process characterized by rough handling and pilferage. Special packaging for overseas shipment may therefore be necessary. Frequently, changes can be confined to the shipping package, avoiding any redesign in the primary package. However, if the product is sold in open-air markets, greater protection may be required.

Regarding promotion, one must consider consumer preferences as to color, size, and appearance; all affect the design and styling of goods and also impact on packaging. Other consumer characteristics, such as disposable income and shopping habits, may also be important. In markets where average income is low, cheaper packaging may be necessary, and goods may have to be packaged in smaller amounts and sizes than elswhere. Thus, in some countries, inexpensive plastic squeeze bottles may be preferred to aerosol cans; razor blades may be packaged and sold individually; and minibars of soap may be required.

In contrast, infrequent shopping by high-income consumers promotes larger sizes and more durable and expensive packaging solutions. More attention to the promotional impact of packaging is also likely. Differences in commonly accepted weights and measures also have an impact on package size. Many beverages sold in pint and gallon containers in the United States need to be sold in liter containers in much of Europe. Even in North America, differentiation may be required since the Imperial pint used in Canada is larger than the U.S. pint.

Labeling

The primary role of labeling is to provide *information*. Frequently, the level of detail required is regulated by the local government; the firm then has limited control. To the extent that government controls exist, labeling standardization becomes a problem. Regulations tend to vary from country to country.

Language differences are also a complicating factor. In most overseas markets, labels and other written materials (instructions and warranties) need to be translated into the local language. Sometimes firms deal with this problem by using a single multilanguage label or by adding internationally recognized symbols to deliver a universal message. However, the use of international symbols pertains mainly to warning and shipping labels. Given the low cost of producing nonuniform labels and the widespread incidence of labeling regulations, a drive to develop a single, international label is not likely to be a high priority in many firms.

Regarding government laws, the most common areas of company concern are descriptions of weight, contents, and ingredients; the name of manufacturer; product dating; and unit price information. An indication of country of origin is also commonly required. The impact of the country of origin of a good was discussed in Chapter 12.

Labels may also have a promotional impact. Graphics are often, but not always, more important than the copy material. Some food manufacturers, hoping to capitalize on France's reputation for fine food, like to use French names and terms on their labels.

Brands and Trademarks

A brand may be defined as a "name, term, sign, symbol or design, or a combination of them, which is intended to identify the goods or services of one seller or group of sellers and to differentiate them from those of competitors."[16] A trademark is the "brand or part of a brand that is given legal protection."[17]

When international firms brand their products for overseas markets, the first issue that they must consider is whether to seek legal protection for these brands. A related problem concerns the mechanics of obtaining a trademark in foreign markets.

Legal protection of corporate brands is generally a desirable objective in those overseas markets with current operations or those identified as potential entry targets. Legal protection constrains actual or potential competitors from copying or othewise exploiting what may be a very valuable corporate asset. The registration of brands also precludes other persons or firms from acquiring local trademark rights to the name. Without such protection, the firm may find it has to purchase the right to use its own brand name if it wishes to enter the market.

Some firms do not seek extensive legal protection outside their major foreign markets because obtaining trademarks is often expensive or because it may not be obtainable prior to use of the brand. Maintenance of protection may also require subsequent use within a given time period. What constitutes "brand use" will vary and may be a tough condition to meet if the market is not considered of special current interest.

Assuming trademark protection is to be sought, managers must seek out expert local legal advice. Where brand ownership is established by priority in use, as in the United States, legal protection can be sought only following introduction of the brand in the marketplace.

In other markets, brand ownership is determined by priority in registration. In these countries, the temptation for opportunists to register other firms' well-known brand names locally is likely to be high. Cases have occurred in which individuals have registered several hundred brand names in a country with no intention of trading under the trademarks that have been acquired. Their goal is to subsequently sell the right to use the trademark.

The steps that have to be followed when registering trademarks vary, and managing the process is usually best left to reputable local attorneys. Although registration fees are often not very high, legal bills can be significant. Even when limited or no brand usage suffices for maintaining trademark ownership, it may be necessary to renew trademark rights periodically.

Obtaining trademark protection is not possible in all countries. A local firm may already be using the brand name or, particularly where brand usage is not a requirement for brand registration, the name may have been registered by an opportunistic brand pirate. In the latter instance, it is probable that the rights to the name can be purchased. When another firm is already using the brand name independently, the issue is more complex. If the brand name is available for sale, the price demanded is likely to be very high. If the asking price is reasonable, it may still not be worth acquiring the trademark because its use on different products is apt to cause confusion among local consumers.

A major issue in international brand management is thus whether or not to develop international brands. The benefits of an international brand are primarily promotional. In an age of extensive international travel, cross-border communication and international media, the advantages of a uniform, globally promoted name are obvious. Tourists recognize familiar products, cross-border advertising does not confuse consumers, and international promotional programs can piggyback on recognized global brands.

Various problems have to be addressed when developing international brand names. Language presents very real problems. The name chosen needs to be easily pronounceable in all relevant languages. It must not have undesirable connotations in countries where it will be used. Names that sometimes sound fine in one language may sound awful in another and, even worse, may have unfortunate meanings. For example, one manufacturer of perfumes discovered that one of its brand names was associated with manure in another language.

The attitudes of foreign governments and local consumer perceptions also need to be considered. Some foreign governments, particularly in LDCs, may oppose the local use of a foreign brand name. Opposition usually reflects nationalist sensitivity and perceptions that international branding may increase the local profits of foreign firms. Use of an international brand may also identify the product as being of foreign origin. Although sometimes beneficial, it can also result in the firm and its product lines being more exposed to nationalist pressures.

When making decisions on international brands, managers must carefully weigh the benefits and costs of uniformity and address the question of feasibility. Apart from carefully considering potential benefits, drawbacks, and barriers to standardization, they should evaluate the significance of branding policy for international sales. Cost savings from a uniform international brand are unlikely to be great. The promotional impact of the policy often deserves more careful attention. If a firm has a well-established and strong local brand name, the cost of discarding it for an unfamiliar uniform brand name can be very high. Generally, the scope for brand name flexibility is greatest only when initially entering an overseas market.

When firms are emphasizing the development of relatively uniform global marketing programs, it is likely that they also attach a good deal of importance to developing internationally recognized brand names. This may involve rationalization of the firm's existing brand names. If so, loss of customer goodwill and the creation of consumer confusion will be very real short-term dangers. Here, widespread publicity of the proposed name change becomes usually desirable, and managing the transition is likely to be expensive and complex.

A good example of a firm deciding that brand name uniformity was indeed worth disruption is provided by the Nissan auto company. In the early 1980s, management decided to change their well-established Datsun brand (which was used in the United States and England) to Nissan which is now used globally. The name Datsun was originally adopted to avoid the possible association of the word Nissan with the word Nippon, used during World War II to identify the Japanese.

The U.S. government is currently pushing hard for greater international protection of intellectual property rights, particularly for patents, copyrights, and trademarks. The aim is to negotiate a multilateral agreement, under the auspices of GATT, to cover protection for all forms of intellectual property. Existing international agreements (discussed in more detail later in this chapter) are of limited effectiveness and do not include countries where the risk of brand piracy is greatest.

Service Policies

Major services that are typically offered in conjunction with physical products can be grouped into presales services (delivery and technical advice) and postsales services (repair services, maintenance, and operating advice). Important service issues include the particular services to be provided overseas, the level and quality of service offered, and the form in which it is provided. Frequently service supports vary between and among markets. Differences in customer needs and behavior, conditions of product use, the firm's ability to deliver, and the availability of local facilities and trained personnel are likely to be significant forces for destandardization.

Where a uniform level of service is considered crucial, as is often the case for aircraft and machine tools, it can usually be attained but the cost is often high. For example, provision of full-service backup for aircraft engines in every national market is likely to be prohibitively expensive. Usually, it is more appropriate for major overhauls to be done in regional service centers, with a provision for some national service capability and mobile engineers to provide needed local support.

A basic problem regarding the maintenance of acceptable standards overseas is that frequently one has to rely on foreign distributors and service agents to provide local services. This weakens a firm's ability to enforce specified service standards. One solution is to develop company-owned distribution and service facilities overseas. This will be expensive and demands trained staff and a network of comprehensive service facilities.

Generally, the more complex the product technology, the greater the demand for pre- and postsales service. There is thus pressure in some firms to offer simpler, more robust products overseas in order to reduce the need for customer support, especially maintenance and repairs. When firms rely on foreign distributors and agents for the provision of service backup, a number of measures can be taken to improve the level of service so provided. The most obvious is to establish adequate training programs for all local service personnel. The level of service provided should be monitored periodically and poor performance penalized. The international firm should also devise systems to effectively monitor inventories of spare parts overseas and it should be prepared to step in and support the local service agents when necessary. A willingness to send in a service engineer and to airfreight vital components when needed is essential.

The emphasis placed behind service support should relate to the importance customers attach to such backup and the firm's competitive strategy. Purchasers of industrial machinery, for example, are often willing to pay heavily for a level of service backup that minimizes machine downtime. A very high priority to providing rapid, high-quality repair and maintenance services is appropriate under such circumstances.

Warranties

Warranties generally provide a written guarantee of manufacturer responsibilities when a product does not perform adequately. Particular attention is usually given to the responsibility for the repair or replacement of defective parts. A warranty thus defines the producer's product liability and may also be used as a promotional tool.

Warranties must comply with local laws and do not supersede any local legislation regarding product standards and manufacturer liability. If local regulations exist, warranty uniformity becomes more difficult to achieve. However, it is doubtful whether much effort should be expended on seeking international standardization. The economic benefits from uniformity are small. In addition, variance in product quality, conditions of product use, and the level of local service backup available all militate against standard international warranties.

Still, warranty uniformity may be desirable for certain customers. Goods sold to internationally mobile consumers may benefit from a standard warranty; consumers may be confused and irritated by differing national warranties. Some customers, notably international firms, purchase products in a variety of locations or intend to use them in different countries, and may actually demand a standard warranty.

Since foreign enterprises may be regarded by local consumers as less dependable than local firms, a strong warranty can compensate for local suspicion. However, the provision of exceptional warranty coverage is expensive and presupposes strong service backup. Offering superior warranty protection is a promotional tool that should be carefully tailored to local customer needs. The firm must be prepared to live up to its promise. Failure to meet warranty responsibilities can generate much consumer dissatisfaction and may stimulate unwelcome attention from host governments.

THE INTERNATIONAL PRODUCT MIX POLICY

Planning the International Product Mix

Planning for and developing the international product mix should occur within the context of a strategic international marketing plan. The significance of strategic planning was discussed in Chapter 11 where the importance of the interrelationship between product-mix decisions and other elements of a firm's international strategy was noted. Policy regarding entry modes, the scope of overseas operations, the diversity of markets entered, and the level of market penetration sought have major implications for product mix strategy.

Other major determinants of international product mix policy are shown in Figure 13-1. Corporate resources and salient characteristics of the operating environment, such as government regulations, consumer needs, and competitive behavior, have a major impact on product policy. Economies of research and development, production, and distribution are also very important. Of particular significance are the likely benefits and costs of the primary strategic alternatives—uniformity, localization and adaptation policies. In some firms, the characteristics of domestic product lines will also have a strong impact. This effect will be greatest in firms with an ethnocentric orientation.

Fundamental issues that need to be addressed are the number of product lines to be offered in international markets, the degree of consistency between these product lines, and their length and depth. In firms emphasizing standardization strategies, a uniform set of international product lines is likely. Where adaptation and localization dominate, the achievement of integrated international product lines is usually not feasible, and national product lines will be the norm.

The Product Portfolio Approach

When developing an international product mix policy, the balancing of all relevant considerations typically involves difficult cost–benefit tradeoffs. Wind[18] has suggested that the development of an optimal international policy can be facilitated by using a product portfolio perspective during planning. This requires focusing on the expected return and risk characteristics of alternative sets of product lines and identifying portfolios lying along an "efficient" frontier. Choice depends on management evaluations of the risk return relationships inherent in each of the portfolios on that "frontier." These ideas are illustrated in Figure 13-2.

The various crosses on the chart indicate feasible product mixes described by expected return and degree of risk. The curve AD represents the efficient frontier since the four portfolios on the curve offer the maximum return for a given level of risk. Those portfolios below the efficient frontier offer less attractive risk-return relationships. If management is risk averse, product mix A is preferred. Risk takers will favor portfolio D because of the higher expected return. It is

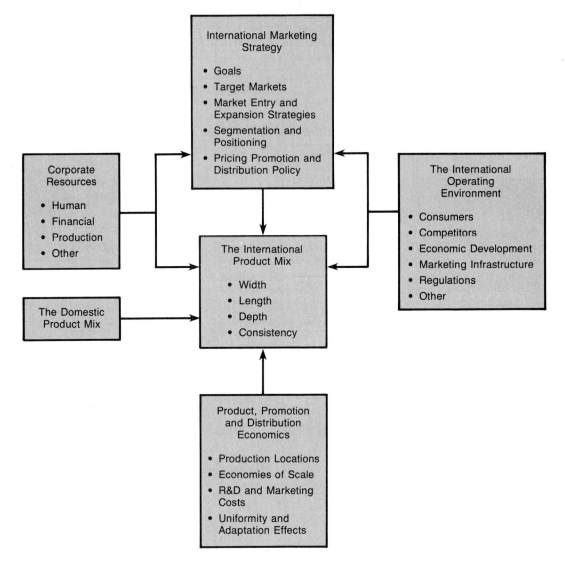

FIGURE 13-1   International Product Mix Policy: Key Determinants

certain, whatever management's objectives, that A will always be preferred to E and that D should always be favored over F.

Although it provides a conceptually appealing analytical framework, the portfolio approach requires the generation and analysis of a lot of information, much of which has to be forecast. Specific steps necessary to develop the required data are briefly noted below:

1. The identification of alternative, viable product portfolios for international markets;

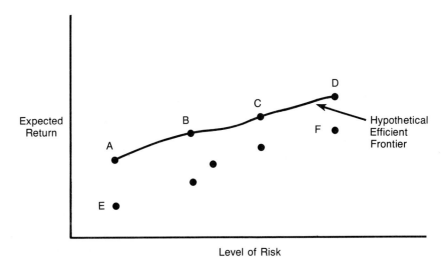

FIGURE 13-2 International Product Portfolios
Note: Each point, such as A, B, etc, represent a given international product mix.

2. Estimation of the cost and revenue implications of each portfolio;
3. Evaluation of the risk profiles of the alternative portfolios.

To accomplish this demanding and time consuming analysis effectively, management should consider several different environmental scenarios. It is to be expected that the efficient frontier will vary by scenario, and this variance will complicate evaluation and decision making. Only firms with well-developed data collection and analytical resources will be able to consider a significant number of alternative portfolios and scenarios. Even in these firms, the time and expense of comprehensive studies is likely to limit the scope of the work undertaken. Despite these problems, this perspective has the virtue of focusing attention on the crucial profit and risk implications of international product-line policy.

Managing International Product Lines

Firms operate in a dynamic environment. There is likely to be a wide variety of pressures acting on an international firm at any one time, pressures that favor product line adjustment overseas. Falling sales, competitive products, product acquisitions, internal product developments and innovation, changes in consumer needs and behavior, and new international objectives and marketing strategies are some of the more common catalysts of change.

As a result of these forces, there is a constant need for ongoing product-line analysis to maintain a flexible and adaptable product line. The primary areas of interest in any ongoing analysis system should be sales and profit performance, market penetration, and product positioning and fit vis-à-vis competing product lines and customer needs. Close attention needs to be paid also to the product lines and policies of competitors and other product threats and opportunities.

For firms operating in numerous foreign markets, evaluating a mass of conflicting data is not easy. Data may, for example, indicate that a product that is doing well in some markets is floundering in others. Should it be dropped in the latter markets, or are basic changes necessary? Would changes conflict with the existing overall strategy? Should significant opportunities be ignored in some markets because expensive product invention and development are needed? Clearly, no magic formula can answer these kinds of questions, but it is imperative that the firm monitor product-line performance and the product environment and realize when action is needed.

There is a strong tendency in many firms to develop long, deep international product lines. The diversity and complexity of international markets and the differential rate of change in these markets encourage firms to increase the number of items in the product mix and to develop multiple product variants. The penalty of such developments are cost increases and unwieldy, undisciplined product lines exhibiting little commonality from market to market.

Additions to international product lines can take the form of *line filling,* whereby more items are added within the current range, or *line stretching,* whereby product additions increase the product line beyond its current range. Even more fundamental changes resulting from the development or acquisition of products not congruent with current product lines may also be contemplated. Whatever the case, a key decision factor is the potential for cannibalization of existing products. Other questions of interest include: In which markets is addition contemplated? Will the new product be made in house? If so, What are the production and other cost implications? How will overall sales and profit performance be affected?

A major problem in international firms is the need to evaluate the overall impact of the product addition on a firm's performance in all overseas markets. The potential for the new product in markets other than the initial target should be reviewed, as should direct and opportunity cost implications for the firm as a whole.

The usual rationale for dropping products is poor profit performance. Insufficient capacity or a belief in a higher profit potential from alternative products may affect the decision to drop. Before making such a decision, management needs to review the reasons for unsatisfactory product performance, and consider possible remedies and the consequences for the firm's activities as a whole. Dropping a product in one market, for example, may result in increased overhead allocations in other markets. Possibilities for reducing cost (such as moving production to low-cost overseas locations or buying out the product from external suppliers) should also be considered.

Dropping and adding products on a market-by-market basis leads to divergence of national product lines. This may be a cause for concern in those firms pushing for a high degree of rationalization and uniformity in international product lines. However, against the dangers of product-line fragmentation must be balanced the dynamic nature of the international market. Situations differ in individual markets, and change occurs at varying rates and in different directions. The prospects for existing products and the need for new products is likely to differ significantly from market to market. Frequently, it is therefore necessary to make drop and add decisions for individual overseas markets rather than across the board.

SERVICES

Much of the discussion in this chapter is based on the assumption that a *tangible* product is being marketed overseas. This assumption is not unreasonable; most international trade and production does involve physical goods. In addition, many of the points made in our analysis apply generally and are not significantly affected by the nature of the product marketed. However, the marketing of services is different in some important respects and we now discuss these differences.

The distinction between a good and a service is not clear cut; most economic output embodies some combination of goods and services. However services mainly involve activities and processes resulting in output that is primarily, but not always, intangible. One definition is that services "represent either intangibles yielding satisfactions (insurance), tangibles yielding satisfactions directly (transportation), or tangibles yielding satisfaction jointly when purchased either with commodities or other services (credit)." [19]

Earlier in this chapter, we noted the importance of service backup when marketing many goods. We now focus on the international marketing of services in their own right and not on service support. Major service sectors characterized by extensive international operations include banking and other financial services, insurance, transportation, travel and tourism, consultancy, accountancy, advertising, construction, and computer services.

The importance of service business cannot be overlooked. In 1983, over 60% of jobs in North America, Japan and the leading West European countries were in service activities.[20] In 1980, it was estimated that service sector trade was worth some $350 billion, or around 20 percent of world trade.[21] The major service exporters are the industrial countries, and the United States and Common Market countries accounted for some 60% of world exports of services.

Special Features of the International Market for Services

Firms engaging in the international marketing of services need to deal with essentially the same types of problems that marketers of physical goods face. However, three significant differences have important implications for marketing policy.

Greater Protectionism

The service sector tends to be less capital intensive and more labor intensive than traditional manufacturing activities; economies of scale are often less important. As such, it is feasible for local entrepreneurs to provide local sevices needed in foreign markets without the high level of investment needed for traditional manufacturing enterprises. In addition, service activities are often viewed by governments as having special cultural or strategic significance. There is a tendency for governments to exhibit strong protectionist tendencies in services. Governments frequently ban foreign providers of services, subsidize local firms, and restrict incoming FDI in service industries. Banking, insurance, transportation, and the communication sectors are particularly exposed to protectionist measures of this type. A common strategy is to not allow foreign firms to make the FDI needed to support their activities, encouraging them instead to share their know-how with local firms through licensing and other similar arrangements.

At present, the United States is putting pressure on countries restricting the free flow of services to reduce their protectionism. It is also urging that GATT give high priority to addressing such restrictions in the Uruguay round of international trade negotiations. If the U.S. strategy succeeds, interesting new opportunities will arise for providers of services to market their products directly overseas.

Direct Contact in Exchange Relationships

Most services exhibit a high degree of intangibility and perishability; service sales typically involve simultaneous production, exchange, and consumption. This results in the need for more direct face-to-face contact when undertaking service transactions, and exchange is often possible only when the buyer and seller are in the same location. Five important implications follow from these points.

First, foreign suppliers of services generally have to supply their product directly in the foreign market. The product cannot be manufactured at home and shipped overseas, as is the case for commodity exports. As a result, service suppliers often find it necessary to establish a physical presence, in the form of a subsidiary and permanent offices, and must undertake direct investment overseas. For example, the provision of banking services in overseas markets is not feasible on any significant scale without the opportunity to establish a network of banks in the foreign market. Of course, some services can still be "exported" in the sense that they are provided by traveling "consultants," based at home, who fly in to meet foreign customer needs and then depart.

Second, the need for direct contact implies that each service transaction is unique, and will be heavily influenced by human variables that are inherently difficult to control. Controlling the quality of services is thus likely to be a major problem, and greater quality variance can be expected in the service business.

Third, most services cannot be produced and then held in inventory in order to meet peaks in demand. Production and consumption of services usually occur either simultaneously or nearly simultaneously. One attraction of international business, therefore, is that it offers an opportunity to reduce variance in the overall level of demand if diversification occurs in markets where the economic cycle follows a different pattern from that in the domestic market.

Fourth, prior customer evaluation of services is difficult because no concrete physical good exists that can be examined prior to purchase. Thus, the reputation and image of international service suppliers is critically important to success.

Finally, it is evident that service industries are more exposed to protectionism in international markets than are most other industries. Governments do not have to directly ban sales by foreign service firms to exclude them. Exclusion can be accomplished simply by not allowing international firms to establish a permanent physical presence.

Economies of Location

There is a stronger tendency for service products to be jointly demanded and supplied than are most goods. This is particularly true for such services as banking, finance, insurance, and tourism. In these service sectors, economies of location result in a high degree of localization (in a geographic sense) of target markets overseas. Thus, the primary market for suppliers of international banking services is likely to be located in cities such as London, Tokyo, New York, and Singapore, where major international financial markets have already developed. Attractive opportunities do exist elsewhere, but these are, once again, centered in local financial centers.

Marketing Services in Global Markets

Significant adjustments in international marketing policy may be required as a result of the factors discussed above. We now review some of the more important issues and actions that may be necessary.

Human Resource Policies

Given the high degree of personal contact involved in service transactions, the quality and effectiveness of the company personnel who deliver the required services to overseas customers is critically important.

Technical competence of a high and *consistent* order is imperative. Unless it is achieved, sharp variance in the quality of the service delivered results. High standards of personnel selection, technical training programs, and the establishment of procedures and quality standards are also important, as is frequent monitoring of personnel performance.

In any international market, cultural sensitivity is crucial. It is not sufficient for managers to be technically competent; they need to be able to deliver the required service in a manner consistent with the foreign customer's sensibilities. It therefore follows that cultural training and, in particular, sensitivity-enhancing programs should be given a very high priority by international service firms. There will also be a strong tendency to mainly employ local natives in foreign markets.

Strategic and Tactical Flexibility

Because of the human-resource intensity of many services, relatively low capital investment requirements, and the versatile nature of the professional staff producing service products, service-based operations are frequently more flexible and less market-specific than are comparable manufacturing activities. For example, professional banking staff are relatively mobile and may be moved from one financial center to another at short notice and relatively inexpensively. In addition, the penalties of failure in any single market are likely to be relatively low. These factors result in many service firms being willing to operate within a broader and more diverse spectrum of overseas markets than is the case for manufacturing firms.

Aggressive internationalization strategies are likely in many service firms. Research in Sweden, for example, indicates that Swedish technical consulting firms are much more likely to initiate foreign operations in unstable developing markets than are Swedish manufacturers.[22] This willingness to enter more overseas markets rapidly is complemented by greater flexibility in dropping markets and shifting resources with changing conditions.

Opportunities for greater flexibility are not limited to strategic policy. At the operational level, service firms may enjoy greater freedom in some areas of policy than do firms marketing tangible goods. Consider pricing policy. The intangibility of most services precludes arbitrage; direct price comparison is rendered more difficult. Price discrimination within and between overseas markets is thus likely to be more viable than is the case for many manufactured products. However this does not always follow, and intense price competition has characterized some service sectors, such as transport and tourism, in times of excess supply.

In the case of distribution policy, service firms enjoy enhanced possibilities for controlling distribution channels. Interaction with and proximity to the customer are required in most service transactions. Short, direct channels are thus the norm. Since service-supplier presence is frequently mandatory, the possibility for successfully using third parties to undertake overseas marketing and distribution are limited. This may be a significant disadvantage for firms that wish to rely on indirect channels.

Service firms wishing to follow an indirect approach will probably sell their expertise to local firms, which then become responsible for providing the service to foreign customers. This requires a transfer of knowledge and skills that is often not easy and is usually accomplished through licensing or franchising.

Differentiation Strategies

Because of the close, direct interface between the service supplier and the foreign customer, there is strong pressure to provide a product tailored to the consumer's special requirements. Given the flexible nature of human beings, it is usually easier and less costly to satisfy such demands than is the case for manufactured goods. It is thus of overriding importance for the service firm to understand very clearly foreign consumer requirements and to respond directly to these demands. Uniformity of the service product is often sought in the sense of meeting desired quality standards, but it is not likely to be a viable strategy for most other characteristics of the service product.

To stand out from its competitors, a service firm may pursue differentiation strategies directed specifically toward satisfying carefully defined international segments of demand. In the area of international management consultancy, for example, McKinsey and Company has specialized in meeting the needs of large enterprises reviewing their basic organization and strategic postures.

The pursuit of strong penetration in market niches by means of offering a superior service package reflects a tendency toward less direct price competition in many service markets. As noted earlier, the intangibility of service products limits the possibility for price comparison and arbitrage. It is thus not surprising that differentiation strategies are likely to be attractive for international service suppliers.

Given nationalist and other protectionist pressures, international service suppliers tend to concentrate on products that demand a high level of supplier resources and expertise. Services of this type are not easily replicated by local firms and are likely to generate high margin business.

Promotion

It has already been noted that company reputation and image in the international marketplace are peculiarly important to service firms. Since tangible samples of the product cannot usually be inspected prior to purchase and direct price comparison is often a problem, effective communication with potential customers is of primary importance. Apart from the use of advertising and other commercial media for reaching customers, noncommercial channels are highly important. Word-of-mouth communication is likely to be particularly powerful. Thus, poor and inconsistent service, even if it is relatively infrequent, may have a devastating impact on a firm's reputation. Consequently, the maintenance of quality control standards and the cultivation of good working relationships with foreign customers is vital. If the customer relationship is sound, occasional problems are tolerable as long as they are reconciled expeditiously and effectively.

Networking Relationships

Many service products are supplied in combination with other goods. For example, architects and firms of engineering consultants work closely with building and engineering firms to supply products such as housing, offices, and industrial plants. Frequently, suppliers of these goods have a major influence on the choice of the service firms with which they will work.

Foreign assignments for service suppliers are thus commonly "mediated" by other firms that have obtained overseas contracts requiring service support (such as construction projects) or who are expanding their own overseas operations by, for example, FDI. Prior contact has often been established at home; many service firms are simply pulled into foreign markets on the coat tails of their domestic customers. Service firms also work together. Typically, initial working relationships and contacts occur with other domestic service firms. However, contact with foreign service firms is likely to become increasingly important as overseas experience increases.

It follows from the preceding points that the number and nature of foreign business opportunities will be heavily influenced by a service supplier's network of relationships with customers and other organizations at home and overseas. In view of the crucial importance of these external relationships, it is important for service firms to carefully evaluate and develop their networks of connections.

The following steps should be undertaken in any evaluation process:[23]

1. Identify and examine the current network of relationships with current and potential clients and other organizations and individuals that could prove useful. Issues of special interest include the genesis, nature, and quality of the relationship.

2. Evaluate ways in which the present network is being and could be used as a platform for generating foreign business. Key questions include: Does it provide good information on overseas business opportunities? Does it result in effective project collaboration? Could these contacts be used more effectively to obtain foreign business?

3. Devise a strategy for network development to facilitate entry into new overseas markets and to increase business opportunities in current markets.

COUNTERFEITING

Product counterfeiting involves the unauthorized use of the various forms of industrial and intellectual property such as patent rights, product design, and trademarks. Traditionally, consumer products such as apparel, records and tapes, jewelry and toys are prime targets for counterfeiters. However, a wide range of other goods (including products such as auto parts and chemicals, many of which are sold to industrial users) are now being counterfeited. Four approaches to counterfeiting may be distinguished:

1. **Piracy** The design and trademark of the original good are copied and the fake is marketed as the genuine product. Rolex watches, Levi's jeans and many brands of auto parts are good examples of frequently pirated products.

2. **Design counterfeiting** The physical attributes of the original good are copied, and the product is then marketed under a different brand name. Apart from looking like the original, the counterfeit product often performs as well as the original. Products such as perfume and electronic equipment are susceptible to this form of counterfeiting.

3. **Trademark or brand-name counterfeiting** The fake is marketed using a well-known brand name but is physically different from the original. Apparel is commonly counterfeited in this way.

4. **Clone strategy** Modification of the design and/or brand name in such a way that the modified product is very similar to the original good. In the case of product design and performance many personal computers are, for example, highly derivative of IBM machines.

Internationally, counterfeiting is a growing problem. It has been estimated that counterfeit goods account for some 2 percent of world trade.[24] In the United States, some $8 billion of domestic and foreign sales are lost annually by U.S. firms to foreign counterfeiters, at a cost of over 130,000 jobs. Although lost sales are the most direct consequence of counterfeiting, other problems are also posed by this activity.

Most counterfeit goods are inferior to the genuine article. This may result in safety hazards, as in the case of replacement parts for cars. Poor quality also damages the image and reputation of the supplier of the genuine article, particularly when trademarks are copied. R&D expenditure and other innovative product development also become less attractive if the results of such efforts cannot be protected.

Anticounterfeiting Laws

Anticounterfeiting laws have been enacted in many countries. However, the scope of the legislation and effectiveness of the enforcement process varies by market.

In Taiwan, for example, there has traditionally been limited opportunity for legal redress against counterfeiters. This has changed somewhat during the 1980s; the government has closed loopholes in laws protecting intellectual property. Changes have been mainly the result of outside pressure from countries like the United States, which has complained about the inadequacy of Taiwanese laws. Despite the new laws and more convictions for infringements of trademarks, patents, and copyrights, enforcement of regulations is still relatively lax. Taiwanese counterfeiting continues to be a big problem for some firms.

In the United States, the Trademark Counterfeiting Act of 1984 increased the penalties for intentional trading in counterfeit goods and services. However the act only applies to the counterfeiting of *registered* trademarks. In the case of imitation products, patent laws offer some protection. But design patents—which concern the design of a good rather than its function—are not available in the United States and many other countries.

Bilateral negotiations offer the opportunity to pressure foreign counterfeiters. In the United States, for example, the Omnibus Tariff and Trade Act of 1988 mandates study of the extent to which a foreign country provides "adequate and effective means under its laws for foreign nationals to secure, exercise and enforce exclusive rights in intellectual property." Import restrictions can be implemented against countries failing to adequately protect intellectual property. There has been particular pressure in the United States to reduce the special duty-free treatment accorded exports from some developing countries, such as Taiwan, Korea, and Brazil, where counterfeiting is alleged to be relatively widespread and minimal government action to counteract it has been taken.

International agreement, in the form of treaties or conventions, offers an attractive route to protecting intellectual property rights. Unfortunately, countries where counterfeiting is widespread are generally not parties to such treaties. International control there is difficult.

The International Convention for the Protection of Industrial Property, or the *"Paris Union,"* is adhered to by some 90 countries, including the United States and most industrial countries. This convention covers trademarks and patents. In the case of patents, a citizen of a participating country has first right to patent registration in other member countries for one year after initial registration. For trademarks, the protection is for only six months.

Under the *Patent Cooperation Treaty,* developed during the 1970s and agreed to in principle by most OECD countries and the Soviet Union, it will be possible to make a single application for a patent in all member countries. Expensive duplication applications are thus eliminated.

The *Madrid Agreement* gives trademark protection in some 20 countries. The United States is not a participant and membership is concentrated in Western Europe. Trademark registration by one member is automatically extended to the other participating states.

Copyright protection is offered by the *Universal Copyright Convention* of 1954, of which the U.S. is a member, and the Berne Convention of 1986. Some 50 countries have acceded to each treaty. An important private initiative to combat counterfeiting has also been taken by the 250 or so firms and trade associations that have formed The International Anti-Counterfeiting Coalition. This group attacks counterfeiting in the high-tech and creative product sectors, mainly through lobbying and educational activities.

Anticounterfeiting Strategies

Lobbying Activities

Individual corporate lobbying at the political and administrative level and collective support of such pressure groups as the Anti-Counterfeiting Coalition may prove very useful. Pressure should be applied in a focused manner in pursuit of three primary objectives:

☐   Tougher *domestic* anticounterfeiting laws and more effective enforcement of existing regulations.

☐   Sanctions against countries where the production and sales activities of counterfeiters are relatively unconstrained either because of weak local laws or ineffective law enforcement. Import restrictions on goods sourced from countries with weak counterfeiting controls are a favorite penalty.

☐   Support for the development of a GATT anticounterfeiting code.

Combatting Counterfeiters

Attacking producers and marketers of counterfeit products is becoming more common. Companies such as Levi Strauss, Ralph Lauren, and Vuitton have hired investigators to track down counterfeiters. Legal action to confiscate fakes and prosecute counterfeiters increases the risk of such activities. Effective action is possible only where patent, trademark, and other anticounterfeiting laws have been enacted.

Other measures should also be considered. Many counterfeit goods are unknowingly marketed by legitimate distributors. Information programs highlighting the counterfeiting problem and facilitating identification of fakes should be targeted at distribution channels. It is important to differentiate between "gray market" products, which are not fakes and are usually not illegal, and counterfeit products.

Product identification can be facilitated by the use of special labeling systems that are difficult and expensive to replicate. Heat-sensitive ink, labels with separate images that vary with the angle of the viewer, and other security measures are possible and have been adopted by such companies as Chrysalis Records, Anheuser-Busch, Puritan Fashions, MGM, and PolyGram. Reward programs for the exposure of fakes may also prove useful. Generally, these are most effective when aimed at encouraging distributors to identify counterfeit goods.

Combatting cloning firms presents special problems because their products, although close copies of other goods, often do not infringe patent and trademark laws. Product-design copying and misleading labeling are particularly difficult to attack. For example, Chateau Montocin Grand Vin, which is bottled ("mis en bouteilles") by the Japanese firm Hamada Vin S.A., is not imported; this fact would surprise four out of ten Japanese purchasers who assumed it to be French.[25]

Product Development

Staying one step ahead of counterfeiters is a valuable but expensive strategy. Frequent product innovation and the development of proprietary product features that are difficult to copy make counterfeiting expensive and more risky. Although performance replication is more difficult, design similarity and trademark copying are often not seriously deterred by this policy. The high cost of innovation designed to deter counterfeiting must also be taken into account by the marketer.

Collaboration

If other policies fail or are not workable, managers may appropriately consider working with rather than against some counterfeiters. When, for example, the counterfeiter is able to manufacturer a clone at a lower cost, that performs as well as the original, a joint venture may make sense. Other forms of cooperation, such as licensing, should also be considered in such situations.

SUMMARY

Standardization is of central importance when formulating international product policy. The topic is controversial and conceptual problems complicate its analysis. Ethnocentric, regiocentric, and geocentric approaches to devising standard policies differ significantly. The first approach involves projecting domestic policy internationally, whereas the latter two take into account the international operating environment and seek to service global or regional market segments.

The major potential advantages of uniformity are cost savings in R&D, production, and distribution; rapid international product diffusion; and the promotional benefits of a consistent global image. Significant drawbacks of standardization include lower sales and penetration in foreign markets and limited automony for overseas marketing staff.

The desirability and viability of standardization strategies is likely to vary sharply according to the aspect of product policy being considered and the nature of the international operating environment. Heterogeneous markets overseas, particularly consumer needs and characteristics, product-use conditions, regulatory contexts, and local marketing practice and infrastructure, often pose serious barriers to uniformity. Variance in the firm's strategy and posture in individual markets is also a problem.

Policies for implementing and facilitating international product uniformity include developing an international product line, modular strategies, the universal and core product strategies, overseas assembly, and buying-out products. The viability and attractiveness of standardization is very situation specific. Often a significant degree of mandatory adaptation of product policy is unavoidable, and careful evaluation of the costs, benefits, and viability of product uniformity is essential prior to making decisions.

Apart from standardization strategies, localization and adaption are also feasible. These pay more attention to specific consumer and local market circumstances but cost more and are less compatible with a global strategic orientation.

Policy in product attributes is influenced by consumer needs and characteristics, product end-uses, conditions of product use, and the legal environment. Frequently, mandatory adaptation of policy is necessary because of significant differences between or among markets.

Packaging has both a protective and promotional role. International distribution, consumer preference, income, climate and other differences overseas may require special packaging solutions. Labeling is often subject to stringent local laws, and language differences also complicate.

Brand and trademark protection in overseas markets may require legal registration of brands in individual markets. Registration can be expensive but is often desirable. The development of uniform international brands is frequently given a high priority in international firms developing global marketing programs. Language, registration, and consumer perception differences can pose problems in this regard. Service and warranty policy are likely to differ from market to market due to variation in the product, conditions of product use, and service infrastructure in overseas markets.

International product-mix policy should be developed in the context of a firm's international marketing strategy and resources. The domestic product mix, the overseas operating environment and the economics of R&D, and production should be carefully evaluated when devising policy. A product portfolio approach can be helpful when assessing the risk–return attributes of alternative product line portfolios.

Management of international product lines requires ongoing monitoring and analysis of product-line performance and competitive behavior. When evaluating the impact of dropping or adding products in international markets, special attention needs to be given to the impact of decisions on the firm's overall activities.

The international marketing of services is significantly affected by the high level of protectionism in many overseas markets, local requirements for physical presence, and direct contact in exchange relationships. Service firms tend to be more flexible than industrial firms when entering and dropping foreign markets. Key success factors include the recruitment of competent, culturally sensitive staff; a willingness to offer a tailor-made service package; and wide and effective networking relationships.

Counterfeiting is a serious problem in international markets. A number of international anticounterfeiting treaties have been developed. However, these have little impact in countries that have not acceded to them. Lobbying activities, new product development, and the aggressive pursuit of counterfeiters can help combat counterfeiting.

DISCUSSION QUESTIONS

1. How would you distinguish between service products and other products? What are the main implications of this difference for the international marketing of services?

2. "Legal constraints in the international market place are insufficient to deter counterfeiting." Comment on this view, describing possible anticounterfeiting strategies.

3. Identify the major barriers to developing international brands.

4. What role should an international product manager fulfill?

5. "Advocates of standardized international product programs fail to take sufficient account of the heterogeneous nature of the international operating environment." Do you agree with this statement? Why or why not?

6. Why is the pursuit of uniformity in international product policy likely to be given a higher priority in most firms than is the case for other elements of the international marketing mix?

7. "Customers in international markets should be offered service and warranty policies that do not differ significantly from market to market." What is your opinion of this advice?

8. Enumerate and discuss the factors that need

to be taken into account when making packaging decisions for international product lines?

ADDITIONAL READING

Boddewyn, Jean J., R. Soehl, and J. Picard, "Standardization in International Marketing," *Business Horizons,* November–December 1986.

Harvey, M. G., and Ilkka A. Ronkainen, "International Counterfeiters," *Columbia Journal of World Business,* Fall 1985.

Kaikati, Jack A., and Raymond Lagance, "Beware of International Brand Piracy," *Harvard Business Review,* March–April 1980.

Keegan, Warren J., and C. S. Mayer, *Multinational Product Management* (Chicago; A.M.A., 1977).

Keegan, Warren J., "Multinational Product Planning: Strategic Alternatives," *Journal of Marketing,* January 1969.

Kotler, Philip., "Global Standardization—Courting Danger," *Journal of Consumer Marketing,* Spring 1986.

Sauvant, Karl P., *International Transactions in Services* (Boulder, Col.: Westview, 1986).

Shainwald R. G., and C. M. Condon, "International Product Counterfeiting," *Business and Economic Review,* October–December 1987.

U.S. Office of Technology Assessment, *Trade in Services, Exports and Foreign Revenues,* 1986.

Walters, Peter G. P. "International Marketing Policy: A Discussion of the Standardization Construct and Its Relevance for Corporate Policy," *Journal of International Business Studies,* Summer 1986.

ENDNOTES

1. A. C. Fatt, "A Multinational Approach to International Advertising, *The International Advertiser,* 1964.
2. Robert D. Buzzell, "Can You Standardize Multinational Marketing?" *Harvard Business Review,* November–December 1968.
3. Theodore Levitt, "The Globalization of Markets," *Harvard Business Review,* May–June 1983.
4. Ralph Z. Sorenson and Ulrich E. Wiechmann, "How Multinationals View Marketing Standardization," *Harvard Business Review,* May–June 1975, p. 167.
5. R. J. Aylmer, "Who Makes Marketing Decision in the Multinational Firm?" *Journal of Marketing,* October 1970.
6. John A. Quelch and Richard J. Hoff, "Customizing

Global Marketing," *Harvard Business Review,* May–June 1986.

7. Howard V. Perlmutter, Yoram Wind, and Susan P. Douglas, "Guidelines for Developing International Marketing Strategies," *Journal of Marketing,* April 1973.

8. Christopher Lorenz, *The Design Dimension: Product Strategy and the Challenge of Global Markets* (New York: Basil Blackwell, 1986).

9. Lorenzo, op. cit.

10. W. J. Kenyon Jones, "Overseas Subsidiaries—How Much Autonomy?" *Planning and Managing an Overseas Subsidiary,* British Institute of Management, 1966.

11. Levitt, op. cit.

12. Sorenson and Wiechmann, op. cit.

13. Peter G. P. Walters, "A Study of Export Operations in the Georgia Forest Products Industry." doctoral dissertation, Georgia State University, 1983.

14. J. S. Downham, Presentation to A.M.A. Annual Marketing Conference, May 1982.

15. E. P. Godden, "Marketing Channels Abroad." op. cit.

16. See *Marketing Definitions: Glossary of Marketing Terms* (Chicago: A.M.A. 1960).

17. Ibid.

18. Yoram Wind, "Research for Multinational Product Policy" in *Multinational Product Management,* W. J. Keegan and C. S. Mayer, eds. (Chicago: A.M.A. 1977), pp. 165–184.

19. R. J. Regan, "The Service Revolution," *Journal of Marketing,* January 1964.

20. J. L. Heskett, *Managing in the Service Economy* (Cambridge, Mass: Harvard Business School, 1986).

21. D. I. Riddle, *Service-Led Growth* (New York: Praeger, 1986).

22. D. Deo Sharma, and Jan Johanson, "Technical Consultancy in Internationalization," *International Marketing Review,* Winter 1987, pp 20–29.

23. Ibid.

24. J. L. Bikoff, New Weapons in the Battle Against Product Counterfeiting," *Toward the Year 2000, ITT Key Issues Lecture Series, 1987.*

25. See *The Wall Street Journal,* December 29, 1987.

Chapter 14
Dimensions of Global Pricing Strategy

Although setting prices in international firms presents problems not faced when establishing domestic market prices, similar factors still need to be taken into account and similar analytical procedures followed. In this chapter, we first focus on a number of pricing issues of special interest to international marketers and then present a general framework for international pricing decisions. Finally, key problems facing decision makers in the price-setting process are discussed in the context of exporting, technology transfer sales, and the operations of global firms.

The Nature of the Pricing Decision

Executives in international firms need to make a variety of pricing decisions, decisions that differ significantly in importance and complexity. Setting international transfer prices, for example, raises issues that, although important, are unlikely to be relevant when establishing end-user export prices. Differences can also be expected according to whether one is pricing a new product or making a change in the price of an existing product.

The extent to which firms are able to control the market price of their products depends, in general, on the competitive environment, industry structure, and the degree of influence a firm exercises over international distribution. In industries characterized by *perfect competition* (where a large number of competing firms produce an identical product, and there are no barriers to entry), the firm will be a price taker. It will not have the power to influence prices unilaterally. In contrast, monopolists—who by definition face no competition—enjoy significant pricing flexibility. In industries characterized by *imperfect competition* (where a relatively small number of firms are dominant), the firm also enjoys some pricing power.

Government regulation and oversight over price setting, particularly by foreign firms, is common in overseas markets. This—and the power that distributors, agents, and other third parties in external distribution channels may have over price setting—limits the pricing flexibility enjoyed by many international firms.

International firms must therefore accept that differences in the structure and dynamics of markets need to be identified and analyzed. Frequently, substantial adjustments in pricing philosophies are required from market to market, as is an acceptance that the firm's ability to set and control prices overseas is often more limited than at home.

Multiple Pricing Environments

International firms typically operate in multiple heterogeneous pricing environments. Some firms choose to simplify international pricing decisions by abdicating responsibility for setting prices abroad. They do so by leaving this task to third parties such as agents and distributors. Those firms interested in controlling and influencing pricing policy in foreign markets must consider many factors which vary from market to market. In some markets, for example, ongoing inflation may require continuous pricing action. In others, the government may impose a price freeze that allows minimal flexibility in pricing.

Major variables in price setting are the patterns of demand and supply in individual markets. The underlying forces determining demand and supply curves can be expected to differ significantly from market to market. On the demand side, differences in consumer needs and behavior and levels of disposable income will be major factors. The availability and price of substitutes and consumer perceptions of the product will also be very important. Supply is impacted by a firm's cost position, which depends heavily on the price of production and production technology.

Other major influences on pricing include market structure, distribution channels, nature of competition, and government oversight and regulation of corporate pricing activities and international flows of trade and capital. Foreign exchange rate movements and the international product life cycle are also important.

Environmental heterogeneity in international markets will not always be mirrored by nonuniform prices. Insofar as governments do not interfere with the operation of market forces and do not attempt to regulate economic relationships with the rest of the world, the concept of an international market and a single international price is meaningful. Under such circumstances, national demand and supply curves can be aggregated into single international demand and supply curves. However, given the extent and nature of government intervention in most countries, particularly with regard to trade restrictions on the outside world, the concept of an integrated international market is theoretical in regard to the pricing of most products.

The Strategic Context

Corporate resources, objectives, and the firm's international strategy and marketing policy must be taken into full consideration when making pricing decisions for overseas markets. Some firms are motivated primarily to obtain a high market share overseas by committing extensive resources to international business and aggressively promoting their products at low prices. Other companies are less interested in developing mass markets overseas; instead, they emphasize "skimming," pricing policies that generate limited, high-margin sales.

Central direction and coordination is necessary to ensure that pricing strategy is developed within a strategic framework and that unnecessary conflicts are avoided. Prices must also be allowed to respond to local market forces, and staff in foreign markets should play a key role in both the collection of relevant price data and in policy making.

INTERNATIONAL PRICING ISSUES

Price Escalation

International distribution usually involves more stages and greater risk than does domestic distribution. Goods shipped over national boundaries are commonly subject to special taxes and other controls. These constraints add additional expense and slow down the distribution process. Because of the distance that products need to be moved and the increased risks for damage and loss incurred in transit, shipping and insurance costs for goods marketed internationally are often very high.

Apart from these additional risk and costs, it may be necessary to offer extra inducements to overseas importers and distributors to persuade them to market products manufactured by foreign firms, particularly when the product is new or unknown to the local consumer. Even when significant market penetration is achieved in foreign markets, it may be very difficult to persuade local distributors to lower profit margins.

For all these reasons, the impact of price escalation can be especially severe for products marketed internationally. A product can rapidly end up costing two to three times the ex-factory price by the time it is finally purchased by the foreign end-user. An example of how escalation occurs is shown in Table 14-1.

TABLE 14-1
An Example of International Price Escalation

Expense Item	Local Market Price (U.S. $)	Foreign Market Price (U.S. $)
Ex-factory price	100.00	100.00
Shipment and insurance costs to local market wholesaler	6.00	
Shipment, insurance, and documentation costs for ex-ported product		22.00
Import tariff (15% of landed value		20.30
Handling and shipping charge—from port of entry to importer		4.00
Importer's margin (12% on cost)		17.60
Wholesaler's margin (10% on cost)*	10.60	16.40
Retailer's margin (35% on cost)*	40.80	63.10
Sales tax (5%)*	7.90	12.20
Price to end user	$165.30	$255.60

* Although the margins and sales taxes used in the example are shown as the same in the domestic and export markets, this is not always the case. Margins vary considerably by country and sales taxes can be considerably higher in other countries.

This example of international price escalation shows that the exported product is subject to additional shipping, insurance, tax and distribution charges which add $90.30 to the export price. The product therefore costs some 55 percent more in the export market than at home.

Frequently, exporters are not aware of rapid price escalation; they are preoccupied with the price they charge to the importer and often quote an ex-factory price. However, the final retail price should be of vital concern; it is this price that plays a major role in determining the level of foreign demand. For example, it is clearly important for exporters of malt whiskey to Japan to realize that the product is subject to a severe liquor tax. A bottle of malt whiskey that sells for $15 in a duty-free shop at an airport will cost over $60 in Tokyo.

If the final end-user price in foreign markets is higher than desired, management has several options. Obvious ones include developing a lower-quality product, implementing domestic production economies, moving to a lower-cost production location, and manufacturing closer to the foreign customer. Savings may also be achieved by reducing the number of links in the distribution chain and persuading foreign distributors to accept lower margins. The firm may also find it necessary to accept a lower export profit margin.

Price escalation is not a problem only for exporters. It affects all firms involved in cross-border flows. Global companies that undertake substantial intracompany shipments of goods and materials across national borders are exposed to many of the additional charges that cause price escalation.

Dumping Regulations

Complaints from industries exposed to foreign competition are frequently based on the argument that overseas competitors are dumping excess output overseas at uneconomic prices. The GATT definition of dumping is "selling below normal market price." Dumping disputes have become more common in recent years. Accordingly, international firms must take care that their pricing policies do not lead to violations of the regulations and controls that most countries have adopted to counteract dumping. It is therefore important to understand the criteria used to measure the incidence of dumping.

In the United States, domestic firms exposed to what they feel to be unfair price competition from imports may complain to the Commerce Department. Which alone with the U.S. International Trade Commission (USITC), will investigate. Recommendations are then made and the President has power to respond to legitimate complaints with a variety of countervailing measures, most commonly tariffs or retaliatory quotas on imports from the offending firm's home country.

Before antidumping measures can be implemented in the United States, the USITC must demonstrate that the contested product is being sold at a price below "fair value" and that such imports are harming or threatening to cause material injury to a domestic industry. Fair value is determined either by reference to the domestic price established by the foreign exporter or by comparing the U.S. price with the exporter's production costs. If the U.S. price is either below that charged in the exporter's home market or below the cost of production, retaliatory action is likely. These two tests for dumping are very commonly used in other countries besides the United States.

Why is a marginal-cost approach to pricing in overseas markets sometimes of interest to international firms? Clearly, dumping can be a key element of a predatory strategy designed to eliminate competition. More commonly, however, it is a convenient means of getting rid of excess output in situations where overseas

EXHIBIT 14-1
Japanese Semiconductor Exports—The Dumping Issue

During 1985, world demand and prices for many classes of memory chips dropped sharply. U.S. prices for 64K memory chips, for example, fell from around $4 in 1984 to as low as 30 cents in 1985. U.S. semiconductor firms were hard hit by this collapse, and many blamed cheap Japanese imports for the dramatic fall in prices. It was claimed that the Japanese manufacturers, who had expanded production capacity rapidly, were selling chips at less than the full cost of production. They were thus able to achieve penetration levels in 1985 of over 60 percent and 75 percent respectively in the U.S. market for 64K and 256K memory chips. Below-cost sales were made possible, according to U.S. critics, by cross-subsidies from other successful products.

The Japanese response to these criticisms was that it is natural to cut prices sharply in competitive industries facing oversupply. Despite price cutting, Japanese manufacturers were estimated to be sitting on sufficient RAM chips in early 1986 to supply the entire U.S. market for three months. They also pointed out that it is very difficult to accurately estimate the marginal cost of chip production.

Antidumping investigations were initiated by the U.S. Department of Commerce, which found that many of the major Japanese manufacturers were selling certain semiconductors at below cost, defined as fully allocated production costs plus an 8 percent profit margin. As a result, there were examples of some chips being sold at prices as low as one-third of those charged in Japan. Many of the Japanese chip exporters are parts of diversified conglomerates and are thus better positioned than many of the more specialized American firms to continue selling chips at a loss. It is alleged that they believed that they would be able to recoup their losses when demand revived as a result of U.S. firms having been driven out of key markets. Other factors account for the ability of the Japanese to reduce prices so sharply. These include a cost advantage from economies of scale, superior production skills that many of the smaller U.S. firms cannot match, and lower financing costs in Japan.

demand is more price elastic than domestic demand or when a firm does not want to disrupt the domestic price structure.

Regardless of motivation, dumping is successful only if the domestic and overseas markets can be separated and if countervailing action by foreign governments is avoided. Market separation is necessary because dumping involves price discrimination that invites arbitrage. Domestic traders may, for example, buy the cheaper export product overseas and then resell it at home at a higher price which is still below the prevailing domestic price. This disrupts domestic prices and profit margins. The threat of retaliatory action by foreign governments or competitors is also very real in markets where the interests of local manufacturers are threatened by cheap imports. An example of price cutting and resulting charges of unfair competition and dumping is provided by Japanese exports of memory chips to the United States.[1] Details of this case are shown in Exhibit 14-1.

Interesting problems arise in the case of dumping from nonmarket economies. U.S. manufacturers have alleged that such has occurred in the case of a variety of products: Hungarian light bulbs, Yugoslavian nails, East German steel, and

EXHIBIT 14-1 (*continued*) —————————————————————————————

Following the Commerce Department report and the threat of countervailing duties, an agreement was reached in July 1986 between the United States and Japan, setting minimum prices for certain Japanese chips sold in any market outside Japan. The pact was designed to halt the allegedly unfair pricing of Japanese chip exports. Although prices did increase in the United States, it was not possible to control prices in many third-country markets where pricing benchmarks were ignored and predatory pricing of Japanese sourced chips was alleged to continue.

The pact created a number of serious anomalies. One result was a glut of chips in Japan that caused Japanese prices to tumble. The resulting disparity between prices in Japan and benchmark prices in third countries created profitable arbitrage opportunities, and a flourishing gray market in chips developed. Brokers bought chips in Japan and dispatched runners who smuggled suitcases full of chips to Hong Kong, South Korea, Taiwan, and other Asian markets. U.S. chip users complained about higher prices in the U.S. as compared with those paid by users in Japan and other Asian markets, and some U.S. buyers started going "to Japan carrying only a suitcase of money, returning on the next flight with another bag holding as many as 40,000 chips worth more than $150,000."

Although the pact was criticized by many as a protectionist measure that deserved to fail, its lack of success caused the U.S. government to announce trade penalties against certain Japanese imports in March 1987. The action taken, punitive tariffs on around $300 million of Japanese electronic goods produced by or containing chips from offending Japanese firms affected only a small proportion of Japan's exports. As the incidence of alleged dumping has declined, the sanctions have been subsequently relaxed.

———————

Sources: Primary sources were *The Wall Street Journal*, February 19, 1986, and February 12, 1987, and *The Economist*, January 11, 1986, p. 59.

—————————————————————————————

Polish golf carts. Such charges are very difficult to investigate using the usual criteria. How, for example, does one determine a fair price in a market where the laws of supply and demand do not operate and where the product may not even be sold domestically? How can costs of production be evaluated when the cost of factor inputs are state controlled?

The most viable approach to dumping from nonmarket economies, albeit a rather crude one, is to examine production costs in what are believed to be comparable market economies. This was done in the investigation of alleged dumping of Polish golf carts exported to the United States. Since these products were not marketed in Poland and Polish cost data was felt to be unreliable, the cost of manufacturing similar golf carts in Spain was substituted as a basis for estimating Polish production costs.

In some cases, firms have been accused of dumping in their home market by bringing in cut-price imports from overseas subsidiaries. In August 1987, for instance, the Commerce Department ruled that Canadian potash was being dumped in the U.S. and among firms accused of dumping were two Canadian subsidiaries of U.S. companies.

Dumping probes are also being launched in some countries where low-priced components are imported for local assembly. The European Community Commission launched an investigation of Japanese manufacturers of electronic typewriters in 1987. European manufacturers claimed that a number of Japanese exporters had set up "very basic" operations in Europe in which cut-rate components imported from Japan were assembled. It was alleged that these "screw driver" assembly operations provided few jobs, added little value, and were only a sophisticated camouflage for dumping.

Government Controls

National governments are able to intervene in a number of different ways that directly or indirectly limit pricing flexibility. Sometimes, especially in the case of commodity exporting countries, governments encourage or require domestic exporters to limit or increase supply on world markets. They do so to influence price levels or to achieve other economic goals. More commonly, restrictions on the flow of imports are implemented; these controls generally have price implications. Direct government intervention to freeze or otherwise limit price increases in foreign markets is also not unusual.

The rationale for government intervention in the flow of exports is usually based on political and strategic considerations. However, efforts to regulate supply on world markets, often in concert with other members of a cartel, are also commonly motivated by a desire to influence prices on world markets. Government controls are likely to have limited impact, however, on goods for which substitutes are readily available.

Generally speaking, import controls are designed to limit the inflow of imports in order to protect domestic producers or to reduce the outflow of foreign exchange. Direct restrictions most commonly take the form of tariffs, quotas and various nontariff barriers. Tariffs directly increase the price of imports, unless the exporter or importer is willing to absorb the tax and accept lower profit margins. Quotas have an indirect impact on prices. They restrict supply; unless demand is perfectly elastic, restriction causes the price of the import to increase. Protectionist measures nearly always result in pressures to increase the price of imports to the final consumer and, even if absorbed by the exporter or importer, reduce price flexibility. Thus, products viewed as low-priced necessities in the home market of the exporter may be forced into the luxury price bracket overseas.

Sometimes import restrictions can have a silver lining for the exporter, particularly if they take the form of quotas. Opportunities to improve profit margins by manipulating product availability and aggressive pricing action present themselves. In many markets, for example, Japanese exports of motor vehicles are subject to quota restrictions. As a result, the Japanese auto firms have tended to export their "fully loaded" models. These carry the highest profit margins. They have also been able to increase export prices more rapidly abroad than at home.

During the period following the implementation of voluntary restraints on Japanese auto exports to the United States in 1981, it is estimated that the price of the average Japanese import increased by some $2,500 more than would have been the case with no restrictions.[2] A similar pattern is apparent when limitations are placed by foreign governments on imports of Japanese television sets, videotape recorders, and industrial machinery.[3]

Action by governments to freeze domestic prices is not limited to developing countries. In the United States, for example, President Nixon imposed a price freeze as part of a package of emergency economic measures in 1971. In 1982, both France and Sweden resorted to price freezes. Usually, such action is a temporary response to inflationary and balance of payments pressures. Fortunately, such measures tend to be relaxed fairly rapidly because of the economic distortions brought about when market forces are not reflected in price movements.

Typically, price controls are part of a package of economic measures. In October 1987, for example, the Argentine government took action to slow inflation, bolster the merchandise trade surplus, encourage investment, and reduce its budget deficit. A wage and price freeze was a prominent element of the economic package. Other measures included a devaluation of the local currency, increased import duties, and higher taxes.

An inability to take pricing action can cause severe problems for firms if the price freeze is maintained for more than a few months. This is particularly true if inflationary pressure is either not dampened by the freeze or if prices are allowed to fall behind increases in costs prior to the imposition of the freeze. To safeguard against the impact of a freeze, firms should continuously review prices in inflationary environments. Action to maintain profit margins is especially vital if a freeze seems likely and this implies taking vigorous pricing action to preempt controls.

If a price freeze does occur and seems likely to last for some time, there is clearly a strong case for accelerating introductions of new products. The absence of benchmark prices for new products, particularly those where few close substitutes exist, makes this policy especially attractive. Governments find regulating the initial price established for new products more difficult. Additional measures that should be considered include the fine tuning of payment terms and other conditions of sale. These may not be controlled and can be changed to improve profit margins. For example, discounts can be eliminated and credit terms tightened.

Even when governments do not freeze prices, they may intervene to regulate inflation by requiring notification and authorization of price increases. Approval processes are often slow moving; significant time lags may elapse before pricing action is authorized. Indexing sytems are sometimes developed in high inflation environments, whereby the rate of price increase allowed depends on the rate of change in cost indicators.

Foreign Exchange-Rate Fluctuations

Since the demise of the Bretton Woods system in the early 1970s, the value of many important currencies have fluctuated day-to-day, and international firms have had to operate in an environment of rapidly changing foreign exchange rates. Not only have currency values become more volatile, they have also become much more difficult to predict. The foreign exchange risk implicit in most in-ternational transactions has increased significantly; this increase has important implications for pricing policy.

The uncertainty facing U.S. firms has been particularly great since the dollar has been allowed to float in a relatively uncontrolled manner against other currencies. Although some countries have pegged the value of their currency against the dollar, this has not been true for the major world currencies. The extent of the change in currency values that can occur in relatively short periods of time can be illustrated by the slide in the U.S. dollar's value from March 1985 to March 1986. During this year, the dollar fell in value by 30 percent and more against the German D-mark, the French franc, the Japanese yen and the British pound. The decline did not take place at an even pace, being most marked after the September 1985 agreement by the United States, Japan, West Germany, France, and Britain to intervene in the currency markets to drive the dollar lower. The dollar lost much less ground against other currencies, such as the Australian dollar, and it actually increased in value against many currencies. For example, compared with March 1985, the dollar's value had, one year later, gained an average of 5 percent against the currencies of the major exporters of textiles and apparel to the United States.

Even in the longer term, significant divergences are apparent. By end 1987, the dollar had skidded by more than 50 percent from its 1985 peak against the yen and the mark and by an average of around 40 percent compared to most West European currencies. However, it has fallen much less or not at all against the currencies of nations involved in around half of U.S. trade.

In the case of Canada and Mexico, which account for some 25 percent of U.S. trade, the U.S. dollar has actually increased in value against their currencies. Dollar appreciation has also occurred against the Chinese yuan. In Hong Kong, the exchange rate has been stable and, at the end of 1987, the dollar had fallen by only some 5 percent, 11 percent, and 27 percent respectively against the currencies of South Korea, Singapore, and Taiwan. This indicates that even when a trend develops in a currency's international value, movements against particular currencies may vary sharply.

Pricing Options

Clearly, changes in exchange-rate relationships pose problems in many areas, not least in pricing decisions. To review the impact of currency movements on prices, let us first consider the situation faced by U.S. exporters since the dollar started its 1985 slide against most major currencies.

In such an environment, a company has essentially three pricing options. These are as follows:

1. Maintain a stable dollar export price which will cause the foreign currency price to fall in line with the dollar's depreciation. This usually results in increased overseas sales.

2. Increase the dollar price of exports in line with the dollar's decrease in value, thereby maintaining a stable foreign currency price and, at the same time, generating higher export profit margins.

3. Combine the two policies. Allow the foreign currency price to fall, but below the rate of dollar depreciation, thereby increasing export margins.

In the early 1980s, the situation was different as the dollar increased sharply in value against many major currencies. U.S. firms faced a severe export pricing dilemma. If dollar prices were maintained, the foreign currency price would increase sharply and sales would be lost to competitors. If dollar prices were reduced in order to maintain stable foreign currency prices, export margins would be squeezed.

To make sensible pricing decisions in an environment of fluctuating exchange rates, managers need to consider the variables discussed below.

Demand

A key variable is the *price elasticity of demand* in foreign markets.[4] In those markets where demand is price inelastic, demand is not very responsive to fluctuations in the local price of the product. Other things being equal, the appropriate response to an appreciating dollar is to allow the foreign currency price to increase. However, the opportunity for increasing prices without an offsetting fall in demand, indicated by inelastic demand, should be explored regardless of what is happening to the value of the dollar. When the dollar is depreciating and demand is inelastic, a policy of allowing the foreign currency price to fall is likely to be inappropriate. Increased dollar revenue will fatten export margins, and can be used to finance additional promotion.

In markets where demand is price elastic, there should be a willingness to react to an appreciating dollar by cutting the dollar price, thereby safeguarding market share. If the dollar is falling, corresponding declines in the foreign currency price are likely to be beneficial; they can be expected to generate substantial increases in demand. However, if local demand is price elastic, local price cutting may well be desirable even when currency values are stable.

Supply

The supply of exports available to source foreign demand and the sensitivity of this supply to price changes, as measured by the elasticity of supply, are critical variables that need to be considered together with the demand situation.[5] If supply is inelastic (indicating a lack of alternative sales outlets for exports and a desire to maintain stable production levels) international firms are likely to favor pricing policies that stabilize foreign demand at current levels, even if home-country based revenues fall and profit margins are squeezed. When export supply is price elastic, this indicates a willingness to adjust export output, and a greater likelihood of more aggressive overseas pricing designed to ensure that export margins are not eroded by currency fluctuations.

Other Considerations

Besides considering the elasticity of overseas demand and the elasticity of supply situations, managers must consider other factors when plotting pricing strategy in an environment of unstable exchange rates. A key variable is expectations for future currency movements. Firms should generally not react to day-to-day currency movements by constantly adjusting their prices. Doing so upsets foreign customers and day-to-day movements frequently cancel themselves out in the short term. Once a definite trend becomes apparent or is forecast, pricing action must be considered. However, it takes time for the effects of adjustment in exchange rates to percolate through the international economy, and there are significant time lags before changes in currency values have a real impact on operations.

Many firms exporting to the United States, for example, did not sharply raise their dollar prices once the dollar began to slide in 1985. This was due in part to many firms not cutting their U.S. dollar prices when the dollar was surging in

1984 and early 1985. They were willing to see export profit margins, which had fattened considerably as the dollar rose in value, shrink in order to maintain market share. However, pressure for action does build when a sustained and significant change in currency values occurs. Toyota Motor Corporation, for example, estimates that it loses some 2.5 billion yen in earnings each time the dollar declines one yen.

The implications of pricing action on a firm's competitive situation overseas and likely competitive responses must also be considered. Firms wishing to gain extensive market coverage and high market penetration find upward pressure on their foreign prices undesirable. Firms with less ambitious sales goals and a strong focus on profitability are more interested in safeguarding profit margins. Prices also need to be consistent with other elements of the marketing mix. Thus, a promotional campaign emphasizing good value may not coexist very happily with rapidly increasing prices for the product.

Some U.S. exporters are reluctant to reduce their prices abroad. Many regard the dollar's depreciation as an opportunity to improve profitability rather than market share. Cutting prices does not always improve competitiveness. Foreign competitors, intent on preserving their market share, frequently match cuts made by U.S. firms. There are also indications that some price cuts never reach final consumers as middlemen in the distribution chain may pocket most of the savings. It has been estimated, for example, that only some 15 percent of the savings from the dollar's decline finally benefit the end user.[6]

Contrasting approaches to increasing Japanese business by exploiting the depreciation of the dollar are provided by Campbell Soups and du Pont.[7] Campbell Soups dropped the store price for a can of soup 16 percent to 185 yen from 220 yen and kept retailer's profit margins stable. Campbell's has also sought to increase distribution of a soup line custom made for the Japanese market. Its primary goal is to achieve long-term growth in market share. Despite the yen price cut, profit margins have also improved. A can of soup that was selling for the equivalent of $0.90 in 1985 yielded over $1.40 a can at end 1987.

Du Pont has not cut its yen prices. Management believes that price cuts will not generate significant new business, and the firm is taking the opportunity to rebuild profit margins and use the additional cash flow to strengthen its presence in Japan. It has invested $85 million in a new technical center near Tokyo, and a 20-story office tower now serves as du Pont's headquarters in Japan.

As the yen has grown stronger, some Japanese firms have faced severe problems in maintaining market share in the United States. Most have been loath to increase dollar prices sharply because of a fear of losing sales to competitors. Healthy profit margins, established when the dollar was strong, enabled many firms to cushion the effect of currency swings in the short term. In the period August 1985 to December 1986, for example, Japanese auto makers increased dollar prices only some 15 percent, despite a 40 percent increase in the value of the yen.[8] In the longer term, as the yen has continued to strengthen against the dollar, further price increases have been forced on importers of Japanese cars. Toyota, for example, raised car prices nine times between late 1985 and January 1988.

Various measures to deal with the pressure of the rising yen have also been put into effect by Japanese firms. These actions indicate the options facing firms with limited flexibility for pricing action when doing business from a high-currency cost base.

Cost reduction measures—both in-house and by external suppliers—are essential. Obvious possibilities include greater efficiency, product design and material savings, overseas assembly and manufacture, and more reliance on sourcing components and raw materials from overseas. These become cheaper because of the lower value of foreign currencies.

Action on product policy is also important. Management's essential goal should be to add more value to product lines; this increases the possibility of significant pricing action. New products embodying technological innovations and more features permit nonexplicit price increases. Moving products up market into less price-sensitive demand segments may also be appropriate. There is evidence, for example, that high-quality food and beverage imports engender high consumer loyalty because they are often used in parties, where the urge to please and impress is of greater concern than price.

To stay competitive in price-sensitive market segments, it may be appropriate to buy finished products from low-cost overseas suppliers for subsequent sale in corporate product lines. Finally, it may be possible to compensate for less profitable overseas sales by paying more attention to domestic business opportunities.

The Impact of Exchange-Rate Fluctuations on Global Firms

For the global company with an extensive overseas manufacturing capacity, foreign exchange fluctuations cause many problems, and all the considerations mentioned so far may apply. However the picture is more complex since a larger proportion of costs are generated in foreign currencies, and global production networks facilitate sourcing flexibility.

To the extent that foreign currency revenue and assets are counterbalanced by foreign currency costs and liabilities, pricing problems resulting from currency movements are mitigated. For example, although local currency depreciation causes the hard currency value of local assets to fall, local revenue and profitability may improve significantly as the price competitiveness of the manufacturing subsidiary improves. An improved performance by this subsidiary may, however, occur at the expense of other subsidiaries or the parent firm. Nevertheless, worldwide manufacturing capability gives a firm the ability to adapt its production activities to shifts in comparative advantage arising from foreign exchange movements.

Transfer Pricing

Transfer prices are those charged for intracompany movement of goods and services. Many purely domestic firms need to make transfer pricing decisions when goods are transferred from one domestic unit to another. However, the scope of the transfer pricing problem and the opportunities for, and interest in manipulating these prices is greatest in global companies. A significant proportion of world trade now occurs between the parent company and foreign affiliates of multinational firms. In the case of U.S. international trade, some 35 to 40 percent is estimated to move within U.S. multinational corporations.[9]

Regulatory agencies in the United States and elsewhere want transfer prices to reflect the free market price arrived at by independent buyers and sellers. In the United States, Section 482 of the Internal Revenue Code gives the Internal Revenue Service (IRS) wide power to review and amend the transfer prices of

U.S.-based firms. Income may thus have to be reallocated between the U.S. parent and overseas subsidiaries in line with the IRS's perspective on appropriate international transfer prices.

Firms need to be able to justify their transfer prices and explain how they have been computed. When evaluating transfer prices, the IRS prefers methods whereby the firm attempts to establish an "arms-length" price for intracompany transfers on the basis of comparisons with transactions for similar goods in the open market. When such a comparison is not possible because of an absence of trade in similar goods between unrelated parties or other reasons, cost-plus approaches are deemed appropriate by the IRS.

Firms may manipulate transfer prices for reasons that include taxes, foreign exchange, and government control. For example, to minimize a firm's global tax liabilities and, in particular, to defer tax payments, there is a strong rationale for manipulating transfer prices in order to maximize profits in low-tax subsidiaries at the expense of earnings in countries where the tax burden is greater. This can be done by establishing high transfer prices for goods and services sold from a low-tax subsidiary to another subsidiary in a high-tax location. Conversely, intracompany shipments from the high-tax country would be charged at a below market price to favor profitability in low-tax subsidiaries.

Foreign exchange risk can be mitigated by manipulating transfer prices to siphon funds from countries where local currency depreciation is expected. Fund flows designed to overcome barriers placed by governments on intercountry movements of dividends, interest, and capital can be accomplished by juggling transfer prices. The parent firm can, for example, overcome a home government ban on FDI by providing financing for foreign subsidiaries by undercharging for goods and services sent to the subsidiary and overpaying for anything bought from the subsidiary. Other reasons for transfer-price manipulation include reducing exposure to tariffs, concealing subsidiary profitability, and increasing the firms' share of profits from joint-venture operations.[10]

Although often very attractive to global companies, transfer pricing manipulation has important drawbacks. First, there is the danger of being found out. Not only do the tax authorities in home and host countries want to guard against tax evasion, but other government institutions such as the customs may also be interested in investigating the legitimacy of transfer pricing charges. Moreover, what is gained in one area by manipulating a transfer price may be counterbalanced elsewhere. Inflated transfer prices to avoid income tax, for example, may result in the payment of a higher import duty.

To the extent that the price of intracorporate traded goods and services deviate from open market prices, the financial performance of the firm is distorted. Control and motivation problems may result. Control becomes problematic because no realistic measure of performance is available. Where the profitability of a subsidiary is understated because of transfer pricing, the reason for poor results may not be understood by corporate control staff and lack of understanding is likely to generate frustration and bitterness among the managers of the subsidiary.

The International Product Life Cycle

Although the international product life cycle model (IPLC) has been criticized,[11] it can provide useful insights into international pricing decisions. According to the theory, a firm's pricing flexibility declines as a product moves through the IPLC. During the innovation stage, demand is typically inelastic for a product that is nonstandard, manufactured at home, and exported by the innovator. As a consequence, the prototype international pricing policy is a high-price, skimming strategy.

During the maturity stage, the uniqueness of the product (as measured by performance and technological attributes) declines, competition increases, and mass markets develop at home and overseas. There is a downward pressure on prices, and cost reductions become important. Domestic output and exports level off and then decline as production increasingly shifts overseas, initially to other relatively advanced, but lower-cost countries. Prices fall significantly and become an important competitive tool.

In the standardization stage of the IPLC, the product and its associated technology are standardized and readily available. Competition is intense and cost control very important. The firm is now a price-taker and output shifts from high-cost countries to LDCs.

In the cycle described above, there is a strong interest in actions promoting pricing freedom. One strategy is to rejuvenate products so that they are pushed back into earlier phases of the life cycle. This requires implementing real product improvements or differentiating the product so that consumers believe it is different from and better than competing products. Effective marketing and a continuous drive to generate an ongoing stream of product and technological innovation—so that products can be replaced as they move into maturity—become very important. By so doing, the firm avoids being in the position of having to accept a market price that it cannot influence.

A FRAMEWORK FOR INTERNATIONAL PRICING DECISIONS

At this point, a general framework for international pricing decisions is presented. This framework emphasizes a number of critical points:

□ The importance of developing pricing policy within the context of strategic market planning,

□ The need to respond to local environmental conditions and the economics of producing and distributing a product,

□ The need to coordinate and integrate pricing policy from market to market,

□ The importance of the associated terms of overseas sales.

Key Variables

Diverse factors are likely to have a significant impact on international pricing decisions. Three major groups of variables can be identified: (1) those specific to the firm, *company factors*; (2) those external to the firm, or *market factors*; and (3) those specific to the product or *product factors*. The interaction of this trio of factors is diagrammed in Figure 14-1, which illustrates key variables in the context of price setting for a specific overseas market.

Figure 14-1 is schematic; it does not pretend to cover every factor that may be relevant in all pricing situations. The figure indicates that the local environment

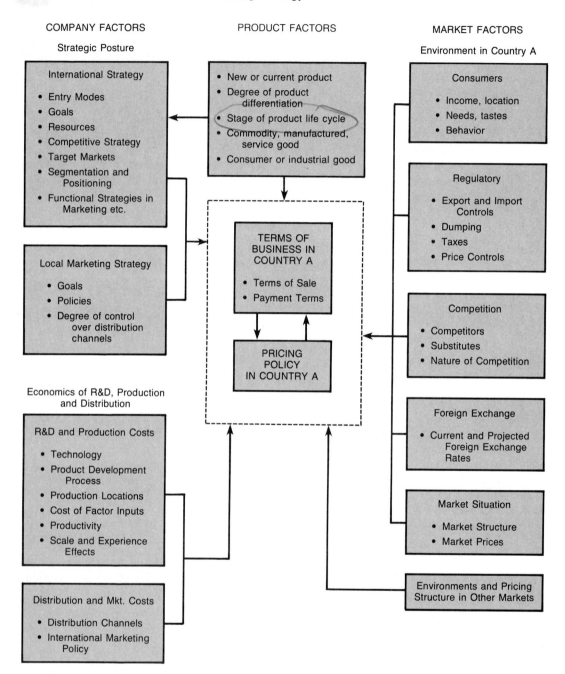

FIGURE 14-1   An International Pricing Framework

is of major importance but that relevant local variables must be evaluated in an international context where the market situation and pricing practice in other markets are also a significant consideration. The firm's international and local marketing strategy and the economic context arising from the corporate cost situation are very important, as are product characteristics.

The variables identified in this scheme will also affect the terms of overseas contracts entered into by a firm. Given the normally close relationship between contract terms and prices, particularly with regard to sales and payment terms, it is evident that decisions in these areas should not be divorced from each other.

Although the forces underlying demand and supply and the dynamics of competition must be analyzed, it is usually not possible to identify specific demand and supply curves. Pricing is an art as well as a science; in most situations, it is not possible to summarize all relevant considerations in the neat diagrams so beloved by economists. Forecasting, intuition, and an ability to see the big picture are essential skills. Typically, these abilities depend on hard-won knowledge, much of it acquired by experience, trial and error, and on-site observation.

Collecting the data needed for effective pricing requires input from production, finance, planning, and marketing staffs, both at home and in foreign markets. Frequently these managers also need to be involved in pricing decisions, but the primary pricing responsibility should lie with marketing. Access to market information is as important for pricing purposes, as is cost data. It is thus important that finance and accounting staffs do not dominate price decisions.

The most obvious market information needed is on the price levels established by firms selling competitive products abroad. Knowledge of the nature and form of competition, consumer characteristics and needs, government regulation, normal conditions of sale, distribution channels, and the outlook for relevant currency movement is also vital. Once relevant data are collected, they must be evaluated in the context of the firm's overall international marketing policy and its strategic posture in particular markets.

The International Pricing Process

The descriptive model of the decision-making process shown in flow chart in Figure 14-2 illustrates the process that should be followed when making international price decisions.[12]

This model assumes that firms have a direct interest in the price of the product to end users. Even if an exporter is quoting a price to an export merchant or some other intermediary, the firm should be concerned that the final end-user prices for its exports are set at levels consistent with the firm's objectives and marketing plan. The firm must be familiar with the pricing environment in overseas markets and must be prepared to take action to influence the pricing policy of distributors. Apart from the price charged by the company to the distributor, possible initiatives include establishing recommended list prices and seeking to control the distribution process.

Prices should be set only after the firm's overall international marketing strategy has been formulated. Likewise, the local marketing plans developed should be consistent with overall policy. Key considerations here include sales, profit and market-share goals; market segmentation and product positioning; and policies on product presentation, promotion, distribution, and service.

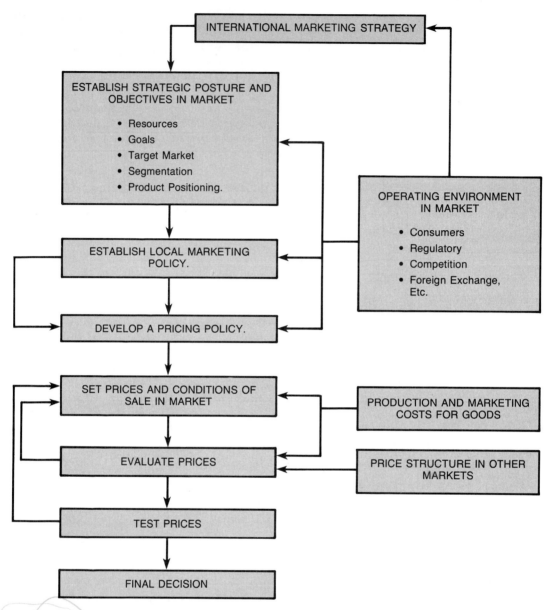

FIGURE 14-2   The International Pricing Decision Process

Once the operating environment has been carefully evaluated, and preliminary prices set that seem appropriate in the context of the firm's strategy and market situation, managers must carefully review initial prices. Review ensures that, given the projected price structure, satisfactory profits at least in the medium term, are feasible. Careful consideration must be used when comparing anticipated revenues, at the given price, with projected costs.

The framework also assumes that costs are only one of a number of key pricing variables; they should not be given special attention in the initial phases of the pricing process. Also, initial prices must be compared with the current or projected export pricing structure in other markets; this allows for the coordination of export prices in overseas markets.

Once prices have been evaluated and, if necessary, adjusted, it is appropriate to undertake a limited market test in which pricing and other marketing variables can be subjected to a realistic trial. Designing such trials can be difficult, and effective testing may not be possible if the product needs to be brought on to the market rapidly. Wherever feasible, though, testing is highly desirable before finalizing prices.

The framework described above is applicable to a wide variety of international pricing situations. However special issues are raised in the case of export pricing, the pricing of technology transfer and pricing in multinational corporations. These are now considered in turn.

EXPORT PRICING

Experience and Channel Control

Key factors affecting the pricing flexibility and power of the exporting firm are the levels of corporate knowledge of and experience in export markets and the degree of control enjoyed over export distribution channels. Knowledgeable, experienced exporters assuming considerable control over export marketing and distribution are well positioned to apply the pricing framework. Inexperienced exporting firms who rely heavily on third parties to undertake export-related activities will have difficulties in gaining the benefits from this approach.

Although the framework implies a significant degree of central control over export price setting, considerable local participation in pricing is necessary. Timely and accurate information on relevant elements of the export market environment are essential and often best generated by local managers. Effective pricing action is also enhanced when those managers immediately responsible for marketing the product have been consulted and have concurred with the pricing policy to be implemented.

The Nature of the Pricing Decision

There are a number of important differences in the price setting process for new products as compared to adjusting the price of existing export products. In the case of new products, key factors impacting the flexibility of the exporter are the degree of product innovation and the level of consumer demand. Exporters of desirable product innovations generally enjoy significant pricing flexibility in the initial stage of the product's life cycle (due to limited supply and competition and characteristically price inelastic demand patterns). However, if the product innovator is new to exporting, ignorance of the overseas operating environment and inexperience will generally limit the firm's ability to capitalize fully on its potential pricing power.

In the case of export price changes, the product is generally more mature, and the experienced exporter often has a better understanding of overseas product-market environments. However, the degree of flexibility enjoyed by decision makers tends to be lower than for new-product pricing. There is a high probability that the product is not unique, faces stronger competition, and is aimed at a broader segment of the market. Consequently, export-price decision makers are forced to pay attention to competitive and cost factors.

When initiating price changes, a firm is generally reacting to some significant change in the market environment or the economics of production and marketing. Exchange rate volatility becomes an important consideration. However, the evident reluctance of exporters to finetune prices in line with exchange rate movements illustrates that there is often a high degree of inertia in the short term. Changing a price poses significant problems because of the signals it sends to foreign consumers and governments, and because of uncertainty regarding competitive reactions from host country and other foreign exporting firms, most of whom the exporter knows little about. Although price leaders may have little to fear from competitors, the likelihood of government oversight is a real deterrent, particularly if consumers complain of being exploited by foreign firms.

For these reasons, many exporters are averse to frequent changes of price. Many firms exporting to the United States have not dramatically changed their dollar price in a see-saw fashion during the 1980s. During the period when the dollar increased rapidly in value, many exporters resisted pressure to reduce prices and maintained stable dollar prices for their exports to the United States, with the result that export profit margins increased sharply. Since 1985, as the dollar has fallen in value, many of these firms have not increased their dollar prices as much as might have been expected.

In place of frequent direct pricing action, many exporters resort to other measures. Initiatives taken by foreign exporters to counter the impact of the decline in the value of the dollar have included cost-cutting measures and the undertaking of more value-added activities, such as assembly operations, in the United States. Other approaches allowing for flexibility without having to change list prices are the offering or removing of discounts and the fine tuning of export delivery and payment terms.

Export Costs

Many firms price exports on a cost-plus basis, with overseas distributors often being given a free hand to set end-user prices. This approach has been summarized as follows: "Take the domestic product price, add insurance and freight, put in a hefty cushion for contingencies and slap on a profit mark-up to the exporter."[13]

The attractions of such a cost-driven approach are readily appreciated. First, it minimizes the need to collect and analyze data on the overseas marketing environment. Second, the policy is convenient and simple to implement. It is prevalent in firms where there is a low commitment to exporting and extensive reliance on third parties to undertake export marketing.

In the pricing framework already outlined, it is apparent that we reject a cost-plus approach to export pricing. However cost data remains an important input in the decision process; exporters need to have a good appreciation of their export cost structure. In the medium and long term, exporting is an activity of interest only insofar as costs are covered and a profit generated. Management also need cost data to measure the attractiveness of export business as compared to alternative uses of resources.

Cost data are important for two other major reasons. Exporters may find that they are accused of dumping their products in overseas markets. Firms developing export prices using a marginal cost approach, in which the direct costs of export output and distribution provide the price floor, are particularly vulnerable to such changes. To anticipate and answer such criticism, firms need to have available appropriate cost data.

The costs and problems arising from shipping products long distances over national boundaries and the additional stages and risk involved in export distribution result in severe price escalation problems for many exporters. Data on overseas distribution costs should therefore be gathered and, if costs are high, remedial action taken to limit the pressure on end-user prices. Possible actions include cost-saving product changes and reduced profit margins for both the exporter and third parties involved in distribution. A reduction in the number of intermediaries in distribution channels plus more effective management and control of logistics may also be feasible.

Indirect exporters and opportunistic firms emphasizing exporting only when domestic business is depressed are unlikely to have well-defined export strategies. Cost-driven pricing often prevails in such firms. The framework developed earlier is applicable only in firms where the establishment of export objectives and strategy is given serious consideration, and where there is sensitivity to responding to local environmental factors. The framework is demand rather than cost driven, and requires the acquisition of current information in overseas markets. This is expensive and time consuming and necessitates the establishment of an explicit export infrastructure within the firm.

Product Factors

The applicability of the framework is not product specific, but the relative importance of particular steps in the decision process and the relevance of environmental factors will vary according to the particular nature of the good or service being marketed. This point may be illustrated by the differences in commodity and service exports.

In the case of many commodity items, market price is given and, in the absence of government interference, does not vary significantly from market to market. Thus many exporters of petroleum, minerals, agricultural products, and goods such as pulp and paper, find that they are price takers in international markets and thus unable to exercise significant discretionary pricing power.

The opportunities for price discrimination are likely to be greatest for intangible products (most service goods) that do not lend themselves to arbitrage. For such service exports, integrating international prices may be relatively unimportant. Measuring the cost of service exports may not be given a high priority either.

Service exporters are less exposed to government regulation in such areas as dumping and transfer pricing. More attention should be given to the notion of "opportunity cost," often the most relevant cost data, if there is flexibility in transferring service operations from market to market.

Terms of Sale and Conditions of Payment

When making price quotations, an exporter must take scrupulous care to make explicit the terms of sale and the conditions of payment. It is very important that the legal implications of the export offer are fully understood before being conveyed to the potential purchaser. Is it an offer that leads to a firm contract of sale at the offer price on acceptance by the purchaser? If so, the opportunity for altering the agreed price because of a subsequent change in market conditions or costs may be very small. On the other hand, a "conditional" offer implies that a firm contract will not be made until the offer is confirmed by the exporter. The terms of a firm contract may also allow for price flexibility in specific circumstances. Given the potential for misunderstanding and disagreement, it is common to specify a particular set of definitions for the international trade terms used in the agreement. INCOTERMS, which have been developed by the International Chamber of Commerce, are an example of widely accepted trade terms.[14]

Regarding price, key factors include the point at which the exporting firm *ceases* to be responsible for the products, the currency of settlement, and the terms of payment. The greater the responsibilities and risk accepted by the exporter, the higher the price that should be charged.

There are five primary alternatives with regard to *export terms of sale*. These are shown in Exhibit 14-2. Exporters should always be prepared to provide C.I.F. quotations; many importers are either unwilling or unable to make the necessary transportation, insurance and other arrangements for shipping a product to their own country. Even if the exporter does not possess the in-house expertise to estimate these costs, freight forwarders can provide the required information and make shipping arrangements once a contract is finalized.

An exporter must also be sure that there is no ambiguity regarding the *currency of settlement*. A price quotation in the exporter's currency will result in the importer's bearing the foreign exchange risk arising from the transaction. If this currency is expected to fall in value against that of the importer, the importer's risk is small. However, if the exporter is pricing in a hard currency that could strengthen before the transaction is completed, the real cost to the importer may be greater than planned. Consequently, importers frequently demand that prices be quoted in their local currency or, if a hard currency is quoted, that they be given significant price breaks. Given the possibility for hedging most export transactions in the forward currency or money markets, there is no reason why exporters should be unwilling to quote in the importer's currency in most situations. However, the exporter should ensure that there is a forward market for the particular currency and should also take care that the cost of hedging, which will be significant for a weak currency, is included in the price quotation.

The *payment terms* specified in a contract also have a bearing on price. The five major forms of payment in international trade are described in Exhibit 14-3.

EXHIBIT 14-2
Terms of Sale

1. **Delivered Duty Paid** The export price quote includes the costs of delivery to the importer's premises. The exporter is thus responsible for paying any import duties and costs of unloading and inland transport in the importing country as well as all costs involved in insuring and shipping the goods to that country.

2. **Cost, Insurance, and Freight (C.I.F.)** The exporter quotes a price that includes coverage of transport and insurance charges to a named overseas point of disembarkation. A number of variations of the C.I.F. quote exists. The most common is the C and F (cost and freight) quote, whereby the exporter is responsible for covering the transport and related charges to the point of disembarkation, but the importer has responsibility for arranging insurance coverage.

3. **Free on Board (F.O.B.)** The exporter's price quote includes coverage of all charges up to the point when the goods have been loaded onto the designated transport vehicle. The designated loading point may be a named inland shipping point or the port of export.

4. **Free Alongside Ship (F.A.S.)** The exporter's price quote includes coverage of all charges up to delivery of the goods alongside the vessel at the named port of shipment. All other charges from this point—such as unloading, loading, wharfage, and transport costs—are the responsibility of the importer.

5. **Ex-Works** The price quoted by the exporter applies at a specified point of origin, usually the factory, warehouse, mine, or plantation, and the buyer is responsible for all charges from this point.

the greater the uncertainty regarding payment, the higher the price wever, if prices are set too high, the greater the likelihood that the unable to sell the product and make payment.

ce terms are not widely used. Such terms are most common ter lacks confidence in the importer's ability to pay, often transactions, or where economic and political instability result in foreign exchange not being made available

little risk for the seller and are widely used LC, where cancellation or modification of thout the mutual agreement of both buyer ble LCs, which can be unilaterally amended used. Confirmed LCs, which are supported also by a bank in the exporter's country are often confirmed LC, the exporter is guaranteed payment even if the foreign bank does not honor its commitments.

Under the terms of a typical LC, the exporter is required to submit documentary evidence that goods have been shipped according to the terms of the credit. Payment is made on receipt of the required documents by the bank that issues the LC. Typically a commercial invoice, a customs invoice, and a bill of lading

EXHIBIT 14-3 _____
Principal Means of Export Payment _____

wanted most by exporter

1. **Cash in Advance** Exporter receives payment before shipment of the goods. This minimizes the exporter's risk and financial exposure.

2. **Letter of Credit** A bank, acting on behalf of the importer, promises to make payment for the exports providing that terms specified in the letter of credit are met. This allows the importer to ensure that the goods are delivered in conformity with pre-set conditions detailed in the letter of credit. Since a bank, rather than the importer, is promising to pay, the exporter can sell on credit terms with little financial risk.

3. **Draft Drawn on Foreign Buyer** A bill of exchange addressed to the importer by the exporter specifying when a given sum of money is due from the importer or his agent. "Sight" drafts are payable immediately upon presentation to the importer or his agent, such as a bank. "Time" drafts are payable at a specified future date. Because of the lag between acceptance and payment they are a useful financing device.

4. **Open Account** The exporter ships the goods first, and bills the importer later in accordance with agreed credit terms. Since the evidence of the importer's obligations are not as well specified as with other instruments of payment, exporters only sell on open accounts to importers who they know very well, or who have excellent credit ratings.

wanted most by importer

5. **Consignment** The exporter retains title to the goods until the importer has sold them. It is thus a highly risky method of payment, usually restricted to dealing with affiliated companies.

are required, and it is important that these documents are exactly as specified in the LC. So long as they are in order, payment must be made to the exporter.

Drafts drawn on foreign buyers are more risky than LCs because the purchaser is still free to refuse to pay the draft after the goods have been shipped in accordance with the original contract. Although the exporter retains title until payment is made or the draft has been accepted, sometimes goods are released to the importer in the foreign country before the importer has accepted the draft. Even if the exporter meets all the conditions of the original contract, it still has to absorb the transport cost of shipping the goods elsewhere if the importer refuses to accept the draft.

Most drafts are "documentary," which means the buyer's obligation to pay is contingent on their receipt of various shipping documents that are needed to obtain possession of the goods. In the case of time drafts, there is an additional risk that the drawee may not make payment at maturity despite having confirmed the draft and received the goods. Time drafts drawn on banks are most desirable because of the strong credit rating of most banks. These "bankers acceptances" can usually be sold at a discount by the exporter prior to maturity.

Drafts have the advantages of providing definitive evidence of a financial obligation and enable the exporter to use its bank as a collection agent. This is not the case with *open account terms*. Although more risky, open account sales are less complex since there are no documentation requirements or bank charges and other fees. But less evidence of buyer obligation is provided which makes it more difficult to collect if the importer defaults.

Consignment sales are highly risky, and are generally limited to intra-company shipments. When sales of this nature are contemplated with independent buyers, the economic and political stability of the foreign country should be examined carefully. Also, it is wise to consider some form of risk insurance. In addition, the contractual agreement should establish who will be responsible for property risk insurance, and freight changes for returned products.

TECHNOLOGY TRANSFER-PRICING PROBLEMS

A variety of international business activities involves the transfer of knowledge and proprietary rights across national boundaries. Typically, these activities require technology transfer in one form or another and embrace elements of at least one of the following: "granting the right to do" or "providing the means and ability to do." In the case of *licensing agreements*, the main possibilities encompass the sale of new or improved technical knowledge and the sale of proprietary rights. Typically, these corporate assets will either be well-guarded secrets or protected by patents.

A second category of contractual agreement is the *management contract*, whereby the firm sells management expertise. Normally this requires the provision of managerial and training resources on an ongoing basis. Franchising arrangements imply a more comprehensive and continuous relationship in which a franchisor grants the franchisee the right to do business and gives assistance in organizing training, merchandising, and management in return for fees.

Although it is often asserted that the costs of transferring knowledge is minimal, studies have indicated that this frequently is not the case, particularly when ongoing assistance is a necessary feature of the transfer package.[15] Of even greater importance than these transfer costs is the value of the proprietary rights and knowledge. Although available to the inventor or initiator at zero marginal cost, the value of such proprietary rights is often very great. However, it is not uncommon for the potential purchaser of technology to assert that it is unreasonable to have to pay a high economic rent over and above the direct marginal costs of technology transfer.

Arguments mobilized in support of this view include the difficulty of comparing the prices of imported technology with those of indigenous technology (no like with like comparison is possible) and the monopolistic character of many suppliers of technology. The problems arising from the absence of pricing benchmarks are accentuated by the difficulty many potential purchasers have in assessing the value of technological inputs that they can only partially evaluate prior to purchase. In LDCs, the limited financial resources of local entrepreneurs may also mean they are not in a position to pay realistic prices for know-how.

The potential supplier to technology, on the other hand, can counter such criticisms by pointing to the high cost and risk of R&D, the risks of future competition from firms acquiring know-how, and the high opportunity costs associated with contractual arrangements. However, because of the problems identified above, prospective sellers of know-how frequently discover that they are unable to negotiate satisfactory prices for their knowledge. Opportunity cost is a key concept, and if potential purchasers of knowledge are unwilling or unable to pay economic prices, the alternatives to contractual agreements will be preferred instead.

PRICING IN MULTINATIONAL COMPANIES

In contrast to many exporters who frequently exercise limited control over the prices set for their products in foreign markets, multinational corporations [MNC] have a physical presence in overseas markets. This means there is a greater potential for, and interest in, controlling end-user prices. In addition, MNCs usually generate substantial intracompany flows of goods and services across national boundaries. The corporate cost base also becomes more diversified since the cost, productivity, and currency denomination of resources deployed in the firm vary from country to country.

In such an environment, problems of determining appropriate transfer prices and coordinating pricing strategies in international markets are likely to loom large. In other respects, setting prices in foreign markets require attention to the same sort of firm- and market-related factors already discussed.

Setting Transfer Prices

The transfer pricing problem is not unique to MNCs and has already been reviewed earlier in this chapter. This section focuses on the crucial issue of how best to determine international transfer prices. Setting prices on an arms-length basis is the safest approach to establishing transfer prices; it minimizes the likelihood of clashes with government agencies. Also, the financial results of the parent company and overseas subsidiaries are not distorted.

Three alternative approaches to arriving at arms-length prices are commonly used. The *comparable uncontrolled* price method favored by the IRS, should be used by U.S. companies when possible. It involves computing the transfer price by reference to the price charged in comparable transactions for a similar good between independent parties. In practice, this method is often impractical, even for very similar goods, because of product quality and other differences, and variance in the transaction in terms of variables like timing and quantity.

The *resale price* method is most appropriate when a product is transferred to an overseas marketing affiliate for resale to an independent buyer. The transfer price is computed by reducing the affiliate's resale price by an amount that covers costs and profit margin. Determining a reasonable markup for the affiliate may be a problem, especially when the reseller adds significant value prior to resale.

Cost-plus methods are the other main alternative. The transfer price is arrived at by adding an appropriate profit markup to the seller's costs. Frequently firms enjoy some discretion in determining full cost, particularly regarding fixed cost allocations, and there is often leeway in regard to a fair markup. Because of these problems, tax officials usually prefer firms to use the first two methods when possible.

When the products and services being traded within the firm are unique, such as when specialized semifinished goods and components that have few close substitutes are traded internally, the cost-plus method seems appropriate. Since this approach allows the firm greatest scope to exercise judgement, opportunities may arise to set prices to further legitimate corporate goals such as minimizing tax liabilities and foreign exchange exposure. Regardless of the policy followed, firms need to be prepared to justify the transfer prices set, must be careful not to contravene the relevant laws of the countries in which they are operating, and should take full account of the possible dangers of transfer price manipulation that were noted earlier.

The issue of setting transfer prices in international firms is controversial, and many MNCs have been accused of setting prices detrimental to the national interest in both host and home countries. Because of the sensitive nature of the topic, managers have been reluctant to discuss it. However, one study of U.S.-based MNCs does shed some light on key influences on transfer pricing decisions.[16] Ten variables were found to have a substantial impact on price setting. These are, in descending order of importance, as follows:

☐ Market conditions in the foreign country

☐ Competition in the foreign country

☐ The need for reasonable foreign affiliate profitability

☐ U.S. income tax

☐ Economic conditions in the foreign country

☐ Overseas import restrictions and customs duties

☐ Foreign market price controls

☐ Taxation in the foreign country

☐ Foreign market exchange controls

Price Coordination

In MNC s, management has an even greater interest than exporters to ensure that there is oversight and coordination of pricing policy at home and abroad. This is especially true when similar product lines are manufactured in more than one location. In the absence of coordination, intracorporate competition and conflicts may inadvertently result from variance in pricing policy.

The problem of price coordination is particularly complex when environmental heterogeneity encourages the establishment of price levels that vary significantly from market to market. This creates opportunities for arbitrage and "gray market" activities (discussed in more depth in Chapters 15 and 17), which are a serious problem for some firms. A good example concerns automobiles, which frequently vary substantially in price between different countries. The price of a number of luxury European cars, such as a Mercedes in Germany, are below the cost of comparable models in the United States. There is therefore good reason for U.S. customers to purchase a new Mercedes in Germany and ship it back to the United States. The cost of shipment and the modifications in the vehicle required to meet Environmental Protection Agency and Department of Transportation requirements have been estimated at around $7,000 for a Mercedes in 1985.[17] Despite this, a cost saving of up to 20 percent was possible at that time. To deal with complaints from U.S. distributors, who were afraid of losing business, Mercedes told its German distributors to refuse to sell cars to U.S. tourists.

For many products, national product standards do not vary as much as in the case of automobiles, and it is thus cheaper and easier to ship the good from one country to another. In these circumstances, even if the average consumer is unaware of the opportunities for profiting from price differences, it will not take long for merchants to exploit the possibilities for arbitrage. The firm then has to either coordinate prices or put into place other barriers that reduce the attractiveness of arbitrage.

One strategy for dealing with coordination problems is to adopt a standardized approach to international pricing policy. Standard overseas prices can be established at corporate headquarters. Flexibility is necessary to allow for foreign exchange movements, differing rates of inflation, and variance in sales and other relevant taxes. However, this means overlooking important elements in the local marketing environment and differences in the firm's strategic position overseas. Given this very serious drawback, it seems that the potential problems associated with standardizing international prices are often likely to outweigh the limited benefits flowing from such a policy.

Insofar as uniformity is desirable, it is in terms of the price category in which the good is to be positioned. For example, even though the absolute product price may vary in line with market conditions, policy could be standardized in the sense that the product is targeted at a similar, well-defined price class.

At the opposite extreme is an approach to price setting where local subsidiaries have freedom to determine prices in the local marketplace. Here, full account can be taken of the local market situation and the subsidiary's particular interests and priorities. The drawback of this perspective is that the interests of the firm as a whole may not be taken sufficiently into account, with coordination problems not being addressed. Thus one subsidiary could end up setting its prices at a level where they attract the attention of customers of another subsidiary. Consequently, one subsidiary could end up facing competition at home and in third-country markets from a sister subsidiary of the same firm.

The third alternative, which for most firms will be the superior policy, is to allow overseas subsidiaries significant freedom within the limits of a global pricing strategy. Thus, pricing decisions are taken within the context of local market forces and needs, but also take full account of overall corporate strategy and interests. Local subsidiaries need to be fully aware of the parameters within which they have decision-making freedom. Usually these are best laid out in a specific statement of the firms' international pricing policy. There should also be a widespread interchange of information within the firm on each subsidiary's pricing structure. In this way, it becomes possible to eliminate suboptimal pricing policies and still respond to local market needs.

SUMMARY

Although international pricing has much in common with domestic pricing, there are a number of important differences. These include the pricing problems and opportunities arising from price escalation, government regulation, foreign exchange movements, transfer pricing, the international product life cycle, and the heterogeneous nature of the international pricing environment.

When making international pricing decisions, management must pay attention to the firm's international strategy, the marketing policies that flow from this strategy, and the economics of manufacturing and distribution. In addition, it must focus on the overall international operating environment and conditions in specific target markets. Major dimensions of interest include consumer characteristics, the regulatory environment, competition, and the foreign exchange situation.

A simple framework for the international pricing decision process indicates that initial prices should be set only after the operating environment has been evaluated. The preliminary pricing structure should then be reviewed and, if necessary, adjusted in the light of the relevant cost data, pricing policy in other markets, and market tests.

This framework can be applied in a wide variety of pricing situations. However, the model is schematic and seeks only to offer broad guidelines that may be adjusted as necessary. Some firms may, for example, wish to give more emphasis to costs at an earlier stage. However, cost-plus approaches to international pricing are dangerous and ignore crucial demand variables.

Deciding prices in the case of international technology transfer arrangements such as licensing, management contracts, and franchising contracts presents a number of special problems. Buyers tend to emphasize the low marginal cost of knowledge transfer, whereas sellers should be most concerned with opportunity costs.

Multinational companies operate in a more complex environment than exporters since they have established international marketing and production networks. Transfer pricing and coordination of pricing policy thus tend to be particularly important issues. Marketing managers in overseas subsidiaries should enjoy a good deal of flexibility when establishing local pricing structures. However, local decision makers should operate within policy parameters developed in the context of the firm's overall international strategy and interests and the global operating environment.

DISCUSSION QUESTIONS

1. Why is it often difficult to compute fair arms-length transfer prices?
2. "In most circumstances, there will be few benefits for international firms implementing standard prices in world markets." Discuss this statement.
3. What are the major causes of international price escalation? Suggest possible courses of action to deal with this problem.
4. The possibility for international arbitrage complicates price decision making in international firms. Explain why this is so and suggest ways to deal with the problem.
5. What relevance has the international product life cycle theory had for pricing strategy in international firms?
6. How have U.S. exporters and foreign exporters to the U.S. market tended to react to the large movements in the value of the dollar that have occurred in recent years? What are the main reasons for the policies implemented?
7. International buyers and sellers of technology frequently disagree on the appropriate price for knowledge. Why?
8. Discuss the importance of the terms of sale and payment terms when making overseas sales.
9. Why are many host governments suspicious of the transfer pricing policies of multinational firms?
10. Price freezes are not uncommon in foreign markets. Discuss strategies to deal with this problem.

ADDITIONAL READING

Arpan, Jeffrey S., "International Intracorporate Pricing," *Journal of International Business Studies,* Spring 1972.

Barrett, M. Edgar, "Case of the Tangled Transfer Price," *Harvard Business Review,* May–June 1977.

Becker, H., "Pricing: An International Marketing

Challenge," in *International Marketing Strategy,* H. Thorelli and H. Becker, eds. (New York: Pergamon, 1980).

Burns, Jane O., "Transfer Pricing Decisions in U.S. MNCs," *Journal of International Business Studies,* Fall 1980.

Elimelech, Raphael L., "Pricing Japanese Success," in *International Marketing,* 2nd ed., S. C. Jain and L. R. Tucker, eds. (Boston: Kent, 1986).

Farley, John U., James M. Hulbert, and David Weinstein, "Price Setting and Volume Planning by Two European Industrial Companies," *Journal of Marketing,* Winter 1980.

Frank, Victor H., "Living with Price Control Abroad," *Harvard Business Review,* March–April 1984.

Grossfield, R., and L. Clague, "Export Pricing in a Floating Rate World." *Columbia Journal of World Business,* Winter 1974.

Leff, Nathaniel H., "Multinational Corporate Pricing Strategy in the Developing Countries," *Journal of International Business Studies,* Fall 1975.

Moustafa, Mohamed E., "Pricing Strategy for Export Activity in Developing Nations," *Journal of International Business Studies,* Spring–Summer 1978.

Samiee, Saeed, "Pricing in Marketing Strategies of U.S. and Foreign Based Companies," *Journal of Business Research,* Vol. 15, No. 1, 1987.

ENDNOTES

1. See *The Economist,* January 11, 1986, p. 59.
2. See "Detroit Rode Quotas to Prosperity," *The Wall Street Journal,* January 29, 1986.
3. See *The Economist,* December 17, 1983, p. 63.
4. Price elasticity of *demand* is defined as the percentage change in the quantity demanded of a good divided by the percentage change in its price. Usually the numerical value of elasticity, which can vary from zero to infinity, will be negative. In practice, the negative sign is ignored. When the numerical value is less than one, demand is said to be inelastic. When the value is greater than one, demand is said to be elastic.
5. Price elasticity of *supply* is defined as the percentage change in the quantity supplied of a good divided by the percentage change in its price. Numerical values less than one indicate a situation of inelastic supply. When the value is greater than one, supply is characterized as elastic.
6. See *The Wall Street Journal,* July 14, 1985.
7. Ibid., May 15, 1987.
8. Ibid., December 15, 1986.
9. See *The Economist,* March 1, 1986, p. 61.
10. Alan C. Shapiro, *Multinational Financial Management* (Boston: Allyn & Bacon, 1986).
11. Ian Giddy, "The Demise of the Product Life Cycle Model in International Business Theory," *The Columbia Journal of World Business,* Spring 1978.
12. This model is adapted from frameworks developed by Cravens and Rao. See: V. R. Rao, "Pricing Research in Marketing: The State of the Art," *Journal of Business,* Vol. 57, No. 1 (1984) p. 42, and D. W. Cravens, *Strategic Marketing* (Homewood, Ill.: Richard D. Irwin, 1982).
13. B. L. Kistler, "Export Pricing in Today's Market," *Business America,* July 9, 1984.
14. *Incoterms* (New York: ICC Publishing).
15. See, for example, D. Treece, *The Multinational Corporation and the Resource Cost of International Technology Transfer,* (Cambridge, Mass.: Bollinger, 1976).
16. Jane O. Burns, "Transfer Pricing Decisions in U.S. MNCs," *Journal of International Business Studies,* Fall 1980, pp. 23–29.
17. See *The Wall Street Journal,* April 22, 1985.

Chapter 15
Dimensions of Global Distribution Strategy

INTRODUCTION

When formulating and implementing its global distribution strategy, the global company's marketing management faces unique problems and issues. These problems and issues exist because the global company is involved in three distinct yet mutually supportive marketing activities, *foreign marketing, international marketing,* and *global marketing,* each of which is characterized by a distribution strategy. This chapter accordingly surveys the importance of distribution to exporter and global companies and the particular problems, issues, and factors that need to be taken into account when making distribution decisions. The chapter also briefly discusses the major distribution differences that exist between global companies pursuing national-market and global-market segmentation strategies or geographic concentration and diversification strategies.

THREE GLOBAL DISTRIBUTION STRATEGIES

All companies involved in foreign marketing generally distribute their products in markets that differ enough from one another to warrant the development of individualized distribution systems and strategies. Even a company with few manufacturing facilities and a larger number of foreign markets must make sourcing, transportation, and inventory decisions that optimally utilize productive resources and supply foreign markets. A global company, particularly a global-market company, needs to coordinate its local and global distribution activities to enhance its competitive advantages while achieving its global and local marketing objectives. To fulfill these various distribution requirements, the global company develops three distinct but related types of distribution strategies; (1) a set of *foreign distribution strategies* that interlock with (2) an *international distribution strategy* and (3) an integrating *global distribution strategy.*

The Foreign Distribution Strategy

Companies involved in foreign marketing often develop distribution arrangements and strategies for each of their foreign markets. There are two major reasons for variations.

The marketing infrastructures of foreign markets differ from country to country. Key variations are: the channels through which particular products flow, the services provided by channel members, the types of outlets patronized by the targeted customers, channel length, channel efficiency, and channel margins. Studying each of these elements is an important managerial task. Only when the strategic implications of these channel differences are understood and accounted for can a company realistically expect to reach its intended market and achieve its marketing objectives.

A company may also play different strategic roles in each foreign market, being the market leader in one while a market follower in another. It may want to develop fully a number of market segments in some countries but be satisfied with servicing just a few in others. Distribution arrangements and strategies will reflect these choices. The resulting strategy is defined as follows:

> A **foreign distribution strategy** is the game plan for attaining corporate distribution objectives in a foreign market. A foreign distribution strategy consists of those decisions associated with the selection, development, and control of channel members in order to meet environmental, market, and competitive conditions and objectives in the host country.

The International Distribution Strategy

A company involved in international marketing must develop an international distribution system suitable for shipping raw materials, semifinished products and components, and finished products and components between countries of manufacture and countries of consumption. Four criteria need to be met when developing such a system: (1) the system must provide for the efficient use of the company's productive resources; (2) it must be economically efficient and reliable; (3) it must be supportive of and responsive to foreign marketing objectives; (4) it must be responsive to changes in external marketing barriers arising from changes in foreign trading policies. The net result of the decisions associated with these four criteria is, in effect, the following strategy:

> An **international distribution strategy** is the game plan for attaining corporate *between-country* distribution objectives. It consists of selecting and managing international channel members and making those sourcing, inventory and transportation decisions associated with the development and control of a logistical system capable of supporting company foreign marketing activities and objectives.

The Global Distribution Strategy

Companies involved in global marketing are interested in developing global distribution strategies that effectively coordinate their foreign and international distribution strategies into one coherent production-marketing effort. The underlying impetus of an overall global distribution strategy is the need to simultaneously achieve marketing objectives while enhancing competitive advantages on all fronts.

When a company is primarily an exporter, it is interested in serving foreign markets in a dependable and cost-efficient manner. This involves selecting international channel members and carriers that ensure the products arrive safely, on time, and at a reasonable cost. When a company begins to produce its products in some countries and markets them in others, however, it can find the physical movement of its products fragmented and costly.[1] Fragmentation may also have an adverse impact on the company's marketing effort in one or more of its foreign markets. The company therefore needs a global distribution strategy to help minimize fragmentation, control costs, and improve coordination.

> A **global distribution strategy** is the game plan for simultaneously attaining the corporate global- and foreign-market distribution objectives. It consists of making those sourcing, inventory, transportation, and local channel decisions

associated with the development and control of an international distribution system and a set of foreign distribution systems capable of simultaneously supporting the company's global- and foreign-marketing objectives.

These three distribution strategies, the associated decisions, and the various factors affecting these decisions, will be discussed in this chapter.

THE IMPORTANCE OF DISTRIBUTION

Distribution is vital to a company. The distribution system is a key link between the company and its customers. Building it requires considerable time and capital, and it is neither easily nor quickly modified. The way the system is structured determines the market segments that can be reached and, in part, the types of marketing strategies that can be created and implemented (particularly in the short run). As a result, the distribution system exerts an important influence on the company's ability to develop new markets or expand existing ones.

Distribution and the Customer

Honda, a well-known Japanese manufacturer of economical cars, created a separate dealership network to handle the Acura, the luxury car it introduced to the United States in 1986. Honda's strategy was partly influenced by a desire to differentiate its high- and medium-priced automobiles. The Rover Group, a British car manufacturer, and Honda joined forces in the 1980s to develop a new luxury car, the Sterling, for the United States. Since 1987, the car has been distributed in the United States by a 151-dealer network created by Sterling Motor Cars. Rover's strategy was then, as now, not to directly associate its name with the car to avoid reviving its one-time reputation among Americans for poor quality.[2]

Distribution and the Marketing Mix

Wholesalers, dealers, and retailers are distribution specialists, serving different functions and providing different services. Their activities also impact the companies they service since they are closer to the end user. The sales and servicing capabilities, financial resources, and market-segment specialization of local channel members therefore need to be taken into account when adding to an existing product line or when making market-expansion and market-segment decisions. Decisions about the company's future competitive position, the product warranty to be offered customers, the level of the sales effort, and the level and quality of after-sales services must also involve distribution channel members, directly or indirectly.[3]

In most cases, the distribution system established a significant long-term commitment by the company, either through contracts or in good faith, to a large number of independent channel intermediaries. The system can take years to build and is not easily or quickly changed. For example, a German car manufacturer or a U.S. refrigerator manufacturer cannot contract with independent distributors in Brazil to sell their products one day and then proceed to buy them out the next day in order to replace them with company-owned outlets. There is, therefore, in channel arrangements a strong tendency toward inertia. Near-term distribution decisions must be made with an eye on the company's future activities and on future market trends.

The international distribution strategy will also affect other elements of the company's foreign marketing strategies. For example, sourcing and international carrier decisions have a direct bearing on pricing decisions made in individual countries, and international distribution decisions impact local inventory levels, product availability, and the timing of new product introductions.

Distribution and Market Development

Since it partially determines the degree of control it has over local distribution, a company's market presence has an impact on market development. For example, if a licensing agreement exists, the development of the distribution system, and thus the market, is generally left in the hands of the licensee. The licensee has primary responsibility for developing and managing local distribution channels and for promoting and pricing products. The same is true of a company that has classified a market as an export market and relies on independent distributors, export merchants, or middlemen to sell its products. The company has more control over market development if it has a physical presence, such as a marketing subsidiary, and local channel members are dealt with directly.

No matter what the original entry strategy, companies often need to change distribution arrangements. Initial and subsequent decisions concerning the route used to reach the foreign market must be made carefully so as not to pre-empt necessary changes later on. Questions similar to the following need to be answered, if only tentatively, when planning distribution: Will the channels be sufficiently effective to generate additional sales should sales targets change, or will they bar the expansion of direct-selling activities when such an approach becomes economically and strategically desirable? Will the selected channels be an efficient transmitter of market information, enhancing the match of products to changing consumer demands? Will they provide the company with future opportunities to develop business contacts?

MANAGING FOREIGN DISTRIBUTION

Foreign distribution is very similar to domestic distribution; it includes all those activities and decisions necessary to get the product to the customer *when* and *where* desired. Since markets differ, however, so do distribution strategies. The factors that determine the degree to which each foreign market distribution strategy must be localized can be grouped under the three headings (1) environmental determinants, (2) market determinants, and (3) competitive determinants. These three groups of factors are external to a company and outside its control. The marketing manager's task is to ensure that local distribution strategies are responsive to local conditions and achieve the company's local marketing objectives.

In the case of a global company, each foreign distribution strategy must also be consistent with and supportive of the company's global marketing strategy and objectives.

Environmental Determinants

The environmental factors of primary importance in the design of a foreign distribution strategy are the country's wholesaling and retailing structures, their relationship, and the rules and regulations that govern channel arrangements and commercial behavior. Environmental factors are outgrowths of historical, socio-cultural, economic, and competitive forces. Comparative studies of channel structures suggest that with economic development:

☐ The number and types of wholesalers increase.

☐ The influence of independent importers such as import agents and import distributors declines, particularly as local manufacturing activity increases.

☐ Channel functions and services become more separated and channel inter-mediaries more specialized.

☐ The financial services provided by wholesalers decline as their markups increase.[4]

Other studies suggest that channel structure and the relationship(s) among channel members are either a function of the relative size of channel members or of their ability to obtain a particular product or technology.[5] That is, channel arrangements may be more strongly influenced by power or technology than by a country's stage of economic development.

The Wholesaling Structure

There is considerable diversity in wholesalers across countries. Their size, services offered, and prices charged for these services differ for any number of reasons—cultural, social, economic, and legal.

The Size of Wholesalers. Table 15-1 presents data on wholesaling in selected countries, subdividing these countries into four groups: industrialized countries, newly industrialized countries, developing countries, and centrally planned economies. The size of wholesalers varies considerably by country and is partially a function of host-country socio-cultural, economic, and political factors. In indus-trialized countries such as Belgium and Sweden, the average wholesaler caters to the needs of fewer than 10 retailers, or less than 1,000 consumers. In newly industrialized countries such as Brazil and South Korea, the average wholesaler caters to the needs of 20 to 60 retailers, and between 1,000 and 3,000 consumers. In centrally planned economies, wholesaling tends to be highly centralized and integrated forward (wholesalers control retailing outlets).

The Role and Social Status of Wholesalers. The role played by wholesalers varies from country to country, as does their status. In the developing countries, wholesalers generally handle a wide assortment of locally produced and imported products. Since the emphasis in developing countries is usually on production, not distribution, wholesalers are often viewed as adding unnecessary costs[6] and

TABLE 15-1
Wholesaling Patterns in Selected Countries

Country*	Number of Wholesalers	Total Wholesale Employment	Employees per Wholesaler	Retailers per Wholesaler	Population per Wholesaler
Industrialized Countries					
United States	416,000	5,355,000	13	5	564
Japan	429,000	4,091,000	10	4	278
Italy	120,366	547,000	5	8	473
United Kingdom	80,104	1,087,000	14	3	698
Belgium	57,079	177,400	3	2	174
Sweden	27,913	193,200	7	3	145
Austria	12,890	148,900	12	3	582
Israel	4,862	36,900	8	8	782
Newly Industrialized Countries					
Brazil	46,000	442,000	10	61	2,820
South Korea	45,568	173,200	4	21	878
Ireland	3,073	42,100	14	11	1,139
Chile	561	15,900	28	42	20,856
Developing Countries					
India	116,000	—	—	32	5,612
Turkey	24,592	87,200	4	20	1,923
Egypt	1,766	42,300	24	1	25,595
Kenya	2,289	30,000	13	1	8,257
Centrally Planned Economies					
Soviet Union	1,000	120,000	120	481	174,922
Yugoslavia	1,110	138,100	124	70	20,000

* Within country groups, countries arbitrarily ranked according to the number of wholesalers.
Sources: *United Nations Statistical Yearbook*, 1983–1984, pp. 866–889, and 1979–1980, pp. 404–419, and *Statistical Abstract of the United States*, 1986, p. 774.

generally held in low esteem. In contrast, wholesalers in industrialized countries tend to be more specialized, both in the products they handle and the types of retailers they serve. Furthermore, they are considered important marketing links.

Services, Costs, and Efficiency of Wholesalers. The services provided by wholesalers are often related directly to competition. For example, in countries where retailers tend to be small and underfinanced, such as India, wholesalers provide a variety of services—from financing to inventory carrying. In industrialized countries, typically characterized by a shift to vertically integrated production-market systems, wholesalers are being squeezed from both ends. As a result, they increasingly provide services tailored to the needs of both major buyers and suppliers.

There is usually little relationship between channel costs and channel efficiency. Channel costs vary considerably from country to country and is primarily a function of channel competition. Channel length, on the other hand, is strongly influenced by the country's retailing structure, channel relationships, geography, and the economic and socio-cultural characteristics of the final consumer. For example, the Japanese distribution system is considered one of the most complicated and decentralized systems found in industrialized countries. It is believed by some to be the result of historical, geographical, and social pressures.[7]

The Retailing Structure

Retailing exhibits even greater diversity than wholesaling. The reasons for this diversity are cultural, economic, and legal.[8] Consumers have certain expectations about the types of outlets in which specific goods are to be found and the services that they will provide, and allowances for these expectations have to be made.

Number of Retailers. Data on the retailing structure of several countries are presented in Table 15-2. Except for Egypt and Kenya, the ratio of retail stores to population varies from a low of 1:42 to a high of 1:21,161. These data suggest that a country's stage of economic development has very little bearing on the number of retailers. Japan, Italy, Belgium, Brazil, and South Korea have similar ratios, as do Austria, India, and the United Kingdom. However, between market and centrally planned economies, there are big differences. In centrally planned economies, the ratio is significantly higher (about 1:300). We can infer that some economies of scale may be obtained, but at the expense of convenience and choice.

Considerable care must be taken when using data on retailing patterns. Samiee has pointed out that unlicensed shops and street vendors, who represent major segments of many developing countries, go unreported in statistics.[9] They are not alone. In order to reduce taxes or avoid payoffs to various government officials, some retail sales are often not reported or are underreported.

Retailing Inventory Practices. Although the number of retailers is not strongly influenced by stage of economic development, retailing practices are. The depth and width of the inventory carried by retailers tends to be smaller in developing countries than in industrialized countries. Most Colombian apparel manufacturers, for example, own clothing stores as real estate investments and generally carry only the limited line of clothing they produce. Generally, because most small retail stores do not have sufficient capital to carry large inventories, goods are often sold on consignment. The retailer lists inventory and, in the event of a sale, takes a sales commission and sends the balance from a sale to the title holder.[10]

Size, Location, and Retailing Practices. Retailing practices in the large metropolitan areas of developing countries, such as São Paulo, Bogotá, and Mexico City, resemble those of retailing stores in the large cities of industrialized countries. Large retailers often carry inventory, offer financial assistance, handle credit purchases, display and promote merchandise, and furnish market information to their distributors. In contrast, small retailers in urban and rural areas carry limited lines of goods, are generally inefficiently operated, and depend heavily on distributors for credit, promotion and display materials, and other types of assistance. Owners of small family-operated stores, especially in rural areas, are reluctant to assume

TABLE 15-2
Retailing Patterns in Selected Countries

Country*	Population (in millions)	GNP per Capita	Number of Retailers	Population per Retailer
Industrialized Countries				
United States	234.5	14,080	1,923,000	126.4
Japan	119.3	10,100	1,721,000	69.3
Italy	56.8	6,390	927,372	61.4
United Kingdom	56.3	9,180	231,674	243.0
Belgium	9.9	9,130	131,798	75.1
Sweden	8.3	12,440	75,709	109.6
Austria	7.5	9,230	37,524	199.8
Israel (1980)	3.8	5,270	40,000	102.5
Newly Industrialized Countries				
Brazil	129.7	1,870	2,817,000	46.0
South Korea	40.0	2,010	945,800	42.3
Ireland	3.5	4,990	32,332	108.3
Chile	11.7	1,890	23,800	491.9
Developing Countries				
India (1980)	651.0	260	3,760,000	173.1
Turkey (1980)	44.2	1,250	491,600	96.2
Egypt	45.2	690	2,136	21,161.0
Kenya	18.9	340	3,335	5,667.2
Centrally Planned Economies				
Soviet Union (1980)	263.4	—	695,700	378.6
Yugoslvaia	22.8	2,490	79,679	286.2

* Countries presented in the same order as listed in Table 15-1.
Sources: Population and GNP per capita information are for 1983 and are from *The World Bank Atlas 1986*. Data on retailing establishments are from the *United Nations Statistical Yearbook*, 1979–1980, pp. 404–419; 1983–1984, pp. 866–890; and *The Statistical Abstract of the United States*, 1984, p. 799.

the risks associated with carrying new products and accepting new retailing ideas and innovations. In many cases, they will not stock a product until the demand for it already exists.[11]

Nomenclature. The local naming of retail stores can be misleading. Although *department stores* and *supermarkets* can be found in many developing countries, it would be misleading to assume that the types of customers they attract are similar to those of supermarkets and department stores in industrialized countries. In many developing countries, they cater primarily to upper- and middle-income families, provide credit, and make deliveries yet stock only a small assortment of products. The U.S. drugstore simply is not characteristic of drugstores in most other countries. For the foreigner who expects to find mostly medicines, the assortment of goods sold in U.S. drugstores can be quite confusing.

Channel Relationships

The distribution of functions and services, the locus of channel power, and the socio-culturally influenced relationships existing between and among channel members all figure in the developing of channel arrangements, making judgments about channel control, and establishing channel objectives, goals and policies.

Functions and Services. Regardless of a country's stage of economic development and general environment, the same marketing channel functions and services take place. For market managers, the critical question is not *whether* these functions and services are performed, but *who* traditionally performs them.

Although selling is common to all wholesalers, the effort exerted on this activity varies considerably from country to country. In Japan, for example, wholesalers are often required to provide retailers with sales personnel and are expected to offer liberal return privileges to small retailers.[12] In centrally planned economies, most wholesalers have national distribution responsibilities and have taken over the selling function from local manufacturers. In general, most wholesalers offer credit. Yet in some countries because of high inflation, the scarcity and cost of money, and other commercial risks, inventories may be kept low.

Channel Power and Conflict Resolution. Many factors determine the power structure in channel arrangements. Three middlemen characteristics central to this issue are *relative size, financial strength,* and *political influence.* In Malaysia, for example, imports are controlled to a great degree by a handful of European commission houses. In Japan, the trading company dominates channels because of financial strength and local and international marketing experience. In Israel, Hamashbir Hamerkazi, a giant wholesaler, has full or partial ownership in 12 major industrial firms.[13] As a consequence, Japanese and Israeli trading companies and wholesalers are major political and competitive forces. In sharp contrast, because of government regulations and poor transportation infrastructures in their countries, Egyptian, Italian, and Turkish wholesalers tend to be small and serve small areas.

Socio-cultural Considerations. The influence of socio-cultural factors on a country's distribution structure and channel practices must not be ignored. In Japan, concern for social welfare has resulted in distribution inefficiencies in order to maintain employment.[14] Also, the very close personal relationships that often link Japanese channel members can be more important in the long run than a particular product's sales volume or profitability.[15] These factors are also present in Brazil and other South American countries.

Legal Factors

In many countries, laws restrict the sale of certain items on particular days of the week and limit the hours and days retailers can stay open. Exhibit 15-1 shows the variations in shopping hours among five European countries.

Channel activities and practices also vary from country-to-country because of differences in turnover and transaction taxes, depreciation allowances, minimum

EXHIBIT 15-1
Shopping in Europe Can Be Frustrating

Federal Republic of Germany

For more than half the weekend, West Germany is a shopper's wasteland. Stores close at 2:00 P.M. Saturday and do not open until Monday morning.

Italy

In Italy, most stores take a 2 hour lunch break.

The Netherlands

In the Netherlands, stores stay open until 9:00 P.M. only one night a week. Those close to the German border often advertise this fact in German newspapers. There is a law before the country's parliament that would permit stores to stay open until 7:00 P.M. on weekdays. Merchants would be permitted to choose their own opening times but be limited to 52 hours per week.

Switzerland

Switzerland has relatively lax rules. Stores may now stay open until 8:00 P.M., and some stores in the larger cities stay open until 10:00 P.M. one night per week.

United Kingdom

In England, it is legal to buy a newspaper on Sunday but not a book. It is also legal to shop for fresh vegetables and fruit, but not the same foods in cans or bottles. Also, shops may legally stay open until 8:00 P.M., and until 9:00 P.M. one night per week. But in most towns and villages, and even in some local shopping districts in metropolitan areas such as London, shops often close for one afternoon a week. In Bath, shops are closed on Monday or Thursday afternoons. In Stratford-on-Avon, early closing day is Thursday.

Source: Adapted from "European Shoppers Push for Changes in 'Blue Laws,'" *Los Angeles Times*, William Tuohy; reprinted in *The State*, Columbia, S.C., December 21, 1986, p. 7-B.

wage and fringe benefit laws, advertising and promotion regulations, and health standards. In some countries, resale price maintenance is legal; in others, manufacturers are forbidden to set resale prices. In addition, channel arrangements are directly affected by liability legislation, franchise laws, legislation affecting middlemen and dealer rights, compensation terms for termination of contractual agreements, territorial restrictions, cartel practices, and reciprocal selling agreements. Examples abound.

A company in the United States has the right to replace a channel member that is not performing to expectations. In other countries, including countries in Europe and Asia, the penalties for severing relations may be sufficiently costly to make buying out the channel member the only viable option. Possibilities for exclusive dealerships also vary. In India the Monopolies and Restrictive Trades Practice Act generally prohibits exclusive dealerships in India. In Europe, however, exclusive dealerships are permitted; companies can restrict dealers from handling competing products and purchasing the company's products from alternate suppliers. In contrast, as a result of fair trade rules announced in 1981, companies in South Korea cannnot restrict their dealers and distributors from these practices.[16]

Market Determinants

Channel decisions are strongly influenced by the market characteristics of host markets. Major determinants are (1) the nature of the product, (2) the nature of the customer, and (3) the nature and location of demand.

The Nature of the Product

Product characteristics play a key role in determining the emphasis given to distribution factors. For example, transportation and warehousing costs are critical issues in the distribution and sale of industrial goods such as bulk chemicals, metals, and cement. Direct selling, servicing and repair, and spareparts warehousing dominate the distribution of such industrial products as computers, machinery, and aircraft. The product's durability, ease of adulteration, amount and type of customer service required, unit costs, and special handling requirements (such as cold storage) also are significant factors.

The Nature of the Customer

The customer, or final consumer, is the keystone in any channel design. Thus, the size, geographic distribution, shopping habits, outlet preferences, and usage patterns of customer groups must be taken into account when making distribution decisions.

Consumer-product channels tend to be longer than *industrial* products channels because the number of customers is greater, the customers are more geographically dispersed, and they buy in smaller quantities. Shopping habits, outlet preferences, and usage patterns vary considerably from country-to-country, and are strongly influenced by socio-cultural factors. French women, for example, tend to be relatively more individualistic than U.S. women and prefer to discover new products on their own. In contrast, U.S. women tend to be members of social groups and depend more heavily on word-of-mouth for product information. At the same time, shopping is a major social activity for French women and takes up a considerable amount of their time.[17] Consumer groups also affect distribution decisions. Supermarkets in developing countries are patronized primarily by upper- and middle-income consumers who own automobiles and refrigerators and can afford to purchase and can transport large quantities of food. The working classes in these same countries tend to shop more frequently, purchase smaller quantities of food items, and patronize farmers' markets and small variety stores.

Considerable variations also exist in the purchase of durable items, variations that are not entirely the result of economic factors. West Germans, for example, are reluctant to purchase durable items on credit, preferring instead to pay cash for such things as refrigerators, cameras and washing machines. They also purchase one quarter of their domestic appliances by mail order. The Dutch, on the other hand, use mail order for about 1 percent of these products.[18]

The Nature and Location of Demand

The nature and location of demand influence distribution decisions greatly.

Nature of the Demand. The perceptions that the targeted customers hold about particular products can force modification of distribution channels. A particular product may be simultaneously perceived as a luxury product, a shopping product, or a staple product in three countries (for example a pocket calculator). Each perception requires modifications in the types of channel used by the company. As discussed in Chapter 6, product perceptions are influenced by the customer's income and product experience, the product's end use, its life-cycle position, and the country's stage of economic development. The channel arrangements to be considered in a foreign market that perceives a product as a luxury will probably differ from those made in a market that considers it a staple.

Location of Demand. The geography of a country and the development of the transportation infrastructure must be factored into distribution plans. Colombia, for example, is divided into three regions by the Andes Mountains; the transportation infrastructure linking these regions is poorly developed. As a consequence, local manufacturing companies have generally remained small; they depend on wholesalers for needed financing, distribution, and storage. Those companies that have managed to develop national coverage for their products have had to pay particular attention to the logistics of inventory and warehousing. In many cases, air freight rather than surface freight must be used. The Philippines and Japan are also divided into natural regions; both countries are archipelagoes. In each country, geographical considerations has resulted in a multi-layered channel system comprised of local wholesalers, agents, and national trading companies.

Competition Determinants

The channels used by competing products and close substitutes are important because channel arrangements that seek to serve the same market often compete with one another. Consumers generally expect to find particular products in particular outlets (specialty stores), or they have become accustomed to buying particular products from particular sources (mail-order houses, street vendors). These expectations are partly the result of competitors educating consumers to a particular channel arrangement. In addition, local and global competitors may have agreements with the major wholesalers in a foreign country that effectively "shuts out" the company from key channels. To overcome channel obstacles, global companies like Tupperware and Avon Cosmetics have developed new channels that they exclusively control.[19]

Developing a Foreign Distribution Strategy

Strategy decisions need to take into account channel *continuity, consistency, adaptiveness,* and amenability to company *control.* Two groups of criteria are used to select from among the channel alternatives available to the company: economic criteria and strategy criteria. Economic criteria include the company's anticipated level of sales and the costs associated with the various channel alternatives. The strategy criteria include a consideration of the foreign market's current and future role in the company's portfolio of foreign marketing activities, and thus the competitive and marketing position the company wishes to establish, maintain, or modify in each foreign market.

Examples of the many kinds of information and data needed to make foreign distribution strategy decisions are shown in Table 15-3.

Market Coverage

The amount of market coverage a channel member provides is important. *Coverage* is a flexible term. It can refer to geographical areas of a country (such as cities and major towns), the number of retail outlets (as a percentage of all retail outlets), or the absolute volume of sales needed to make marketing profitable. Regardless of the market coverage measure(s) used, the company has to create a distribution network (dealers, distributors, and retailers) to meet its coverage goals.

Selection of Channel Members

Once the strategic objectives for the foreign market have been established, management's task is to decide which channel members and arrangements can best fulfill these objectives. Forging a working relationship with channel members so selected should then be given a high priority.

A company may not be able to create optimal channel arrangements in many foreign markets because the desired types of channel might not exist or are unavailable. For example, mass marketers like large department stores and supermarkets do not exist in some developing countries. It is not uncommon for companies to select distributors or dealers without sufficient care.[20] For example, a highly successful and well-known company with branded consumer electronics products in Europe and the United States decided to enter Asian markets. As part of its expansion plans it undertook a "whirlwind tour" of several Asian countries to select distributors who had been identified on the basis of their bids or their unit orders. As a result of this approach, the distributor that was selected to handle this new "key market" had no consumer electronics market experience, no service capability, no experience in managing advertising or promotion campaigns, no important government connections, and no retail trade record. In addition, the company failed to ask for financial or performance references. After several years, the company is still suffering from this decision.[21]

To avoid similar mistakes, Business International recommends using the 13 basic criteria presented in Table 15-4 when selecting foreign dealers or distributors.[22] These criteria can be used to screen potential channel members and build channel arrangements, ensuring that future marketing success is not jeopardized by decisions based on short-term expediency.

The weights assigned each criterion and the ratings given potential channel members depend on the nature of the company's business and its distribution

TABLE 15-3
Examples of Factors Affecting the Foreign Distribution Strategy

	Channels of Distribution	*Physical Distribution (logistics)*
Environment	☐ Trends in economic factors affecting market demand	☐ Geographic dispersement of market (urban/rural)
	☐ Financial/capital climate	☐ Transportation infrastructure (ports, railroads and roads)
	☐ Consumer or user buying habits and location preferences	☐ Frequency and quantities handled by intracompany shipments and by local channel members
	☐ Local attitudes and rules concerning the establishment of foreign subsidiaries vs. use of local agents and/or distributors	
Competition	☐ Distribution arrangements and strategies of local and foreign competitors and their performance	☐ Physical distribution habits of local and foreign competitors and the costs associated with each
	☐ Relative effectiveness and productivity of external and internal channel arrangements of competitors	☐ Relative efficiency of each type of carrier used, inventory levels maintained, and warehousing facilities used
Channel Institutions	☐ Types of wholesalers and retailers, their qualifications, reliability, capabilities, and availability	☐ The logistical alternatives available and their costs, individual and in combination
	☐ Existence of government-controlled channels such as in centrally planned economies and some developing countries	☐ The reputation of each carrier for reliability, punctuality, and geographic coverage
	☐ Existence of cartel arrangements	
Legal	☐ Government regulations on the marketing activities of foreign subsidiaries	☐ Special rules pertaining to safety, packaging, markings, size of vehicles, etc.
	☐ Government regulations governing selection and dismissal of channel members	☐ Other legal constraints on transportation activities
		☐ Legal formalities and their costs

objectives in given markets. For example, the hypothetical consumer packaged goods company used in Table 15-4, to illustrate the method presented, considered the distributor's marketing management expertise and financial soundness as of greatest importance. In the example, Distributor 1 would be for this company. Alternatively, an industrial goods company may consider the distributor's product compatibility, technical know-how, and technical facilities and service capabilities of high importance, and the distributor's infrastructure, client performance, and attitude toward its products of low importance. A high-tech consumer goods company, on the other hand, may favor financial soundness, marketing-management expertise, reputation, technical know-how, technical facilities and service support, and government relations.

TABLE 15-4
Examples of Distributor (Dealer) Selection Criteria

Criteria (no ranking implied)	Weight	Distributor 1		Distributor 2		Distributor 3	
		Rating	Score	Rating	Score	Rating	Score
1. Financial soundness and depth of channel member	4	5	20	4	16	3	12
2. Marketing management expertise and sophistication	5	4	20	3	15	2	10
3. Satisfactory trade/ customer relations and contacts	3	4	12	3	9	3	9
4. Capability to provide adequate sales coverage	4	3	12	3	12	3	12
5. Overall positive reputation and image as a company	3	5	15	4	12	4	12
6. Product compatibility (synergy or conflict?)	3	3	9	4	12	4	12
7. Pertinent technical know-how at staff level	—	—	—	—	—	—	—
8. Adequate technical facilities and service support	—	—	—	—	—	—	—
9. Adequate infrastructure in staff and facilities	1	5	5	3	3	3	3
10. Proven performance record with client companies	2	4	8	3	6	3	6
11. Positive attitude toward the company's products	1	3	3	3	3	3	3
12. Mature outlook regarding the company's inevitable progression in market management	1	3	3	3	3	3	3
13. Excellent government relations	1	4	4	3	3	3	3
Score			111		94		84

SCALES	Rating		Weighting	
	5	Outstanding	5	Critical success factor
	4	Above average	4	Prerequisite success factor
	3	Average	3	Important success factor
	2	Below average	2	Of some importance
	1	Unsatisfactory	1	Standard value

Source: Based on *Finding and Managing Distributors in Asia,* New York: Business International, 1983, p. 92.

Control of Channel Arrangements

Channel control is of critical concern to global-market companies wanting to establish global brands and a consistent image of quality and service worldwide. It may be of less importance to companies marketing multibrand products to national markets.

The company must decide how much control it wants to have over how each of its products is marketed. The answer is partly determined by the strategic role assigned each market. It is also a function of the types of channel members available, the regulations and rules governing distribution activity in each foreign market, and—to some extent—the roles traditionally assigned channel members.

Adaptive Criteria

Long-term commitment has as a corollary some loss of flexibility. For example, contracts with independent distributors in Indonesia are required by law to be for a minimum of three years. Also, long-term contracts are generally costly to drop. In general, the longer a contractual commitment, the greater the control a company should exercise over the actions and activities of its channel members.

The Cost of Alternative Channel Arrangements

Establishing and operating channel arrangements requires the careful comparison of relative costs of alternative distribution structures. The final configuration of each foreign market's distribution structure is generally the result of a compromise between costs and other objectives.

Once objectives have been clearly and quantitatively established and the type of channel members selected, management is ready to run an economic analysis of alternative channel arrangements. Of the three channels illustrated in Figure 15-1, the sales force of the company's subsidiary is the preferred channel choice if total cost is the main criterion and if sales are expected to be large. However, since the marginal costs of the three alternatives may not be strictly comparable,[23] a breakdown of costs is needed. The breakdown of costs obtained as a result of completing cost forms similar to that presented in Table 15-5 is very helpful.

Two other problems face the company that decides to undertake distribution. It is assuming the risk for the movement of its products within the foreign market. It is also exposing at least some of its assets to the economic and political risks associated with foreign direct investments.

MANAGING INTERNATIONAL DISTRIBUTION

International distribution strategy consists of all those decisions and activities necessary to move products from a company's production facilities to its foreign markets. These decisions include: (1) selecting and managing international channel members and facilitators; (2) selecting an international carrier; and (3) making storage, inventory, and material-handling decisions.

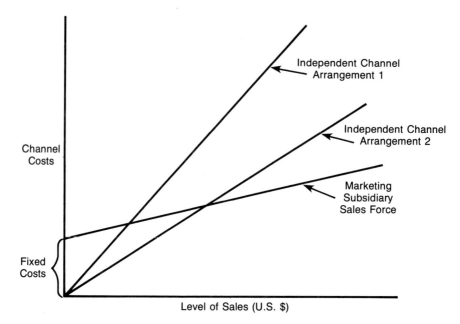

FIGURE 15-1   Example of an Approach for Selecting a Channel Arrangement Using Level of Sales and Costs as Criteria (Source: Adapted from Philip Kotler, *Principles of Marketing*, 2nd ed. [Prentice-Hall, Inc., 1983].)

International Channel Members and Facilitors

Two groups of external international intermediaries are generally used by exporters and companies marketing in foreign countries. The first group consists of firms and individuals who *facilitate* the flow of products between countries, such as freight forwarders, banks, international carriers, and insurance companies. The second group consists of firms and individuals who actively participate in the international marketing effort. For our purposes, and to distinguish them from facilitators, they will be referred to as *international channel members*.

Both groups of intermediaries are shown in Figure 15-2, which illustrates the relationship between a global-company's production activity in foreign country A (the production facility could be in the company's home country) and its international and foreign marketing activities. It represents two channel structures for moving products from foreign country A to buyers in foreign markets B and C. In foreign market B, the company has established a foreign-sales subsidiary; that market is therefore probably of strategic importance to the company. The firm is interested in being close to the market and wants direct control of the marketing activities there. In foreign market C, the company has decided to use an indirect form of exporting; it therefore relies on external independent intermediaries. An independent channel arrangement such as the one shown for market C tends to be used by exporters or by large global companies in their smaller foreign markets. Market C is then probably of low strategic value.

TABLE 15-5
Form for Costing External Channel Alternatives

Channel Level	Foreign Marketing Subsidiary	Primary Wholesalers	Secondary Wholesalers	Retailer
Possible functions of each level				
Storage needs				
Inventory				
backward ⎫				
Credit ⎬				
forward ⎭				
backward ⎫				
Transport ⎬				
forward ⎭				
Technical services (including after-sales service)				
Promotion				
Collections				
Price maintenance				
Accounting				
Risk carrying (such as insurance, product performance)				
Packaging				
Characteristics of each level				
Degree of specialization				
Size				
Geographical coverage				
Performance				
backward ⎫				
Tie-in ⎬				
forward ⎭				
Exclusivity				

Source: Adapted from Richard D. Robinson, *International Business Management* (Hinsdale, Ill.: Dryden, 1978), p. 80.

International Facilitators

The several types of facilitators on which a company can depend for assistance in exporting its products are briefly described in Table 15-6.

One of the most important types of facilitators is the *freight forwarder.* These specialists arrange and expedite the *physical movement* of products from country to country. Their services usually include selecting economical transportation routes and carriers, consolidating shipments for several exporters in order to receive lower transportation charges, and preparing the many documents that are required when goods are shipped between countries, and clearing such shipments through the customs agencies of the exporting and importing countries. The knowledge and experience provided by freight forwarders, together with their

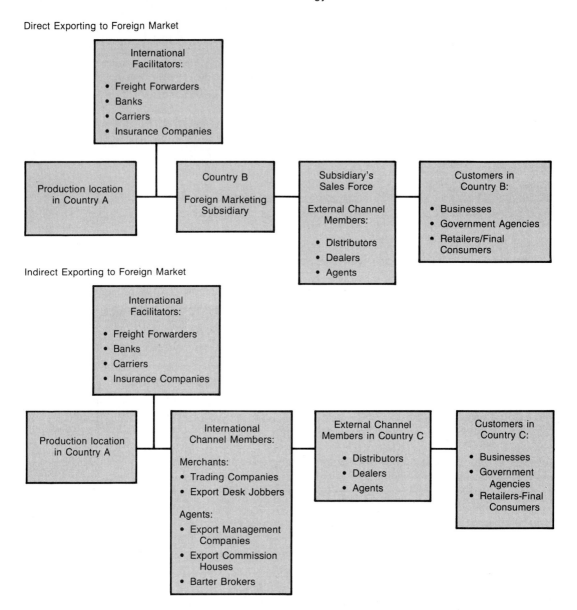

FIGURE 15-2   Examples of Distribution Channels: International and Foreign

ability to spread costs among a number of clients, often means it is cheaper and more efficient to employ them rather than try to perform such functions in house. For example, a recent survey of active ocean shippers revealed that 94.6 percent of the respondents used freight forwarders.[24]

International Channel Members

There are five basic types of international channel members: international trading companies, export desk jobbers, export management companies, export commission houses, and barter and countertrade brokers. The first two take title, or legal possession of the company's products, and are usually classified as *merchant* middlemen. The other three do not take title, are usually classified as *agent middlemen, domestic exporting middlemen,* and market the company's products under a contractual arrangement and generally receive a commission based on the value of sales. Each type of international channel member provides a different package of services, and advantages and disadvantages.

As a particular foreign market develops and matures, an indirect exporter may want to move closer to the market, even to the point of direct selling through its own sales force. To facilitate this move, the company requires a flow of information related to (1) export packaging, documentation, freight, insurance, handling, and tariffs, (2) the identity and preferences of the end user, (3) the local channels through which the product flows, (4) the devices used to promote sales, (5) usual trade margins, and (6) feedback from both the distribution channels and the final customer with respect to product quality, design, terms of sale, delivery, and servicing. Thus, it behooves the company to arrange for these types of information to be passed on by its international channel members.

International Trading Companies or Merchants. International trading companies typically purchase manufactured products from a number of firms and market the products in foreign markets, often through wholesalers and retailers operated by the trading company. Many of these trading companies are large-scale organizations that frequently become involved in shipping and financing in addition to marketing. They may also develop products for particular markets and assist companies by offering marketing research or technical assistance.

International trading companies provide the manufacturer several important advantages. They are generally large, well-resourced companies; they can provide the manufacturer with capital, working cash, and marketing information on overseas markets (trends, fashions, quality standards, and the like). By assuming title of the products the manufacturer produces, they can also reduce the manufacturer's risks. However, the transfer of risk is not without disadvantages for the firm. Since the trading company is between the manufacturer and its foreign markets, the manufacturer is dependent on it for foreign sales and may therefore not develop the experience and contacts necessary for exporting directly to its foreign markets. It may also have little influence over where and how the trading company markets its products.

Export Desk Jobbers. These export middlemen specialize in marketing staple commodities like agricultural goods, raw materials, lumber, and basic metals. They purchase these commodities for resale and generally aim to match their purchases with orders already in hand. Although they do take title of the goods they purchase, they normally do not take physical possession. Goods are shipped directly to the customer.

TABLE 15-6
Examples of International Facilitators*

Types of Facilitators	Description
Government Agencies	Government agencies provide many services to assist exporters and promote exporting. The U.S. Department of Commerce provides publications detailing trade regulations, local competition and economic conditions in a large number of countries. Governments also offer a number of trade-promotion programs designed to help exporters explore foreign markets, participate in trade fairs, and locate foreign agents and distributors.
Export Financing	Many exporting countries have programs to reduce exporting risks and incentives by providing insurance and credit for export sales, sometimes with reduced interest rates. For example, the Export-Import Bank of the United States (EXIM) was created in 1934 as an independent U.S. government agency to aid in financing and facilitating exports. It extends direct loans to foreign buyers of U.S. goods and provides guarantees for repayment of medium-term credit extended by U.S. banks to foreign buyers.
Private Banks	Private banks are a major source of both secured and unsecured short-term financing of exports. They can also be useful by providing commercial leads, and checking on the credit worthiness of foreign buyers.

The advantages and disadvantages of using export desk jobbers are very similar to those mentioned for trading companies. However, because these intermediaries deal in homogeneous goods, there are fewer risks than in the case of trading companies.

Export Management Companies. Export management companies (EMCs), also referred to as *combination export managers,* act essentially as external exporting departments for companies whose exporting volume or experience may be too limited to justify an in-house export department. Although the main responsibilities of EMCs are to locate foreign markets for their clients' products and to arrange for sales in these markets, they sometimes become involved in promotion and financing, and they may arrange transportation for overseas shipments.

EMCs bestow several advantages. First, the producer can start to export its products with little or no international experience. Second, commitments in human resources and other start-up costs are avoided. Third, relationships can be severed once the producer has gained the necessary experience and volume of sales needed to establish an economically successful export department.

There are some disadvantages to EMCs, however. A major one is, as with other intermediaries, the producer's dependency. An independent, profit-seeking company may not be willing to spend the time and money necessary to fully develop its client's foreign market. Also, EMCs may not have the capabilities necessary to provide the level and quality of after-sales service the producer wants to offer.

Export Commission Houses. Export commission houses act as purchasing agents for single buyers or groups of buyers located in other countries. They generally have established purchasing arrangements with local manufacturers, who then act as suppliers for their foreign buyers. An example is a commission house

TABLE 15-6 (continued)

Types of Facilitators	Description
Foreign-Trade Zones and Bonded Warehouses	Foreign-trade zones are secure areas legally outside a country's customs territory where goods destined for importation may be stored, exhibited, broken down, repacked, assembled, sorted, graded, or otherwise processed further without paying import duties until or unless they legally enter the country. Customs bonded warehouses have some of the attributes of a foreign-trade zone. Dutiable goods may enter duty free (under bond) into a customs bonded warehouse and remain there for up to three years. Import duties are levied when the goods are withdrawn from the warehouse for local consumption.
Freight Forwarders	The services provided by freight forwarders include, among other things, advise on carriers, packaging and documentations, negotiation of carrier rates, preparation of shipping documents, and expediting cargo from inland shipping points to ports of export.
Customhouse Brokers	The functions provided by customhouse brokers include advise on import classification (to save on import duties), preparing all necessary documents for quick customs clearance, advising on the types of bonds and arranging for required bonds, expediting cargo transfers, arranging for delivery to inland destinations, storage, and advising on foreign trade zones.

* An excellent source of detailed information on international facilitors is R. Duane Hall, *International Trade Operations: A Managerial Approach* (Jersey City, N.J.: Unz & Co., 1983).

in Hong Kong collecting clothing products from local manufacturers to fill orders received from U.S. and European retail stores. Such houses often provide the local manufacturers with the designs and fabrics and help them meet the standards of quality required by their foreign buyers.

Barter and Countertrade Brokers. In recent years, there has been an upsurge in barter and countertrade transactions in international trade. It has been prompted by countries attempting to conserve scarce foreign exchange reserves by offering locally produced goods or commodities in exchange for foreign goods. For example, in 1984, Saudi Arabia was unable to purchase additional aircraft because of insufficient cash, so Boeing arranged a switch-trade with an oil importer. The importer received more than $1 billion of crude oil from Saudi Arabia and reimbursed Boeing in dollars.[25] The increasing use of barter and countertrade deals has created a need for intermediaries to help companies sell goods and commodities accepted in exchange for their products. When barter or countertrade is common, as in the case of McDonnell Douglas, companies will create separate organizations to handle the sale of the goods and commodities they receive.

Developing an International Distribution Channel

The two major elements of an international distribution activity are the management of the company's logistical network and the management of its exporting activities.

Management of the International Logistical Network

Logistics, or physical distribution, includes transportation, storage, packaging, order taking and processing, and inventory control. The management of an international logistical network is considerably more complicated than for national networks for several reasons. These include the geographic distances involved; the various costs that need to be taken into account when making decisions; and the company's dependency on carriers, customs officials, and many others who can assist or hinder the flow of goods between countries.

The Logistical Infrastructure. Management of the international logistical network can be divided into two parts, the development and management of the various units that make up a company's logistical infrastructure and ensuring that the logistical network provides for the effective and efficient movement of shipments between countries.

Physical Distribution Costs. As many as 14 tangible and intangible costs can be associated with the shipment of goods across national borders. These are listed in Exhibit 15-2. For a particular production-facility–foreign-market combination, the task of the marketing manager is to select from the various international carriers most suitable for the company's purposes.

Management of the Company's Exporting Activities

The management of the company's export markets is of sufficient importance to be covered as a separate topic (see Chapter 17). At this point, our discussion

---

EXHIBIT 15-2 _____

International Distribution Costs (Physical Distribution) _____

   1. Buffer inventory at production facility

   2. Packing costs

   3. Transportation and loading costs (point of departure)

   4. Paperwork associated with shipment

   5. International carrier charges

   6. Insurance costs

   7. En route inventory costs and customs waiting costs

   8. Customs broker charge and associated paperwork

   9. Import duties

10. Repackaging costs, if necessary

11. Inspection, point-of-sale, and shrinkage or damage costs

12. Delivered inventory costs

13. Import deposits

14. Quota and local content laws (offsetting exports)

_____

Source: Adapted from David Rutenberg, *Multinational Management* (Boston: Little, Brown and Company, 1982), pp. 153–154.

centers on the selection and control of the international channel members that best support the company's global marketing strategy.

Selection of International Channel Members. International and foreign channel members serve the same basic functions for a company; both link the company with its export markets. International channel members are responsible for identifying and exploiting marketing opportunities for the company's products in overseas markets. However, since the company is very distant from export markets served indirectly it must place greater reliance on these channel members. As a consequence, the exporting company should pay particular attention to the motivation, compatibility, technical know-how (if relevant), and maturity of these channel members.

Control of International Channel Members. Since increased involvement is generally associated with increased management and financial costs. The need to control channel members is neither equal for all foreign markets nor uniform across all marketing activities. The degree of control advisable depends on the company's strategic objectives in each market. The company may opt for one of three types of control: a conventional channel approach, an administrative channel approach and a contractual channel approach.[26]

In a conventional approach, the company and its channel members act strictly as independent sellers and buyers with no concern for overall distribution issues and problems. In an administrative channel approach, the company and its channel members cooperate and coordinate their activities through informal noncontractual agreements. In a contractual channel approach, the company and its channel members integrate their activities through a formal contract to obtain channel economies and to maximize market impact. Under this last approach, distribution activities tend to be standardized for efficiency and coordinated to reduce operational risks for each member.

Each approach has advantages and disadvantages for the exporting company. Although the conventional channel approach is a low-risk approach for tapping foreign markets, the channel member's marketing effort may not be optimal for the company. Channel members generally have a large number of suppliers and carry an assortment of products with different margins; no long-term commitment involved. Thus, this approach is best suited for those companies whose products are readily and inexpensively adaptable to foreign markets and do not require aggressive marketing.[27] It is often used by companies that export infrequently or place low priority on exports.

The administrative approach provides the company with many of the efficiencies associated with contractual arrangements without long-term commitments. Thus, the company retains channel flexibility while minimizing the cost and effort often required by exporting. This approach is well suited for companies requiring flexible yet efficient entry to foreign markets, but is not always feasible because of local laws and a desire of intermediaries to have formalized relations.

The contractual arrangement benefits both the company and the channel member. Marketing efforts can be standardized for greater efficiency and coordinated for greater effectiveness. However, this approach is suitable only for companies "with the capability and willingness to perform contractual commitment over a long period of time."[28]

MANAGING GLOBAL DISTRIBUTION

The purpose of a global distribution strategy is to ensure that the company's foreign and international distribution strategies are consistent with and supportive of the company's global marketing strategy and objectives and its productive resources. The five dimensions of the company's global marketing strategy discussed in Chapter 11 need to be individually and collectively considered when making global distribution decisions. Each dimension, particularly the company's *geographic expansion* and *global segmentation strategies,* has a direct affect on the types of channel members used, the criteria used to select these channel members, and the time and resources expended in developing local distribution networks.

The coordination of overseas distribution activities should be undertaken by all companies. Even small exporters and companies in the initial stages of international involvement need to periodically weigh the strategic and economic costs of not explicitly managing their international and foreign distribution activities as a co-ordinated and mutually supportive system of strategies.

The Company's Geographic Expansion Options

Ayal and Zif have suggested that a company interested in expanding internationally explicitly or implicitly adopts one of three geographic expansion strategies: *geographic concentration, geographic diversification,* or some *combination* of the two. Within these strategies, the company also elects to use either a *segment concentration* or a *segment diversification* strategy. The former involves limiting the company's marketing activities to one or just a few market segments within each country. The latter involves extending its marketing activities across a number of market segments. Each geographic-segmentation strategy combination, presented in Figure 15-3, has implications for the company's foreign distribution strategies and its allied international distribution strategy.[29]

Strategy 1—Geographic and Segment Concentration

This strategy entails concentrating on a few market segments in a limited number of countries. It is particularly appropriate when local competition is intense but the market segments are large, have high or stable growth rates, or are widely dispersed. It is also appropriate when considerable marketing resources are needed to educate market segments to the value of the product, to develop brand loyalty, to develop a reliable and effective distribution system, or to exploit economies of scale in distribution.

Within Country Market Segments

	Concentration	Diversification

	Concentration	Diversification
Concentration	**STRATEGY 1** Geographic concentration and segment concentration	**STRATEGY 2** Geographic concentration and segment diversification
Diversification	**STRATEGY 3** Geographic diversification and segment concentration	**STRATEGY 4** Geographic diversification and segment diversification

Country-level expansion

*Possible combination strategies are not shown. Diversified, multi-divisional companies could be using two or more of the above strategies at the same time.

FIGURE 15-3   Geographic Expansion Strategy Alternatives*

Strategy 2—Geographic Concentration and Segment Diversification

This strategy is suitable for a product or product line that appeals to several market segments. The company concentrates on developing foreign distribution arrangements in a few countries that can reach a variety of consumers. These consumers typically use a variety of outlets, have different shopping habits, and expect different types of services. Geographic concentration and segment diversification are particularly effective and efficient when the company can exploit economies of scale in promotion and distribution.

Strategy 3—Geographic Diversification and Segment Concentration

This strategy is particularly suitable for global-market companies with specialized products of potential appeal to customers in many countries. The economic return of this strategy is considerable when country entry costs are lower than internal distribution costs and when the company enjoys economies of scale in production or benefits from accumulated experience. In many cases, the strategy requires the development of effective distribution arrangements in each country, and thus may rely on the availability of qualified independent distributors and dealers.

Strategy 4—Geographic and Segment Diversification

This dual diversification strategy is generally used by larger, aggressive global-market companies with product lines that appeal to a large number of national markets. The strategy can also be used by companies with limited resources provided that (1) foreign distribution costs are not excessive, (2) channel members do not need a lot of attention, or (3) a limited or superficial coverage of national markets is satisfactory to the company. National-market companies seldom use a dual diversification strategy; their global marketing strategy is to serve the unique needs or requirements of specific national markets, a goal that consumes considerable resources.

The Company's Global Segmentation Strategy

As alluded to above, the design of foreign distribution channels is contingent on a company's global segmentation strategy. The relative emphasis placed on external and internal distribution factors depends on whether the company is pursuing a global or a national segmentation strategy. In the following discussion, we use *global-market company* to mean a company seeking to satisfy a need or requirement of a market segment *not* defined by national boundaries. A company seeking to satisfy a need or requirement defined by national boundaries is a *national-market company.*

Global-Market Companies

Since companies using global-market strategies are generally competing with other global companies, their foreign distribution strategies need to take into account both local market conditions and global competitive requirements. In contrast to companies using national segmentation strategies, global-market companies generally require:

1. A high degree of control or influence over the marketing activities of channel members, such as the quality of their promotional and servicing activities, the timing and level of their selling efforts, and the end-market pricing of their products;
2. Considerable efficiency in the delivery and order processing of their products to ensure that local inventory levels are maintained and that channel margins, channel payment terms, and customer prices are competitive;
3. Uniformity in the types and quality of outlets used to ensure that the same customer groups are reached across national markets;
4. Uniformity in the after-sales services provided by retailers or service centers across national markets.

At the same time, however, these companies generally benefit from customer groups:

1. That perceive the company's products as specialties or shopping goods and that are therefore more likely to make price and quality comparisons, and are willing to risk time and effort in locating a desired product;
2. That are willing to deviate from traditional shopping patterns in order to obtain a desired product; and
3. That come from the more affluent sectors of the country.

To meet channel requirements and to exploit their advantages, global-market companies often find it necessary to help channel members develop their capabilities and strengthen or improve their activities and practices. Many companies conduct training programs for their distributors and dealers and often provide financial and managerial support to enhance the efficiency of their major channel members. For example, Levi Strauss, when faced with increased competition in Europe, developed a strategy to gain or retain distributor loyalty that included offering retailers support and incentives in exchange for their placing greater emphasis on Levi products.[30] Levi also provided retailers assistance in developing local advertising campaigns, provided point-of-sales promotional materials, and offered them in-house computerized management information systems to check on the availability of products and to place orders electronically.

Global-market companies also find it necessary to spend considerable time and resources in developing efficient delivery systems. To cut distribution costs in Europe, Philips centralized its warehousing operations, standardized the 400,000 components used to service its products into 133,000 computerized code numbers, installed a computerizing ordering network that linked national distribution organizations to the central warehouse, and introduced new order-processing systems to ensure that most orders are dispatched within one working day.[31]

National-Market Companies

The foreign channel arrangements adoped by national-market companies tend to be *market driven* rather than company driven. (In sharp contrast, the channel arrangements adopted by global-market companies tend to be company driven.)

To be successful in foreign markets, companies serving national-market segments need to be relatively more efficient and effective in serving their local target markets than do local and global competitors. In contrast to global-market companies, the foreign distribution systems of national-market companies need to be:

1. More sensitive to local market conditions, such as the outlet and service expectations of local customers;

2. More sensitive to local competitive conditions, such as channel domination, channel promotion, and changes in the services provided wholesalers and retailers; and

3. More flexible in switching channel arrangements (the types of outlets used) to match shifting retail shopping patterns of local consumers.

National-market companies feel strong local pressures to use traditional channels and to rely heavily on local channel members. This is especially true for those products with national brand names. However, innovation in channel arrangements need not be ruled out. Channel design is a competitive weapon that can have significant marketing value if used skillfully.

National-market companies are more likely than global-market companies to join forces with a local joint-venture partner in order to gain entry to a particular foreign market. Doing so gives them on-site insight into local competition and regulations. Local partners can provide the market knowledge needed and probably have access to the requisite channels of distribution. Disadvantages of joint-venture arrangements (discussed in Chapter 10) can be localized. Since each country is seen to represent a single opportunity, the need to coordinate marketing activities across countries is given a low priority. Pillsbury has followed this line of reasoning in adopting a geographic diversification strategy in Central and South America.

The Company's Global Sourcing Decision

Global sourcing decisions involve more than a comparison of the costs associated with shipping goods from production sites to markets (see Exhibit 15-1). Four broad categories of variables need to be considered when making or modifying such decisions: (1) plant-market factors, (2) cost factors, (3) government relations and restrictions, and (4) miscellaneous other considerations. Examples of the variables that need to be considered in each category are presented in Exhibit 15-3.

Plant-Market Factors

Several plant-market factors need to be considered when making a sourcing decision. The more obvious factors include the proximity of the plant to the

---

EXHIBIT 15-3
Examples of Factors Affecting Global Sourcing Decisions

Plant-Market Factors

□ Proximity of plant to market
□ Speed of delivery
□ Available plant capacity
□ Quality of local subcontractors
□ Acceptability of source to customer(s)
□ Ability to Supply parts
□ Ability to grant adequate sales financing

Government Relations and Restrictions

□ Local content rules
□ Export requirements (and desires)
□ Social and political factors (layoffs at plants not given order)
□ Ability to overcome nontariff barriers (product codes, specifications)
□ Bilateral and multilateral agreements
□ Exports and market expansion relationship
□ Antitrust implications

Cost Factors

□ Landing costs (freight, tariffs, import taxes)
□ Import obstacles (surcharges, import deposits)
□ Exchange-rate effects
□ Opportunity costs to other plants
□ Plant utilization rate

Other Considerations

□ Joint-venture partner interests
□ Ability to benefit from special import-duty incentives (tariff preferences)
□ Tax advantages (within and across countries, effects on income)
□ Investment and market strategies (new plant)

Source: Adapted from *201 Checklists: Decision Making in International Operations* (New York: Business International, 1980), pp. 247–248.

market, the speed of delivery, and the availability of productive capacity to handle an order or provide the products needed to satisfy market demand. Less obvious factors sometimes also need to be considered. For example, what is the customer's perception of the products produced by the plants under review? Will the customer or potential customer consider a product produced in Switzerland of better quality than a product produced in another country, even though the product is produced by the same company and meets the same specifications? (As discussed in Chapter 13, product perceptions can be influenced by country-of-origin effects.) Another factor often overlooked is the ability of the plant to supply spare parts, provide repairs, and service installed equipment (when required). In some cases, since sales may depend on the financial package the seller can offer the potential buyer, the financial factors may also affect the decision. Although this is especially true for large-price items such as aircraft and large-frame computers, the ability to provide financial assistance in cases of large-volume transactions may have an impact on the decisions of foreign distributors.

Cost Factors

Two types of costs are involved in choosing which production facility supplies a particular market, transit costs and production costs. *Transit costs* are incurred as a result of shipping products from one country to another. *Production costs* are incurred in order to produce the products to be shipped. They are preshipment costs, and depend on such things as utilization rates, depreciation allowances, productivity rates, wages and salary scales, and the cost of materials. There can thus be considerable variation in plant costs from country to country. Consequently, the advantage one plant may have because of market proximity and reduced transit costs could be lost because of relatively higher production costs.

Government Relations and Restrictions

Sourcing decisions can affect government relations in several ways, all of which need to be weighed carefully. General Motors had to modify its sourcing plans for the Australian market in order to meet local content laws. By agreeing to offset imports of fully assembled automobiles by exporting component parts, GM was able to provide employment and thus satisfy both social and political pressures. Such compromises are, of course, not always possible. The sourcing decision that favors one location has the potential to penalize another, especially if plants are not operating at or near capacity. Penalties may involve the laying-off of workers and the loss of any foreign-exchange earnings the exports would have generated.

In addition, the ability to expand marketing activities in a particular country may be contingent on a company's exporting activities. For example, a company may be required to export an agreed-upon percentage of its production; its ability to serve the local market is thus directly tied to its exports. When exports are not forthcoming, the government may intervene and stop local expansion of the company.

A growing phenomenon in international trade is the use of voluntary bilateral and multilateral trade agreements that, by quota, restrict imports from specific countries. Many companies have therefore set up assembly plants in countries with unfilled quotas. For example, in the 1980s, many Asian companies have set up operations in the Caribbean Basin to supply their U.S. markets and thereby bypass the increasingly stiff quotas applied to products manufactured in their own countries.

Other Considerations

Sourcing decisions can be influenced by many other issues, a number of which are presented in Exhibit 15-3. We now discuss these "other considerations" briefly.

An increasing number of global companies have joint-venture partners in some or all of the countries in which they operate. Since most joint-venture partners have a stake only in the local activities of a global company, they are more interested in the implications that sourcing decisions may have on the joint-venture's performance than in the sourcing decision's effects on the global company's overall performance. Similar problems also arise when the company's overseas activities have been divided into regional profit centers. Sourcing decisions need to take into account the marketing and production plans of these regional groups.

Sourcing decisions also have a bearing on local and corporate income taxes. Unless transfer prices are used to minimize income effects, the plant receiving the order will generally end up having to pay local income taxes on the order. Decision makers need to study and weigh these tax effects.

Notwithstanding the potential snags just detailed, a company may have overriding strategic reasons for using a particular plant even if the decision results in a relatively poor short-term performance. For example, as noted in Chapter 11, a company may be interested in developing a particular market that necessitates the use of a particular plant, such as was the case with IBM in Mexico. Also, a company may have long-term plans that require the closing of some plants for modernization and the utilization of others, regardless of short-term penalties.

THE GRAY MARKET AND THE GLOBAL COMPANY _____

Because some global-market companies are simultaneously marketing standardized products in several foreign markets, they and their authorized channel members are vulnerable to a growing phenomenon often referred to as *the gray market,* or *parallel market.*

> A **gray market** generally consists of those unauthorized distributors and dealers that circumvent authorized channel arrangements by buying a company's products in low-price markets and selling them in high-price market at prices lower than those offered by authorized channel members.

Although these activities are not always viewed as illegal by governments, global companies are concerned with gray markets. They reduce sales for legitimate channel members and disrupt distribution and pricing strategies.[32]

The gray market has become especially serious in recent years. As recently as the late 1970s, it occurred in just a few select products—typically cameras, watches, and perfumes. By the mid-1980s, it had grown to include such diverse products as automobiles, tires, and crystal.[33] The number of foreign-made automobiles entering the United States through gray-market channels grew from 5,500 units in 1982 to 70,000 units by 1985.[34]

Reasons for the Gray Market

There are several reasons for the rapid growth of the gray market which include (1) the growth in the number of global products, (2) fluctuating exchange rates, (3) price discrimination, and (4) excess supply.

Growth in Global Products

In recent years, an increasing number of companies have found it profitable to market standardized products simultaneously in several foreign markets. An increase in the number and variety of products sold on a worldwide basis automatically increases opportunities for profit by experienced international traders. Since global companies find it difficult to modify their inventory and pricing strategies in individual countries in response to daily changes in demand and foreign exchange rates, gray market problems are compounded. The gray market responds more quickly to market fluctuations than do global companies.

Fluctuating Exchange Rates

Fluctuation in the relative value of foreign currencies is a major reason for the growth of the gray market. When companies settle on foreign-market pricing strategies, they generally set prices with certain exchange rates in mind. These prices are not changed every time exchange rates vary; to do so would be disruptive. Sophisticated gray market traders take advantage of any disparities. They carefully watch foreign exchange rates and inventory levels; when the difference between or among selected currencies is sufficient, they enter the market and make their purchases. Gray market dealers are, in effect, arbitraging in products the same way foreign exchange traders deal in foreign currencies.

Price Discrimination

An alert international distributor can take legal advantage of price differences between markets. For example, the wholesale prices of Japanese cameras in Hong Kong tend to be much lower than in other countries. An independent U.S. camera retailer can often get cameras more cheaply from a Hong Kong distributor than from a company-authorized U.S. camera retailer. The major difference between this situation and the situation resulting from foreign-exchange fluctuations is that here the price differences between markets is set by the manufacturer as part of its pricing and distribution strategies.

Excess Supply

Both demand and supply can fluctuate in response to market conditions. Thus, a distributor or dealer in one country with an unexpected oversupply of a particular product may be quite willing to sell its excess supply for less than the normal margin in order to recover his or her investment. In addition, when all import duties and local value-added taxes are rebated on reexport, as in European Community countries, there is an added incentive to sell the surplus stock to an international distributor.

Reactions to the Gray Market

Global-market companies faced with gray-market problems have at least three options: they can ignore the problem, seek legal redress, or modify their marketing strategies. We now briefly discuss this trio of options.

Do Nothing

Some manufacturers and their authorized foreign dealers hesitate to take legal action against gray-market traders. There are several reasons for this reluctance. First, a company's customers or potential customers may switch to competing brands if unable to obtain the company's products at the lower, unauthorized price. Second, collecting evidence to take gray-market traders to court can be difficult and costly. Third, some companies just hope that the problem will disappear. Indeed, it might—if the price differential is the result of foreign-exchange-rate changes.

Seek Legal Redress

Although the legal option can be time consuming and expensive, some companies and their authorized dealers have chosen to prosecute gray-market traders. For example, Seiko won an injunction against Alexander's department store in New York. Alexander's had been giving the impression that Seiko provided a similar warranty for gray market watches as for watches sold by authorized dealers.[35] Not all manufacturers are as fortunate in the courts as was Seiko. Courts do not always decide in favor of the manufacturer. In 1983, Duracell International complained to the U.S. International Trade Commission that gray-market traders in the United States were importing Duracell alkaline batteries made in Belgium. Although the ITC ruled in favor of Duracell and recommended a ban on the importation of gray-market Duracell batteries, the ruling was overturned by President Reagan.[36] President Reagan believed the ruling violated the principles of free trade.

Change Marketing-Mix Strategies

The quickest and most direct way to confront a gray-market problem is at its source, the marketplace. Companies can modify their marketing strategies in four distinct areas: (1) product strategy, (2) pricing strategy, (3) advertising strategy, and (4) distribution strategy.[37]

The *product strategy* involves localizing the product for a specific overseas market. This is possible only when the foreign market is sufficiently large to keep production and marketing costs within reasonable limits. For example, Olympus used this strategy when it introduced a new camera made exclusively for the U.S. market.

In a *pricing strategy,* the prices charged are changed to minimize price differentials between markets. For example, Canon A-1 cameras were being sold to authorized U.S. retailers for $396 when the gray-market price was $370. Canon reduced its U.S. retailer price to $362.[38] Nikon and Hasselblad have also used this option to reduce gray-market activities in their products.

Unlike the first two marketing-mix options, which are proactive, the *advertising strategy* is reactive. The effect on profits of losses to the gray market are minimized by cutting cost. This approach, of course, can be dangerous and depends on competitive conditions at the time of the decision. Hasselblad used this strategy when it cut its 1983 U.S. advertising budget by $100,000 to increase its U.S. profits.

In the final option, *distribution strategy,* the company's relationship with its channel members is modified particularly with the retailer. Two approaches based on coersion and incentives have been used.[39] For example, Vivitar publically threatened to cancel its contracts with any legitimate distributor found to be dealing in gray-market products. Minolta, on the other hand, provides only a one-year warranty on gray-market Minolta cameras, not its usual two-year warranty. However, that one-year warranty does not extend to gray-market cameras sold in the United States. Seiko warned its dealers that it would do business only with those retailers who refused to handle gray-market Seiko watches.

SUMMARY

Distribution decisions are among the most complex and challenging facing the global company for an ineffective distribution arrangement can nullify the most carefully developed global marketing strategy. The global company needs to develop three types of distribution strategies, each of which supports a corresponding marketing strategy. The foreign distribution strategy ensures that the company's products are available when and where the customer wants them. Into this strategy are factored the changing expectations and location of the customer; changing demand patterns; competitive conditions; and local regulations, laws, and distribution practices. When it becomes necessary to supply foreign markets from production facilities located in other countries, the international distribution strategy ensures that these markets are supplied efficiently and reliably. The company must be responsive to market demand and production conditions. Companies involved in global marketing activities develop global distribution strategies to coordinate foreign and international strategies into cohesive and mutually supportive production-marketing efforts that implement local and global objectives.

The international and foreign distribution arrangements created by companies consist of an elaborate yet synchronized network of internal units and independent channel intermediaries. The five basic types of international channel members are international trading companies, export desk jobbers, export management companies, export commission houses, and barter and countertrade brokers. In many cases, external arrangements represent a significant long-term commitment by the company, take many years to build, and cannot be quickly or easily changed. Also, since independent channel intermediaries tend to offer specialized capabilities, they effectively introduce constraints that can curtail a company's ability to modify its short-term marketing strategies and market development plans.

International sourcing decisions impact several of the company's others activities, particularly production functions. Synchronizing the company's production and marketing activities without jeopardizing its position in the foreign markets being served presents a special challenge.

The five dimensions of the company's global marketing strategy discussed in Chapter 10 have a significant bearing on international and foreign distribution strategies. For example, the company's geographic expansion strategy and its global segmentation strategy individually and in combination influence the selection of channel members and whether channel arrangements are primarily proactive or reactive.

A phenomenon of growing importance in international markets is the gray market, which consists of unauthorized traders buying and selling a company's product in different countries. The gray market is of particular concern to companies using global segmentation strategies and manufacturing and marketing highly standardized, globally branded products. Companies confronted with a gray-market situation can react in one of three ways. They may decide to ignore the problem, take legal action, or modify elements of their marketing mix. The option chosen is strongly influenced by the nature of the situation and its expected duration.

DISCUSSION QUESTIONS

1. Distinguish between foreign-market distribution and international distribution.
2. When would it be feasible and advisable for a global company to centralize the coordination of its foreign-market distribution systems? When would decentralization be more appropriate?
3. Under what circumstances would a geographic and segment diversification strategy be appropriate for a national-market company?

4. Identify and discuss the implication of three legal barriers for the foreign and international distribution strategies of a global-market company.
5. Explain how selected data on wholesalers and retailers from *United Nations Statistical Yearbook* could be used by a company planning a market-entry strategy. What are some of the advantages and disadvantages of using such data?
6. "The more developed a country's economy, the shorter its channels of distribution." Explain why this statement is true in some cases but not in others. (What other factors, for example, influence channel structure?)

ADDITIONAL READING

Anderson, Erin, and Anne T. Coughlan, "International Market Entry and Expansion via Independent or Integrated Channels of Distribution," *Journal of Marketing,* Vol. 51, January 1987.

Goldstucker, Jac L., "The Influence of Culture on Channels of Distribution," in *Marketing and the New Science of Planning,* Proceedings of the Fall Conference (Chicago: American Marketing Association, 1968).

Kacker, Madhav, "Coming to Terms with Global Retailing," *International Marketing Review,* Vol. 3, Spring 1986.

Stock, James, and Douglas Lambert, "Physical Distribution Management in International Marketing," *International Marketing Review,* Vol. 1, Autumn 1983.

ENDNOTES

1. Students interested in pursuing this topic should see David Rutenburg, *Multinational Management* (Boston, Mass.: Little, Brown and Company, 1982).
2. "Shh! Please don't call his car a Rover," *Business Week,* January 12, 1987, p. 59.
3. E. Raymond Corey, *Industrial Marketing: Cases and Concepts* (Englewood Cliffs, N.J.: Prentice-Hall, 1976), p. 263.
4. Jac Goldstucker, "The Influence of Culture on Channels of Distribution," American Marketing Association *Proceedings,* Fall 1968 pp. 468–473, and George Wadinambiaratchi, "Channels of Distribution in De-

veloping Economies," *The Business Quarterly,* Winter 1965.

5. Susan P. Douglas, "Patterns and Parallels of Marketing Structures in Several Countries," *MSU Business Topics,* Spring 1971, pp. 38–48.

6. John Borrell, "Anti-Asian Sentiments in East Africa Worry the Region's Indian Communities," *The Wall Street Journal,* September 2, 1982, p. 20.

7. Michael R. Czinkota, "Distribution of Consumer Products in Japan," *International Marketing Review,* Vol. 2, No. 3, Autumn 1985, pp. 39–51.

8. See footnote 4.

9. Saeed Samiee, "Retailing Structure in the Distribution Network of Less Developed Nations," unpublished paper, p. 16.

10. Jerome B. Kernan and Montrose S.Sommers, *Comparative Marketing Systems* (New York: Appleton-Century-Crofts, 1968), p. 398.

11. William P. Glade, James E. Littlefield, William A. Strang, and Jon G. Udell, *Marketing in a Developing Nation* (Lexington, Mass.: Lexington Books, 1970), p. 55.

12. Czinkota, op. cit., p. 43.

13. Philip R. Cateora and John M. Hess, *International Marketing,* 4th ed. (Homewood, Ill.: Richard D. Irwin, 1979), p. 588.

14. Czinkota, op. cit., p. 40.

15. Ibid., p. 42.

16. *Finding and Managing Distributors* (New York: Business International, 1983).

17. Robert T. Green and Eric Langeard, "A Cross National Comparison of Consumer Habits and Innovator Characteristics," *Journal of Marketing* 39 (July 1975), pp. 34–41.

18. Vern Terpstra, *International Dimensions of Marketing* (Boston: Kent, 1982), p. 51.

19. "Business Briefs," *World Press Review,* February 1981, p. 55.

20. Derek F. Channon with Michael Jalland, *Multinational Strategic Planning* (New York: AMACOM, 1978), p. 284.

21. *Finding and Managing Distributors* (New York: Business International, 1983).

22. Ibid, p. 92.

23. Richard D. Robinson, *International Business Management* (Hinsdale, Ill.: Dryden, 1978), p. 72 and 76.

24. "Freight Forwarders: The Export Experts," *Distribution,* March 1980, p. 38.

25. "Boeing Gets Order from Saudi Airline For $1 Billion in Jets," *The Wall Street Journal,* August 16, 1984.

26. L. W. Stern and A. I. El-Ansary, *Marketing Channels* (Englewood Cliffs, N.J.: Prentice-Hall, 1982).

27. Daniel C. Bello and Nicholas C. Williamson, "Contractual Arrangements and Marketing Practices in the Indirect Export Channel," *Journal of International Business Studies,* Vol. 16, No. 2 (Summer 1985), pp. 65–82.

28. Ibid, p. 80.

29. This section is based on the marketing expansion model proposed by Igal Ayal and Jehiel Zif, "Market Expansion Strategies in Multinational Marketing," *Journal of Marketing,* Vol. 43 (Spring 1979), pp. 84–94, and discussed in Chapter 10.

30. *Cutting Marketing Costs in Europe* (Geneva, Switzerland: Business International S.A., 1985), pp. 6–7.

31. Ibid., pp. 5–6.

32. Ann Hughey, "Gray Market in Camera Imports Starts to Undercut Official Dealers," *The Wall Street Journal,* April 1, 1982, p. 29.

33. Roger Neal, "See the Nice, Gray Cat," *Forbes,* May 6, 1985, p. 31.

34. William J. Hampton and Jerome Zukosky, "The Gray Market: Mercedes Tries to Slam on the Brakes," *Business Week,* September 2, 1985, p. 34.

35. Michael Blumstein, "Seiko Wins Order to Get Alexander's to Change Its Ads," *New York Times,* August 4, 1982, p. 24.

36. Anthony Baldo, "Score One for the Gray Market," *Forbes,* February 25, 1985, p. 74.

37. Gay Jervey, "Gray Market Hits Camera, Watch Sales," *Advertising Age,* August 15, 1982, p. 19.

38. Ibid.

39. Mark Harrington, "U.S. Retailers Find Themselves Up Against the Gray Market," *Merchandising,* January, 1985, pp. 19–23.

Chapter 16
Dimensions of
Global Promotion
Strategy

INTRODUCTION _____

Promotion is the most visible and probably the most controversial marketing activity routinely undertaken by a firm. In this chapter, we examine global promotional needs, emphasizing the major issues and problems that affect promotional activities abroad. Toward this end, we have divided the chapter into six sections. The first three sections deal with the issues and problems inherent in involvement in one or more foreign markets. The next two sections address the issues and problems arising from the need to match company promotional strategies simultaneously *within* and *across* national markets. The last section deals with multinational advertising agencies.

The company involved in foreign marketing is faced with at least two promotional problems. First, the company may have to develop a customized or modified promotion strategy for each foreign market to take into account differences in such things as product offerings, brands, prices, distribution activities, and sales goals. Second, the promotion strategy may also have to be adjusted because of local differences in the socio-cultural, educational, and economic attributes of the targeted buyers, the regulation of promotional activities, and the availability of particular types of media.

In the case of global companies, promotion is further complicated by the need to coordinate promotional activities across markets. The aggregate demand resulting from intracountry promotional activities must be managed efficiently. At the same time, the company may be interested in developing global brands and a consistent image for quality, prices, and service *across* countries.

Any promotion strategy involves purposeful and explicit communication by a company with several publics: the markets it serves, the general public, government agencies, financial institutions, and so on. Since we are concerned primarily with marketing, we will limit our definition as follows:

> **Promotion strategy** is the blending of the *advertising, publicity, personal selling,* and *sales promotion* activities of a company to achieve a particular response from one or more of the markets it intends to serve. These four elements of the *promotion mix* are generally used to enhance the company's image vis-à-vis its competitors and/or to inform, educate, and influence the attitudes and buying behavior of the individuals, companies, institutions, and/or government agencies that make up a targeted market.

THE GLOBAL COMMUNICATION PROCESS _____

The purpose of promotion is essentially the same for national and global marketing companies: inform, educate, persuade, and stimulate an appropriate and timed response from a particular market or market segment. *What* is communicated, and *how, where,* and *when* it is so communicated should not be left to chance. Effective market communication is not an easy task, especially when the company and its market(s) are from different cultures.

The Promotion Mix

The promotion mix consists of four major activities: *advertising, publicity, personal selling* and *sales promotion*. These elements exist in various combinations in all commercial situations, regardless of the country, its stage of economic development, and its competitive milieu. In most countries, the marketing of industrial goods relies heavily on personal selling; the marketing of consumer goods depends more heavily on advertising and sales promotion. Factored into these elements are the pragmatic concerns of style, price, and packaging and sales location. The entire marketing mix must be synchronized to send one, clear and forceful message.[1]

The four promotion-mix elements can be viewed as communication tools. The relative emhasis placed on each varies with type of product, management's perceptions of the merits of each element, and the practices generally adopted by companies in different countries.

The Four Elements of Market Communication

All effective communication has three elements: a *sender,* a *receiver* (audience), and a *message.* Marketing communication adds a fourth element, a *communication channel.* The sender encodes the message and transmits it through a channel. The receiver decodes the message. The target market provides a *feedback link.* A large number of factors external to the company affect communication; language, the local economy, laws, and other socio-cultural phenomena. The communication components, activities, and influencing factors are illustrated in Figure 16-1.

The communication process shown in Figure 16-1 underscores the key attributes of effective communication anywhere. To be effective, the sender or communicator needs to have a clear understanding of the message's purpose, the audience to be reached, and how this audience will interpret and respond to the message. To ensure that the message is decoded and acted on by the receiver as intended, the sender must use socio-cultural cues and symbols familiar to the receiver and select a medium that is socio-culturally and legally appropriate.

Factors Affecting Global Communication

In practice, the factors charted in Figure 16-1 are not in and of themselves barriers to effective communication. More correctly, the problems can be attributed to discrepancies between and among the company's home market and its foreign markets. For example, as we have seen in earlier chapters, differences in socio-cultural and economic factors give rise to differences in buyer behavior, product perceptions, and product attribute preferences.

Language Differences

Some problems of language diversity in global marketing were discussed in Chapter 6. However, the subtleties of language differences go well beyond a strict translation of the message. It is axiomatic that language suffers in translation. Thus, the tradenames, brands, slogans, sales presentation materials, sales promotion

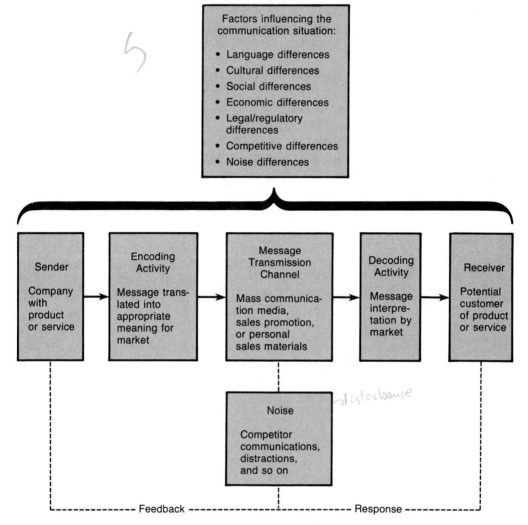

FIGURE 16-1   Elements of a Global Communication Process

materials, and advertising content used by companies in their domestic markets may have to be *changed* as well as *translated* when used in other markets. A slogan or advertising copy that is effective in one language may mean something offensive or even ludicrous in another language. Many companies insist that the translation must not only be accurate, it must convey a similar, if not identical, meaning.

Gillette, for example, found it necessary to change the Trac II name to GII after market studies revealed that "trac" in some of the Romance languages denotes fragility.[2] As Rodney S. Mills, executive vice-president of Gillette International put it, "We wanted our target audience—men—to know that they could count on a good strong razor and not on one that would easily break." Another example involves the brand name for Playtex's line of haircare products, Jhirmack. Playtex discovered that the French had difficulty in pronouncing the word. The name was therefore changed to Algelée. "Both smack of professionalism and have no other meaning."[3]

Cultural Differences

Almost anything in an ad can adversely affect a market. Values, color preferences, and gestures all resist mere "translation." For example, Chileans may buy their coffee strictly on the basis of price; Germans may be willing to pay almost any price to get what they consider good coffee. A laundry detergent emphasizing "whiteness" may not be effective in Brazil; Brazilians tend to wear multicolored patterns.[4]

Amoco wisely educated itself on the connotations of color in an Asian ad campaign. In 1981, the firm decided to launch a corporate awareness campaign in the People's Republic of China to improve its chances of obtaining drilling rights. It developed seven advertisements to describe different aspects of Amoco's capabilities. Each advertisement exploited Chinese color preferences, emphasizing bold bright colors such as red, gold, and purple. In China, red stands for life, purple connotes quality, and gold implies brilliance. Amoco also incorporated the moon in two of its seven advertisements since the moon is traditionally viewed as a symbol of good luck.[5]

Social Differences

Differing attitudes among business executives and consumers toward promotion in general and advertising in particular may be rooted in historical and social biases. For example, a survey of European executives found that, while the sampled executives expressed a strong belief in the usefulness of advertising, they were concerned about the effects advertising may have on social values.[6] The concerns voiced in one country are not necessarily valid in another. For example, German and Norwegian consumers tend to interpret statements more literally than do Italian or Spanish consumers.[7] Beatson found that though a majority of Finns (75 percent) and Norwegians (80 percent) feel that advertising is helpful, only 48 percent of the Danes and 41 percent of the French sampled concurred.[8]

Economic Differences

Prevailing economic conditions also affect communication. The literacy level, and the degree of urbanization have a significant influence on communication. In developing countries, households may have radios but not television sets. Markets may be widely dispersed, thus adding to the costs of promotional coverage. In countries with relatively low levels of literacy, written communication may not be as effective as visual or oral communication. Instead of using newsprint, a company may have to use demonstrations or a car with a loudspeaker. The discretionary income of individuals and families directly affects their attitudes toward products. Necessities in one country are luxuries in another. For example, products used for recreation in one country, such as snowmobiles and outboard motors, may be viewed as means of transportation and work in another. All the factors above impact the structure and content of the advertiser's message and the media used.

Legal and Regulatory Differences

Local advertising regulations and industry codes directly influence the selection of media and content of promotional materials (choice of words, type of comparative statements, whether or not coupons and samples can be used). For example, Gillette may never introduce its Trac II razor to certain countries in Latin America, the Middle East, and Africa. In general, countries in these areas consider shaving a luxury socio-culturally unredeeming, or not sanctioned by religion, and either do not allow the importation of the product or assess a prohibitive tariff.[9] Such restrictions, of course, affect Gillette's ability to develop standardized regional promotional campaigns. Playtex also ran into a sales promotional problem when it discovered that door-to-door couponing and sampling was illegal in France. As a result, the company had to modify its promotional strategy to include in-store demonstrations where its representatives were permitted to give samples away. Since couponing and sampling are prohibited in Denmark,[10] Playtex uses print advertising there.

Competitive Differences

The nature of the competition—whether it is national, regional, or global—also has a significant influence on promotion. Promotional expenditures, the frequency of the communication, and the types of promotional approaches used are determined in great part by local factors such as the intensity of competition; the rate at which product innovations are introduced: and the national, regional, and global communication strategies of competitors. Since competitors vary from country-to-country in terms of number, size, type, and promotional strategies used, a company may have to modify its local promotional strategy and the timing of its promotional efforts.

Although the level of promotional expenditures and the distribution of these expenditures across the promotional mix in a particular market are partly determined by the company's marketing goals and the characteristics of the market, they are also a function of competitor reaction. For example, if Nestlé were to launch a massive promotional campaign in Europe, it would have to anticipate some retaliatory action from its major competitors.

In conclusion, there may be considerable variation in promotional patterns from one country to the next. Furthermore, variations across countries are primarily the result of the individual and combined effects of three forces:

1. Economic and socio-cultural differences,
2. Legal and regulatory constraints,
3. Differences in the marketing practices and strategies of competitors.

GLOBAL PROMOTION PATTERNS

The considerable variation among countries in the role played by promotion in the marketing mix is examined in this section. The discussion is focused on a few selected countries and is grouped according to the three major elements of the promotion mix: the role of advertising; the role of sales promotion; and the role of personal selling.

The Role of Advertising

The prevailing level of promotional expenditures in a particular national market provides the marketing manager measures for determining the relative importance of the promotional activity. There are at least three measurements: (1) total advertising expenditures; (2) advertising expenditures by industry; and (3) advertising expenditures by media.

The first set of data provides an overall measurement of the general competitive environment in a particular country. Also, when these data are compared across countries, they give the marketing manager some rough measure of the relative intensity of advertising competition across countries. The second set of data focuses more sharply on advertising at an industry level. These data can be used initially to determine promotional policies *within* and *across* markets. Finally, the third set of data can provide some insight into the importance of various types of media in particular markets. They are a useful initial, albeit rough, indicator of the media strategies used by potential competitors.

Global Advertising Expenditures

In 1983, global advertising expenditures were estimated to exceed $150 billion.[11] About 50 percent of that sum was spent in the United States, 25 percent in Europe, and 25 percent in the rest of the world. The significance of these expenditures for different countries are compared in Table 16-1 for nine selected countries.

Advertising expenditures on a per capita basis and as a percentage of GNP are relatively small in most countries and vary considerably across countries. For example, in 1982 advertising expenditures on a per capita basis and as a percentage of GNP varied from a high of $285.75 and 2.18 percent in the United States to a low of $6.08 and 0.23 percent in Portugal.

The industrialized countries of Europe, North America, and Asia account for most advertising expenditures. In general, per capita advertising expenditures in Central and South American countries, as in developing countries in general, are much less than in more industrially advanced countries. We can infer from this that there is a positive correlation between advertising expenditures and stage of economic development. Advertising expenditure per capita tends to increase as personal income increases. There are at least two possible reasons for this. First, an increase in GNP per capita generally results in an increase in the disposable income of individuals and families and patterns of spending that are more flexible and subject to corporate influence. Second, as a country's GNP per capita increases, so does the assortment of competing products. Thus, there is increased pressure for companies to promote individual brands.

Regardless of the actual reasons for increased advertising activity, the data in Table 16-1 suggest that firms competing in the relatively more affluent economies can expect to spend a greater portion of their marketing dollars on promotional activities. However, this general tendency is not axiomatic. The relationship does not always hold. For example, Belgium and the United Kingdom, Portugal and

TABLE 16-1
Advertising Expenditures Per Capita and As a Percentage of GNP and GNP Per Capita

Country	Per capita (in U.S.$)	% GNP	GNP per capita (in U.S.$)
North America[1]			
Canada	149.79	1.27	12,280
United States	285.75	2.18	14,080
European Community[1]			
Belgium	49.47	0.40	9,130
Denmark	114.17	0.84	11,540
France	76.38	0.60	10,480
Germany, West	87.22	0.63	11,400
Greece	18.96	0.41	3,910
Ireland	36.61	0.86	4,990
Italy	55.40	0.77	6,390
Luxembourg	66.00	0.60	14,620
Netherlands	131.26	1.08	9,870
Portugal	6.08	0.23	2,230
United Kingdom	115.41	1.24	9,180
Central and South America[2]			
Argentina	29.02	1.27	2,510
Brazil	13.22	0.71	1,870
Colombia	10.20	0.98	1,410
Mexico	9.26	0.55	2,180
Venezuela	30.54	0.95	3,830
Asia[2]			
Hong Kong	29.70	0.74	6,070
Japan	96.10	1.00	10,100
Singapore	41.25	1.00	6,660

[1] Advertising data for North America and the European Community are for 1982. GNP per capita data are for 1983.

[2] Advertising data for Asian, and Central and South American countries are for 1980. GNP per capita data are for 1983.

Source: Data on advertising expenditures are from *World Advertising Expenditures*, New York: Starch INRA Hooper Group of Companies, and the International Advertising Association, 1981 and 1984. Data on GNP and GNP per capita are from *The World Bank Atlas 1986*, Washington, D.C., 1986.

Mexico, and Argentina or Venezuela and Greece have very different levels of advertising expenditures although each pair of countries has similar GNP per capita. These disparities suggest that within-country advertising practices are affected by a number of other factors. As previously mentioned, a country may have a negative attitude toward advertising, local businessmen may not see it as useful, and local advertising regulations may be quite restrictive.

Industry Advertising Expenditures

The type of industry in which a company competes also has an impact on advertising practices. As can be seen from the data presented in Table 16-2, not

TABLE 16-2
Advertising Expenditures and Media Usage by Industry:
The United States, Australia, and Japan for 1976
(Millions and Percentages)

Product Group	United States			Australia			Japan		
	Total	Print (%)	TV (%)	Total	Print (%)	TV (%)	Total	Print (%)	TV (%)
Food & beverage	1,913.3	24	76	66.4	23	77	646.1	19	81
Tobacco	383.8	95	5	9.2	57	43	(included in above)		
Clothing	203.2	39	61	14.6	29	71	110.0	50	50
Banking & insurance	n.a.			6.7	40	60	130.3	79	21
Government	n.a.			7.4	67	33	58.1	39	61
Automotive	836.2	42	57	34.1	52	48	n.a.		
Toiletries & detergents	1,197.2	12	88	33.6	13	87	277.1	26	74
Household furnishings	454.1	35	65	15.1	25	75	168.7	38	62
Entertainment	296.8	42	58	n.a.			278.5	58	42
Pet food & products	177.5	6	94	5.3	9	91	n.a.		
Pharmaceuticals	462.4	12	88	8.2	18	82	195.4	33	67
Publishing	76.8	34	66	9.5	20	80	n.a.		
Watches, jewelry and cameras	95.6	18	82	3.1	54	46	n.a.		
Office equipment	n.a.			1.8	89	11	127.3	52	48
Electronic equipment	n.a.			14.6	33	67	161.1	44	56

Source: William H. Davidson, *Global Strategic Management* (New York: John Wiley & Sons, 1982), Table 4-4, p. 153.

only does the level of advertising expenditures vary by industry and country, it also varies by media.

The reasons for these variations are many but include the nature of the product, regulation of the various types of media for commercial uses, exposure of the various markets to the various types of media, and business practices. In the United States, television is the dominant medium for advertising watches, jewelry, and cameras. The dominant medium for advertising these products in Australia is print. Likewise, media differences exist between banking and insurance advertising expenditures in Australia and Japan. In Australia, the dominant medium is television; in Japan, print.

Other important differences can also be gleaned from the data in Table 16-2. The percentage of total advertising expenditures spent by a particular industry may vary from one country to the next. The percentage of total advertising expenditures spent by the Japanese office equipment industry is greater than that spent by the Australian industry. Also, the U.S. entertainment industry spends relatively less on advertising than does the Japanese entertainment industry. Differences such as these need to be taken into account when developing promotional strategies and allocating promotional resources.

Not only do industry data provide marketing managers with some understanding of the role played by promotion in a particular market, but they also help managers tailor promotional strategies to specific countries. For example, the relatively lower advertising expenditures in the U.S. entertainment industry (relative to those in Japan) suggest that the U.S. company marketing in Japan must allocate more resources to advertising than it does at home. The U.S. company may, of course, decide to use U.S. practices. However, if local industry practices are to be violated, the reasons for a particular pattern needs to be thoroughly investigated, and the implications of spending above or below local industry standards understood. Data on the promotional activities of foreign competitors in their home markets may also provide domestic competitors some insights into the promotional practices of these competitors.

Types of Media and Their Availability

Considerable variation exists between and among countries in the types of media traditionally used. In some countries, cinema is used extensively; in others, television. In some countries, wall posters and kiosks substitute for billboards. The relative effectiveness of each medium varies considerably and is a function of educational, economic, and socio-cultural factors and the advertising expectations of customers arising from business practices.

Table 16-3 presents data on advertising expenditures for the three major media (print, radio, and television) for various regions of the world. The data indicate that print is still the major media worldwide. About 41 percent of the

TABLE 16-3
Advertising Expenditures by Media and Region for 1980
(Millions of U.S.$ and Percentage of Total by Region)

Region	Media						% of Total Advertising Expenditures Spent on These Media*
	Print		Radio		Television		
	Amount	(%)	Amount	(%)	Amount	(%)	
North America	21,861	38	4,106	7	11,878	21	66
Western Europe	16,206	52	966	3	4,035	13	68
Asia	4,990	38	742	6	4,348	33	77
Latin America	1,255	27	632	14	1,667	36	77
Middle East and Africa	648	36	104	6	192	10	52

Source: *World Advertising Expenditures* (New York: Starch, 1981), pp. 40–41.
*Note: The unaccounted for balances were spent on posters, cinema, direct mail, sales promotions, exhibits, and trade fairs.

total reported advertising expenditures in 58 countries in 1980 was spent on newspaper and magazine advertisements. Television was second, accounting for 21 percent of total advertising expenditures. Radio, with 6 percent, was a somewhat distant third. Worldwide trends indicate that the importance of television is increasing and that of print and radio decreasing.

Patterns of expenditures do not just reflect socio-cultural factors and customer and business preferences. As we will soon see, local laws exert an influence. For example, many countries place restrictions on the use of television and radio for commercial advertising.

Advertising, which is the most important form of promotional expenditures relies on the mass media. These media are thus expected to become increasingly important. Information on print, radio, and television for selected countries grouped by region is presented in Table 16-4.

Considerable variation exists in the availability of media, which is not just a function of the relative economic status of individual countries. For example, in 1980, the number of radio receivers per 1000 population in the Netherlands was only one-third of that in the United Kingdom, and one-half that in France. There is a better correlation between the economic status of countries and the number of TV sets per capita.

Print. The number of newspapers and magazines is one indicator of the availability of print as an advertising medium. However, coverage and readership are also important to market analysts. In 1980, the United States had 1,744 daily newspapers, whereas the United Kingdom only 125.[12] However, most American dailies do not have national coverage. Most of the 125 British newspapers have national circulations. If anything, a proliferation of papers renders ad decisions more difficult. On what basis does a manager decide where to place advertisements? The problem of placement is not just a matter of number of readers.

One constant problem facing advertisers is how to define what constitutes quality. Trade journals like the *International Advertiser* devote frequent and considerable space to this topic. In one study published in the *International Advertiser* about Europe's quality dailies, noted that dailies in the United Kingdom are classified according to the socio-economic class of the readership.[13] In other European countries, the classification of dailies is less specific. Accordingly, managers of advertising need to take care when selecting newspapers or local magazines.

Another issue concerns the use of national rather than multinational publications, particularly when a product enjoys good distribution in a country.[14] Extreme care needs to be exercised, however, since the readership can vary considerably across countries, particularly across developing countries. That is, comparisons are difficult to make.

Radio and Television. Radio enjoys worldwide popularity because of its relatively widespread ownership. Television, although the major mass media in most industrialized countries, is not so widely used in others. Fewer people can afford TVs, and, in many countries, the use of television for commercial advertising is prohibited (especially in developing countries). In addition, certain categories of products cannot be advertised on television in some countries. For example, in

TABLE 16-4
Availability of Mass Media for Selected Countries in 1970 and 1980

| Country | Newspapers | | | | Magazines | | | | Television Sets Per 1000 Population | | Radio Receivers Per 1000 Population | |
| | Dailies | | Nondailies | | Consumer | | Trade* | | | | | |
	1970	1980	1970	1980	1970	1980	1970	1980	1970	1980	1970	1980
North America:												
Canada	115	115	1031	1111	879	384	136	601	332		742	
United States	1773	1744	9490	7876		10236**			412	609	1412	2031
Europe and Scandinavia:												
Belgium		38		30		94	759	995	216	296	350	455
Denmark							312		266		325	
France	106	83	1007	898		190		6930	216	303	315	640
Germany, Fed. Rep.	1093								272		318	
Italy	73	92	147	—		943	423	746	181	303	218	367
Netherlands	95	110	167	574		67		—	223	298	278	324
Sweden	114	125	57	25		30	155	300	312	386	410	422
United Kingdom	109	125	581	1056		1152		1700	293	361	623	905
Central and South America:												
Argentina	261	700**				657	49	53	144	202	370	229
Brazil			730		644		36		66		60	
Colombia	36	36	16	13	58	23	3	19	38	65	105	212
Mexico	200		288		1963				59		276	
Venezuela	42	72	21	59		55		143	70		164	
Asian Countries:												
Hong Kong	57	127**	17		179	296**	16		109		107	
Japan	178	415**				430**	827		219	547	551	769
Singapore	12	11	2	1		19	17	38	77	161	122	186

* Trade includes technical magazines

** These data are totals for daily and nondaily newspapers or consumer and trade magazines.

Source: *World Advertising Expenditures* (New York, N.Y.: Starch, INRA, Hooper and International Advertising Association), various issues. Also, *UNESCO Statistical Yearbooks*, 1971–1976 editions, (Paris, France: UNESCO), 1972–77.

Britain, cigarettes, contraceptives, female sanitary products, and certain alcohol products cannot be advertised. Nor can religions nor political parties advertise. Also, members of the medical profession and their look-alikes cannot be used.[15]

Cable and Satellite Operations. Two other media that are exerting considerable influence on international advertising are cable and satellite systems. A number of cable and satellite projects are now in operation or under preparation throughout Europe and the United States. Some are national, others international. The increased geographic, or market, overlap of cable-satellite advertisements creates a need to find ways to enhance message receptivity in transnational targeted markets.

As shown in Table 16-5, satellites already provided commercial users considerable coverage by 1985. In December 1984, the European Commission summed up European developments to date as follows:

> Tens of millions of Europeans already receive up to a dozen national or foreign television channels by cable daily. A few million tune in to programmes broadcast by satellite, such as Sky Channel, an independent British undertaking, or TV-5, a joint initiative by Francophone national television stations. But this is only the beginning. It has been estimated that by the end of the decade, viewers in most European countries will be able to watch, apart from their usual stations, up to five satellite TV channels, 30 national stations transmitted by cable and a host of other progammes, broadcast from countries throughout the continent. By the 1990s, at a touch of a button, millions of Europeans may be able to choose between an English soccer match, a French news progamme or an Italian documentary, with translations into their own language, either on sound or through teletext subtitles.[16]

Besides North America and Europe, other regions of the world are developing cable and satellite capabilities. In 1981, Univision, a joint venture of SIN, Mexico's Televisa and Spain's Radio-Television Española started satellite television broadcasting

TABLE 16-5
European Satellite Channels Currently Carrying Advertising

Channel	Language	Homes Reached	Countries of Reception
Sky Channel	English	4,051,178	Netherlands, Switzerland, West Germany, Finland, Norway, UK, Austria, Sweden, Luxembourg, France, Denmark, Belgium
Music Box	English	2,544,000	Netherlands, Switzerland, UK, Finland, West Germany, Sweden, Austria, Denmark
TV-5	France	2,000,000	Belgium, Finland, France, West Germany, Netherlands, Norway, Sweden, UK, Switzerland
SAT-1	German	460,000	West Germany
Children's Channel	English	110,000	UK
Screen Sport	English	100,000	UK, Sweden, Finland
RAI	Italian	N/A	Belgium
New World Channel	Multilingual	—	—

Source: From Rein Rijkens and Gordon E. Miracle, *European Regulation of Advertising*, (Amsterdam: North Holland, 1986), p. 175 quoted from *Campaign* August 30, 1985, Vol. 35, as reported by David Wood.

to 270 million Spanish-speaking viewers in 18 Latin American countries, Spain, and the United States.[17]

The Role of Sales Promotion

Sales promotion is a common practice in most developed countries; it is generally treated as a supplement to mass communication and personal selling. In most cases, it is designed to accomplish specific short-term marketing objectives. However, in those countries where mass communication is weak because of literacy levels or restrictive regulations, or where the targeted market is difficult to reach, managers should consider increasing monies allocated to sales promotions. In some developing countries, sales promotions constitute the major form of communication in rural and remote areas.

Particular sales-promotion devices take on added importance in some national markets. For example, West Germany has a 700-year-old tradition of trade fairs. Buyers depend on these for information. Before placing an order, many German buyers will wait until they have seen the product and have talked with the seller's technicians and management.[18]

The regulation of sales-promotion activities varies across countries. In many countries, the use of the word *free* is restricted and the size and value of premiums and samples controlled. For example, Belgium strictly regulates clearance sales and prohibits premiums. In West Germany, the use of giveaways is limited to items of low value. There and elsewhere, the prudent manager checks for local restrictions on sales-promotion devices.

The Role of Personal Selling

Personal selling is probably the most prevalent promotional method used internationally. Regardless of stage of economic development and level of affluence, the salesperson is found in all societies. The extent to which a company is involved in personal selling in foreign markets is a function of its market presence, local marketing objectives, and the local distribution network. For many exporters and global companies, the primary selling function is performed by an external distribution network. As a result, the company has very little direct control over selling. It does or can exert some influence by establishing sales guidelines and providing technical assistance, sales training, and sales materials.

When a local sales force is used, sales personnel may be *expatriates, third-country nationals, local nationals,* or some mix. Let us briefly illustrate these terms. A German working for a German company in the United States is an expatriate. The same German working for a U.S. company in Germany is a local national. If assigned to France, he or she is a third-country national.

Expatriates and third-country nationals may be used for short periods to upgrade a subsidiary's selling performance; fill management positions; and transfer sales policies, procedures, and techniques. However, most companies use local nationals as their sales personnel. They are familiar with local business practices and can be managed according to local practices.

Expatriates and third-country nationals are seldom used in sales capacities for long periods of time. Why not? There are two main reasons. The costs associated with assigning these personnel to overseas assignments are high. An in-depth understanding of the local culture and business practices is required to be effective. In addition, they and their families face adaptation problems. Personnel administration becomes complex. Career planning, compensation, pension planning, taxation issues, and local visa and work-permit requirements are added complications.

GLOBAL PROMOTION ISSUES

The major external promotional issues confronting marketing managers operating in foreign markets can be grouped under two headings, ethics and social benefits. Both groups of issues have a strong influence on the regulations imposed by governments on advertising practices and on the self-regulation of advertising.

Ethics

Although most business executives would agree that it is important to maintain high ethical standards, there is little agreement on what standards should be used, particularly as one moves from principles to everyday situations. "The issue becomes even more complicated when an organization operates in various international markets, and the executives must define human welfare, ethical standards, or accepted modes of conduct across shifting cultural boundaries."[19]

Many global companies operate in countries that represent a wide spectrum of ethical standards and modes of behavior. Christian values may operate in one of the company's markets; in another, Islam may prevail, or Hinduism, or Buddhism. Even when two countries share the same predominant religion, such as Mexico and the United States, denominational (Catholicism and Protestantism), economic, and sociocultural value differences may greatly limit similarities. The practical problems associated with disparate value systems and philosophical differences have been described as follows:

> The situation is not black and white . . . It is clouded by the question of what is "proper." Practices illegal in one country may be accepted ways of doing business in another. A company that adheres strictly to a policy of restraint may find itself at a serious disadvantage in some countries. A company that goes along with the accepted practices in a country may find it has a different problem. A number of American companies have been criticized at home for engaging in practices (abroad) that are quite legal and above board in those countries where they were used but are illegal in the United States.[20]

Ethical and philosophical differences are indeed of particular relevance in promotions. For example, Saudi Arabia bans advertising that include women, veiled or unveiled, and Malaysia bans the portrayal of women in sleeveles dresses.[21]

Social Benefits of Advertising

Considerable debate exists about the role promotion (in general) and advertising (in particular) should play in economic activities. Debate falls into three areas: (1) the economic value of advertising, (2) what constitutes acceptable competitive practices, and (3) the protection of consumers.

The Economic Value of Advertising

The governments of some countries view advertising as an additional and unnecessary cost to be carried by the customer. To budget for it, in this view, is a misallocation of economic resources. In developing countries, in particular, this view has certain merit. Advertising outlays may well be wasteful and nonproductive when the assortment of products is limited or the demand created by advertising is for imported products. Given indigenous income and demand structures, any ad-facilitated transfer of alien consumption patterns may well be inappropriate, even divisive.

In contrast, governments of developed countries tend to take a more positive view toward advertising. They generally assume that the economic stimulation it triggers offsets expenditures incurred. Advertising has the advantage of reducing unit costs through scales of economy and distribution, and may provide useful information to consumers.

Acceptable Competitive Practices

What constitutes fair or unfair competition is determined by many factors: the prevailing value structure of a country, attitudes toward the roles played by large and small firms, and toward the role of competition in everyday business life. Until recently, for example, West Germany forbade any form of comparative advertising, explicit or implicit. Comparative advertising was considered an unacceptable form of competition.

Cooperative advertising, too, may be disapproved, being viewed as providing an unfair advantage to large companies or to a group of companies. In general, the regulations and industry codes in many countries are aimed at protecting companies from unfair competitive attacks.[22] However, what constitutes unfair advertising practices varies by country. It is not safe to assume that all member nations of an economic region such as the European Community have adopted a particular regulation or that they enforce it with equal vigor.

Consumer Protection

Most countries impose some regulations on advertising practices to protect the consumer against misleading and false advertising. Generally, these regulations assume that consumers must be protected both from the wrongful practices of business and their own gullibility.[23] It is thus generally assumed that the customer needs complete information and a means for redress. Details of local regulations and industry codes and the degree to which they are enforced obviously vary by country. The regulations and their enforcement reflect local value structures, attitudes toward competition in the economy, and the relative power of industry, consumers, and government.

Global Regulation of Advertising

In recent years, many countries have increased their regulation of promotional activities. Boddewyn has identified twelve major regulatory forces warranting close monitoring.[24] These major forces, listed in Table 16-6, include vocal consumer advocates who have criticized the media for various reasons. Has advertising unfairly targeted especially vulnerable groups—the young, the old, and the sick? Do cable television and automated telephone services unfairly exploit impulse buying? Do billboards jeopardize our environment? What separates fair advertising from discrimination or victimization? Can profit and ethics mix?

TABLE 16-6
Twelve Major Global Forces Stimulating the Regulation of Advertising

Regulatory Force	Description	Example of Regulatory Action or Abuse
Consumer protection	Real and imagined business abuses have motivated protective regulations against false and misleading advertising for decades.	Many countries regulate the use of words such as *gratis, free, low calorie, fat/fatty*, etc.
Growth of a service industry	As developed economies have become more service-oriented, governments are increasingly aware of a need for increased regulation since services are less standardized.	Truth in lending, fair credit reporting, privacy protection, prospectus content, etc.
Fairness and vulnerable groups	Advertising to vulnerable groups such as the young, the old, and the sick.	Canada and the European Community (EC) restrict TV ads directed at children. The EC bans ads that abuse the consumer's trust, credulity, or lack of experience.
New media technologies	Trends in the use of videocassette recorders, cable TV, automatic telephone service, interactive TV and TV marketing.	"Cooling off" period too short. Blurs distinction between advertising and information. Capital requirements limits competition.
Trade protection	Unfair trade practices—denigrating persons, methods, or products. Providing advantages to groups of companies.	Comparative advertising regulations. EC courts extending unfair practices to include consumers.
Environmentalism and conservation	Distracting, cluttering billboards. Wasteful use of energy.	Belgium bans the use of electricity for ads between midnight and 8:00 A.M. Similar restrictions in at least 14 other countries.
Civil rights and privacy	Ethnic jokes and sexist portrayal of women. Exclusive use of one sex in ads. Infringement of privacy (direct mail, unsolicited phone calls, etc.).	France and Sweden regulate transborder flow of mailing lists and data about citizens. Japan restricts compilation of computerized mailing lists.
Religion, morality and taste	Religion has always been a vocal source of advertising restrictions. Defines what is proper and fitting.	Canada requires all feminine hygiene ads be prescreened.

TABLE 16-6 (*continued*)

Regulatory Force	Description	Example of Regulatory Action or Abuse
Nationalism	Desire to keep or create jobs for local labor, to preserve national cultural heritage.	In order to enhance national culture, Peruvian regulations forbid the use of foreign materials. South Korea bans plagiarizing of foreign-inspired messages.
Recession and inflation	Recession often leads to trade-protection measures. Recession and inflation often result in companies placing increased emphasis on price, value, and other comparative appeals.	Recent moves by the French government to legalize comparative ads have been slowed by fears that Japanese auto makers would increase their share of the French market.

Source: Compiled from Jean J. Boddewyn, "Advertising Regulation in the 1980s: The Underlying Global Forces," *Journal of Marketing*, Vol. 46 (Winter 1982), pp. 27–35.

The pressures listed in Table 16-6 suggest that governments will continue to regulate advertising. Examples of regulations already existing in selected Western European countries are presented in Table 16-7.

As Table 16-7 indicates, many categories of restrictions exist. They include ownership restrictions of media and advertising agencies, limitations on media time for advertisements, restrictions on the kinds of products that can be advertised, restrictions on advertising techniques, and restrictions on the use of foreign languages. Restrictions on particular forms of promotion exist in many countries. For example, Austria, Belgium, France, Italy, the Netherlands, and West Germany all prohibit or restrict the use of comparative advertising. Switzerland, Scandinavian, and Anglo-American countries are not too strict and permit critical comparisons of products. Restrictions are limited by common sense; the use of superlatives claiming that a product is the best of its kind is often permitted on the grounds that the consumer will not take hyperbolic claims seriously and that such advertisements do not affect competition.[25]

Self-Regulation of Advertising

The worldwide trend toward increased government regulation of advertising has not gone unnoticed by industry. There is, in business, a growing awareness of the need for self-regulation. The types of self-regulation are quite varied and are based on local needs, cultural and social values, and level of economic development. There are basically two forms of self-regulation, (1) industry-imposed regulation and (2) company-imposed regulation. Examples of self-regulation are presented in Table 16-8.

In a number of countries, advertisements need to be reviewed and cleared by a self-regulatory body before they can appear. Monitoring of potential problem categories of advertising is also done in the form of spotchecks, and questions of veracity and ethics are raised. Examples include questions concerning the

TABLE 16-7
Examples of Regulations on Advertising in Western Europe

The Most Sensitive Areas				
Country	**Tobacco**	**Alcohol**	**Pharmaceuticals (general public)**	**The Use of Superlatives**
West Germany	Forbidden to make any suggestion that smoking is not dangerous; to encourage young people to smoke; and to use the terms "pure" or "natural."	No restrictions so far, but this is now under review.	Banned	Allowed where the superiority can be proved, though the rules are stricter in some areas.
Belgium			Banned for products aimed at cancer, TB, polio and diabetes; Some other restrictions.	
France	Any reference to health is banned.	Forbidden entirely when it comes to drinks with a high alcohol content; less strict for others.	Forbidden for any product the cost of which is refunded by Social Security.	Forbidden on TV to all intents and purposes.
Italy	Banned.	The brand name can be promoted, but not the product.	Must have special clearance; no ads for contraceptives.	
Netherlands	Voluntary restraint.	Voluntary restraint.	Voluntary restraint.	Accepted where it is backed by facts. Since no law exists, advertisers tend to be cautious.
Great Britain	"Every packet carries a government health warning," has to be mentioned in all advertising.	No legal controls, but voluntary restraint.	Forbidden in the case of cancer. Restrictions on others. Firms are not allowed to claim that they can cure a disease.	
Sweden	Some form of warning is being studied, as is a total ban.	Forbidden to mention the price or the catalog number.	Allowed, but with very strict controls.	Forbidden when excessive. Allowed if presented as a subjective opinion.

Source: *Transnational Corporations in Advertising* (New York: UN, 1979), p. 52.

misuse of opinion leaders, the misuse of warranties (to protect the manufacturer rather than the buyer), and the risks associated with hazardous products (understated). In addition, particular media are the objects of special attention by self-regulatory bodies in some countries. In Belgium, for example, mail-order advertising is self-regulated.[26]

TABLE 16-7 (continued)

The Most Sensitive Areas (continued)		False Advertising Claims		
Mention of Rival Firms	**TV Advertising**	**Burden of Proof**	**Penalties**	**The Right of Consumer or Associations to Bring a Law Suit**
Theoretically not allowed, but many exceptions.	Voluntary restrictions on tobacco advertising.	On the plaintiff in the case of unfair competition (with prima facie evidence from the defendant). It stays with the government for foods and medicines.	Both penal and civil. In some cases, consumer associations can ask for imprecise claims to be withdrawn.	Only where the cases do not involve either foods or medicines.
Banned if misleading, denigratory, or not relevant.	Does not exist.	On the plaintiff.	Both penal and civil. Injunctions possible.	On condition that they are members of the Consumer Council.
Banned if denigratory.	No advertising.	Under study; on the plaintiff, but advertisers must produce any evidence on demand.	Both penal and civil. Under study: ads containing corrections.	Under study.
Forbidden to mention names.	More careful vetting than in other media	On the plaintiff.	Both penal and civil.	None.
Acceptable if no names are given, and if it is not denigratory.	Boards of control check pharmaceutical products and drinks.	On the plaintiff.	Both penal and civil.	None.
Banned if denigratory. Must contain facts which can be proved.	Cigarette advertising is banned and drinks advertising restricted.	On the plaintiff.	Both penal and civil (fines of up to £400).	None.
Forbidden if defamatory or injurious.	Does not exist.	In civil cases, on the defendant. In criminal cases, on the relevant government department.	Penal and civil; sometimes the rapid withdrawal of the manufacturing license.	In general, through Ombudsman; otherwise, consumer associations can go to law.

GLOBAL PROMOTION STRATEGY DECISIONS

The development and implementation of any promotinal strategy requires that several questions must be answered. These include:

1. Toward what segment of the market is the promotion directed?
2. What is the objective of the promotional campaign?

3. What should be the message(s) communicated?

4. How much of the promotional budget should be spent on the campaign?

5. How should this budget be allocated across the promotional-mix elements, media, in geographic areas, on particular products, and over time?

TABLE 16-8
Examples of Self-Regulation in Selected Countries

Country	Central Self-regulatory Bodies	Volume of Activity	Other Self-regulatory Activity	Trends
North America				
United States	National Advertising Review Board (NARB) National Advertising Division of the Council of Better Business Bureaus (NAD) Local Advertising Review Boards (LARBs) (22 regions)	250 + cases per year	Major companies and agencies have legal counsel to check advertisements; all important industry associations have codes and committees. Media have individual and group codes, review mechanisms.	High level of controversy, strong consumer pressures for increased legislation and government action NARB/NAD still establishing itself.
Canada	Canadian Advertising Advisory Board (CAAB), top level with two review bodies: Advertising Standards Council; regional councils in Winnipeg and Vancouver	1,440 cases in 1973	None	All quarters report satisfactory situation.
European Countries				
Belgium	Jury d'Ethique Publicitaire	70 cases in 1973	Comité de la Publicité pour les Médicaments (Pharmaceuticals self-regulation)	Toward more government regulation, due to consumer pressures
Denmark	Dansk Reklame Nævn (Danish Advertising Standards Authority)	Very active	None	Consumer Ombudsman as result of consumer pressures
France	Bureau de Vérification la Publicité	1003 cases in 1973	None	Increasing government regulation, including "corrective advertising" law
West Germany	Zentralausschuss der Werbewirtschaft e.V. (ZAW)	30 cases in 1973	Various industries have own codes; agency legal staffs check conformity.	Reluctance to increase volume of self-regulation; increasing legislation

TABLE 16-8 *(continued)*

Country	Central Self-regulatory Bodies	Volume of Activity	Other Self-regulatory Activity	Trends
Other Countries				
Japan	Japan Advertising Review Board currently being formed.	None yet	While Review Board is being formed, nine major advertising industry associations continue to handle complaints according to own codes.	Further government regulation
Philippines	None	None	Advertiser and agency associations handle complaints via committees.	Government body is preparing a code, with advertising industry cooperation.
Venezuela	None		No report	Policy of new government is not yet defined; no plans for self-regulation.

Source: Adapted from "Transnational Corporations in Advertising," *Technical Paper* (New York: UN 1979), pp. 53–57.

6. What procedures should be used for pretesting the message(s) and monitoring of campaign response?

These six decisions and their supporting decisions need to be made regardless of market and are the core of the promotion strategy process (shown in Figure 16-2). However, the process and the strategies created by it are influenced by many company factors, some of which are shown to the left of the diagram in Figure 16-2. Not included in the diagram but also significant are such issues as the selection of an advertising agency, the location of research and other creative activities. (Although affecting the final content of promotional strategies, these decisions are more concerned with the management of the promotional activity and will be discussed later).

The model presented in Figure 16-2 provides a framework for key decisions associated with the development of global-company promotional strategies. It will be assumed that the company has control over—or can influence to some degree—what is promoted, how it is promoted, when it is promoted, and where it is promoted.

Corporate Influences

The corporate factors directly impacting the scope, content, and thrust of a company's promotional strategy consist of (1) its corporate geographic focus, (2) the attitudes its corporate marketing managers have toward foreign marketing, and (3) local corporate conditions. These will be discussed in the order mentioned.

Corporate Factors
Influencing the Process

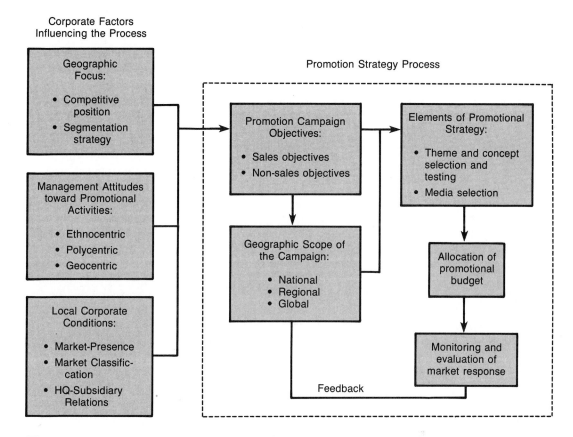

*This model is schematic in form and content and does not pretend to include every decision that needs to be made when developing a particular promotional strategy.

FIGURE 16-2   A Global Promotion Strategy Formulation Process*

The Company's Geographic Focus

One of the most controversial areas debated by marketing scholars and practitioners alike concerns the degree of uniformity to be maintained in advertising themes, copy, and media across countries. One side argues that the a standard campaign, message, media, and/or theme should be used in all countries. Proponents of this viewpoint point to a number of single-theme successes and the benefits that a global approach yields. The company, they maintain, can develop a highly consistent message across markets. Cost savings accrue from limiting the amount of original work required in each market and from exploiting scale economies across markets. The company's promotional campaigns can be integrated into one cohesive effort by centralizing worldwide promotional activities at corporate headquarters.

Opponents of standardization point to differences in market characteristics, media availability, media costs, business practices, and government regulations. They argue for a localized, or differentiated, approach. As one executive put it: "If you go with a marketing strategy that will work in all the different markets, you end up going for the least common denominator."[27] Supporters of localization stress that localized campaigns improve communication because they are rooted in specific markets. Another benefit often mentioned is the greater willingness of subsidiary managers to market new products when given the authority to develop their own promotional campaigns.

Policy should be based on a carefully researched and reasoned *geographic segmentation strategy* and *competitive market-positioning strategy*. As discussed in Chapter 11, the combination of a company's geographic segmentation strategy and product strategy yields four basic, or core, marketing strategies: a *pure global marketing strategy,* a *global product positioning strategy,* a *pure national marketing strategy,* or a *mixed marketing strategy.* The adoption of one of these four basic strategies strongly influences a company's general stance on standardization.

For example, companies that have adopted a pure global marketing strategy often adopt a standardization policy. A company using this strategy believes its markets are identical in terms of product function and condition of use. It assumes that its potential customers will attach similar importance and respond in a similar fashion to the product attributes emphasized in the company's promotional campaign. Global-market companies are also very conscious of costs and wish to coordinate and integrate their promotional activities across markets. Needs such as these further pressure the company to standardize promotion.

A standardization policy also tends to be favored by companies seeking similar competitive positions and marketing the same product or product line in most of their markets. Companies choosing a global product positioning strategy are under some pressure to develop a global corporate image and global brand names across markets.

In contrast, companies that adopt a pure national marketing strategy are inclined toward differentiation. Experience and/or marketing research has demonstrated that their national markets are significantly different in terms of customer product preferences and attribute perceptions. Communication with particular markets thus needs to be localized in order to encompass these differences. The case for differentiation is further strengthened when different competitive positions are sought.

Finally, companies pursuing mixed marketing strategies have found the perceptions and preferences of potential customers in each market sufficiently varied to warrant a mix of promotional strategies. Thus, in some cases, standardization may be successful; in others, differentiation may be required.

Management Attitudes

In Chapter 10, we noted that marketing managers can be classified according to the attitudes they have concerning their companies' foreign marketing activities. *Ethnocentric* marketing managers tend to view all foreign markets as similar to and extensions of domestic markets. They are therefore inclined to assume that promotional campaigns successful in their home markets will be equally successful in foreign markets. Marketing research and theme and content testing may be either considered an unnecessary waste of time, or be ignored, or misinterpreted. By making unsupported assumptions about the marketplace, such managers shorten the time normally required for formulation of promotional strategy.

At the other extreme, *polycentric* marketing managers view all foreign markets as highly individualistic. Successful campaigns in other markets are ignored; a campaign is developed for each market. Accordingly, polycentric managers socialize and make few general assumptions about the marketplace.

Of course, both approaches may be successful. However, the ethnocentric approach depends on market similarity and a polycentric approach may be unnecessarily costly to create, prepare, and test. In both cases, there is no built-in incentive to learn from the company's successes and failures in other countries.

A more middle-of-the road stance characterizes the *geocentric* manager, who is generally aware that there are similarities and differences across markets. He or she expects to distinguish between these similarities and differences, and to learn from the company's promotional successes and failures. Consequently, the strategy formulation process may be short in some situations and long in others.

Local Corporate Conditions

The degree of standardization or differentiation adhered to at the national level is partly determined by the company's local operations. Three of the more important considerations for managers are (1) the company's market presence, (2) its classification of the market, and (3) its relations with subsidiary management.

The local affiliate's ability to assume the responsibilities of mounting a national promotional campaign is partly a function of its status within the company. For example, the staff of a sales branch may consist only of a manager and a few salespeople. The branch, therefore, neither has the time nor the skill to develop, test, and implement promotional strategies. It can either depend on the services of its regional or corporate office or hire an international or local advertising agency. In the first two cases, the local manager will probably be under some pressure to adopt a standardized promotional strategy or will be limited in the degree to which the strategy can be localized. In the third case, that of a local agency, the manager has greater latitude but may still be restricted by budget.

If the affiliate is a joint venture, who is responsible for local promotional decisions will depend on the conditions of the joint-venture agreement. Most large global companies with local partners generally have control over local promotional decisions. Whether the local partners contribute to the decision process depends on their relationship and the products being marketed locally.

When a national market is small or deemed of minor strategic importance, it probably will be treated as part of a larger, regional market. In such cases, to minimize promotional costs, even a company that has adopted a general differentiation policy may use a standardization policy on occasion. On the other hand, if the market has considerable potential, is exceptionally large, or has been classified as strategically important, the local affiliate may be given both the authority and the budget to develop localized promotional campaigns. Such a company may use its larger affiliates to develop and test campaigns that are then used in its smaller markets.

When local conditions are politically or economically volatile and the local management is successful, strong willed, or both, the local management may be given considerable latitude in how its subsidiary operates. For example, one U.S.-based company in Brazil permits the local manager, an American, to exercise total autonomy in the daily operations of the company's business. He has been extremely successful, and the company sees no economic reasons for making him toe the line on corporate policies and procedures.

Promotion Strategy Decisions

Once the core decisions of deciding on the geographic scope of the promotional campaign and the promotional objectives to be achieved have been made, the company can decide on specifics of the campaign, the resources to be allocated, and the degree of attention appropriate for monitoring and evaluating market response. We will discuss these five decisions in the order presented. In practice, however, decisions are not iterative and may have to be made simultaneously. For example, the geographic scope of the campaign or the choice of media, may have to be changed because of resource limitations.

The Geographic Scope of the Campaign

Promotional campaigns can be either national, regional, or global in scope. The geographic scope of each campaign establishes the territorial boundaries within which the campaign is to be conducted. It also provides some guidelines concerning the types of activities that need to be undertaken. The development and testing of advertising themes and messages and their transferability, for example, are partly determined by the campaign's geographic scope. However, geographic scope does not always affect whether a standardization or differentiation approach is appropriate.

Objectives of the Campaign

The company's global, regional, and national marketing objectives have a strong and decisive influence on the promotional objectives of a particular campaign. For example, two of Coca-Cola's marketing objectives are to develop several global brands and to be the dominant competitor in all its markets. On occasion, it may also want to enter a new market or introduce a new or modified product on a global, regional, or national basis. Marketing objectives such as these underpin and give direction to the company's promotional activities. Ultimately, they are the objectives against which the company's promotional activity is measured. Marketing objectives also play a key role in the globalization-localization decision. This does not mean, however, that marketing and promotional objectives are always identical. For example, an increase in market share in one or more markets is a valid marketing objective. But what promotional objective is consistent with and supportive of this marketing objective?

In practice, promotional objectives can be divided into sales and nonsales objectives. *Sales objectives* entail the generating of immediate or near-term sales of a particular product or group of products (for example, "a 10 percent share of this year's 20 to 25-year-old market"). *Nonsales objectives* concern developing an awareness and interest in a product or group of products ("within 5 years 85 percent of the targeted market should be aware of our product, and 50 percent should have some knowledge of the product's uses").

Dividing promotional objectives into sales and nonsales objectives has utility in resource allocation and performance measurement, particularly across markets in different stages of the product's life cycle. For example, the effectiveness of promotional activities associated with achieving sales objectives is more easily measured than the effectiveness of promotional activities associated with nonsales objectives. Also, nonsales objectives are generally seen as complementary promotional objectives, involving a longer time horizon to achieve than sales objectives. Thus, if market share is a major objective in several markets (some with high product awareness, and some with low product awareness), the promotional strategies for both types of markets will be different, as will the allocation of resources to sales and nonsales promotional activities. Furthermore, if the campaigns are successful, market-share increases will probably be more immediate in high awareness markets than in low awareness markets.

Elements of Promotion Strategy

The most difficult promotional campaign is one pitched at several national markets, as with regional and global promotional campaigns. The difficulties stem from the need to (1) effectively communicate to multiple targeted audiences and (2) to minimize the amount of resources, creativity, and management time involved.[28]

Many global companies have responded to these difficulties by adopting what is commonly referred to as "prototype standardization," or a core strategy.[29] These companies are interested in determining the transferability of promotional strategies and in identifying techniques useful in developing and testing multimarket messages.

The Core Strategy Approach. This approach involves developing an advertising strategy amenable to extensive modification. Although its value is primarily economic, other savings can be realized, such as the creative work associated with developing two or more localized advertising campaigns.

For example, assume that a company is interested in introducing a new or modified product to several national markets. In this situation, it would be interested in (1) creating product awareness and (2) creating an interest in and desire for the product. The first objective can probably be achieved using one advertising campaign. However, the second objective requires localized advertising campaigns. Product interest and desire are strongly influenced by a customer's perceptions and preferences, which are, in turn, the outgrowth of socio-cultural factors. Thus, a company using the core strategy concept wants to develop an advertising campaign that increases awareness *across* countries yet is sufficiently flexible to allow country-level modifications.

The Transferability of Promotion Strategies. The effectiveness of standardized promotion campaigns and the ability to profitably use a core strategy depend on the transferability of the campaign. Transferability, in turn, depends on many environmental factors, some of which are idiosyncratic to individual markets.[30] Eight environmental factors that have been found to be important in the effective transfer of promotional strategies are presented in Exhibit 16-1. They are listed in order of decreasing importance and were ranked by marketing executives of large U.S.-based companies.

Not all the environmental factors listed in Exhibit 16-1 are of equal importance for all companies. For example, consumer products companies probably consider factors 1, 3, 4, 6, and 8 relatively more important than the others when deciding on the transferability of promotional campaigns. Industrial products companies, on the other hand, would probably find factors 1, 2, 3, 5, and 8 more important.

Message Development and Testing. The transferability of promotional campaigns also depends on the perceptions customers have concerning such things as the function the product will serve and the conditions under which it will be used.[31] Thus, all advertising themes and content should be subjected to extensive testing. For example, when Gillette introduced its Trac II razor to the European market under the brand name GII it decided that a sports analogy would have universal appeal.[32] However, it recognized that U.S. sports may not have the same appeal to European customers as they do for U.S. customers. Thus, it produced more than 50 commercials, variously using tennis players, boxers, or soccer players.

EXHIBIT 16-1
Eight Environmental Factors Affecting the Transferability of Promotional Strategies

(in order of decreasing importance)

1. Level of education; level of literacy;

2. Attitudes toward risk taking, achievement and work, and wealth and monetary gain;

3. Experience and competence of personnel in foreign agency or branch of U.S. agency; experience and competence of personnel in foreign subsidiary or distributor;

4. Degree of nationalism in country; attitudes toward the U.S.;

5. Rate of economic growth of country; per capita income and distribution of income; import duties and quotas in country; development and acceptance of international trademarks and trade name;

6. Eating patterns and customs; importance of self-service retailing;

7. Attitudes toward authority; social class structure; applicability of product or slogan to other markets;

8. Independence of media from government control; availability of satisfactory media.

Source: Reprinted from S. Watson Dunn, "Effect of National Identity on Multinational Promotional Strategy in Europe," *Journal of Marketing,* Vol. 40, (October 1976), pp. 50–57, published by the American Marketing Association.

These commercials were then subjected to consumer receptivity tests. Gillette used the core theme of its successful U.S. advertising campaign and then adapted it.

Playtex also tests consumer receptivity when introducing products to foreign markets. For example, the selling strength of Jhirmack haircare products was tested in several markets by (1) opening miniature stores stocked with many products, (2) exposing potential customers to product messages, and (3) giving the customers money to spend on these products. Because of the positive results, the company decided to use the Jhirmack message in all the markets included in the tests.[33]

A multicountry, regional advertising strategy[34] was used by Ford in Europe. The technique, shown in Figure 16-3, assumes customer product perceptions and preferences are measurable and comparable, that they are determinants of message transferability, and that the costs associated with gaining an in-depth understanding of customer perceptions and preferences are acceptable.

For less expensive, nondurable products, Ford's approach might be too costly and time consuming. Major assumptions might have to be made to reduce marketing research costs. For example, a less elaborate marketing research effort may be possible if the company has accumulated appropriate experience in the targeted markets. If product perceptions and preferences are quite similar, a regional advertising strategy may have to accomodate only language differences. A hypothetical example of this last point is the introduction of a new brand of coffee by a company to its Spanish-speaking South American markets. The message and the way it is presented may not need to be altered. It may require only the dubbing of local dialects and slight changes in idioms or slang. Reinforcement and reminder advertising can also be developed on a regional basis provided a regional brand name has been used.

Media Selection

The selection of the media to be used for advertising campaigns needs to be done simultaneously with the development of message theme, concepts, and copy. A key question in media selection is whether to use a mass or target approach. The mass media (television, radio, and newsprint) are effective when a significant percent of the general public represents potential customers. This percentage varies considerably by country for most products; the approach may be effective in some countries and ineffective in others. For example, the income level of the targeted population may be well above the average in one country and about average in another. Thus, targeted media (specific magazines, radio stations) would be appropriate in the first country, and mass media would be appropriate in the second. Thus, in some countries, printed media, particularly magazines, are more likely to play a more significant role because of an inherent "targeting feature."

The selection of the media to be used in a particular campaign typically starts with some idea of the target market's demographic and psychological characteristics, regional strengths of the product, seasonality of sales, and so on. The media selected should be the result of a careful fit of local advertising objectives, media

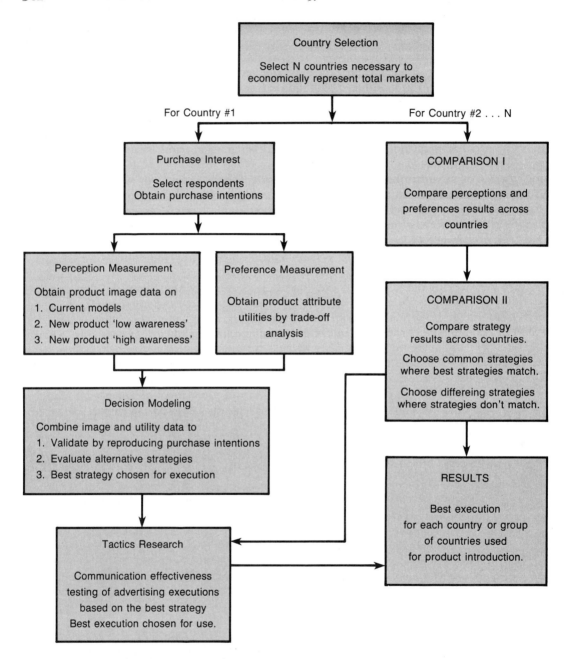

FIGURE 16-3 **A Model for Developing Multi-Country Advertising Campaigns** (*Source:* Adapted from Michael Colvin, Roger Heeler, and Jim Thorpe, "Developing International Advertising Strategy." *Journal of Marketing.* Vol. 44 [Fall 1980], pp. 73–79, published by the American Marketing Association.)

attributes, and target market characteristics. The media attributes generally compared within and across countries are discussed in the following sections.

Objectives in Media Selection[35]

Although the ultimate objective of promotional activity is to influence sales, media are usually selected on the basis of some exposure or "opportunity to see" measurement. Three measures often used are reach, frequency, and impact. *Reach* is a measure of the number of people in the target market exposed to at least one advertisement in a given time period. *Frequency* is the average number of advertisements for the product seen by members of the target market. *Impact* is a measure of the total effect of the campaign on the targeted audience.

Reach, frequency, and impact vary by media and by country. Thus, different media may be needed in different countries if similar results are sought across countries. In some countries, television may be used; in other countries, print may be used.

Media Scheduling across National Markets

Once the media have been selected, how they are to be used must be decided. Traditionally, media scheduling is based on a single measure, such as the cost per thousand (obtained by dividing the cost of the media by the size of the audience). However, when dealing with two or more national markets, a method is required that can take into account (1) differences in the company's market objectives across countries and (2) differences in media effectiveness across countries. One possible method is to adjust the traditional cost per thousand measure by a number of quantitative and qualitative factors that take into account these differences. These factors can be conveniently grouped into five categories and assigned weights according to their relative importance across countries: *target market weight, vehicle appropriateness weight, vehicle exposure weight, perception weight,* and *cumulative frequency weight.*[36] These five factors, together with audience estimates, are combined with estimates of total impact to arrive at some estimate of the cost effectiveness across and within national markets.

Target Market Weight. Not all national markets are of equal importance to the company. The same is also true of markets within countries. Thus, weights may be assigned to the various markets on the basis of their relative importance to the company. For example, across-country weighting could be in terms of a single variable such as each market's contribution to total sales, or a combination of variables such as immediate sales and market growth potential. In a similar fashion, within-country media weighting could be based on a single variable or a combination of variables such as age, social class, and income class.

Vehicle Appropriateness Weight. Promotion vehicles are not equally effective within and across countries. Such things as credibility, editorial climate, technical capabilities of the vehicle, and so on, can be assigned weights that reflect the company's assessment of each factor's relative importance.

Vehicle Exposure Weight. The probability that an individual will be exposed to a particular advertisement is a function of the vehicle used; it may not be the same across countries. For example, the number of people who actually watch television ads varies by country.[37]

Perception Weight. Not all individuals exposed to an advertisement will be conscious of its content. Thus, weights based on recall or recognition tests can be assigned to the media being used. For example, the number of people who recall seeing a particular advertisement in a particular magazine.

Cumulative Frequency Weight. These weights measure the effect of increasing the number of exposures of an advertisement to a particular individual. For example, an individual exposed to an advertisement only a few times may not become aware of the message; after a large number of exposures, he or she may be sufficiently saturated to ignore the message.

Promotion Strategy Problems in Developing Countries

Promotional activities in developing countries often require significantly different approaches from those used in more advanced or industrialized countries. The reasons for these differences have been discussed in many places in this book, but they bear restating:

1. The illiteracy rate in many developing countries is often very high; written communication is of limited value.
2. The media infrastructure is often underdeveloped, and media frequently used elsewhere, such as television, may be limited or not used for advertising purposes.
3. Some countries may be multilanguage countries; translation costs may be very high.
4. The company's products, brands, and so on, may be unknown.
5. The markets may be narrow because of wide variations in income and extremes in income distribution.
6. The markets may be geographically diverse and dispersed and therefore difficult and expensive to reach.

A checklist compiled by Business International for advertising activities in developing countries is presented in Exhibit 16-2. Their recommendations stress the need for flexibility, originality, and adequate market research.

Allocation of the Promotional Budget

The size of the promotional budget and its allocation across markets, across promotional-mix elements, across media, and over time are strongly influenced by the company's marketing planning process, its competition, and the national characteristics of its markets.

EXHIBIT 16-2

Recommendations for Advertising in Third-World Countries

1. Develop advertising campaign from the host country perspective.

2. Beware of cultural and governmental taboos.

3. Use of the visual and colorful whenever possible.

4. Seek to establish product identification, and brand loyalty through non-verbal means (illiteracy)

5. Entertain rather than lecture.

6. When country lacks effective media, create your own (traveling cinema vans in Ghana, audiovisual equipment in Saudi Arabia)

7. Pick media with broadest penetration into countryside (e.g., radio)

8. In multilanguage countries use government broadcasting systems when possible (generally available for a fee).

9. Identify decision-makers of families or village groups in each country.

10. Use of Western images can be helpful for status and modernization themes (however, considerable care needs to be exercised).

Source: Adapted from "Advertising in LDCs: How to Fit Techniques to Market and Culture," *201 Checklists: Decision Making in International Operations* (New York: Business International, 1980), p. 118.

The Marketing Planning Process

Promotional budgets are directly or indirectly subject to corporate control via the annual budgetary process to be discussed in Chapter 19. The marketing plans and promotional activities of the company's foreign affiliates are usually reviewed both at the regional and corporate levels. The company thus has the opportunity to review spending plans and to influence both their size and thrust. Unless regional and/or global promotional campaigns are contemplated, the distribution of the budgets over the planning period and across the promotional-mix elements and media are usually left to the discretion of the local marketing manager.

The Effects of Competition

The high cost of promotional activities and the economics of promotion tend to favor companies with large market shares.[38] For example, the total cost of reaching a particular market using television is the same for all firms, but the cost per customer is lower for companies with large customer bases. Consequently, companies with small market shares have to spend a higher percentage of their promotional budgets to reach customers than do companies with large market shares. Thus, the larger share companies will tend to have a bias toward larger mass communication expenditures than the smaller share companies. Small market share companies tend to piggyback on the generic demand created by the larger market share companies and to focus on more narrow market segments through careful media selection, particularly if they are following niching strategies. Small market share companies may also opt to reduce promotional expenditures and to pass on these savings in the form of lower prices, larger discounts, and improved product features.

Budget Allocation

A number of methods commonly used to arrive at the size of the promotional budget include *percentage of sales, competitive parity,* and *a minimum spending rate.* The easiest method for setting the promotional budget is the percentage of sales method. Its major advantage is that expenditures are directly linked to the volume of sales. However, the method can be severely criticized, especially when several foreign markets are involved. Three criticisms are commonly leveled against it. The method (1) uses historical performance rather than future performance, (2) does not take into account variations in the company's marketing goals across countries, and (3) docs not take into account differences in such things as media availability, costs and regulations within countries. Also, the method is of little value when a new product is to be introduced, or when competitors make adjustments to their strategies. Similar criticisms can be leveled against the other methods traditionally used in domestic situations.

A more appropriate allocation technique is one based on the approach suggested for selecting media across and within countries. That is, weights can be assigned to the various promotional-mix elements and media choices according to their effectiveness in achieving the company's marketing objectives expressed in sales and non-sales objectives for each market. The total budget and its allocation across countries can then be determined using such techniques as a linear programming technique.

Another problem faced by companies involved in multicountry promotional activities is how to distribute the budget over the planning period. For example, seasonality in buying patterns varies across countries, thus influencing when promotional activities are undertaken. Timing is of particular concern when developing a regional or global campaign involving consumer products. For example, in the United States, the weeks preceding Christmas are a major sales period for retailers, manufacturers of toys, household appliances, and many other products. In South America, the buying period often falls after Christmas, since Epiphany is the time when gifts are exchanged.

Monitoring and Evaluating Market Response

To establish the size of the budget and its allocation across promotional strategies, markets, promotional-mix elements, and media the company requires knowledge of the relationship between profits, or sales, and promotion in each of its markets. However, measuring the relative effectiveness of promotional activities is extremely difficult. One reason for these difficulties stems from the wide variation in the size of the company's foreign markets. Many markets may be quite small and cannot afford to undertake large-scale assessments; many countries may lack the facilities needed to make the assessments; the media used may be different across markets, and the emphasis placed on advertising and personal selling may differ. Thus, ingenuity has to be exercised, and cross-country experience is vital.

MANAGING GLOBAL PROMOTIONS ———————————————————

Organizing Promotion Activities

There is considerable diversity of opinion on how a company should best organize and control its global promotional activity. Some executives believe that the task needs to be decentralized to ensure that local promotional campaigns do indeed reflect socio-cultural and economic factors. Other executives are of the opinion that the task needs to be coordinated and centralized from headquarters.

Global companies can choose from three alternatives: (1) centralize all decision making at the corporate level; (2) completely decentralize the decision-making process; or (3) use some blend of the first two alternatives. The alternative selected cannot be separated easily from the company's overall organization for international business. For example, a company using a centralized global product structure is not likely to use a decentralized geographic structure for its promotional activities. Regardless of the alternative selected, there is some consensus among executives on the points presented in Exhibit 16-3.

Executives generally agree that control of the promotional decision-making process should be centralized. However, they advise flexibility to ensure global and national campaigns are integrated effectively. Foreign affiliates should also be required to seek corporate approval when selecting local advertising agencies. Although the corporate staff should be responsible for setting geographic and product objectives and developing core campaigns, these objectives and strategies need to take into account local differences in such things as sales patterns and buying habits. Furthermore, local marketing research facilities should be used when possible, and all translation should be done locally. Finally, the corporate staff should be responsible for providing advice and for seeing that the company's experience in its home and foreign markets is transferred to affiliates.

Choosing an Advertising Agency

Although many marketing activities are performed by the company and its staff, promotion is one activity where the company depends heavily on outside expertise—in the form of the advertising agency. In many cases, the agency provides the company with creative services and information and data on its target markets, media availability, and costs. The agency is also often responsible for the bulk of the company's promotional expenditure. Thus, the selection of an agency (or agencies) is of critical importance. A global company can choose from one of four alternatives: (1) use its domestic agency; (2) use an agency with branches in its foreign markets; (3) use local agencies in its foreign markets; or (4) use some combination of the above alternatives.

Corporate Factors and Choice of Agency Approach

The approach used by a particular company is heavily influenced by several factors, including its level of international involvement, its organization, and its policy regarding standardization.

Level of International Involvement. This includes the company's form of market-presence, and its level of marketing activity in specific foreign markets

EXHIBIT 16-3
Managers Opinions on The Management of Global Advertising

Control

1. Centralize control, but maintain built-in flexibility.

2. Develop a uniform worldwide company image, particularly for multiproduct companies.

3. Combine international and local campaigns to the greatest possible degree.

4. Establish advertising policy at HQ.

5. Keep most planning and coordination responsibilities at HQ.

6. Maintain budget control at HQ.

7. Have subsidiaries and branches obtain HQ approval before selecting advertising agency.

Campaign Planning

1. Prepare a written marketing plan. Establish geographical and product objectives for each foreign market. Allow for differences arising from variations in such things as sales, buying habits, and seasonality of buying.

2. Design international copy for international consumption that truly reflects company image.

3. Fit prototype campaigns developed at the local level to the overall corporate strategy and policy.

Administration and Operations

1. Have international advertising manager report to international operations manager.

2. Have international advertising manager work closely with HQ and foreign subsidiaries.

3. Make use of local marketing research facilities.

4. Do translations of copy and related materials in foreign offices, but with HQ verification.

5. Ensure that home and third-country experience is transferred as much as possible.

Media

1. Provide advice and techniques for selecting and evaluating local media.

2. Provide HQ with justification for media selected.

3. Coordinate local advertising campaigns with HQ.

4. Maintain complete dossiers on foreign media, circulation claims, and price schedules at HQ.

Source: Adapted from *201 Checklists: Decision Making in Internation Operations* (New York: Business International, 1980), pp. 117–119. This table is the result of a survey of a large number of companies concerning their beliefs regarding the organization and control of worldwide advertising campaigns.

influence the agency choice. For example, in joint-venture arrangements, the global company may have to cater to the preferences of its local partner when selecting an agency. Also, in situations where the company depends heavily on an external distribution system, the company may relinquish control, even influence, over the choice.

Company Organization. Highly centralized companies such as Caterpillar, IBM, and Procter & Gamble will generally assume responsibility for local agency selection. Decentralized companies such as 3M and Pillsbury prefer to leave agency selection to the managers of foreign affiliates.

Standardization Policy. Global companies that have adopted a general policy of standardized promotions will be strongly influenced by their need to centralize decision making in order to coordinate and integrate promotional activities within and across countries and to develop product, brand, and image uniformity. They will be inclined to seek the services of an international agency with affiliates in most of their important markets. Local managers might not have very much influence in the decision. Global companies who have adopted a differentiated promotional approach will be more strongly influenced by market-related criteria.

Market Factors and Choice of Agency Approach

The choice of agency approach adopted by a global company is also influenced by the economic and socio-cultural diversity of its foreign markets.

Economic Level and Importance of Market. Companies that spend most of their promotional budgets in third-world countries are inclined to use international agencies. Common reasons for this approach are the lack of qualified agencies in some countries and the fact that a centralized decision-making process is used by these companies.[39]

Socio-cultural Differences. Global companies marketing products and services that are sensitive to socio-cultural differences are more inclined to leave agency selection to their local managers than are companies marketing products or services insensitive to socio-cultural factors.[40]

Agency Selection Criteria

Once an approach has been adopted, the choice of a particular agency will depend on its suitability for specific situations. A company will generally use several criteria when selecting the agency, or agencies, with which it will work. Since most criteria are specific to the needs of a company and the marketing goals it wishes to achieve, three general criteria serve as guidelines for the kinds of questions that need to be asked:

Market Coverage Does the agency, or group of agencies, provide the geographic coverage required by the company in foreign markets?

Quality of Coverage Are the quality and breadth of coverage provided by the agency, or group of agencies, adequate to meet the company's needs? If not, can these requirements be developed?

Supporting Activities Does the agency, or group of agencies, have the necessary coordination capabilities, marketing research facilities, and creative services required by the company? Does the agency, or group of agencies, have ready access to media, and are media and government relations satisfactory?

MULTINATIONAL ADVERTISING AGENCIES

The multinational advertising agency is not a recent phenomenon. For example, J. Walter Thompson opened its first overseas office in London in 1899. However, the overseas expansion of U.S. advertising agencies did not become significant until the late 1960s and early 1970s, in response to the rapid spread of U.S. multinational manufacturing companies and the high growth of advertising expenditures overseas. Between 1961 and 1971, for example, over 291 offices were opened in foreign countries by U.S. advertising agencies. European agencies and, more recently, Japanese and Brazilian agencies, have opened or merged operations with agencies in other countries to an increasing degree over the last 20 years.

Geographic Spread and Penetration of Foreign Markets

The international advertising business is dominated by U.S. advertising agencies, as illustrated in Table 16-9. In 1985, only three of the largest fifteen agencies in the world were not from the United States. Dentsu and Hakuhodo, both Japanese, ranked third and fourteenth in 1985, and Saatchi and Saatchi was British. The next largest foreign agency was Eurocom, which ranked eighteenth.

Since 1985, the rankings have changed considerably, partly as a result of mergers and takeovers. For example, in 1987, SSC&B: Lintas Worldwide merged with the Campbell-Ewald Company,[41] BBDO International, Doyle Dane Bernbach Group, and Needham Harper Worldwide also merged, and the J. Walter Thompson Group was acquired by WPP, a British group.

Although the network of these large advertising agencies is worldwide, the bulk of their activities is located in the industrialized countries of Europe, North America, and Asia. For example, in 1977, over 85 pecent of the income reported by the world's largest 50 advertising agencies was generated from activities in

TABLE 16-9
The World's Fifteen Largest Advertising Agencies in 1987 (Millions of U.S.$)

Rank (1985)	Rank (1977)	Agency	Country of Origin	Gross Income (1985)	Gross Income (1977)	Number of Countries (1978)	% 1979 Billings of U.S. Agencies from outside the U.S.A.
1	3	Young & Rubican	U.S.A.	536.00	164.70	21	29.2
2	5	Ogilvy & Mather	U.S.A.	481.10	127.90	27	48.9
3	1	Dentsu Inc.	Japan	473.10	212.60		
4	9	Ted Bates Worldwide	U.S.A.	473.10	98.80	22	45.7
5	2	J. Walter Thompson	U.S.A.	450.90	189.00	29	53.5
6		Saatchi Saatchi	U.K.	440.90			
7	6	BBDO International	U.S.A.	377.00	118.60	23	36.5
8	4	McCann-Erickson Worldwide	U.S.A.	345.20	162.60	58	72.3
9		D'Arcy Masius Benton & Bowles	U.S.A.	319.50			
10	11	Foote, Cone and Belding	U.S.A.	284.20	89.10	14	30.3
11	7	Leo Burnett	U.S.A.	269.40	116.00	22	32.7
12	10	Grey Advertising	U.S.A.	259.30	97.20	18	29.8
13	13	Doyle Dane Bernbach Group	U.S.A.	231.80	74.80		29.8
14	16	Hakuhodo International	Japan	198.90	70.10		
15	8	SSC&B: Lintas Worldwide	U.S.A.	190.90	100.50	31	78.2

Note: In 1985, the largest foreign advertising agency after Hakuhodo International was Eurocom Group, France. It ranked 18th. Eurocom ranked 25th in 1977.

Source: *Advertising Age*, various issues, and "Transnational Corporations in Advertising," *Technical Paper* (New York: United Nations, 1979).

the industrialized countries. In the same year, the bulk of their income from developing countries came from Latin America.[42]

Another characteristic of these large agencies is their dominance in markets other than their home countries. Again using 1977 data, they accounted for nearly 50 percent of the total advertising expenditures in industrialized countries. In most developing countries, their share was even higher. In Latin America they accounted for 58.2 percent of total advertising expenditures, in the Caribbean, 91.8 percent, and in Africa, 83.3 percent.[43]

The dominance of the U.S. advertising agencies is quite apparent in many countries. For example, in Austria, Belgium, Germany, Italy, Spain and the U.K., the top four agencies are U.S.-owned. In Latin America, at least three of the top five agencies in Argentina, Brazil, and Venezuela are U.S.-owned, while in Mexico eight of the top ten are U.S.-owned. In Asia, the markets of Malaysia, Singapore, and Indonesia are dominated by SSC&B; in Hong Kong, six of the top ten agencies are U.S.-owned.[44]

The Role of Multinational Advertising Agencies

The existence of multinational advertising agencies provides global companies with three major advantages. First, they permit the global companies to deal with their worldwide advertising needs at one central location. The agency assumes the responsiblities and burdens of communicating with its field agencies and coordinating the global company's promotional activities across markets. Second, agencies can provide the company with creative services, information about media availability, costs and coverage, and socio-cultural and economic data for each market in which it has an agency or where it has established working relations with local agencies. Third, agencies can efficiently test advertising themes, presentations, and formats within or across markets, thus reducing considerably the global company's management of promotional activities.

There are, however, some risks and costs associated with dealing with a multinational advertising agency. Dependence on a third party, particularly a third party that is handling the company's image, reputation, and marketing plans, is always risky. The association requires a high degree of confidence and personal involvement by both parties; the global company is the central party in the agency's communications network and promotional activities. Its representatives must be kept informed of all decisions and actions taken by the agency and its foreign affiliates. At the same time, the company must keep its own affiliates informed on the decisions and activities that have transpired between it and the agency and be ready to respond to ideas, recommendations, and arguments raised by these affiliates. The company must also convey to the agency any strategic changes that may be made in its corporate, regional, or national marketing plans and the implications these changes may have on the agency's activities.

SUMMARY _____

Domestic, foreign, and global promotional strategies are similar in that they consist of one or more of the four promotional-mix elements (advertising, personal selling, sales promotion, and publicity) and are aimed at obtaining a predetermined and timed response from a targeted market. However, the development and the implementation of foreign and global promotional strategies are considerably more complicated than domestic promotional strategies. These complications arise because of differences in (1) the company's external environment across and within national markets and (2) its global, regional, and national marketing objectives and corporate practices.

The external factors distinguishing foreign and global promotional strategies from domestic promotional strategies can be divided into two groups, socio-cultural and econo-political factors. Since the core of promotion is communication, there is considerable pressure for a company to differentiate its promotional strategies to conform to the language, cultural, and social characteristics of its foreign markets. A company's foreign promotional activities and the types of media it can use to communicate with its markets are also affected by many local factors, including the country's stage of economic development, its value structure, local promotional practices, competition, and promotional regulations. In many situations, there is enough variation in these factors across national markets to require the company to adjust its promotional strategies on a country-by-country basis, regardless of market characteristics.

The internal factors that complicate the development and implementation of promotional strategies across and within national markets can also be divided into two groups, company factors and marketing objectives. Because of its geographic focus, management attitudes, and local operating conditions the company may want to use a standardized or differentiated promotional strategy across national markets. For example, companies marketing to global-market segments may want to use the same promotional strategy across national markets, regardless of environmental differences. Marketing managers with poly-

centric attitudes may want to use customized promotional strategies, even if additional costs are incurred. Second, marketing objectives may be similar or different across national markets. For example, in some markets the company may be attempting to build market share, whereas in others it may be attempting to maintain market share.

Despite external and internal pressures to standardize or differentiate promotional strategies, we have recommended that the company's general policy toward standardization or differentiation should be based on its overall objectives, including its geographic segmentation strategy and its competitive positioning strategy. The company's general policy also should be sufficiently flexible to permit specific promotional strategies to be modified on the basis of their geographic scope and objectives. Moreover, all multicountry promotional strategies need to be tested to determine their transferability in terms of their themes and messages. Finally, when selecting and scheduling the use of media, the media's reach, frequency of use, and impact needs to be determined, and weights assigned according to the relative importance of such things as markets, vehicle, and exposure.

The choice of advertising agency is heavily influenced by the company's level of international involvement, its organization, and stance on standardization. If the company has adopted a global, or standardized, promotional policy, it will be inclined to hire the services of a multinational advertising agency. This type of agency is better able to provide the company with the degree of promotional integration and coordination needed across a large number of markets. Such an agency is also more likely to provide a consistent level of quality and coverage across these markets. If, on the other hand, the company has adopted a national, or differentiated, promotional approach, it will be more inclined to use a local or regional advertising agency. These agencies are more likely to be sensitive to the local socio-cultural characteristics of the markets that are important to the company and the products it is marketing.

DISCUSSION QUESTIONS

1. Identify and discuss problems associated with allocating the company's promotion budget across several foreign markets.

2. Identify and discuss problems associated with assessing advertising effectiveness in foreign markets.

3. Identify the environmental constraints that act as barriers to the development and implementation of standardized global advertising campaigns.

4. Why does translating an advertisement sometimes entail changing the message itself? Explain and illustrate your explanation with examples.

5. Discuss the core strategy approach to advertising.

6. An executive of a large U.S. conglomerate once commented that a multinational company should use only local advertising agencies. Comment on this opinion.

7. Discuss the influence that management attitudes may have on the formulation, implementation, and control of promotion strategies. When would ethnocentric and polycentric management be appropriate?

ADDITIONAL READING

Belk, Russell W., and Richard W. Pollay, "Materialism and Status Appeals in Japanese and U.S. Print," *International Marketing Review,* Vol. 2, Winter 1985.

Plummer, Joseph T., "The Role of Copy Research in Multinational Advertising," *Journal of Advertising Research,* October–November 1986.

Samiee, Saeed, and John K. Ryans, Jr., "Advertising and Consumerism in Europe: The Case of West Germany and Switzerland," *Journal of International Business Studies,* Vol. 13, No. 1, 1982.

Tilien, Gary L., and David Weinstein, "An International Comparison of the Determinants of Industrial Marketing Expenditures," *Journal of Marketing,* Vol. 48, Winter 1984.

Wills, James R., Jr., and John K. Ryans, Jr., "Attitudes toward Advertising: A Multinational Study," *Journal of International Business Studies,* Vol. 13, No. 3.

ENDNOTES

1. M. Wayne DeLozier, *The Marketing Communication Process* (New York: McGraw-Hill, 1976).
2. J. Talan, "Yankee Goods—and Know-How—go Abroad," *Advertising Age,* May 17, 1982, p. M-14.
3. Ibid., p. M-16.
4. Ibid., p. M-21.
5. Ibid., pp. M-20 and M-21.
6. D. Christian, "European Views of Advertising," *Journal of Advertising,* (Fall 1974), pp. 23–25.
7. Rem Rijkens and Gordon E. Miracle, *European Regulation of Advertising* (Amsterdam: North Holland, 1986), p. 361.
8. Ronald Beatson, "The Image of Advertising In Europe," a presentation to the Annual Meeting of the American Association of Advertising Agencies, Palm Springs, California, March 19, 1984.
9. Talan, op. cit., p. M-16.
10. Ibid., p. M-18.
11. Rijkens and Miracle, op. cit., p. 10.
12. "Ready Reference to Europe's Quality Dailies," *International Advertiser,* September–October 1982, pp. 22–29.
13. Ibid.
14. Thomas B. Gething, "How Experts Reach the Latin Business Elite," *International Advertiser,* January–February 1982, pp. 22–24.
15. Sylvia Quenet, "Television in the U.K.—Today and Tomorrow," *International Advertiser,* December 1982, pp. 14–16.
16. Rijkens and Miracle, p. 176; quoted from "Towards a European Television Policy," *European File,* (Brussels, 1984), p. 3.
17. Rhoda Daum, "Univision Unites the Spanish-Speaking World," *International Advertiser,* January–February 1982, p 30.
18. Ingrid Boyd, "In Germany, Trade Fairs Are Sales Fairs," *International Advertiser,* December 1982, pp. 10–12.
19. G. R. Laczniak and J. Naor, "Global Ethics: Wrestling With the Corporate Conscience," *Business,* July–September 1985, p. 3.
20. S. Watson Dunn, M. F. Cahill, and Jean J. Boddewyn, *How Fifteen Transnational Corporations Manage Public Affairs* (Chicago: Crain Books, 1979).
21. These examples are taken from Jean J. Boddewyn, "Advertising Regulation in the 1980s: The Underlying Global Forces," *Journal of Marketing,* Vol. 46 (Winter 1982), pp. 27–35.
22. Ibid., pp. 30–31.
23. See Jean J. Boddewyn, "Advertising Regulation . . ." See also, Jean J. Boddewyn, "The Global Spread of

Advertising Regulation," *MSU Business Topics,* Spring 1981, pp. 5–13, and James R. Wills, Jr. and John K. Ryans, Jr., "Attitudes Toward Advertising: A Multinational Study," *Journal of International Business Studies,* Winter 1982, pp. 121–130.

24. Boddewyn, op. cit.

25. See, for example, Jean J. Boddewyn and K. Marton, *Comparison Advertising: A Worldwide Study,* sponsored by the International Advertising Association, Hastings House: New York, 1978.

26. *Effective Advertising Self-Regulation* (New York: International Advertising Self-Regulation, 1976).

27. B. G. Yovovich, "Maintaining a balance of planning," *Advertising Age,* May 17, 1982, p. M-21.

28. Michael Colvin, Roger Heeler, and Jim Thorpe, "Developing International Advertising Strategy," *Journal of Marketing,* Vol. 44, Fall 1980, pp. 73–79.

29. Deem M. Peebles, John K. Ryans, and Ivan R. Vernon, "A New Perspective on Advertising Standardization," *European Journal of Marketing,* Vol. 11 (1977), pp. 569–576.

30. S. Watson Dunn, "Effect of National Identity on Multinational Promotional Strategy in Europe," *Journal of Marketing,* Vol. 40 (October 1976), pp. 50–57.

31. Warren J. Keegan, "Multinational Product Planning: Strategic Alternatives," *Journal of Marketing,* Vol. 33 (January 1969), pp. 58–62.

32. Endnote 2, p. M-14.

33. "Playtex conditions its strategies," *Advertising Age,* May 17, 1982, p. M-18.

34. See endnote 28.

35. For a summary and discussion of some of the techniques used to select media see Peter T. FitzRoy, *Analytical Methods for Marketing Mangement* (London: McGraw-Hill Book Company, 1976), pp. 178–189.

36. The proposed method is based on one suggested by FitzRoy, *Analytical Methods,* pp. 179–180.

37. See, for example, G. A. Steiner, "The people look at commercials: a study of audience behavior," *Journal of Business,* Vol. 39 (April 1966), pp. 272–304. This study revealed that only about 14 percent of the audience watches all or almost all of a TV commercial.

38. William H. Davidson, *Global Strategic Management* (New York: John Wiley & Sons, 1982), p. 149.

39. J. N. Donnelly and John K. Ryans, Jr., "Agency Selection in International Advertising," *European Journal of Marketing* (1972), pp. 211–215.

40. Ibid.

41. "Agency nets merge, trims, consolidate," *Advertising Age,* October 19, 1987.

42. *Transnational Corporations in Advertising* (New York: United Nations, 1979), p. 4.

43. Ibid., p. 9.

44. Ibid.

Chapter 17
Dimensions
of Exporting
Strategy

The preceding chapters have discussed many of the topics with which export marketing managers should become familiar. This chapter extends those discussions, covering in more detail issues that are especially relevant to exporters: government regulation of trade flows; export promotion programs; the place of exporting in internationalization; the development of a strategic market plan for export operations; distribution, organization, and financing issues; countertrade; and importing and the gray market.

GOVERNMENT POLICY AND EXPORTING

Home- and Host-Country Control

All governments wish to monitor and regulate the movement of goods, technology, and services into and out of their territories. Major reasons for seeking control were detailed in Chapter 3, among them were the protection of local industries and jobs with regard to imports; and political, strategic, "domestic added value" and national security arguments with regard to exports.

The propensity of governments to intervene is generally greater for imports than for exports. Consequently, host-country controls are likely to be a bigger problem for most exporters than are home-government regulations. However, exporters of high-tech and strategically sensitive products (such as computers and armaments) may find home-country oversight and regulation strict. Certainly, the cumulative impact of home- and host-country regulation is likely to be significant for many exporters. Regulations can translate into loss of business opportunities overseas; less evident "costs" arise from red tape and bureaucratic delays.

Export Regulations

For purposes of illustration, we will now discuss export regulations using the United States as an example. U.S. export controls were used during World War II to ensure an adequate domestic supply of important commodities. Controls were maintained after the war; the Export Control Act of 1949 authorized the regulation of exports to the U.S.S.R. and other communist countries for political reasons as well as to ensure adequate domestic supply. Major revisions were subsequently made in the Export Administration Acts of 1969 and 1979 and in the Export Administration Amendments Act of 1985.

The regulations authorized by these successive acts enable the U.S. government to control which domestic products may be exported and to what destinations. In addition, the U.S. government seeks to control both the re-export of American goods from overseas and the non-U.S.-origin exports of the foreign subsidiaries of U.S. firms. The export controls also apply to technical data, defined as "information of any kind that can be used or adapted for use in the design, production, manufacture, utilization or reconstruction of articles or materials."[1] Three major reasons for export control may be identified regardless of nation of origin:

1. **National security:** When exports of goods and technology could make a significant contribution to the military capability of a foreign country and detrimental to national security.
2. **Foreign policy:** Control facilitates foreign policy and diplomatic goals.
3. **Short supply:** Control limits the loss of scarce materials from the home economy.

In the United States, the implementation of control regulations is primarily the responsibility of the Office of Export Administration in the U.S. Department of Commerce. However, other government departments may be involved and have primary responsibility for some products (the Department of State for armaments, the Department of the Interior for endangered wildlife, and so on).

A licensing control system has been established by the U.S. Department of Commerce. Two types of licenses are available to authorize exports, a general license and a validated license:

General license Most products exported to non-communist countries may be exported under the authorization of a general license. A formal application for the license is not required. All that is necessary is that the exporter check that the good can be exported without a validated license and note on the "Shipper's Export Declaration" form (which must be filed with customs prior to shipment) that the product is being exported under a general license.

Validated license These can be obtained *only* in response to a *formal application* to the Department of Commerce. Upon approval, the exporter is issued a license permitting exportation within the conditions specified on the license. The validation process allows for governmental review—on a case-by-case basis—of controlled or restricted commodities and technical data.

To determine whether a validated license is required, exporters should consult the Commodity Control List (CCL) supplement to the Export Administration Regulations. This list identifies all commodities that require a validated license to some or all destinations. Overseas markets are classified into country groups. For each controlled commodity, the CCL lists the country group(s) requiring a validated export license. Major country groups (these groups are subject to change) are shown in Table 17-1.

The CCL control system is the target of criticism from a number of directions. On the one hand, some argue that control is too lax, and that large amounts of strategically sensitive embargoed material (such as sophisticated computers) have been allowed to reach communist countries. Others maintain that the controls are often too tough, particularly those imposed for reasons of foreign policy. A 1987 National Academy of Sciences study found that over 50 percent of U.S. exporters claimed to have lost overseas sales because of "excessive" U.S. controls. Supposedly, these controls cost U.S. exporters an estimated $10 billion worth of "lost" U.S. exports each year.

Efforts by the U.S. government to extend export controls extraterritorially have resulted in friction with foreign governments. Costs are not only monetary. The restrictions placed on the export of products manufactured by U.S. overseas subsidiaries and licensees in Western Europe for the Soviet European natural gas

TABLE 17-1
U.S. Export Control Country Groups*

Country Group	Countries	
Canada	Canada	Least control; almost all goods exportable without a validated license
Country Group T	Western Hemisphere (except Cuba)	
Country Group V	Western Europe, Middle East, Africa, non-Communist Asia, China	
Country Group Q	Romania	Increasingly tight control over U.S. exports
Country Group W	Poland, Hungary	
Country Group Y	Soviet Union, East Germany, Czechoslovakia, Mongolia, Bulgaria, Albania	
Country Group S	Libya	
Country Group Z	North Korea, Cuba, Vietnam, Cambodia	Virtual embargo on exports of U.S. goods and technical data

Source: Export Administration Regulations, 1983.
*Note that frequent changes are made in this classification.

pipeline in 1982 were ineffective; they resulted in open conflict between the United States and its NATO allies. The monetary cost of these restrictions to U.S. companies has been estimated at some $4 billion over six years.[2]

In an effort to address some of these costs, the Export Administration Amendment Act of 1985 loosened licensing requirements on some exports to NATO allies and Japan and reduced the processing time for license applications by an average of about 30 percent. At the same time, the Act increased the enforcement powers of the Department of Commerce and of customs. Details of the old and revised processing deadlines are shown in Table 17-2.

In the United States, further recent measures to streamline export controls include provisions that free U.S. firms from having to obtain validated licenses for exports of sensitive products to certain already approved, reliable buyers in allied countries. The United States has also eased restrictions on exports from other countries of foreign made products containing U.S. parts. These measures alone should reduce the Department of Commerce's yearly caseload of 120,000 license applications by an estimated 20 percent and shorten the average license-processing time from 20 to 14 days.

In January 1988, the Department of Commerce unveiled a computerized system designed to expedite the processing of licenses for high-tech exports. The system avoids mail delays by allowing officials instant access to all information needed to act on licence requests. It is estimated that the system is able to process licenses for exports to allied countries in just three days. Thirteen days is the expected average for exports to other nonsocialist countries.

TABLE 17-2
U.S. Export License Application Processing Deadlines

	EAA 1979	EAAA 1985
Licensing: Non-COCOM Countries		
Issue or deny a license if it does not require outside referral.	90 days	60 days
Licensing: Non-COCOM Countries and Outside Referral		
Refer a license to another agency or department if outside position required.	30 days	20 days
Outside agency must return its recommendation to Commerce. (If recommendation not received, Commerce assumes approval.)	30 days	20 days
Maximum extension an outside agency may request to provide its recommendation.	30 days	20 days
After receipt of outside agency recommendations, Commerce must issue or deny a license.	90 days	60 days
TOTAL	180 days	120 days
Licensing: COCOM Countries		
Issue or deny license for COCOM country.	NA	15 working days*

* Commerce can request an additional 15 working days for review.
Source: Olson, W. J. "Export Administration Amendments Act of 1985," *Business America*, September 2, 1985, p. 4.

The United States has also improved its surveillance of high-tech exports to communist countries. Export control is coordinated through the Coordinating Committee for Multilateral Export Controls (COCOM), based in Paris. The agency has 16 members (the 15 NATO members and Japan) who have agree to enforce COCOM decisions regarding a list of goods and technologies restricted from export to the East.

Revelations in 1987, of exports by Japan's Toshiba Corporation and Norway's Kongsberg Vaapenfabrikk of sensitive equipment and technology that enabled the Russians to build quieter submarines, lead to greater efforts by COCOM members to control the leak of technology to communist countries. In 1988, it was agreed that COCOM members would stiffen penalties for violations of export controls, increase export surveillance, and share intelligence on suspicious traders. It was also agreed to reduce the number of items on the control list and focus on truly sensitive goods and technology.

Facilitating Exports

Most governments have a strong commitment to promoting national exports and have accordingly developed a variety of programs to encourage exporting. In central-command economies and countries where there is a significant nationalized industrial sector, such government intervention can be very direct. For example, publically held firms may be directed to develop export activities even if this is not economically attractive.

In the case of market-oriented economies, governmental support usually takes a more indirect form. The most common initiatives to facilitate exporting include government subsidies, tax benefits for exporters, government assistance in financing and insuring export business, and the provision of government-funded market research and other export services. We will now survey the major forms of export support in market economies.

Subsidies

Subsidies to individual firms or industries are commonly not given just to exporters; such support would blatantly violate GATT regulations. However, general subsidies frequently enable domestic producers to become price-competitive overseas. Let us look briefly at two European subsidy efforts. At the present time the United States is highly critical of the Common Market's agricultural policy, a policy that guarantees many European farmers artificially high prices for their produce. This support has encouraged overproduction and resulted in the exporting of grain and other produce to third markets at low prices that compete directly with U.S. farm products. Government subsidies also support the European Air Bus consortium, which produces the Jumbo jets competing in export markets with aircraft manufactured by Boeing and McDonnell Douglas. Over the last 17 years, European taxpayers have provided launch aid of some $10 billion for Air Bus jets. Without this aid, the Air Bus consortium would have folded.[4]

The Europeans have responded to U.S. complaints in kind. They point out that the United States also spends billion of dollars subsidizing its farmers, and maintain that R&D expenditures of many U.S. firms, in particular aircraft companies like Boeing, are heavily subsidized by government-funded military contracts. These contracts, it is argued, often generate important commercial spinoffs. Differences, such as these, generate conflict. Besides the threat of direct retaliation resulting from such disputes, exporters receiving government subsidies are highly exposed to dumping investigations in markets where their cheap exports adversely affect the business of local manufacturers.

Tax Benefits

The nature and extent of the tax benefits enjoyed by exporters varies from country to country. Topping the list are deferred taxes on export earnings, long-term tax "holidays" for export profits, and low export-profit tax rates.

In the United States, the primary means of generating export tax benefits from 1972 to 1985 was through the Domestic International Sales Corporation (DISC). DISC allowed U.S. firms to defer taxes on part of the profit from export sales. By 1982, there were some 9,000 active DISCs, and over 70 percent of U.S. exports were channeled through them. However, the DISC system was frequently criticized as inconsistent with GATT rules, and it was largely replaced in 1984 with an alternative incentive program compatible with GATT. In that year, a Foreign Sales Corporation (FSC) tax incentive scheme was approved. Exporters can still elect to use a DISC, but only for export revenue of up to $10 million per annum and they have to pay an interest charge on the tax being deferred.

The Foreign Sales Corporation

FSC tax incentives have been an option since January 1, 1985. Exporters can establish an FSC either to operate as a principal, buying and selling on its own account, or as a commission agent. Individual manufacturers or groups can set up an FSC subsidiary as can independent export brokers and merchants. Just as through a DISC, export sales may be made on a buy-sell or a commission basis, and FSC export income is subject to tax breaks. The 1985 FSC rules allow for *permanent* exemption from federal tax for part of the profit on FSC export sales. A corporate tax exemption is allowed for up to 32 percent of export earnings. The proportion of earnings exempted depends on the manner in which transfer prices are computed and whether the FSC buys from independent or related suppliers.

Unlike the DISC, an FSC must be incorporated in and have its main office in territories outside the U.S. customs area in either a U.S. possession (the U.S. Virgin Islands, American Samoa, Guam, or the Northern Marianas) or a foreign country having an exchange-of-information agreement with the United States. At least one director must be a foreign resident, and books of account have to be maintained at the offshore office. Various management activities must take place off shore, and the FSC must undertake a substantial level of marketing activity outside the United States. Small exporters may elect to set up "small" FSCs, which allow for tax relief on export receipts up to $5 million. Small FSCs are substantially less expensive to establish; they do not have to meet all the foreign management and foreign economic and sales conditions of a regular FSC.

The increased administrative costs of organizing an FSC may render the program less attractive than the old DISC program for small- and medium-sized exporters. Given the choice between the "interest charge" DISC or an FSC, most exporters with export sales of less than $1 million should not set up an FSC unless exports are very profitable. For most exporters with sales between $1 million and $5 million, the small FSC option is best. In the case of larger exporters, the regular FSC is generally preferable.[5]

A "shared" FSC—one owned and operated by up to 25 unrelated exporters— is a useful means of spreading the costs of organizing and operating a FSC. It has been estimated that small exporters can realize up to a 7 to 1 payoff for money spent operating a shared FSC.[6] Shared FSCs may be sponsored by state or regional authorities, a trade association, banks, export management companies and shippers, or groups of firms. Since a shared FSC is only created for administrative purposes, it does not get involved in the export business of participants. Also, export profits and proprietary information are not shared among the member companies.

Government Support Services

In many countries government agencies give extensive assistance to current and potential exporters. Apart from financial and tax-related benefits, governments provide a wide range of export services free or at low cost. These include the collection and analysis of overseas market information, assistance in locating foreign consumers and distributors, the organization of trade missions, facilitating attendance at trade fairs, and consulting and educational programs.

In the United States, the primary federal agency providing export assistance is the Department of Commerce (reviewed in the next section). The U.S. Small Business Administration, which has a chain of field offices throughout the United States, also plays a role in providing counseling, export training, legal advice, and financial support for current and potential small exporters. The U.S. Department of Agriculture offers assistance to exporters of agricultural products.

State development agencies and, in some cases, county, city, and other local bodies are frequently providers of valuable services to local exporters. The aid offered is typically focused on education programs and marketing assistance. Some states have also created export financing agencies and offer export-related state tax benefits. In New Jersey, for example, the governor announced plans in 1988 to encourage exporting by small firms by means of loans, tax breaks, and a state-sponsored export trading company.

U.S. Department of Commerce Programs

A wide range of services are provided to exporters by the Department of Commerce, primarily through the International Trade Administration Division. This organization has a network of 48 district offices and 24 branch offices located throughout the United States. Services available via the district offices and district export councils include individual export counseling, export seminars, and access to a mass of overseas market information. Help is also available from specialists in Washington, D.C. Country desk officers (Country specialists), for example, are a good source of information on trade potential in specific markets.

Some of the primary market intelligence and export promotion services available from the Department of Commerce include:

- **Market Identification Statistics:** This data highlights attractive export markets and newly emerging markets.

- **Market Research Studies:** These are detailed evaluations of promising markets by country and by product.

- **Market Contact Services:** These services provide sales leads, names, and background data on overseas buyers.

- **Product and Services Promotions:** These facilitate overseas promotion through international publications, catalog and video exhibitions, government- and industry-organized trade missions and trade shows, and foreign-buyer missions to the United States.

THE DEVELOPMENT OF EXPORT OPERATIONS

The Initiation of Export Operations

Although there are differences between the process of becoming aware of export opportunities and the decision to export. In practice, awareness and involvement are frequently intertwined. Figure 17-1 summarizes major influences on initial export involvement.

It is apparent that outside agents and fortuitous events play a major role in the decision to export.[7] Many studies indicate that the unsolicited export order is often the primary catalyst. Other significant factors in promoting export interest include governmental export promotion agencies, industry associations, banks, chambers of commerce, the behavior of competing firms, the media, and foreign travel by employees.[8]

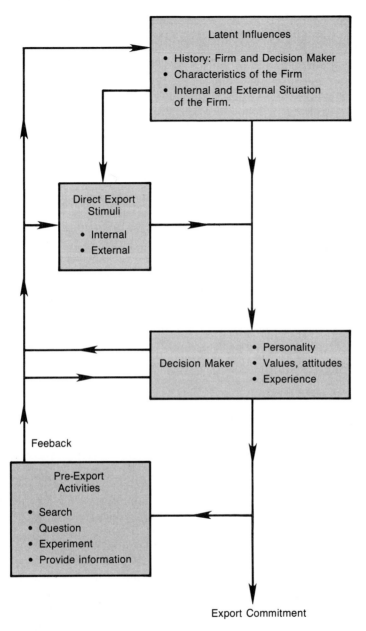

FIGURE 17-1 **Influences on Initial Export Involvement** (*Source:* L. S. Welch, "Managerial Decision Making: The Case of Export Involvement," *Scandinavian Journal of Materials Administration,* Vol. 9, No. 2, 1983.)

Pre-export activity in firms is an important influence on subsequent export behavior.[9] Key variables are the firm's pattern of regional expansion in the home market; the availability of relevant information; and the attitudes, perceptions, and predisposition of export decision makers. The degree of management interest is particularly important; managers who have been exposed to overseas markets by virtue of foreign birth, education, travel, or work experience are most likely to initiate export operations.

The immediate context in which the decision maker is operating also has an important effect on initial and subsequent export invovlement. Internal factors identified as favorable to exporting include technological innovation, successful product differentiation, excess capacity, and ambitious corporate goals. Influential external influences include a limited and competitive home market, seasonal demand, government incentives, dynamic overseas markets, the behavior of competitors, and unsolicited orders.

In many firms, initial exporting is largely an unplanned reaction to random events; that is, it is not based on a strong foundation of management commitment. Initial exporters thus often rapidly cease exporting if special problems arise or if business is not successful in the short term.

Export Operations in the Internationalization Process

For most firms, export operations are the first step in internationalization. There is evidence that many firms develop their export business only gradually. Stages that have been identified include a pre-export phase, and experimental, active, and committed exporting stages.[10]

Although exporters often do not go through all these stages, the acquisition and evaluation of knowledge, especially experiential knowledge, plays a key role in the internationalization process. Firms tend to initially export to those markets which are familiar, where barriers to information retrieval are low, and resource commitment typically proceeds incrementally.[11] External change agents play an important initial role in triggering export interests, as do internal management attitudes. In this learning situation, there is a tendency to focus on markets which are close in a cultural, economic and geographic sense. It can also be expected that extensive use will be made of third parties, both at home and overseas, to undertake export related activities. As experience and export resource commitment increases, so does the ability and desire to take direct control over export marketing.

Once export operations have started, there is no necessary congruence between the reasons for initiating and maintaining export activities. Research has uncovered a wide range of motivations for continuing ongoing exporting. It is apparent that rational objectives such as export profit, sales potential, and the advantages of market diversification are significant reasons for continuing operations.

Export Barriers and Risks

A wide variety of barriers to successful export operations have been identified. Some mainly affect export startup; others, exporting itself. Critical factors hindering export startup include a large home market, ignorance of overseas opportunities, and insufficient resources. Inadequate information on potential foreign customers, competition, and foreign business practices are key barriers. Obtaining adequate representation for overseas distribution and service, ensuring payment, import tariffs and quotas, and difficulties in communicating with foreign distributors and customers are also major concerns.

Operational problems are also commonplace. Production disruptions may occur, and result from a need for nonstandard export products. These will increase the cost of manufacture and distribution. Obtaining export financing is another major difficulty.

Exporting, at least at the outset, is a fairly high-risk activity because of these problems and market ignorance. Extensive use of third parties and conservative strategies, such as demanding payment in advance for export shipments, can help limit risk. However, high payments and lost business often result. Export-related risks may be divided into two groups, financial and political. Financial risks result primarily from the sources listed below. Political risks result mainly from government intervention.

Financial Risks

☐ Exchange-rate fluctuations when contracts are made in a foreign currency.

☐ Failure of export customers to pay because of a contract dispute, bankruptcy, refusal to accept the product, and fraud.

☐ Cost escalation due to high export manufacturing, distribution, and financing expenditures.

☐ Delays and damage in the export shipment and distribution process.

Political Risks

☐ Export controls imposed by the home government.

☐ Foreign-exchange controls imposed by host governments, limiting opportunities for foreign customers to make payment.

☐ Host-government import restrictions.

☐ The disruption of markets by civil strife, revolution, and war.

Various risk-management strategies are open to exporters. The most obvious is to avoid doing business in high risk markets. Another is to diversify export markets so that the firm is not overdependent on any single country. Insurance may be available in the case of some risks; government schemes are particularly attractive. Also, export business may be structured to transfer risk to the buyer (for example, pricing exports in a hard currency and demanding cash in advance), but this will make it harder to get export orders.

THE STRATEGIC EXPORT MARKETING PLAN

A wide variety of strategies can lead to export success. However, firms operating from high-cost countries, such as the United States, often do best targeting specialty niche markets with high-quality products. Demand in these market segments is often relatively price inelastic, and consumers are willing to pay more for a superior product that has few direct substitutes.

In recent years, West Germany has overtaken the United States as the world's leading exporter, and many German exporters have prospered as a result of concentrating in specialty areas rather than mass markets. High product quality and motivated, effective overseas dealers are common components in the export strategy of many German firms. An export tradition, which implies a long-term commitment to exporting, plus flexibility, such as a willingness to manufacture some products in foreign markets when necessary, are also critical success factors.

Many U.S. exporters also succeed in mass markets as a result of effective cost leadership or differentiation strategies, and it is not always appropriate to seek out niche markets. Thus U.S. exporters of commodity products, such as paper and grain, and of high-tech items, such as commercial aircraft and computers, have carved out large shares of mass world markets.

Key Elements of the Plan

Most of the concepts and principles of strategic planning reviewed in Part III apply as much to exporting as to other forms of servicing overseas demand. Consequently, the following discussion is designed to highlight only those points that are particularly important for export activities.

Prior to developing a detailed plan, managers should evaluate the operating environments of potential export markets and the firm's present and future export potential. The evaluation should include an analysis of the firm's resources, goals, products, and experience. These should be examined in relation to the salient characteristics of the firm's likely competitors in overseas markets. Within each market, the aim of the evaluation should be to identify the relative strengths and weaknesses of the firm and, in particular, determine the company's distinctive competence. (U.S. industries identified as having high export potential are shown in Exhibit 17-1.)

Overseas export opportunities must be carefully assessed. This requires an evaluation of foreign customers, competing products, and the structure of foreign markets. Broad environmental trends also need to be considered, along with a focus on market segments of particular interest. Once this has been done, the

---

EXHIBIT 17-1
U.S. Industries with High Export Potential*

1. Computers and peripherals
2. Telecommunications equipment and systems
3. Computer software and services
4. Medical instruments, equipment, and supplies
5. Electronic parts
6. Analytical and scientific laboratory instruments
7. Industrial process control instruments
8. Aircraft and avionics equipment
9. Automotive parts and equipment
10. Electronic production and test equipment

*Ranked in descending order
Source: Small Business Administration.

aim of the assessment should then be to seek out "windows of opportunity" where there is a fit between the distinctive competence of the exporter and market opportunities. Careful consideration needs to be given to the resource demands, export barriers, and risks likely in exploiting the opportunities identified. The direct and opportunity costs of exporting, likely benefits and the degree to which such export business is compatible with the firm's strategic posture and goals also need to be reviewed.

If it is decided to proceed with export operations, it will be necessary to develop an export plan based on top management's expectations regarding the firm's export mission and business. This requires making decisions concerning the role exporting will play in the firm, the scope and nature of the export product lines and overseas markets, specific export performance goals, and the level of corporate commitment to export operations. Once done, functional plans for the achievement of export objectives need to be developed. Finally, detailed budgets for export operations should be drawn up. These will be financial statements of the resource, cost, revenue, and profit implications of the functional strategies that have been developed.

A plan is only as good as the quality of the data gathered and the analysis undertaken during the planning process. It is important to involve all levels of management in this process and a corporatewide commitment to exporting is vital for long-term success.

The Export Marketing Mix

The export marketing plan should focus on market objectives; market segmentation and positioning; export product-line characteristics; distribution channels; and export pricing, advertising, and sales policies. Its goal should be a comprehensive, integrated marketing strategy that maximizes the effectiveness of the overall export effort. The plan needs to be detailed. It should include targets, budgets, action schedules, and the assignment of responsibilities for implementing the plan.

The identification of attractive export markets and accurate estimation of their export potential are crucial for success. High-quality market research and forecasting is therefore very important. Many small- and medium-sized exporters are unable to afford expensive primary data. This means a heavy reliance on secondary source material. Familiarity with the wide range of secondary source material available for many overseas markets is therefore important, as is an understanding of the techniques needed to evaluate these data. When developing estimates of market size, for example, data extrapolation methods may be useful. However, the short-comings of such methods and the inevitable "cost-accuracy" tradeoff must be taken into account.

Most of the primary issues that exporters need to consider when setting marketing policy have already been reviewed in preceding chapters. In product policy, a key issue is the adaptation of export product lines. Is change needed in product attributes and, if so, what must be changed, where, by how much? Some firms will export only those products requiring no modification. Others are more flexible, though product changes are clearly a major barrier for many exporters, particularly those with limited resources. (For the major variables that should be addressed when determining product policy, see Chapter 13.)

In the area of pricing, common problems are cost-plus export pricing, insufficient attention to the pricing environment in individual markets, and excessive overseas distributor price margins. Promotional policy in overseas markets is often the prime responsibility of foreign distributors and agents. Exporters should support this activity by providing financial and other assistance. They should also closely monitor the policies implemented.

Most exporters rely heavily on independent channel intermediaries. Managing export distribution channels therefore requires particular attention. We now turn to that topic.

EXPORT DISTRIBUTION

Most exporters make extensive use of external distribution channels and because independent channel intermediaries, particularly those located overseas, undertake much more than physical distribution, their effectiveness critically affects a firm's export performance. An overseas distributor, for example, typically is responsible for local market research, forecasting, promotion, and selling, as well as for holding inventory and providing service backup.

Unfamiliarity with the environment in foreign markets and geographic and cultural distance can complicate the tasks of selecting and managing channel intermediaries. Key areas of concern include the following:

☐ Establishing channel structures and organizational relationships appropriate to the firm's export strategy and market context.

☐ Identifying and recruiting qualified and motivated agents and distributors.

☐ Establishing monitoring systems that can distinguish between distributor performance and market performance (since the latter measure is often heavily affected by factors beyond the control of the distributor).

Common problems arising in agency relationships include distributors and agents who represent too many products or are unwilling to push the exporter's particular product line, clashes due to cultural misunderstanding, excessive markups and declining performance due to executive turnover in distributors, and a loss of key local contacts. Negotiations to terminate agency agreements with minimum disruption and cost is therefore an essential task for the export manager.

Direct and Indirect Exporters

The degree to which exporters seek to manage and control the marketing and distribution of their products to and in foreign markets varies greatly. In the case of indirect exporters, extensive use is made of external third parties at home and overseas. The exporter's primary responsibility is confined to producing the goods to be exported.

This approach has strong attractions for exporters with limited knowledge of exporting and overseas markets and for firms wishing to economize on export resource commitments. However, relinquishing control over export marketing activities can result in serious problems.

Many intermediaries represent numerous exporters; they tend to concentrate their efforts on those product lines that are well established and do not require extensive marketing support and promotion. If intermediaries work hard to market products overseas, high fees are reasonable. These fees, however, export profits.

Most exporters tend to seek more involvement in managing and controlling their export operations as overseas sales and experience grows. This requires an investment in establishing a corporate export infrastructure staffed by export specialists. However, most direct exporters continue to make extensive use of intermediaries such as freight forwarders and foreign distributors. The distinguishing characteristics of a direct exporter, therefore, are the assumption of substantial corporate responsibility for export marketing and distribution and the provision of in-house resources for managing these activities.

Domestic Export Distribution Channels

Six important types of intermediaries available in the home market that work with exporters to generate foreign sales include:

1. **Export commission agents** operate as the representative of foreign firms. They seek out products required by their principal and negotiate the purchase of these goods, in return for a commission, on behalf of their foreign clients.
2. **Resident foreign buyers** are controlled by an overseas buyer and locate and purchase goods needed by their owners. They are frequently controlled by foreign governments or quasi-governmental agencies.
3. **Export brokers** bring together buyers and sellers of exports in return for a fee. They assume no financing or shipping responsibilities.
4. **Export agents** act on behalf of exporters as a selling agent. They do not take title to products and rarely finance orders. They may handle shipment and operate on a commission basis.
5. **Export merchants** buy goods directly from the manufacturer for sale overseas. They assume all risks, usually sell in their own name, and control overseas marketing. Some export trading companies share many characteristics with merchants. Their role, and the U.S. legislation designed to encourage their activities, is considered in more detail later.
6. **Export management companies** act as the export department for one or more firms in related fields. They solicit business overseas and handle export marketing and shipment activities in the name of the manufacturer. They may also undertake export financing. Typically, they are paid a commission augmented by a retainer.

Foreign Export Distribution Channels

The exporter may sometimes sell directly to the foreign end user, particularly in the case of commodity and producer goods. Generally, though, use will be made of one or more of the following four channels of distribution:

1. **Sales agents** fulfill a role equivalent to that of the manufacturer's representative in the home market. Their major function is to identify foreign customers and promote the exporter's products. Generally, they are paid a commission

and work under contract for defined periods of time. They assume no risk, but may advise on pricing and provide limited after-sale service.

2. **Distributors** operate as a merchant, buying for their own account and undertaking their own marketing of the goods in the local market. They usually carry inventory and are frequently responsible for providing service support. The relationship with the manufacturer is regulated by contract. Distributors normally seek long-term relationships because of the investment they must make in developing their business. Terminating distributor arrangements can be difficult and expensive.

3. **Foreign retailers** may buy directly from exporters. This approach is generally limited to consumer product lines. It is a means of reducing markups in the distribution chain. Big orders generate transaction cost economies.

4. **Overseas sales branch or subsidiary:** More experienced exporters frequently find it worthwhile to set up a corporate-controlled marketing and distribution system in the local market. Control is increased, direct access to customers is achieved, and experience quickly gained. However, a significant investment is often required, and ongoing expenses are substantial. The choice between a branch office or a subsidiary may have important tax and legal implications.

Prior to making overseas distribution decisions, the exporter should be very familiar with consumer needs and the local distribution system (channel availability, channel use, laws affecting sales and distribution) and have determined the basic goals of the firm's export distribution strategy. Basic issues relating to the export distribution strategy include degree of corporate control desired, geographic and consumer coverage desired, the level of sales and service support required from intermediaries, distribution logistics, and the degree of support available to distributors for training, finance, and promotion.

Legal Issues

Generally, it is essential to have a clearly drafted legal agreement that sets out the duties and obligations of the exporter and the channel intermediary. This is especially important overseas, where cultural differences, differing business customs and laws, and geographic distance can greatly complicate everyday business relationships.

A key problem in many countries is the existence of local laws that heavily penalize foreign firms for terminating or failing to renew agency or distributor agreements. These laws are often ambiguous, tend to heavily favor the foreign agent or distributor, and typically override the provisions of any contract. As a consequence, the ending of undesirable business relationships with foreign intermediaries may result in protracted litigation and high settlement costs. This is particulary likely when the exporter seeks to terminate a contract prior to its expiration date, for many countries have enacted contract termination laws that make it difficult to end agency relationships without substantially compensating the local agent or distributor.

Exporters can best minimize the risks of contract termination by evaluating the relevant local laws, by carefully selecting agents and distributors, and by taking great care when drawing up agency agreements. *A written contract is essential,* and should be drawn up with the following points in mind:

☐ The benefits to both parties should be clearly delineated. The agreement should not impose an excessive or profitless burden on either party.

☐ The contract should contain a clear statement of the rights and duties of each party; the nature, character, and duration of the relationship; and, if possible, the conditions under which the agreement may be terminated.

☐ Clear definitions of contract terms are important. For example, an agreed-on English version of the contract, to have priority in cases of conflict, is desirable for the U.S. exporter.

☐ Jurisdictional and arbitration clauses are very useful. Frequently, however, local laws require that disputes be referred to local courts. Any arbitration clause should identify the arbitration forum and procedures.

In most common law countries, special laws penalizing or precluding the termination of agency agreements are unusual. In other markets, relatively more care needs to be exercised. However, it may be possible to waive restrictions placed on the agency contract by prior agreement with the foreign agent or distributor.

Export Trading Companies

Export trading companies (ETCs) engage in and facilitate international trade. They share many of the characteristics of an export merchant but play a wider role. In addition to their primary role as an exporter, ETCs may also engage in importing and barter, arrange sales between third parties, and offer export services to outside parties.

In the United States, the Export Trading Company Act of 1982 has been an important stimulus to the formation of ETCs. The act has provided two major benefits for exporters. First, it offers exporters greater protection from U.S. antitrust laws, and antitrust preclearance can be granted by the Commerce Secretary for specified joint export activities. Second, bank holding companies and other eligible financial institutions are permitted to own and control ETCs. More financial muscle can therefore be mobilized for export activities.

The antitrust protection afforded by the act encourages joint export ventures in the form of an ETC. This protection allows for the exploitation of economies of scale, the pooling of expertise, and risk diversification. Prior to the ETC Act, exporters had enjoyed limited antitrust immunity from the Export Trade Act of 1918 (more commonly called the Webb-Pomerene Act), which allows firms to form export associations. However, the protection offered was ill defined and limited in scope. As a result, by 1979, only 33 Webb-Pomerene associations were operative; their exports accounted for under 2 percent of the U.S. total. Firms are still free to join other exporters in Webb-Pomerene associations, thereby gaining limited antitrust protection, bargaining leverage, and an opportunity to share many export costs.

One of the stimuli for passage of the ETC Act was the success of a number of large Japanese general trading companies. However, most U.S. ETCs have not followed the Japanese model; instead, they tend to be relatively small, market specialized product lines, and have emerged as extensions of existing manufacturing companies. Most have not functioned as independent general traders and are not as large and diversified as the Japanese firms.

The U.S. Department of Commerce has given antitrust preclearance to some 300 firms and individuals. Aggregate exports reported by these ETCs total more than $300 million.[12] This is not particularly impressive growth. It is unlikely that the act has yet produced the $3 billion in export sales expected in the first year alone. In general, performance of U.S. ETCs has been mediocre.[13]

An indication of the problems experienced by U.S. ETCs in the mid-1980s is provided by the closure, after four years of existence and losses of $60 million, of Sears World Trade in 1986. The firm was planned as a global trading giant patterned after the Japanese trading firms, but it found its activities were limited by the then strong dollar. Subsequently, a weaker dollar and more experience have improved prospects for other U.S. ETCs somewhat.

Export Shipment

The three primary export shipment objectives are speed, economy, and safety. It is rarely possible to achieve all three goals concurrently. Exports have to be shipped long distances over national boundaries and are typically liable to high physical distribution costs and delays.

Most U.S. exports move by sea or air to the foreign market, and nearly all exporters make some use of international freight forwarders to expedite shipment. Freight forwarders act as an external traffic department for the exporter. Acting as the exporter's agent, they oversee the movement of goods to the foreign customer. In the process of ensuring the pickup, storage, movement, and delivery of exports, the freight forwarder often neither sees nor handles the merchandise. The forwarder principally chooses the most suitable transport mode; books space; negotiates the best rates and services for the exporter; prepares the shippers' commercial invoices, packing lists, and other documentation required for customs clearance; controls the movement of goods to the foreign destination; and arranges for cargo insurance. Forwarders can also assist with packing and advise on such matters as letters of credit and obtaining export licenses.

When selecting a freight fowarder, consideration should be given to the range of services offered by the forwarder; their specialization in terms of destination, classes of merchandise, and transport mode; their reputation; and the cost of their services.

For most export shipments, three types of document are required: shipping documents, import documents, and collection documents. Although freight forwarders commonly prepare many of these documents, the exporter is ultimately responsible for the completeness and accuracy of the information provided. Details of the required documentation are shown in Exhibit 17-2.

Foreign Trade Zones

Many countries have established secured areas within their territory that are not subject to normal customs regulation. Firms are permitted to import merchandise

EXHIBIT 17-2
Export Shipping Documents

Shipping and Export License Documents

These are required in order to clear U.S. customs, and for loading and transportation to the foreign market. Key documents include:

☐ *Validated Export License* (if required).

☐ *Shipper's Export Declaration Form* Filled with U.S. customs prior to shipment; used by customs to ensure that regulations are met and for statistical purposes.

☐ *Bill of Lading* Provides evidence of the transport contract between the shipper and carrier and is a negotiable instrument through which title to the goods can be transferred; a key document in establishing legal ownership; thus an essential element in financial transactions concerning the goods.

☐ *Insurance Certificate* Describes insurance coverage for the goods.

☐ *Packing List* Detailed description of merchandise shipped by type, quantity, weight, type of packing, and identifying marks.

Collection Documents

These are documents that must be submitted to the customer or his agent to receive payment. Precise requirements vary by country and payment arrangements. Key documents include the bill of lading (described above) and:

☐ *Commercial invoice* Descriptions of goods, quantity, price, date of order, shipment date and mode, delivery and payment terms.

☐ Other Documents that may be needed in some countries include:
   a) *Certificate of origin* Evidence of the origin of the goods.
   b) *Consular invoice* Invoice certified by the resident consul, in country of export.
   c) *Inspection certificates* Certification that the shipment meets the order terms with regard to quantity and quality.

☐ *Draft* A written, unconditional order—usually issued by the exporter—ordering the importer or the importer's agent to pay, on demand (sight draft) or at a fixed future date (time draft), the amount specified.

Import Documents

These are required to clear merchandise through customs in the foreign market. Shipping and collection documents will invariably need to be shown, along with the special documents, such as import licenses and import declaration forms, required in the country of destination.

---

into these foreign trade zones (FTZ) without paying import duties. Typically, this merchandise is either stored or used inside the zone in value-added activities such as processing, assembly, and manufacture. Eventually, this merchandise is either shipped from the FTZ to third-country markets, without ever being subject to duties in the FTZ, or imported into the customs territory of the country where the FTZ is located, at which time regular import duty must be paid.

In the United States, FTZs have been permitted since 1934. Initially, only limited activities such as storage, repacking, and transhipment were allowed. Subsequent changes in the law have sanctioned manufacture in the FTZs and excluded domestic processing costs from U.S. duties.

The Foreign Trade Board, within the Department of Commerce, reviews and approves applications to establish FTZs. All official ports of entry are entitled to a general purpose FTZ. Most FTZs are administered by states or port authorities and all are supervised by customs officials. Subzones may be established by individual firms at their own production facilities, but approval conditions are very tight.

In the United States, FTZs have been established mainly near primary ports of entry, industrial parks, and major warehouse facilities. The number of FTZs has expanded rapidly, from only 27 in 1975 to 247 in 1987. Many big U.S. companies use FTZs. The value of goods moved through them was nearly $40 billion in 1986, some 60 times greater than in 1975.[14] The rate of FTZ growth in the United States is likely to slow. Opposition to FTZs has emerged. Critics claim that FTZs harm the U.S. economy because they facilitate cheap imports at the expense of U.S.-made goods.

The primary reasons countries establish FTZs are to attract international trade and to generate local employment. For exporters and importers, use of FTZs can provide a number of advantages. It becomes possible to ship exports in bulk to FTZs where times can sort, package, and exhibit merchandise, or hold it in inventory without payment of import duties. All these capabilities generate financial savings and improve cash flow. Within FTZs, exporters can also establish processing, assembly, and manufacturing operations, all of which add value to imported components and commodities. This is particularly the case when the local cost of these value-added activities is low. As an example, low labor costs have attracted some firms to establish assembly activities in Panama's FTZ. The finished products are then re-exported, with no payment of Panamanian duties, to third-country markets in Latin and North America.

Assembly operations within FTZs are also attractive when import duties are lower for a fully assembled product than for components. Smith-Corona Corporation, for example, found that it was paying duty of up to 7 percent on imported parts used in its U.S. typewriter manufacturing operations; Japanese typewriters entered duty free. To meet this challenge, operations were consolidated into a single facility that was granted trade zone status. Components can now be imported duty free, and the finished products are not dutiable when shipped to customers in the United States.

Toyota has also pressed for foreign trade subzone status for its new auto plant in Kentucky. Subzone status will enable Toyota to avoid average duties of 3.3 percent on imported parts, and the firm will have to pay only the 2.5 percent rate for finished cars. Toyota estimates this will allow savings of up to $40 a car.[15]

Bonded warehouses share many of the characteristics of FTZs. Imports may be held, duty free but under bond, in a customs bonded warehouse for up to three years in the United States. The merchandise becomes dutiable only in this period if taken into the United States; no duty is paid if the goods are exported from the warehouse. During storage, the goods may be cleaned, sorted, and repackaged, and limited manufacturing is also sometimes allowed.

EXPORT ORGANIZATION

Indirect exporters, who rely extensively on help from intermediaries such as export management companies, may not find it necessary to establish an export infrastructure within the firm. However, as export business grows, serious exporters will need to establish a suitable organization for managing and controlling export operations and will have to recruit capable personnel to staff export functions. Over time, as the firm's export business and key strategy evolve, corresponding charges in the export organization can be expected.

Characteristics of the most commonly used approaches to organizing export operations are shown in Exhibit 17-3.

The export task force and *built-in* modes tend to be characteristic in the pre-export and experimental phases of export development or in those firms where the volume of export sales is low. The advantage of such structures are that they require little overhead. However, extensive use must be made of external inter-mediaries, and domestic managers with export responsibilities are frequently neither qualified for nor interested in these tasks.

With increasing export sales and experience there is often increased top management commitment to exporting. More resources are made available, greater direct control over export operations is sought and export departments are formed. Higher overhead costs result, but the advantages arising from increased export specialization and coordination often more than outweigh these expenses.

Continued growth of exports and other forms of international business often

---

EXHIBIT 17-3
Organizing for Export Operations

Export task force Usually made up of representatives from major functional areas. Typically responsible for assessing export potential and developing an export strategy, it is not a formal structure. It is most commonly used in the pre-export and experimental stages of export development.

Built-in export department No separate export department is established and most export related activities are a part time responsibility for domestic managers. However, an export manager is appointed who commonly concentrates on obtaining and processing export orders and who also seeks to coordinate export related activities.

Export department All major export activities are concentrated in a single specialized department. The role and status of the export manager and the resources available to this executive are greatly increased.

Export sales subsidiary/division A separate sales subsidiary or division, divorced from domestic operations, is assigned full profit responsibility for export and other international operations. Although it remains controlled by the parent company, it is normally given a high degree of autonomy. This allows for better measurement of export profitability and can reduce friction with domestic departments. Tax advantages may also accrue from the separate identity of the subsidiary. In the United States, for example, it may be appropriate to establish FSC or DISC status.

lead to the establishment of a separate international division responsible for all overseas activities. As export profits climb, U.S. exporters are likely to set up DISC or FSC subsidiaries through which export business is channeled and overseas branches and marketing subsidiaries may be established. Continued overseas growth may also require the development of more sophisticated organizational structures. By this time, many firms will be undertaking other forms of international business alongside exporting and it becomes less relevant to focus on export organization in isolation. More urgent is the need to develop structures appropriate for operating and controlling the firm's total portfolio of international operations.

Key variables to be evaluated when making decisions on export organization should include:

☐ Corporate export strategy

☐ Current and forecast level and scope of export operations

☐ Resource availability, especially of qualified export managers and financial resources

☐ Level of top management interest in exporting

☐ Degree of corporate control desired over export marketing and distribution

☐ Availability of export intermediaries at home and overseas, the nature of export distribution channels

☐ The financial, legal, and tax implications of alternative organizational structures.

EXPORT FINANCING _____

Raising Export Finance

The principal forms of export payment have already been reviewed in Chapter 14 where we noted that exporters prefer to make overseas sales on cash or near-cash terms to minimize risk and the need for export financing. In practice, cash or letter-of-credit terms are often unrealistic because of the high cost to the importer and the better competitive pressures that mandate more attractive terms. Importers who have proved their creditworthiness will be particularly insistent on obtaining credit terms.

When seeking financing, exporters generally have two objectives in mind, (1) to obtain working capital and (2) to guarantee payment for the goods shipped overseas. (Use of the exporters' own financial resources and existing bank lines of credit may be sufficient to finance some export production but does not meet the second objective.) Principal means of providing short-term financing for export contracts include the use of overdrafts, bank drafts, and letters of credit. These approaches were reviewed in Chapter 14. Other methods include buyer credit arrangements, factoring houses, and government-supported programs. The last method is discussed in detail later in this chapter.

Buyer credits involve making arrangements with a bank in the exporting country for the provision of credit to the prospective importer. In the case of export leasing, the exporter sells on cash terms, to a leasing company, which then leases the product to the foreign customer. *Factoring houses* purchase exporters' account receivables for cash. The arrangement is often of a nonrecourse nature, where the factorer assumes all the risk and collection problems associated with particular receivables. This service is not cheap, but it does assure prompt payment for export sales.

For many small- and medium-sized U.S. exporters, obtaining adequate export financing support from banks is not easy.[16] Many banks have reduced or eliminated their export finance departments in recent years. Morgan Guaranty Trust, for example, provided extensive export finance services in the 1970s. Now Morgan and many other big banks concentrate on financing big export deals; they are not interested in providing small loans. Many small banks are unfamiliar with foreign trade financing and are wary of making export loans.

The reasons for these problems are simple. Providing trade finance is expensive, time consuming, and risky. The return from this business is unattractive, particularly when dealing with smaller exporters. Providing finance for exports to indebted developing countries is particularly unattractive.

Bank trade financing tends to be more available in Japan, West Germany, and Britain than in the United States, essentially because profit margins there are greater. Foreign banks also provide around a third of the export credit granted in the United States. However, foreign banks also favor big exporters and concentrate on financing exports to countries they know well.

Government Programs

Government supported export financing is a major source of inexpensive credit that has generated considerable controversy and dispute. An ability to provide cheap, government subsidizied credit is often a crucial factor in major export contracts. As such, there has been a tendency for governments to underwrite below-market interest rates for export credits and to support the provision of loans to noncreditworthy foreign customers. Although efforts have been made to regulate the use of subsidized export credit terms as a means of obtaining business, it remains a serious source of friction.

The problems faced by U.S. exporters when seeking export finance from commercial banks are a big reason for recourse to government programs. This is particularly the case for smaller firms.

The principal U.S. agencies specializing in the provision of export finance or insurance which are similar in nature to the institutions found in other big trading nations, are discussed briefly below.

The Export-Import Bank (EXIMBANK)

The bank is an independent agency of the U.S. government that supplements and encourages commercial bank financing of U.S. exports of goods and services. The bank's budget exceeds $10 billion per annum, and some 15 percent of U.S.-manufactured exports receive some EXIMBANK support. Assistance is available mainly in the form of loan guarantees. The U.S. exporter obtains loans from commercial banks, which are then guaranteed by EXIMBANK. Guarantees are available for export working-capital loans, and for medium- and long-term export credit extended to foreign buyers by U.S. banks. A discount loan program supports U.S. banks making medium-term fixed-rate export loans. The bank makes some direct loans to foreign purchasers of major capital equipment, such as mining machinery and aircraft, where long-term financing from 5 to 15 years is required.

In recent years, EXIMBANK has incurred substantial losses of some $250 million per annum. These are principally due to loans made at uneconomic interest rates to customers of big U.S. exporters. Most of these loans were made prior to 1982, when the export credit agencies of many countries were offering subsidized export financing. Since 1982, when the industrial countries agreed to limit credit subsidies, this form of competition has been less intense. However, EXIMBANK losses reached a record $387 million in 1987. In 1988, the bank was in need of a $3 billion bailout.

The Foreign Credit Insurance Association

When exporting goods on credit, managers should obtain coverage against both commercial and political risk. The Foreign Credit Insurance Association (FCIA), which is an association of major insurance companies, administers the U.S. government's export credit insurance program in cooperation with private insurance companies and on behalf of EXIMBANK. Protection against *commercial risks,* such as buyer insolvency or protracted default, are underwritten by FCIA. Insurance for *noncommercial risks*—risks due to political events such as war, revolution, expropriation, and cancelled import licenses—is provided by EXIMBANK, which also reinsures some commercial risks.

Other U.S. Agencies

The U.S. *Overseas Private Investment Corporation* (OPIC) provides political risk insurance for U.S. firms making direct investment in developing countries. Loans for investment in LDCs are also available, and these may be used to finance the purchase of U.S. exports needed for implementing projects abroad. The *Commodity Credit Corporation* (CCC), an agency of the Department of Agriculture, provides export financing for eligible agricultural products. The *Agency for International Development* (AID) provides loans and grants to LDCs for development projects. AID funds are often used to finance imports from the United States. The *Small Business Administration* (SBA) has introduced a revolving line of credit for firms developing foreign markets and for pre-export financing. Under this program, the SBA guarantees a line of credit to small business exporters.

Medium-to-long export-financing loans are also available from the *Private Export Funding Corporation* (PEFCO), which is owned by some 50 U.S. banks and industrial firms. PEFCO provides long-term supplementary loans to foreign buyers of U.S. exports.

The financial sources and institutions discussed immediately above are specifically linked to exporting. However, many more internal and external sources of funds, that are note export specific, are used extensively to finance export operations.

COUNTERTRADE

Exporters are increasingly finding that it is necessary to engage in countertrade transactions when doing business overseas. It is estimated that well over 10 percent of world trade now involves countertrade deals. Historically, countertrade has been most associated with East–West trade, and over 35 percent of this trade is accounted for by countertrade transactions. Countertrade has expanded rapidly over the last 15 years and is increasingly common when doing business in the developing world and in major industrial markets. A 1983 survey by the National Foreign Trade Council [NFTC] of 110 U.S. firms engaging in countertrade,[17] indicated that the number of countries where countertrade transactions were requested increased from 15 in 1972 to 88 by 1983. The incidence of countertrade appears to be greatest in the case of large exporters engaged in military equipment, high technology, and capital project sales. A survey by the U.S. International Trade Commission found that in 1984 over $7 billion of U.S. exports were linked to countertrade arrangements, and that armaments accounted for 80 percent of these sales.

Each countertrade transaction is different; all, however, normally require extensive negotiation between buyer and seller. A general definition of *countertrade* is "commercial transactions in which the exporter agrees to accept products instead of cash as full or partial payment for exports."

There is no definitive classification of countertrade transactions, primarily because of the uniqueness of each transaction and the hybrid nature of many deals. Five primary forms of countertrade are identified below:

Barter A direct exchange of goods for goods. Cash payments are not required, and the exporter normally has the responsibility for selling the goods received in the transaction. Barter is unpopular with many firms because they may end up with goods that are difficult to sell, heavy financing costs, and storage costs (while the bartered goods are held in inventory).

Counterpurchase (Parallel Barter) A common form of countertrade in which the exporter agrees to make reciprocal purchases from the buyer within a given time—usually within a year. It requires the negotiation of two contracts, the first directly contingent on the second. The first contract is for the initial sale; the second, for the reciprocal purchase. Each contract requires payment mainly in cash. Counterpurchase allows the exporter to be paid in cash and gives time in which to find customers for the goods that they are required to buy. Counterpurchase transactions are not necessarily balanced, and there is often considerable flexibility regarding the products that the exporter is required to purchase.

Compensation or Buy-back In return for selling capital equipment, technology, and other proprietary rights, the exporter receives payment, in full or in part, from the output generated by the resulting production facilities established by the buyer. For example, a number of Western firms have built chemical plants in the Soviet Union under terms allowing the Russians to make partial payment (through resulting chemical exports) for periods up to 20 years.

Offset These are complex and often long-term transactions, particularly common in the case of military contracts (which typically include subcontracting, co-production, and counterpurchase). Governments are often involved in negotiating offset contracts. The contracts arrangements made in the sale of F-16 jet fighters to a number of foreign governments in Europe are a good example of an offset deal. During the life of the contract, F-16s are to be assembled in Europe in cooperation with local firms; major components are manufactured, under license, in Europe; and the U.S. exporter has agreed to buy components from firms in purchasing countries.

Switch Trading This is a means of facilitating transactions in which the exporter is unwilling or unable to market all or part of the goods received in a countertrade deal. Switch traders are specialized third-party trading houses that have developed extensive international networks of contacts and are willing, in return for a fee, to find buyers for countertraded goods. Although goods that are marketed by switch traders have reduced value to exporters, because of the need to pay substantial fees to the trader, this arrangement reduces the risk of the original transaction. Switch-trade deals often play an important role in facilitating bilateral barter-clearing deals between countries; they can lead to complex transactions involving many parties.

In the case of U.S. firms involved in countertrade, the 1983 NFTC survey indicated that the most prevalent forms of transaction were counterpurchase and offset. An overview of the frequency of the primary alternatives is shown in Figure 17-2. These data are from the NFTC survey. Industries in which the proportion

FIGURE 17-2   **Countertrade Methods: Incidence of Usage in U.S. Firms** (*Source:* National Foreign Trade Council, *Survey of Problems in U.S. Countertrade;* Fall 1983; data gathered from 64 firms.)

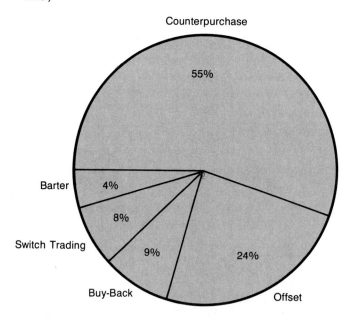

of exports requiring countertrade arrangements are particularly high include aerospace, construction, electronics and defense, where the percentage of export affected was 47, 27, and 20 percent, respectively. Frequently the goods offered in compensation are difficult to market either because of low quality or excess supply on world markets. Also, marketable products are often not offered in sufficient quantity to meet the compensation value. Bureaucratic problems, especially when negotiating with government agencies, and insufficient experience on the part of the firm and its foreign customers are also a source of delay and difficulties. The survey also indicated that substantial price discounts averaging around 12 percent were often necessary, along with fee payments to intermediaries when disposing of countertrade goods.

Despite these difficulties, over 80 percent of the firms in the 1983 survey reported breaking even or making a profit on countertrade transactions. Extensive use was made of third parties, notably trading houses and international banks, when evaluating and making countertrade transactions. Some 30 percent of the firms either employed a countertrade specialist or had established an inhouse trading subsidiary.

Most exporters do not willingly enter into countertrading, at least initially. Generally, the major reason for entering into countertrade deals is that they are a necessary requirement for an otherwise attractive business deal. However countertrade may also open access to low-cost sources of raw materials, components, and finished products that can either be used internally or sold for a profit. A willingness to undertake countertrade deals may also have a favorable public-relations impact in the foreign market.

The traditional reason why importers are interested in countertrade is a shortage of foreign exchange. This factor is still of major significance, particularly in Eastern Europe and in many developing markets. Countertrade also offers purchasers who have limited marketing skills the opportunity to utilize the contacts, distribution channels, and marketing capabilities of their suppliers. In the case of counterpurchase deals, the supplier of the manufacturing plant has a vested interest in helping the overseas customer to make maximum use of the imported technology and equipment and to upgrade product quality.

Countertrade also facilitates the maintenance of balanced bilateral trade. It can be used to disguise the exporter financing the transfer of funds out of the importing country, and dumping activities. In the case of dumping, for example, the nominal value for the countertraded goods is stated at an inflated price; in reality, the true exchange rate lies below this nominal rate. This tactic is also attractive for countries wishing to disguise the fact they are selling goods at a real price that lies below some agreed-on benchmark. An obvious example is that of the oil producer who wishes to disguise selling oil at a price below that agreed on in OPEC negotiations.

Countertrade deals are often inefficient and expensive because exporting firms are either forced to become traders—a role for which many are ill prepared—or to use expensive intermediaries. Risk is also high. Countertraded goods may be delivered late, be of poor quality, or have to be held in inventory for long periods, during which their value may decline sharply. Oil, for example, which is involved in many countertrade deals in the Middle East, fluctuates in value from day to day.

Countertrade is often highly complex. For example, one transaction by the U.S. firm Caterpillar, involved shipping construction equipment to Venezuela. Venezuela then exported iron ore to Romania which, in turn, shipped men's suits to Britain, receiving cash that was paid to Caterpillar.

The incidence of countertrade seems likely to increase. Exporters therefore need to be prepared to deal with countertrade proposals. Big exporters may find it desirable to set up inhouse trading organizations. In smaller firms, internal expertise is also necessary, even when extensive use is made of outside intermediaries for managing countertrade transactions. Although countertrading will normally increase the cost, time, and risk of exporting, an ability to countertrade is a prerequisite for achieving significant export sales in some overseas markets. Opportunities to profit from such transactions need to be recognized and exploited.

IMPORTING

The scope of importing activities is tremendous. At one end of the spectrum are small entrepreneurs like the Charleston, South Carolina, importer of $400,000 of traditional giftware from England every year. The firm buys directly from various British manufacturers and consolidates shipments into containers shipped to Charleston every week. Marketing is done mainly at some 30 major gift shows every year. Every day up to 50 boxes of goods are shipped to retailers. In operations such as this one, it is crucial to have good contacts with overseas producers and to have an effective domestic marketing program. Access to efficient international and domestic transport systems is also important. In the case of our example, this was provided by liner service to Charleston, an effective port system, and rapid U.S. distribution by truck lines. Financial resources and know-how sufficient to meet purchase, shipment, and inventory-holding costs and changes in exchange-rate relationships are essential.

At the other end of the scale, big importers face many of the same basic problems. There are some significant differences, however, particularly for big domestic retailers like Sears and domestic manufacturers like Wilson Sporting Goods, both of which import large volumes of merchandise. These firms have well-developed domestic distribution channels and are mainly interested in acquiring inexpensive products (from either independent firms or their own manufacturing subsidiaries) to sell under American brand names or as components for goods assembled in the U.S.

A good example of this type of importing is provided by the Schwinn Bicycle Co. of Chicago. Schwinn imports around 1 million bikes, annually some 70 percent of sales, from Taiwan's Giant Manufacturing Company. The design, paint, and all other details are specified by Schwinn, and the bikes are sold using U.S. brand names. In this situation, the importer exercises a much higher degree of control over the importation and marketing process than is the case for small entrepreneurs.

Import Regulation

A major priority for importers is rapid customs clearance of imports. Frequently, this is a time-consuming and costly process; arbitrary enforcement of complex regulations can result in many problems. Sometimes nations erect a web of regulations and controls purposely designed to exclude all but essential imports. These nontariff barriers often present insurmountable problems. Importers are well advised to steer clear of product lines heavily impacted by such protectionist measures. (The impact of these and other forms of protectionism has been reviewed in Chapters 3 and 4.)

Effective management of the importation process requires that the importer has knowledge of and a sound understanding of national import laws, import taxes, and control procedures. Areas of special concern include:

- Entry documentation
- Import duties and regulations
- Restricted merchandise
- Dumping regulations
- The import control process

Customs services usually play a major role in the implementation of import regulations and control procedures. Primary responsibilities of U.S. Customs include the assessment and collection of import duties and the enforcement of U.S. laws and treaties regarding imports. All merchandise entering the U.S. must be cleared by customs in a process involving review of entry documents and inspection, valuation, and assessment of merchandise.

In the entry process, documentation must be presented. Various documents describe the nature of the imported merchandise, present evidence of the right to entry, and include commercial invoices for valuation purposes. Surety, usually a bond, must also be posted to cover potential duty payments. For most products, the U.S. importer does not require an import license. However, permits or licenses issued by an appropriate agency are needed for the importation of specified products. Among these are alcoholic beverages, firearms, petroleum products, trademarked goods, and many agricultural products. Many products, including clothing, automobiles and television sets also have to satisfy special labeling, marking, and certification requirements.

In many countries, the services of a custom-house broker is useful in expediting importation. In the U.S., such brokers are licensed by customs. Many freight forwarders undertake this role. Custom-house brokers lease with shippers lease to ensure the rapid transit of goods, receive and prepare documents necessary for customs clearance, make arrangements for storage and inland shipment, advise on ways of minimizing import duty, and arrange bonds.

Importing and the Gray Market

In situations of price discrimination, opportunities for profitable arbitrage can open up if the cost of product transhipment is less than the price differential between markets. A number of barriers exist to discourage such gray market opportunities. Barriers to product transhipment posed by differences in product regulations or product use conditions, transport costs, import duties, opposition from the manufacturer and their overseas distributors, and the difficulty of achieving access to distribution channels will often limit arbitrage activity. Despite these hurdles, price differentials are sometimes large enough to encourage unofficial importing from low price into high price markets. This is particularly true when the product has a relatively high value in relation to its weight or volume (such as cameras) or when barriers to trade are not very significant (as is the case for some intra-Common Market trade).

Gray-market sales are likely to be a major irritant to authorized distributors in the importing country. They will lose sales to unauthorized distributors who market the cheap imports. Because of the reaction of official distributors and the loss of control over the distribution process, the original manufacturer of the good is also likely to be involved. Customers who have purchased the full-price product are likely to be irritated if cut-price products appear on the market. Local marketing plans may be disrupted by an inflow of cheap imports.

For these reasons, manufacturers often resort to a variety of measures to combat unofficial importing. The most obvious action is to tightly control the distribution process in low-price markets, ensuring that only bona fide distributors and customers can obtain the good. Where this is not feasible, it may be possible to attack unofficial distributors in the high-price markets by threats of legal action and extrapromotional support for authorized dealers. Warranty and service support may not be provided for goods purchased outside the usual channels, and efforts may be made to differentiate the product offered in markets where the price is low. The usual approach followed is to make inexpensive and minor cosmetic changes, such as in model name or number.

The exporter may also consider a world price policy. The price in all markets could be based on a base price which is only adjusted from market to market for such variables as transport cost, duties and the cost of order fulfillment. However, doing so limits the firm's opportunity to exploit differences in the pattern of demand and supply in overseas markets.

SUMMARY

Governments exhibit a high propensity to regulate international flows of trade and services, and exporters must be familiar with relevant laws and control procedures both at home and in overseas markets. In the United States, export controls regulate both the type of good that may be exported and the destination of exports. In the case of certain goods and destinations, a formal application for validated export licenses is required.

The encouragement of exporting is a major priority for many governments and public agencies. The most common initiatives include export subsidies, tax benefits for exporters, governmental assistance in financing and insuring export business, and the provision of government-funded services for exporters.

Subsidies invite retaliation and usually conflict with GATT obligations. Exporter tax breaks are common, as are government programs designed to assist exporters collect and evaluate information on foreign markets. The primary federal agency providing export assistance in the United States is the Department of Commerce. In the United States, tax incentives are available to firms setting up a Foreign Sales Corporation. This program has largely replaced the benefits available under the old DISC system.

Many firms begin exporting in an unplanned, random fashion. Outside agents and fortuitous events play a major role in the export startup. The availability of relevant information, patterns of domestic expansion at home, and the attitudes and perceptions of decision makers have been identified as major factors influencing the development of export activities.

Export development has been characterized as a learning situation in which management focuses first on overseas markets where barriers are minimal, and then gradually increase its resource commitment.

Because of the many barriers faced by exporters, exporting is commonly seen as a high-risk, low-priority activity. A strategic planning perspective is important when developing export operations. Explicit export objectives, functional strategies, and detailed export budgets need to be developed. The marketing plan should be a comprehensive, integrated, and detailed statement of export marketing strategy based on high-quality market research and forecasting.

Many firms make extensive use of third parties to manage the export marketing and distribution process. These indirect exporters benefit from the experience of external export facilitators and do not have to invest in an inhouse export organization. Direct exporters establish an internal export infrastructure capable of managing and controlling overseas business. Some exporters make extensive use of domestic intermediaries such as resident foreign buyers, export management companies, and export brokers, agents, and merchants. Major export distribution channels overseas include sales agents, distributors, foreign retailers, and a foreign sales branch or subsidiary.

Setting up appropriate export distribution channels and effective management of channel intermediaries is very important. Great care needs to be taken when selecting overseas intermediaries and when negotiating legal agreements. The Export Trading Company Act of 1982 encourages the formation of ETCs by waiving anti-trust implications and allowing banks to corporate in the formation of these ventures. However, to date, the Act has only had a limited impact.

Freight forwarders play an important role in facilitating the efficient shipment of exports. They are used extensively by most exporters.

Foreign Trade Zones have been established in the United States and elsewhere for processing, sorting, and holding goods in inventory—*without* paying import duties.

Most export sales require financing. Major possibilities include bank overdrafts, bank drafts, letters of credit, factoring, buyer credit arrangements, and government programs. The latter are often very attractive because of favorable financial terms and the use of less stringent measures of buyers' credit standing. In the United States, principal public agencies providing export finance or insurance include EXIMBANK and the FCIA.

Countertrade transactions are an increasingly important element of international trade. Five primary forms of countertrade may be identified: barter, counterpurchase, compensation, offset, and switch-trade deals. Usually exporters are unwilling participants in such transactions. However, countertrade is a prerequisite for certain export business and can also open access to low-cost products that may either be used internally or sold for a profit.

It is vital that importers are familiar with relevant import regulations and control procedures. In the United States, the customs service is primarily responsible for controlling imports. Many imports have to satisfy special requirements regarding labeling, markings, and certification. Customshouse brokers expedite the importation process for some.

When exporters adopt price discrimination policies, potential problems can arise on the gray market. Authorized distributors will lose business to these gray-market importers; action by the exporter may be necessary.

DISCUSSION QUESTIONS

1. What are the major provisions of the Export Trading Company Act of 1982? Why do you think U.S. ETCs have, to date, been less successful than the big Japanese trading companies?

2. Why do many international traders make extensive use of the services of freight forwarders and customshouse brokers?

3. Why is it essential to take great care when selecting foreign market channel intermediaries such as distributors and agents?

4. "U.S. export controls are unnecessarily strict and their cost to U.S. exporters and the economy is very high." Comment on this statement.

5. Why is it not always in the interest of a small exporter to set up an individually owned Foreign Sales Corporation? How might such firms best reduce their tax liability on export earnings?

6. How is the export development process affected by resource constraints and limited knowledge of foreign markets in exporting firms?

7. "The establishment of Foreign Trade Zones helps importing firms at the expense of local manufacturers." Do you agree with this view?

8. "EXIMBANK is a luxury that U.S. taxpayers are unable to afford." Comment on this statement.

9. Why have barter deals been superseded by more sophisticated forms of countertrade?

10. Why are many firms interested in eradicating the gray market? Identify retaliatory strategies.

ADDITIONAL READING

Czinkota, Michael R., and George Tesar, *Export Management* (New York: Praeger, 1982).

Delacroix, J., "Export Strategies for Small American Firms," *California Management Review,* Spring 1984.

Green, Robert T., and A. W. Allaway, "Identification of Export Opportunities: A Shift-Share Approach." *Journal of Marketing,* Winter 1985.

Hall, R. Duane, *International Trade Operations* (Jersey City, N.J.: Unz, 1983).

Malekzadeh, Ali R., and Samuel Rabino, "Manufacturers' Export Strategies," *International Marketing Review,* Winter 1986.

Nollen, Stanley D., "Business Costs and Business Policy for Export Controls," *Journal of International Business Studies,* Spring 1987.

Rosson, Philip J., and Stanley D. Reid, *Managing Export Entry and Expansion* (New York: Praeger, 1987).

U.S. Department of Commerce, *A Basic Guide to Exporting* (Washington, D.C.:, 1987).

Walters, Peter G. P., "A Study of Planning for Export

Operations," *International Marketing Review,* Autumn 1985.

Wood, Van R., and Jemy R. Goolsby, "Foreign Market Information Preferences of Established US Exporters," *International Marketing Review,* Winter 1987.

Yaprak, Attila, "An Empirical Study of the Differences between Small Exporting and Non-Exporting U.S. Firms," *International Marketing Review,* Summer 1985.

ENDNOTES

1. See Export Administration Regulations, Article 379, 1(a).
2. Stanley D. Nollen, "Business Costs and Business Policy for Export Controls," *Journal of International Business Studies* Spring 1987.
3. See *The Wall Street Journal,* February 10, 1987.
4. See *The Economist,* February 14, 1987.
5. R. North, and R. Feinschreiber, "From DISC to FSC: What, Why and How," *Export Today,* Spring 1985.
6. J. J. Korbel, and C. M. Bruce, "Shared FSCs: An Innovative, New Benefit for Small and Medium-Sized Exporters," *Business America,* January 20, 1986.
7. Lawrence S. Welch, "Managerial Decision Making: The Case of Export Involvement," Norwegian School of Management, Working Paper Series 1982, N. 14.
8. Warren J. Bilkey, "An Attempted Integration of the Literature on the Export Behavior of Firms," *Journal of International Business Studies,* (Spring–Summer, 1978).
9. Paul, F. Wiedersheim, Hans C. Olson, and Lawrence S. Welch, "Pre-export Activity: The First Step in Internationalization," *Journal of International Business Studies,* Spring–Summer 1978.
10. S. Tamer Cavusgil, "Differences Among Exporting Firms Based on Their Degree of Internationalization," *Journal of Business Research,* June 1984.
11. Johanson, J. and Vahlne, J. E. "The Internationalization Process of the Firm—A Model of Knowledge Development and Increasing Commitments." *Journal of International Business Studies,* Spring/Summer, 1977.
12. J. V. Lacy, "The Export Trading Company Act is Alive, Healthy, and Promoting U.S. Exports." *Business America,* February 16, 1987.
13. See, for example, Lyn S. Amine, S. Tamir Cavusgil, and R. I. Weinstein, "Japanese Sogo Shosha and the U.S. Export Trading Companies," *Journal of the Academy of Marketing Science,* Fall 1986.
14. See K. Slocum, "Import Battle," *The Wall Street Journal,* September 30, 1987.
15. See *The Wall Street Journal,* November 17, 1987.
16. See *The Wall Street Journal,* May 14, 1987.
17. See results from "Survey of Problems in U.S. Countertrade," Fall 1983, the National Foreign Trade Council Foundation under the direction of W. A. Bussard.

PART FOUR CASES
8. RXR Computers Ltd.

In looking over the sales figures for 1987, Bob Dupuis, a senior manager for RXR Computers Ltd., a maker of personal computers (PCs) in Atlanta, Georgia, noticed an increasing number of unsolicited export orders from France and a number of sales to foreign students (apparently European) from local universities. Michelle Platard, one of his part-time assistants, a French MBA intern at Georgia State University, had frequently mentioned the growing French computer market and the lack of any competition for the IBM, Amstrad, Honeywell-Bull, Tandon, and Olivetti PCs that dominate the market. Dupuis wondered if there was a possibility of expanding operations overseas into the European market, particularly in France, and decided to put Platard to work on a feasibility study.

COMPANY HISTORY

RXR Computers began in 1978 as a mail-order electronic-supply house. It was started by two friends, James Richman and Steven Wilder. Both attended electrical engineering school at Georgia Tech and had worked for large computer companies after graduation. Dissatisfied with the stifling and rigid atmospheres prevailing at these companies, they saved money, quit their jobs, and started RXR Computers. Originally begun as a mail-order outlet offering supplies and components to the electronics hobbyist, RXR found a niche in the PC market and began marketing an IBM PC-compatible clone through the mail and its local showroom. RXR started assembling IBM PC-compatible clones in 1983 after it became clear that IBM had set the industry standard for personal computing and after observing the success of other clone makers in meeting business and home users' demands for a more affordable alternative. The owners were ex-

This case was prepared by Professor Frank L. DuBois, The American University, Washington, D.C.

tremely pleased with the success to date. RXR had minimal outstanding debt and a large cash balance. The owners were anxious to reinvest the excess cash into market expansion.

RXR's PRESENT SITUATION

Sales of PC clones had soared in the four years since they had been introduced. Wilder and Richman had moved ahead quickly in the face of a rapidly growing market both in the Atlanta area and the United States. It was apparent that consumer resistance to the purchase of PCs for home and office use was falling rapidly as people became familiar with their capabilities and features, systems became standardized, and high-quality applications software became widely available. The company was now spending a significant amount of money on splashy full-color ads in computer magazines such as *PC World*, *PC Week*, *PC Magazine*, and *Computer Shopper*. Ads in the *Atlanta Constitution*'s weekly business section attracted walk-in business at the company's showroom in downtown Atlanta, and RXR had received a good response from an occasional ad in the *Wall Street Journal*. A major New York discount camera and electronic supply house also carried RXR's product line.

THE PRODUCT OFFERING

At a retail price of $700, the lowest-priced RXR machine, the T9000, was essentially a carbon copy of the basic IBM PC XT that first appeared in 1984. However, the T9000 had several advantages over the XT. Its turbo motherboard increased processing speed from 4.77 MHz to 8 MHz. This allowed the T9000 to process complicated spreadsheets and other applications software much faster than the basic XT. Also, the T9000 came standard with 640 KB of random access memory (RAM), giving it still more speed and processing capacity. Two 360 KB 5.25″ floppy disk drives came standard on the base model with the possibility of substituting a 20 or 30 MB hard drive for one of the floppy drives at an additional charge of $150 and $200, respectively. Most users opted to add the fixed disk drive. A color monitor and graphics adapter could be added to the RXR system for an additional $300. A 3.5″ 720 KB floppy drive could also be substituted for a 5.25″ drive for an additional $75. The 3.5″ drive allowed compatibility with the new generation IBM System 2 PCs.

The System 2 IBM line was introduced with much fanfare in April 1987. These machines offered better graphics capabilities than the competition through a more sophisticated graphics adapter, and they took up about half the desk space of the original IBM PC thanks to the use of surface mount technology.[1] Despite these improvements, some critics claimed that the new line was not a great improvement over the earlier IBM PCs and suggested that buyers would receive greater value from the purchase of a PC-compatible clone.

The newest RXR model, the T9500, was introduced in late 1986 and featured the Intel 80286 microprocessor on the motherboard. This gave it a processing speed of 12 MHz, which was slightly faster than the industry standard IBM AT but at a considerably lower price than the AT and its System 2 counterpart, the Model 50. The T9500 sold for $1,100 in its base configuration with one 1.2 MB floppy drive. IBM model 50s started at $2,500 and included a 20 MB hard drive; prices increased rapidly as new features were added. Hard drives and color monitors for the RXR T9500 were available for the prices stated earlier.

RXR had no product offerings in the upper end of the PC performance range. However, the firm was exploring the possibility of assembling a machine based on the 80386 microprocessor. This

was the most powerful microchip then available but there was a serious shortage of these chips. RXR did not feel that they could justify designing and manufacturing a 386-based computer until the microchip supply improved.

RXR is what is known in the computer industry as a Value-Added Reseller (VAR). VARs differ from mainline PC manufacturers in that they are not involved in the manufacture of any computer components; instead, they assemble computers using components sourced from both domestic and foreign manufacturers. For example, the T9000, RXR's most popular model in the United States, uses components sourced through a variety of manufacturers. (See Exhibits 1 and 2 of the feasibility study at the end of this case.) RXR purchases these components essentially off the shelf and then assembles them into a finished personal computer in a facility on the outskirts of Atlanta. The Georgia location was originally chosen because of its excellent transportation facilities and its proximity to a major source of electrical engineering talent. RXR was able to minimize investment in components and finished goods because of numerous transportation options in the Atlanta area. Because their buying volume was often relatively low, RXR typically worked through a distributor to source components. For some components, such as cases, monitors, and some molded parts, RXR sourced directly from the manufacturer.

Sales had grown to the point that the firm exercised some clout with its suppliers and could negotiate reasonably favorable price and delivery terms. Because of the numerous manufacturers of the different components, the firm was not wedded to a single supplier for any of its purchased items. Components, for the most part, were totally compatible across brands. This helped to ensure excellent service from vendors and distributors.

RXR's success was based on a reliable product that offered the most commonly demanded options backed by a very favorable warranty. Software was provided through the normal channels, for RXR machines were 100 percent compatible with the applications software written for the IBM PC. This meant that Lotus 1-2-3, Wordstar, Wordperfect, DBaseIII Plus and other application packages could be used on RXR machines with no problem. The only major piece of software RXR provided with its machines was the MS-DOS version 3.2 operating

---

[1] Surface mount technology allows the manufacturer to pack more components onto a printed circuit board than did older thru-board technology. Thru-board technology involved drilling holes in the circuit board and then soldering components such as capacitors, resistors, and diodes into place. Surface mount technology entails simply tacking specially designed components to the surface of the board.

Export ?!s to focus on

system. Even this was a $99 option. The mail-order channel counted on sales to users that were already familiar with PCs through work or school. These users typically knew exactly what they wanted and did not require much after-sales service other than a toll-free call to a staff technician when setting up the machine for the first time.

The majority of RXR sales were through the mail, but the company was having some success in establishing distribution beachheads with smaller, regional computer stores. The larger chains were still the domain of the larger IBM-compatible makers such as Epson, Kaypro, Compaq, and Tandy had sole control of their large distribution network of Radio Shack stores. The key to success in gaining more traditional distribution channels was the ability to offer favorable credit terms to outlets that were able to promise a certain guaranteed amount of display space for RXR's wares. The most popular of these outlets were the independent computer sellers that could always be found in every large city and in university towns.

Management was pleased with this arrangement but was having trouble expanding this segment of the distribution chain because of intense competition. Due to the ease of becoming a VAR, RXR had to compete with what seemed like an infinite variety of clone makers. The foreign threat was also an issue; much of RXR's most serious competition was coming from clone makers in South Korea and Taiwan. For this reason, RXR wanted to investigate other markets.

The firm felt that the European market might provide an opportunity for growth by providing computer users with a less expensive but still high-quality alternative to the more costly products offered by mainline computer manufacturers. How should they go about doing this? Should the company export its standard machine from the United States? Would a foreign sales company arrangement be advantageous? Should RXR set up assembly operations in Europe, perhaps in Spain or Portugal, where wages are the lowest in the Common Market? Or, should it look into the use of a foreign trade zone[2] on the East Coast to set up assembly operations for export sales? What adaptations would have to be made to the computers? And what legal regulations, such as export licensing, would the firm have to contend with in getting the machines from the United States to France? Finally, what would be the best way of financing export sales? These questions and more were sure to arise in the market-expansion discussions that were scheduled to be held after the senior managers in the company had received and had a chance to comment on Michelle Platard's feasibility study.

---

[2] A Foreign Trade Zone (FTZ) is a special area designated by the U.S. Department of Commerce that allows firms to import components duty free if the component is assembled into a final product that is destined for export. Thus, by manufacturing in an FTZ or by having a facility designated an FTZ subzone, a company can avoid paying duty on any components that will eventually be exported to another country in a final product. Savings are also possible through the deferral of import duties. If the final product is sold in the U.S. market, the manufacturer pays duties on the imported components only when the final product actually leaves the FTZ and enters the U.S. market.

The Feasibility Study

To: Mr. Robert Dupuis
From: Michelle Platard
RE: Market Feasibility Study–France
Date: March 15, 1988

I. *Current Market Analysis*

Ia. *Market Characteristics*

The French market for personal computers is thriving, with all indicators pointing to continued growth of sales. The majority of French PCs are imported from outside suppliers. In 1983, PC imports were valued at $166 million. By 1987, imports of PCs at the lower end of the cost scale were expected to reach $517 million, a growth rate of 211 percent in four years! By far, the leading supplier country was the United States, with 59 percent of the imports in 1983 and an expected 77 percent import share in 1985 (see Tables 1 and 2 for details).

TABLE 1
Market for Micro Computer Systems in France
1983 and 1987 (estimated)
(in millions of U.S. $)

	1983	1987
Micro Computers—		
transportable/professional		
Production	24	110
Imports	137	332
Exports	8	50
Market Size	153	392
Micro computers—home/hobby		
Production	5	70
Imports	29	185
Exports	2	30
Market Size	32	225

Note: Computer segments are based on purchase price in U.S. dollars (in 1983) as follows: transportable/professional segment $1,000–$5,000; home/hobby segment, under $1,000.

Source: *Country Market Survey: Mini and Micro Computer Systems in France*, U.S. Department of Commerce, December 1985.

The Commerce Department's forecasts in Tables 1 and 2 are rather cautious. More recent data indicates that PC sales increased over 30 percent in 1986 to sales of some $250 million.[3] At any rate, growth in this market is sure to be strong over the next few years as French users become more computer literate and demands for computing power from small businesses increase. With some 77 percent of PC imports coming from the United States and with imports accounting for about 80 percent of the market, this represented a $155 million market for U.S. computer manufacturers in 1986 with a probable growth rate of at least 25 percent annually over the next several years.

The French popular magazine *L'Expansion* estimated an annual growth rate for microcomputer deliveries of 19 percent from 1985 to 1991 with the number of units delivered reaching 831,510 units in 1991 (see Table 4). This would put France in third place behind the United Kingdom and West Germany with regard to the total number of personal computers installed.

Ib. Market Segments

The French Market for personal computers can be characterized as fragmented into two parts, IBM plus IBM compatible and the rest. Much to the discomfort of French hardware makers, IBM has managed to carve out an increasingly dominant position in this lucrative market, thanks to their long-term presence in the European Community. Similar to what happened in the U.S. market, manufacturers of personal

---

[3] "World Market Report: France," *Electronics*, January 13, 1986, p. 44.

TABLE 2
French Imports of Micro Computer Systems by Leading
Supplier Countries
(in Millions of U.S. $)

	1983	1985
Micro Computers— **transportable/professional**		
United States	96 (70%)	188 (76%)
Japan	7	25
Italy	4	8
United Kingdom	3	5
Netherlands	2	3
Other	25	19
Total	137	248
Micro computers—home/hobby		
United States	19 (32%)	59 (81%)
Japan	4	6
United Kingdom	2	2
Germany	1	2
Other	3	4
Total	59	73

Source: *Country Market Survey: Mini and Micro Computer Systems in France*, U.S.
Department of Commerce, December 1985.

computer systems have been forced to adopt the IBM PC standard operating system
or suffer declining market shares and eventual obsolescence.

The PC is no longer in the introductory stage of the product life cycle in the
United States, and it has become established as a mature product. IBM has played
a leadership role in developing the PC into a standardized product with an industry
standard operating system. The few manufacturers that have survived with non-

TABLE 3
Micro Computer Market Shares in
France, 1985

Company	# of Units Installed	Share (%)
Apple	137,000	26
IBM	101,000	19•
Bull	42,000	8
Olivetti-Logabox	36,000	7
SMT-Goupil	25,000	5
Victor	16,000	3
Hewlett-Packard	15,000	3
Other Makers	162,000	29
Total	534,000	100

Source: *L'Expansion*, September, 1986.

TABLE 4
Comparative Growth Rates: Micro Computer Deliveries in Europe, 1985 and 1991

	Units Delivered Each Year		Annual Growth Rate (%)
	1985	**1991**	
Spain	86,880	406,870	29.4
Austria	29,370	121,930	26.8
Italy	192,200	664,000	22.9
West Germany	266,660	921,150	22.9
Netherlands	100,280	287,830	19.2
France	*291,050*	*831,510*	*19.1*
Finland	30,530	86,900	19.1
Sweden	67,430	173,700	17.1
Belgium	58,570	146,250	16.5
Switzerland	49,030	120,300	16.1
Norway	35,180	84,720	15.8
United Kingdom	397,150	950,460	15.6
Denmark	52,620	114,370	13.8
Total	1,656,990	4,909,990	19.8

Source: *L'Expansion*, September, 1986.

IBM standard systems have been able to carve out small specialized niches in the market, but they have not been able to compete on the same scale as IBM and the IBM compatible.

In France, the largest French PC maker, Honeywell-Bull, introduced its first IBM compatible in 1983 and has seen sales increases, thanks to the availability of a "Made in France" alternative to the IBM PC.[4] IBM was also helped by Bull's switch because of the respectability that their operating system now has with French users. However, IBM dominates the market because of local production facilities and an extensive dealer network.

The exception, Apple, has managed to capture much of the education market and a significant portion of the home market in France. With its vast array of educational software and with a strong marketing focus in these two segments, Apple, has developed an easy-to-use product of widespread popularity in the schools. In fact, in 1985, Apple had a market share in France of 26 percent with an installed base of 137,000 machines (see Table 3). However, in the university and professional market segments, Apple's domination ends and IBM and IBM-compatible clones predominate. Apple has never been able to exploit the upper end of the PC market as has IBM because it lacks computing power and software development for professional applications. For PCs that use IBM's operating system, software can be easily transferred from one machine to another. This fosters a trend towards standardization that feeds on itself.

---

[4] "It's Still Big Blue in Any European Language," *Electronic Business*, October 1, 1986, p. 132.

II. *Opportunities and Issues*

Based on the above discussion, the French market stands out as a potentially lucrative market opportunity for RXR. Development of an Apple compatible has thus far been stymied by Apple's reluctance to part with the technical details of its proprietary operating system. Thus, the following discussion is focused on the assumption that RXR markets its basic IBM compatible machines in France. Market growth in this segment is strong and there is every indication that it will remain so in the future. With regard to domestic competition, the local subsidiaries of the large U.S. multinationals are the largest threats.

In particular, IBM—with its large manufacturing presence in France and 19 percent of the market—is the largest and most dangerous competition in this market segment. Looking at strictly French competition, the list is brief, Bull and the others. "Others" refers to SMT-Goupil, with 5 percent of the market, and Leanard, with an even smaller share. There are more manufacturers in France (close to 30), but their market shares are so small that they are relatively insignificant when compared to Apple and IBM. Other competition comes from Olivetti (Italy), Victor (England), and Hewlett-Packard (United States). As is apparent from Table 4, none of these firms has more than 7 percent of the French market.

A potential problem is selling computers in the French market is the "Buy French" attitude that pervades the market. In many cases, the French purchaser will overlook a superior imported product in favor of a French-made item. In the computer segment, this was a problem until IBM's dominance was asserted in the early 1980s and French computer buyers found it increasingly hard to justify purchase of a more costly, inferior French product.

Also important is the issue of consumer resistance in the French—and for that matter, the European—computer markets. In comparison to the United States, the French and the Europeans are probably 2 to 3 years behind in the adoption of information technology and office automation. This lag has nothing to do with lack of technical sophistication of the French consumer; it is more a manifestation of European reluctance to change until the benefits of change are proven. In the light of predictions that indicate faster growth and a growing acceptance of the computer as an everyday part of French life, it appears that this resistance has diminished considerably.

Contributing to increased acceptance of computerization in everyday life is a unique program sponsored by the French Postal, Telephone, Telegraph Company (PTT) that hopes to put a toaster-sized computer console into the home of every telephone subscriber in the network. The Minitel, as it is called, is provided at a nominal charge and allows subscribers to tap into various privately owned databases and online information sources via telephone lines. The user pays by the amount of time spent accessing the database (about $9 per hour). With the Minitel, the user can find telephone numbers, pay bills, purchase airline tickets, make theater reservations, get weather reports, and even access dating services. As of late 1986, the network was comprised of 2 million units with expectations of 3 million units by 1987.[5]

With widespread acceptance of the Minitel, consumer resistance to PCs should diminish even further and the use of computers to increase productivity and to save time will become as common as using a telephone. For the French consumer, a PC offers capabilities in word processing, spreadsheet analysis, professionals, and games

---

[5] "Punching Up Wine and Fois Gras," *Time*, December 1, 1986, p. 65.

and education. A PC coupled with a Minitel interface provides the user with Minitel capability plus PC flexibility. While the PTT offers the Minitel for a nominal charge to subscribers, it is also expected to pique the curiosity of the French consumer and lead to increased PC sales.

With respect to other sources of concern to a U.S. exporter, one must consider the presence of barriers to trade that might exist in the French computer market. According to the market profile report done in 1984 for the U.S. Department of Commerce[6] "France erects no nontariff barriers (NTBs) against intake of computers and peripheral equipment and none are yet foreseeable." The absence of French NTBs probably reflects a noncompetitive PC industry; it does not appear that the situation will change soon.

However, this was not true in the case of VCR exports from Japan in the early 1980s. At that time, French Customs was guilty of de facto protection of its failing VCR industry. It unnecessarily complicated the import process for Japanese VCR manufacturers by requiring all VCR imports to be cleared through a small understaffed point of entry in Poitiers, a town in rural France. Such is not expected to be the case with personal computers because of the weakness of the domestic industry, and it is unlikely that France will restrict the import of anything as important to the vitality of its economy as computer equipment. Some concern has been felt in France about U.S. export controls for computers with possible military applications. However, any controls enacted will target machines at the upper end of the price and sophistication spectrums and should not spill over into the low-cost commodity PC segment. The only apparent barrier to trade is the common EEC external tariff of 4.9 percent.

III. Market Strategies and Sales Objectives

IIIa. Product Strategy

In the light of the above discussion it is proposed that RXR begin exporting and launching their IBM-compatible personal computer clone on the French Market. This computer will be similar in form and function to the IBM PC and PC XT but will carry a lower price tag and, if possible, will be available with an optional tie into the Minitel network. In order to combat IBM's dominance in the French market, the product will compete essentially on price. However, with the available technology and the presence of commodity components, a machine superior to the IBM product could easily be manufactured in the United States and exported to France at a profit. Thus, the proposed offering is as follows:

An IBM PC XT clone configured with
- ☐ 640K memory based on the Intel 8088-2 microprocessor
- ☐ 2 360K 5.25″ floppy drives
- ☐ Monochrome monitor with color optional
- ☐ IBM "AT" style keyboard adapted to French character set
- ☐ 8 expansion slots
- ☐ 220-volt power supply
- ☐ Phoenix BIOS (Basic Input/Output System)

---

[6] "Profile Report on the Mini and Micro Computer Systems Market in France," *Tactical Marketing Limited*, London, April 1984.

- Full IBM compatibility
- One-year warranty on parts and labor

Various options would be made available through the dealer network, such as a 20 or 30 MB hard disk, the interface card for the Minitel network (which would have to be sourced through a third party manufacturer), and a choice of color or black-and-white monitors. Options in terms of software would not be available through RXR but would be taken care of by software vendors for the French market. The only product adaptations that needs to be made is substitution of a modified keyboard to accommodate the French character set, a power supply to accommodate a 220-volt 50-cycle power system and, optionally, translation of the instruction manual from English to French.

Translation of the supporting manuals and instructions is not mandated by the normally stringent French Language Restrictions because of an exception in the code that excludes "... computer, business machine, and aerospace components and products since the use of the English language in these sectors is the accepted norm and French equivalents do not always exist."[7] However, to obviate potential warranty problems and to ensure acceptability of the product to potential users, it is suggested that all supporting documentation and manuals be translated into French. This could be done reasonably inexpensively through a university language department. French versions of the MS-DOS operating system are also readily available in the French market.

IIIb. Pricing Strategy

The product should be priced as low as possible in order to gain market share and user acceptability as rapidly as possible. In the U.S. market, RXR is able to offer a similar product at a cost of 30 percent lower than a comparable IBM product. It is well known that IBM avoids price competition and prefers to concentrate on competing on the basis of quality and service support. As the quality of components has become more or less standardized, this is no longer the legitimate issue that it was in the early stages of the PC product life cycle. Also working to the exporters' favor are the high price levels in the French market.

Relative to the U.S. market, the French PC market in early 1988 is in the final stages of the introductory phase of the product life cycle. Firms competing in this market are charging prices almost double what would be paid in the United States for the same item. One estimate puts the cost of one dollar of computer hardware in France at 12 to 14 francs.[8] With the exchange rate now stabilized at around 5.8 Ffr to the dollar, this gives considerable pricing flexibility to the U.S. exporter while putting pressure on the French manufacturer that does not have the same access to sources of supply as in the well-developed U.S. market. The various costs relevant to the manufacture of a basic IBM-compatible PC in the United States are shown in Exhibit 3.

Assembly in an FTZ with export to France is another possible alternative to serving the market. This would allow some savings to be made in components

---

[7] *Exporter's Encyclopedia: 1986*, Dun and Bradstreet Corporation, p. 2.518.

[8] "Cocorico à Lilliput," *L'Expansion*, 12:25, September 1986.

directly sourced from overseas manufacturers. Presently, tariffs on computer components run anywhere from 0 percent to 5 percent. There are no tariffs on components sourced from countries that have a most-favored nation trading status with the United States. Depending on sales projections, RXR could increase its direct sourcing from overseas manufacturers and set up operations in the Atlanta FTZ.

Given a production cost of $640 and a 20 percent markup from the plant, the final price required in the French market is as follows:

f.o.b. plant price (20% markup)	$768.00	
Air freight and insurance	50.00	
Landed c.i.f. value		$ 818.00
4.9% E.E.C. duty	40.08	
18.6% value-added tax (VAT)	152.15	
Cost to distributor		1,010.23
25% importer/distributor markup	252.56	
VAT on markup	46.98	
Retailer cost		1,309.77
25% retailer markup	327.44	
VAT on markup	60.90	
Final price in dollars		$1,698.11

This final price corresponds to a selling price of approximately 9,850 Ffr at an exchange rate of around 5.8 Ffr to the dollar. Of course, this is a tentative price and is based on a number of assumptions (airfreight costs and the required markups and VAT at each stage of the distribution channel). The typical selling price for this type of system in the United States is in the neighborhood of $1,100 to $1,200 if purchased through a retail outlet. This compares very favorably given the earlier estimate of computer hardware selling in France at close to double U.S. prices. To reiterate, a final selling price in France of 9,850 Ffr would allow for reasonable markups at every stage of the distribution channel while still offering considerable value to the purchaser. Based on the 12–14 Ffr per one dollar of hardware assumption, an equivalent machine would probably sell for around 13,200 Ffr in France. However, since this computed price may be on the low side, before setting a final price, it is suggested that potential retailers be consulted.

IIIc.   *Distribution Strategy*

Direct sales by foreign manufacturers to French users are extremely rare, even for large computer systems. Buyers demand a local presence in the market to ensure service support. Thus, it is common practice in France that all sizes of microcomputers be sold through an importer/agent and smaller micros be sold to private consumers and small businesses through a dealer network. The pattern of distribution for personal computer sales in France breaks down as follows.[9]

---

[9] "Country Market Survey: Mini and Micro Computer Systems in France," *U.S. Department of Commerce: International Trade Administration*, December 1985.

Channel	% of Sales
Specialist dealer	84
Department store	7
Mail order	5
Other	4
	100%

The key to a successful entry into the French market is establishing a relationship with a nationally known and accepted dealer. French users are wary of after-sale complications and possible lack of support, so marketers must cultivate French dealers and distributors. This requires assistance in making contact with potential dealers in France and entering into negotiations with them. The most probable avenues for this approach are the use of U.S. Department of Commerce assistance in contacting French distributors, and attendance at one or more of the many computer trade shows that take place annually in France and Europe.

The distributor selected would be expected to offer service support for the product and should be well qualified to assist the buyer with any problems and to provide a full range of system software. This requires provision of spare parts and technical service by the distributor.

IIId. Promotional Strategy

Concurrent with the introduction of the product in France, print media should be used to stimulate interest in the RXR PC. Advertising touting the product's price and performance advantages should be purchased in the major French computer magazines. If possible, the product should be introduced through a nationwide chain of distribution outlets to build on the synergy that a national introduction would create.

Advertising should be targeted with a specific customer in mind, specifically, small businesses, professionals, students, and other consumers seeking to move up from smaller, less powerful machines. Also important is the first-time buyer who uses a PC on the job and wishes to have one at home. The professional market should be particularly lucrative. In Europe, which has a white-collar population roughly equal to that of the United States, there were only 3.05 million PCs installed by the end of 1985, while the U.S. equivalent was 9 million.[10] The consumer sector, which in 1987 was expected to snap up 63 percent of the 480,000 microcomputers sold in France (see Table 5), should also not be ignored.

Adaptation of the promotional message will not be required as the same product characteristics that serve to generate sales in the United States—low cost, high performance, and IBM compatibility—will draw customers. One point, though, does need to be stressed, the availability of a local service outlet in the event that any problem requiring warranty service occurs.

IIIe. Sales Objectives

Without a first hand look at the market and discussions with potential distributors, it is difficult to make exact sales forecasts for a product. However,

---

[10] "Europe: Expanding in Year of Optimism," *Electronic Business*, July 1, 1986.

TABLE 5
Expenditures in France for Micro-Computer Systems by Major
Institutional and Professional/Consumer Sectors
(1983 and Projected 1987, in $ Millions)

	1983 Units	Value	1987 Units	Value
Institutional sectors				
Government	767	3	2,726	7
Finance and insurance	3,522	14	9,860	25
Manufacturing	1,606	6	6,380	16
Utilities	201	1	580	1
Transportation	1,205	5	4,350	11
Communications	730	3	3,480	9
Retailing and wholesale	4,501	16	13,340	33
Health care	785	3	1,740	4
Education	2,829	11	10,440	26
Research institutions	1,533	6	3,480	9
Other	1,021	5	1,624	4
Subtotal	18,250	73	58,000	145
Professional/consumer sectors				
Physicians	2,183	9	8,472	21
Attorneys	2,910	12	12,708	32
Accountants	10,185	41	25,416	64
Mgmt. consultants	10,185	41	29,652	74
Other professions	12,368	49	42,360	106
Consumer	34,290	139	304,992	762
Subtotal	72,751	291	423,600	1,059
Total	91,001	364	481,600	1,204

Source: *Country Market Survey: Mini and Micro Computer Systems in France*, U.S.
Department of Commerce, December 1985.

assuming that all goes well and the product is well received in the marketplace, an assumption of a 0.5 percent market share in the first year is not unreasonable. The following estimates are based on the assumption of a market size of $252 million in 1986 with 25 percent growth in 1987 to give a total market of $315 million in 1987.

Probable growth from 1987 to 1988 of 20 percent will result in a $378 million market in 1988. Continued 20 percent growth will produce a total market in 1989 of $454 million. Recall from Table 4 that the 1985 to 1991 growth rate is expected to be 19 percent. With an introduction date in late 1988, we could expect sales volume for 1988–1989 to be around $2,270,000 based on an approximate final price at the retail level in U.S. dollars of $1,700. This would require the export and sale of about 1,335 units of the RXR PC exclusive of any add-ons.

With demand growth in 1988–1989 to the levels that the Department of Commerce estimated for 1987 (see Table 1) sales might well reach 1600 units or more. Thus, given these assumptions and some tentative conclusions about the size of the market, we could conservatively expect to sell between 1,200 and 1,600 units in 1988–1989. This would result in first-year revenues on an f.o.b. (plant) basis of between $921,000 and $1,228,800. These revenues would produce a pretax income of $153,600 to $294,800 respectively, assuming a manufacturing cost of $640 per unit (manufacturing costs could undoubtedly be decreased as sales volumes rise). Looking ahead to 1989–1990, it would not seem unreasonable to expect sales to increase rapidly if the product is well accepted in the market. This is contingent, however, on the assumption of stable exchange rates and limited competitor retaliation. For 1989–1990 sales between 2,500 and 4,000 units are expected.

At this time, however, much depends on the availability of a good supplier network to facilitate the sales effort. Given that this requirement can be fulfilled, entry into the French market should proceed as soon as possible. It appears quite obvious that the French will be receptive to a well-made, competitive, and low-cost alternative to IBM's product line. Every attempt should be made to secure a reliable distribution channel and sales network.

EXHIBIT 1
Major Personal Computer Components

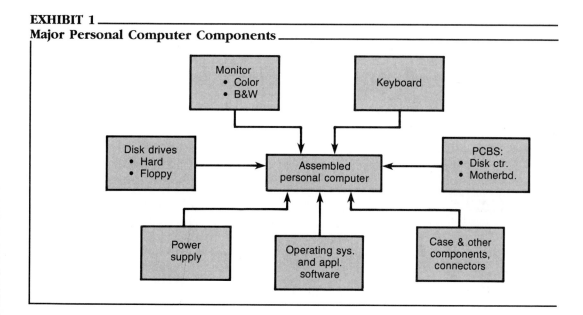

EXHIBIT 2
RXR Personal Computer Component Sourcing

Component	Source	Nationality
Monitor	Taxon, Samsung	South Korea
Power supply	NTK Electronics	California
Disk drives	Toshiba (floppies)	Japan
	Seagate (hard disk)	California
Keyboard	Keytronic	Washington State
Motherboard	AST Research	California
Controller boards*	Various manufacturers	Worldwide
Case	Johnson Electronics	Dallas, Texas
Cables and connectors	AMP Incorporated	Pennsylvania
	Burndy Incorporated	California

*Controller boards are necessary to coordinate the operation of the floppy and hard disk drives.

EXHIBIT 3
Standard PC Manufacturing Costs

1 Central processor board	$265
2 Disk drives	100
1 Power supply	65
1 Monochrome monitor	60
1 Keyboard	25
1 Chassis and case	100
Final assembly and testing	25
Total cost	$640

Source: "PCs Turning Back the Far East Tide," *Electronic Business*, August 15, 1986, pp. 54–55.

9. HSK Medical Supplies Company

BACKGROUND

Bill Green started the HSK Medical Supplies Co. in 1963. The firm concentrated on the manufacture and marketing of renal equipment.[1] At first, Green oversaw production and sales for the company, but he soon realized that working both jobs was too much for him to handle alone, and he hired George Alverson as manufacturing manager in 1968. HSK has concentrated on developing and producing state-of-the-art equipment, and the firm's major product line is continuous ambulatory peritoneal dialysis (CAPD) equipment.

In 1972, Bill Green hired Sarah Crosswell to help him with marketing. With the continued success

This case was prepared by Thomas M. Rogers at the University of South Carolina.

[1] Renal equipment is used to flush the kidneys and surrounding areas of impurities when the body is not able to do so on its own. This process is called kidney dialysis.

of HSK, Bill Green placed Sarah Crosswell in charge of sales, moved himself to the position of chief executive officer (CEO), and made George Alverson executive vice-president in charge of manufacturing.

HSK—PRESENT

The problem facing HSK Medical Supplies Co. is that they were able to push their sales to 5 percent of the U.S. renal equipment market by 1985 but have subsequently been unable to increase their market share. Bill Green is anxious to explore opportunities for increasing the firm's growth, and he feels that HSK is strong enough financially to consider expansion opportunities. The balance sheet below suggests adequate strength.

To address growth possibilities, Green arranged a meeting of himself, George Alverson, and Sarah Crosswell in mid-1987. During this meeting, Green asked for recommendations. Alverson advocated expanding the product lines to include X-ray equipment and stated that he would be able to start production within two years. Green responded that HSK had been in the business of renal equip-

ment for 24 years; and he would rather not change the focus of the company.

In the light of Green's evident wish to stick with the CAPD line, Sarah Crosswell suggested that, while she believed room existed for growth in the U.S. market, HSK might make some inquiries concerning overseas sales opportunities. Green believed the idea had merit and, over the next several weeks, gave some thought to identifying promising overseas markets for HSK.

When they got back together, Sarah Crosswell suggested penetrating the West German market. George Alverson pushed for the penetration of the Japanese medical market. He argued that the Japanese market was large and stated that, given HSK's commitment to producing quality products and staying on the leading edge of technology, it should be able to stay ahead of any Japanese competitor. Green was more interested in Canada, but he admitted he was biased by Canada's geographical location.

After some debate, it was decided to investigate the Japanese market. Initial inquiries were made with the U.S. Department of Commerce and the U.S. embassy in Tokyo concerning the possibility

HSK Medical Supplies Co.
Balance Sheet
December 31, 1987

ASSETS			LIABILITIES		
Current			Current		
Cash	620,658		Notes payable	311,448	
Marketable securities	325,055		Long-term debt	13,152	
Inventories	1,525,017		Accounts payable	1,330,586	
Prepaid expenses	157,017		Accrued taxes	597,297	
Subtotal		2,627,747	Subtotal		2,252,483
Property, plant, and equip.			Long-term debt	92,967	
Land and improvements	368,718		Deferred income tax	312,561	
Buildings	1,705,551				
Machinery and equip.	3,678,646		Stockholders equity		
	5,752,915		Common stock	187,071	
Less allowance for			Capital surplus	336,999	
depreciation	(300,000)		Retained earnings	4,898,581	
				5,422,651	
Subtotal		5,452,915	Subtotal		5,828,179
Total Assets		8,080,662	Total Liabilities		8,080,662

of penetrating the Japanese market. The information HSK received is summarized below.

JAPAN

Japan is slightly smaller than California. Much of its population is concentrated in the urban areas of Tokyo (the capital), Yokohama, Nagoya, Sapporo, Osaka, and Kyoto. Japanese GNP was $1.7 trillion (U.S.) in 1986 with a per capita income of $13,987. Some 48 percent of the Japanese workforce is employed in service activities; a further 34 percent works in manufacturing. Japanese exports totaled $210.8 billion in 1986 and imports were valued at $127.6 billion that same year. The United States is Japan's largest trading partner. Exports from Japan to the United States accounted for 37.1 percent of Japanese exports; imports from the United States to Japan were 20 percent of total Japanese imports.

Of the 121 million people living in Japan, 10 percent are over 65 years of age. The life expectancy of males is 74.2 years; of females, 79.8 years. A Department of Commerce report on the Japanese medical equipment market noted that:

> In Japan, as in other parts of Asia, care of the sick, aged, and infirm until recently has been the responsibility of families, employers, or private organizations. However, to meet the needs of an urbanized, modern industrial society, this system has changed greatly, and the government conducts a broad range of modest, but successful, social welfare programs. In response to the rapid growth of the number of elderly in Japan—where in fiscal 1980, some 10 percent of Japanese over the age of 65 accounted for nearly one-third of all national health care expenditures—the Government has adopted several laws to promote health care for elderly citizens.[2]

Renal Equipment

The growth of the renal equipment market in Japan is obvious from several statistics. In five years, 1975 to 1980, some 36,000 patients received dialysis treatment and some 19,000 dialysis systems were installed.[3] Growth is expected to continue in this market because of efforts by the Japanese government to subsidize the expenses incurred by dialysis patients. The Japanese government is also making efforts to subsidize the training of dialysis technicians.

In 1982, sales of domestic renal equipment in Japan were $204 million, with imported equipment accounting for some $40 million of this total. The Japanese renal equipment market was expected to increase by 40 percent from 1982 to 1987. Overall sales of $286 million and imports of some $55 million are projected for 1987 and U.S. firms are expected to hold a 60 percent share of this import market.[4]

Competitive Assessment

While Japanese producers in the various areas of the medical equipment market retain the lion's share of their respective domestic markets, U.S. manufacturers hold over half of the import market. Technology and quality are the main criteria used by Japanese end users to judge foreign products,[5] and the quality of competing Japanese equipment is very high.

The inquiry with the U.S. embassy in Tokyo spawned an unexpected contact. Ikuro Yamamoto, a representative for a Japanese import agent, called Bill Green concerning the possibility of handling HSK's product line in Japan. Yamamoto told Green that his firm would be interested in handling all aspects of introducing the product in Japan, marketing the CAPD line to the Japanese medical community, and moving the product through the proper distribution channels to the end user. His firm was interested in an exclusive agency relationship.

[2] *Country Market Survey: Medical Equipment—Japan*, U.S. Department of Commerce, International Trade Administration, January 1984, p. 14.

[3] *Country Market Survey: Medical Equipment—Japan*, U.S. Department of Commerce, International Trade Administration, January 1984, p. 9.

[4] Ibid, p. 7.

[5] Ibid, p. 2.

Green's view of this unsolicited contact was that it demonstrated that there is a market for the product in Japan. However, he was worried that HSK would lose control over marketing in Japan. He had also heard that Japanese distribution channels were very complex, and he wondered whether it would be desirable to attempt to circumvent the usual channels, selling either directly to the end user or at least avoiding use of some intermediaries commonly used. Circumventing the usual traditional channels would maximize HSK's control and allow it to internalize the margins otherwise paid to external distributors.

Distribution Channels

The general advice received from the Department of Commerce on distribution decisions was as follows: "In order to determine which method of distribution is best for your requirements, you must assess the potential market size, the structure of the market, the degree of complexity of existing distribution channels, your resources, and your willingness and ability to make a commitment to the Japanese market."[6] The major options identified regarding Japanese distribution channels included the four defined immediately below.

Sole Import Agent A sole import agent has exclusive Japanese marketing rights and undertakes negotiations with the many intermediaries in the Japanese distribution system. Such agents are able to undertake a wide range of promotional activities, provide ready access to distribution channels, and sometimes shoulder responsibility for after-sales service. However, using a sole agent limits control, and if the agent loses interest or is ineffective, rapid termination of the relationship is generally difficult and expensive.

General Trading Company The general trading companies, or *sogoshosha,* play a key role in internal and external Japanese trade; the aggregate sales of the top nine sogoshosha account for around 25 percent of Japan's GNP. General trading companies cover a large geographic area and deal with a wide range of products; this geographic and product diversity gives them their economic strength. General trading companies can provide financing for users, funnel information between suppliers and users, and absorb risk. They are also able to guarantee stable supplies to their customers by purchasing the products from the seller and storing them until needed. There have, however, been complaints that the sogoshosha specialize in shuffling papers and don't have any real knowledge of the products themselves. A firm considering a relationship with a General Trading Company must weigh the strength of the sogoshosha against the certainty of being just one of many firms and product lines handled by the company.

Specialized Trading Company The marketing activities of specialized trading companies, or *senmonshosha,* are focused by product, industry, or geographic area. The senmonshosha typically generate sales revenues from a few specialized product lines or, alternatively, a broader range of product lines in a limited region of Japan. Like general trading companies, specialized trading companies are willing to purchase and store products until needed by their customers. They will also undertake joint product development with the exporter. These smaller specialized trading companies offer a more focused and personal service than do the sogoshosha.

Licensing Entering into a licensing agreement with a Japanese firm may be the most feasible way to enter the Japanese market at a minimum cost. Licensing can also improve price competitiveness, since Japanese producers can capitalize upon efficient production methods, and barriers arising from import controls, tariffs, and transport costs are avoided. The quality of imports to Japan may also be enhanced; Japanese quality-control techniques are often better than those in the United States. The licensee is also able to modify the product to better meet local end-user's needs and the conditions of product use. The licensee has responsibility for registration and government approval and should be familiar with local distribution channels. It may also be possible for the licensee to negotiate better terms with Japanese distributors and other intermediaries.

---

[6] "Tips on Exporting to Japan," prepared by Kathleen S. White for the International Trade Administration, pp. 8–9.

QUESTIONS

1. Do you believe HSK should enter the Japanese market at this time? What is your rationale.
2. Assuming HSK does enter the market, which distribution arrangement offers the greatest promise?
3. If they decide to appoint a Japanese agent, what steps should HSK take during the selection process?

10. Technologies CI, SA

In August, 1985, Randall Zats, financial director of Technologies CI, SA, thought about a recent conversation with Patrice Fleming, managing director of Technologies' Belgian subsidiary. Patrice had said, "How can I meet a growing target profit for my subsidiary while selling memory chips that reduce my profits?" She also pointed out that both the subsidiary's target profit and her bonus would be larger if she stopped selling memory chips altogether.

Randy knew that the transfer price at which Patrice bought memory chips from the parent company was higher than the current market price. But she needed to sell memory chips to customers who bought the profitable integrated circuits to keep them from buying memory chips from suppliers who might become competitors for the integrated circuit business. Further, corporate strategy required that Technologies maintain their market share in memory chips in Europe.

Randy reflected that he could solve the problem by lowering the transfer price for memory chips. However, this would mean losses for the French subsidiary which manufactured the memory chips. It might also spell trouble with the French taxation authorities and Customs for chips shipped outside the common market.

THE COMPANY

Technologies CI, SA (TCI) is a large French company that manufactures integrated circuits, memory chips, and similar computer-related products. It manu-

This case was prepared by Jack Gray (with the assistance of Randy Zats), Case Development Center, Carlson School of Management, University of Minnesota.

factures in Nantes, France, and corporate headquarters and central research facilities are in Versailles, France. TCI markets products throughout Europe through subsidiaries operating in each major European country.

TCI was founded in 1971 to manufacture memory chips for the rapidly growing microcomputer industry. By the late 1970s, the company produced memory chips in large volume. This large-volume production permitted very efficient production, making TCI a low-cost producer that could profit on memory chips, despite falling selling prices.

In the early 1980s, the manufacture of memory chips became even more competitive as many Japanese producers entered the market. This forced prices down even more rapidly, making the manufacture of memory chips unprofitable for TCI as well as most other industry members.

Following the industry pattern, TCI continually developed larger memory chips. In 1985, 64K memory chips were produced in large volume, but 256K memory chips were in large-scale production and would be dominant by 1988. Even larger memory chips were being developed in 1985, but TCI believed it was keeping pace with the Japanese in developing larger chips.

After gaining a major position in memory chips, TCI turned most of its research toward developing integrated circuits, small computers on a chip that perform specialized control functions in larger products. For example, many kitchen appliances have integrated circuits that control speed, timing, and other aspects of their operation. Automobiles have as many as 10 chips to control engines and other functions. These chips were custom designed to a particular application. While many companies were able to design and manufacture integrated circuits, TCI proved itself adept at designing and producing custom integrated circuits more rapidly than its competitors. This unique ability protected TCI somewhat from price competition and helped them earn attractive margins on the integrated circuits.

Manufacturing

All manufacturing was done in Nantes in northwest France. This region provided a pool of skilled workers and adequate materials. The company employed 1,500 people in manufacturing. TCI shipped to all West European countries from Nantes. Distances were short, and transportation reliable enough that even customers reducing their inventories could be served easily from Nantes.

Just-in-time purchasing of integrated circuits, which became popular in the mid-1980s, added to TCI's traditional market strength. Just-in-time purchasers develop close relationships with suppliers and involve them more heavily in product planning and design. This permitted TCI to better customize products and take advantage of its reputation as a reliable supplier. And price competition was not as severe with just-in-time purchasers.

Marketing

TCI marketed its products through wholly-owned subsidiaries in each Western European country. Subsidiaries were expected to maintain close contact with customers and feed information back to Nantes on new products that customers were designing so that proposals could be developed for new integrated circuits.

When a subsidiary found an existing or potential customer considering design of a new product, it maintained close ties. Working with the Versailles research group the subsidiary developed a preliminary integrated circuit proposal and presented it to the customer.

If the customer indicated substantial interest, the subsidiary could authorize more extensive design work and, ultimately, production of prototype integrated circuits for customer testing. Most customers were experts in production of their products, appliances, automobiles, etc., but lacked expertise in electronics. Therefore, they were usually happy to have TCI take over major design work. Design, and patents if developed, were the property of TCI. If the product met customer needs, TCI was virtually assured of sales of the circuit to the customer for at least several years and often for the life of the customer's product.

To control design costs, TCI had developed the following policies:

1. All design work would be done in the central research facilities in Versailles, France.
2. The cost of preliminary design work, which lead to a proposal to the customer, was borne by the manufacturing facility. This encouraged development of proposals for all product opportunities that seemed profitable to the sales subsidiaries.
3. When product design passed the proposal stage to the detailed design and development of prototypes, design costs were borne by the subsidiary, which expected to sell the product to the customer. This policy was intended to assure that only the most promising projects were chosen for the more extensive (and expensive) design stages. If the subsidiary did not expect sales of the product to the customer, they would not authorize the design and pay the costs.

These policies seemed to work quite well for the design and marketing of integrated circuits.

When the product was ready for production, manufacturing was done at Nantes. The subsidiary billed for the products and administered all other customer relations from its own country. Subsidiary managers were responsible for their own marketing programs, product pricing, and profitability. The subsidiary was charged the cost of the design work it authorized for products developed for its customers. Subsidiary profit depended on developing appropriate products, setting appropriate selling prices, controlling marketing expenses, and maintaining a sales volume high enough to meet profit targets.

Transfer Prices

Transfer prices for integrated circuits and memory chips were standard cost of production plus 12 percent. TCI management occasionally discussed alternatives to cost-based transfer prices. A market-based transfer price has some advantages. But a market-based transfer price was not feasible for most TCI products since independent market prices do not exist for custom designed integrated circuits. Given the decision to use a cost-based transfer price, TCI management chose standard rather than actual cost as the base.

Both the manufacturing subsidiary and the marketing subsidiaries are evaluated as profit centers. The manufacturing subsidiary has no direct control over sales volume, but indirectly influences sales by designing quality new products that serve customer needs. The manufacturing subsidiary can also add to its profits by keeping costs at or below standard. Cost reduction is important in this industry because of the intense price competition.

The marketing subsidiaries earned a profit by understanding their customer's needs and designing integrated circuits to meet those needs. For legal reasons, TCI permitted each subsidiary to sell only in its home country. This also reduced competition between subsidiaries for the same customer. As annual planning started, marketing subsidiaries requested transfer prices on existing products, and planned sales volume, sales mix, and marketing expenses to achieve their annual target profit.

Besides marketing, each subsidiary was charged with maintaining good government relations in its country as well as monitoring the country's political and economic environment. The subsidiary was to be particularly alert to potential legislation that would restrict TCI's ability to ship its product freely from France into the subsidiary's country.

Subsidiary management had to be familiar with customs procedures in its country and able to arrange customs clearance as needed. Subsidiaries revised procedures in response to changes in customs regulations.

A transfer price has to be accepted as objectively determined by tax authorities in France and in each subsidiary's country. Transfer prices cannot be used to transfer income to a country with more favorable tax rates. TCI's transfer prices resulted in profit in both the countries of manufacture and sale. Taxing authorities tend to accept cost-based transfer prices as objective. Rarely was a TCI transfer price challenged by tax authorities.

Strategy

By 1985, TCI earned all its profits on integrated circuits business. Price competition in memory chips was severe and this business was unprofitable. However, TCI management committed to remain in the memory chip business and maintain its European market share. TCI management believed that smaller chip manufacturers would eventually be forced out of the memory-chip markets and that manufacture of memory chips would again be profitable.

In the early 1980s, Malaysia, Singapore, and Indonesia were major competitors in memory chips. Many major chip manufacturers assembled chips in these countries because of the relatively low wage rates. A worker in Malaysia can assemble 120 chips per hour. However, equipment available in 1985 makes it possible for a skilled worker to supervise eight machines that can assemble 5,120 chips per hour. With lower transportation costs, overseas production no longer has a cost advantage.

Fairchild Camera and Instrument Corporation, a U.S. chip manufacturer, reported "many, many customers to whom [we] can ship zero days late and no more than one day early."[1] Meeting this shipping schedule from overseas factories meant carrying larger inventories than if chips were produced in domestic factories. Mostek Corporation had closed an assembly plant in Kota Bahru, Malaysia, and had reduced its work force at its plant in Penang, Malaysia. National Semiconductor Corporation was also closing a plant in Seremban, Malaysia. Other companies were closing or reducing production at plants in Singapore and Indonesia.

Besides these favorable developments, another reason TCI wanted to stay in the large and relatively stable memory chip market was because it contributed to the company's image with investors. In contrast, most of TCI's integrated circuit customers produced consumer durable goods that closely followed consumer income cycles.[2]

---

[1] "U.S. Semiconductor Makers Automate, Cut Chip Production in Southeast Asia," *The Wall Street Journal*, August 21, 1985, p. 26.

[2] There are cycles in memory chip business as larger capacity chips replace smaller chips, but there is a strong upward trend in demand independent of the consumer economic climate.

TCI also thought that its credibility as a supplier of computer components was enhanced by a strong presence in the memory chip market.

Company strategy was to maintain European market share in memory chips until 1988, even if it meant incurring some losses on the product line. The profitability of the integrated circuits would be sufficient to meet profit targets until 1988, when memory chips should again contribute to profits.

Annual Budgets

TCI top management believed in what they called "guided" decentralization. The company and its subsidiaries operated on a calendar year. Each Au-

Budgets were prepared by the subsidiaries in standard formats and presented by the managing director of each subsidiary to TCI top management in November. If the budgets met the year's targets, they were usually approved with only minor revisions. Once approved, the budgets were the standards for subsidiary performance.

THE PROBLEM IN 1985

In spite of its stated objective of maintaining market share in the memory chip business, TCI discovered that from 1982 to 1984 its sales and estimated European market share for 64K memory chips had fallen as follows:

	TCI Sales	*Total Market Sales*	*Market Share %*
1983	12,816,000 Ffr	106,800,000 Ffr	12
1984	25,454,000 Ffr	231,400,000 Ffr	11
1985*	21,360,000 Ffr	213,360,000 Ffr	10

* estimated

gust, all subsidiaries received three major kinds of objectives to guide preparation of budgets for the next year. They were:

1. A target growth rate in total sales;
2. A target profit for the coming year; and
3. Target market shares by product and customer type.

Target market shares were established for sale of memory chips and integrated circuits to various industries in each country. For example, the Italian subsidiary had target market shares for sales to the automobile industry and laundry appliance manufacturers. TCI already played an important role in these industries and expected the subsidiary to maintain or increase market share. Beyond these industries, the Italian subsidiary had a small market share goal for Italian telecommunications equipment where TCI had no market share in 1985. Using the market share targets, TCI top management guided subsidiaries into markets that management thought had great potential or where the company had success in other countries.

The decline in sales and market share occurred in all European countries. While the growth of the market for 64K memory chips stopped, the picture for total memory chips was brighter. The 256K memory chip was introduced in 1984. Between 1985 and 1990, unit sales of the 256K chip were predicted to grow at a compound annual rate of 64 percent. The 64K memory chip had followed the same type of growth curve as it replaced the older 16K memory chip in the early 1980s.

Discussions with several subsidiary managers revealed heated emotions. Subsidiary managers resented being expected to budget a constant market share in memory chips. They pointed out that the sale of memory chips was unprofitable with the present cost-based transfer price and depressed selling prices for memory chips.

Indeed, how could individual subsidiary managers meet a growing target profit while selling memory chips that reduced profit? Recall Patrice Fleming's statement (at the start of the case), whose profit and bonus would be larger if she ceased selling memory chips altogether.

Other subsidiary managers agreed that if top

management wanted them to sell memory chips, then European headquarters should reduce transfer prices. All subsidiary managers questioned why the manufacturing subsidiary made a 12 percent profit on memory chips while the sales subsidiaries lost 40 percent on all they sold.

Ernesto Placida, managing director of the Spanish subsidiary argued, "If they want us to sell memory chips, let them reduce the transfer price on memory chips so that they are a profitable product."

The practical result was that subsidiaries budgeted enough sales to maintain market share, but did not try to sell the budgeted number of memory chips. Marketing efforts were concentrated on integrated circuits. They sold memory chips to integrated circuit customers at market price to provide full service but did not cultivate new customers for memory chips. At year end, most subsidiaries achieved their profit targets while falling substantially below budgeted unit sales of memory chips. Bonuses were based on the profitability of the subsidiary and were improved by failure to maintain market share in memory chips.

A Potential Solution

TCI management appreciated the subsidiary managers' dilemma. In the long run, subsidiaries would benefit from remaining in the memory chip market. But short run profits suffered.

TCI considered reducing the transfer price of memory chips to make them profitable for the subsidiaries. TCI management estimated that in 1985, a market-based transfer price of 10 French francs would make it profitable for subsidiaries to sell the 64K chip. TCI calculated its cost-based transfer price for 1985 as follows:

Direct materials	4.45 Ffr
Direct labor	4.01
Manufacturing overhead	7.30
Total	15.76 Ffr
Mark up @ 12%	1.89
Transfer price	17.65 Ffr

The manager of the French subsidiary argued that a 10 French franc transfer price would create

significant losses for the subsidiary. Since all production was done in France, the French subsidiary would bear all losses. With the current market and transfer prices, losses were distributed among the various marketing subsidiaries and therefore not nearly as large for any one subsidiary. Of course, management recognized that from the corporate point of view, the total loss on sale of memory chips was the same regardless of in which subsidiaries they occurred.

Having all the loss borne by the French subsidiary created a potential problem with French tax authorities. They would be unhappy with the reduction of French income and income taxes. The corporate tax manager also pointed out that if the lower transfer price was accepted by customs authorities, lower customs duties would be paid on chips shipped outside the European common market. But the lower transfer prices might be challenged by customs officials in importing countries.

TCI's managing director was likely to ask Randall Zats to recommend a solution to this problem before budgeting began for next year. Randall decided to list and evaluate all alternative solutions. If he recommended reducing the transfer price for memory chips, he knew he would have to propose and justify a price.

GLOSSARY[3]

Bit An abbreviation of binary digit, one of the two numbers—0 and 1—that record data in a computer. A bit is expressed by a high or low electrical voltage.

Byte A group of eight bits used to represent a single letter, number or symbol.

Chip A small piece of silicon that is a complete semiconductor device, or integrated circuit.

Integrated Circuit A semiconductor circuit combining many electronic components in a single substrate, usually silicon.

K Usually an abbreviation for kilo (1,000). A 1 K memory chip, however, contains 1,024

[3] Adapted from "The Chip: Electronic Mini-marvel," *National Geographic*, Allen A. Boraiko, October 1982 (Washington, D.C.: National Geographic Society), p. 439.

bits because it is a binary device based on powers of two. Thus, a 64K memory can store 65,536 bits of information (64 × 1,024).

Memory Chip A semiconductor device that stores information as electrical charges.

Microprocessor An integrated circuit that interprets and executes instructions and usually incorporates arithmetic capabilities and some memory in a single chip.

Semiconductor An element whose electrical conductivity is less than that of a conductor such as copper and greater than that of an insulator such as glass.

11. Norstar Plastics Ltd.

In May 1985, Director Ole Berg was faced with a number of serious problems. Increased production capacity for rigid plastic film was coming on stream at the same time as demand had weakened. Profitability in the "film" department, which he headed, was threatened and there was an urgent need to increase sales. A partial solution to some of his problems had arisen in the form of a proposal for a comprehensive barter arrangement with his biggest customer, a state-controlled trading company in the German Democratic Republic (GDR). The East German trading company was currently Norstar's biggest customer for plastic film, and the barter deal offered the chance of substantially increasing this business.

However, barter was something Norstar had not done before, and for this reason, and because other departments of the firm would be involved, Berg felt that the situation needed careful analysis and a rather diplomatic approach.

COMPANY BACKGROUND

The Norstar concern is a well established family company located in Oslo, Norway. The firm is over 100 years old and has grown rapidly in the postwar period. Norstar is quite large, by Norwegian standards, with a 1985 turnover of some Nkr 620 million (around $100 million).

Major fields of business activity, and their recent development, are shown below.

Percentage of Annual Sales

	1980 (%)	1982 (%)	1984 (%)	1985 (est.) (%)
Building products	22	20	21	20
Agricultural products	17	14	16	19
Consumer goods (mainly food)	23	22	23	21
Plastic products	24	30	30	25
Miscellaneous	14	14	10	15
	100	100	100	100
Turnover in million Nkr	420	480	545	620

This case was written by Professor Bjarne Bakka, The Norwegian School of Economics and Business Administration, Bergen, Norway.

The firm is organized along product division lines, with each division enjoying significant autonomy as an independent profit center. One-year operating plans are developed within the context of a five-year strategic plan. Planning is primarily undertaken in the divisions under the coordination of a limited Corporate planning staff. All plans have to be accepted by the Corporate board, but once acceptance is achieved, the divisions have considerable freedom in running their business.

THE PLASTICS DIVISION

The Plastics Division started with the production of floor tiles in 1952 at a factory near Oslo. Ready markets were found, both in Norway and overseas. For many years, floor tiles were the main breadwinner of the division. Profits were, to a large extent, plowed back into new plants, machinery and development. In fact, Norstar became a tech-

packaging materials. A factory was erected at the Moss site, sharing energy and transport facilities with the pipe plant. Again, turnover grew quite quickly, and in 1984 new equipment was installed at a cost of Nkr 25 million, doubling production capacity. From the start, the film business was dependent on overseas markets, and exports accounted for around 80 percent of revenue.

Raw materials (primarily PVC) for the plastic production was mainly bought from Norwegian suppliers, such as Norsk Hydro. The Norwegian petrochemical industry was based upon Norway's plentiful North Sea oil resources, and the ready availability of domestically produced PVC was seen by Norstar as a source of competitive strength.

The recent development of the major product lines produced by the plastics division is shown below:

Plastics Division
Percentage of Annual Sales

	1980 (%)	1982 (%)	1984 (%)	1985 (%)
Flooring materials	76	66	54	58
Pipes	22	26	30	28
Film	2	8	16	14
	100	100	100	100

nological leader in this field. Gradually, the assortment was widened to include other types of floor coverings, including tufted carpets, some of them bought from other producers.

In the beginning of the 1970s, the Plastics Division entered a new field of activity, the production of rigid PVC* pipes for sewage, draining, water supply, etc. A new plant was built at Moss, a small town on Oslo Fjord, not far from the Swedish border and with easy access to rail, road, and sea transport. This business grew quickly, and after five years its turnover had reached 20 percent of the yearly sales of flooring materials. Again, profits were plowed back into further development, resulting in better processes, more stable quality, and a patented production system sold internationally, for instance to Turkey and Thailand.

In the late 1970s, a third field of activity was taken up: the production of rigid PVC film for

Over the last year, results in the division have not been up to expectations, mainly due to international and local overcapacity and sharp price competition. The three fields of activity were considered separate profit centers and the divisional organization chart is shown at the top of the next page.

Each department has parallel structures with sections for production, marketing and administration (working in close contact with the Corporate staff). The marketing section of each department concentrates on planning, product development and inland sales. Export sales are coordinated in a separate department under which are placed three foreign sales companies.

THE FILM DEPARTMENT

The film department is headed by Ole Berg (45), a graduate in chemistry and engineering with 15

---

* Polyvinylchloride is raw material for plastic production.

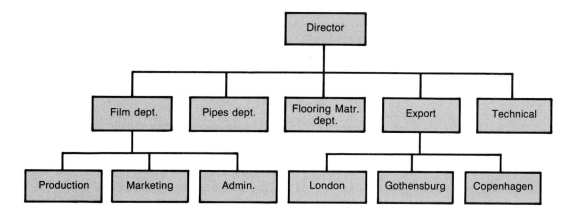

years experience of plastic manufacturing before he joined Norstar in 1980. Berg felt that the department's crucial need was to gain a firm foothold in a limited number of markets. He had appointed an export manager to work from Moss, had utilized actively the foreign sales offices, and had placed his own sales representative in the London office.

Sales of PVC film had shown the following growth (tons):

1981	1982	1983	1984	1985 (est.)
400	1,400	2,500	2,400	2,300

The start up of the film business was considered an impressive achievement by everyone in the company. Unfortunately, international overcapacity and price competition were spoiling the chances to make a reasonable profit. In fact, after the addition of new equipment in 1984, increasing the yearly capacity from 2,500 to 5,000 tons, there had been only a modest contribution from the film business.

The production of PVC film comprised the following operations:

☐ Mixing of PVC and other raw materials

☐ Heating and stirring

☐ Rolling over heated and cold rollers

☐ Further rolling of narrow bands to a thin film (0.1–0.7 mm)

Production was, to a large extent, tailor made to clients' specifications as to width, thickness, color, etc. Typical examples were white film for butter and margarine packs, opaque film for pharmaceutical products, clear film for toothbrush blister packs, and so on.

The film was delivered in large rolls, weighing 30–100 kilos. Storage required ample floor space. Delivery took place mainly by road, but exports to more distant markets relied on sea transport.

Sales of PVC film required extensive personal contact with clients, and not just with the purchasing department. Contact with the product development and production people in client firms was usually more important. It was extremely important to find the correct "quality balance" in the film, to give the right protection, while securing a smooth packing operation and good display effects. Berg and his sales colleagues felt that they had succeeded in building up excellent relations with their major clients in Western markets. In Eastern Europe it had proved much more difficult to develop relations with the end user because business was done with bureaucrats in the relevant state trading agency.

From the start in 1980, sales efforts had been directed towards a limited number of markets. In 1985, the turnover was expected to be distributed as follows:

Norway	20
Sweden	20
Denmark	10
East Germany [GDR]	25
United Kingdom	20
Secondary markets	5
	100

Norstar's main competitors were large concerns in West Germany, Italy, and France. In the United Kingdom the only PVC film producer of importance, Commercial Plastics Ltd., had withdrawn from the market in early 1985.

THE GDR BARTER REQUEST

Exports of PVC film to the GDR had grown from 100 tons in 1982 to nearly 600 tons in 1985 (est.). Prices were a bit below the regular international level, but because of the prospects of long-term contracts, and low credit risk, the business was considered worthwhile, and was moderately profitable. Berg had involved himself personally in this important relationship and felt that there was room for further growth.

During his last contacts with the GDR trading company in April, a senior German official had aired the following proposal for a barter operation:

1. The GDR would continue to buy Norstar's film for pharmaceutical, agricultural and possibly other types of packaged goods. Yearly quantity between 1,000 and 2,000 tons. Priced at today's prices adjusted for documented changes in costs. Duration of contract, 2–3 years.

2. In return, Norstar would buy from the GDR another type of rigid plastic film showing promising qualities for larger packing operations, and it might be feasible to use it to replace corrugated paper boxes (for instance, for fish products). Quantities corresponding to one-third of the GDR purchases from Norstar. Prices and conditions to be negotiated. Norstar would be free to re-export the film to other Scandinavian markets and the United Kingdom, but not to other countries owing to existing arrangements with sole distributors.

3. Norstar would also buy from the GDR quantities of PVC raw materials corresponding to 10 percent of their total PVC needs of some 15,000 tons per annum for their tile, pipe, and film production. Prices and conditions to be negotiated.

4. At a later stage, Norstar would also undertake negotiations for the purchase of GDR products from other East German trading companies.

Likely products included steel for their building division and vegetables for their soup products.

5. All transactions between Norstar and the GDR would be included in one single contract. Debits and credits would be regulated as per April 1st and October 1st each year and balances paid within four weeks.

The GDR trading company wanted to start negotiations as soon as possible, with the aim of signing a contract in September 1985.

PRELIMINARY DISCUSSIONS

After returning from the GDR, Berg considered the issue important enough for a preliminary discussion with the Corporate management and his colleagues in other divisions. He felt that the various views could be summed up as follows:

> Corporate management emphasized Norstar's long term interests vis-à-vis the Norwegian oil/petrochemical/plastics sector. The North Sea resources might become decisive for regular and possibly low priced supplies. Considerable national efforts should be put into research and development and Norstar might benefit from taking an active part in this. If Norstar's importance as an end user of PVC grows it will achieve more influence in the Norwegian industry.
>
> The director of the Plastics Division agreed that these long-term considerations were important, but pointed out that the division needed better profitability quickly. Western markets were plagued by overcapacity, fierce competition from multinational producers, low prices, and no signs for optimism. Markets in Eastern Europe might be easier and the GDR would be a natural starting point.

On the departmental level, the managers tended to look at more specific factors relating to their own businesses:

> The flooring materials people were rather skeptical of the GDR proposal. The very fact that the GDR wanted a barter arrangement might indicate that their products were difficult to sell. It was also argued that Norstar's limited sales capacity should not be

used to market bartered goods. In addition, only the film people had any experience with the GDR as a trading partner and it would seem overly optimistic to expect the GDR to rapidly expand their demand for other Norstar exports.

The pipe department was not enthusiastic about the idea of having to use PVC from the GDR in their production. Even small foreign particles in the PVC might cause the pipes to burst and, anyway, comprehensive pilot production would be needed to adjust to the new quality of PVC. They also pointed out that if you start bartering, there might be no end to new requests.

Berg felt that his colleagues' skepticism was to some extent justified. The GDR products might be problematic to use and difficult to sell. On the other hand, his exports to the GDR were crucial for his department and might be lost if there is no barter agreement. (Berg sensed political pressure behind the GDR proposal owing to foreign currency problems.) From the GDR's five-year plan, Berg knew that the country needed considerable imports of many types of finished plastic products until their own capacity had been developed around 1990. A barter operation might pave the way for further business, better contact with the end users, sales of technology, and so on. And after all, could not barter operations be left to specialized brokers in London, Vienna, and Zurich? Of course they would have to be paid a commission, but they could take care of any marketing problems.

As to the properties of the GDR packaging film, it was thicker and more rigid than the Norstar versions, and Berg felt that it might represent a worthwhile widening of the Norstar assortment. Berg had no details about its technical specifications, but limited tests and practical judgement from Norstar's laboratory people were positive. The fish cases received from the GDR as samples were rather simple, but indicated sufficient strength and good handling and stacking properties. After some product development they might be OK for trial sales to the fishing industry—a market which was new for Norstar, both in Norway and overseas. Other Norwegian producers had already launched plastic fish cases, and Berg had the impression that demand was growing rapidly.

Berg had no previous experience with barter operations and realized that the GDR proposal raised many important questions. Unfortunately, there was not much time for contemplation, as the summer holidays were drawing near and the GDR trading company wanted serious talks rather soon.

Specific issues that Berg felt demanded immediate attention included:

☐ How should he respond to the German proposal?

☐ What were the implications of such a barter deal for the film department, the plastics division and the Norstar company?

☐ What strategy should be followed when negotiating with the officials from the GDR?

12. Makhteshim Chemical Works

"To say that we are unhappy with our progress to date would be an understatement," admitted Mr. Ilan Leviteh, vice-president of Makhteshim Chemical Works, a small Israeli specialty chemicals company.

This case was prepared by Patricia P. McDougall and Earl H. Levitt of Georgia State University and Kendall J. Roth of the University of South Carolina.

Now in 1987, Makteshim faced a key decision: "Our penetration of the U.S. market has not gone well, and we have to decide what to do about it. We have to be here," he emphasized. "The U.S. market is just too important."

Makhteshim's management still saw the large U.S. market for flame-retardant chemicals as an inviting opportunity for expansion. Although they believed Makhteshim had a strong technology and an excellent manufacturing cost position, they were frustrated by the company's inability to establish a significant position in the U.S. market.

For the last three years, M&T Chemicals, a U.S. company, had marketed the F-2000 Series of brominated polymeric flame retardants for Makhteshim. If Makhteshim wanted to exercise its cancellation option in its contract with M&T for the sale of its flame-retardant product line in the United States, it had to do so soon. Should Makhteshim cancel and find a new U.S. representative, or should it try to continue working with M&T in the hopes that sales performance would improve? Another major U.S. flame retardant company has asked Makhteshim to produce a generic product for them. Could Makhteshim enter into some sort of joint arrangement for that product as well as the F-2000 line? Or, should Makhteshim just expand their New York office, and do the marketing and sales jobs itself? Faced with several alternatives, Makhteshim was determined to reassess its entry strategy in this vital market.

U.S. FLAME RETARDANT INDUSTRY OVERVIEW

The flame retardants industry in the United States is an $850 million business growing in excess of 15 percent per year (see Tables 1 and 2). With the continuing increase in the use of new materials and new applications for existing materials, the flame-retardant chemical industry is expected to grow to over $2 billion by the year 2000.

TABLE 1
Sales of Flame Retardant Substances, 1986

	Pounds (millions)	Sales ($ millions)
Organic		
Chlorinated	199	70
Brominated	150	260
Inorganic		
Aluminum trihydrate	400	80
Antimony oxide	40	60
Other	350	380
TOTAL	1,040	$850

TABLE 2
Flame-Retardant End-Use Market Growth Rates

	Percent
Carpet backing	(5)
Wire/Cable	>15
Unsaturated polyester	8–10
Thermoplastics	6–10
Flexible PVC	>10
New applications/ Polymers	>20

The purpose of flame retardants is to slow down the development and spread of a fire, allowing sufficient time for people to react to the fire situation. Flame retardants are used in a multitude of end-use applications, from electrical wire insulation, connectors, and circuit boards to carpet backing, children's clothing, plywood paneling, and plastic plumbing.

U.S. Flame Retardant Industry

The industry has three major characteristics. It is (1) created by regulation, (2) driven by technology, and (3) sustained by supplier commitment. Without a firm understanding of these characteristics, successful competition in the industry is impossible. Regulations are important because few consumers of flame retardants would use them if they were not required to do so. Flame retardants add cost to the end product, change and degrade properties of the base polymer, and are generally inconvenient to work with. However, with the increasing rash of highly publicized fires taking their toll in both lives and property, and the increasing use of polymers in critical applications, flame and fire retardants are increasingly demanded by building codes, insurance regulators, the military, large buyers, and government bodies at all levels.

Most industry analysts foresee increasing regulation as a certainty, with more and more governmental entities concerning themselves with the issues of smoke and toxic gasses from burning plastics.

The customers for flame retardants have a single objective—to meet a specific flame retardant performance requirement at the lowest possible cost, giving them a competitive advantage in a specific application. They are relatively indifferent to the product or technology which gives them this level of flame retardant performance. However, the flame retardant user has a variety of performance requirements which they are attempting to satisfy simultaneously and the industry is *technology driven* in its search for suitable products. Thus, a product that gives them flame retardancy alone, but degrades other performance characteristics they are trying to achieve, is unacceptable.

There is usually a close working relationship between the flame retardant manufacturer and the customer. The marketing and business people of the supplier are expected to know the end users of the products and the characteristics of the industry being served by his customer. They, too, must be sufficiently knowledgeable in the industry technology to understand and deal with the technical issues.

The third major characteristic of successful flame retardant businesses is the importance of the customer's perception of a long-term *commitment* from the supplier. A customer's new products may require years of research to develop. They are highly proprietary and rarely patentable. It can take at least a year and over $200,000 to get the necessary UL or MILSPEC certifications before the product can be sold for a specific application. Once the official testing is completed (usually a UL test is required), it can take an additional year or more before the customer certifies the product and incorporates it into its product line. A customer will not likely undertake the development of a new product with a supplier that the customer feels lacks either the commitment or staying power to ensure the new product's continued availability.

FLAME RETARDANT INDUSTRY SITUATION

Marketing

The flame retardant industry is a specialty chemicals business which sells a performance characteristic, rather than a chemical product. Sales of flame-retardant products to the polymers industry in the United States in 1986 were on the order of $850 million, with an industry growth rate in excess of 15 percent. Prices ranged from a low 15 cents per pound in aluminum trihydrate to specialty fluoropolymers costing $15.00–20.00 per pound. Examples of product pricing are presented in Table 3. Operating profit in the flame retardant specialty additives business is high, typically running 20–40 percent on sales.

TABLE 3
Flame Retardant Product Pricing (1986)

Type	$/Lb.
Flourine compounds	15.00 – 20.00
Chlorine/Bromine compounds	.50 – 3.05
Phosphorus compounds	1.10 – 1.80
Antimony	1.50 – 1.90
Aluminum trihydrate	.10 – .30

There are currently three trends which are radically changing the character of the industry and redefining the opportunities available to the participants.

The first is the *increasing politicization* of the regulatory standards in which the flame retardants industry must function. Toxic gas and smoke emissions in a fire environment are becoming critical to the nontechnical community due to the rather spectacularly publicized deaths in recent hotel fires. The MGM Grand Hotel in Reno, Nevada in 1981, and the DuPont Hotel fire in Puerto Rico in 1986 are particularly vivid examples of publicized horror. The public is demanding a "safe" fire environment, and is demanding that technology provide a solution. Some flame-retardant systems will be regulated out of existence, not on the scientific merits of their products, but on the political issues at hand. Primarily at risk are some brominated products which are also under attack in Germany as dioxin creators. All halogen-based systems are at risk due to their high smoke levels and their evolution of acid gases. Companies which fail to address the political, as well as the technical issues, will find themselves regulated out of business.

The second major trend is that of recent *industry consolidation*. As can be seen from Table 4, major players are consolidating their strengths. By combining technologies, obtaining synergism in their sales and marketing programs, and increasing their "critical mass," these companies are reinforcing their commitments for the future.

TABLE 4
Industry Consolidations

Buyer	Acquired
Great Lakes Chemicals	Velsicol
Ethyl Corporation	Saytex
	Dow
Tenneco	Albright & Wilson
Albright & Wilson	Mobil
Anson, Inc.	McGean Rehco, Inc.

Finally, the issue of *market obsolescence* due to technological change will have a profound effect on certain market segments. Ten years ago, Occidental Chemical sold several million pounds of their product, Dechlorane® Plus to the polypropylene market. Today less than one-tenth of that amount is sold in that segment due to new polymers being used in the previous applications and to engineering redesigns to remove the need of flame retardancy altogether. A similar situation is occurring in carpet backing, as major carpet manufacturers are conducting research and development to make the carpet fiber itself flame retardant.

Technology

Technology, brought to play in the marketplace, is considered by most industry experts to be the single most important factor for success in the flame retardant business. New regulations for smoke and toxic gas emissions require technological improvements in existing products. The acid gases (HCl, HBr) that develop during a fire not only pose a threat to lives, but may do considerable damage to expensive electronic equipment. When a New York City telephone switching station burned, over $50 million of equipment was destroyed, not by flames, but by the acid gases released in the fire. Also, because halogens act primarily in the vapor phase, large amounts of smoke are generated, hampering escape from the fire. For these two primary reasons, regulators and consumers are driving the flame retardant industry away from halogen systems. Aluminum trihydrate is the main

beneficiary of this effect, as its primary mechanism is that of a heat sink in the early stage, and later decomposing into innocuous water vapor.

New polymers are constantly being brought to market, replacing other construction materials (wood, metal) as well as other polymers. With these new polymers come increasing challenges for flame retardancy, such as higher processing temperatures, polymer and copolymer compatibility, and smaller particle size for thinner sections. The flame retardant companies are addressing these technology issues with significant research programs in surface modifications and coatings, fine particle-grinding technology, encapsulation techniques, concentrates, and chemical/matrix modifications.

Manufacturing

Manufacturing plants for fire-retardant chemicals tend to be small (annual capacities of 10–50 million pounds) and flexible. (Several products are made using the same equipment.) Their $5–$20 million capital cost is considered low by chemical industry standards. The plants often require specialized equipment, and production is usually campaigned, resulting in significant inventory levels. A plant's location is usually not a factor in competition because transportation costs, even from overseas, are small relative to value added. For example, Occidental's Dechlorane® Plus sells for approximately $2.60 per pound. Transportation, duty, and handling costs to most parts of the world rarely exceed 5 cents per pound. Product quality and consistency, however, are critical. Raw materials tend to be a small part of the overall cost of the products (15–25 percent) and, while a strong raw materials base may be a competitive advantage, it is not a requirement for success.

Other Key Points

Several other key points must be made in order to understand the current industry situation. First, the flame retardants business is a *worldwide business,* both in terms of markets and producers. Companies based in West Germany, Israel, and Japan have established strong marketing presences in the United States, just as U.S. companies have done overseas. Applications technology is the name of the game, and technology transfers are rapid and efficient. As most major producers have learned, it is necessary that strategy, marketing, pricing, and technology be centralized with a worldwide overview.

Second, while the industry is large in dollar terms, it is a *very small industry* in people and organizational terms. Everyone in the industry knows everyone else, what they are doing, and with whom they are doing it. There are very few secrets for very long. This requires that market participants have strong leadership, with clearly defined plans and objectives, as execution of plans must be clean and sure. False starts or hesitation in execution can cause the loss of an opportunity or of a competitive position.

Finally, the *rapid change* of the rules by which the industry has lived for the last 30 years has thrown it into confusion. Managers who are used to dealing with technical performance issues are somewhat at a loss in dealing with political regulatory bodies. Newer managers seem to face these issues more effectively. However, industry management is currently in a generational transition and remains, for the most part, ill equipped to deal in this new arena. Thus companies that can deal with the public policy makers have an opportunity to influence regulation in the direction most beneficial to their products and technologies.

MAKHTESHIM CHEMICAL WORKS

Makhteshim-Again is a part of Koor Industries, Ltd., Israel's largest industrial manufacturing firm. Koor Industries had worldwide sales of over $2.1 billion in 1986, and ranked 262 on the *Fortune*-500 list of non-U.S. companies. It has over 100 manufacturing facilities, and over 180 marketing, financial, and commercial companies within the Group.

Makhteshim Chemical Works and Again Chemical Manufacturers, Ltd. are both parts of the chemical branch of Koor Industries. They operate three manufacturing facilities in Israel, employing 1,750 workers. Outside Israel, Makhteshim and Again operate as a joint company, sharing offices, staffs, and communication facilities. Makhteshim-Again has three regional sales offices which are located in Europe, the United States, and Brazil, and achieves the distribution of its products in 65 countries through more than 40 distribution centers

on five continents. Sales in Israel account for 30 percent of their sales revenue and only 10 percent of Makhteshim-Again's production. Sales in 1985 were $160 million, with export sales accounting for 70 percent of the sales revenue. The distribution of sales among the company's main product groups is shown in Table 5.

TABLE 5
Main Product Groups

Product	% of Revenues
Agrochemicals and household pesticides	87.0
Fine chemicals and intermediates	5.0
Polyester and flame retardants	3.0
Photographic chemicals	2.0
Industrial chemicals	3.0
TOTAL	100%

In Israel, Makhteshim Chemical Works and Again are run as basically two different companies, each with separate headquarters and staffs. They compete with each other and other Koor subsidiaries for resources from the parent company. Again, by far the larger of the two groups, deals primarily in agricultural chemicals and household pesticides. Makhteshim, on the other hand, produces fine chemicals, flame retardants, polymer intermediates, and other industrial chemicals. Because of their different product focuses, the marketing approaches and operating philosophies of these two organizations are different.

The agricultural chemical business tends to be more tightly focused, with fewer suppliers competing in a relatively homogeneous marketplace for chemicals. The number of customers tends to be smaller and more stable, and ongoing relationships can be built up on the business side of customer companies. Because Again sold primarily chemical compounds of known technology and enjoyed widespread recognition for providing quality products, there was little need for interaction between Again's R&D staffs and the customers' technical people. In most parts of the world, Again's technical people generally limited their contacts to demonstrating the application of herbicides and pesticides, along with general agromic techniques. Again thus had developed a marketing approach that did not require great technical sales expertise, but relied on price. This strategy has been successful for Again.

Makhteshim, on the other hand, was a smaller organization that sold a diverse product line in many markets. One common element in these markets was their strong technological orientations. Makhteshim's management believed the company enjoyed a strong technological position based primarily on its work in bromine and phosgene chemistry. They considered Makhteshim's technical staff to be of excellent quality and its laboratory facilities to be "world class." They had backed these resources with an $80 million capital investment program begun in 1986 and were confident that Makhteshim did fine technical work when it was aware of a problem or issue confronting a customer industry.

A second common element in Makhteshim's markets was the incorporation of the chemicals, such as flame retardants, in the customer's end product. In this environment the customer's technical staff, who specified the components of the end product, play a key role in the purchasing decision. A supplier must maintain close contact with potential customers' technical staffs if its products are to be tested and eventually specified. Suppliers typically hire technically trained sales people, and competitive pressure requires that these sales people be familiar with the product technology and various issues facing the customer's industry. Knowledge of a customer's technology and the nature of its end product are also important since rival sellers of flame retardants often used alternate technologies to perform the same function.

In the opinion of its management, Makhteshim operated at a disadvantage on this second element. The company's technical staff were not part of its marketing program. Instead, they remained in their laboratories with limited interaction with customers or industry peers, leading to isolation from industry issues and trends. Their contact with Makhteshim's sales force was limited too, generally consisting of responding to the latter's requests for specific technical information. Management believed that this state of affairs made it difficult for the technical staff to develop an overall picture of industry trends

or an understanding of how they might make better commercial use of their technical skills.

Some elements of Makhteshim's management believed the company had failed to recognize opportunities and to obtain the resources required to implement its own strategy because its overseas activities were combined with the much larger Again. Instead, Makhteshim had been forced to adopt a low-cost strategy that limited the resources committed to its technical sales function and to the regulatory and political conflicts that surrounded some of its products. Sometimes this meant bringing new products to market with limited technical support. In entering the U.S. market, Makhteshim attempted to overcome this shortcoming by arranging for M&T to market its F-2000 flame retardant product line. According to industry sources, M&T had a good technical staff that called regularly on customers and could easily handle the F-2000 line. However, this arrangement had brought disappointing results and Makhteshim's management was considering a new strategy.

In particular, they now doubted the efficacy of distributor marketing when it is not backed with knowledge of the market and strong support from their own manufacturing operations. It was in this light that Makhteshim was reassessing its basic strategy in the U.S. flame retardant market.

ALTERNATIVES FOR MAKHTESHIM EXPANSION INTO THE U.S. MARKET

Makhteshim has four basic strategy alternatives for expanding its flame retardant business in the U.S. Each has benefits and drawbacks, with varying levels of risk and potential reward.

The M&T Option

Continuing to work with M&T, a known factor, and increasing the support to this distributor, is possibly the simplest choice for Makhteshim. The assessment of M&T as being unsuccessful in promoting the flame retardant line may be misleading due to a longer lead time in the normal introduction of a new product into a skeptical marketplace. It may be that the three years of less than desired sales are no more than the normal entry cost of convincing customers of the firm's commitment to the U.S. marketplace. After all, Makhteshim is a rather small company by U.S. standards, it is based in a volatile area of the world, and it has only a limited track record in flame retardant technology. Maybe Makhteshim expected too much, too quickly, of its U.S. market. This is certainly the position of M&T. It points to a recent major customer order as a "breakthrough" in the marketing program. Although the initial order was small, the fact that the customer has developed a new product line based on Makhteshim's product offers the potential of continuing sales for a long time.

This option of staying with M&T also provides little capital risk to Makhteshim. Little additional resources would be needed to pursue this option, and if, indeed, a major upturn is around the corner, why confuse the marketplace and customers with a change now? Possibly, only minor changes to their agreement, such as additional incentives to M&T for increased sales or more support from Israeli technical personnel to support the sales effort, are all that is really needed.

However, is M&T really the right company for Makhteshim to be using? It is not one of the strongest players in the flame retardant marketplace, and manufactures its own product line (Thermoguard) which is competitive in some respects. Additionally, the outlets for additional technology in the polymers area Makhteshim may develop might be somewhat limited by using M&T as its only market channel. The sorry fact is that M&T has not performed up to expectations so far. Can Makhteshim continue to accept this performance level?

The New Distributor Option

The option of finding a new distributor/agent in the United States for Makhteshim's product is an attractive one from the Israeli standpoint. A new distributor would bring both enthusiasm and new ideas to the marketing of the product, without the old baggage of several years of a frustrating lack of success. Additionally, a new distributor might be motivated by the potential of additional new products, and serve as an outlet for further Makhteshim technology. However, the education and technical training of the new distributor in the

Makhteshim product line would be both time consuming and expensive. How much progress would be lost and how would the customers perceive Makhteshim's commitment with this change of horses in midstream? More practically, who would this new agent be? The bromine flame retardant industry has been consolidating, and there are now only 4 to 5 major players. Would one of them really be willing to take on a competitive line and give it the required service in this highly competitive industry? Could a deal really be structured which would be beneficial to Makhteshim? What would Makhteshim bring to the table?

Finally, given Makhteshim's unhappiness with their current distributor, why would they do any better with a new one? It will take time and effort to understand each other in a new relationship. Would the results be any different?

Expand International Organization

The most logical way to control its own fate in the marketplace would be for Makhteshim to expand its New York office with its own sales and marketing force. There is already an organization in place for the agricultural business which could be expanded to the flame retardant industry. This would serve the purpose of raising its profile in the flame retardant industry, as well as give it a base on which to expand into other polymers areas. But this would be expensive. The number of customers in the industry, and the amount of technical support required to be successful, would require several sales people, all technically trained. Additionally, some technical capabilities would be required in the United States to support applications work with the customer. While the actual laboratory facilities could remain in Israel, additional resources from the labs would be necessary to come to the States on a regular and frequent basis. The limited initial product line would not support this flow expenditure in the short run. In the long run, more products would have to be added to support the expenditure level required.

Additionally, the question of who the personnel should be, and whether home or host country, is a critical one. The U.S. chemical industry tends to be a rather closed society characterized by long-term personal relationships. Most successful foreign entries into the U.S. chemical market have chosen to enter by acquisition of a U.S. company, leaving the organization relatively intact and making changes only at the top. Those companies that have tried to control the U.S. organization too tightly have had limited success. Makhteshim, having been successful in its European and Far East operations with Israeli nationals, has trouble understanding why a similar method of operation does not work in the United States. It is reluctant to hire a large number (by its standards) of Americans for its U.S. operations. Additionally, Americans are an expensive labor force.

There is also a question of cultural and political naiveté by Makhteshim related to marketing in the United States. Makhteshim has been successful in its worldwide marketing of flame retardants using a low cost–low hire strategy. In the U.S., however, the price of the flame retardant is only a secondary issue. Marketing of specialty chemicals revolves around technology and customer service. The Israelis have only limited experience in this type of marketing in the United States.

Finally, since future success in the flame retardants industry will depend a great deal on how a company manages the political and regulatory environment, it is critical that Makhteshim examine its own record in this area. Makhteshim's success in the U.S. political and environmental regulatory arena is suspect. While Israel was successful negotiating a free trade agreement with the United States, a notable exception to this success was in the area of bromine chemical and flame retardant chemicals. Industry sources have described Israel testimony and efforts as "surprisingly poor." As the atmosphere surrounding the use of flame retardants becomes increasingly political, and emotional, should Makhteshim spend the resources to attempt this effort on their own?

Joint Venture Possibilities

Makhteshim has approached several U.S. companies in search of a suitable partner for expansion into the U.S. market. The most serious discussions have been held with a company (company A) which wishes Makhteshim to use its cost position in raw materials, and its flexible manufacturing facilities, to produce a flame retardant neither company now

makes. Company A would then market the product in the U.S. Company A has proposed a straight sales deal, with Makhteshim producing the product, selling it to A, and A reselling it in the U.S. market. The Israelis, however, would like a more extensive arrangement. They see this company as a valuable outlet for their product technology, and a possible long-term partner. Makhteshim would like to consider a joint venture, not only on this new product, but on the whole F-2000 line. Eventually, the Israelis could see this joint venture expanding to include other polymer products they might develop. As the Israelis see it, a joint venture would gain for them the sales and marketing expertise they do not have, and would insure the commitment of their partner which they felt was lacking with M&T. They feel they could provide a joint venture with strong technical R&D capabilities, new products, a flexible manufacturing facility, and a strong raw materials position. Additionally, its free-trade position with the EEC could provide cost advantages for the joint venture.

Company A has a strong market presence in flame retardants, being active in all major industry organizations and well respected for its customer commitment. It has a strong sales and marketing force, provides good coverage of the United States, and an excellent marketing strategy. It is active, but considerably weaker, overseas. And, finally, company A has an aggressive management, willing to take risks, and with a proven record of profit growth and performance. While it has some potentially competitive products, its product line is limited, but growing. Makhteshim's new technology would be complementary in some future products.

But there are serious problems to be resolved, the most serious of which is that the U.S. company is not really convinced that they want to be partners with Makhteshim, let alone joint venture partners. They would prefer a straight purchase of product, avoiding any more permanent arrangement until they see "how this works out". They see in Makhteshim a company with considerable technological skill, excellent manufacturing facilities, and potential new products which could significantly expand their product line. But the Israelis have a reputation for following a low-cost strategy, and company A is nervous about associating itself with that kind of thinking. This nervousness is apparent in their "let's try it for a while" attitude.

Both companies are cautious about sharing control in a joint venture. Both are skeptical about the mode of operation of the other, and the effect it would have on the combined venture. The Israelis are additionally concerned about the expense of this kind of joint venture, being unfamiliar with a large sales force, and the expenses entailed in doing business in the U.S. marketplace. They are not used to large bills for dinners, tend to stay in less expensive hotels, and control entertainment expenses tightly. Whether to pursue this option with its control, expense, and cultural mindset problems and how a joint venture could be structured, is causing serious debate within Makhteshim.

Increasingly, the management of Makhteshim has recognized that the current mode of operation in the United States will not be successful. More resources will be required in any new strategy, whether it be additional technical support to distributors, building its own sales and marketing organization, or managing and functioning in a joint venture environment. The decision will undergo intense scrutiny by Koor management, and will be questioned vigorously by other groups within Koor, who are all competing for the same limited resources. A clear consensus is, at present, not available.

13. Prima Diapers

BACKGROUND

Late one afternoon in October 1988, Ahmet Tankut, product manager for Ender Baby Products, Inc.'s (EBP) disposable diaper "Prima" was wondering how to approach his biggest professional challenge to date, rejuvenating the introduction of Prima in the Swiss market. Prima, a high-quality disposable diaper introduced successfully into the Turkish market in 1985, had been introduced in March 1988 in three Swiss cities to test European-market potential. The sales results of the initial six-month test-marketing period and the consumer survey that followed had been discouraging.

When the decision to expand abroad was made, EBP marketers had initially considered only two markets, the European Community (EC) and the Middle East (ME), represented by Turkey. They believed that Turkey, EBP's home country, formed a natural bridge between Western Europe and the Middle East historically, geographically, and culturally. The acceptance of the company's star product in either the EC or ME market could serve, they thought, as a later route of entry for other Ender

products. Given Turkey's associate member status in the EC and the advanced state of negotiations about her full membership, EBP marketers chose to test market Prima in the European market first.

Having decided on Europe as the general test area, EBP then chose Switzerland as the test-market country. While not a member of the EC, Switzerland was, they thought, an excellent microcosm of Europe. It had French, German, and Italian subcultures; multilingual capabilities; and a cosmopolitan outlook. Many international organizations were domiciled there. Located at the heart of Europe, it would be an excellent nucleus of expansion if the test marketing of Prima were to prove successful. To ensure ready acceptance of the product, EBP had even commissioned a Swiss import *grosshandler* (large distributor) who specialized in the distribution of children's clothing and furniture. This grosshandler, Jouvaille and Stadtmüller (J&S), distributed products from many Mediterranean countries. Given Turkey's impending full membership in the EC, they had shown particular interest in distributing Ender's products.

In the light of its own market research and in consultation with J&S, Ender had selected Geneva, Basel, and Zurich as test-market cities. J&S distributed Prima to department stores (such as Nouvelles), supermarkets (such as Migros), pharmacies, and institutional cooperatives (superstores where

This case was prepared by Attila Yaprak, Associate Professor of Marketing, Wayne State University, for class discussion and not as an example of either effective or ineffective managerial decision making.

employees of a given institution such as the armed forces often shopped for bargains). Prima was shelved in each of these retailers alongside world brands such as Pampers, Luvs, and Huggies, and with national brands from France, Italy, and Germany.

When evaluating the discouraging sales figures from the first six months of test marketing, Ahmet Tankut asked himself the six following strategic questions:

1. Why was Prima, a successful product entry into the Turkish market, so much less successful in the Swiss market? Was the positioning of the product as a direct competitor to internationally known-brands a poor choice of strategy? Had the distribution outlets been inappropriately chosen? Should Ender phase out marketing indirectly through J&S and gradually build its own sales force to diffuse the products more directly? Would the cost of developing such a sales force be prohibitive?

2. Was the advertising campaign that had accompanied Prima's introduction ill conceived? Was the quality of the product questionable? Was Prima suffering from country-of-origin bias (against Turkish-made products)? Was Prima incorrectly priced?

3. Was Switzerland the wrong country for test marketing Prima in Western Europe?

4. Was the European market for baby products not growing as fast as the Turkish market?

5. Could Prima be positioned as a product with unique product attributes and accordingly targeted at a niche market?

6. What competitive strategies could Prima use to brighten the gloomy sales picture to date?

7. Should EBP forgo the opportunity to market Prima in Europe in favor of marketing it in other Middle Eastern countries?

ENDER BABY PRODUCTS, INC.

EBP had been incorporated in Izmir, Turkey, in 1984 by Ramiz Okyay. Okyay, a wholesaler and retailer of a line of baby shoes, had, in the late seventies, diversified into the manufacture of infant clothing and sleepwear. Inspired by the exploding baby product market in Turkey and neighboring Middle Eastern countries, Okyay had sought out for partnership other baby product manufacturers. In 1983, he had succeeded in acquiring Alper Baby Products, a medium-sized manufacturer of plastic and cleaning items such as bibs, training bottles, cleansing creams, and baby wipes.

After the acquisition of Alper by Okyay Products was announced in various trade media, Okyay was approached by Pura Babywear Company, a manufacturer of infant clothing and nursing pads and a supplier of disposable diapers to large Turkish consumer-product companies. Particularly interesting was Pura's claim that the company, aided by a pediatrician, had succeeded in developing a high-quality disposal diaper worthy of competing head on with such internationally known brands as Luvs, Pampers, and Huggies.

Convinced that Pura's products were indeed of high quality but that the firm lacked the resources for effectively marketing the much touted new diaper, Okyay successfully persuaded Alper and Pura to form a new corporation in 1984 to sell several lines of baby products under the Ender's name as well as individual brand names. Upon incorporation, EBP started manufacturing and marketing plastic baby items, infant clothing, baby sleepwear, and disposable diapers. Each year after its introduction in 1985 into the disposable diaper market, Prima showed startling sales growth in Turkey.

THE TURKISH BABY PRODUCTS MARKET

The Turkish baby products market had grown rapidly since the early 1970s. Ender's marketing staff attributed this growth to (1) rapid population growth, especially in rural Anatolia; (2) accelerated urbanization; and (3) a revolution of rising expectations in both urban and rural areas.

EBP marketers had also determined that disposable diaper usage as a proportion of total diaper usage was rising rapidly, particularly among urban dwellers. They believed this share would rise from about 30 percent in 1985 to about 50 percent in 1990.

The quality of disposable diapers was also rising, both as a result of advancing technology and the explosive growth in the number of Turkish yuppies in urban coastal areas. Demand was also growing. Accordingly, the average retail price of disposable diapers had been rising faster than the rise in raw material and manufacturing costs, and the margins offered to wholesalers and retailers expanded. Between 1988 and 1990, EBP marketers expected an 8 to 10 percent per year growth rate for units of disposables sold and 14 to 20 percent per year growth rates for lira sales.

Given this encouraging market picture and confident of the superior quality of its product, EBP did indeed introduce Prima in Turkey to compete head on with such well-known brands such as Pampers, Luvs, Huggies, Mon Bébé, and Cottonelle. Prima was introduced at a relatively lower per diaper retail price and was distributed through wholesalers to department stores, supermarkets, pharmacies, and institutional stores. To build a "premium" image for Prima, low-volume retailers such as grocery stores, smaller markets, and convenience stores were intentionally excluded.

EBP's bold strategic move appeared to be succeeding. By 1988, sales figures showed encouraging penetration of Prima into the market shares enjoyed by foreign "designer" brands such as Ultra Pampers Plus, Super Luvs and Super Absorbent Huggies. Prima also successfully cut into the market shares of such premium brands as Ultra Pampers, Mon Bébé, and Cottonelle (see Exhibit 1).

Market trends clearly showed a shift away from basic brands toward the higher quality disposables. Whatever their nationality, consumers had become more demanding in their expectations of product attributes. For example, the attributes they were now demanding included advanced absorbency, thicker padding, leak resistance, convenience (for example, refastenability) ease in multiple checking (of the baby's bottom for wetness) attractive package design, safety information, and high value for the money (see Exhibit 2). Prima's attributes compared very favorably with both the premium and the super premium brands. Indeed, Prima's waist shield was moisture proof. It guaranteed leak resistance; its waistline tapes lined up on colorful characters such as teddy bears, koala bears, and stars. Ahmet Tankut and his staff hypothesized that these product attributes, in addition to the premium positioning of Prima and a slight price advantage over other premium brands, may have been responsible for its strong market penetration in three years.

EXHIBIT 1
Market Shares for Disposable Diapers (%) Turkish Market

Brand	1980	1985	1987
Pampers	10	12	12
Ultra Pampers[1]	3	8	19
Ultra Pampers Plus[2]	0	4	6
Luvs	8	10	11
Super Luvs[2]		3	5
Huggies	8	11	12
Super Absorbent Huggies[2]	0	2	4
Prima[1]	0	1	5
Mon Bébé[1]	12	14	12
Cottonelle[1]	12	13	12
Yumak	18	12	8
Cici Bébé	16	8	3
Others	13	2	1

[1] "Premium" Brands

[2] "Designer" (super premium) brands

Yumak, Cici Bébé, and Others were Turkish private label brands positioned as low-cost alternatives to manufacturer's brands.

EXHIBIT 2
Product Attributes of Disposable Diaper Brands

Attribute	Absorbency/Dryness	Padding
Brand		
Pampers	Absorbent	Regular padding
Ultra Pampers	Advanced absorbent	Thick padding
Ultra Pampers Plus	Very absorbent	Thick, fluffy to cushion baby
Luvs	Absorbent	Thick padding
Super Luvs	Advanced-absorbent, deluxe-fitting leg gathers	Extra-thick baby-shaped padding
Huggies	Absorbent	Dry-touch inner liner
Super Absorbent Huggies	Very Absorbent	Extra-thick absorbent padding
Prima	Absorbent	Thick, baby-shaped padding
Mon Bébé	Absorbent	Thick padding
Cottonelle	Absorbent	Regular padding
Yumak	Not quite absorbent	Regular padding
Others (private brands)	Not quite absorbent	Regular padding

INTRODUCTION INTO THE SWISS MARKET

Encouraged by its Turkish success, EBP management explored the European market potential of Prima. Switzerland appeared to be the wisest choice of test market for the reasons mentioned earlier and reviewed below.

First, Switzerland was a microcosm of France, Germany, and Italy. It contained three of the major subcultures within the EC. Testing Prima in this EC microcosm seemed wise. By December 31, 1992, the Community would be a single economic unit encompassing 320 million people with a single communitywide currency. People, goods, capital, and services will move across national boundaries as they now do across state lines within the United States.

Second, Switzerland was one of the wealthiest countries in the world and enjoyed one of the world's highest standards of living. Surrounded by France, West Germany, Austria, Liechtenstein, and Italy, and at the heart of Europe, it symbolized European coexistence.

EXHIBIT 2 *(continued)* _____

Waist Panel	Refastenability	Leak Resistance	Safety Tips on . . .	Package Design
Tapeless	With pin	Some leaks	—	Attractive
Line-up tapes	Yes	Leak resistant	Burns	Very attractive
Line-up tapes on colors for multiple checking	Yes	Taping panel for guaranteed leak resistance	Burns, choking	Very attractive
Refastenable tapes	Yes	Leak resistant	Burns, choking	Very attractive
Line-up tapes allow multiple checking	Yes	No-tear taping surface for guaranteed leak resistance	Burns, choking	Very attractive
Very thin tapes	Yes	Leak resistant	Burns, choking	Very attractive
Gentle elastic waist/no-tear panel	Yes	No-tear taping surface for guaranteed leak resistance	Burns, choking	Very attractive
Line-up tapes on characters for multiple checking	Yes	No-tear taping surface Moisture-proof waist shield and leg gathers for guaranteed leak resistance	Burns, choking Disposing diaper	Attractive
Line-up tapes	With pin	Leak resistant	No	Very attractive
Line-up tapes	With pin	Leak resistant	No	Very attractive
Tapeless	With pin	Leak resistant	No	Somewhat attractive
Tapeless	Some with pin; others without	Not quite leak resistant	No	Attractive to not attractive

Third, with a highly educated population of 6.4 million (1987) and as the home base of some 150 international organizations employing hundreds of thousands of non-Swiss citizens, Switzerland was a wonderful nucleus from which to spread the Prima concept and brand name.

Fourth, a nascent marketing presence for Prima already existed in Switzerland. While an MBA student in Lausanne, Ahmet Tankut had developed a feel for the Swiss market and had established close business relationships with several Swiss businesses, including J&S distributors. Tankut believed that J&S had an excellent network of wholesalers and retailers on which to piggyback other EBP products.

Fifth, EBP's research indicated that Swiss women were entering the work force at a slightly higher rate than the European average. This was particularly true for such white-collar professions as banking, the sciences, and communications. Tankut read into this statistic a greater need for disposable diapers. Annual population increase through live births (including immigrants) had averaged around 1 percent between 1980 and 1985. This too augured well for the market for disposable diapers.

Sixth and last, Switzerland's leading trading partners were all EC member countries. Easy diffusion opportunities into those countries seemed assured.

Basel, Geneva, and Zurich—French and German cities—were chosen as the test market cities. While Mr. Tankut had intended to include in the test marketing effort the heavily Italian Ticino. Inclusion of this canton was postponed for cost-efficiency reasons.

Basel, Switzerland's third largest city (367,000 in 1987) and its only direct link to the Atlantic Ocean (through the Rhine River), accounted for over 35 percent of Swiss foreign trade in 1987. Located where France, West Germany, and Switzerland come together, it is also home to a large pharmaceutical industry and to international commerce. The per capita income in Basel is twice the Swiss national average; it is a major R&D center for pharmaceutical companies, and its consumers are considered very demanding.

Geneva (323,000 in 1987 and home to over 100 international organizations) had always been a progressive city. It was here that John Calvin had delivered his fiery Protestant teachings in the Reformation; have that the International Red Cross, the League of Nations, and the United Nations were established; and have that the first Swiss female mayor had been elected (in 1968). Geneva supported perhaps the most cosmopolitan population in the world, a very high per capita income, and the greatest proportion of opinion-leading consumers. The city was heavily French in culture and attitudes.

Zurich, the largest Swiss city (707,000 in 1987), was decidedly German in outlook and lifestyle. While Zurich's population was also cosmopolitan, it had a greater proportion of foreign workers and immigrants than did Geneva and Basel. It was home to large banking, precision instrument, watch, insurance, electronic component, food and beverage, and personal and medical care industries. Its per capita income was slightly higher than the Swiss national average, but its consumers had relatively modest product expectations and conservative values. Zurich provided a realistic counterbalance to Geneva and Basel.

EBP introduced Prima into Basel, Geneva, and Zurich in March 1988 through the J&S's distribution network. As in Turkey, Prima was shelved alongside well-known premium and super premium brands in department stores, pharmacies, supermarkets, and institutional stores. It was positioned as a premium product that delivered better value for the money spent (see Exhibit 3). Prima's superior value was communicated to Swiss consumers through advertisements in two newspapers, *Der Blick*, the largest Swiss daily, and *Journal de Genève*, the third largest Swiss daily. Advertising in women's magazines was considered, but had to be scrapped due to high cost. Radio advertising was ruled out because it could not demonstrate Prima's superior attributes. Television advertising, while great for demonstration, was simply too expensive to support an introductory campaign. A two-minute film was being produced in Zurich to be shown in cinemas before feature films.

J&S's July 1988 report to Tankut showed that, while they had effectively distributed Prima to the retail endpoints of their channel network, retailers were not reordering the product at the expected pace. J&S advised Tankut not to be discouraged, but he felt that a market survey was necessary to pinpoint the cause of Prima's poor performance. He authorized a Swiss firm to do such a survey.

THE AUGUST 1988 SURVEY

In July 1988, EBP commissioned Giresse Market Research (GMR) of Geneva to conduct an August market-awareness survey of Swiss consumers. Telephone interviews with 1,200 women of childbearing age and personal interviews with 450 women shoppers in pharmacies and supermarkets in Basel, Geneva, and Zurich showed that:

1. Only about 3 percent of all interviewees had heard of Prima; less than 1 percent had tried it.

2. Users had liked it, but were not sure whether it was in fact superior to other premium brands.

3. Eighty-eight percent of those interviewed said that they were not willing to try Prima; 90 percent indicated brand loyalty to other, primarily European, brands.

4. Once told that Prima was a Turkish-made product, 76 percent said that they would have

EXHIBIT 3

Swiss Retail Prices of Different Package Sizes of Disposable Diaper Brands

Brand	Package Count	Package Price (in Sfrs)
Pampers	96	37
Ultra Pampers	48	21
	96	40
Ultra Pampers Plus	28	22
	32	24
	48	26
	64	42
Luvs	96	38
Super Luvs	32	23
	64	44
Huggies	18	8
	24	12
	48	20
	96	39
Super Absorbent Huggies	18	9
	48	22
	64	40
Prima	18	7
	24	9
	32	14
Mon Bébé	32	15
	48	23
Cottonelle	32	14
	48	22
Private Brands (average)	18	6
	32	12

expected it to be priced lower (closer to the private brands); 18 percent would not buy a Turkish-made diaper; the 12 percent who were willing to try it were skeptical about whether Prima would be as good a product as internationally known brands.

GMR's survey also showed that:

1. Leak resistance and absorbency were the most desired attributes, followed by padding, waist panel, and refastenability. Package design was somewhat important; safety information not.

2. Most interviewees were willing to buy relatively cheaper brands for everyday use. They pur-chased the premium brands for overnight use or for special occasions such as evening visits with friends and relatives and to alleviate skin rashes. Most mothers used 5–7 disposables per day, only 1–3 of these being the premium brands.

3. Purchasing agents and buyers believed that (a) Swiss women were very "value conscious"; (b) Prima was in fact a "value" product, but this was not communicated effectively to the consumer; and, (c) pricing Prima as an economy product, might make it more competitive.

4. Approximate "European" market shares (averaged over only West German, French,

EXHIBIT 4

Market Shares for Disposable Diapers (%)

European Market

Brand	1987	1990 (est.)
Pampers	13	10
Ultra Pampers	8	9
Ultra Pampers Plus	5	8
Luvs	10	8
Super Luvs	4	6
Huggies	10	7
Super Absorbent Huggies	3	6
Mon Bébé	15	16
Cottonelle	15	16
Private Brands	15	8
Newcomers	2	6

and Italian markets) were as displayed in Exhibit 4.

Based on these findings, GMR made the following recommendations to the EBP management:

☐ It would be difficult to crack the European consumer market with the current strategy. EBP may want to reposition Prima toward the economy end of the market by cutting its price and including smaller retailers in its distribution network.

☐ EBP may also want to explore niche markets such as hospitals, nursing homes for the elderly, and—most of all—the growing number of child-care centers. Successful wholesale distribution to any or all of these markets might provide the initial working capital margins with which EBP could later try to penetrate the consumer market.

☐ Why not try other Middle Eastern markets? With explosive birth rates and cultural similarities to the Turkish market, marketing Prima in, say, Saudi Arabia, Egypt, or Pakistan, might be less costly than Switzerland, France, or West Germany.

14. General Consumer Products, Inc. (A)

In late 1981, General Consumer Product's (GCP) special *Strategic Task Force* (STF) faced three critical decisions as it considered a set of proposals from Global Consultants, Inc. Global was recommending a drastic overhaul in foreign-marketing planning and management approaches in the international division of the company's Household and Personal

This case was prepared by Brian Toyne.

Care division (HPCID). These were the decisions to be made:

☐ Should GCP adopt the long-range planning approaches recommended by Global, including the portfolio and strategic-business-unit concept (SBU), which had recently become popular within large diversified firms in the United States and Europe?

☐ If so, should the portfolio concept be viewed

as a tool to be used in the analysis of certain situations, or more comprehensively, as a complete system for the strategic management of HPCID's marketing activities?

☐ What planning and organizational implications would these decisions have for the management of individual subsidiaries and other forms of international involvement? For example, to what extent should the managers of individual foreign subsidiaries retain the authority to decide which new products should be introduced to their markets and the general level of effort expended on their markets?

BACKGROUND

Domestic Activities

In the years following World War II, GCP of Newark, New Jersey, had become a significant company in the U.S. household cleaner industry. By 1960, this core business accounted for about 70 percent of the company's total sales of $102 million. These sales were concentrated mainly in three product groups: bar soaps, laundry detergents, and kitchen cleaners. Personal-care products, such as toothpastes, toothbrushes, and shampoos, accounted for the remaining $18 million in sales.

Between 1960 and 1980, the company grew rapidly and added several new product lines; by 1980, HPC's household product lines included liquid soaps, dishwashing liquids, and fabric softeners. Its personal care business had been expanded to include hand and body lotions, bath and shower foams and oils, hair-coloring and hair-grooming products, shaving products, and deodorants. By the end of 1980, these businesses accounted for 39 percent and 23 percent, respectively, of total sales of $1,020 million.

To reduce its dependency on these two businesses and to provide a more solid base for growth, GCP began to diversify in the mid-1960s, primarily through acquisitions. Between 1966 and 1974, the company acquired the following four companies:

1966 Health Care Company, Madison, Wisconsin, a manufacturer of skin-care products, including moisturizing and suntanning products (1980 sales of $81.6 million).

1969 Douglas Paper Products Company, Portland, Oregon, a manufacturer of household paper products and packaging materials (1980 sales of $102.0 million).

1971 Berger Health Appliances, Inc., Houston, Texas, a manufacturer of premium-quality exercise equipment, primarily for health clubs (1980 sales of $153.0 million).

1974 Natural Nutrition Company, Newwark, New Jersey, a small producer of health foods and beverages (1980 sales of $51.0 million).

These acquisitions were treated as virtually independent and autonomous operating units, or divisions. Apart from the regular submission of annual plans and budgets, the general manager of each division continued to operate in much the same way that they had prior to acquisition. Each general manager reported directly to Andrew Saxon, GCP's president. An abbreviated organization chart of GCP as of 1980 is presented in Figure 1.

The general managers of the four acquisitions also expanded their product lines as markets developed and consumer needs changed. For example, Douglas Paper Products introduced a line of disposable diapers in the late 1960s, and Health Care Products added a successful line of sun-protection products in 1980. Berger Health Appliances, responding to the growing interest in home exercising equipment, planned to introduce a line of exercise equipment specifically designed for home use early in 1982. Natural Nutrition added vitamins and other food supplements to its product offerings.

International Activities

Since the early 1950s, GCP had been involved in sporadically expanding its foreign business as attractive opportunities were brought to the attention of its marketing management. GCP's foreign sales were initially the result of exports to Western Europe and Latin America; they relied heavily on commission agents, wholesalers, and large retailers in those regions.

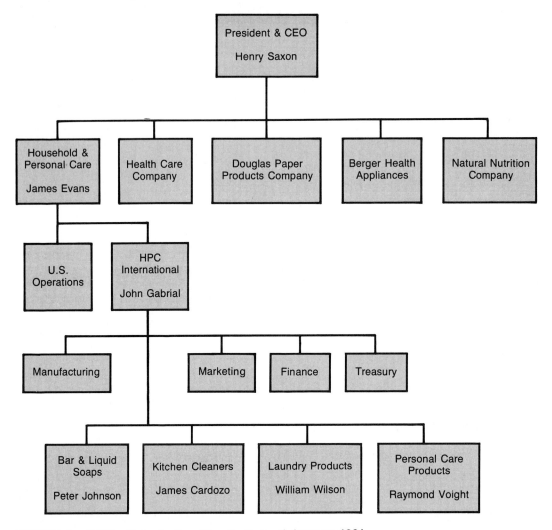

FIGURE 1   GCP's Organization Structure as of January 1981

While total foreign sales grew fairly steadily during the 1950s and 1960s, the company discovered that particular products were not equally attractive in both regions. GCP also found that foreign demand for its newer products appeared several years after introduction into the United States and began to decline relatively shortly thereafter.

Notwithstanding these problems, foreign sales represented 15 percent of total sales by 1970 and increased to 32 percent of total sales by 1980. This expansion was partly attributed to HPC's decision

to establish manufacturing subsidiaries in Canada in 1960, Great Britain in 1963, West Germany in 1967, Brazil in 1973, and Costa Rica in 1977. Within each of these subsidiaries, a general manager was responsible for overall operations. These included manufacturing, marketing, and sales activities. HPC also established sales and marketing offices in the other countries of the European Community, Spain, and several South American countries. The sales and marketing activities of these offices were the responsibility of local marketing managers. In compliance with GCP's standing policy, these affiliates were entirely owned and operated by HPC. GCP's management was of the opinion that their competitive strength was not in the patents they held but in the production and marketing of the company's products, which needed direct and tight control.

In order to coordinate these foreign manufacturing, marketing, and exporting activities, HPC's management created an international division late in 1968. As of 1980, John Gabrial was the executive responsible for HPCID's operations. Reporting to him were four product group managers: Peter Johnson, responsible for bar and liquid soap products; James Cardozo, for kitchen cleaner products; William Wilson for laundry products; and Raymond Voight for personal-care products.

The reasons for establishing the international division were several. Management was increasingly concerned over its dependency on foreign earnings to finance domestic growth plans and foreign activities were not receiving the managerial attention they warranted. HPC's dependency on foreign earnings had become clear when domestic earnings had dropped sharply in the late 1960s because of an unexpected decline in consumer spending.

Another reason for the growth in GCP's foreign sales was the company's other businesses. These had also expanded into overseas markets after acquisition—initially through exports, but eventually as a result of foreign manufacturing activities and exports. However, in these cases, there were considerable differences in overseas performance. For example, in 1980, foreign sales represented 10 percent of Health Care's total sales, 20 percent of Douglas Paper's sales, 3 percent of Berger Health Appliances' sales, and less than 2 percent of Natural Nutrition's sales. Of these four divisions, only Douglas Paper had adopted an international division structure and operated manufacturing facilities in Canada, Great Britain, and Brazil. Sales and marketing offices were located in West Germany in Europe and in Colombia and Venezuela in South America. Health Care operated one foreign manufacturing facility (located in France) and had sales and marketing offices in Great Britain and in Mexico. Although Berger Health Appliances had an offshore manufacturing arrangement in Taiwan, its foreign sales were mainly the result of exports to Europe.

Natural Nutrition's foreign sales were also the result of exporting, primarily to West Germany.

THE STRATEGIC TASK FORCE (STF)

Creation of the STF

After consulting with Gabrial and Evans, Henry Saxon circulated a memorandum in late 1979 to key members of GCP's management. The memorandum announced the formation of a special team to study the long-term approach to be taken in HPC's markets. It stated in part:

> Over the last twelve months, each of the foreign manufacturing and sales operations of HPC has presented us at headquarters with marketing programs for their individual markets. As in the past, these plans raise questions concerning the overall long-range strategy for HCP's foreign activities. I am appointing a Strategic Task Force to review this matter and to provide us with a set of recommendations for the future. The Task Force will be comprised of Mr. John Gabrial, Vice President of HPCID, the four product managers responsible for HPC's major product lines, and several additional company executives. Representatives from GCP's other divisions will be assigned to observe the activities of the Task Force.
>
> The Task Force is charged with identifying alternative approaches for developing affiliate marketing strategies consistent with HPC's resources, and the long-range plans for its products and product groups. At a minimum, these alternatives should:
>
> 1. Help management make decisions regarding the matching of product and cash-flow potentials with resources and establish the sequencing and timing of product and resource transfers among affiliates and the various products and product groups they handle;
> 2. Enable management to select the most appropriate marketing strategies for its product groups and products, thereby gaining maximum market penetration and profitability; and
> 3. Ensure that HPC's foreign affiliates re-

ceive a regular flow of relevant information on products and competitive activity.

Activities and Recommendations of the STF

After studying the foreign operations of HPC for a number of months, the STF decided to hire Global Consultants, Inc., a well-known strategic management consulting company, to assist them in generating alternative recommendations for the restructuring of the division's marketing planning and management activities. Global was given 12 months in which to study the situation and make recommendations. At the end of this time, the consulting company met with members of the STF and the local managers of HPCID's foreign operations. It produced a lengthy report covering the problems of the foreign side of the division's business. The report contained a number of observations on HPC's foreign marketing operations, observations that could be summarized as follows:

1. The foreign-marketing function had become much too complex and diffuse to be managed effectively by HPCID at the local level. Opportunities were being missed and errors in resource commitments being made. Among the opportunities missed was an aggressive pushing of HPC's liquid soap products in Europe and its sun protection products in Latin America. Among the errors cited was the failure of HPCID to develop a systematic procedure for collecting and analyzing information needed to assess trends in foreign markets, to determine their competitive positions in these markets, and to make decisions concerning the allocation of resources among these markets.

2. The general managers of HPCID's affiliates were much too preoccupied with generating cash flows from a limited number of well-established, high-margin products, and were too little concerned with developing HPC's overall competitive position. Parallel with this, they were also slow in mounting costly campaigns to introduce new products that were deemed by Global to have considerable potential in several of HPCID's foreign markets.

3. The marketing plans received by HPCID from its foreign affiliates were inconsistent in quality and in the way product and product group potentials were measured. The affiliates also exhibited little regard for the overall resources available for budgeting, and their marketing plans displayed little knowledge of the range of new products made available by HPC, and did not address the strategic objectives of the division. These problems were due partly to the autonomous and single-cycle planning approach used by the foreign affiliates and partly to the considerable variations in the market and competitive characteristics of these affiliates. In the case of HPC's sales and marketing affiliates, little attention was given during planning to the productive capabilities of the manufacturing subsidiaries upon which HPC depended.

As a first step, Global Consultants, Inc., proposed that HPCID be broken up into several geographic areas. Coordination of area activities, the allocation of resources, transfer of products, and the approval of all marketing programs at the area and country levels were to be handled at HPCID's headquarters. To ensure that resource allocation, product transfer, and marketing program decisions were consistent with HPCID's overall plans, HPCID was advised to adopt a three-cycle planning process built upon the portfolio concept.

These recommendations were buttressed with lengthy arguments and detailed analyses of HPCID's operations and markets.

THE STF'S RECOMMENDATIONS

Reorganization of HPCID

On the basis of an analysis of HPCID's operations, Global concluded that three area groups should be formed: Europe and Africa, Latin America and Canada, and the Pacific. Export business done with African countries, primarily South Africa, was relatively small, so those countries did not warrant inclusion as a separate subdivision. On the other hand, the export business done with Australia, New Zealand, and several other Pacific countries provided sufficient sales to warrant separate attention. In addition, these markets offered HPCID opportunities that Global feared might be overlooked by managements concerned only with developing HPCID's European and Latin American businesses.

To ensure that HPC's four product groups received equal attention by the three area groups. Global recommended that each area should be subdivided into product groups. The resulting groups were to replicate HPC's domestic operations.

The factors taken into account in reaching this conclusion included the geographical proximity and similarity of foreign markets, the location of manufacturing subsidiaries and sales and marketing offices, the volume of intracorporate shipments, the frequency of communications between HPCID and its affiliates and among affiliates, and the nature and size of local competition. Figure 2 indicates how these areas would be structured after reorganization.

To ensure that the activities of the three newly created area groups were coordinated in support of HPCID's objectives, a new layer of HPCID head-quarter managers was to be created. (These are also shown in Figure 2.) The manager in charge of the manufacturing unit would be responsible for coordinating the manufacturing activities of HPCID's facilities in Brazil, Canada, Costa Rica, Great Britain, and West Germany, and would also ensure

that HPC's U.S. facilities met the export needs of HPCID. The marketing manager would be responsible for coordinating the marketing and exporting efforts of HPCID's three area groups. He or she would have line authority over the allocation of HPCID's marketing resources, final approval over all marketing programs and strategies down to the country level, and would be charged with ensuring that new product information was disseminated and acted upon by local managers. The manager responsible for the finance unit would have duties similar to those of the manufacturing and marketing managers. Basically, that manager would be responsible for gauging the performance of the three area groups, managing the financial structure of the division, handling international financial transfers, and budgeting. The person in charge of the treasury unit would be responsible principally for handling such issues as taxes, blocked funds, and currency fluctuations. Initially, the manager in charge of product R&D would be responsible for coordinating the development and testing of those new products specifically designed for HPCID's markets (to ensure that all affiliates benefitted from these activities). Eventually, however, the R&D manager would be responsible for all product R&D activities. The affiliates would retain the testing and refining of products for their national markets.

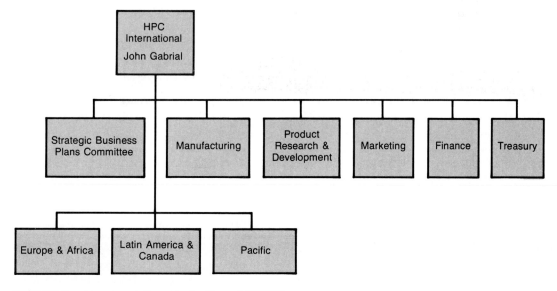

FIGURE 2   Proposed Reorganization of HPCID

The overall long-range direction of HPCID's activities was to be decided upon by a Strategic Business Plans Committee. This committee would consist of the vice-president in charge of HPCID, the three area group managers, and the four managers of the newly created headquarter units. In addition to setting the long-range goals for the division, the SBPC was to provide the guidance needed to ensure that the shorter range plans adopted by the three areas and their country managers would help the division achieve its basic business goals.

The Three-Cycle Portfolio Planning Approach

Global also concluded that HPCID's planning process could be described as a "two-cycle" process in which local managers first prepared functional plans for their operations and then developed sales and budgetary forecasts based on these plans. Except for the initial input of objectives from HPCID's headquarter staff, local managers were free to select the product lines and the products within these lines and to develop marketing programs they believed appropriate. The general managers of HPCID's manufacturing subsidiaries had the added responsibility of developing production schedules; the sales and marketing managers located in other countries were dependent upon these managers for the timely delivery of products. Also, when interested in adding to their product lines, they had to coordinate these marketing plans with subsidiaries or with HPCID directly. For example, the Mexican marketing manager was forced to delay the introduction of a new bar soap because the Costa Rican manager did not have sufficient capacity to meet his own demand, let alone the Mexican demand. The Costa Rican manager had experienced some production start-up problems, and had made commitments that now exceeded his facility's capacity. In addition, HPC's U.S. facilities were operating at capacity; they could not supply the Mexican market.

Global attributed the market problem in Mexico (and many others like it) to the lack of a three-cycle planning process, which it recommended should be adopted. In a three-cycle process, functional plans are preceded by strategic market planning. First, choices are made about the definition

and mission of each market. Next, plans are formulated to accomplish the chosen strategies. Third, sales forecasts and budgets are developed. Global stressed that any shift from a two-cycle to a three-cycle process was not to be just a change in the mechanics of planning. It required that the managers involved in the planning process think strategically and coordinate planning activities during each of the three cycles.

To ensure that the three areas (down to their country levels) developed plans consistent with and supportive of HPCID's long-range goals, Global recommended that the division's four product groups be treated as SBUs for planning purposes at all three levels: country, area, and headquarter levels. Countries with only sales and marketing offices would have to coordinate their plans and activities with those of the subsidiary from which they received their inventories. Export plans would be the responsibility of the country of origin.

To demonstrate this approach, Global prepared three growth-share matrices (see Figure 3) for presentation at the STF meeting. The first matrix showed HCP's market position on a worldwide basis (excluding the U.S. market) for each SBU. Global suggested that this matrix could be used to classify the four SBUs according to their growth potentials and competitive positions and be of some assistance in deciding on the overall strategic objectives for each SBU and the resources assigned to each.

Global was careful to point out that the matrix was only illustrative. The allocation of HPCID's resources on the basis of the worldwide positions of these four SBUs could be misleading. For example, the worldwide positions of the four SBUs did not indicate the relative positions of these groups within particular areas. Although a particular SBU could be classified as a cash cow on a worldwide basis, because of the international product-life cycle and local competitive differences, it could also be classified as a potential star in some markets. To illustrate its point, Global presented two additional matrices, also shown in Figure 3. The first illustrated the relative market positions of the four SBUs in Europe and Africa; the second presented the situation for the laundry products SBU in individual countries within Europe and Africa.

Global concluded this part of its presentation by recommending that the portfolio procedure described be used to systematically assess HPC's

The World-Wide Market Positions of HPCID's Major Product Groups:

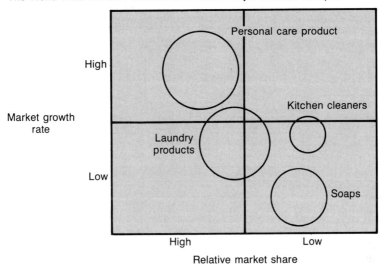

Market Positions of HPCID's Major Product Groups in the Europe & Africa Area:

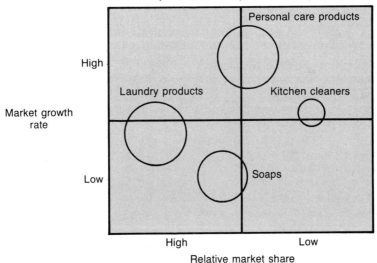

FIGURE 3   Illustrations of HPCID's Activities Based on a Portfolio Concept

market position on worldwide, regional, and country bases for each SBU and its product lines and products. This information could then be used by HPCID, the regional managers, and the country managers to develop guidelines, to allocate resources, and to suggest the most appropriate marketing strategies. John Gabrial considered the following extracts from Global's report most compelling:

Market Positions of Laundry Products in Major European & African Markets

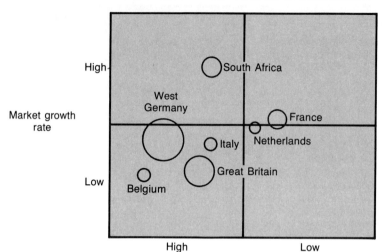

FIGURE 3   Illustrations of HPCID's Activities Based on a Portfolio Concept

☐ Use the portfolio approach to provide a uniform and qualitative assessment of each SBUs direction and needs.

☐ By using this concept for each SBU, members of the Strategic Business Plans Committee would be able to "see" the cash flow and net income implications of HPCID's overall and area plans—for HPC in particular and GCP in general. For example, HPCID management would benefit from its ability to rank the relative desirability of each SBU's international plans in terms of profitability, cash requirements, and strategic fit.

☐ Local affiliate managers would benefit simply from the process of formalizing their product plans along a portfolio concept.

REACTIONS TO GLOBAL'S PROPOSAL

Most of HPCID's local managers reacted negatively to the proposal. They saw the recommended shift from a decentralized to a highly centralized approach as reducing their authority and, thus, their ability to respond quickly to changing market conditions. Also, general managers would have to report to area managers, and sales and marketing managers would have to get approval for their plans from general managers.

In addition to these issues, several others surfaced that members of the STF considered particularly relevant. These are summarized below.

1. Global's proposal assumed that HPC's international markets were not sensitive to national differences (they could be segmented without regard to local differences). Consequently, marketing decisions would emphasize product uniformity rather than market variations. For example, it had been claimed by one member of the STF that many of HPCID's products were insensitive to local market structures and conditions. In fact, however, most of HPCID's affiliates had found it necessary to develop new products and to modify existing products for local consumption and use patterns.

2. Global's proposal also placed considerable emphasis on market share. This emphasis had been challenged by one of the managers, who had argued that market share was not the only

criterion to guide marketing strategies. Competitive environments varied considerably; a company's position need not be the same, or should not be the same, in all of the countries in which it competes. While some affiliates were well established and were faced with the task of protecting their positions, others faced the major task of establishing HPC in their national markets.

3. Global's proposal also implied regionalization, if not globalization, of HPCID's marketing approaches. This was in sharp contrast to the philosophy of product adaptation that had successfully been pursued in the past. For example, in recommending the centralization of product R&D, Global had apparently assumed that "washing is washing" worldwide, and that the market-by-market evaluations and localized marketing strategies undertaken by HPCID's affiliates were unnecessary.

4. Finally, Global had assumed that, with the effective centralization of HPCID's coordination and planning activities, the management of daily activities would be equally effective. However, the reaction of the local managers to Global's recommendation suggested that they would resist only attempts to reduce their authority.

Part V
Organization and
Control of Global
Marketing Activities

Marketing efforts must reflect company concerns and advance company goals. Accordingly, in these last two chapters, we focus on ways to organize, control, and assess these efforts: alternative organizational structures, the planning process, resource allocation approaches; and performance evaluation measures.

Chapter 18: examines the various organizational structures used by companies and factors influencing choice of those structures. The advantages and weaknesses of each alternative are discussed.

Chapter 19: examines the processes by which national and global marketing activities are controlled. Also explored are typical issues and problems encountered in any effort to coordinate, integrate, and evaluate global and national marketing activities.

Case Studies: International Engineering
General Consumer Products, Inc. (B)

Chapter 18
Organization
of the Global
Marketing Effort

_____

As its international activities grow, the organizational structure of a company invariably become more complex. This change is partly in response to the growing strategic importance of the company's overseas operations and partly in response to the complex problems associated with managing operational and geographic diversity.

Two conflicting pressures emerge as a result of international growth that require management action. Growing overseas operations create pressures to centralize for optimal coordination, integration, and control. At the same time, the growth in the number and diversity of the environments in which a company competes and the need to match strategies to these environments create pressures to decentralize.

In the 1960s, a third pressure emerged. This was the appearance of globally competitive industries. Companies competing in global industries found they needed to develop global strategies to protect worldwide market positions, to gain global-scale efficiencies, and to develop global-scanning capabilities to monitor environmental changes and competitors.

Since organization design is one of several management tools used to ensure that a company's resources are effectively used to attain corporate objectives, these evolving and conflicting pressures often resulted in the periodic reorganization of a company's activities. In most cases, this involves a restructuring of a company's domestic and international activities, a realignment of its authority and reporting relationships, adjustments in its resource allocations, and human and material transfers, and adjustments in its planning activities.

In this chapter, we answer some of the major questions raised when a firm reorganizes for international growth: What organizational structure should it use? Who should make what decisions? What planning approach should it use?

KEY ELEMENTS OF INTERNATIONAL ORGANIZATION DESIGN _____

Organization design requires more than the selection of a structure for a company's subunits. It also involves creating a goal-oriented social entity to accommodate and focus the efforts of individuals and groups: to collect and pool information, skills, and capital; to engage in agreed-on actions toward the achievement of predetermined objectives and goals; to monitor performance; to initiate corrective actions; and to facilitate the defining of new objectives and goals.[1]

Major Organization-Design Decisions

Many major decisions need to be made when creating an international organization for a particular company. Key questions are: (1) Which strategic dimension(s) of the company's activities should be emphasized? (2) What type of formal structure should be used to organize the company's activities? (3) To what extent should decision making be centralized? (4) What type of planning process should be used?

The organization design, or structural map, of a company should be consistent with and supportive of its overall strategic goals. The company with a *global strategy* focus will want to develop an *integrated,* or headquarters-directed, organization. One that has a *national strategy* focus will want to develop a foreign-affiliate-influenced design.[2] To a considerable extent, these differing approaches determine the relative emphasis a company will place on its functional activities, its product or business-related activities, and its regional, country, and market activities. As Prahalad and Doz point out, the formal structure reveals (1) the locus of power (to allocate critical resources), (2) consensus on strategic orientation, and (3) the mindset of the management.[3]

Structure dictates function. Because the structure selected determines the formal relationships that will exist within a particular organization, it also helps shape the corporate culture and the types of informal relationships established between and among managers.

A formal structure also influences the ease with which decision making can be centralized or decentralized. Other factors at work include specific marketplace and industry characteristics, the capabilities and job descriptions of its managers, and the information and reporting relationships established.

The planning process has a direct impact on the relative importance ascribed to the company's functional, product, and regional activities. In effect, it determines the kinds of information received by particular managers and, as a result, the influence these managers have on the future activities of the company.

Factors Influencing Organization-Design Decisions

The organization design adopted by a particular company grows from the type of business it is in, its strategic goals, and management capabilities; and reflects the company's history, its resources, its competitive environment, and the preferences and personalities of its management. For a company with international operations, the design also reflects the relative importance ascribed to key activities and the various forms of market presence established in overseas markets.

Essentially, an organization design needs to account for the six basic capabilities identified in the center of Figure 18-1. These basic capabilities are largely determined by environmental, market, and company factors, some of which are shown in the left-hand column of boxes. The six "organizational capabilities," and the company's "corporate activity focus," determine the formal structure, the decision-making structure, and the planning structure of the company, shown in the lower right-hand corner boxes.

The six organizational capabilities are (1) coordination and integration; (2) management control; (3) product, technology, and resource transfer; (4) communications; (5) resource development; and (6) competitive scanning (monitoring). As indicated by the title of Exhibit 18-1, organization design can be viewed as a management tool. It is the means by which a company achieves its corporate, business, and functional strategies at the parent, regional, and local levels.

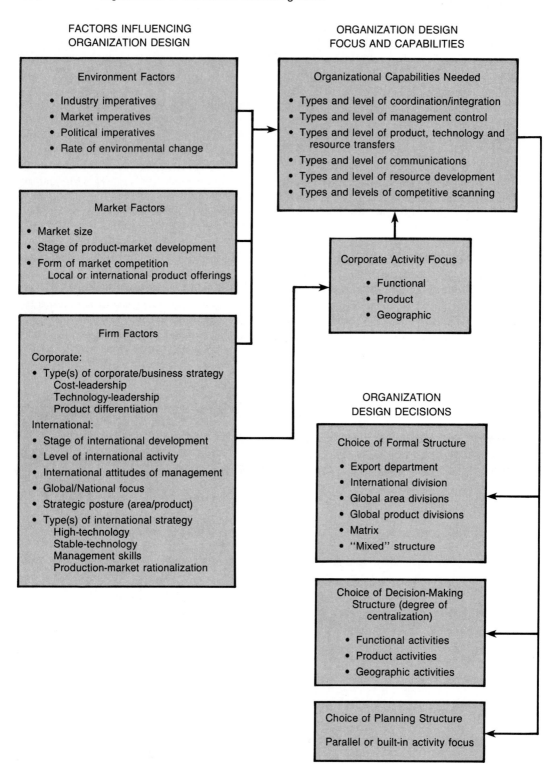

FIGURE 18-1   **Factors Influencing Choice of Formal Organizational Structure**

EXHIBIT 18-1————————————————————————————————————
Organization Design As a Strategic Management Tool————————————————————

The organization design created by a company can be viewed as a tool for accomplishing the following:

□ Implementing and subsequently achieving a company's strategic objectives and goals by facilitating the planning, monitoring, and control of its activities;

□ Establishing the relative importance of domestic and international markets;

□ Gaining strategic balance between the company's functional, product, and geographical interests by ensuring that appropriate importance is placed on and attention given to the coordination, integration, and control of the company's functional activities, product diversification activities, and markets.

□ Deploying resources (transferring appropriate technology, skills, and expertise and allocating financial and other resources) and accumulating appropriate human and material resources for future activities;

□ Establishing appropriate reporting relationships by explicitly creating information flows, and assigning responsibility for coordinating, integrating, monitoring and controlling activities

□ Fostering and reinforcing a particular social structure and climate through dependency relationships, values, and compatible reward- and performance-measurement systems.

□ Providing an ability to respond appropriately to competitive challenges in the company's various markets.

Environmental Factors

Strategic foci are not chosen in a vacuum. Corporate and business strategies are partly determined by factors external to company control. Many, often conflicting environmental factors have a strong influence on the types of organizational capabilities needed by a company competing in many national markets. These factors can be grouped under four major headings: (1) industry considerations, (2) market considerations, (3) political considerations, and (4) rate of environmental change. These considerations will determine the organization design of a particular company, singly or in combination. They are defined here and then discussed briefly:

Industry considerations The degree to which the competitive characteristics of the company's industry are national, regional, or global.

Market considerations The degree to which the salient characteristics of the markets in which the company competes are nationally, regionally, or globally determined.

Political considerations The degree to which governments determine the extent and form of the company's local involvement.

Environmental considerations The rate of change in critical market and environmental dimensions, such as consumer preferences, technology, and economic and political conditions.

Industry Considerations. Companies in global industries compete primarily with other global companies across national markets. As a result, they need organization designs that provide worldwide coordination, integration, control, planning, and competitor-scanning capabilities. These global-strategy companies experience strong competitive pressures to adopt structures that facilitate *centralization*. They also experience pressures to create organization designs that ease the transfer of products and technology between and among their various overseas operations and encourage the collecting of detailed information on the worldwide performance of their products.

Market Considerations. Companies competing in market-driven industries, on the other hand, generally compete with local companies and other global companies within specific national markets. Such companies experience strong pressures to adopt *decentralized* decision-making and planning structures; local manager discretion is a critical element in responsiveness to local markets and conditions. These national-strategy companies also have a relatively greater need to pool and subsequently transfer knowledge and experience among and between local marketing operations. Accordingly, they must develop or acquire an information system that provides considerable information on local and regional market and environmental developments or risks.

Political Considerations. Organization design must provide companies with the ability to respond appropriately to the demands of local governments. In some cases, this requires a particular form of market presence, especially if the company is entering the market for the first time. In other cases, it may require merely a modification of an existing market presence. Either response requires a design flexible enough to handle a number of different legal and operational contingencies. For example, prior to 1978, IBM required 100 percent ownership of all foreign subsidiaries. However, starting in 1978, it began to accept joint-venture arrangements in some markets, initially in response to government demands. It has subsequently found that joint ventures can be used for strategic gain.

Environmental Considerations. The rate at which salient dimensions of the environment change also has a direct impact on organization design. High-tech companies generally need an organization design that permits a quick response to change. In contrast to low- or stable-technology companies, they tend to have organization structures with relatively fewer levels of management and to use a more decentralized decision-making structure. The same is true of companies faced with other rapidly changing environmental conditions, such as rapid changes in consumer preferences or economic and political volatility.

In general, a company subject to rapid environmental change needs organizational capabilities that are flexible and responsive to those key environmental and market dimensions that are of competitive importance. These capability requirements are reflected in the organization and decision-making and planning structures adopted by the company. In addition, the structural relationships between managers so affected also tend to be shorter than those between managers in a more stable market environment.

IBM, for example, considers product development, technology development, and marketing critical success factors. As a result, they are focal points of the company's activities and have been given group (divisional) status. However, because of different competitive and marketing environments, the geographic scope and responsibilities of the groups and their divisions vary. The product development and technology development groups have worldwide responsibilities. The marketing and manufacturing activities, as of 1983, were divided into four basic geographic groups. One group was responsible for the United States; another for the Americas; a third for Europe, the Middle East, and Africa; and the fourth for Asia and the Pacific.

Company Factors

Although environmental and market conditions are important, the organization design adopted by a company is also determined—sometimes exclusively—by *firm-specific* factors. Some of the more important factors include:

1. The strategic importance of company's present and future international activities;
2. The company's background and international experience;
3. The product and market diversity of the company's international operations;
4. The traits and philosophies of the company's management as they relate to international activities;
5. The international skills, experience, and capabilities of the company's management; and
6. The capacity and ability of the company's existing organization to adjust to the requirements of new organization design.

Importance of International Operations. The absolute and relative sizes of a firm's international activities are closely related to the choice of organization design. Initially, when international activities are small, the company may be influenced by a desire to increase these activities. This is generally done by separating foreign from domestic activities. In some cases, the company may also give considerable autonomy to the managers of individual foreign activities. Later, the company will be more interested in consolidating its international activities (1) to reduce duplication, (2) to pool its international experiences, and (3) to ensure that these activities are consistent with the company's overall long-term interests. When the size of international activities begins to approach that of domestic activities, the company again modifies its position vis-à-vis these international activities. The strategy then shifts from consolidation to integration. That is, the international and domestic activities are merged. As will become clearer in a subsequent section, the three strategies of *growth, consolidation,* and *integration* often require different organization designs.[4]

Company Background. The choice of organization design appears to be affected by the company's home base. The structure of U.S. companies has typically evolved from export department to international division to either an area or product form of global structure. European companies have often followed a different pattern, generally creating functional structures for domestic operations and highly decentralized holding companies for international activities.[5] The decision-making and control systems used by these two groups of global companies also differ significantly. U.S. companies typically delegate considerable decision-making freedom to lower levels of management but compensate to some degree by exerting considerable formal control. European companies generally delegate considerable decision-making freedom with very little formal control.

Operational and Market Diversity. The choice of organization design is also closely related to the diversity of the company's product offerings and to the markets in which it competes. Companies with few product lines satisfying more or less universal needs or wants unaffected by national and geographical differences and trends tend to favor organization designs that emphasize functional expertise and efficiency. Companies with limited product lines catering to universal needs and wants but strongly affected by national or regional differences favor organization designs that emphasize local and regional market diversity. Finally, companies with diverse product lines that use different technologies or serve different market segments where success is not highly dependent on national or regional differences favor organization designs that allow for operational diversity.

Management Traits. The traits and philosophies of managers, particularly regarding overseas business, and their mindset about things "foreign" have a considerable impact on organization design. As noted above, European companies have been found to favor organization designs that facilitate decentralized decision making and control and commonly emphasized a holding company approach. In contrast, U.S. companies tend to favor organization designs that provide greater potential for decentralized decision making but strong central control. Historically, they have also emphasized product innovation.

The attitudes of management toward international activities affects choice of organization design. Managers with ethnocentric tendencies are more likely to favor organization designs that support the centralization of functional activities (marketing, coordination, integration, and control), decision making, and planning. Managers with polycentric tendencies tend to favor organization designs that permit a decentralized approach. Managers with geocentric tendencies favor organization designs that encourage a global approach at both the corporate and foreign-affiliate levels.

Human Resources. The successful implementation of any organization design is heavily dependent on the presence of well qualified managers. All companies, as they reorganize to meet the challenges of international growth, need internationally experienced managers. It is increasingly recognized that the requisite managerial characteristics vary with job responsibilities. For example (using the portfolio terms covered in Chapter 9), managers responsible for market growth strategies need to be entrepreneurs, risk takers, and open to change. Managers need to be careful yet aggressive; their job is to succeed without jeopardizing an established market position. Managers implementing for cash-cow strategies generally avoid risk while seeking consistent and efficient performance.[6]

Organization designs emphasizing national or regional differences generally need a greater number of general managers with country or regional experience. Organization structures emphasizing particular product groups or businesses need general managers with broad international business experience and experience in the particular products. Functional structures need to be staffed with functional managers with considerable international experience. Thus, a shortage of a particular type of manager may keep a company from adopting a particular organization design.

Capacity for Change. The final factor influencing a company's choice of international organization design is the capacity and willingness of the present management to adjust to organizational change. This depends to some degree on the company's culture, the influence that key managers have had in developing domestic and international activities, and the approach used to implement reorganization.

STRATEGIC DIMENSIONS OF ORGANIZATION DESIGN

Creating an international organization design is difficult mainly for the three following reasons:

1. *A company's corporate, business, and functional strategies change over time.* Its competitive environment changes, its products and resources change, and its markets grow in number and evolve. Although these changes may be predicted, management must periodically adapt the company's organization to its current strategic needs and build in allowances for future changes in those needs.

2. *The organization design appropriate for one type of product may be quite different than that for another.* For example, the firm that produces both household appliances and industrial generators may need two distinct organization designs. The technology used and the production and marketing activities associated with these two product groups may be sufficiently different to warrant different groupings of functional specializations and different decision and reporting relationships.

3. *The organization design appropriate for one national or regional market may be quite different from that needed for another.* For example, environmental and market conditions in European and South American countries pose sufficiently different problems for management that the reporting, decision, and planning structures of the organization for each region may need to be substantially different.

Because of considerations such as these, any company operating internationally needs to take into account three basic dimensions, or activities, when creating an organization design.

The three strategically important dimensions of a company's activities are often identified as *function, product,* and *geography.*

Function is generally defined in terms of activities such as production, finance, marketing, control, personnel, research, and government relations. The function dimension is primarily concerned with occupational specialization and the company's functional efficiency such that the appropriate functional specializations are developed and that knowledge, experiences, and skills are pooled and used when and where required.

Product is generally defined as groups of products or businesses grouped according to some key product characteristics (such as technology, customer group, or manufacturing technology). Any particular group is relatively homogeneous with respect to the key characteristic. The product dimension is primarily concerned with the coordination, integration, and control of activities such as technology, production, product design, and research necessary to attain business strategy objectives and goals.

Geography is generally defined as groups of markets grouped according to some key market characteristic (geography proximity, socio-cultural traits) or the potential to maximize homogeneity. The geography dimension primarily encompasses the development of capabilities to handle considerable variation in key environmental factors (that is, *external diversity*) and achieves business strategy objectives.

 The goal of organization design is to create an organization that strategically balances and focuses these three dimensions in such a way that the company's objectives and goals are achieved. However, these three dimensions are inherently in conflict. For example, by placing relatively more importance on *function,* the firm may enhance the efficiency and effectiveness of it's worldwide marketing, production, and financing activities. However, it does so at the cost of geographic coordination and the transfer of product and technical expertise within its global network. An emphasis on *product* may enhance the firm's cost efficiency and scanning capabilities, but it does so at the cost of geographic coordination and the duplication of functional activities. Finally, an emphasis on *geography* may enable the firm to better coordinate its business interests in particular countries or regions—at the cost of inhibiting product coordination and integration and with duplication of functional expertise and effort.[7]

Notwithstanding these issues, the company's competitive environment, strategies, and administrative capabilities are such that the general structure of the company is often predetermined. Historically, organization design tends to be one-dimensional and to reflect built-in biases affecting decision making, resource transfers, information flows, and functional activities.

Bias need not be negative; it can be beneficial. For example, a company with a national strategy, such as Pillsbury, is involved in producing and marketing highly localized products to meet the tastes and shopping habits of specific national markets. Such a company needs to pay considerable attention to local and regional activities and to develop the capability to spread its cumulative marketing knowledge and experience among its local operations within particular regions. A geographic emphasis is thus in order. On the other hand, a company with a *global strategy,* such as Caterpillar or Xerox, is involved in producing and marketing highly standardized products that meet recognizably universal needs. Such companies are interested in obtaining global production and management economies, a global-scanning capability, and the ability to transfer product and technical knowledge and experience worldwide. They also often use somewhat standardized marketing programs. A *product* emphasis is in order for this type of company.

INTERNATIONAL ORGANIZATION STRUCTURES

Although the organization structures used by companies for overseas operations are as diverse as their international corporate, business, and functional strategies, the number of basic, or fundamental structures used by companies as they evolve from domestic to global enterprises can be identified. These six basic structural forms:

1. An export department,
2. An international division,
3. A global area structure,
4. A global product structure,
5. A matrix structure, and
6. An umbrella, or shell, structure.

These six options are not unique to international business. Rather, they are modifications of structures commonly used by national companies. This section discusses the appropriateness of each of these distinctive forms for international activities.

Functional versus Divisional Structures

The first five structures identified in the section above are based on two primary structural models, the *functional* model and the *divisional* model. Generally, the functional structure is used by companies with a few closely related products. These companies focus on a narrow range of customers, products, or technologies. Functional structures emphasize such activities as marketing, manufacturing, and finance.

The divisional structure is generally used by companies with a number of unrelated product lines or business activities. Examples of companies that are divisionally organized include General Foods, Hewlett-Packard, and United Technologies. These companies have a wide range of products with different customers, technologies, and distribution channels. Consequently, they have a relatively greater need for strategic coordination, integration, and control. The divisional structure gives these types of companies the ability to separate their activities into distinct units (divisions) according to customer, product, or technology groups. Each unit or division has its own staff for marketing, finance, production, and so on. There generally is a corporate staff whose purpose is to provide companywide expertise and assistance to the product groups. Another corporate-level group, which generally includes the managers responsible for each division, determines the overall direction for the company, allocates resources, and generally coordinates and integrates divisional activities to ensure that the separate divisions are working toward corporate goals.

The Functional Structure

A typical functional structure is shown in Figure 18-2. Activities are grouped on the basis of the functions performed. The three principal advantages of this structure include the opportunity to (1) centralize decision making, (2) gain functional efficiency (as a result of in-depth specialization), and (3) emphasize the importance, power, and prestige of key functions.

However, the functional structure also has several important disadvantages: (1) it concentrates profit responsibility at the top; (2) tends to develop a narrow functional viewpoint among managers; (3) hampers interfunctional coordination and management development (because of occupation bias); and (4) fragments company growth (function, not strategy, reigns). From an international perspective, the major weaknesses of the functional structure include difficulties in efficiently handling geographic and operational diversity, one-dimensionality, and inflexibility in responding to internal and external changes. The latter point is of particular concern when the company's national markets are diverse and undergoing rapid environmental change.

The Divisional Structure

A typical divisional structure is shown in Figure 18-3. This type of structure is generally adopted by companies as a response to increasing size and complexity. It has been found to be an effective means for allocating resources for companies operating in a number of diverse businesses or for those handling a number of diverse product lines. A major advantage of the divisional structure is its ability to handle diversity arising from the company's operations, customers, or competitive environments.

Managers adopting a divisional structure believe that it provides for a better exploitation of a company's distinctive competencies in product, market and technology. This *synergy*—coordination, integration, and control of the company's

FIGURE 18-2 Typical Functional Structure

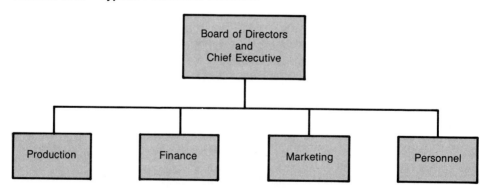

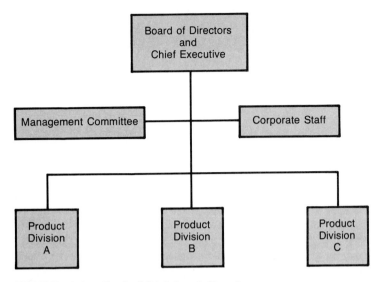

FIGURE 18-3   Typical Divisional Structure

corporate dimensions (markets, costs, technology, and management)—can result in a cumulative performance that surpasses that expected from the sum of the individual parts.[8] Of course, functionally structured companies also exhibit synergy. However, theirs is generally the result of techniques and approaches of task teams and committees.

A divisional structure facilitates the employment of specialized capital and technology and makes easier the coordination of functional specialization and knowledge within divisions. Profit responsibility for a division can also be given to the divisional manager, thereby focusing the manager's attention on market performance and the efficient use of capital and other resources. At the same time, the divisional structure requires a large staff of persons with general managerial abilities, and it tends to increase costs through duplication of functional activities, control services, and staff activities. The degree of coordination, integration, and control that should be exercised by the corporate staff over the divisions also presents problems.

The major weakness of a divisional structure, from an international perspective, is that the structure is unidimensional. Functional activities suffer from excessive duplication, and geographic and product needs may be ignored. Other problems occur because this type of structure tends to foster independence of the division managers. This independence can result in an overemphasis of divisional welfare— to the detriment of corporate welfare. Company growth will be fragmented unless adequate control is retained at the corporate level.

Although divisional structures are generally established by business or product line, a number of other subtypes are possible. Options include divisions according to (1) geography, (2) customers, and (3) process. Of these, the geographical structure is the most common international form.

International Structures

Export Department

The export department is often the first organizational structure used for overseas activities, but is also found in mature global companies and their affiliates. In these cases, they are used for intracompany transfers and to serve markets in which no local manufacturing facilities exist.

Two typical organization diagrams are illustrated in Figure 18-4. The first is for a company organized along functional lines; the second, for a company organized along product lines. In both cases, the export department is managed by an export manager responsible for overseas sales.

Initial export involvement by U.S. companies is often modest and handled by a domestic sales department. Eventually, however, successful exporters find it necessary to coordinate activities in order to better exploit newly perceived foreign market opportunities and need to develop in-house export management expertise.

In response to coordination needs, the company may use either an export management company or establish an internal export department. Generally, the export department is established to ensure that the export activity is given increased attention. It also creates the structure necessary for the development and accumulation of requisite expertise.

However, when exports take on increased importance, conflicts often arise between the export department and the domestic arm(s) of the firm. For example, the export department may have difficulty in filling export orders promptly, if at all. This often occurs because the export and domestic sales departments are not coordinated and must share company output. Problems such as this are accentuated because the power of the export manager is usually subordinate to that of other managers in the company.

Because of the growing frequency and seriousness of these conflicts, management often decides that licensing and direct investment are better strategies for handling foreign markets. These developments, plus the conflicts noted, create pressures that often push a company toward an international division structure.

International Division

A typical organization structure for a firm using an international division structure is shown in Figure 18-5. It is generally an autonomous division operated by a vice-president who reports directly to the chief executive. In larger companies, the international division may be operated as a separate company with a president. In both cases, it is linked to the company's domestic structure.

The purpose of the international division is to concentrate foreign-market expertise in one subunit where responsibility for running all international business operations, not just exporting, is concentrated. Doing so tends to ensure that the international activities of the company receive the attention. Bristol-Myers, IBM, 3M, and du Pont are examples of large, mature global companies that rely on international divisions to manage their international operations. These companies believe that a cadre of internationally experienced executives which a geographic focus add important competitive dimensions to overseas operations.

(a) EXPORT DEPARTMENT—FUNCTIONAL STRUCTURE

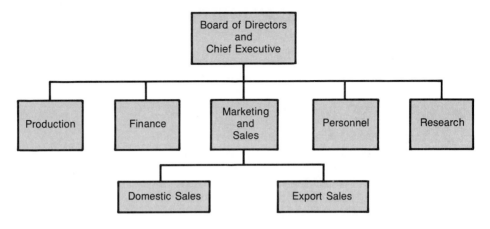

(b) CENTRALIZED (POOLED) EXPORT DEPARTMENT—DIVISION STRUCTURE

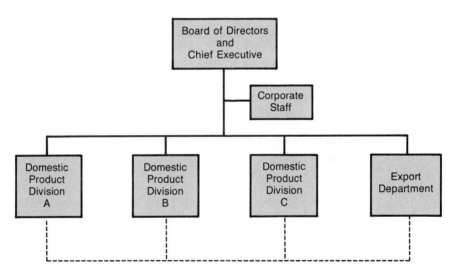

FIGURE 18-4 **Examples of an Export Department Structure for Functional and Divisional Organizations**

In most cases, the international division's activities are geographically grouped and include responsibility for all the company's exports, licensing arrangements, and overseas manufacturing and marketing activities. It may or may not be responsible for the international product-development activities; this depends to some extent on whether the company follows a global strategy or a national strategy. As mentioned earlier, IBM's product group is responsible for all product innovation;

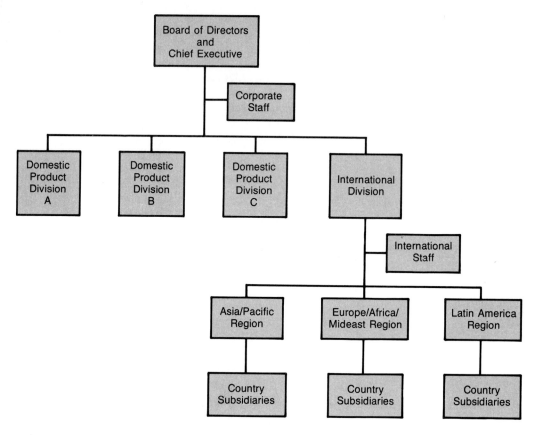

FIGURE 18-5   Example of an International Division for a Product Division Organization

three geographically organized international divisions are currently responsible for overseas manufacturing and marketing activities within their regions.

Most companies using an international division structure locate product development at home. The international division is thus heavily dependent on domestic product divisions for new products. Furthermore, these domestic product divisions are often reluctant to give priority to foreign needs. For example, IBM's office products division once turned down a request from its international division to develop a desktop copier more suitable for many foreign markets.[9]

The international division tends to be an unstable or transitory structure. For a majority of U.S. firms, it gives way to another, more global structure. The choice is generally between a global-product and a global-area structure. Frequently, it mirrors the basic structure used domestically.

Pressures for a change in structure arise from several sources. In the case of change from an international-division structure to a global-product structure, there is an inability to handle simultaneously diverse of domestic activities (generally organized along product lines) and the diversity of national markets. The global-product structure is viewed by management as providing these particular capabilities.[10]

In the case of change from an international-division structure to a global-area structure, there is often devisive rivalry between the international and domestic divisions for capital, R&D budgets, and managerial talent. As the international division grows and becomes more equal in size to the largest domestic division, this rivalry intensifies. In some cases, domestic managers have been known to form coalitions to break up the international division. The domestic divisions benefit in several ways: they share in the allocation of the international division's resources, revenues, growth potential, and power.[11]

Global Structures

Global-Area Structure

In general, the global-area structure is used when a limited number of products are taken overseas, or when only the dominant product or business is internationalized.[12] A typical *global-area division* structure is shown in Figure 18-6. In

FIGURE 18-6   Example of a Global Area Organization Structure

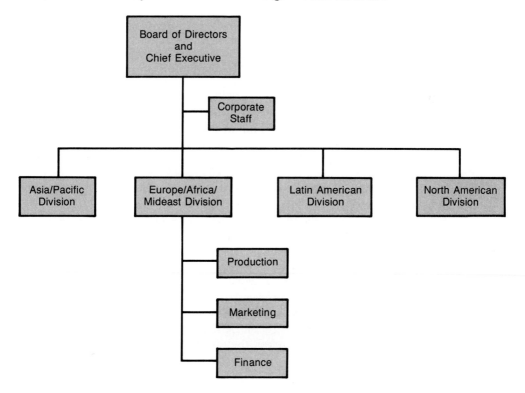

this case, the world's markets have been divided into four groups, or regions. Each group is usually headed by a vice-president or group president responsible for all functional- and national-market activities within a given region.

The major advantage of the global-area structure is an improvement in handling the diversity arising from multiple markets. By focusing management responsibility at the regional level, it emphasizes local markets and improves coordination between regional markets and national markets within regions. The area structure also takes advantage of economies of operating locally, improves communication between local managers because of their local and regional interests, and provides for the development of managers with general manager capabilities and skills.

A major problem with the area structure is the need for a relatively large number of persons with general manager abilities, particularly with country- or region-specific experience. The structure also makes it more difficult to gain economies from centralized services, increases control problems for top management, and results in the duplication of functional activities across national and regional markets. Another major shortcoming of the area structure is that it emphasizes only one of the three dimensions. Because of its geographic orientation, an area structure tends to promote integration of functional and product activities at the affiliate level, or regional level, to the neglect of the integration of these activities across countries and regions. For example, Davidson points out that:

> In pure area-based structures, individual country managers will determine manufacturing and marketing activities for each affiliate. As a result, product lines will proliferate, product standards will deteriorate and competition for export markets between affiliates will occur. The manufacturing configuration resulting in such a structure can be highly inefficient as each affiliate produces the same product at low volume levels.[13]

Global-Product Structure

A typical global-product division structure is presented in Figure 18-7. This structure is generally used by multiproduct companies wishing to internationalize all of their products.[14] It is frequently adopted by global-strategy companies; they see it as well suited for implementing strategies that depend on global economies, experience in manufacturing, and the centralization of specialized functional activities within divisions. These companies also believe that the global-product structure provides a more effective competitor-scanning capability.

The major advantages of a global-product structure is management's ability to efficiently handle operational diversity. It focuses attention and effort on achieving the company's objectives and goals for its various product lines. It also places profit responsibility at the division level, improves coordination of functional activities within divisions, and permits growth and diversity of products and services within the strategic scope of each business division.

Unfortunately, the structure requires more persons with general manager abilities than does the functional structure. It tends to hamper economies of centralized services. It increases the problems associated with corporate control. More important, perhaps, for the globally oriented firm, the global-product structure can foster excessive duplication of corporate and affiliate activities in sales, marketing, finance, coordination, and integration. It also tends to fragment international

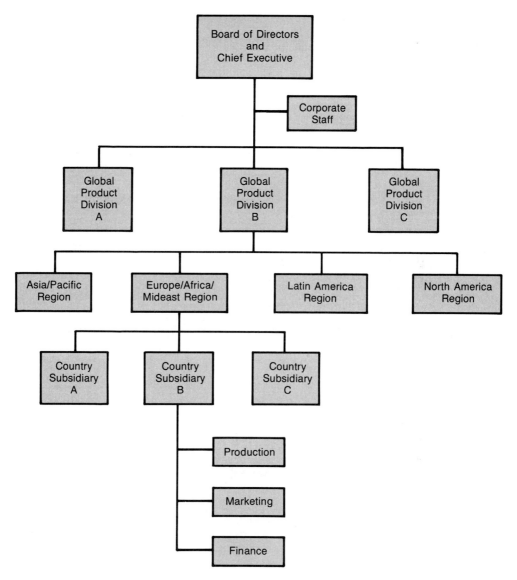

FIGURE 18-7   Example of a Global Product Organization Structure

expertise and experience, and achieving coordination between product divisions is a big problem.[15] Finally, comparative studies suggest that product structures do not facilitate the transfer of technology. New technologies introduced by companies organized along product lines were found to be transferred overseas more slowly than by companies using other organization structures, and they tended to resort more frequently to licensing rather than direct investment when developing foreign markets for new products.[16] However, international product diffusion tends to be more rapid in product division structures.

The Matrix Structure

As listed in Table 18-1, the two global structures tend to emphasize diffferent organizational needs of vital interest to a global company. The global-product structure tends to offer better capabilities to rationalize production across countries thus gaining production cost efficiencies. It also provides better capabilities for more efficient sourcing, consistency in marketing, and the attainment of global strategic coordination within product lines. On the other hand, the area structure provides for more effective host government relations and a better use of affiliate infrastructures, and it is more responsive to local market trends and needs and allows for more coordinated and focused regional policies. The area structure also provides better capabilities for determining local opportunities and threats. Since some global companies pursue corporate strategies that require all these capabilities, a few companies have adopted a more complex structure, the *matrix structure*.

The matrix structure is used by some global companies to increase the number of strategic dimensions receiving management attention. It is an attempt to give equal weight to at least two of the three dimensions. The typical international matrix structure is a two-dimensional structure that emphasizes *product* and *geography*. In the example shown in Figure 18-8, the general manager of a subsidiary in a Latin American country reports to the company's Product Division B office and to the company's Latin American Regional office. Similar reporting responsibilities are imposed on general managers of subsidiaries in other regions of the world.

Generally, each product division has worldwide responsibilities for its own business, and each geographical or area division is responsible for the foreign operations in its region. Less frequently encountered in an international context are matrix structures that emphasize *function* and one of the other dimensions. However, Business International reports that some European firms use a *product-function* structure.[17]

Because the two dimensions of product and geography overlap at the affiliate level, both enter into local decision-making and planning processes. It is assumed

TABLE 18-1
Major Differences in Global-Area and Product Structures

Organizational Needs	Area Structure	Product Structure
Production Rationalization	Weak	Strong
Sourcing Efficiency	Weak	Strong
Marketing Consistency	Weak	Strong
Global Strategic Coordination	Weak	Strong
Effective Host Government Relations	Strong	Weak
Local Market Responsiveness	Strong	Weak
Use of Affiliate Infrastructure	Strong	Weak
Monitoring Local Opportunities and Threats	Strong	Weak

Source: Adapted from William H. Davidson, *Global Strategic Management* (New York: John Wiley & Sons, 1982), pp. 285–286.

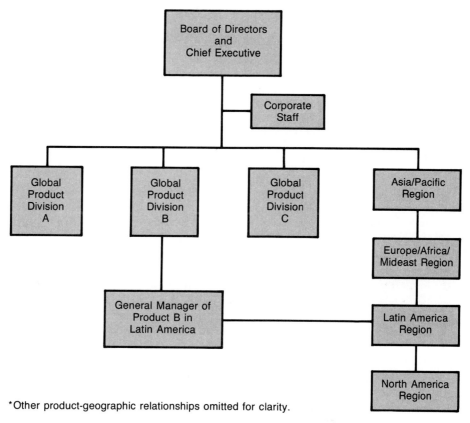

FIGURE 18-8   **Example of an International Matrix Organizational Structure***

that area and product managers will defend different positions. This will lead to tensions and "creative" conflict. Area managers will tend to favor responsiveness to local environmental factors, and product managers will defend positions favoring cost efficiencies and global competitiveness. The matrix structure deliberately creates a dual focus to ensure that conflicts between product and area concerns are identified and then analyzed objectively.

A good example of a matrix structure that emphasizes the product and area dimensions is the structure adopted by General Electric:

General Electric Company effectively joins product-related and geographic concerns. The firm is working toward a product SBU organization in which each SBU has worldwide strategic planning responsibility. GE has identified a number of priority countries. Each product SBU head sets forth what he plans to accomplish in each country within a certain time frame. The country executive develops a comprehensive country opportunity plan to cover all products and strategies. This is a difficult task, because the country manager lacks the expertise to decide authoritatively what is optimal for each product and strategy—but it is important that he contribute to the planning effort. The country plan is then compared with the individual product SBU plans for that country. The outcome is a merging of informational and strategic input from both sources. Conflicts are identified and proposals made for their solution. Some conflicts may be resolved at the country level, others at the area or even the sector level. Each party may push issues up its relevant hierarchy for higher-level review.[18]

The matrix structure enables the company to address the inherent conflicts existing between *function, product,* and *geography,* and thus resolve these conflicts in the best interests of the company. It also stimulates the sharing of managerial experience, resources, expertise, and information, and balances and integrates technology and market-related factors as a result of the planning process needed for such structures.

The matrix structure does have weaknesses that make its use for some companies problematic. These weaknesses arise because of structural and political duality.[19] *Structure duality* refers to the need for some managers to report to two superiors. *Political duality* refers to the relative influence, or power, these superiors have in the decision process. Since the decisions are not based on a single line of formal authority, they may be influenced as much by interpersonal and political considerations as by technical considerations. As stated by Prahalad and Doz, "A matrix is not a structure. It is a decision-making culture where multiple and often conflicting points of view are explicitly examined."[20] Consequently, the adoption of a matrix structure requires a fundamental change in management behavior and the company's culture. Managers subjected to the pressures of dual reporting relationships require extensive training, considerable maturity, and wide or deep experience; they must clearly recognize and accept the underlying premise of this type of structure.

The Mixed Structure

To overcome, or at least reduce, some of the strategic disadvantages of the area- and product-division structures and the complications arising from the duality of the matrix structure, some companies use a combination of structures. A company with multiple products or businesses may create an organization that caters to the individual strategic peculiarities of each product group or business. For example, mature product lines that make significant contributions to revenue may be organized along global-T product or area lines, while those in the introductory or growth stages of development may have an international division structure.

For example, most of Uniroyal's products are handled by an international division. At the same time, however, chemicals and plastics are organized as global-product divisions. IT&T also uses different organization structures for its telecommunications, electric appliance, hotel, and insurance divisions.

A mixed organization structure is shown in Figure 18-9. In this example, divisions A and B have very little experience overseas, need to accumulate this experience, at headquarters. The products produced by divisions A and B are marketed by the company's international division, which is structured along geographic lines. On the other hand, Division C is organized as a global products division.

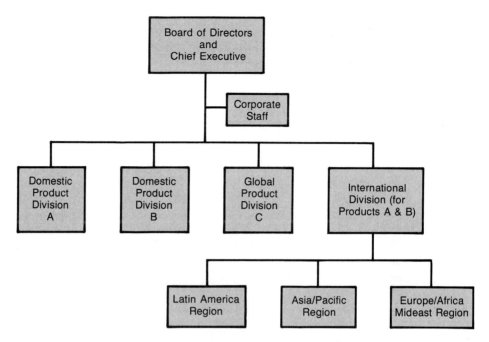

FIGURE 18-9   Example of an International "Mixed" Structure

The Umbrella (Shell) Structure

A problem sometimes encountered by companies using a global-product division structure is the presence of several divisional operations in a single country, particularly countries with large, diversified markets such as Brazil, the United Kingdom, and West Germany. This can lead to legal and fiscal difficulties and duplication of administrative activities (in cash management, accounting, taxes, and negotiations with government and labor organizations). These difficulties have led some companies to use local holding companies, often called umbrella, or shell, companies. These umbrella companies house the affiliates of their companies in one country; however, the affiliates report to different divisions.

A typical umbrella company is shown in Figure 18-10. In this illustration, the operations of three divisions fall under the "umbrella" of the local Japanese company. The presidency of such an umbrella company is generally rotated among the country managers to provide them with experience in negotiating with governments and labor organizations. Also, the local affiliates of the divisions rent their administrative services from the umbrella company.

Prior to its reorganization in the early 1980s, IBM used umbrella companies in many countries to retain a single-company image. These local umbrella companies were used to house IBM's local computer and general business products operations. At the same time, these operations reported directly to their respective divisions. In the case of computers, reporting was to one of IBM World Trade's two regional organizations; in the case of general business products, it was to the international division of this product group.

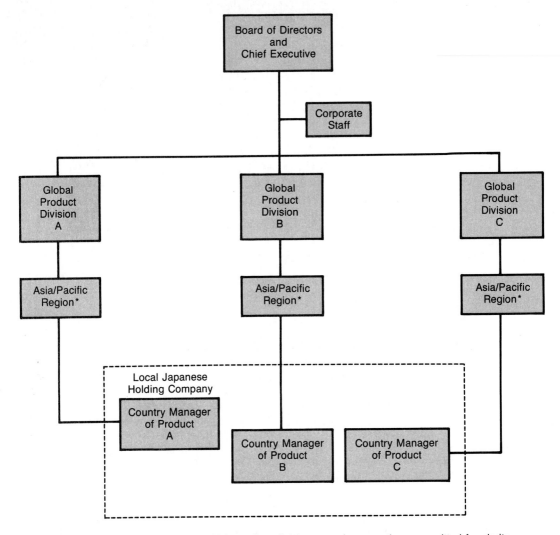

*Other regions and countries in which product divisions may be operating are omitted for clarity.

FIGURE 18-10   Example of a Local Umbrella (or Shell) Company Structure

THE DECISION-MAKING PROCESS

Although a considerable amount of attention has focused on the organizational structure, other important aspects of operations need to be incorporated in organization design. These include, but are not limited to, processes of decision making and planning. This section discusses some of the factors that affect the decision to centralize or decentralize authority and thus directly impact the structure of the decision-making process. A later section discusses some of the organization design issues related to international planning activities.

The *degree* to which authority within a company is delegated to regional or even national managers determines the extent of centralization or decentralization. Interestingly, the organizational structure does not necessarily reveal whether authority is centralized or decentralized. (Job descriptions and the scope of decision-making authority of each position often must be reviewed to determine this.) However, the organizational structure does hint at the extent to which decentralization *might* occur. For example, divisional structures usually encourage greater decentralization of authority than functional structures.

There are many factors that affect the decision to centralize or decentralize decision making. One group of factors deals with the characteristics of specific affiliates, such as age, size, and profitability. (Managers of large, profitable, and long-established affiliates are likely to have considerable autonomy.) The confidence corporate management has in the abilities of the local management, the degree to which other affiliates are dependent on the affiliate's output, and the degree to which local economic and political forces require local and possibly unique treatment add to this list of factors.

Yet other factors deal with the company's plans for the affiliate. Affiliates considered critical to the achievement of the company's long-term objectives and goals will be closely monitored, even directly controlled. Conversely, affiliates unimportant to the company's primary strategy frequently receive considerable autonomy. Operative factors include the need for coordination and integration arising from the competitive structure of the company's industry, the rate at which the company's basic technologies are changing, and the need for rapid communications and the dissemination of techniques. These factors work toward centralization.

Generally, the centralization or decentralization of authority varies by function. In most companies, centralized decision making occurs when the company has a global strategy or integrated perspective and economies of scale are involved. Although scale economies are most apparent in the area of production, they can also arise in the functional and management areas and in the use of expensive specialists. Also, finance commonly receives considerable corporate attention, particularly in capital expenditures and budgeting. Marketing, on the other hand, is generally centralized by global strategy companies, but decentralized at the local level by national strategy companies. At the same time, however, the degree of autonomy given managers responsible for different marketing activities may vary. For example, product development, research and development, and purchasing may be on a global, regional, or national level depending on whether opportunities exist to optimize these activities. Pricing, distribution, and promotional activities, on the other hand, tend to be mostly decentralized at the region or national levels because of market pressures.[21]

OTHER ASPECTS OF ORGANIZATION DESIGN[22]

Most companies operating internationally tend to seek solutions to complexity by periodically restructuring operations. For example, IBM reorganized its World Trade Corporation in 1973 and again in 1985 in response to changes in the relative importance of its overseas markets. Between 1970 and 1984, Hewlett-Packard also underwent three reorganizations to remain responsive to changes in its domestic and foreign markets and to meet challenges posed by various competitors. However, reorganization is not always used. Some companies, as the examples below suggest seek solutions by modifying the human side of organization design.

For example, Timken, Corning Glass, Baxter Travenol, Bristol-Meyers and several other companies have not made a habit of restructuring every time external or internal conditions change. Instead of reacting in either-or terms to the three pressures discussed at the start of this chapter, they have tried to create organizations which are simultaneously responsive to the *function, product,* and *geography* dimensions of their operations.

When faced with a growing threat of Japanese competition, Timken chose to retain its organizational structure; it standardized its product lines to gain efficiencies on a regional basis. At the same time, it retained a local focus on customer services, felt to be of critical importance.

In an effort to overcome the unidimensional bias built into the decision-making process of most organization designs, some companies upgrade their personnel and provide them more responsibilities. They modify job descriptions of selected positions to eliminate decision-making biases inherent in specific organization structures. Redefinition, for example, can reduce the ability of a product or area manager to make unilateral decisions without a superior's approval and it can increase the influence that other managers have in the decision process.

An adjustment in decision making and responsibilities cannot be made in isolation. Corresponding changes must be made in information transfer systems. For example, when Corning Glass decided to upgrade the roles of its product and functional managers, it modified its information system. Prior to the decision, Corning had consolidated data only by geographic entity; this had resulted in conflicting product definitions, and in some cases, double counting.

Other mechanisms that are used to eliminate or reduce the biases inherent in each organization design include attempts to influence the informal structure. In some cases, this has involved the use of meetings, the formation of task teams, and the assignment of specific managers to various positions requiring frequent colleague contact. For example, Baxter Travenol uses frequent meetings to encourage managers to develop informal relationships. It also increased the scope of its annual general managers' meetings to include product and functional managers.

THE INTERNATIONAL PLANNING PROCESS

International planning differs significantly from planning for purely domestic operations. As noted in Chapter 10, external differences include distance, currencies, culture, language, and market and environmental conditions exist. Other differences are found in the accounting conventions used in different countries and in the reliability and accuracy of the market information and data to be used. Because of factors such as these, it is difficult to develop and use consistent planning assumptions.

Planning is further complicated because of internal variations in such things as the company's organizational structure, and the decision-making and control processes employed. As noted earlier, these have a direct bearing on the types of information and data collected and forwarded to other units within the company. For planning to be of most value to the global company, uniform approaches need to be used in order to permit comparability and evaluation.

Because of variations such as those described above, there is no best approach to planning in global companies. However, most planning approaches used by such companies try to ensure that the functional, product, and geographic dimensions of the company's activities are strategically integrated and that transnational complications are dealt with efficiently.

The Types of Planning Processes

Among the many factors influencing the type of planning process a particular company adopts are the following:

1. The degree and type of product diversity;
2. The interdependency of the company's affiliates in terms of cross-border transfers of resources, inputs, and products;
3. The scale and experience economies associated with production and functional activities;
4. The organization structure and the decision-making process adopted by the company, particularly as these relate to the relationships established between affiliates, area, and/or product divisions, and corporate headquarters; and
5. The balance needed between the strategic requirements of function, product, and geography.[23]

The international planning needs of a particular company, and thus the type of planning process used, parallels its level of involvement in international activities. This can best be described in terms of the company's international strategic perspective, its organizational structure, and its information needs. We now discuss these.

Planning and the International Strategic Focus

A company with a global strategy generally adopts a centralized, or integrated, planning approach. Its foreign affiliates' involvement in planning is limited and supportive in nature. Their main function is to supply the information and data requested by corporate headquarters. A company with a national strategy generally adopts a more decentralized, or group-planning, approach. Foreign affiliates of such companies play a more significant role. The role of corporate headquarters is to try to blend affiliates' plans into one overall corporate plan.[24]

High-tech and capital goods companies tend to use integrated planning. Consumer goods firms tend to use group planning. Companies in between often experiment with combinations of these two approaches. The integrated approach tends to be very time consuming for local managers; it does not provide them with motivation; and it tends to emphasize product. The group approach, while providing local managers motivation for planning, can degenerate into a set of fragmented strategies; it emphasizes geography.

Organization Structure and the Planning Process[25]

Planning is also affected by the company's stage of international involvement. As the company's involvement expands and becomes more diverse in terms of product and geographic, the scope, the complexity of international planning increases. Planning within the framework of the company's organizational structure, and reflects the strategic dimensions emphasized therein.

A company whose primary involvement overseas is through exports is generally budget oriented. That is, the company's international strategy is determined primarily by the development of the capital budget, which serves as the means for allocating resources. Resource allocation decisions are based on anticipated rates of return. Consequently, planning is often contained within the comptroller's review.

For both large and small companies with export departments and international divisions, the strategic focus is primarily domestic. Thus, domestic activities dominate planning. When overseas manufacturing facilities exist to serve the needs of local markets, these affiliates often enjoy considerable planning autonomy.

Companies with international divisions characterized by considerable product diversity tend to have more sophisticated planning activities. This is especially true when a high degree of interdependence exists between the international division and the domestic area or product divisions. For example, General Electric uses the strategic business unit (SBU) approach discussed in Chapter 9. Strategic plans are developed at the level of the SBU to cover function, product, and geographic areas; they are then consolidated and coordinated at corporate headquarters. Control is exercised through resource allocation.

In the case of companies using global-area structures, the company sets overall objectives, such as expectations in ROI and profit growth. These overall objectives are then parcelled out among domestic and overseas groups. The overseas groups, in turn, break down their own targets by country. Each country develops its plan using its own targets and the planning assumptions decided on by its region. In the case of large affiliates, the country plans are frequently developed by local staffs. In the case of smaller affiliates, the regional staff is often called on to assist.

In the case of companies using global-product structures, the planning process is somewhat different because of the strong need for coordination and integration. Each product division's corporate office is generally responsible for developing product plans that meet the corporate objectives established by headquarters. These objectives often include a rate of profit growth, sales-growth targets, market-share targets, ROI, and targets for new product introductions. Country managers are generally limited to providing accounting and other financial measurements. Each product division's plan is a comprehensive statement of the division's anticipated functional and staff activities, sales expectations for each of the division's national markets, expected production levels for each of its plants, and necessary intracompany flows.

Structuring the International Planning Process

Who should be responsible for the company's planning activity? Where in the hierarchy should the activity be located? These are key decisions that will strongly influence the importance given to planning by management. Planning activities can be organized separately from, yet parallel to, the operational structure or as a built-in unit.[26]

A *parallel* planning structure is independent from the operational activities of the firm from top to bottom. Thus, the company's planners report to planning managers at each level of the organization. This approach is used when a strong and objective planning function is needed; it can be developed and implemented quickly. However, the fact that line managers are not actively involved is the main disadvantage of the parallel approach. The planning process and the resulting plans may not be accepted by these managers.

The *built-in* approach generally has a top-level manager responsible for the company's corporate and business planning. Below this level, however, all the planners report to lower-level line managers. The primary advantage of this approach is the confidence it engenders in line managers; the resulting plans are likely to be accepted. The major disadvantage of this approach is that objectivity may be tainted. Also, the use of a "standardized" planning approach depends on the support of the planners and the line managers to which they report. If the activity is placed too high in the organization hierarchy, planning can be viewed as a control mechanism, not a support mechanism.

SUMMARY

As a company's international activities grow geographically, and operationally, significant changes generally occur in organization design. These changes normally include a restructuring of domestic and international activities, a realignment of authority and reporting relationships, and adjustments in planning activities.

Reorganization can be viewed as a three-stage process, particularly in the case of U.S. companies. The initial, or growth stage, involves the creation of an export department. The manager of this department is given line authority to aggressively pursue overseas opportunities. The second stage, consolidation, involves the creation of an international division in which all the company's international expertise and experience is housed. This generally occurs when the international commitment has reached a level that justifies a senior management position, the company needs to coordinate its overseas activities, and managerial economies can be achieved through centralization. The third stage, integration, generally involves replacing the international division with some sort of global-division structure. Companies that make this structural change have decided that for strategic reasons their international and domestic activities can no longer be treated separately. Companies that internationalize all or most of their diversified products tend to use worldwide-product structures. Companies that internationalize few product groups or have limited product offerings tend to use global-area structures.

The organization design's activity focus has a significant influence on the choice of organization structure, the type of decision-making process adopted, and the type of international planning implemented. This organizational focus involves deciding which of the three dimensions of a company's activities is to be emphasized, function, product, or geography. For example, a functional focus has the benefits of integrating marketing, finance, and production across national markets and developing considerable expertise in these areas. However, these benefits are generally gained at the cost of local market sensitivity, regional coordination, and increased difficulties in transferring product and technological expertise. A product focus reduces the difficulties of transferring product and technology expertise and knowledge and improves the company's ability to gain global-scale economies and to compete effectively across markets. However, a product focus results in the duplication of functional activities, difficulties in corporate coordination and control, and some insensitivity to local market conditions and local company interests. A geographic focus, on the other hand, tends to increase regional coordination and heightens company sensitivity to local market conditions. But it does so at the expense of functional duplication and product coordination. It also results in difficulties in corporate coordination and control.

Notwithstanding these biases, most companies will favor one of these three organization designs. For example, global-strategy companies generally favor a product focus. This results in the use of a product structure, decentralized decision making, and information and planning systems that emphasize product performance across national markets. At the same time, these companies tend to centralize the coordination and control of those activities providing global economies of scale, such as production, R&D, and product development. National-strategy companies normally favor a geographic focus because of end-market diversity. Thus, they are characterized by the use of a global-area structure, decentralized decision making, and infor-

mation and planning systems that emphasize national differences and conditions. Those companies that need to be simultaneously responsive to global competitive forces and differences in national marketing forces favor a two-dimensional structure such as the matrix. Some firms use a mixed structure, thus emphasizing geographic considerations for some product lines, and product considerations for others. The shell or umbrella structure is used to reduce administrative costs and the confusion that can arise when two or more divisions of the same company operate in a single country.

DISCUSSION QUESTIONS

1. What is meant by a *global organization structure*?
2. Discuss how the organization of a company may affect its planning process.
3. Is there an ideal organization structure for international business? Why or why not?
4. Discuss why some mature global companies continue to use an international divisional structure and not another structure.
5. Identify the three dimensions of a company's activities and explain how they can influence its organizational design. Focus on one particular company.
6. This chapter suggests that an international company's growth can be divided into three stages. Identify these stages and discuss their relationship to company reorganization.

ADDITIONAL READINGS

Bartlett, Christopher A., "Building and Managing the Transnational: The New Organizational Challenge," in *Competition in Global Industries,* ed. Michael E. Porter (Boston: Harvard Business School, 1986).

Buatsi, Seth N., "Organizational Adaptation to International Marketing," *International Marketing Review,* Vol. 3, Winter 1986.

Davidson, William H., and Philippe Haspeslagh,

"Shaping a Global Product Organization," *Harvard Business Review,* July–August 1982.

Hulbert, James M., and William K. Brandt, *Managing the Multinational Subsidiary* (New York: Holt, Rinehart, and Winston, 1980).

Ouchi, William G., *Theory Z* (Reading, Mass.: Addison-Wesley, 1981).

ENDNOTES

1. See Raymond Vernon and Louis T. Wells, *Manager in the International Economy,* 3rd ed. (Englewood Cliffs, N.J.: Prentice-Hall: 1976), p. 31.
2. The terms *global strategy* and *national strategy* are explained in Chapter 10. They approximate those used by Michael Z. Brooke and Mark van Beusekom in *International Corporate Planning* (London: Pitman 1979), Chapter 2.
3. C. K. Prahalad and Yves L. Doz, *The Multinational Mission: Balancing Local Demands and Global Vision* (New York: Free Press, 1987), pp. 178–179.
4. See Business International, *New Directions in Multinational Corporate Organization,* Chapter 1, for additional details on growth, consolidation, and integration as they relate to structure.
5. Ibid., p. 1.
6. John H. Grant and William R. King, *The Logic of Strategic Planning* (Boston: Little, Brown and Company, 1982), p. 188.
7. *New Directions,* pp. 1–2.
8. Jay R. Galbraith and Daniel A. Nathanson, "The Role of Organizational Structure and Process in Strategy Implementation," *Strategic Management,* ed. Dan E. Schendel and Charles W. Hofer (Boston: Little, Brown and Company, 1979), p. 255, for an excellent summary of research on organization structure.
9. "IBM World Trade Corporation," a case copyrighted by the President and Fellows of Harvard College and distributed by Intercollegiate Case Clearing House, Boston.
10. Galbraith and Nathanson, op. cit.
11. Ibid.
12. John Stopford, "Growth and Organizational Change in the Multinational Field," doctoral dissertation, Harvard University, 1968.
13. William H. Davidson, *Global Strategic Management* (New York John Wiley & Sons, 1982), p. 284.
14. Stopford, op. cit.
15. Davidson, op cit., p. 284.
16. William H. Davidson and Philippe Haspeslagh, "Shaping a Global Product Organization," *Harvard Business Review* July–August 1982, pp. 127–128, and William H. Davidson, *Global Strategic Management* p. 302.
17. John Stopford and Louis T. Wells, *Managing the Multinational Enterprise* (London: Longmans, 1972).
18. Business International, *New Directions* p. 132.
19. Stopford and Wells, op. cit.
20. Prahalad and Doz, *The Multinational Mission,* p. 177.
21. R. J. Aylmer, "Who Makes Marketing Decisions in the Multinational Firm? *Journal of Marketing,* October 1970, pp. 25–30.
22. This section draws heavily from Christopher A. Bartlett, "MNCs: get off the reorganization merry-go-round," *Harvard Business Review,* March–April 1983, pp. 138–146.
23. Derek F. Channon with Michael Jalland, *Multinational Strategic Planning* (New York: AMACOM, 1978), p. 52.
24. Brooke and van Beusekom, *International,* pp. 26–27.
25. For a more detailed discussion of this topic, see Channon and Jalland, Chapter 3.
26. For a more detailed discussion of the points covered in this section, see Brooke and van Beusekom, Chapter 10.

Chapter 19
Control of the
Global Marketing
Effort

Marketing management exercises control over two distinct yet interdependent groups of activities. One group consists of those tasks necessary to create, implement, monitor, and adjust *marketing strategies*. These activities and decisions focus on satisfying a particular market at a particular point in time; they are both *market specific* and *time specific*. The other group of tasks consists of those activities and decisions required to create, maintain, and control the *process* by which marketing strategy decisions are made, supported, and evaluated. This group includes marketing-opportunity analysis, marketing research, staffing, and the planning, structuring, coordination, budgeting, evaluation, and control of the overall marketing effort.

These two groups of activities are required of marketing management whether their responsibilities are domestic or global. The first group of activities has been the focus of the preceding chapters. In this last chapter, we focus on the scope and complexity of *global marketing management*. Our discussion includes a review of the scope of and issues associated with the process, the factors that directly impact on it, and certain of the more important features, or elements, of the process itself. The *global marketing management process* is both the framework for and the conduit through which specific marketing strategies are developed, implemented, and controlled. It dominates, even constrains, the actions of global marketing management. The process and the marketing strategies produced by the process are inextricably interwoven. When synchronized, the company functions competitively in the marketplace; when not, they can work against each other and render the company ineffective.

This chapter is divided into four major parts. The first part discusses the various devices used by global companies to integrate their marketing activities. The second part discusses the roles of planning and resource allocation in directing and controlling global marketing. The third part looks at the three most commonly used methods for evaluating marketing performance abroad. The fourth and final part discusses key issues and problems associated with standardizing the global management process.

INTEGRATION OF THE GLOBAL MARKETING EFFORT

The way a company markets its products, the tasks performed in-house and purchased from outside agencies, and the managerial techniques, approaches, and practices vary considerably from country-to-country but are potentially under the direct control of the company. A major responsibility of the global marketing manager is to coordinate, control, and support these activities to advance company objectives while remaining responsive to local conditions and competitive pressures.

The integration of the company's foreign marketing activities into a cohesive marketing effort is achieved in several ways. Examples include modifying organization design, the use of various integrative devices, the centralization of various support services, the judicious location of decision-making, the establishment of policies and procedures, and the assignment of particular tasks to the corporate, regional, and national management teams. Each of these approaches to the integration and control of the global marketing effort will be discussed below.

The Company's Organization Structure

It was pointed out in Chapter 18 that each of the basic company organization designs has particular strengths and weaknesses. Each structure often needs to be modified to fit a particular marketing situation in order to further corporate goals. To effect such modification, there have evolved a number of integrative mechanisms: corporate and divisional staff groups, specialized product managers, and the like. The precise nature of each mechanism depends on the type of organization design within which it functions, the company's stage of development, the characteristics of its products, and its state of technology.

The International Division

The international division structure is normally used by companies during the *growth stage* of their international activities. There is considerable diversity in the types of integrative mechanisms used. However, they do have some features in common.

One of the major reasons for using the international structure is to provide a centralized location for international expertise and experience. Many companies create new marketing units, located either at the corporate or regional level, to assist foreign affiliates in the coordination and development of their marketing strategies. These units also act as communication centers that stimulate and expedite two-way flows of technological and marketing know-how. The coordination and consultancy activities that they provide promote the integration of various affiliates to insure that they do not deviate far from company objectives and goals. More than likely, they follow the policies and procedures developed by the parent company.

For example, American Can created a marketing- and business-development unit whose key task was to help foreign affiliates develop five-year strategic plans. The unit also assisted these affiliates in the development of marketing information systems. In another case, a large U.S. consumer products company presently uses a highly decentralized international division approach for its overseas activities. Its corporate staff is minimal, providing only coordination functions for various regional management centers. To strategically gain from its international activities, it has created an International Administration and Marketing (IA&M) department with four purposes: (1) to disseminate information, particularly new product information; (2) to handle requests from affiliates for information and materials; (3) to serve as a training ground for new international management personnel; and (4) to route key documents from the affiliates for signing by designated corporate or regional managers. In addition to these communication services, the department is responsible for the company's export activities, the introduction of new products to the company's foreign affiliates, the supply of product samples, and the dissemination of domestic marketing-research results.[1]

Global Organization Structures

Global product and area structures tend to emphasize either product or geography. As a consequence, one important responsibility of global marketing management is to ensure that the other dimensions of a company's activities are neither overlooked nor neglected by regional and local marketing teams. Companies structured along global product lines will therefore often create organizational units at corporate headquarters that house regional or area coordinators. In contrast, companies that employ area structures often have product coordinators. Whichever is the case, it is the responsibility of these coordinators to ensure that the interests and problems of their particular dimensions of company activities are not overlooked when marketing strategies are formulated and evaluated.

The role of these coordinators can best be described by example in companies using a geographic or regional structure, the marketing and manufacturing functions are organizationally dispersed; this creates coordination problems. For example, a marketing manager responsible for a particular product who is stationed in Brazil probably reports to the Latin American regional marketing manager. This manager's counterparts in Europe and the United States probably report to European and U.S. regional marketing managers at divisional headquarters. Thus, to coordinate and oversee product planning for this particular product an additional management layer is required. Its responsibilities are likely to span the European, Latin American, and U.S. regions. Thus, global-area organizations often are complemented by worldwide planning groups authorized to dictate to areas on such matters as pricing, production, and overall geographic planning. These groups may also have the power to ration output when production problems (bottlenecks and breakdowns) arise.

In the case of global-product organizations, the opposite type of problem exists: a lack of coordination in the countries where several divisions may be represented. As a result, these organizations often have a country or regional management superimposed with responsibilities for coordinating and managing product division activities. These responsibilities can include coordinating sales-force activities to ensure that potential customers are not inundated and confused by visits from several divisions, joint marketing-research projects when appropriate, and the assembly or packaging of products from various divisions into customer-designed "systems."[2]

Other Integrative Marketing Devices

Other devices used to effect the coordination, integration, and control of foreign marketing activities include *special meetings, standing committees, ad hoc committees,* and *task forces.* One type of coordinating technique used by some companies (Baxter Travenol, for example) is to hold worldwide operating reviews at some convenient location, such as corporate headquarters. These meetings provide attendees an opportunity to hear the plans of the home office, regions, and countries and to address common problems. To ensure a balanced perspective, the meetings are often attended by representatives from production and finance as well as marketing.

Some companies use standing committees composed of individuals from the product groups, international and regional groups, and functional staffs. Others use ad hoc committees (composed of members from the various groups just mentioned) to develop long-term strategic plans, and in-depth country plans.

For example, Procter & Gamble has established "so-called Euro Brand teams that analyze opportunities for greater product and marketing program standardization. Chaired by the brand manager from a 'lead country,' each team includes brand managers from other European subsidiaries that market the brand."[3] Other team members include personnel drawn from Procter & Gamble's European technical centers and its European divisions responsible for a variety of brands. The company used a similar approach when developing a liquid detergent for its U.S. and Japanese markets. In this case, the product development team was made up of staff from the United States and Japan.[4]

Centralized Marketing-Support Services

In addition to the creation of integrative mechanisms, there is a strong tendency among global companies to develop centralized support systems. These systems are charged with covering such things as competitive assessments, market research, advertising, promotion, packaging design, and training. The location of these services depends, to a considerable extent, on the company's overall organization design and strategic thrust. In international-division companies, these services tend to be located at the division headquarters. In global structures, they tend to be housed at the divisional level when the divisions are profit centers and at corporate headquarters when they are not.

For example, Caterpillar Tractor is essentially a one-product company that has favored a tightly knit managerial group with a unified global perspective. Its major thrust is product standardization and the resulting interchangeability of components and parts. A functional approach is emphasized, and functional activities are broken down as "general offices" (GOs) on a highly centralized basis. Within the scope of the marketing activity, there are two general offices. The product GO is responsible for economic analysis, pricing and scheduling, product control, and product source planning; the marketing GO is responsible for worldwide sales and sales development.[5]

The ability to provide centralized support services depends in part on whether the company has a single business (such as Caterpillar Tractor) or a number of businesses (3M, General Electric, General Foods). The greater the diversity of countries and businesses, the more difficult it is to provide centralized services. In diversified companies, these services may come from widely dispersed locations.[6] Global companies often must concentrate major activities in regional affiliates. For example, a particular subsidiary may be given the responsibility for the development of certain products, the manufacture of part of the company's product line, or the sale and distribution of all of the company's products. To fulfill this latter responsibility, it must become involved in the procurement of products from other subsidiaries and in regional export distribution.

The Location of Marketing-Mix Decisions

Any company seeking to integrate its global marketing efforts must determine where particular marketing-related decisions will be made. The centralization or decentralization of decision-making activities involves balancing the particular needs of the company and its markets. Consequently, no global company either centralizes or decentralizes all decisions, and although marketing decision-making structures vary from company to company, broad similarities exist, especially among companies in the same industry.

Since the issues surrounding the location of marketing-mix decisions have already been treated extensively in earlier chapters, at this time, we will simply note that *the location of marketing decision-making activities has a direct bearing on which competitive advantages can best be developed and exploited.* For example, one study of 9 consumer durable companies and 26 of their foreign affiliates showed that local management was responsible for 86 percent of advertising decisions, 74 percent of pricing decisions, and 61 percent of channel decisions. However, as shown in Table 19-1, decisions concerning product design were imposed or jointly made with corporate headquarters in 70 percent of the programs studied. As already discussed, the study also determined that organizational factors affect the location of the decision-making activities.[7]

A study involving 27 companies marketing consumer packaged goods found that product characteristics, brand names, and packaging were the most highly standardized elements of the marketing mix. Reasons given for the high degree of standardization of these elements included economies of scale in production, better legal protection of trademarks, and better control over intangible advantages such as worldwide brand identity. In contrast, pricing and distribution decisions

TABLE 19-1
Degrees of Foreign Marketing-Management Autonomy

Degree of Foreign Marketing-Management Autonomy	Local Marketing Decision			
	Product design	Advertising approach	Retail price	Distribution outlets (per 000 population)
Primary authority rested with local management	30%	86%	74%	61%
Local management shared authority with other levels in organization	15	8	20	38
Decision primarily imposed upon local management	55	6	6	1
N (marketing programs observed)	N = 86	N = 84	N = 84	N = 86

Source: Adapted from R. J. Aylmer, "Who Makes Decisions in the Multinational Firm?" *Journal of Marketing,* October 1970, p. 26, published by the American Marketing Association.

tended to be relatively more localized because of the considerable variation in local conditions.[8]

The Distribution of Marketing Responsibilities

Closely related to the location of decision-making activities are the assignment of responsibilities and the establishment of policies and procedures. Some idea of how companies go about coordinating and controlling global marketing responsibilities can be gained from Exhibit 19-1.

The distribution of the responsibilities listed in Exhibit 19-1 reflects the integrative tasks facing top marketing management. Responsibilities retained at corporate headquarters and divisions impact most heavily on the maintenance of the company's worldwide activities, company identity, strategic-planning activities, intracompany transfers of resources, and production. The responsibilities assigned to subsidiaries enable the company to be responsive to local conditions, competitors' moves, and changes in the marketplace. This distribution of responsibilities closely approximates geocentric management (see Chapter 10).

EXHIBIT 19-1
Examples of Marketing-Management Responsibilities at Three Levels in a Global Company

Corporate

- ☐ Policies on intercorporate pricing
- ☐ Policies on warranties and servicing of company products
- ☐ Policies on selection of advertising agencies
- ☐ Policies on trademarks and other corporate identification
- ☐ Supervision and policies on prices and customer discounts for affiliates
- ☐ Control over company image (institutional advertising)
- ☐ Conduct of general economic and political forecasting
- ☐ Coordination of distribution channels
- ☐ Policies and instructions on government sales

Divisional

- ☐ Develop marketing plans for export markets
- ☐ Joint development of marketing plans with subsidiaries
- ☐ Product management assistance to subsidiaries
- ☐ Review of marketing performance and action recommendations
- ☐ New Product planning

Subsidiary

- ☐ Management of all line marketing and sales operations
- ☐ Market research on country level
- ☐ Advertising and promotion activities within policy guidelines

Source: 201 Checklists: Decision Making in International Operations (New York: Business International, 1980), pp. 19–20.

INTEGRATION AND THE PROCESS OF GLOBAL MARKETING PLANNING

Planning is essential to the effective integration of marketing and policy. The process brings together representatives of finance, marketing, and production units at various levels of management, requiring them to set mutual short- and long-term goals. The plans that flow from this process become the basis for the allocation of the company resources. Through the judicious allocation of these resources, the company influences which competitive advantages to develop, which skills to add to, and which specific marketing opportunities to exploit.

Global Marketing Planning

Global marketing planning is normally part of a more comprehensive corporatewide planning process designed to provide the kinds of information necessary to allocate resources and to plan for the future activities of the firm, both short and long term.

The role played by global marketing management in overall planning—and thus the degree to which its marketing activities need to be integrated with domestic activities—is determined by the company's diversity of product offerings, its cross-border product and resource flows, the economics of production, and the key characteristics of its marketing policies. The process is also affected by (1) the hierarchical relations of subsidiary, area, and product divisions and corporate headquarters and (2) the desired balance between product and geography.[9]

For example, *multibusiness* companies tend to use global-product or matrix structures. Planning in these companies entails the development of plans covering functions, product markets, and geographic areas and the means for integrating them. The relationship between planning and integration is diagrammed in Figure 19-1. On the other hand, *single-business* companies, such as Corn Products Company, tend to provide their foreign subsidiaries with considerable planning autonomy except where cross-border product flow occurs. The greater the cross-border product flow, the greater the need to centralize the planning activity to ensure coordination of production and distribution (as in the case of Caterpillar Tractor).[10]

The Content of Global Marketing Plans

The planning of the global marketing and domestic marketing efforts differs significantly. Involvement in foreign and international marketing activities add complexity. As stressed through out this book, markets are not homogeneous. They are fragmented and diverse. Competitive, economic, and political conditions vary substantially across markets. Geography and cultural difference add substantially to market differences. All these factors contribute to the differences in opinion that invariably arise during planning.

The range of items that should be considered in the global marketing planning process includes key variables presented in Exhibit 19-2. Such information is

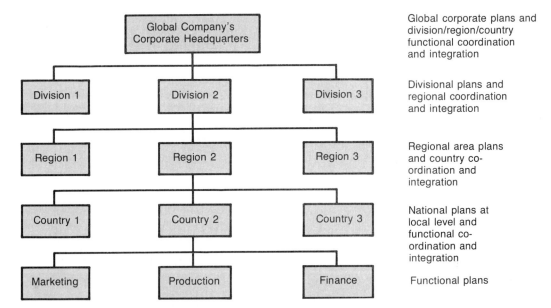

Global Company's Corporate Headquarters	Global corporate plans and division/region/country functional coordination and integration
Division 1 — Division 2 — Division 3	Divisional plans and regional coordination and integration
Region 1 — Region 2 — Region 3	Regional area plans and country co-ordination and integration
Country 1 — Country 2 — Country 3	National plans at local level and functional co-ordination and integration
Marketing — Production — Finance	Functional plans

FIGURE 19-1   Example of the Planning-Integration Relationship in a Multi-Business Global Company

required of all foreign and international operations and can be classified as self-appraisal, industry appraisal, intercompany dependency appraisal, market appraisal, and competitor appraisal. Each affiliate and region should also develop a set of ranked alternative plans and the resources required to support them. Each succeeding level of management can then evaluate the economic impact of the plans on company operations if situations change and an alternative plan must be adopted.

The degree of sophistication of each marketing planning effort reflects the relative importance of the foreign affiliate and the availability and caliber of local personnel. Some affiliates receive assistance from their regional headquarters; others are expected to complete planning assignments locally.

Allocation of Resources to Foreign Markets

The procedures used for allocating scarce corporate resources is a key control mechanism used by a company to achieve its overall strategic objectives. Control is exercised through (1) the persons involved in the procedure, (2) the importance assigned the procedure in the planning process, and (3) the funds actually allocated the various activities of the company. For example, managers directly involved in allocation can influence resource allocation decisions.

The location of the process is also important because it partially determines the kinds of information used to make allocation decisions and the roles played by the various departmental units in the collection and preparation of information.

EXHIBIT 19-2 _____
Elements of the Global Plan: Examples of Country
Information Requirements _____

Environmental Appraisal

□ Government regulations on price, advertising, channel relations

□ Government fiscal and monetary policies

□ Political and economic stability

□ Attitudes of company's publics (e.g., financial, media, general)

Self-Appraisal

□ Marketing objectives and goals

□ Competitive strategies (e.g., market leader, market challenger, market follower, market nicher)

□ Form of market presence

□ Patent protection (e.g., process, products)

□ Degree of product standardization by product category

□ Rate of technical change (e.g., major change in production and/or product by category, moderate change, little change)

□ Rate of new product development or introduction

□ Market position overall and by product categories

Industry Appraisal

□ Rate of technical changes (e.g., production processes, product categories—major, moderate, little)

□ Industry concentration (e.g., percentage of sales accounted for by four largest competitors)

□ Exports as percentage of industry sales

□ Imports as percentage of industry sales

□ Growth rate of industry over past ten years (in value and unit terms)

□ Instability of industry unit sales over past ten years

□ Composition of major competitors (e.g., local vs. foreign)

Finally, the resources allocated determine whether or not given activities are to be expanded, maintained at current levels, or cut back.

The Marketing Resource Allocation Process

There are two types of resource decisions, the allocation of *capital resources* and the allocation of *operational resources.* In most companies, capital resource decisions are part of strategic planning and the operational resource decisions are part of budgeting. Many global companies, especially those pursuing global-market strategies, are increasingly making the operational resource decision an integral part of the strategic planning process; they refer to it as operational planning.[11]

When the operational resource decision is handled as part of budgeting, it is based on sales, costs, and profit forecasts prepared by the financial department. Country managers and their staffs play a key role in identifying, defining and estimating the level of activity expected in their respective markets.[12] They therefore have considerable influence over capital and operational expenditure decisions. On the other hand, when the resource decision is handled as operational planning, it is controlled more closely by corporate management. Heavier emphasis is placed on the strategic merits of capital and operational resource decisions and on their long- and near-term implications, respectively.

EXHIBIT 19-2 (*continued*) _____

Supplier Appraisal

☐ Percentage of total purchases from largest local suppliers

☐ Percentage of these suppliers' total sales

☐ Availability of alternative supply sources (e.g., easy, difficult, none)

☐ Degree of vertical and horizontal integration of suppliers

☐ Government restrictions on local and foreign suppliers

Intracompany Dependency

☐ Percentage of total purchases from other company affiliates by location

☐ Percentage of total sales to other company affiliates by location

☐ Percentage of shared plant and equipment, etc., with other parts of company

☐ Percentage of sales to same customers of other company affiliates

☐ Percentage of sales using same sales force, advertising, and marketing programs

Market Appraisal

☐ Size of market and market segments served (e.g., sales volume in units and value)

☐ Geographic location of major segments of markets

☐ Number of competing brands

☐ Entry and exit of competitors

☐ Customer concentration (e.g., number of accounts accounting for 50 percent or more of sales)

☐ Percentage of sales by type of channel

☐ Percentage gross margin by wholesaler and/or retailer

☐ Market share by product category, by market segment

Competitor Appraisal

☐ Relative product quality by product category

☐ Relative selling prices by product category

☐ New product introductions by product category

☐ Relative marketing expenditures by type of activity

☐ Relative performance measurements

Exhibit 19-3 presents an example of the planning cycle used by a global paper company and highlights the *timing* and *interdependency* of the two resource allocation decisions. In this case, resource allocation guidelines are established every spring and are based on targeted ROI levels and growth rates. These guidelines then become the basis for setting capital and operational resource levels. Capital expenditure levels are fixed in late summer; operational expenditure levels, in December.

The factors that affect the procedure used and the latitude managers have in staying within their resource allocations reflect the organizational structuring of the company, its global-market segmentation strategy, and its geographic expansion strategy. For example, the structuring of the organization has a strong influence on the relative importance given product and geographic considerations and thus the relative power of product and area managers in determining resource allocations.

The corporate management of a global-market company generally expects local managers to stay within resource allocations. Corporate management is highly involved in such allocation decisions. In contrast, the corporate management of national-market companies recognize that local managers need to be responsive

EXHIBIT 19-3 _____
**Example of the Resource Allocation-Global Planning Process in a
Global Company** _____

    I. Distribution of guidelines
   II. Preliminary meetings (spring)
      A. Strategic planning
        1. Review of mission and general strategy
        2. Identification of strategic issues
        3. Establishment of guidelines
          a. R&D levels
          b. Growth rates
          c. Resource allocation
      B. Operational planning
        1. Identification of operating issues
        2. Establishment of guidelines for expected performance
  III. Planning analysis (summer)
      A. Situation analysis
      B. Formulate issue resolution approaches
      C. Preliminary financial projections
  IV. Interim meetings (late summer)
      A. Review of developing plans
      B. Limiting of alternatives to be evaluated
      C. Setting of first year's capital allocations
   V. Plan development (September and early October)
      A. Action programs
      B. Contingency plans
      C. Financial projections
  VI. Final review meetings (November)
 VII. Budget preparation (December)

Source: Adapted from an example of the planning cycle used by an international paper company and presented in *Strategic Planning for International Corporations: Organization, Systems, Issues & Trends* (New York: Business International, 1979), pp. 51–52.

to rapidly changing market conditions and so must not be rigidly held to resource expenditure goals.[13] Local marketing teams have an accordingly greater latitude in determining resource needs when their markets necessitate significant modifications to products and entail the formulation of unique marketing activities.[14]

    The resource allocation procedures used by companies driven by geographic diversification strategies differ from those used by companies with geographic concentration strategies. If following diversification strategies, corporate management generally has considerable influence over capital and operational resource decisions. The opposite is true of companies using concentration strategies. The need to defend their competitive position and gain a reasonable market share increases the influence of the local marketing management team.

Methods for Allocating Marketing Resources

    Many analytical methods have been developed to help managers make marketing resource allocation decisions. Models have been developed as aids to managers making advertising budget decisons,[15] promotional expenditure decisions,[16] media selection and allocation decisions,[17] sales effort decisions,[18] and other marketing-mix decisions.[19] Although such methods have value, they can be used only once management decides what resources to allocate to each of the company's foreign markets.

When making these resource allocation decisions, management treats new market ventures and existing operations separately. Entry into new markets involves problems that are of a one-time nature; existing operations are known entities with fairly well-defined performance characteristics. The following discussion centers on the more common problem of allocating company resources to existing operations.

For companies using product or area structures, the three-step allocation procedure illustrated in Figure 19-2 is appropriate. In the simplest situation, the company first allocates available resources to its product or area units, then to the foreign markets within these units, and finally, to the various functional units within foreign markets. Complications arise if the foreign markets are operated as joint ventures or as market clusters. For single product companies, such as Caterpillar, a two-step approach is more appropriate. Available resources are allocated directly to foreign markets and then to their various functional units.

The following discussion relates to multiproduct or multiarea companies, and focuses on the first two steps of the three-step approach. For illustrative purposes, only two allocation methods are presented, one for each step. The choice of technique ultimately depends on the company's objectives, the allocation criteria used, and the level of sophistication desired.

Allocating Corporate Resources to Business Units. The initial problem facing management is to fund a variety of resources (n), which then need to be assigned to a number of business units (m) with different profit generating possibilities

FIGURE 19-2   Resource Allocation Procedures for Global-Market and National-Market Companies

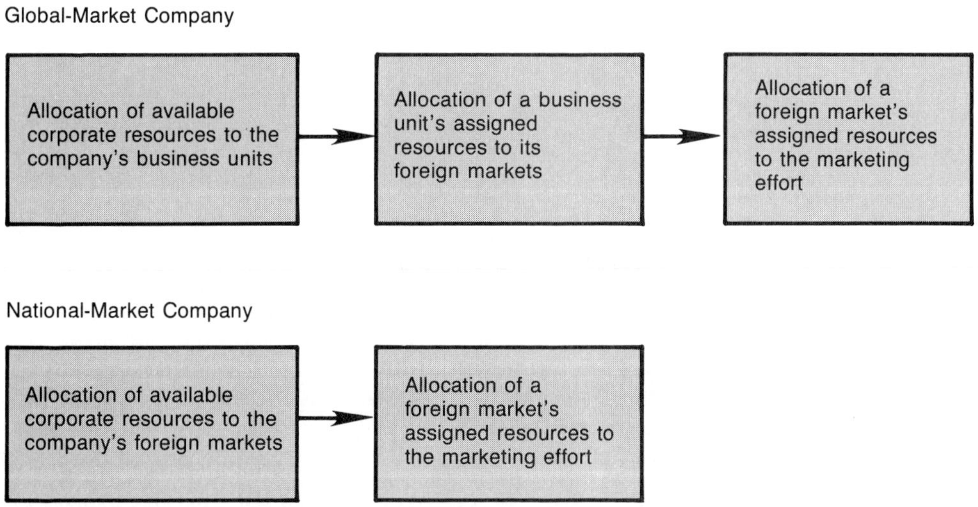

Global-Market Company

National-Market Company

and objectives. The funds are generated in one time period, and the resources are then used in the next time period by the business units to meet their profit generating responsibilities. For example, a company may have four divisions (such as General Foods' packaged grocery products, grocery coffee, processed meats, and food services), each with a different potential for generating cash (profit). The company may also make use of several types of resources (R&D, product development, advertising, selling, administrative and technical staffs, and so on), each of which has a direct and distinct impact on the profitability of each division. Management must decide on the funding levels for each of the n resources and allocate these resources accordingly to each m division.

Allocation can be divided into two tasks. The first task is to *adjust the resources* upward or downward according to the influence they have on the profit rate of individual business units. For example, General Foods' packaged grocery products division may depend much more on product development for its profitability

---

EXHIBIT 19-4
The Allocation of Available Corporate Funds to *N* Resources and *M* Business Units

A multibusiness unit company needs a method for allocating available funds to a variety of resources: these, in turn, must be allocated to business units. The following method assumes that the funds, resources, and profitability of these units are interdependent.[1]

Adjustment to Corporate Resources

The level of resources available to a company is not constant; it can be adjusted upward or downward according to the profit rate of the individual business units and the available profits (funds). A model of this resource adjustment process is

$$r_i(t + 1) = r_i(t) + f_i[b_i(t)\pi(t)] \blacktriangle t \qquad (19.1)$$

where

$r_i(t)$ = level of resource i at time t

$\pi(t)$ = total profit at time $t = \Sigma_j \pi_j(t)$, where $\pi_j(t)$ is the profit from business unit j

$b_i(t)$ = proportion of total profit allocated to resource i

f_i = functional relationship between profit and resource level

Equation 19.1 may be expressed as the differential equation

$$\frac{dri(t)}{dt} = \dot{r}_i(t) = f_i[b_i(t)\pi(t)] \qquad (i = 1, 2, ..., m) \qquad (19.2)$$

Profitability Objective of Business Unit

Profitability of unit j is assumed to be a function of the level of resources allocated to it at time t. So, if $\pi_j(t)$ is the profit for business unit j at time t, this can be expressed as

1. The method presented here is based on the normative model of strategic product planning proposed by Peter T. FitzRoy, *Analytical Methods for Marketing Management* (London: McGraw-Hill, 1976), pp. 277–279.

than does the food service division. The grocery coffee division may depend much more on advertising than does the processed meats division. Final adjustments are limited by the amount of cash available.

The second task is to *allocate a mix of the adjusted resources* to each of the company's business units to achieve profit objectives. The decision is complicated; the optimal mix of resources may be different for each business unit, as noted above.

Allocations of funds to the various resources and of the resources to the different business units need to be made simultaneously. An example of one way to do this is presented in Exhibit 19-4.

Allocation of Resources to Foreign Markets. The second step in the allocation process involves allocating the resources assigned a particular business unit among its foreign markets. A simple method is to allocate the resources on the basis of

---

EXHIBIT 19-4 (*continued*) _____

$$\pi_j(t) = g_1[a_{j1}(t)r_1(t)] \tag{19.3}$$
$$+ \cdots + g_m[a_{jm}(t)r_m(t)] \qquad (j = 1, 2, ..., n)$$

where

$a_{jk}(t)$ = proportion of resource k allocated to business unit j at time t

$r_k(t)$ = level of resource k at time t

g_k = response function of profit to resource k

At any time t, the following constraints hold:

(i) $\quad \displaystyle\sum_{j=1}^{n} a_{ij}(t) = 1 \qquad (i = 1, 2, ..., m)$ **(19.4)**

(ii) $\quad \displaystyle\sum_{i=1}^{m} b_i(t) = 1$ **(19.5)**

Constraint (i) states that all of resource i is to be allocated to some unit. Constraint (ii) states that all of the total available funds is to be allocated to some resource.

Equations 19.1 to 19.5 are a system of equations that describe the dynamic characteristics of the business-unit mix over time. The problem is to find the coefficients (the *a*s and *b*s) that will maximize total profit over a given planning horizon:

$$\pi = \sum_{t=1}^{T} \pi(t)$$

This is a complex optimization problem that may be solved using dynamic programming.[2]

_____

2. S. E. Dreyfus, *Dynamic Programming and the Calculus of Variance* (New York: Academic Press, 1965).

each market's profitability. This involves calculating the ratio *r* for each market *i*, as shown below:

$$r = \frac{c_i}{C}$$

where c_i is the contribution ratio for market *i*, and *C* is the contribution ratio for the business unit. A market with low values of *r* is less profitable than the business unit as a whole and may deserve fewer resources than a market with a higher ratio. It may also require additional analysis to determine the reasons for below-average performance.

The problem with such a simple procedure is that the profit potential of the business unit's foreign markets are not equal. A more realistic but more complicated procedure is to factor in the business unit's profit objectives for each market, the market's responsiveness to various marketing stimuli, and the market's competitive conditions. A method that attempts to take these factors into account is presented in Exhibit 19-5.

The advantage of this approach is the explicit inclusion of each market's sales potential and response characteristics when making allocation decisions. The limitations include the expense of determining the values of the salient factors for each market. This requires considerable country-specific marketing knowledge, generally the result of experience and marketing research.

Budgets and Pro Forma Estimates

The global marketing budget and pro forma estimates are the result of the foreign and international marketing plans finally adopted. They serve as part of the integration and control process, not only for the various regional and foreign marketing efforts but also for company production plans and, in turn, financial plans. Plans are normally developed for the following year's activities, and estimates are made for subsequent years using contingency and scenario planning techniques.

The precise nature of the items to be budgeted vary considerably from company to company and within company by product. Examples of some of the common budget elements are presented in Table 19-2.

GLOBAL MARKETING PERFORMANCE

How marketing performance is evaluated is important for the three levels of marketing management generally found in global companies. It impacts future activities, budget allocations, and careers. Performance evaluations can be used by the global marketing management to coordinate and influence foreign marketing activities. Arriving at fair and reliable measurements of performance is, however, very difficult for four reasons. First, the national, and as a consequence, the regional markets in which the company competes, are not identical. They vary in terms of potential, competitive intensity, marketing infrastructure, and responsiveness to different types of stimuli (such as media, advertising messages, samples, and packaging). Second, the company's foreign affiliates vary in terms of market presence

In order to allocate a fixed amount of resources to n foreign markets, we must take into account the market's profit objective, its responsiveness to various marketing stimuli, and its competitive conditions. A resource allocation method that is responsive to the differential marginal response to marketing effort is presented below.*

Let the unit sales of market i be given by the expression

$$q_i = k_i(1 - e^{-a_i x_i}) \qquad (19.6)$$

where

q_i = unit sales of market i $\quad (i = 1, 2, ..., n)$
k_i = measure of market potential
x_i = level of marketing resources allocated to market i
a_i = response parameter for market i

It is further assumed that the business unit has a total budget, X, which is to be allocated to n markets; thus

$$\sum_{i=1}^{n} x_i = X \qquad (19.7)$$

The Lagrangian expression of the profit equation

$$L = \sum_{i=1}^{n}(P_i - d_i)k_i(1 - e^{-a_i k_i}) - \lambda\left(\sum_{i=1}^{n} x_i - X\right) \qquad (19.8)$$

where

P_i = price of units sold in market i
d_i = unit variable cost of units sold in market i
λ = Lagrange multiplier

Differentiating equation 19.8 with respect to x_i, we obtain

$$\frac{\delta L}{\delta x_i} = (P_i - d_i)k_i a_i e^{-a_i k_i} - \lambda = 0$$

For any two markets i and j, the relative allocation of the budget is thus given by

$$\frac{e^{-a_i k_i}}{e^{-a_j x_j}} = \frac{(P_j - d_j)k_j a_j}{(P_i - d_i)k_i a_i} \qquad (19.9)$$

Additional insight can be obtained if the firm's business unit has two foreign markets. From equations 19.7 and 19.9, it can be shown that the optimal allocation is given by:

$$x_2 = \frac{1}{a_1 + a_2}\left\{ \ln\left[\frac{(P_2 - d_2)k_2 a_2}{(P_1 - d_1)k_1 a_1}\right] + a_1 X\right\} \qquad (19.10)$$

$$x_1 = X - x_2$$

As can be seen from equation 19.10, the allocation to the second market is increased as its contribution increases and its market potential increase.

---

* This approach is a modification of a technique for allocating a fixed amount of resources to a number of products suggested by Peter T. FitzRoy, *Analytical Methods for Marketing Management* (London: McGraw-Hill, 1976), p. 268.

TABLE 19-2
Examples of Budget and Forecasting Requirements
(required at each ascending level: subsidiary/region/division)

Broad Category	Item
Marketing	Overall product volume for served market (value and units)
	Expected market shares
	Sales by product category
	Selling prices
	Marketing expenditures
Production	Volume of output required by product category
	Production capacity required
	Plant utilization rates
	Materials, fuel, and manpower required
	Production costs per product category
Distribution	Volumes to be shipped from other affiliates
	Distribution facilities required
	Distribution costs
	Manpower required
Research and Development	Planned improvements in production efficiency
	Planned product development
	R&D costs
Manpower	Overall manpower requirements
	Management requirements

Source: Reprinted, by permission of the publisher, from *Multinational Strategic Planning*, p. 79 ©1978 Derek F. Channon with Michael Jalland, Manchester Business School. Published by AMACOM, a division of American Management Association, New York. All rights reserved.

and the roles they are expected to play in the overall marketing effort. Some markets may be large, sophisticated, and employ highly specialized personnel. Others may be small, understaffed, and overworked. Some may exist only to respond to competitor threats. Third, separating local performance from corporate influence is not easy; local marketing effort is often strongly influenced by corporate and regional decisions not under its control or even its influence. Fourth, performance—when measured in terms of revenues, costs, or profits—is affected by fluctuations in exchange rates and in currency and capital flow controls.

Three general measures of performance have evolved. A survey conducted by Business International indicates that the most widely used of the three is *performance against budget.* Two other measures frequently mentioned are *market share* and *profitability.*[20]

Performance against Budget

Performance against budget is considered the most reliable method for measuring marketing performance. Of the several budget measures available, the two most widely used are *ratio of marketing costs to sales* and *rate of increase of sales versus rate of increase of costs.* These are considered the most reliable for comparing marketing activities across several national markets. Since percentages are used, both measures avoid the problems associated with translating local currencies into home-country currency.

The surveyed marketing managers feel that the ratio of marketing costs to sales measurement minimizes the distortions caused by differences in the size and sophistication of markets and affiliates. The rate of increase of sales versus rate of increase of costs measurement is also considered a reliable cross-national measurement of market performance. In the case of the latter measure, costs of introducing new products and the resulting sales are not included. Managers believe that new product introductions generally require extraordinary outlays that distort performance.

Market-Share Performance

Although marketing share is frequently used to measure marketing performance, it is really a measure of overall company results. For example, market-share growth can be attributed to production if production savings are passed on to the consumer in the form of lower prices. A low price strategy for a new marketing campaign could also result in growth in market share, which in turn, could reflect marketing performance, manufacturing performance, or both. Market share can also be obtained at the cost of profits.

Market-share calculations for foreign markets raise other problems. Their validity depends on the availability of comparable market statistics, even market definitions, across markets. Also, the reliability of estimates depends on the accuracy of the available data. In addition to the problems discussed in Chapter 5, business statistics (a major data source for market-share estimations) are affected by local taxation structures and tendencies toward tax evasion.[21] Output, even sales by the manufacturer or retailer, may be deliberately undervalued to reduce taxes. Also, government statistics may be unavailable, only rough estimates, or classified in ways not useful for determining market share. Smuggling may also result in an underestimating of market size. For example, it is estimated that smuggling accounted for more than 20 percent of the clothing purchased in Mexico in 1985.

Profitability

Because of the difficulties associated with measuring market share, *profitability* measurements are considered to be of more value by most companies. However, there are still problems with this measurement because of foreign exchange rates, cost allocation issues, and other local differences. These differences are of primary importance when attempting to compare marketing performance across national and regional markets.

GLOBAL MARKETING MANAGEMENT AS A STANDARDIZED PROCESS

In the opening paragraphs of this chapter, we pointed out that the marketing process is marketing-activity specific. In contrast, marketing strategy is market specific and time specific. This means that the marketing process is relatively more responsive to the firm's strategic needs and the marketing strategy is relatively more responsive to marketplace conditions. That is, the practices, techniques, and approaches used by marketing personnel to fulfill their responsibilities are not as directly influenced by the expressed needs, or wants, or conditions of a particular market at a particular point in time. As a result, many of the tasks included in the marketing process can be standardized and centralized. Marketing *strategy,* on the other hand, must be developed to satisfy a particular set of expressed needs and wants of the market(s) identified, analyzed, and selected by the marketing process.

As Shuptrine and Toyne emphasize, a standardized marketing process should seek to "provide a conceptual framework, a way of thinking, together with a methodology for implementation rather than specific, detailed guides for action."[22] The basic advantage of using a standardized marketing process for foreign marketing activities is the assurance it gives that marketing and strategic goals mesh. Any standardized marketing plan satisfies the following four criteria:

1. It is based on a systematic and objective identification and analysis of each foreign market, and the factors and mechanisms influencing how and what needs are to be satisfied.

2. It is based on the company's pooled marketing knowledge and best marketing practices.

3. It is compatible with the company's corporate, business, and marketing objectives.

4. It is compatible with the company's human and material resources.

As Walters has noted, the most obvious elements of the process to be considered include the data to be collected, the method of data collection, how the data are to be used, the steps to be taken, the analytical methods to be employed, decision-making criteria, and who is to be involved in making decisions.[23]

A standardized marketing process also overcomes some of the inherent problems associated with a decentralized foreign marketing effort, namely, inconsistent brand identities, a limited product focus, and slow new-product launches.[24] In these cases, the influence of standardization is felt in the policy and procedures established by the corporate or divisional marketing managements and in the use of the coordination and integration devices described earlier.

Nestlé is an example of a company that has adopted a standardized data-gathering system.[25] Each subsidiary utilizes a similar approach to forecasting and planning. Information collected by all foreign affiliates is broadly comparable across markets and can be used to plan production, distribution, and promotional activities and to help avoid duplication of common activities. Standardization thus facilitates the development and implementation of a global approach to marketing-information and planning.

SUMMARY

The integration and control responsibilities of the global marketing manager can be divided into two distinct yet interdependent groups of activities. One group consists of those tasks necessary to create, implement, monitor, and adjust marketing strategies. The second group consists of those activities needed to create, maintain, and control the marketing process by which marketing strategy decisions are made, supported, and evaluated.

Integration and control of these two groups of activities is accomplished in several ways. Typical methods include the creation of integrative marketing units superimposed on the organizational structure adopted, the centralization of marketing-support services, and the judicious location of marketing-mix and other marketing-related decision-making activities.

Planning, resource allocation, and performance evaluation also help integrate and control marketing activities within and across national markets. The planning process is the means by which management meshes short- and long-term marketing activities across national markets. In addition, the plans that flow from this process become the basis for the allocation of the company's resources and act as a benchmark for evaluating market performance.

Standardizing the marketing process rather than marketing strategies has merits. Marketing strategies are market and time specific. Therefore the standardization of process is more feasible than standardization of strategy. The benefits to be gained from standardizing marketing processes include consistency in the quality of the marketing approaches and techniques used within national markets. A certain degree of standardization in the marketing process also reduces the problems associated with the development and implementation of a global marketing-information system. For example, it expedites the accumulation and dissemination of marketing research based on common collection and classification techniques, rendering comparative data more valid.

DISCUSSION QUESTIONS

1. Identify the major integrative weaknesses inherent in the international division structure. Describe two types of integrative marketing units that could be used to overcome these weaknesses.

2. The global-area structure is used by some companies to ensure responsiveness to national or regional differences. Describe at least two methods that these companies could use to ensure that the marketing activities undertaken in different regions of the world are indeed supportive of the company's overall objectives.

3. Identify and discuss the major integration problems confronting a company pursuing a national-market strategy. How can the company solve these problems without reducing its responsiveness to national differences?

4. Identify and discuss which dimensions of a global-market company's marketing effort should be centralized and which decentralized. What criteria should be used for each decision?

5. Discuss how the planning process can be used to control the marketing effort in a particular country. What role does resource allocation play?

6. Discuss the pros and cons of standardizing the marketing management process. Is a standardized process of more benefit to the company pursuing a national-market strategy or a global-market strategy?

ADDITIONAL READING

Daimantopoulos, A., and Bodo B. Schlegelmilch, "Comparing Marketing Operations of Autonomous Subsidiaries," *International Marketing Review*, Vol. 4, Winter 1987.

Douglas, Susan P., and C. Samuel Craig, "Examining Performance of U.S. Multinationals in Foreign Markets," *Journal of International Business Studies*, Vol. 14, Winter 1983.

Doz, Yves L., and C. K. Prahalad, "Patterns of Strategic Control within Multinational Corporations," *Journal of International Business Studies*, Vol. 15, Fall 1984.

Gray, David, "Control and Coordination in Multinational Corporations," *Journal of International Business Studies*, Vol. 15, Fall 1984.

Hall, George E., "Reflections on Running a Diversified Company," *Harvard Business Review*, January–February 1987.

Piercy, Nigel, "The Corporate Environment for Marketing Management and Marketing Budgeting," *International Marketing Review*, Vol. 1, Spring–Winter 1984.

ENDNOTES

1. *Designing the International Corporation Organization* (New York: Business International Corporation, 1976), pp. 91–93.
2. Ibid.
3. John A. Quelch and Edward J. Hoff, "Customizing Global Marketing," *Harvard Business Review*, May–June 1986, p. 66.
4. Christopher Lorenz, *The Design Dimension: Product Strategy the Challenge of Global Marketing* (New York, Basil Blackwell, LTD., 1986.), p. 137.
5. *Designing*.
6. Yves Doz and C. K. Prahalad, "Patterns of Strategic Control within Multinational Corporations," *Journal of International Business Studies*, Fall 1984, p. 57.
7. R. J. Aylmer, "Who Makes Marketing Decisions in Multinational Firms?" *Journal of Marketing*, October 1970.
8. Ralph Z. Sorenson and Ulrich E. Wiechmann, "How multinationals view marketing standardization," *Harvard Business Review*, May–June 1975, p. 39.
9. Derek F. Channon with Michael Jalland, *Multinational Strategic Planning* (New York: AMACOM, 1979), p. 52.
10. Ibid., pp. 57–61.
11. *Strategic Planning for International Corporations: Organization, Systems, Issues and Trends* (New York: Business International Corporation, 1979), p. 22.
12. See, for example, William H. Davidson, *Global Strategic Management* (New York: John Wiley & Sons, 1982), p. 338, and Ibid., p. 48.
13. *Strategic Planning*, p. 48.
14. William H. Davidson, *Global Strategic Management* (New York: John Wiley & Sons, 1982), p. 340.
15. See, for example, Alfred A. Kuehn, "A Model for Budgeting Advertising," in *Mathematical Models and Methods in Marketing*, ed. Frank M. Bass et al., (Homewood, Ill.: Richard D. Irwin, 1961), pp. 302–53.
16. See, for example, John D.C. Little, "A Model of Adaptive Control of Promotional Spending," *Operations Research*, November 1966, pp. 1075–97, and Lawrence Friedman, "Game Theory Models in the Allocation of Advertising Expenditures," *Operations Research*, September–October 1958, pp. 699–709.
17. See James F. Engel and Martin R. Warshaw, "Allocating Advertising Dollars by Linear Programming," *Journal of Advertising Research*, September 1964, pp. 41–48 and Mario J. Picconi and Charles L. Olson, "Advertising Decision Rules in a Multibrand Environment: Optimal Control Theory and Evidence," *Journal of Marketing Research*, February 1978, pp. 82–92.
18. See Philip Kotler, *Marketing Management: Analysis, Planning, and Control*, 5th ed. (Englewood Cliffs, N.J.: Prentice-Hall, 1984), p. 692, and A. Parasuraman and Ralph L. Day, "A Management-Oriented Model for Allocating Sales Effort," *Journal of Marketing Research*, February 1977, pp. 22–33.
19. Robert Dorfman and Peter O. Steiner, "Optimal Advertising and Optimal Quality," *American Economic Review*, December 1954, pp. 826–836, and Peter T. FitzRoy, *Analytical Methods for Marketing Management*, (London: McGraw-Hill, 1976).
20. *201 Checklists: Decision Making in International Operations* (New York: Business International, 1980), pp. 116–117.
21. Susan P. Douglas and C. Samuel Craig, *International Marketing Research*, (Englewood Cliffs, N.J.: Prentice-Hall, 1983), p. 79.
22. F. Kelly Shuptrine and Brian Toyne, "International Marketing Planning: A Standardized Process," *International Marketing: Strategy and Planning*, Vol. 1 (1981), pp. 16–28.
23. Peter G. P. Walters, "International Marketing Policy: A Discussion of the Standardization Construct and its Relevance for Corporate Policy," *Journal of International Business Studies*, Summer 1986, p. 60.
24. Same as Endnote #3.
25. Same as Endnote #8.

PART FIVE CASES
15. International Engineering Corporation _____

Per Olsen, Marketing Director of IEC, is concerned about IEC's current situation in world markets. His view, which is being presented to IEC's Managing Director at a regular Monday morning meeting, is as follows:

> Our sales performance abroad is strongly influenced by the fact that Eastern European manufacturers are copying parts of our dewatering equipment, and there seems to be very little we can do to stop them legally. Sales are dropping, and the outlook for 1987 is anything but promising. However, the situation may not be all that critical. If we can successfully move from selling individual products to complex problem solving, then competition in the markets for individual components will be of minor importance.

Managing Director Hans Berg pondered for a second:

> I have studied your recent report on marketing strategy, in which you bring up the possibility of system selling as a future strategy for IEC. Basically, I agree with your conclusion, but I see a number of problem areas which should be studied carefully. I would like you to undertake a thorough evaluation of system selling as soon as possible.

BACKGROUND

IEC started producing fish meal and fish oil at a factory located in Western Norway in 1905. The company developed into an engineering enterprise internationally renowned for its innovations and know-how in developing machines for the chemical and fish industries.

The production of fish meal is very much a question of dewatering the raw materials. IEC had improved existing dewatering technology by effective R&D activity. The firm was divided into two main divisions:

1. *The Factory Division*, responsible for the operation of the fish meal factory;
2. *The Engineering Division*, by far the largest and most dynamic division, both in terms of growth in sales and manpower; where most product development and innovation occur.

The technological nature of IEC's activities necessitated the extensive use of engineers and technicians, who made up most of the engineering division's employees. The organizational structure and manpower of the Engineering Division as of March 1986 are shown in Exhibit 1.

The relative importance of the Engineering Division increased markedly in under a decade. In 1978, it accounted for 76 percent of total sales. By 1986, the comparable figure was 90 percent. And, whereas the sale of fish meal and oil was decreasing, the Engineering Division was currently enjoying an annual growth rate of approximately 20 percent.

THE MARKET FOR DEWATERING EQUIPMENT

The supply of dewatering equipment was not limited to fish-processing industries. A number of other industries had similar dewatering problems and could benefit from the use of IEC's dewatering services. The twin-screw press (see Exhibit 2) had, for example, proved its efficiency for such wet fibrous materials and pulps as:

- Sugar-beet pulp
- Distillers' spent grains
- Brewers' spent grains
- Starch residues
- Cottonseed residues

_____
This case was written by Bjarne Bakka and Inge Skjelfjord, the Norwegian School of Economics and Business Administration, Bergen, Norway.

- Alginates
- Pectines
- Fruit and fruit residues

Based on the industries ordering the equipment, it was possible to distinguish between three major types of sale:

- Sales to fish industries
- Sales to sugar-beet industries
- Sales to other industries

The sale of dewatering equipment to the fish-meal industry had accounted for the major part of the company's revenue in the past. But, as early as the 1950s, efforts had been made to expand sales to other industries as well. During the 1970s, the sugar-beet industry had developed as an attractive market.

Development of sales showed the following pattern in the period 1976–1986:

matter of selling individual dewatering components. The agents possessed a relatively good general knowledge of IEC's machinery.

The *ideal agent* would, according to Per Olsen, have an engineering background, have some knowledge of international marketing, and be culturally comfortable in the market. These criteria could not easily be satisfied by one individual. It was particularly difficult to find agents with adequate engineering expertise.

Consequently, IEC had to draw on its own engineering staff to organize export marketing, and a team of ten sales engineers had been established. The role of the agent became more diffuse, but their main function was that of a cultural go-between, especially in markets culturally distant from Norway. A discussion had been under way for some time as to what extent agents should be given product/engineering training at the Nor-

	Fish-Meal Industries	*Sugar-Beet Industries*	*Other Industries*	*Total (Million Nkr)*	
1976	71%	29%	0%	100	138
1977	63	37	0	100	145
1978	64	35	1	100	156
1979	63	35	2	100	146
1980	40	50	10	100	151
1981	44	44	12	100	171
1982	51	36	13	100	180
1983	43	46	11	100	192
1984	44	38	18	100	230
1985	39	39	22	100	227
1986	52	41	7	100	252

EXPORT BACKGROUND

Contacts were established in the early 1950s with a Swedish company, GLOBE Trading Company, that had developed a worldwide network of agents. With the help of GLOBE, IEC had supplied dewatering equipment to more than 400 companies in 40 countries. Export sales in 1986 were valued at some Nkr 200 million ($32.5 million).

Personal Sales were the key element in IEC's marketing strategy. The total world number of fish-meal producers was approximately 500, 80 of which were located in Norway. The use of GLOBE's agents had functioned well as long as it was mostly a

wegian headquarters to help integrate their work with that of the sales engineers.

A sales engineer from IEC enjoyed strong professional backup from all organizational levels of the company. If necessary, a sales unit could call in IEC people from chemical processing, construction, production, management, and marketing. Customers were usually impressed by IEC's technical capability.

A *sales unit* consisted of 2 or 3 sales engineers. After a preliminary survey of markets and customers, one would focus in on potential targets. The company in question would be approached, and generally one tried to establish contact with the production management. Not only would one "speak the same language," but communication with the production side of the company would give the IEC people direct insight into the complexity and the extent of the operation, what problems existed, and so on.

Spare-parts service, which IEC stressed in the company's marketing efforts, seemed to have contributed to a strengthening of IEC's image with the customers. Offering effective assistance and speedy supply of parts, IEC succeeded in reinforcing its positive image. The extent of the spare-parts service was illustrated by the fact that several of the customers had 20 to 30 year-old machines in operation, and each piece of machinery contained a substantial number of parts requiring periodic replacement. Hence, IEC promised their customers that "they could call at any time of the day and that IEC's people would go out of their way to help."

The *customers* seemed often to be interested in purchasing an extended product, not just pieces of production equipment. Fish-meal producers in developing countries, for instance, had to buy foreign expertise and know-how in order to obtain up-to-date production facilities. It was also the official policy in many of these countries to stimulate purchase of foreign know-how to bridge the knowledge gap.

Markets in Eastern Europe were in many respects in a similar situation. It was clear that these countries wished to catch up with the superior technology and production techniques existing in the West. Through their five-year plans, one could get an idea of what industries and economic domains were favored for development by means of know-how bought from outside.

Some large international companies often turned to IEC for the supply of mechanical equipment. Their professional management placed increasing emphasis on efficient use of company resources and preferred to engage specialists in areas where the company itself did not have a particular competence.

A number of IEC's customers were small local producers of fish meal who did not have enough resources or experience to develop and to install processing equipment. These producers had no other alternative but to purchase hardware, components, and know-how from outside.

One sales engineer summed up his impressions from a trip to South America like this:

> Sure we can sell presses, boilers, and screws, but what the fish meal producers are really needing is system engineering. Take this Chexouga plant in Guatemala, for example. The plant is old and uneconomically operated. We found, during our visit, that by replacing three central subsystems, operating cost would be halved, production capacity would increase by 65 percent, and profit would double. Señor Garcia, who owns the factory, was very excited about what we told him and would like us to draw up plans to modernize the entire plant. Other examples like this support my feelings that IEC should concentrate on systems. The problem is often not on the technical side, but more a question of mismanagement and poor training of production personnel. We could easily develop standardized programs for training of personnel and implementation of production and management routines.

Per Olsen had felt for some time that IEC's basic strategy was too dominated by its tradition as a supplier of mechanical equipment—despite the fact that the market largely perceived IEC as an innovator in food processing. Olsen was also influenced by IEC's attempts to establish a competence in chemical processing. Recently, a young chemist had joined the company to coordinate IEC's internal R&D and projects that IEC had going with external research institutions.

Consequently, Per Olsen had started to study system selling as a new marketing strategy for IEC. He saw the strong impact such a move would have on the entire organization. New demands would be placed on manpower, finance, and the allocation of resources in general.

Pricing

Traditionally, IEC followed a uniform price policy that in principle implied that customers would pay the same prices, receive identical discounts, credit offers, and so on—irrespective of what industry or geographical area the customer operated in. IEC's products were in a higher price bracket than most competitive equipment. High prices were complementary to high product quality. However, it had become increasingly difficult to maintain a high price level. Foreign competitors were copying IEC's dewatering equipment and were underbidding IEC in traditional markets.

The price of an all-inclusive package would disguise the prices of single components. Customer acceptance of the overall price would, in part, depend upon their perceptions as to the dependability and trustworthiness of IEC. Per Olsen felt that the company's development from fish-meal producer to supplier of mechanical equipment established a certain goodwill in the market that most competitors did not enjoy. The issue of honesty ought, therefore, to work in IEC's favor.

The price of individual dewatering components ranged from Nkr. 300,000 to 500,000. According to Per Olsen's calculations, the prices of an entire production unit would be in the neighborhood of Nkr. 14–20 million, depending on how far IEC went in adding technical and administrative know-how to the sale of hardware components.

Preliminary discussion with the sales teams revealed strong differences in opinion as to how far IEC should develop system selling at this stage. Some of the engineers were very much opposed to the idea, arguing that it would deviate too much from IEC's basic mission as inventor and developer of mechanical equipment. There were also some doubts as to whether IEC could compete as a "systems seller."

COMPETITION

In the past, IEC enjoyed significant technological protection from competitive producers. IEC's products were superior to existing dewatering equipment, and were patented worldwide. Moreover, sales of this type of equipment were relatively insignificant compared to the overall size of the market, and larger corporations did not find it lucrative to bother with IEC. The individual installations often had to be tailored to suit the needs of respective customers; the scope for large scale mass production was thus limited.

This situation supported the idea of advantageous niche operations or, more specifically, market segmentation. This meant allocating company resources toward specific segments that pro-

vided the right competitive climate for a midsize company.

However, competition had taken a turn for the worse. In addition to the problems of competitors copying IEC's products, the company also struggled with high and increasing labor and material costs. Competitors were often located in low-cost areas, which gave them a general cost and price advantage.

The sale of entire production lines and systems would mean the inclusion of know-how and engineering expertise in the supply package. IEC was not a complete novice in this area and on one occasion IEC had been responsible for building a fish-meal factory in Peru. Even though it was a small plant, the company gained valuable experience in coordinating and carrying through such an extensive project. An ad hoc project group had functioned as a connecting link between the various activities during this project, and discussion had taken place as to whether this group should be made a permanent part of the organization.

The Peruvian experience exemplified what some fish-meal producers felt about purchasing entire production systems. The owner of the plant had this to say after IEC handed over the plant:

> The creation of an entire fish meal factory is best left to experts in system engineering. As producers of fish meal, we should primarily be concerned with the physical production process, the supply of raw materials, improving the quality of fish meal, and the marketing of the finished products.

During his efforts to look into the strategic move from single product selling to system selling, Per Olsen had met with several of his colleagues from both the sales and production sides of the company to learn their opinions. In one of the meetings, he had tried to sum up some of the consequences he saw system selling would have for IEC:

> We are facing a severe challenge in our traditional markets. In my opinion, we can best meet this threat by turning our resources towards extensive engineering problem solving and by offering complete engineering services. In the long run, I visualize that the system package must be enlarged to also include additional administrative and marketing services, so that IEC

EXHIBIT 1
International Engineering Corporation's Engineering Division: Structure and Manpower

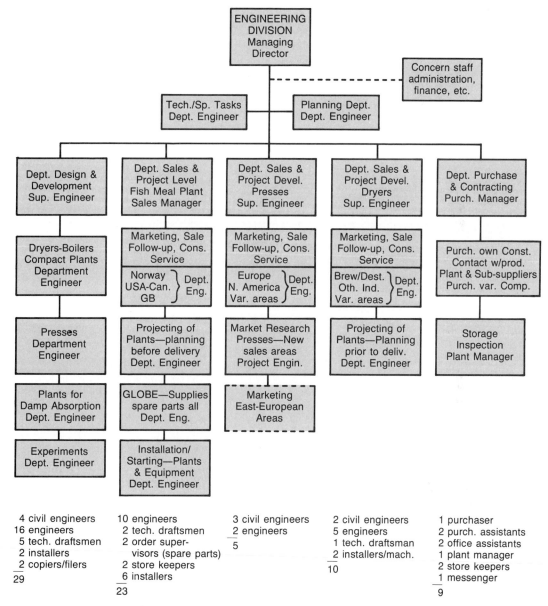

4 civil engineers	10 engineers	3 civil engineers	2 civil engineers	1 purchaser
16 engineers	2 tech. draftsmen	2 engineers	5 engineers	2 purch. assistants
5 tech. draftsmen	2 order super-	5	1 tech. draftsman	2 office assistants
2 installers	visors (spare parts)		2 installers/mach.	1 plant manager
2 copiers/filers	2 store keepers		10	2 store keepers
29	6 installers			1 messenger
	23			9

eventually will supply entire production systems, and also provide extensive management consulting services, both for production as well as administrative functions.

Sales engineer Lars Larsen had worked with Per Olsen in establishing a discussion platform for a possible move to system selling. He had this to say:

> I agree that we should start thinking in terms of system engineering, as our future

EXHIBIT 2
The Twin-Screw Press

Perhaps the most ingenious product invention was the Stord Twin-Screw Press. The press basically provided dewatering by means of mecanical pressing, at a cost as low as 10 percent as that of thermal drying. A company brochure lists the following as reasons for the success of the Stord Press:

1. High substance content, savings in drier fuel consumption, reduction in drying capacity required;
2. Robust design, modest space requirements, easy installation and access to vital parts, low maintenance cost;
3. Reliable and economic operation;
4. Low power consumption per unit of capacity and moisture reduction;
5. Available for a wide range of capacities;
6. Applicable to a variety of processes and industries.

THE TOTAL DEWATERING SYSTEM

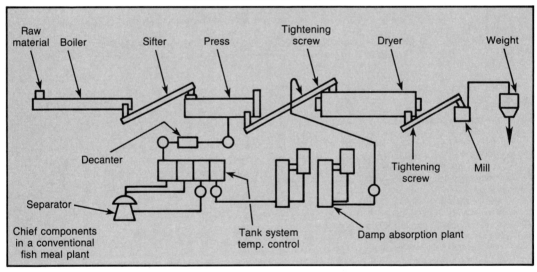

marketing strategy. This will be the logical continuation of the particular competence developed over the years. We can draw on our knowledge from past experiences to study the organizational and marketing effect of a general switch to system selling. As a point of origin for our debate, I think we should start to regard ourselves as engineering problem solvers rather than suppliers of mechanical equipment.

Jens Pedersen, head of the department for Design and Construction, did not share Per Olsen's enthusiasm for system selling:

The problem of competitors copying our products represents nothing new. As in the past, I believe we can beat off future competitors moves by producing better and more sophisticated dewatering equipment. The reduction in sales we have experienced during the last quarter is more a reflection of recession rather than of competitors cutting in on our markets. System selling means entering into agreements with suppliers of a number of different products and types of equipment that have nothing to do with our business. Further, it means tying up resources in countries where the political and economic environment may represent a genuine risk for a loss of funds invested.

Hans Hansen, from the company's administrative staff, also expressed some anxiety:

I feel that the marketing people are underestimating the economic and financial implications of system selling. The average order size will increase drastically, we shall need much more time for filling any individual order, our clients will need larger and longer credits, etc. Even if our capital situation and banking relations are good, we may run into serious problems. And

what about our cost level? I fear that we shall need more engineers and draftsmen, more training and traveling, and that we shall have a terrific unemployment problem in slack periods.

Per Olsen felt that he had essentially two problems. One, on the organizational and psychological level, concerned converting the hard core of product-oriented engineers, who argued against system selling on the principle that it was not in line with IEC's basic profile.

Secondly, Per Olsen felt that he should establish some guidelines as to what IEC should (and could) include in a system package at this point. What customers and markets should the company first aim at? and How? What price policy should one follow? How would one have to allocate company resources? What role would the marketing function have to play in case of a change in strategy? These and several other questions needed immediate attention.

16. General Consumer Products, Inc. (B) ——————

Six months into his new job as vice-president in charge of HPC, Peter Welch reviewed the progress made by HPCID in implementing the changes recommended three years earlier by the Strategic Task Force. Although some difficulties had been encountered, most had been anticipated, and the general consensus had been that the changes were quite successful. HPC's foreign sales as a percentage of total sales had increased dramatically from 32 percent in 1980 to 48 percent by 1984. Welch wondered if it was time to make a major change to HPC's organization structure.

Peter Welch had been hired by James Evans in January 1984 to replace him on his retirement in January 1985. Hired from the outside, he had no loyalties to any particular product group, nor had he become involved in internal politics. He felt that he could be quite objective in the decisions

———
This case was prepared by Brian Toyne.

he had to make. Prior to joining GCP, he had been the Marketing Vice-President for Latin American at Jason, Inc., one of GCP's major competitors. One reason Evans had hired Welch was his growing belief that HPC had to become totally global if it were to continue to be successful.

Welch believed that the worldwide product structure concept adopted by Jason, Inc. in 1979 had proven very effective. He himself had been instrumental in the reorganization of Jason's businesses and had been involved with the problems that had arisen during implementation.

An analysis of Jason's product lines, markets, and competitors had resulted in the creation of six worldwide product groups, each of which served as an SBU. The reorganization had lessened the considerable overlap in the company's product lines, resulted in administrative cost reductions, focused the company's resources on its critical markets, and enabled the six product-group managers to prepare strategic plans consistent with the company's resources and long-range objectives. At the same time, however, Jason's top management had found it necessary to train managers at all levels of the company in the use of strategic-planning techniques, to revamp planning procedures, and to create new control mechanisms.

Because of his previous experience, Peter Welch was predisposed to a worldwide product-group structure similar to Jason's. Such a decision he knew would be welcomed by the managers responsible for HPC's domestic activities. In general, these managers viewed the growing strength of HPCID as threatening and were increasingly resentful of the growing proportion of HPC's resources being allocated to support its activities. Rightly or wrongly, they believed that HPCID was draining off resources needed to strengthen their competitive positions in the U.S. market. At the same time, however, Welch was aware of John Gabrial's strong objections to such a decision. Gabrial believed that the area focus now provided by HPCID would be lost if a product-dominated structure were adopted. He was convinced that HPCID's success was due to its ability to respond differentially to the differences in its national markets. Gabrial was also of the opinion that a global perspective could be achieved by modifying HPC's planning and management information systems. He recommended the creation of a Strategic Business Plans Committee similar to the one used by HPCID. It would provide HPC's various operational units with guidelines, coordinate their activities, and allocate resources according to the company's long-range objectives.

Before making his decision, Welch decided that he needed additional information and comments from his operational managers. These needs were summarized in a comprehensive memorandum sent to all operational managers on July 10, 1985. Extracts from this memorandum follow:

1. A report has been requested detailing market trends/changes and the competitive environments in HPC's major markets in the United States, Canada, the European Community, Latin America, and the Pacific. The responsibility for this task has been given to Arnold Steppes,

one of my full-time assistants. Mr. Steppes has been asked to have the report ready for presentation at a meeting—to be attended by all operational heads—beginning September 16, 1985. The reason for the meeting is to initiate discussion on the possible restructuring of HPC's businesses and the strategic allocation of resources. Please assist Mr. Steppes by supplying him with any information he may need to accomplish his assigned task.

2. My other three assistants, Thomas Bevan, Susan Casas, and Jaimé Vasquez have been asked to develop proposals outlining the advantages and disadvantages to HPC of (a) adopting a worldwide product structure, (b) adopting a worldwide area structure, and (c) remaining with the current structure but modifying the planning and management information systems to comply with the portfolio concept. Since the underlying objective of these proposals is the enhancement of HPC's competitive position on a worldwide basis, the advantages and disadvantages of each alternative must be developed with this goal in mind. Again, please assist these people by supplying them with any information they may need.

3. The agenda for the September meeting is as follows:

   a. Presentation and evaluation of HPC's current competitive environment and market conditions on a global basis.

   b. Discussion of alternative definitions and missions for our business activities. On the basis of the conclusions reached as a result of our discussion of the above point, should HPC revise the definitions of its four major product groups? What should HPC's mission be in each of its markets? On a worldwide basis?

   c. Presentation and evaluation of the pros and cons of the three organizational proposals. Which proposal best satisfies HPC's strategic requirements for the next five years? Would it be better to combine these proposals?

Index